AGRARIAN CHANGE IN LATE ANTIQUITY

Agrarian Change in Late Antiquity
Gold, Labour, and Aristocratic Dominance

JAIRUS BANAJI

OXFORD
UNIVERSITY PRESS

OXFORD
UNIVERSITY PRESS

Great Clarendon Street, Oxford OX2 6DP

Oxford University Press is a department of the University of Oxford.
It furthers the University's objective of excellence in research, scholarship,
and education by publishing worldwide in

Oxford New York

Athens Auckland Bangkok Bogotá Buenos Aires Cape Town
Chennai Dar es Salaam Delhi Florence Hong Kong Istanbul Karachi
Kolkata Kuala Lumpur Madrid Melbourne Mexico City Mumbai Nairobi
Paris São Paulo Shanghai Singapore Taipei Tokyo Toronto Warsaw

and associated companies in Berlin Ibadan

Oxford is a registered trade mark of Oxford University Press
in the UK and in certain other countries

Published in the United States
by Oxford University Press Inc., New York

First published 2001
First published in paperback 2007

British Library Cataloguing in Publication Data

Data available

Library of Congress Cataloging in Publication Data

Banaji, Jairus, 1947–
Agrarian change in late antiquity : gold, labour, and aristocratic dominance /
Jairus Banaji.
p. cm. — (Oxford classical monographs)
Includes bibliographical references and index.
1. Land tenure—Rome. 2. Land tenure—Byzantine Empire. 3. Administration
of estates—Rome. 4. Administration of estates—Byzantine Empire. 5. Rome—
History—Empire, 284–476. 6. Rome—Economic conditions—30 B.C.–476 A.D.
7. Byzantine Empire—History—To 527. 8. Byzantine Empire—Economic
conditions. I. Title. II Series.

DG105 .B36 2002
937—dc21 2001021140
ISBN 978-0-19-924440-9 (Hbk.) 978-0-19-922603-0 (Pbk.)

1 3 5 7 9 10 8 6 4 2

Typeset by Regent Typesetting, London
Printed in Great Britain on acid-free paper
by Biddles Ltd, King's Lynn, Norfolk

For Rohini, Shaku, and Murad

PREFACE

When Santo Mazzarino announced, in 1942, 'For us moderns it appears impossible to return to Gibbon's interpretation', he could scarcely have anticipated the sheer speed with which long-established conceptions of late antiquity would soon be overturned by the rapid proliferation of a wide range of new sources and by the appearance of new historiographical perspectives, which were less positivistic in their obsession with causality and closer, in some ways, to Gibbon's own intuition that late antiquity had brought a profound cultural transformation. Today it is impossible to conceive of the period between Diocletian's overhaul of Roman imperial structures and the Islamic expansion as one of persistent decay, let alone dramatic decline. No one who thinks late antiquity can think about it outside the framework established by Mazzarino's own work, or that of Tchalenko, for that matter, or Peter Brown. (See the brilliant review of Jones by Peter Brown in 'The Later Roman Empire', *EcHR* 2nd ser. 20 (1967) 327 ff.) At another level, however, the old historiographical visions survive and continue to shape the interpretation of the late antique world, both in detail and in more general and subtle ways, and it may be worth asking why this is so. The most general explanation, perhaps, is that old paradigms never die completely and continue to exert a pervasive influence, especially in fields like the social sciences and history, long after new and better ways of understanding have emerged. But this is probably also the weakest explanation, for it does not explain why many scholars familiar with the new evidence and new models of historical thinking should still cling to moribund dogmas. (I recall one of them, for example, challenging the credibility of the numbers contained in Byzantine papyri when these were read to him at a conference in Milan some years ago!) In the case of Roman or 'late Roman' economic history, this persistence of the old pessimism is linked, in my view, to two other factors which have been of considerable importance: on the one hand, the sheer strength of primitivism in continuing to influence the ways we think about 'ancient' (and medieval?) economies, and, on the other, the powerful influence of Max Weber in constructing an internally coherent economic explanation of decline which seemed to elide the late antique into an emerging medievalism and, in this way, provide the economic underpinnings of the otherwise largely political and moral story of the late empire. Weber forged his ideas in the 1890s, when papyrology was still a nascent science and local evidence thin on the ground, when the historian's interest in money rarely extended beyond the third century, and when, scientifically, it was still possible, indeed respectable, to rely on a few scraps of evidence to sustain generalizations stretching over centuries. None of this would be acceptable today but primitivist and Weberian legacies remain pervasive, and *what is surprising is how rarely they have been challenged.*

This book sets out to do just that by upgrading, or less ambitiously, perhaps, beginning to upgrade, our vision of late antique economy through the rich infrastructure of evidence available to historians writing at the end of the twentieth century by contrast with those who may have thought about these issues a century earlier. It began, obscurely, as an interest provoked in the mid-1970s by my first reading of Gunnar Mickwitz's brilliant book on the fourth century, and grew more precise when I finished reading the late Geoffrey de Ste. Croix's *The Class Struggle in the Ancient Greek World* with, like everyone, obvious awe, but also a sense of latent dissatisfaction at what seemed, still, a traditional picture of late antiquity (based unremittingly on legal and textual sources). Those were years when, against the background of lively intellectual discussions about the nature and epistemological claims of economic laws and whether any such set of laws could explain the 'decline' of the Roman empire, I began to think increasingly about the intelligibility of the notion of decline, both in its own terms and with reference to the classical world. Motivated in a general way by the slogan of 'going back to the things themselves', I undertook a D. Phil. at Oxford in the late 1980s, and the book below is a revised version of the thesis I presented in 1992. Interrupted by other commitments and a different field of study in the 1990s, the revisions had to be made at various times throughout that decade. If I were to write the whole thing from scratch, assuming that were possible, some parts of the argument would hopefully emerge with greater clarity, more would be said about institutional landholders, and there would be a more detailed consideration of the origins of the eastern aristocracy. With these qualifications, there is nothing in the argument I would want to present differently.

The writing of this book over the late 1980s and 1990s owes a great deal to the many friends, colleagues, and supervisors who interacted with different portions of it. Without the assistance of the librarians of the Ashmolean and various reading rooms in the Bodleian, it would not have been possible, however, and I would like to thank all of them first of all. I am particularly grateful to Alan Bowman, Elio Lo Cascio, and Nicholas Purcell for their invaluable support over several years, and to them as well as Michael Metcalf, Chris Howgego, and Clementina Panella, for commenting on earlier drafts of individual chapters. So too John Lloyd, whom I shall always remember with the greatest affection. Jane Rowlandson was extremely kind in sharing her comprehensive list of leases with me in the late 1980s. Richard Hodges and Amanda Claridge made my stay at the British School at Rome in the early 1990s one of the most interesting experiences of my life. Bryan Ward-Perkins and James Howard-Johnston have been generous with lunches and ideas. I have also learned a great deal from Gavin Williams, Barbara Harriss-White, and Terry Byres, all of whom have spent much of their professional lives writing and thinking about agrarian issues. I was fortunate to have John Matthews as my main supervisor in the formative years of this book and owe much to his encouragement and stimulation. Cathy King and John Rea extended specialist supervision, in late Roman numismatics and papyrology respectively, and were always accessible in terms of time as well as ideas. Their contribution is so comprehensively embedded in this book that I owe each of them more than I could possibly express in this acknowledgement. My greatest debt is to Fergus Millar, who more than anyone encouraged me to write this book, contributed to its general shape, and saw the project through to completion. Without his involvement it is not just possible but very likely that the arguments which follow would forever slumber quietly in the basements of the Bodleian. I should also like to thank Hilary O'Shea and her colleagues at Oxford University Press for expediting publication with remarkable thoroughness and efficiency. Finally, I am immeasurably indebted to my family for their love and support, and for putting up with the 'fourth century' for what sometimes seemed to them almost 400 years!

J.B.

Oxford
June 2000

NOTE TO THE REVISED EDITION

Agrarian Change was revised and updated over most of my first semester as a Member of the Institute for Advanced Study, Princeton, in 2006–2007. The rapid pace of work would not have been possible without the excellent facilities proffered by the Institute, for which I should like to thank both its director, Peter Goddard, as well as the library staff there and at Firestone. I am especially grateful to Glen Bowersock, Peter Brown and Patricia Crone for being so encouraging and such good company, to Patricia for the chance to work with her, and to all of them and John Haldon for a constant flow of intellectual stimulation!

Princeton
March 2007

CONTENTS

ABBREVIATIONS

AArchHung	*Acta Archaeologica Academiae Scientiarum Hungaricae*
Aegyptus	*Aegyptus: rivista italiana di egittologia e di papirologia*
AIIN	*Annali dell' Istituto Italiano di Numismatica*
AJ	*The Archaeological Journal*
AJA	*American Journal of Archaeology*
AE	*L'année épigraphique*
ANRW	*Aufstieg und Niedergang der römischen Welt*
AntAfr	*Antiquités africaines*
APEL	A. Grohmann, *Arabic Papyri in the Egyptian Library* (Cairo, 1934–62)
APF	*Archiv für Papyrusforschung u. verwandte Gebiete*
ARHE	*Amphores romaines et histoire économique: dix ans de recherche. Actes du colloque de Sienne (22–24 mai 1986)* . . . Collection de l'École Française de Rome, 114 (Rome, 1989)
BASP	*Bulletin of the American Society of Papyrologists*
BCTH	*Bulletin archéologique du Comité des travaux historiques*
BGU	*Berliner griechische Urkunden (Ägyptische Urkunden aus den königlichen Museen zu Berlin)*
BIFAO	*Bulletin de l'Institut français d'archéologie orientale*
BL	*Berichtigungsliste der griechischen Papyrusurkunden aus Aegypten*
BollNum	*Bollettino di Numismatica*
BSFN	*Bulletin de la Société française de numismatique*
Byzantion	*Byzantion: revue internationale des études byzantines*

BZ	*Byzantinische Zeitschrift*
Catalogue	J. Banaji, 'Rural Communities in the Late Empire AD 300–700: Monetary and Economic Aspects', 2 vols. (Oxford University D. Phil., 1992), 2, p.51 ff.
CE	*Chronique d'Égypte*
CPR	*Corpus Papyrorum Raineri Archiducis Austriae*
CR	*Classical Review*
CRAI	*Comptes rendus de l'Académie des Inscriptions et Belles-Lettres*
CRIPEL	*Cahiers de recherches de l'Institut de Papyrologie et d'Égyptologie de Lille III*
CSBE	R. S. Bagnall and K. A. Worp, *The Chronological Systems of Byzantine Egypt* (Zutphen, 1978)
DOP	*Dumbarton Oaks Papers*
EOS	*Epigrafia e ordine senatorio* (*Tituli* 4–5), 2 vols. (Rome, 1982)
Eranos	*Eranos: acta philologica Suecana*
GCC	S. Lancel (ed.), *Actes de la Conférence de Carthage en 411*. Sources Chrétiennes, 3 vols., 194–5, 224 (Paris, 1972–5)
Hahn, *MIB*	W. Hahn, *Moneta Imperii Byzantini*, 3 vols. Osterreichische Akad. Wiss., Phil.-Hist. Klasse, Denkschriften, 109, 119, 148 (Vienna, 1973–81)
Hardy, *Large Estates*	E. R. Hardy, *The Large Estates of Byzantine Egypt*. Studies in History, Economics and Public Law No. 354 (New York, 1931)
Hesperia	*Hesperia: Journal of the American School of Classical Studies at Athens*
Historia	*Historia: Zeitschrift für Alte Geschichte*
HREB	*Hommes et richesses dans l'Empire byzantine*. 1: *IV–VII siècle* (Paris, 1989)
Hultsch, *Metr. script. rel.*	F. Hultsch, *Metrologicorum scriptorum reliquiae*, 2 vols. (Leipzig, 1864)
IEJ	*Israel Exploration Journal*
Iura	*Iura: rivista internazionale di diritto romano e antico*
JA	*Journal asiatique*
JEA	*Journal of Egyptian Archaeology*

JESHO	*Journal of the Economic and Social History of the Orient*
JHS	*Journal of Hellenic Studies*
JJP	*Journal of Juristic Papyrology*
JNG	*Jahrbuch für Numismatik und Geldgeschichte*
Jones, *LRE*	A. H. M. Jones, *The Later Roman Empire 284–602. A Social, Economic and Administrative Survey*, 2 vols. (Oxford, 1964, repr. 1973)
JRA	*Journal of Roman Archaeology*
JRS	*Journal of Roman Studies*
Klio	*Klio: Beiträge zur alten Geschichte*
KRU	W. E. Crum and G. Steindorff, *Koptische Rechtsurkunden des achten Jahrhunderts aus Djême (Theben)* (Leipzig, 1912)
LS	*Libyan Studies*
MDAI	*Mitteilungen des Deutschen Archäologischen Instituts*
MEFRA	*Mélanges d'archéologie et d'histoire de l'École Française de Rome, Antiquité*
Mickwitz, *Geld und Wirtschaft*	G. Mickwitz, *Geld und Wirtschaft im römischen Reich des vierten Jahrhunderts n.Chr.* (Helsinki, 1932)
NAC	*Numismatica e antichità classiche: Quaderni Ticinesi*
NC	*The Numismatic Chronicle*
NCirc	*The Numismatic Circular*
NZ	*Numismatische Zeitschrift*
P. Abinn.	H. I. Bell, V. Martin, *et al.*, *The Abinnaeus Archive: Papers of a Roman Officer in the reign of Constantius II* (Oxford, 1962)
P. Amh.	B. P. Grenfell and A. S. Hunt, *The Amherst Papyri* (London, 1990–1)
P. Amst.	R. P. Salomons *et al.*, *Die Amsterdamer Papyri* (Zutphen, 1980)
P. Ant.	*The Antinoopolis Papyri*
P. Apoll.	R. Rémondon, *Papyrus grecs d' Apollônos Anô* (Cairo, 1953)
P. Bad.	*Griechische Papyri . . . aus den badischen Papyrus-Sammlungen*
P. Beatty Panop.	T. C. Skeat, *Papyri from Panopolis in the Chester Beatty Library Dublin* (Dublin, 1964)

P. Berl. Zill.	H. Zilliacus, *Vierzehn Berliner Griechische Papyri* (Helsinki, 1941)
P. Bod.	R. P. Salomons, *Papyri Bodleianae I* (Amsterdam, 1996)
P. Cairo Isid.	A. E. Boak and H. C. Youtie, *The Archive of Aurelius Isidorus* (Ann Arbor, 1960)
P. Cairo Masp.	J. Maspero, *Catalogue général des Antiquités égyptiennes du Musée du Caire; Papyrus grecs d'époque byzantine* (Cairo, 1911–16)
P. Charite	K. A. Worp, *Das Aurelia Charite Archiv (AD 325–348)* (Zutphen, 1980)
P. Coll. Youtie	A. E. Hanson, *Collectanea Papyrologica: Texts published in honor of H. C. Youtie*, 2 vols. (Bonn, 1976)
P. Flor.	D. Comparetti and G. Vitelli, *Papiri greco-egizi* (Milan, 1906–15)
P. Flor. XVIII	R. Pintaudi and P. J. Sijpesteijn, *Tavolette lignee e cerate da varie collezioni (Papyrologica Fiorentina XVIII)* (Florence, 1989)
P. Freer Aphrod.	J. Gascou and L. MacCoull, 'Le cadastre d'Aphroditô', *Travaux et Memoires* 10 (1987) 103–58 (= *SB* XX 14669)
P. Giss.	E. Kornemann and P. M. Meyer, *Griechische Papyri . . . zu Giessen* (Leipzig, 1910–12)
P. Grenf.	B. P. Grenfell and A. S. Hunt, *New Classical Fragments and other Greek and Latin Papyri* (Oxford, 1897)
P. Hamb.	P. M. Meyer, *Griechische Papyrusurkunden der Hamburger Staats- und Universitätsbibliothek* (Leipzig and Berlin, 1911–24)
P. Heid.	*Veröffentlichungen aus der Heidelberger Papyrussammlung*
P. Iand.	*Papyri Iandanae*
P. Köln	*Kölner Papyri* (1976–)
P. Landlisten	P. J. Sijpesteijn and K. A. Worp, *Zwei Landlisten aus dem Hermupolites* (Zutphen, 1978)
P. Laur.	R. Pintaudi, *Dai papiri della Biblioteca Medicea Laurenziana* (Florence, 1976)
P. Lips.	L. Mitteis, *Griechische Urkunden der Papyrussammlung zu Leipzig* (Leipzig, 1906)

P. Lond.	*Greek Papyri in the British Museum* (London, 1893–1917)
P. Med.	S. Daris, *Papiri milanesi* (Milan, 1966–7)
P. Mich. XIII	P. J. Sijpesteijn, *The Aphrodite Papyri in the University of Michigan Papyrus Collection* (Zutphen, 1977)
P. Michael.	D. S. Crawford, *Papyri Michaelidae* (Aberdeen, 1955)
P. Mon.	A. Heisenberg and L. Wenger, *Byzantinische Papyri der Bayerischen Staatsbibliothek München* (2nd edn.; Stuttgart, 1986)
P. Oxy.	*The Oxyrhynchus Papyri*
P. Prag.	R. Pintaudi *et al.*, *Papyri Graecae Wessely Pragenses* (Florence, 1988)
P. Ross.-Georg.	*Papyri russischer und georgischer Sammlungen* (Tiflis, 1925–35)
P. Strasb.	*Papyrus grecs de la Bibliothèque Nationale et Universitaire de Strasbourg*
P. Tebt.	*The Tebtunis Papyri*
P. Thead.	P. Jouguet, *Papyrus de Théadelphie* (Paris, 1911)
P. Turner	*Papyri Greek and Egyptian edited by various hands in honour of Eric Gardner Turner* (London, 1981)
P. Vars.	G. Manteuffel, *Papyri Varsovienses* (Warsaw, 1935)
P. Vatic. Aphrod.	R. Pintaudi, *I Papiri vaticani greci di Aphrodito* (Vatican City, 1980)
P. Vindob. Sal.	R. P. Salomons, *Einige Wiener Papyri* (Amsterdam, 1976)
PCAA II	J. M. Blázquez Martínez and J. Remesal Rodríguez (eds.), *Produccion y Comercio del Aceite en la Antigüedad. Segundo Congreso International (Sevilla, 24–28 Febrero 1982)* (Madrid, 1983)
PERF	*Papyrus Erzherzog Rainer. Führer durch die Ausstellung* (1894)
PSI	*Papiri greci e latini, pubbl. della Società Italiana . . .* (1912–)
QAL	*Quaderni di archeologia della Libia*
RAL	*Rendiconti della Classe di Scienze morali, storiche e filologiche dell' Accademia dei Lincei*

RBN	*Revue belge de numismatique et de sigillographie*
REA	*Revue des études anciennes*
REG	*Revue des études grecques*
RN	*Revue Numismatique*
Rostovtzeff, *SEHRE*	M. Rostovtzeff, *The Social and Economic History of the Roman Empire*, 2 vols. (2nd edn.; 1971)
SB	*Sammelbuch griechisher Urkunden aus Aegypten* (1915–)
SEBGC	W. Hahn and W. E. Metcalf (eds.), *Studies in Early Byzantine Gold Coinage* (ANS, New York, 1988)
SNR	*Schweizerische numismatische Rundschau*
SPP	C. Wessely, *Studien zur Palaeographie und Papyrusurkunde* (1902–)
SRIT	A. Giardina (ed.), *Società romana e impero tardoantico*. Istituto Gramsci, 4 vols. (Rome and Bari, 1986)
TAPhA	*Transactions and Proceedings of the American Philological Association*
Till, 'Koptische Arbeitsverträge'	W. Till, 'Die koptische Arbeitsverträge', in *Symbolae Raphaeli Taubenschlag dedicatae* = *Eos* 48 (1956) fasc.1, 273–329
Timm, *CKAAZ*	S. Timm, *Das christlich-koptische Ägypten in arabischer Zeit* (Wiesbaden, 1984–)
Tyche	*Tyche: Beiträge zur Alten Geschichte, Papyrologie und Epigraphik*
Weber, 'Soziale Gründe'	M. Weber, 'Die sozialen Gründe des Untergangs der antiken Kultur', *Die Wahrheit*, 1896, repr. in *Gesammelte Aufsätze*, 289–311
Weber, *Gesammelte Aufsätze*	M. Weber, *Gesammelte Aufsätze zur Sozial- und Wirtschaftsgeschichte* (Tübingen, 1924)
YClS	*Yale Classical Studies*
WChr	L. Mitteis and U. Wilcken, *Grundzüge und Chrestomathie der Papyrusurkunde*, 2 vols. (Leipzig and Berlin, 1912)
ZPE	*Zeitschrift für Papyrologie und Epigraphik*

INTRODUCTION

Ancient economic history remains a largely undertheorized field of study, not because ancient historians have ignored theory in the general pursuit of 'facts', but for the opposite reason, because they have ignored the evidence. In other words, the proliferation of evidence stands in curious disproportion to the atrophied models that rule in this field of enquiry, and the gap is becoming worse with each passing year. Behind this curious paralysis lie the massive and sombre legacies of the late nineteenth century, and behind those the deadweight of other, earlier generations which looked on the past with the patronizing attitudes of a world in unbridled expansion. The triumph of capitalism was also the downgrading of every preceding epoch with its supposedly increasingly primitive forms of technology and social interaction, and its inability to achieve a rational organization of the world. These ideologies of the past are so deeply rooted in our own mental frameworks that most history that passes for a scientific enquiry is simply a rationalization of their explicit and implied claims. The late nineteenth century is in fact the best example of this. In historicizing the notion of capital Marx left the intellectuals of the later nineteenth century with the general problem of knowing in what terms one could, correspondingly, 'think' the world before the full flowering of capitalism. Weber was obsessed with the issue, and out of his obsession came a rich, complex, and deeply ambiguous set of reflections which have been discussed by many scholars since. Weber's introduction to the 'Agrarverhältnisse im Altertum', the third and substantially revised edition of which, we now know, he drafted with great rapidity in 1907,[1] reflects these ambiguities in a condensed form. It contains the extraordinary admission that he had underestimated the quantitative importance of free labour as well as the scale or extent of money economy in previous work on antiquity.[2] These were significant concessions to the modernism of Eduard Meyer and his pupil Wilcken's researches on Egypt, but if so they were made grudgingly. The use of hired labour was largely confined to harvesting and

[1] See H. Bruhns, Review of *Max Weber Briefe 1906–1908*, ed. R. Lepsius and W. J. Mommsen (Tübingen, 1990), in *Annales ESC* 53 (1998) 404 (drafted in four months, 'in extremely difficult psychological and material conditions').

[2] Weber, 'Agrarverhältnisse im Altertum', in *Gesammelte Aufsätze*, 1–288, at 11.

various forms of public employment. 'Otherwise their employment was generally scattered and irregular.'[3] Moreover, Egypt, where Wilcken had found both money economy and free labour, was 'untypical'. Finally, even more interesting, Weber implied that none of this applied to the late antique period. In a terse passing reference he claimed that 'in late antiquity (third century onwards) the aristocratic estates (*Grundherrschaften*) and a state economy which was run on "household-economy principles" were increasingly driven by *Naturalwirtschaft*.'[4] The bigger problem here was the general issue of the conceptual and historical boundaries of our notion of 'capitalism', and the paradox of these admissions and their grudging qualifications was to confine the efflorescence of ancient capitalism to the heyday of the slave-based enterprises. Thus ancient capitalism was inextricably bound up with slavery (more than with free labour). What mattered here was not the forced character of labour but the fact that it was purchased *en bloc* with the clear aim of commercial enterprise. On the other hand, the agrarian enterprises of late antiquity, Weber suggested, could not be construed as capitalist in the full sense (despite the existence of markets in produce and land), because the labour-power deployed on those estates was not the object of commercial transactions, either through the spot purchases of workers (as with slaves) or via recruitment in the labour market. 'The enterprise is in this case an intermediate entity', wrote Weber,[5] further complicating the issue since 'natural economy' had been claimed as the crucial constraint on the economic character of the late Roman estates.

In fact, the model that Weber sketches in the complex pages of the *Einleitung* is one that may well have surpassed the divide between modernists and primitivists, for it was in Gummerus's book on the Roman estate, published a year before Weber drafted the third edition, that two cardinal theses of Weber's historiography of the ancient world were clearly formulated—and that in the work of a pupil of Meyer: the assertion, on the one hand, that 'in antiquity capitalism was inextricably bound up with slave economy',[6] and

[3] Weber, 'Agrarverhältnisse im Altertum', 12.

[4] Weber, 'Agrarverhältnisse im Altertum', 11 ('Ebenso beherrschte die Naturalwirtschaft aber auch zunehmend die Grundherrschaften und die "oikenwirtschaftlich" betriebene Staatswirtschaft der antiken Spätzeit (seit dem 3. Jahrh.)').

[5] Weber, 'Agrarverhältnisse im Altertum', 14 ('Der Betrieb ist in diesem Fällen ein Mittelding; er ist "kapitalistisch", sofern für den Markt produziert wird und der Boden Verkehrsgegenstand ist,—nicht kapitalistisch, sofern die Arbeitskräfte als Produktionsmittel sowohl dem Kauf wie der Miete im freien Verkehr entzogen sind.')

[6] H. Gummerus, *Der römische Gutsbetrieb als wirtschaftlicher Organismus nach den Werken des Cato, Varro und Columella* (Leipzig, 1906) 94, 'Der Kapitalismus war im

the dogma, on the other, that over time Roman aristocratic estates (*Grundherrschaften*) were subjected to increasing economic isolation.[7] Gummerus, like Weber, saw the labourers on those estates as 'serfs' of some kind, and clearly accepted the view, universal in those days, that the late antique world was one of commercial and economic decline. Weber's thesis of the re-emergence of forms of natural economy was not seriously questioned even by Rostovtzeff,[8] who gave a peculiarly Russian twist to the drama of late antiquity, portraying its essential catastrophe as one of a classical civilization besieged by an expanding tide of peasant barbarism, with the revolutionary emergence of the new militarized state expressing the grievances of an oppressed peasantry,[9] and reflecting, with the displacement of classical culture by Christianity, both cultural and economic decay. Since the 1930s, however, these grand pictures of the late Roman centuries have been subjected to extensive revision, largely under the pressure of new evidence, even if, as the case of archaeology shows, the rules of evidence are not always clear, and this book defines its own starting-point in such historiographical revisionism, accepting the truth of Mazzarino's claim that historiography has moved irrevocably beyond Gibbon,[10] and extending this advance, hopefully, to the last bastion of the earlier legacies.

Chapter 1 sets the stage for this enquiry in a general way, underlining the variegated nature of the Roman countryside and adducing some of the archaeological evidence for a reoccupation of the countryside in the late Roman period. The general economic revival of the fourth century was linked to a new period of monetary expansion and had an important impact on the rural sector, with a massive wave of investment in rural estates and the beginnings of a sustained demographic surge. Chapter 2 contrasts Weber's understanding of the late antique economy with the picture developed by Mickwitz barely three decades later—a period marked by a veritable explosion of source material, which laid the basis for a major transformation in the historiography of the late empire. In an important sense, then, this study takes off from the perspectives established

Altertum unauflöslich mit der Sklavenwirtschaft verbunden', and his ref. on the same page to 'Die Sklaverei des Kapitalismus'.

[7] Gummerus, *Der römische Gutsbetrieb*, 97, 'Die allmählich fortschreitende wirtschaftliche Isolierung der römische Grundherrschaften'.

[8] Though Rostovtzeff claimed never to have read Weber's famous lecture of 1896, cf. *SEHRE* 2.751 n. 9.

[9] Cf. Fergus Millar, 'The World of the *Golden Ass*', *JRS* 71 (1981) 63–75, at 68: 'Nothing could be further from the truth than Rostovtzeff's idea that the army of the Imperial period somehow represented an oppressed peasantry. On the contrary, the soldiers were a privileged official class whose presence was feared by ordinary people.'

[10] S. Mazzarino, *Stilicone. La crisi imperiale dopo Teodosio* (Rome, 1942).

by Mickwitz's dissertation of 1932, even though a major part of his argument is rejected. In particular, Mickwitz's admirable integration of papyrological and numismatic sources helps to integrate the general scheme of this book. Thus Chapters 3 and 5 are unified conceptually by an argument about the accumulation of gold in the hands of new bureaucratic groups and about its long-term investment in land, with a resultant restructuring of agrarian production. Presupposed here is a recasting of the 'political economy' of the late empire on the lines of Mazzarino's critique of the Mickwitzian argument that state employees were in the forefront of a drive for payments in kind, and thus the social bearers of a massive (but now more circumscribed) *Naturalwirtschaft* (Chapter 2). These themes are replayed, with less abstraction, in Chapter 3, where it is argued that the late Roman state exerted a progressive or modernizing influence by driving forward the forces of monetary economy, both through its inflexible and, in many ways, extraordinary commitment to the gold coinage and, through that, to a gold-based system of currency, and, with more counterfinality, through the bargaining pressures that swelled up in its own ranks among powerful new groups in the army and bureaucracy. At any rate, monetary expansion is the pivotal framework within which one has to assess the peculiar vitality and resilience, or lack of them, of the late antique centuries, and any theory that seeks to account for the 'transition' while ignoring monetary phenomena (as a long tradition has done, from Weber to Perry Anderson and beyond) is simply lacking in credibility.

Chapters 5 and 6 present a story of social change in the eastern Mediterranean countryside—against the backgrounds sketched above. It is well known that the local élites who ran the town councils were under considerable pressure in the fourth century, and seem, eventually, to have collapsed. I argue that these municipal élites who were the dominant local landholders down to the middle decades of the fourth century were subsequently largely displaced by major new groups of landowners, and that in the eastern Mediterranean, at any rate, the social physiognomy of the countryside was profoundly altered by the main part of the fifth century. What emerged in the course of those decades was a more complex and deeply stratified rural society, hegemonized at different levels by the landed middle bureaucracy of the provincial towns—the core of a new urban-based agrarian middle class—and by the new imperial aristocracy of the eastern Mediterranean. Of course, these groups have to be reconstructed from a hugely scattered mass of evidence and are almost never presented to us with any sense of the collective identities by which undoubtedly they were defined. What the sources do not enable us to see is how far these agrarian classes had purely commercial counterparts in the large urban centres such as Alexandria, where their presence is surely presupposed by the close economic linkages between (late antique) town and (late antique) countryside. For, while it is just possible to get some sense of the nature of rural activity from an essentially urban and commercial archive,[11] the reverse so far has proved impossible.

Finally, I break with the widespread orthodoxy that wage labour has been of only marginal importance in so-called 'pre-capitalist' forms of economy. In Chapters 7 and 8 I suggest that for reasons related at least partly to demographic growth the late antique world saw a significant expansion of wage employment, and that this had an obvious influence on the organization of labour on the new aristocratic estates of the fifth and sixth centuries. There is a powerful if often latent consensus among late Roman historians that land was hardly ever managed in large integrated units and that Roman landowners invariably preferred tenancy to direct management. These assumptions are challenged and discarded in Chapter 7, which suggests that the larger estates were typically structured around compact settlements comprising the kind of 'peasant labour force' found in the Egyptian *ezbas* in more recent times.[12] Given the high degree of formality that is evident at every level of late antique society and not least in its economic relations, it is certainly disappointing that almost no evidence survives as to the kind of contracts through which these rural labourers were 'attached' to their employers.

[11] A. L. Udovitch, 'International Trade and the Medieval Egyptian Countryside', in A. K. Bowman and E. Rogan (eds.), *Agriculture in Egypt from Pharaonic to Modern Times*. Proceedings of the British Academy, 96 (Oxford, 1999) 267–85.

[12] Roger Owen, *The Middle East in the World Economy 1800–1914* (London, 1981) 148, referring to the ability of *ezba* proprietors to 'extract cheap labour from a well-disciplined peasant labour force'.

CHAPTER 1

The Rural Landscape of the Late Empire

Landscapes of Diversity

When the merchant Ibn Ḥauqal described the countryside of Egypt around the middle of the tenth century, the distribution of cash crops was dominated by a certain specialization, with Assouan (Syene) noted for its abundance of date palms, Ashmunein for flax, 'Fayyum' (the former Arsinoe) for fruit orchards and rice cultivation, Bahnasā (Oxyrhynchus) for its diversified textile industry, and so on.[1] There is no doubt that even in antiquity the areas immediately surrounding a city or urban centre were among the richest, most intensively cultivated parts of the countryside. Ammianus refers to the 'rich, cultivated farms' surrounding Amida *c.*359.[2] They must have suffered terribly in the destruction of the town in that year. His *Res Gestae* are in fact full of vivid references to landscape, especially urban countrysides. He refers to the wine estates on the banks of the Euphrates, *villae* which stored their produce in large 'bladders',[3] to the well-cultivated and neatly kept fields (*terrae*) of Palestine,[4] to the 'rich villages' (*vicos uberes*) of Thrace,[5] to 'fertile estates' 'sprawling' around Heraclea,[6] to the 'exceptionally rich suburban countryside' near Lepcis[7] where the Austoriani encamped briefly in 363, 'fearing to come near Lepcis'. A lot of these descriptions seem to suggest either that Ammianus had personally seen the

[1] Ibn Ḥauqal, *Configuration de la terre* (*Kitāb Ṣūrat al-ʿarḍ*), tr. J. H. Kramers and G. Wiet (Beirut and Paris, 1964) 1.155–7. He left Baghdad in 943 and may have been in Egypt in the 950s (though he also drew heavily on the work of al-Iṣṭakhrī).

[2] Ammianus 19.2.2, 'agros pingues cultosque'.

[3] Ammianus 30.1.9.

[4] Ammianus 14.8.11, 'cultis abundans terris et nitidis'.

[5] Ammianus 31.6.5.

[6] Ammianus 31.16.3, cf. V. Velkov, 'Les campagnes et la population rurale en Thrace au IVe–VIe siècle', *Byzantino Bulgarica* 1 (1962) 31–66, esp. 37.

[7] Ammianus 28.6.4, 'suburbano eius uberrimo'.

countrysides he was writing about (which is impossible for most of them) or based his account on the evidence of others who had (which is not unlikely). These are valuable passages, for they constitute a sort of imaginary photography, substituting the power of condensed description for a physical image.

In his narrative of the campaign against Firmus, in Mauretania, in 373, which must count as one of our most sustained descriptions of an indigenous late Roman landscape, Ammianus refers to a series of 'castella'. Four are described by the use of this word, one is called a *munimentum* when we have evidence to show that it too was called a *castellum*, and a sixth was probably also a *castellum* judging by his description of the site.[8] The only other rural settlements in this landscape were *fundi*—massive estates owned by various members of a single 'indigenous' family. In the early empire Pliny had described the *castella* as the dominant form of rural settlement in Africa.[9] By the late Roman period *castellani* had to share their countryside with an exceedingly large number of private estates. The typical Roman African landscape combined *fundi* or *villae* with *castella* (more than with *vici*) even in the largely 'ethnic' regions west of the Grande Kabylie. When Constans' emissary Macarius set out to crush the recalcitrant bishops of Donatism in the summer of 347 he stopped over at an estate (*possessio*) called Vegesala, in southern Numidia, now identified as Ksar el-Kelb where Courcelle excavated the remains of a church commemorating this group.[10] The next major toponym in the passion which recounts these events is the *castellum* of Nova Petra where Marchulus was, it seems, specially taken for a dramatic—if clandestine—execution. This settlement is described as 'conjoined to the precipice of a steep mountain both through its name and by virtue of its location'.[11] To

[8] Ammianus 29.5.25 (Tingitanum = El Asnam, *Itin. Ant.* 37.7), 44 (Audiense), 49 (Duodiense), 55 (Subicarense), all *castella*; 29.5.45, 'munimentum nomine Medianum', which appears in the *Notitia provinciarum et civitatum Africae* (*CSEL* 7) Maur. Caes. 86, as *castellum Medianum*; 29.5.39, 'ad civitatem nomine Contensem . . . ubi captivos nostros Firmus ut in munimento abstruso locarat et celso' (to a town called Conta which resembled some remote and towering fortress in which Firmus had placed those of our men whom he had captured), probably a *castellum*. In general, see S. Gsell, 'Observations géographiques sur la révolte de Firmus', *Recueil des Notices et Mémoires de la Société Archéologique de Constantine* 36 (1903) 21–46.

[9] Pliny, *NH* 5.1.1, 'populorum eius oppidorumque nomina vel maxime sunt ineffabilia praeterquam ipsorum linguis; et alias castella ferme inhabitabant' (the names of its peoples and towns are largely unpronounceable except in their own languages, and for the rest they mostly reside in *castella*).

[10] P. Courcelle, 'Une seconde campagne de fouilles à Ksar-el-Kelb', *MEFR(A)* 53 (1936) 166–97, cf. Y. Duval, *Loca Sanctorum Africae: le culte des martyrs en Afrique du IVe au VIIe siècle*, 2 vols. (Rome, 1982) 1. 159f. (no.75).

[11] *Passio Marculi* 6 (ed. J.-L. Maier, *Le Dossier du Donatisme*. 1: *Des origines à la mort de Constance II (303–361)*. TU 134 (Berlin, 1987) 282), 'castellum Novae Petrae, quod

reach his actual place of execution the bishop had to be escorted through a landscape where terraces rose one above another as far up as the water could be made to reach them.[12] Again, the *castellum* of Fussala was the main actor in the drama caused by the errant bishop Antoninus and the hectic bargaining which erupted over attempts to get rid of him. These events occurred in the rural areas to the south and south-east of Hippo.[13] Fussala was located, probably, in the mountainous region of Reguegma which has altitudes from 300 m. in the valley bottoms to 900 m. on the peaks. The territory of the *castellum* must have included several *fundi*, for Augustine refers to one owned by the church which was 'in eodem Fussalensi territorio constitutum'.[14] The *fundus Zubedi* owned by a military official was also *in territorio Fussalensi*.[15] And 'close to' Fussala was the *fundus Thogonoetensis*, whose owner was a *clarissima* who intervened repeatedly in the affair to keep the frightening bishop out of her estate.[16] All this happened at a time when rural congregations were defecting to the Catholic church under the pressure of increased coercion, with the systematic attempt to break the stranglehold of Donatism. These rural communities, the *castellani* who (with the estate workforces) had formed the chief base of the 'alternative' church in Numidia and rural areas further west, were remarkable expressions of the tremendous spirit of independence which characterized all such communities, certainly in North Africa, whether they resided in *castella* or formed estate workforces like the 'coloni' of the *fundus Thogonoetensis*. One expression of this

ardui montis praecipitio et nomine et vicinitate coniunctum est' (the settlement of Nova Petra, which is linked to the precipice of a steep mountain both through its name and its physical proximity).

[12] *Passio Marculi* 11 (Maier, *Dossier*, 286–7), 'Iter quoque ipsum quo ad supplicium ducebatur tale illi fuerat procuratum ut, exstructis undique versum terrae molibus ac paulatim in altum aggeribus elevatis, ad passionis suae insigne fastigium perveniret, ipsa montis famulante natura ut primo humilia collis iuga, dehinc arduous vertices calcans, velut per gradus quosdam in sublime conscendens' (The very pathway by which he was led to his execution had been so arranged for him that he made his way to the lofty pinnacle of his passion with masses of earth piled up in every direction and the gradual elevation of terraces. The very nature of the mountain played a role in this, since he would first trample the gentler slopes of the hill, and then the steep summits, as if he were climbing to the firmament by a staircase of some kind). 'They rise one above another etc.' is borrowed from R. L. Playfair, *Travels in the Footsteps of Bruce in Algeria and Tunis* (London, 1877) 75, describing the villages around Menaa in the Aurès. The date was 29 Nov. 347, so Monceaux, *Histoire littéraire de l'Afrique chrétienne depuis les origines jusqu' à l'invasion arabe*, 7 vols. (Paris, 1901–23) 5.74.

[13] See S. Lancel, 'Études sur la Numidie d'Hippone au temps de saint Augustin. Recherches de topographie ecclésiastique', *MEFR(A)* 96 (1984) 1096 f., 1102 f.

[14] Augustine, *Ep.* 20*.29.2 (*CSEL* 88.110).

[15] Augustine, *Civitas Dei* 22.8 (*CSEL* 40.602).

[16] Augustine, *Ep.* 20*.10.1 (*CSEL* 88.100), 'Iste autem fundus ita castello propinquus est ut, etc.'

independence was simply the fact that most rural communities (in regions like Africa) insisted on having their own bishop. One of our last references to the *castella* as a type of human settlement comes, in fact, in a circular of Pope Leo I which told the Mauretanian bishops in 446 that from then on bishops should no longer be consecrated in 'any old settlement or *castellum*' ('non in quibuslibet locis neque in quibuscumque castellis'), since the ministry of priests was quite sufficient for such communities. Leo reserved the prerogative of having a bishop for *civitates*.[17]

Of course, the *castella* survived. They had predated the Roman conquest[18] and would outlive it by centuries. In the Arab period a whole region south of Gafsa was called *Qasṭīliya*.[19] These *castella* of southern Byzacena were simply rural settlements of the sort the Arabs came to call *ksour*.[20] In the North African landscape, the *ksour/castella* represented the communal anarchism of the Berber mountains, huge fortified granaries which coalesced with villages or physically dominated them[21] and in any case held them together.[22] It is not certain, therefore, that the *castella* reported from other regions of the Mediterranean countryside or further afield (Noricum ripense,[23] Spain,[24] Asia Minor[25]) would have had exactly

[17] Leo, *Ep.* 12.10 (*PL* 54.654), dated 446.

[18] e.g., Livy 42.23, 'oppida castellaque agri Carthaginiensis', about 172 BC.

[19] See L. Poinssot, 'Note concernant Castella (Qastîlîa)', *BCTH* 1938–40, 415–19.

[20] Thus al-Bakrī, *Description de l'Afrique septentrionale par Abou-Obeïd-el-Bekri*, tr. Mac Guckin de Slane, ed., rev., and corr. (Paris, 1965) 101, tells us that the villages around Gafsa were called the *ksour* of Gafsa ('On désigne ces villages par le nom de *Cosour Cafsa*, "les bourgades de Cafsa"'). These had existed for centuries, for Sallust refers to the *loca munita* around Capsa and to Capsa itself as one, *Bell. Jug.*, 97.1. Strabo 17.3.12 describes Capsa as *τὸ γαζοφυλάκιον τοῦ Ἰουγούρθα*. Finally, T. Lewicki, 'Une langue romane oubliée de l'Afrique du Nord. Observations d'un arabisant', *Rocznik Orientalistyczny* 17 (1951–2) 415–80, at 463 f. (no. 61), points out that Arabic sources also referred to Ḳaṣṭīliya as al-Ḳuṣūr. (According to al-Idrīsī, most of the inhabitants of Gafsa spoke *al-latīnī al-āfarīqī* as late as the 12th cent., *Description de l'Afrique et de l'Espagne par Edrîsî. Texte arabe publiée pour la première fois . . . avec une traduction, des notes et un glossaire*, ed. R. Dozy and M. J. de Goeje (Leiden, 1866) 122, cf. Marçais, *Revue Afric.* 85 (1941) 47 and of course Lewicki's fundamental study.)

[21] A. Louis, *Tunisie du Sud: Ksars et villages de crêtes* (Paris, 1975) discusses the different relationships between *ksar* and *kalaa*, esp. 37 f.

[22] See J. Despois, 'Les greniers fortifiés de l'Afrique du Nord', *Cahiers de Tunisie* 1 (1953) 38–60 (building on previous work), and the classic monograph by Robert Montagne, *Un magasin collectif de l'Anti-Atlas: l'Agadir des Ikounka* (Thèse complémentaire présentée à faculté des lettres de l'Université de Paris) (Paris, 1930). 'Berber mountains' but with the qualification in F. Millar, 'Local Cultures in the Roman Empire: Libyan, Punic and Latin in Roman Africa', *JRS* 58 (1968) 126–34, at 128.

[23] Eugippius, *Vita Severini* 12.1 for the *castellum Cucullis* (Kuchl), and the more general reference in 17.1 to *oppida vel castella*.

[24] Hydatius, *Chron.* 91 (Tranoy, 1.130), 'plebem quae castella tutiora retinebat', in Gallaecia; obviously rural settlements not 'forts' as in Thompson, *Nottingham Medieval Studies* 21 (1977) 22, 26; cf. Hydatius, *Chron.* 49, 'Hispani per civitates et castella

[*See following page for n. 25*]

these characteristics. They were, in any case, rural settlements, the indigenous heart of the Mediterranean, and when a westerner like Jerome wished to refer to villages in Egypt he could think of no Latin term more natural than 'castellum'.[26]

In the east, villages had a more urban character. The average *kōmē* was probably far bigger than most rural settlements in the west. In the early empire Josephus claimed that even the smallest village in Galilee contained a population of over 15,000, explaining the density by the level of productivity.[27] Contrast this with Despois's assertion, in 1931, that among the huge villages of the Sahel (in Tunisia) 'some even exceeded 10,000'.[28] In Egypt, Aphrodito is certainly our best-documented example of a very large independent village in the Byzantine period. A papyrus from there refers to the 'brilliant residences of the village's long-established great landowners'.[29] These were clearly substantial houses, large and solidly built, with a certain resemblance, no doubt, to the more substantial 'villas' noted by Tchalenko on the limestone massif (in Syria). In Syrian terms Aphrodito was probably more like Brād or al-Bāra than like Dalloza or Refāde or even Ruweiha.[30] It had a total cultivated area of *c.*5,900 arouras, over 10 per cent of the district acreage.[31] Eighty-eight per cent of this was arable cultivation

residui', *Leges Visigothorum* 9.1.21, 'civitas, castellum, vicus aut villa'; John Biclar. s.a. 572.2 (*Chronica minora* 2.213), 'Leovegildus rex Cordubam civitatem diu Gothis rebellem nocte occupat . . . multasque urbes et castella interfecta rusticorum multitudine in Gothorum dominium revocat', s.a. 577.2 (p. 215), 'civitates atque castella'. For their medieval counterparts, see the fascinating book by A. Bazzama, P. Cressier, and P. Guichard, *Les Châteaux ruraux d'al-Andalus. Histoire et archéologie des ḥuṣūn du Sud-Est de l'Espagne*. Publications de Casa de Velázquez, sér. Archéologie 11 (Madrid, 1988), who note that the majority of toponyms associated with the *ḥuṣūn* are pre-Islamic (296).

[25] Pliny, *NH* 5.94: 'cetera castella XLIV inter asperos convalles latent', about Isauria; Livy 37.56: 'oppida, vici, castella, agri, qui ad Pisidiam vergunt', about the eastern parts of Caria. Livy may have known little about the Greek helots but he described them as 'iam inde antiquitus castellani, agreste genus' (a rural people who had been country dwellers from remote antiquity), cf. Briscoe, *A Commentary on Livy Books XXXIV–XXXVII* (Oxford, 1981) 92, '*castellani* are simply rural inhabitants, not defenders of strong points', and Walbank, *CR* NS 1 (1951) 99, 'country folk'.

[26] Jerome, *Ep.* 22.34: 'Habitant autem quam plurimum in urbibus et castellis' (for the most part, however, they reside in towns and *castella*).

[27] Josephus, *BJ* 3.43.

[28] J. Despois, 'Essai sur l'habitat rural du Sahel tunisien', *Annales de Géographie* 40 (1931) 259–74, esp. 259–60.

[29] *P. Cairo Masp.* I 67002 ii 23 f. (567), φανερὰ 'οἰκήματα' λαμπρὰ τῶν ἀρχαίων κτητόρων μεγάλων τῆς κώμης (the splendid houses of the long-established large landowners of the village, which stand out from the rest).

[30] G. Tchalenko, *Villages antiques de la Syrie du Nord. Le Massif de Bélus à l'époque romaine*, 3 vols. (Paris, 1953–8) 387–9.

[31] *P. Freer Aphrod.* (= *P. Freer* 08.45 a+b) 294 with *P. Cairo Masp.* I 67057 for the district figures.

(dependent on the flood). Orchards were the leading summer crop with as much as 35 per cent of the total garden area of the district. Aphrodito was full of churches, had numerous monasteries, a range of occupations, and above all a strong sense of its own autonomy.[32] The crucial fact about villages like Aphrodito is that unlike the smaller villages and estate settlements they were on the whole free from the domination of the aristocracy. The most important aristocrat known from the village was Count Ammonius. Yet in 525 his holdings on the urban account amounted to a mere fraction of the area controlled by the monastery of Apa Sourous.[33] Both *ousiai* were deeply fragmented; the monastery's holding was dispersed over forty-nine separate parcels, Ammonius' over eighteen parcels. Such fragmentation may have been a characteristic of the bigger villages. Both Theodoret and Libanius describe the large villages of the eastern Mediterranean as communities of numerous landholders, and Libanius directly contraposes these to others dominated by a single *despotēs*.[34] Tchalenko's work on the *massif calcaire* generated a typology reflecting similar divisions between rural settlements.[35] At any rate, in the east entire villages could be described as 'belonging to' a single owner. This was as true in the first century, when Josephus referred to the *kōmē* of Arous as a *ktēma* of Ptolemy, as in the sixth, when the *Life of Theodore of Sykeon* refers to whole villages (*chōria*) (in Galatia) 'belonging to the church' (τῶν διαφερόντων χωρίων τῇ ἐκκλησίᾳ).[36] In contrast to these, however, were the smaller estate-controlled settlements called *epoikia*. In the papyri employees frequently refer to the 'villages' of their landlords as 'your *epoikion*' or 'the *epoikion* of your Excellency'.[37] These were on the whole small settlements[38] so that even if there were small

[32] J. G. Keenan, 'The Aphrodito Papyri and Village Life in Byzantine Egypt', *BSAC* 26 (1984) 51–63, esp. 55 (churches), L. MacCoull, 'Notes on the Social Structure of Late Antique Aphrodito', *BSAC* 26 (1984) 65–77, esp. 71–2 (monasteries), 65–71 (occupations), *P. Cairo Masp.* I 67019 and Bell, 'An Egyptian village in the age of Justinian', *JHS* 64 (1944) 23–4 (autonomy).

[33] About 67 arouras against over 308, see *Catalogue*, Aphrodito 6c.

[34] Theodoret, *Phil. Hist.* 17.3 (*SC* 257, 2. 38), about a 'very large' village near Emesa, οὐδὲ γὰρ εἶχεν ἡ κώμη δεσπότην· αὐτοὶ δὲ ἦσαν καὶ γεωργοὶ καί δεσπόται (Nor did the village have a controlling landowner, for they themselves were both owners and cultivators), Libanius, *Or.* 47.4 (Norman, 2. 502, 510), Εἰσὶ κῶμαι μεγάλαι πολλῶν ἑκάστη δεσποτῶν (There are huge villages, each comprising many landowners), contrasted in 11 with others οἷς εἷς ὁ δεσπότης (but also others owned by a single landlord).

[35] Tchalenko, *Villages antiques*, esp. 383 ff.

[36] Josephus, *BJ* 2.69; *Vie de Théodore de Sykéon*, 75 (Festugière, 63).

[37] *P. Merton* 36.6–7 (360), *SB* VIII 9907.8, 13–14 (388), *BGU* II 364.9 (553), *SB* XVI 12485.5–6 (6c.), cf. *P. Turner* 44 (331/2) where the owner Eulogius kept Sakaon and others out of his *epoikion* which was naturally called *epoikion Eulogiou* (l.8).

[38] According to *CPR* X 45 (6c.) the *epoikion* of Eustochius (in the Fayum) contained roughly 150 inhabitants. Compare this with the Naqlun monastery a few kilometres to

villages which were not controlled by estates[39] Libanius' distinction on the whole seems valid.

The structural counterparts of the *epoikia* in the western provinces were the *vici*.[40] There is a vast amount of evidence (from Africa in particular) to associate *vici* with individual estates.[41] A famous passage in the *agrimensores* describes private owners (*privati*) in Africa controlling 'large working populations and *vici* around the central estate (*vicos circa villam*)'.[42] The *organization* of estates must have been determined crucially by their use of labour, and it is hard to believe that owners would have adopted a single pattern of labour-use across diverse ecological zones where different crops predominated and labour requirements varied correspondingly. Olive cultivation required large inputs of seasonal labour but only a small permanent staff.[43] Estates like the *fattoria* at El-Beida housed their labour force in habitations described by Catani as 'cramped and poor'.[44] Presumably these were like the *casae* of the Casas Villa Aniciorum further along the coast.[45] Arable production

the east (at a site near the present Monastery of Archangel Gabriel); *c*.631 this was said to comprise 120 monks and 200 lay inhabitants, cf. T. Derda, *Deir el-Naqlun: The Greek Papyri (P. Naqlun I)* (Warsaw, 1995) 22, J. Dobrowolski, 'The Monastic Complex of Naqlun—Topography of the Site', in P. O. Scholz, *et al.*, *Orbis Aethiopicus: Studia in honorem Stanislaus Chajnaki* (Albstadt, 1992) 309 ff.

39 G. Tate, 'La Syrie à l'époque byzantine: essai de synthèse', in J.-M. Dentzer and W. Orthmann (eds.), *Archéologie et histoire de la Syrie. 2: La Syrie de l'époque achéménide à l'avènement de l'Islam* (Saarbrücken, 1989) 97–116, esp. 106 (against Libanius).

40 See Amanda Claridge, 'Il vicus di epoca imperiale: campagne di ricerche 1987–1991', in M. G. Lauro (ed.), *Castelporziano III. Campagne di scavo e restauro 1987–1991* (Rome, 1998) 115–36, for a summary of the excavations at Vicus Augustanus Laurentium at Castelporziano near Ostia.

41 e.g. the *Tabula Peutingeriana* is full of *vici* which belonged to private landowners (*Vicus Aureli*, *Vicus Iuliani*, *Vicus Valeriani*, etc.). The *vicus Iuliani* in *Tab. Peut.* 4.2, 25 miles south of Hippo, has now turned up in Augustine, *Ep.* 23A* (419), cf. J. Desanges and S. Lancel, 'L'apport des nouvelles Lettres à la géographie historique de l'Afrique antique et l'Église d'Afrique', in *Les Lettres de Saint Augustin découvertes par Johannes Divjak* (Paris, 1983) 87–99, esp. 89. *PLRE* 1.477–9, Julianus 23, 25, 26, 37 are all possible candidates for ownership. The 'loca magnarum domorum seu fundorum' in *CTh.* 16.6.2.1 (377) were simply *vici*, cf. the *interpretatio* to *CTh.* 1.16.11 where 'per singulos agros et loca' paraphrases 'per omnium villas vicosque'.

42 *Corpus Agrimensorum Romanorum*, ed. Thulin, p. 45, 'habent autem in saltibus, privati[s] non exiguum populum plebeium et vicos circa villam in modum municipiorum' (in the *saltus*, private individuals control a substantial population of rural folk as well as village settlements around the central estate, on the pattern characteristic of entire towns).

43 See J. Poncet, *La Colonisation et l'agriculture européennes en Tunisie depuis 1881. Étude de géographie historique et économique* (Paris and The Hague, 1961) 463–73 (French estates in the Sahel).

44 E. Catani, 'I frantoi della fattoria bizantina di El-Beida', *QAL* 8 (1976) 435–48, esp. 445.

45 *Itin. Ant.* 61.2 (Cuntz, *Itineraria Romana*, 1, 1929). For the location cf. Cpt. Le

required more stable inputs of labour and a greater continuity of relationships. The 'science' of agricultural management was basically devised for owners of vineyards and arable estates who faced a more complex schedule of labour demands, combined different categories of labour, and were preoccupied with the average level of effort, problems like whether fields were properly ploughed. Arable cultivation and viticulture presupposed careful production-scheduling where delay in the completion of tasks could 'disrupt the entire task sequence'.[46] In these regions stable working communities were essential, and creating such communities was doubtless one of the major hurdles large landowners faced in countrysides still dominated by pastoralism. They seem on the whole to have succeeded, for in the late empire the countryside of Numidia, where transhumance had been strongest, comprised countless numbers of estate communities who, indeed, even identified themselves by their employer's name or the name of the estate, much as workers do in modern companies.[47] Donatism drew on the strength of these communities and gave them a wider sense of solidarity both among themselves and with the towns. With the harvest gangs who resided on the estates on a seasonal basis, they played a decisive role in the religious conflicts of the fourth century.

The North African rural landscape was a rich and complex tapestry of agricultural forms. Traditional nomadism had been hemmed in and rigidly circumscribed, so that Tertullian described the *Maurorum gentes* and the *Gaetulorum barbariae* as living 'under siege'.[48] The carving up of their lands had certainly begun by the

Boeuf, 'Notes et documents sur les voies stratégiques et sur l'occupation militaire du Sud tunisien à l'époque romaine', *BCTH*, 1903, 283–4. Isidore defines *casae* as 'agreste habitaculum palis atque virgultis arundinibusque contextum' (a rural habitation covered with stakes, cuttings, and reed-canes) (*Etym.* 15.12.1). The *mapalia* used by the transhumants who provided much of the seasonal labour were usually described as *casae*, cf. Jerome, *Commentaria in Amos*, Prol. (*PL* 25.990) 'agrestes quidem casae et furnorum similes, quas Afri appellant mapalia' (Certain rural habitations which look like ovens, which the Africans call *mapalia*), Festus 132 (Lindsay, p. 133), 'Mapalia casae Poenicae appellantur' (the indigenous African huts are called *mapalia*).

[46] Columella, *RR* 11.1.30, 'omnisque turbatus operis ordo spem totius anni frustratur' (and when the task sequence suffers a general disruption, that dashes our hopes for the entire season).

[47] Sulpicius Severus, *Ep. ad Salvium* (*CSEL* 1.254 f.) 'Volusianenses' for employees of the *fundus Volusianus*, *ILAlg.* 1.3636, Bir Bouraoui, 230s, Vesatenses (or Vasatenses) from the estate of C. Annius Anullinus.

[48] Tertullian, *Adversus Iudaeos* 7.8, 'Maurorum gentes et Gaetulorum barbariae a Romanis obsidentur, ne regionum suarum fines excedant' (The Berber tribes and Gaetulian tribesmen are under siege from the Romans, confined within the boundaries of their respective regions), recalling Berque's judgement on the French: 'And now the French advance subdivided the mountain into "bureaux", imposed rules and fixed limits; it broke up the pasture for the flocks and the sky for human beings', Jacques Berque, *French North Africa: The Maghrib between the Two World Wars*, tr. J. Stewart

early second century,[49] and would no doubt continue without respite for the remaining centuries of Roman rule. Transhumance survived and was probably—next to seasonal labour—the essential means of subsistence of the *castellani*. Within the agrarian structure the emphasis was on large-scale agricultural activity, substantial properties which were frequently controlled by members of the senatorial aristocracy.[50] These reflected varying levels of investment. The *ousia* of Count Heraclian, *comes Africae*, was valued at 2,000 lb. of gold.[51] Many African estates were associated with, or actually called *turres*. The *turris* described a form of rural architecture that was purely indigenous. Diodorus Siculus refers to the *pyrgoi* as strongholds of the native aristocracy which were located near sources of water and used basically for storage.[52] *Turres* could be confused with *castella,* doubtless because of their actual affinities, but Livy was careful to note that on one occasion Hannibal fled to his *turris* on the coast between Acholla and Thapsus,[53] and Appian notes that the African countryside was full of *pyrgoi* and *phrouria*, i.e. *turres* and *castella*.[54] It seems likely that the architectural traditions of the indigenous *pyrgoi* survived in a diffuse form to shape building styles when Roman landowners began to construct 'villas'.[55] Mosaics like one from Tabarka and the Julius mosaic from

(London, 1967) 118, referring to the Middle Atlas; see P. Trousset, 'Les bornes du Bled Segui. Nouveaux aperçus sur la centuriation romaine du Sud Tunisien', *AntAfr* 12 (1978) 125–77, for the partitioning of the tribes within 'tightly defined territorial and administrative units' (163).

[49] *ILTun.* 1653 = *CRAI* 1923, 72 (Kalaat es Senam), a 'terminatio' *inter Musulamos et Valeriam Atticilam*, part of the massive series of operations handled by L. Minicius Natalis in his drive to stabilize circuits of transhumance across the steppe region; *CIL* 8.270 = J. Nolle, *"Nundinas instituere et habere". Epigraphischen Zeugnisse zur Einrichtung und Gestaltung von ländlichen Märkten in Afrika und in der Provinz Asia* (Hildesheim, 1982), 89 ff. (Hr el Begar); the dates are 105 and 138 respectively.

[50] e.g. M. Overbeck, *Untersuchungen zum afrikanischen Senatsadel in der Spätantike* (Kallmünz, 1973).

[51] Olympiodorus 23 (*FHG*, 4.62, Blockley 2.186). This was the value of 'immoveables' and was equivalent, for example, to roughly 248 churches in the same class as the basilica of Khirbet Hassan in the Jebel Bariša (in Syria), J.-P. Sodini, 'Les églises de Syrie du Nord', in Dentzer and Orthmann (eds.), *La Syrie de l'époque achéménide*, 347–72, at 348.

[52] Diodorus Siculus 3.49, *τοῖς δὲ δυνάσταις αὐτῶν πόλεις μὲν τὸ σύνολον οὐχ ὑπάρχουσι, πύργοι δὲ πλησίον τῶν ὑδάτων, εἰς οὓς ἀποτίθενται τὰ πλεονάζοντα τῆς ὠφελείας* (their chiefs have absolutely no cities but inhabit towers located near water sources, in which they store all their surplus wealth).

[53] Livy 33.48.1, 'postero die ad mare inter Acyllam et Thapsum ad suam turrem pervenit' (he arrived next day at his *turris* on the coast between Acholla and Thapsus).

[54] Appian, *Libyca* 101 (Viereck, Roos, Gabba, 1.270), *Λἰβύων δὲ τοῖς ἐς πύργους καὶ φρούρια, ἃ πολλὰ ἦν ἐν τῇ χώρᾳ, καταφεύγουσιν κτλ.* (some of the Africans took refuge in the numerous towers and castles strewn throughout the countryside).

[55] Cf. T. Sarnowski, *Les Représentations de villas sur les mosaïques africaines tardives* (Warsaw, 1978).

Carthage give us a rough idea of what these domesticated *turres* may have looked like in the late empire, since these mosaics are usually dated to the late fourth or early fifth century.[56] But the character of estates as well as their layout, appearance, size, etc. must have varied enormously. Ammianus describes the *fundus Petrensis* in the Soummam valley as 'built in the style of a city'.[57] To understand this description one has to look at the *agadir* of Morocco,[58] or read the Arab geographer Idrīsī's description of Qalaʿa in the eleventh century, before its destruction.[59] The *fundus Gaionatis* likewise was an *agadir*-type estate, 'muro circumdatum valido, receptaculum Maurorum tutissimum'.[60] The families who controlled these estates were clearly a sort of aristocracy exercising influence over a vast region between the Chélif and the Soummam valleys.[61] Yet it is hard to imagine a world more remote from the dazzling coastal villas of Silin, which in turn differed completely, according to Ricotti, from the type of villa depicted at Tabarka or Carthage.[62] It seems important to retain this sense of diversity, and not flatten the countryside in abstractions like 'fortified estate'.

The 'Cycle' of the Late Empire

The late empire has traditionally been seen as a period of economic decline. Thus Rostovtzeff wrote:

> The salient trait of the economic life of the late Roman Empire was gradual impoverishment. The poorer the people became, the more primitive grew the

[56] K. M. D. Dunbabin, *The Mosaics of Roman North Africa: Studies in Iconography and Patronage* (Oxford, 1978) 119–22 and 252, 271 in the Catalogue.

[57] Ammianus 29.5.13, 'quem Salmaces dominus (Firmi frater) in modum urbis exstruxit' (which its owner Salmaces, Firmus' brother, had built in the style [or, on the scale] of a city); cf. Ch. 7, n. 5.

[58] J. Jacques-Meunié, *Greniers citadelles au Maroc*, 2 vols. (Paris, 1951), with excellent photographs.

[59] Al-Idrīsī, *Kitāb nuzhat al-muštāq fi'ikhtirāq al-āfāq*, ed. R. Dozy and M. J. De Goeje (Leiden, 1866) 91 = *Description de l'Afrique et de l'Espagne par Edrîsî. Texte arabe publiée pour la première fois . . . avec une traduction, des notes et un glossaire*, tr. R. Dozy and M. J. de Goeje (Leiden, 1866) 106–7. Qalʿa (of the Beni Hammād) lay further south, in the Hodna region, cf. Gsell, *Atlas*, f.25 (Msila), 92. Idrīsī describes it as 'adossée à une grande montagne qui la domine et qui est entourée de tous côtés par les murailles de la ville' (p. 107). The site is described in Playfair, *Handbook for Travellers in Algeria and Tunis*, 251.

[60] Ammianus, 29.5.25, 'surrounded by a strong wall, a remarkably safe haven for the Mauri'.

[61] See G. Camps, 'De Masuna à Koceila. Les destinées de la Maurétanie aux VIe et VIIe siècles', *Histoire et Archéologie de l'Afrique du Nord. IIe Colloque Internationale* = *BCTH* 19B (1983) 307–25, esp. 309.

[62] E. Salza Prina Ricotti, 'Le ville maritime di Silin (Leptis Magna)', *RPARA* 43 (1970–1) 135–63, esp. 162.

economic life of the Empire. Commerce decayed, not only because of piracy and barbarian inroads, but mainly because customers disappeared. The best clients, the city *bourgeoisie*, decreased constantly in numbers and in purchasing power. The peasants lived in extreme poverty and reverted to an almost pure 'house economy', each home producing for itself what it needed.[63]

In 1980 Hopkins wrote, 'The Late Empire witnessed a significant downturn in trading, deeper in the third century A.D. ... than in the fourth century A.D.'; 'The decline in the exaction of money taxes brought about a decline in trade.'[64] In the 1970s Perry Anderson argued: 'Throughout most provinces, urban trade and industry progressively declined: *there was a gradual but unmistakeable ruralization of the Empire*.'[65] In fact, Rostovtzeff even characterized the late empire as a 'new state based on the peasants and the country'.[66] The assumption here is that landowners pulled out of the urban economy. The dogma that the aristocracy and ruling classes abandoned the cities in a historical rearguard action, a sort of huge primordial return to the countryside, is improbable in itself and unsupported by much of the archaeological evidence for continued urban vitality. But the 'moment of truth' in that theory is the renewed growth and expansion of the late Roman countryside. Our most detailed survey of rural establishments in the western provinces refers to the 'rapid development of rich and sumptuous country establishments' and the 'spectacular' and 'feverish' activity of construction which brought an 'extraordinary apogee' to the rural areas of Spain and Portugal in the early decades of the fourth century.[67] Surveying similar establishments in a very different part of Europe, Biró states that 'In the fourth century the concentration of agricultural estates spread all over the territory of Pannonia.' 'Large villas built earlier are used in the fourth century as well; they were expanded and provided with mosaics . . . *The flourishing of Pannonian villa-farms took place in the years between 300–370*.'[68] In the countryside around Carthage, rural settlement seems to have expanded in the fifth century and reached a peak in the sixth.[69] At

[63] Rostovtzeff, *SEHRE* 1.523–4.

[64] K. Hopkins, 'Taxes and Trade in the Roman Empire (200 B.C.–A.D. 400)', *JRS* 70 (1980) 105, 116.

[65] P. Anderson, *Passages from Antiquity to Feudalism* (London, 1974) 93 (emphasis mine).

[66] Rostovtzeff, *SEHRE* 1.506 (calling it a 'new phenomenon in history'). On the background to Rostovtzeff's 'peculiar vision of antiquity', see B. D. Shaw, 'Under Russian Eyes', *JRS* 82 (1992) 216–28.

[67] J.-G. Gorges, *Les Villas hispano-romaines. Inventaire et problématiques archéologiques* (Paris, 1979) 47–9.

[68] M. Biró 'Roman Villas in Pannonia', *AArchHung* 26 (1974) 23–57, esp. 53, 52.

[69] J. A. Greene, 'Une reconnaissance archéologique dans l'arrière-pays de la Carthage

the other end of the Mediterranean, the fourth to sixth centuries were a period of remarkable rural expansion. In Greece, a series of regional survey projects have demonstrated a clear pattern of the reoccupation of the countryside in the late Roman period.[70] Further east, the Hauran would see 'major Byzantine period occupation'.[71] For example, the Hesban region in central Transjordan 'witnessed more widespread occupation in the Byzantine period than in any other era'.[72] In the villages of the southern Hauran there was a rapid proliferation of church building in the third quarter of the sixth century, signifying the astonishing prosperity of the areas around Bostra throughout the sixth and early seventh century.[73] In southern Syria, villages like Nawa and Kafr Shams saw the construction of substantial rural houses in the Byzantine period, described by Villeneuve as 'grandes maisons rurales'.[74] The Hauran as a whole flourished under Justinian, recovering rapidly from the plague.[75] Further north, in the massifs between Antioch, Chalcis, and Apamea, cash poured into the villages through the large-scale trade in olive oil. There was enough wealth in circulation, in fact mainly in the late sixth/early seventh centuries, for the churches to accumulate vast quantities of precious metals with donations drawn 'from people of every social level'.[76] Tchalenko notes that despite the repeated disasters which struck the urban sector in the course of the sixth century there was still considerable prosperity in the

antique', in A. Ennabli (ed.), *Pour sauver Carthage. Exploration et conservation de la cité punique, romaine et byzantine* (Paris and Tunis, 1992) 195–7, esp. 197.

70 S. Alcock, *Graecia Capta: The Landscapes of Roman Greece* (Cambridge, 1993) ch. 2; J. Bintliff, 'The Roman Countryside in Central Greece: Observations and Theories from the Boeotia Survey (1978–1987)', in Graeme Barker and John Lloyd (eds.), *Roman Landscapes: Archaeological Survey in the Mediterranean Region* (London, 1991) 122–32, esp. 126 ff.; M. H. Jameson, C. N. Runnels, and T. H. van Andel, *A Greek Countryside: The Southern Argolid from Prehistory to the Present Day* (Stanford, Calif., 1994) 400 ff., 554.

71 G. King, C. J. Lenzen, and G. O. Rollefson, 'Survey of Byzantine and Islamic Sites in Jordan. Second Season Report, 1981', *ADAJ* 27 (1983) 385–433, esp. 430.

72 R. D. Ibach Jr., *Archaeological Survey of the Hesban Region: Catalogue of Sites and Characterization of Periods* (Berrien Springs, Mich., 1987) 183.

73 M. Sartre, *Bostra. Des origines à l'Islam* (Paris, 1985) 119 ff., esp. 135.

74 F. Villeneuve, 'L'économie rurale et la vie des campagnes dans le Hauran antique (Ier siècle av.J.-C.–VIIe siècle ap.J.-C.). Une approche', in J.-M.Dentzer (ed.), *Hauran I. Recherches archéologiques sur la Syrie du Sud à l'époque hellénistique et romaine. Première partie* (Paris, 1985) esp. 106 ff., 113.

75 M. Sartre, 'Le peuplement et le développement du Hawran antique', in Dentzer (ed.), *Hauran I* 197 ff.

76 M. Mundell Mango, 'The Origins of the Syrian Ecclesiastical Silver Treasures of the Sixth–Seventh Centuries', in N. Duval, F. Baratte (eds.), *Argenterie romaine et byzantine. Actes de la Table Ronde, Paris 11–13 octobre 1983* (Paris, 1988) 165. 'The majority of the donors were probably ordinary people' (p. 168). On p. 168 she notes that the Syrian village treasures come mainly from 540–640.

countryside; something like a third of the monuments (on the limestone massif) were constructed, expanded, or reconstructed in the sixth century.[77] Thus revenues from oil were obviously still flowing. In Cyrenaica, too, Catani's careful reconstruction of the Byzantine *fattoria* at El-Beida implies continuing investments in the third quarter of the sixth century (and, as he says, no apparent reason to suppose that production declined or was discontinued in the first half of the seventh century).[78] A similar reorganizaton occurred at the late Roman villa of Vilauba in north-eastern Catalunya since 'Phase III' there involved the 'building of a more efficient press, with the levelling of the surrounding buildings', again in the later sixth century. 'The pressing arrangements demonstrate the continuing importance of olive oil to the villa.'[79] At the Favara villa in contrada Saraceno, on Sicily's southern shore, the earthquake of 365 had precipitated the conversion of a largely residential complex into an 'industrially organized farm', and this transformation was later re-emphasized by further reorganization and investments in production in the first half of the sixth century.[80] On this estate, the staple commodity was grain. In Egypt the huge wine factory excavated in the centre of Marea on the southern coast of Lake Mareotis was surely active in the sixth century.[81] The intense boom which stimulated investments in wine growing throughout the Byzantine period[82] lasted well beyond the sixth century, however. Remote

[77] Tchalenko, *Villages antiques,* 430. For the opulence of the towns, see J.-Ch. Balty, 'Apamée au VIe siècle. Témoignages archéologiques de la richesse d'une ville', in *HREB* 79–96, and 'Notes sur l'habitat romain, byzantin et arabe d'Apamée: rapport de synthèse', *Actes du III Colloque Apamée de Syrie* (Brussels, 1984) 471–503.

[78] Catani, 'I frantoi della fattoria bizantina', esp. 446, 'il frantoio epigeo e quello costruito nella terza fase di ampliamento della villa, essendo contemporanei, risalirebbero entrambi al terzo quarto del VI secolo . . . La loro attività *perdurò sicuramente nella prima metà del VII secolo*, fino alla conquista dell'intero territorio da parte degli Arabi (643 d.C.) e forse anche dopo tale evento'. El Beida now figures as Siret el Giamel in E. Catani, 'Lucerne fittili dalla fattoria bizantina di Siret el Giamel in Cirenaica: tipologia ed inquadramento cronologico', *L'Africa Romana* 6/2 (1988) 459–74, where the complex is said to have been in a state of 'advanced decline' by the period of the Arab conquest (p. 470).

[79] R. F. J. Jones, S. J. Keay, *et al.*, 'The Late Roman Villa of Vilauba and its Context: A First Report on Field-Work and Excavation in Catalunya, North-East Spain, 1978–81', *The Antiquaries Journal* 62 (1982) 245–82, esp. 278–9, 'Phase III saw the probable introduction of a press for oil in the fifth century but the later sixth century produced an even more radical reorganisation and the building of a more efficient press etc.'

[80] G. Castellana and B. E. McConnell, 'A Rural Settlement of Imperial Roman and Byzantine Date in contrada Saraceno near Agrigento, Sicily', *American J. of Archaeology* 94 (1990) 25–44, esp. 35 ff., 42–3.

[81] F. el-Fakharani, 'Recent Excavations at Marea in Egypt', in *Das römisch-byzantinische Ägypten. Akten des internationalen Symposions 26.–30. September 1978 in Trier* (Mainz am Rhein, 1983) 175–86.

[82] Two-thirds, 67 per cent, of all wine leases which survive on papyrus are from the 6th or 7th cent.

villages in Middle Egypt exported wine to Constantinople as late as the second quarter of the seventh century.[83] In Palestine, these 'late' investments are represented by the large wine presses of the Byzantine period[84] and the remains of substantial or middle-sized estates.[85] The country around Ascalon became the centre of a flourishing wine industry.[86] Wine dominated the slopes of the Jebel Hauran to the east,[87] was found along the banks of the Euphrates,[88] was widespread in the seventh-century Fayum,[89] and dominant in the Mareotic region, extending 'well beyond along the coast to the west'.[90] Silk became a major enterprise in the course of the seventh century and exemplifies the complex forms of integration between

[83] M. J. Luzzatto, 'P. Vat. gr. 52: trasporto di vino dall'Egitto a Costantinopoli nel VII sec. D.C.', *ZPE* 114 (1996) 153 ff., brilliantly elucidating *P. Flor.* XVIII 3 (7c.). From Alexandria the cargo would be carried in a 'dekahemerion', presumably a swift, small vessel. The type of jars used may also be surmised. *P. Vat. gr.* 52.15–16 refers to a freight charge of one solidus per batch of 750 *knidia* of wine. As the total quantity involved was 5,826 *knidia* of pure wine (l. 6), this would have meant a total freight cost of 7.768 solidi. At a hypothetical wine price of 30 *knidia* to the solidus, this was exactly 4 per cent of the value of the cargo. Second, assuming that the *knidion* in question had an average capacity of 5 *sextarii*, i.e. that the real price was 150 *sextarii* to the solidus (e.g. *P. Oxy.* XVI 1920.17, late 6c.), the total capacity of the cargo would have been 15,934.11 litres of wine. This quantity could have been carried in *c.*5,900 (5,901½, to be precise) Egloff 174 amphorae (capacity = 2.7 litres) or in 3,000 Egloff 173 amphorae (with an average capacity of 5.3 litres). Both wine jars have a date range in the 7th cent. (see M. Egloff, *Kellia. La poterie copte. Quatres siècles d'artisanat et d'échanges en Basse-Égypte*, 2 vols. (Geneva, 1977) 1.114–15), but the Upper Egyptian provenance of the former may make it a more likely candidate. In either case, one is dealing with the famous 'carrot-shaped' wine containers which are 'regularly present in small quantities' in the excavations at Saraçane in Istanbul, J. W. Hayes, *Excavations at Saraçhane in Istanbul* (Princeton, 1992) 2. 66–7.

[84] Y. Hirschfeld, 'Ancient Wine Presses in the Park of Aijalon', *IEJ* 33 (1983) 207–18; I. Roll and E. Ayalon, 'Two Large Wine Presses in the Red Soil Regions of Israel', *Palestine Exploration Quarterly* 113 (1981) 111–25, and their statement, 'The size and number of these sites increased greatly in the late Byzantine period (sixth–seventh centuries A.D.)' (at 123).

[85] Y. Israel, 'Ashqelon', *Excavations and Surveys in Israel* 13 (1995) 100–5 (substantial), Y. Hirschfeld and R. Birger-Calderon, 'Early Roman and Byzantine Estates near Caesarea', *IEJ* 41 (1991) 81–111, esp. 100 ff. (middle-sized). The so-called third mile site near Ashkelon exemplifies the in-house manufacturing of jars 'in very large workshops on the premises', see the general survey by Hirschfeld, 'Farms and villages in Byzantine Palestine', *DOP* 51 (1997) 33–71, esp. 69 f.

[86] B. L. Johnson and L. E. Stager, 'Ashkelon: Wine Emporium of the Holy Land', in S. Gitin (ed.), *Recent Excavations in Israel* (Boston, 1995) 95 ff. (My thanks to Sean Kingsley for this reference.)

[87] Villeneuve, 'L'économie rurale', 123 f.

[88] See n. 3 above.

[89] See *Catalogue*, Fayum 7c.

[90] W. A. Daszewski *et al.*, 'Excavations at Marina el-Alamein 1987–1988', *MDAIK* 46 (1990) 15–51, at 46. See M. Rodziewicz, 'Classification of Wineries from Mareotis', in J.-Y. Empereur (ed.), *Commerce et artisanat dans l'Alexandrie hellénistique et romaine. Actes du colloque d'Athènes . . . 11–12 décembre 1988*. BCH Supplement 33 (École Française d'Athènes, 1998) 27–36, and Feisal el-Ashmawi, 'Pottery kiln and wine-factory at Burg el-Arab', in the same volume, 62 ff.

private capital and the Byzantine regulatory system. It has been claimed that the trade was run by 'wealthy individuals at the head of powerful economic organizations'.[91] In short, from one end of the Mediterranean to the other, the late empire signified a 'late' expansionary cycle which persisted (if one sees it as a 'long' cycle) till the middle decades of the seventh century. If the aristocracy returned to its estates, as Rostovtzeff believed, this was certainly not for lack of urban markets.

The general implication of the late Roman expansion of settlement is a demographic upswing. In his recent book *The Roman Near East*, Fergus Millar has drawn attention to the extraordinary fact of 'extensive rural settlement' throughout the Roman Near East, the 'dense network of villages and small settlements which can be shown to have covered large parts of the region'.[92] The archaeological record is now beginning to suggest that settlement densities increased sharply through most of late antiquity. Thus Palestine appears to have witnessed a demographic peak in the late sixth/early seventh centuries, if site ratios are a reliable indication.[93] In Egypt, the evidence of pottery in the area around Tell el-Fara'in/Bouto, in the central Delta, suggests 'a fairly dense occupation in the Byzantine period'.[94] Jordan, it has been said, was 'intensively settled in the Byzantine period', e.g. for the wadi el-Ḥasā, south of the Dead Sea, 'The Byzantine period was apparently the one of greatest population and the greatest number of settlements in the area surveyed.'[95] In Syria, in the villages of the limestone massif, the mid-fourth to mid-sixth centuries were a period of general demographic advance; Tate has calculated that the number of rooms in the houses he surveyed increased by a factor of four and a half between 330 and 550.[96] Finally, the 'resurgence' of the late Roman

[91] N. Oikonomidès, 'Silk Trade and Production in Byzantium from the Sixth to the Ninth Century: The Seals of Kommerkiarioi', *DOP* 40 (1986) 33–53, esp. 33–43.

[92] F. Millar, *The Roman Near East 31 BC–AD 337* (Cambridge, Mass., and London, 1993) 16–18.

[93] C. Dauphin, *La Palestine byzantine: peuplement et populations*, 3 vols. (BAR International Series 726, 1998), 1.79, who refers to a 'demographic explosion'. Dauphin's consecutive notion of a large-scale demographic collapse in the decades following the Persian invasion of 614 and in the 'Arab epoch' is less certain, however, for reasons related to the dating of sites, e.g. P. Mayerson, 'Some Observations on the Negev Archaeological Survey', *IEJ* 46 (1996) 100–7.

[94] P. Ballet and T. von der Way, 'Exploration archéologique de Bouto et de sa région (époques romaine et byzantine)', *MDAIK* 49 (1993) 1–22.

[95] M. Piccirillo, 'Rural Settlements in Byzantine Jordan', in A.Hadidi (ed.), *Studies in the History and Archaeology of Jordan*, 2 (Department of Antiquities, Amman, 1985) 257–61, citing B. MacDonald, 'The Wadi el Hasa survey 1979: a preliminary report', *ADAJ* 24 (1980) 179.

[96] G. Tate, 'Les campagnes de la Syrie du Nord à l'époque proto-byzantine', *HREB* 63–77, esp. 74–5, and his book, *Les Campagnes de la Syrie du Nord du IIe au VIIe*

countryside under the impact of wider economic forces[97] and the powerful restructuring of social relations[98] is also evident in the much greater continuity of habitation between the late antique and post-Roman/post-Byzantine phases. This is clear from Geoffrey King's work on Jordan,[99] and the scattered evidence of individual sites.[100]

To sum up, the sources describe a richly variegated countryside with different kinds of villages and smaller settlements. *Castella* were widespread in the western and central Mediterranean, indigenous to their rural pattern, which necessitated substantial storage facilities. By contrast, the *vici* were usually estate villages, under private or imperial ownership, as the *casae* certainly were. The eastern countryside was both more densely settled and more fertile, with large villages which were difficult to distinguish from towns. The expansion of Roman business and landed interests contributed to a dramatic growth of agricultural enterprise, but again, estates differed considerably in their physical characteristics and form, from, for example, the huge integrated farms on the wheat plains of northern Gaul (the rich plains of the Paris basin)[101] or the massive 'walled' estates in the mountains of Kabylia to the irrigated orchards around Arsinoe, in the seventh century,[102] and the wine estates

siècle. Un exemple d'expansion démographique et économique à la fin de l'antiquité (Paris, 1992).

[97] See Ch. 3 in particular.

[98] See Chs. 5 and 6.

[99] G. R. D. King, 'Settlement Patterns in Islamic Jordan: The Umayyads and their Use of the Land', in *Studies in the History and Archaeology of Jordan*, 4 (Amman, 1992) 369–75; G. R. D. King, C. J. Lenzen, *et al.*, 'Survey of Byzantine and Islamic Sites in Jordan. Third Season Preliminary Report (1982). The Southern Ghōr', *ADAJ* 31 (1987) 439–59, esp. 451; King, Lenzen, and G. O. Rollefson, 'Survey' (see n. 71) 430; and H. I. MacAdam, 'Settlements and Settlement Patterns in Northern and Central Transjordania, ca. 550–ca. 750', in G. R. D. King and Averil Cameron (eds.), *The Byzantine and Early Islamic Near East. 2: Land Use and Settlement Patterns* (Princeton, 1994) 49–93, esp. 91.

[100] e.g. R. F. J. Jones, 'End of the Roman Countryside in the Iberian Peninsula', in R. F. J. Jones, J. H. F. Bloemers, S. L. Dyson, and M. Biddle (eds.), *First Millennium Papers. Western Europe in the First Millennium AD* (BAR International Series 401, 1988) 159–73, esp. 163 (Catalan villa sites); H. Broise and Y. Thébert, *Recherches archéologiques franco-tunisiennes à Bulla Regia,* 2/1 (Rome, 1993) 394 f.; J. B. Ward-Perkins, J. H. Little, and D. J. Mattingly, 'Town Houses at Ptolemais, Cyrenaica: A Summary Report of Survey and Excavation Work in 1971, 1978–1979', *Libyan Studies* 17 (1986) 109–53, esp. 152.

[101] Pliny, *NH* 18.296, Palladius, *Opus agric.* 7.2.2 ff., both referring to the use of superior harvesting machines 'on the large farms of the Gallic provinces' (Pliny) or the 'flatter parts of Gaul' (Palladius). See G. Raepsaet, 'Les prémices de la mécanisation agricole entre Seine et Rhin de l'antiquité au 13e siècle', *Annales ESC* 50 (1995) 911–42, esp. 918–28, for the technologies and a possible geographical reference.

[102] *SB* I 4483 (29.5.621, *BL* 8.309), *P. Ross-Georg.* III 55 (24.4.630, *BL* 8.291), *SB* XVI 12481 (28.11.668, *BL* 9.284).

along the Euphrates. These contrasts were embedded in other, larger, juxtapositions[103]—of landscape, climate, the management of water,[104] the concentration or dispersal of human activity, and the incessant shaping and reshaping of the land, as well as cultural factors. Against these backgrounds, the fourth century inaugurated a period of remarkable rural expansion, which showed no significant let up till well into the seventh century, strongly indicating that the once dominant pessimist historiographies of the late empire blended the intellectual transcription of history with a large element of cultural construction. The next chapter looks at two major influences on the modern history of late antiquity, contrasting their conceptions of the period as well as their particular ways of seeking to understand the past.

[103] See esp. P. Horden and N. Purcell, *The Corrupting Sea: A Study of Mediterranean History* (Blackwell, 2000), on the peculiar fragmentation of the Mediterranean and the human responses to it.

[104] J. Birebent, *Aquae Romanae: recherches d'hydraulique romaine dans l'Est algérien* (Algiers, 1964); P. Trousset, 'Les oasis présahariennes dans l'antiquité: partage de l'eau et division du temps', *AntAfr* 22 (1986) 163–93; C. Meuret, 'Le règlement de *Lamasba*: des tables de conversion appliqueés à l'irrigation', *AntAfr* 32 (1996) 87–112; P. Squatriti, *Water and Society in Early Medieval Italy, AD 400–1000* (Cambridge, 1998).

CHAPTER 2

Weber, Mickwitz, and the Economic Characterization of Late Antiquity

Weber's 'Die sozialen Gründe des Untergangs der antiken Kultur'

In 'Finance, Coinage and Money from the Severans to Constantine', which he published in 1975, Michael Crawford summed up the economic background of the late empire in the following terms: 'Empire-wide, the debasement of the silver coinage brought about a move to the collection of taxes and the payment of soldiers and officials largely in kind . . . *The monetary circle simply became increasingly meaningless*. It was doubtless completely abolished in the end by Theodosius I.'[1] Crawford's assertion illustrates an important fact: the crux of the theory of a late imperial economic decline has always been some set of postulates about the monetary history of the fourth century. Inflation and debasement symptomized the inexorable decline of monetary economy, the reversion to a more primitive stage, precursor of some medieval barbarism. The deep-rooted character of this conception, its almost axiomatic nature, is strikingly obvious in the fact that even Eduard Meyer (who, of course, was otherwise only too inclined to advocate a wholesale 'modernization' of the Ancient Economy) accepted the theory. For him there was a direct causal link between the monetary regression of the late empire and the evolution of that generalized compulsion which was the hallmark of late imperial political and social life.[2] Like his own generation and the following one, Meyer could only perceive the 'late antique' through classical eyes. At any rate, if the economic basis of this 'methodological classicism' is the theory of late imperial economic decline, the systematic rejection of its premises

[1] M. Crawford, 'Finance, Coinage and Money from the Severans to Constantine', *ANRW* 2.2 (1975) 560–93, at 570f., emphasis mine.

[2] E. Meyer, 'Die wirtschaftliche Entwicklung des Altertums', *Jahrbüchern für Nationalökonomie und Statistik IX*, repr. in *Kleine Schriften*, 1^2 (Halle, 1924) 79–168, esp. 158.

must start with this theory and with its monetary postulates. It is obvious, however, that no inversion will be possible—one cannot supersede the pessimism of traditional historiography with some untenable optimism. The problem seems insoluble and we should perhaps begin by asking: is there a way out of this dilemma?

That way, I believe, was first outlined in the study which Gunnar Mickwitz published in 1932. Mickwitz, it has been claimed, was a Weberian. The claim is not true, however. *Geld und Wirtschaft* does refer to Weber at one point, but in a footnote, and that says, 'The theory of a third century reversion to natural economy actually stems from Weber's *Römische Agrargeschichte*'[3] (i.e. the published version of Weber's thesis, which Mommsen supervised). Now Mickwitz himself was totally opposed to any theory of this sort, for that or for the succeeding century. He emphatically rejected the theory that the late antique world was characterized by generalized economic decline. Weber had been decisively influenced by Bücher, who in fact believed that the modern categories of 'commodity', 'price', 'wages', 'profits', etc. were entirely inapplicable to the ancient world.[4] Bücher's construction lacked any empirical basis, but then, as he explained to Meyer, an economist was under no obligation to take history seriously, for economics was more interested in pure concepts. The 'concept' which Bücher developed, that of the 'closed' 'Household Economy', drove a deep gulf between the ancient and modern, and made it difficult to see how ancient economic history could be studied at all. In fact, it was Weber who gave life and respectability to Bücher's fantasies about economic evolution. Even in his last (and greatest) work, Weber described Bücher's *Entstehung der Volkswirtschaft* as a 'fundamentally important work'.[5] He had always taken Bücher seriously. Bücher was aware of this and in later editions of *Die Entstehung* there are, diplomatically enough, references to Weber as the obvious authority on the Roman world. Bücher's influence was to prove

[3] Mickwitz, *Geld und Wirtschaft*, 3 n. 4.

[4] K. Bücher, *Die Entstehung der Volkswirtschaft. Vorträge und Versuche* (4th edn.; Tübingen, 1904), 133 = 84–5 (1st edn.), 'keine Waren, keinen Preis, keinen Güterumlauf, keine Einkommensverteilung und demgemäss keinen Arbeitslohn, keinen Unternehmergewinn, keinen Zins als besondere Einkommensarten'. Moreover, when Bücher says earlier in the same passage that 'If . . . the expression capital is restricted to means of production, then it must in any case be limited to tools and implements, the so-called fixed capital. What modern theorists usually designate circulating capital is in the independent household economy *merely a store of consumption goods* in process of preparation' (*Industrial Evolution*, tr. S. M. Wickett (London, 1901) 112), he simply forgets moneylending.

[5] Max Weber, *Economy and Society: An Outline of Interpretive Sociology*, ed. G. Roth and C. Wittich, 2 vols. (University of California, 1978) 1.114–15.

a catastrophic limitation on Weber's ability to distil an accurate picture of the Roman economic background. Weber's most coherent exposition was undoubtedly the Freiburg lecture of 1896, the essay entitled 'Die sozialen Gründe des Untergangs der antiken Kultur', and though Weber modified some of his emphases later, he never abandoned the essential argument propounded there. In the following summary, I have isolated the propositions which I think are crucial to his argument (abstracting from the numerous subsidiary channels the essay drives into) and indicated these by numerals in square brackets.[6]

In Weber's topography of classical culture, the countryside is a merely latent background, a reservoir of natural economy behind the pure forms of ancient life, the great cities of the Mediterranean which were the active centres of its cultural and economic evolution.[7] So Weber refers to 'die Naturalwirtschaft der barbarischen Bauern des Binnenlandes' (p. 292), and supposes that the reassertion of this world, suppressed by urban economy, will only come with the decline of antiquity. This image strikes him as so obvious that it functions, in some sense, as his only axiom. Classical civilization was urban, coastal, and slave-based. Weber thus argues, [1] 'the organisation of slave labour forms the indispensable basis (*Unterbau*) of Roman society' (p. 296). The generalization is massive, unqualified. [2] Because rural estates are the essential form of wealth in this society, the basis of all other economic activity, the great agricultural establishments of the late republic and early empire are supreme models for the study of this type of organization (p. 296). In the economy of these estates, high-value crops (vines, olives, etc.) displaced arable production to soils of inferior quality. Production of foodgrains was generally unprofitable, Weber claims,

[6] G. E. M. de Ste. Croix, *The Class Struggle in the Ancient Greek World* (London, 1981) 85 calls the 'Soziale Gründe' Weber's 'best piece of historical writing'. D. Vera, 'Forme e funzioni della rendita fondiaria nella tarda antichità', in *SRIT* 1, 373–4 refers to Weber's 'celebrated essay on the fall of ancient civilisation' and says he accepts its theses for the western part of the empire. Mazzarino has a sympathetic but balanced review in *La fine del mondo antico* (Milan, 1959) 147–61. The best English translation of the essay is C. Mackauer's in *The Journal of General Education* 5 (Oct. 1950) 75–88.

[7] For recent discussions of Weber's work on antiquity, see E. Lo Cascio, 'Appunti zu Weber "teorico" dell'economia greco-romana', *Fenomenologia e società* 5 (1982) 123–44, and 'Weber e il "capitalismo antico"', in M. Losito and P. Schiera, *Max Weber e le scienze sociali del suo tempo* (Bologna, 1988) 401–21; L. Capogrossi Colognesi, *Economie antiche e capitalismo moderno. La sfida di Max Weber* (Rome and Bari, 1990), especially interesting; and J. Love, *Antiquity and Capitalism: Max Weber and the Sociological Foundations of Roman Civilization* (London and New York, 1991). Momigliano discussed Weber repeatedly in various essays, notably, 'Max Weber and Eduard Meyer: Apropos of City and Country in Antiquity', in *Sesto Contributo alla Storia degli Studi Classici e del Mondo Antico*, 2 vols. (Rome, 1980) 1.285–93, and 'After Gibbon's *Decline and Fall*', ibid. 1.265–84.

besides, slave labour was psychologically unsuitable for these types of cultivation.[8] This entailed a differentiation of the forms of organization which governed the two sorts of production: landowners would lease out the arable but produce the high-value crops on a centralized basis. Now, it is this 'centralized' production which interests Weber. So, [3] 'The estate establishment is of a plantation-type (Der Gutsbetrieb ist plantagenartig) and the estate workers are slaves (und die Gutsarbeiter sind Sklaven)' (p. 297). [4] The internal life of this plantation-like estate is organized on the model of a barracks (p. 297), with labour subjected to a rigid military discipline (p. 298: 'Die Arbeit ist streng militärisch diszipliniert'). This is the decisive feature of work organization in Roman landownership. The slave workforce leads an existence deprived of family life. The crucial consequence of this is the inability of the workforce to reproduce itself. With high levels of exploitability [5] this entails a rapid absolute consumption of labour power and the crucial need for a slave market as the 'indispensable presupposition of slave barracks geared to market production' (p. 298). And here, significantly, Weber adds, 'We thus come to a turning-point in the evolution of ancient civilisation' (p. 299). That is to say, the great problem of the decline of Roman power is already looming on Weber's horizon. So let me halt the summary at this point and return to the image Weber has developed.

Weber's notion that the type of work discipline which characterized the Roman estate was specifically determined by its use of slave labour, I think, misconstrues the logic of Roman estate organization. Tight control over the execution of jobs and maximal supervision of the workforce were more general principles of Roman work organization and implied a type of discipline which extended to all sections of the labour force, including hired labour.[9] But by reconstruing the underlying logic of this managerialism in the more specific guise of a logic peculiar to the deployment of slave labour,

[8] See W. Scheidel, 'Grain Cultivation in the Villa Economy of Roman Italy', in J. Carlsen (ed.), *Land Use in the Roman Empire* (Rome, 1994) 159 ff. for a rebuttal of this argument, and M. S. Spurr, *Arable Cultivation in Roman Italy c.200 BC–c.AD 100* (JRS Monographs No. 3, 1986) 133–40, on 'slave-staffed arable estates'.

[9] Columella, *RR* 3.13.11–13 wanted tighter controls through sample checks and the use of measuring devices; for one of these, which local farmers called *ciconia*, he produced a design modification that would enable landowners to argue their case for a better quality of trenching. In Columella's example the contractor seems to have no latitude in determining the way the job is done; the method is predetermined and the work (based on contract labour) tightly supervised. Cf. Columella, *RR* 2.4.3 (ploughing), Palladius, *Opus agricult.* 2.3.2 (ploughing), 2.10.4 (hoeing), and Carlo Poni's fundamental work on Bologna in the 18th cent., *Gli aratri e l'economia agraria nel bolognese dal XVII al XIX secolo* (Bologna, 1963), for the struggle over ploughing.

Weber was able to posit a form of enterprise which never actually existed. He called this type of organisation 'plantation-like' and throughout his life referred repeatedly to 'the Roman plantation'. It is important to realize, however, that Weber was discussing a purely imaginary entity, since there is no evidence to show that any form of large-scale enterprise even approximately resembled the plantations of early modern mercantilism. The physical concentration of large groups of unfree workers into common production sites does not, of course, add up to a 'plantation'.

Weber's assumptions about foodgrains as a subsistence economy are also hard to reconcile with the systematic landowner opposition to price controls (*vilitas*). The size of the marketable surplus in foodgrains is an area of total obscurity, but a simple example illustrates the point. We know from the 'Cadastre d'Aphroditô' published recently by Gascou and MacCoull that the arable area of Aphrodito *c.*525 was 5,200 arouras.[10] Since much of this land was ἄνυδρος, that is, without irrigation equipment and dependent solely on the flood, it would not be unrealistic to estimate average arable productivity at, say, not more than 10 artabas to the aroura.[11] With the usual rate of deduction for seed, this would yield a total net output of 46,800 artabas. Now at this date Aphrodito's cash payments (by way of taxes) were 352¼ solidi.[12] If the whole of this amount were met from wheat sales and the entire arable area was sown to wheat, then at the average price levels of this foodgrain (say, 12 artabas to the solidus) Aphrodito would have to sell 9 per cent of its wheat stock. That would be the level of its 'gross marketed surplus'. However, *P. Cairo Masp.* 67002 shows that by *c.*567 Aphrodito was paying more than 1,017 solidi in taxes[13] so that the marketed surplus would have had to be 26 per cent. In fact, since some of the arable area was sown to other crops which were not mainly sold, the actual level would have been substantially higher, perhaps close to a third, at any rate within the range usually cited for villages in India today.[14]

[10] *P. Freer Aphrod.*, col. ix 294, cf. J. Gascou and L. MacCoull, 'Le cadastre d'Aphroditô', *Travaux et Mémoires* 10 (1987) 103–58, at 118.

[11] Cf. D. J. Crawford, *Kerkeosiris: An Egyptian Village in the Ptolemaic Period* (Cambridge, 1971) 126, 10 artabas as the average yield of wheat. In the Khiṭaṭ al-Maqrīzī cited the normal range of variation (for wheat) as 2–20 ardabs per feddan, 'suivant les terres', *Description historique et topographique de l'Égypte*, 290.

[12] *P. Flor.* 297 iv verso.

[13] See R. Rémondon, 'P.Hamb. 56 et P.Lond. 1419 (notes sur les finances d'Aphrodito du VIe siècle au VIIIe)', *CE* 40 (1965) 401–30, at 428.

[14] The classic study by D. R. Gadgil and V. R. Gadgil, *A Survey of Farm Business in Wai Taluka* (Poona, 1940) 92, Table 20, calculated a marketed surplus of 30.6 per cent but on crop production as a whole and largely due to money crops such as groundnut

To transform the fluctuations of the slave market into a dynamic determining the evolution of the empire, Weber supposes that as the supply sources dried up, Roman landowners were confronted by a chronic shortage of labour. (He ignores the fact that the Mediterranean economy was characterized by persistently high levels of underemployment and that free workers were always available.) At any rate, [6] landowners made a fundamental response to the problem they faced—one which produced profound changes in the morphology of the lower orders. Where they still utilized slave labour, those workforces were progressively disintegrated by their settlement on the land as separate households, forming a common mass of dependants with the former *coloni*, as the latter were increasingly transformed from tenants into employees (pp. 300 f.). With these sweeping changes in the organization of estates, the latent "feudalism" of the late empire simply asserted itself more openly.[15] For [7] it proved quite impossible to sustain existing levels of market production with the new kind of dependent labour force, since—and now a crucial assumption—production for exchange presupposed slave barracks bound by rigid discipline (p. 303: 'Für die Absatzproduktion war die disziplinierte Sklavenkaserne Vorbedingung'). Weber did not explain *why* he thought so and was of course not unaware that east of the Elbe the 'second serfdom' had coexisted with consistently high levels of market activity. At any rate, once the restructuring of estates made market production impossible, this shattered the fragile structures of exchange which lay superimposed on the latent background of natural economy ('die naturalwirtschaftliche Unterlage'). Thus Weber derives the renewed dominance of natural economy from changes in the organization of the estate, through some causal link which he leaves unexplained. The mentality of the estates is purely autarchic now, their economic policy one of isolationism. As Weber says, 'The large estates cut themselves off from the urban market' (p. 304: Die grossen Güter lösen sich vom Markte der Stadt). Finally, [8] since the exchange basis of the late imperial economy was drastically curtailed, the financial system of the late empire, Weber argues, was forced back into the mould of *Naturalwirtschaft*. For the lack of private capital development and the dwindling capacity of landowners to meet cash payments undermined the

and turmeric. Nadkarni, *EPW* xv, March 1980 (Review of Agriculture) 13–24 calculates 37.2 per cent for wheat, 24.4 per cent for millet. Olsen has comparable figures in her thesis of 1984.

[15] Weber, 'Soziale Gründe', 303: 'Die Entwicklung der feudalen Gesellschaft lag in der Luft schon des spätrömischen Reiches.'

state's ability to sustain any other sort of financial system (p. 306). Weber concludes: 'The disintegration of the empire was the necessary political result of the gradual disappearance of market exchange and the progressive rise of natural economy. Basically, it only signified the collapse of an administrative apparatus and monetary-political superstructure less and less adapted to the substructure of natural economy' (p. 308).

Weber's 'Soziale Gründe' is a more compact, cohesive account of Roman economic development than the corresponding sections of his *Agrarverhältnisse*. But the cohesion is achieved at the cost of considerable abstraction—he almost never cites sources, generalizes massively, and generates causal connections which are rarely self-evident. Above all, Weber's picture of the late antique estate economy is seriously flawed by his presumption of the dominance of *Naturalwirtschaft*, and for this I can find no explanation other than, perhaps, a certain ignorance. Three years later, another of Mommsen's pupils, Ulrich Wilcken, would produce his massive *Griechische Ostraka*, subtitled 'An essay on ancient economic history'. The picture Wilcken assembled through patient but seminal labour on the ostraca and papyri could not have had less in common with Weber's general account. Above all, Wilcken had no illusions, as Weber seems to have done, about the significance of monetary economy in the main periods of Hellenistic and Roman history. For example, even as he conceded the dogma of a fourth century dominated by its reversion to *Naturalwirtschaft* (under Meyer's influence, and Meyer's presumption can be traced back to a misunderstanding of Mommsen),[16] he could write, 'It is of some relevance to the stability of money economy that even in this century of government bankruptcy and shocking debasement of currency [he means the third], people generally continued to make their payments in money.'[17] The interval between Weber's essay and Wilcken's work is so narrow that the defects of the former can hardly be explained away by the imperatives of 'German abstract thought'. Indeed, in the revised and extended version of the *Agrarverhältnisse* which he published in 1909, Weber had an ideal opportunity to modify some of his positions, but he reaffirmed his underlying notion that the basis of ancient economy was the *Naturalwirtschaft* of the hinterlands.[18] 'The expansion of large

[16] Meyer, 'Wirtschaftliche Entwicklung', 158 cited Mommsen, *Geschichte des römischen Münzwesens* (Berlin, 1860) 827 ff. for the strange idea that in the crisis of the third century 'das Geld wieder zur Ware wird'.

[17] U. Wilcken, *Griechische Ostraka aus Aegypten und Nubien*, 2 vols. (Leipzig, 1899) 1.680 n. 1.

[18] Weber, 'Agrarverhältnisse im Altertum' (3rd edn.), in *Gesammelte Aufsätze*, 273,

holdings progressed further,' he wrote, 'and with it their gradual but simultaneous cutting loose from the market' (p. 272).

Thus Mickwitz was surely right to ignore Weber's essay almost totally, except for the passing reference which ascribed the dogma of the reversion to *Naturalwirtschaft* to Weber himself. Let me return for a moment to Weber's conception of a late imperial *Privatwirtschaft* which progressively reverts to the autarchic isolation of the closed 'household' economy. One fact should be immediately obvious. Clearly, Weber knew next to nothing about the monetary history of the empire. It is significant, for example, that inflation is nowhere mentioned. He has no notion of the levels of liquidity and wealth in the late empire, and no idea of the close control exercised by landowners over accounting and cash flows. Nor was his logic either obvious or inexorable. The conclusion that the fall of the empire was the 'necessary political result' of the disappearance of trade ignores his own consistent assumption that exchange relationships were of only superficial importance in the Roman economy. How could a process described as a mere shell, as the 'thin fabric on the background of natural economy', have such decisive political consequences? Again, the contraction of slave workforces was decisive for the process of evolution, yet Otto Neurath, Weber's contemporary (and friend), would later develop precisely the opposite logic when he argued, in *Antike Wirtschaftsgeschichte*, that the more an exchange economy developed, the less feasible it became for Roman landowners to retain slave labour forces. Neurath's logic had an unimpeachable economic basis. He argued, 'The exchange economy generated all sorts of conjunctural fluctuations, even slumps and periods of crisis. Free workers could easily be dismissed in such periods, to cut employers' losses. But the situation was different when slaves were employed. By generating crises, the exchange economy contributed to the *elimination of slavery*.'[19] Thus for Weber the reversion to *Naturalwirtschaft* was in some sense rooted in the decline of slavery, whereas for Neurath, more convincingly, I think, the evolution of a commercial economy was a powerful factor in the declining employment of slaves. For Neurath, commercial involvement was a peculiarity of Roman landownership as such; for Weber, it was simply the distinctive

'Diese Verkehr ist ein dünnes Fadennetz über der naturalwirtschaftlichen Unterlage'. Hopkins, *JRS* 70 (1980) 104, repeats this dogma in almost the same words: 'The monetary economy constituted a thin veneer of sophistication spread over and tied to the subsistence economy by the liens of taxes, trade and rent.' Contrast Millar, 'The World of the *Golden Ass*', 72–3, with more realism.

[19] O. Neurath, *Antike Wirtschaftsgeschichte* (2nd edn.; Leipzig and Berlin, 1918) 91, emphasis mine.

feature of one type of enterprise, the so-called 'plantation' based on unfree labour. Neurath's conception reflects a deeper understanding of Roman economic reality, whereas Weber's plantation can safely be dismissed as a historical myth.

Despite the tortured complexity of much of his work, in Roman history at least Weber acquired the general reputation, by the 1920s, of a firm believer in the autarchic 'household' character of the ancient economy. Rostovtzeff classified him with Bücher and Salvioli as the leading exponents of the belief that 'the ancient world never emerged from the forms of primitive house-economy (*Oikenwirtschaft*)'.[20] When Dopsch published his defence of *Geldwirtschaft* in 1930, Weber figured as the propounder of the theory of the alleged regression to natural economy in the late empire.[21] Yet in the work Dopsch was referring to Weber had said almost nothing about the stages of this process. His method was antithetical to historical detail. Its presumed strength was its ability to abstract and generalize, not the capacity to generate "specific" historical characterizations. Dopsch pointed out that Weber's thesis had been accepted uncritically and that even Stein subscribed to it. Two years later, a young Finnish scholar came out with a book on the fourth century which was destined to transform the terms of the problem, refute the whole orthodoxy of the monetary collapse and inaugurate a new period of Roman economic history.

Mickwitz

'Il n'avait pas trente-cinq ans et il semblait cependant que, depuis longtemps, sa pensée lucide avait imposé son empreinte à l'histoire des derniers siècles de l'empire romain', Claire Préaux wrote about Mickwitz when he died in 1940.[22] He was probably the first historian to try systematically to integrate numismatic evidence into a more general form of argument about the economic evolution of the late empire. His fusion of numismatics and papyrology remains even today a distinctive and highly original contribution to ancient history. If the underlying assumptions of Cambridge 'minimalism' are partly rooted in Weber's refusal to come to terms with what Meyer called 'the fundamental importance of trade and money in ancient history',[23] the supersession of those legacies must have its

[20] Rostovtzeff, *SEHRE* 1.537.

[21] A. Dopsch, *Naturalwirtschaft und Geldwirtschaft in der Weltgeschichte* (Vienna, 1930) 21 n. 80, referring to Weber's *Die römische Agrargeschichte* of 1891.

[22] Cl. Préaux, 'Gunnar Mickwitz', *CE* 31 (1941) 298–300.

[23] Meyer, 'Wirtschaftliche Entwicklung', 88.

starting-point in Mickwitz. Numismatic analysis has more to contribute to our understanding of the late empire than sociological abstraction. Yet precisely Mickwitz shows that the opposition between these levels need not survive. It is characteristic of Mickwitz's method that he discerns in a purely numismatic problem a deeper economic process. For example, in a separate study where the essential problem was that of silver weight standards (and he advocated systematic use of the standard deviation), he would argue, 'Once our judgements about the silver coinage of the fourth century, which even then formed an important part of the monetary system, can be put on a more secure footing, we have a basis for saying something about the way the state related to the economy of the period and about its financial policy.'[24] This ability to penetrate to a 'social' level behind and beyond the confusing monetary process of the fourth century is, of course, what makes *Geld und Wirtschaft* such an exciting work.

I shall summarize this study as rapidly as I can. For Mickwitz it is typical of the orthodoxy about the late empire that even Meyer and Rostovtzeff accepted Bücher's picture of Constantine's century as a period of *Naturalwirtschaft*.[25] Stein revised this orthodoxy with the notion that there was a revival of money economy towards the latter part of the fourth century. This at least was a step forward because it helped to reinstate monetary phenomena at the heart of the problem.[26]

Mickwitz then devotes several pages to a purely abstract exposition of the concept of money.[27] This is important because by defining the preservation of value as a decisive function of the money commodity, he is able to reintroduce the state into his argument. This is possible because, when we look at money as a preserver of value, what matters most are the value-fluctuations of the coinage. Now it is precisely the value of the currency which, Mickwitz claims, is generally subject to the sharpest fluctuations, not least because of the intervention of the state. So if the alleged contraction of monetary economy is eventually rooted in the internal relationships of the monetary system, we would have to search for the causes of that contraction in two sorts of fluctuations—in the value-relations of the coinage and in the standards of minting. Mickwitz thus proposes to focus his study on changes in the value of money.

First Mickwitz states reasons for rejecting Mommsen's view of

[24] Mickwitz, *Systeme des römischen Silbergeldes im IV Jhdt. n. Chr.; ein Beispiel zur Anwendung der variationsstatistischen Methode in der Numismatik* (Helsinki, 1933) 2.

[25] Mickwitz, *Geld und Wirtschaft*, 3 f.

[26] Ibid. 6.

[27] Ibid. 9–17.

the fiduciary character of the third-century silver coinage (which he—Mommsen—called 'Kreditmünze'). He characterizes the monetary system of the middle and late empire as a bimetallism, and asks whether the currency debasement of the middle period can be explained by this feature. The essential defect of bimetallism is its vulnerability to fluctuations in the price of gold and silver as metallic substances. The fluctuations of value that this engenders can then be neutralized in two ways: either by altering the value-ratio between the gold and silver coinages or by increasing or reducing the number of coins minted from one of the metals. Now, for Mickwitz, who endorsed the quantity theory of money, these adjustments cannot in themselves precipitate an inflation process. He is careful to specify that debasement (that is, a deterioration in the quality of the metal used for coining) does not by itself lead to inflation. (It is worth stressing this because Bagnall has recently constructed a whole explanation of the fourth-century inflation which rests precisely on this misunderstanding.[28]) For, as Mickwitz explains, 'If, instead of the coins withdrawn from circulation and melted down, precisely the same number of debased coins were struck and consequently the quantum of money remained the same, no one would have a higher income and no one would have to pay higher prices than before. Demand would not rise and therefore the level of prices would remain constant. What the government decides to do with the extra metal is a matter of no importance . . . The only thing that matters is that it is not coined' (p. 47). On the other hand, of course, governments go in for debasement precisely because they stand to gain by pumping more money into circulation from a given stock of metal. In the middle empire and into the fourth century, this generally involved 'recycling' and strenuous government attempts to reabsorb older coins from circulation. But Mickwitz notes that the gold coinage was the crucial exception to this pattern (p. 66).

Chapters 3 and 4 of *Geld und Wirtschaft* are about inflation directly, with the general argument (1) that the inflation of fourth-century billon was less serious than the collapse of third-century silver; that in some purely monetary sense the fourth century was in fact more stable than the third; (2) that the inflation had no major discernible impact on the economic life of Egypt (whose price movements we know best)—at most, Mickwitz claims, there was a limited tendency for the extension of payments in kind, though even this was reversed later; (3) that inflation is in any case much less

[28] R. S. Bagnall, *Currency and Inflation in Fourth-Century Egypt* (ASP, The Scholar's Press, 1985).

serious with a metallic currency than with paper money. The reason for this is that whereas the age of a note makes no difference to its devaluation (i.e. inflation affects all notes equally), coins retain an intrinsic or metallic value. Now this in some sense is the only concrete, empirical way of testing the hypothesis of a reversion to natural economy—for the contractual evolution of the late empire should show an absolute predominance of payments in kind, if that hypothesis is true. Mickwitz concludes that *despite* inflation the monetary system survived and the theory should, consequently, be rejected (p. 137).

Thus, so far Mickwitz has been able to develop a nuanced and consistent picture of the monetary process. Inflation progressed in cycles caused by periods of heavy debasement (due to the expanded supply of money); its impact was limited, however: gold was exempt from the process, and there is no evidence for a generalized regression to *Naturalwirtschaft.* In chapter 6 Mickwitz transforms monetary history into political economy. This is the important chapter which describes the social process at work in the inflation of the fourth century, but as the title of the chapter indicates ('Die staatliche Naturalwirtschaft'), this is also the one part of his study which makes a crucial concession to the theorists of natural economy, thus drastically limiting his analysis of that process. The concession Mickwitz makes is to divide the late imperial economy into public and private sectors and attribute to the public sector a largely *naturalwirtschaftliche* character. A monetized private economy thus coexists with a state whose own organization is increasingly dominated by payments in kind. This dualism—or the specific form that Mickwitz gives it—dooms his whole discussion of the Theodosian Code.

The late imperial state had a formidable fiscal appetite. Its survival depended on its ability to extract the requisite amount of revenue from the public. The decisive issue was the form in which this should be done. Mickwitz argues that state employees were the worst sufferers in an inflation and thus strongly motivated to identify their interests with payments in kind. Such payments, he supposed, were the surest protection against future debasements and price rise. But by the same logic taxpayers would prefer to meet their obligations in cash. Thus if the assessments were collected in kind (and not just determined as such), taxpayers would want to press for commutation. The social process Mickwitz describes is this conflict over the specific form of payment, with landowners pressing for *adaeratio* and the bureaucracy aligning itself with *Naturalwirtschaft.*

Thus Mickwitz's theory of the late imperial *staatliche Naturalwirtschaft* (pp. 165 ff.) presupposes the model of the *Staatsangestellten*, the bureaucracy and the army, fighting off the impact of inflation and doing so by rejecting the monetary economy. It is this model which Mickwitz uses to interpret the constitutions in the Theodosian Code which deal specifically with *adaeratio*. Since, as I believe, Mickwitz's study offers us a basis for a more integrated model of late Roman economic relationships, it is important to demolish those parts of his analysis which in some sense contradict its essential tendency. This, in fact, is what Mazzarino did in the central chapters of *Aspetti sociali del quarto secolo*, published in 1951. For Mazzarino, Mickwitz's book was the great turning-point in the deadweight of historical pessimism about late antiquity. What Mickwitz had offered us, through his decisive proof of the continued monetary vitality of private economy, was 'an "optimistic" judgement about the "style" of the late empire'.[29] This is a marvellous image, for it exactly captures the exciting aspect of Mickwitz's work. But Mazzarino knew the legal and historical sources too well to admit the interpretations in chapter 6. Mickwitz systematically misinterprets the constitutions he deals with, because he wants them to confirm the preconceived notion of a bureaucracy fighting for payments in kind. Let me take only one example of this (reserving others for a more detailed discussion). The early 380s saw a succession of harvest failures, with the inevitable impact on prices. Mickwitz correctly saw this as the background presupposed in *CTh.* 11.2.4, posted at Beirut at the end of January 384. This says, 'Regarding the produce which is normally scheduled for payment by way of regular taxes or arrears, the produce itself shall be paid, not its cash equivalent (*non sunt pretia specierum, sed ipsae quae postulantur species inferendae*), obviously so that (for this is the crucial point and the source of the whole grievance) their payments consist of the actual produce scheduled under this type of payment and they do not acquiesce in fluctuations which cause losses because of the rates which are fixed (*in annonario quoque titulo species annonarias solvant neque sub taxationibus pretiorum dispendiosis occasionibus adquiescant*).' Mickwitz interprets this as an attack on the general preference of taxpayers for cash payments and their manipulation of *adaeratio* (p. 169). But this is obviously not what the constitution means.[30] The grievances referred to are precisely those of the *collatores*. It is they, the taxpayers, who must refuse

[29] S. Mazzarino, *Aspetti sociali del quarto secolo. Ricerche di storia tardo-romana* (Rome, 1951) 24.

[30] See ibid. 141 ff.

to put up with losses. The *taxationes pretiorum* are the rates of commutation which the bureaucracy arbitrarily imposes on landowners, in this case on the basis of market prices which had skyrocketed when the harvest failed. The ruling is a government intervention to protect landowners from officials or army officers who have extorted payments in the commuted form of money, at rates which are considerably above average market levels. *Occasio* has the specific sense of a price conjuncture, as in other passages.

Mickwitz's failure to grasp the precise sense of this or other interventions was rooted in certain assumptions he made about the late empire. There are four assumptions specifically, of which possibly only the last corresponds to a real intuition about power relationships in the late antique world. The other three are, it seems to me, hard to sustain. (1) Mickwitz sees the late imperial state as a homogeneous bloc, a conception which crucially ignores its 'socially autonomized' character—the fact that the army and the bureaucracy had specific social interests which they enforced through the positions of power and authority which their jobs entailed.[31] Thus much of the legislation of the late empire is precisely an attempt to curb or repress this process, and it becomes meaningless to assimilate state employees and the legal state under a single concept. (2) Mickwitz ascribes a purely defensive psychology to state personnel. He sees them reacting to inflation in defence of emoluments and doing so by wanting payments in kind. But if we examine the groups involved in the bargaining and conflict over commutation, they turn out to be the backbone of the late Roman military and administrative apparatus, the crucial middle levels of the hierarchy—the *duces*, *tribuni*, *praepositi*, collectors of military supplies, *officia praefecturae*, and so on. The psychology of these groups was anything but defensive. (3) Crucially, Mickwitz rules out the possible option of shifting to more stable currencies in reaction to the debasement and inflation of the base-metal coinage. I believe it was this option, and not payments in kind, which the upper and middle levels of the late Roman bureaucracy went in for. The triumph of the solidus was the economic reflection of

[31] This was clear to contemporaries, e.g. Jerome, who refers in his commentary on Ezekiel (*Commentar. in Ezechielem* VI, 18, *PL* 25.175) to the 'violence' of the bureaucracy, which 'oppresses people by virtue of its official authority' (ut taceam de militantium et iudicum violentia, qui opprimunt per potentiam). Eunapius, fr. 49 (*FHG* 4.36) said the *archontes* were 'more hostile (to people) than the enemy', *οἱ ἄρχοντες τῶν πολεμὶων ἦσαν πολεμιώτεροι*. Cf. T. S. Brown, *Gentlemen and Officers: Imperial Administration and Aristocratic Power in Byzantine Italy A.D. 554–800* (The British School at Rome, 1984) 63: 'It was the military profession as a whole, and not just the commanding officers, who were regarded by contemporaries as forming a distinct social category' (about the new military élite which governed Byzantine Italy).

their social dominance. The logic of commutation was the reverse of the Mickwitzian hypothesis—the pressure for *adaeratio* came from the ruling professional groups, as Mazzarino emphasized, and the *possessores*, who, ideally, would have preferred to discharge their obligations in a debased money, would, since that was not possible, certainly have preferred payments in kind to the exaction of gold and silver.

The monetary and numismatic implications of this argument were an area Mazzarino refused to venture into. Whereas Mickwitz believed that the quantity theory of money was a sufficient explanation of the successive inflations, Mazzarino was content with the general observation that once Constantine discarded the monetary illusions of the third century, 'economic life would be dominated by the specific relation between the solidus and the fractional coinages'.[32] The penetration is typical. The inflation of the late empire was a 'stratified inflation'. The differential destinies of the gold and base-metal coinages and the permanent stability of the solidus meant that holders of gold assets were not in fact exposed to an inflationary process at all. The Anonymous understood this central fact about the Constantinian order and registered a covert protest.

Finally (4) Mickwitz assumes, correctly I think, that the army and the bureaucracy were the most powerful classes of the late empire (p. 190). It is worth noting that he calls them 'classes', thus acknowledging that the late Roman state had developed socially autonomized forms. Their organized, professional existence gave them a massive superiority over the other strata, who, despite their private accumulations of wealth, remained serialized and incapable of resistance.

The upshot of all this may be summarized as follows: conversion to gold was the decisive economic movement of the late empire, as I argue in the following chapter. Far from being a massive reservoir of expanding 'natural economy', it was the state and its impact on the rest of late Roman society which led to the powerful diffusion of an economy based on gold. The solidus became the essential preserver of value, means of payment, medium of circulation, and eventually, indeed, by the end of the fifth century, money of account. Constantine's social order reveals its peculiar stability in the fact that for the first time in 150 years the Mediterranean had a mass currency which was infinitely stable. Understanding the social costs of this economic mechanism presupposes some conception of

[32] Mazzarino, *L'impero romano*, 3 vols. (2nd edn; Bari, 1976) 3.668.

how fourth-century 'bimetallism' actually generated the cyclical inflation of the abandoned base-metal coinages. Financial mechanisms obviously dominated monetary history, but at least one recent contribution (by Lo Cascio) has been able to supersede the orthodoxy which locates a manipulative intervention at the heart of the inflationary process. In other words, the conflicts of the fourth century may have had more to do with the intrinsic nature of metallic money, the fact that gold is both a commodity and money and governed by different laws, than with the results of financial policies, such as the fact that debasements coincided with periods of intensified government expenditure.

CHAPTER 3

The Monetary Economy of the Late Empire and its Social Presuppositions

> I possessori d'oro si trovarono, d'un tratto, gli effettivi signori della società del quarto secolo
>
> Mazzarino[1]

Introduction: Features of the Monetary System

Gold and Silver

In *Aspetti sociali del quarto secolo* Mazzarino argued that the Constantinian monetary order differed fundamentally from Diocletian's. He saw the differences mainly in terms of social ones. Constantine promoted the interests of the owners of gold. The basis of this is the idea that Diocletian, on the contrary, held the price of gold artificially low.[2] The evolution of Constantine's system destroyed these value relations with inexorable permanence.[3] In other writings Mazzarino described these changes as 'revolutionary'.[4]

Though the Prices Edict (20 Nov.–9 Dec. 301) refers to the gold coinage as 'solidi', '(aurum) obryzae in regulis sive (in) solidis pondum unum D LXXII',[5] it is clear that no gold coin of this name

[1] Mazzarino, *Aspetti sociali*, 114.

[2] *P. Beatty Panop.* 2.215–21 (16.2.300) shows that in February 300 the *aureus* was already tariffed at 1,000 denarii.

[3] The best recent survey of the fourth century is C. E. King, 'The Fourth Century Coinage', in *L' "Inflazione" nel quarto secolo d. C. Atti dell' incontro di studio, Roma 1988* (Rome, 1993) 1–87. The most stimulating analytical pieces are the cycle of studies by Elio Lo Cascio, 'Teoria e politica monetaria a Roma tra III e IV D. C.', *SRIT* 1. 535–57, 779–801, 'Prezzo dell'oro e prezzi delle merci', in *L' "Inflazione" nel quarto secolo d. C. Atti dell' incontro di studio, Roma 1988* (Rome, 1993) 155–88, and 'Aspetti della politica monetaria nel IV secolo', *Atti dell' Accademia Romanisitica Costantiniana, X Convegno Internazionale* (Naples, 1995) 481–502.

[4] Mazzarino, *L'impero romano*, 3.666 f., and 674 ('rivoluzione monetaria costantiniana').

[5] R. Naumann and F. Naumann, *Der Rundbau in Aezani, mit dem Preisedikt des Diokletian* (Tübingen, 1973) 57 (30, 1a).

was struck to the weight standard, established by Constantine, of 72 to the pound. (1) The post-294 reform aureus/solidus of Diocletian, struck at 60 to the pound, was tariffed at 1,000 denarii both before and after the revaluation, which seems to have affected only the silver denominations.[6] The Constantinian solidus, on the other hand, was a coin with no fixed denominational value but a price which fluctuated constantly in the market, and which could only be expressed in some currency other than gold itself.[7] Lo Cascio has argued that the fixing of a maximum price for gold, whether in coin or in bullion, shows that the aureus could not have had the same attributes as money as either the silver argenteus (under Diocletian) or the gold solidus (under Constantine). This argument seems to me both persuasive and fundamental.[8] (2) Prices in the Diocletianic system were expressed mainly in denarii in striking contrast to the monetary system which evolved in the later fourth century, where, as Kent notes, 'values are expressed exclusively in terms of gold'.[9] It is worth stating the conceptual meaning of this more clearly. The assertion that gold became the measure of value (and thus standard of price) does not mean that no prices would be expressed in any money of account other than gold. What it does mean is that the expression of prices in traditional units of account or in silver, coined or uncoined, always presupposed the value of these lower currencies in terms of gold. That is to say, these currencies were simply symbols for gold and their price functions simply ways of representing different quantities of gold.[10] Gold was the immediate representative of value.

Diocletian attempted to work the system in terms of fixed relationships between the metals. This could only succeed as long as government ignored the market. Of course, the Prices Edict was a way of doing just that, but both it and the currency reform failed. In *P. Beatty Panop.* 2.215 (AD 300) the price of gold for state

[6] E. Ruschenbusch, 'Diokletians Währungsreform vom 1. 9. 301', *ZPE* 26 (1977) 193–210, esp. 203. J. Jahn, 'Zur Geld- und Wirtschaftspolitik Diokletians', *JNG* 25 (1975) 91–105, esp. 94, thinks the *aureus* was revalued by 20 per cent.

[7] This expresses the metaphysics of money rather beautifully: in expressing the price of the solidus, it is copper, not gold, which functions as the specific equivalent commodity—as money.

[8] Lo Cascio, 'Teoria e politica monetaria', 546. Jahn, *JNG*, 1975, 103 draws the opposite conclusion despite his own observation 'Es sei darauf aufmerksam gemacht, dass sich im Preisedikt *kein Hinweis auf den Wert eines Pfundes Silber in Münzen, sondern lediglich eines Pfundes Feinsilber findet'* (p. 97).

[9] J. P. C. Kent, 'Gold Coinage in the Later Roman Empire', in R. A. G. Carson, C. H. V. Sutherland (eds.), *Essays in Roman Coinage presented to Harold Mattingly* (Oxford, 1956) 190–204, esp. 191. See n. 47 below.

[10] In other words, these monies could not define the value of a commodity without the underlying reference to their own value in gold.

purchases was 40 talents per lb., i.e. 60,000 denarii. In *P. Oxy.* 2106, *c.*304–6, the Oxyrhynchite nome was asked to supply 38 lb. of gold at 100,000 den. per lb.[11] Thus, if the latter papyrus is correctly dated, the official requisition price of gold had increased by two-thirds in the space of some five or six years. Now the only basis for such an increase would have been the unwillingness of private holders of gold to part with their assets at the hopelessly unrealistic levels of February 300. Rémondon thinks that the price of gold expressed in terms of the ratio of gold to silver rose steadily through the reign of Constantine and then remained at the high level of 1:18 till the end of the century.[12] This argument presupposes that the exactions of bullion listed in *SB* 6086 date from the last years of Constantine's reign. But in *P. Vindob.* G 13174 verso (dated to 323–*c.*337) gold and silver are paid in a ratio of 1:12.[13] Adelson has argued that gold increased in value in response to 'the increased demand for gold coinage during the fourth century'.[14] However, he also thinks the last years of the reign of Constantius II saw a sudden shift in the ratio with gold collapsing in favour of silver. On the general presumption that the gold/silver ratio had thus far reflected the role of demand factors, this sudden reversal must clearly have meant not that the demand for silver had suddenly shot up relative to gold and to its own supply, but that the supply of gold had increased or was increasing dramatically relative to the (generally strong) demand for it. In short, the market was suddenly flooded with gold, putting pressure on the price of the solidus and forcing an alteration in the ratio. The assumption (behind the arguments of Rémondon and Adelson) is that the state actually intervened to modify the value relations of the two metals and that it did so on some perhaps regular basis. But the idea that the late Roman state would have adopted or enforced a higher or lower valuation of gold or silver fairly frequently is difficult to accept. To do anything of the sort would have been immensely disruptive, and it was sufficient that short-run fluctuations, even ones

[11] See J. R. Rea, 'P. S. I. IV 310 and Imperial Bullion Purchases', *CE* 49 (1974) 163–74, at 164, with a date 'somewhat earlier than 11th August A.D. 301'.

[12] R. Rémondon, 'À propos du papyrus d'Antinoé n° 38', *CE* 32 (1957) 130–46, at 138–40.

[13] *P. Vindob.* G 13174 verso (= P. J. Sijpesteijn and K. A. Worp, 'Ein neues Archiv: Hermias und Maximos, Söhne des Sarapion', *ZPE* 32 (1978) 250f., no. 6), receipt for the *aurum coronarium*, re-publ. as *SB* XIV 12215. *SB* III 6086 is a 'Steuerliste', which was originally dated to the start of the 4th cent.

[14] H. A. Adelson, 'Silver Currency and Values in the Early Byzantine Empire', in H. Ingholt (ed.), *Centennial Publication of the American Numismatic Society* (ANS, New York, 1958) 1–26, esp. 25.

of considerable amplitude such as the collapse of silver prices in Antioch in 540,[15] should be left to their natural determination in the open market. This is illustrated by the Arcadian price documents of the early fifth century, *P. Oxy.* 3628 ff., where 'The equation 1 lb. silver = 5 solidi remains stable throughout this series of documents'[16] by contrast with (minor) fluctuations in other commodity prices.

Perhaps it is worth emphasizing what we do and do not know about the ratio. First, we do not know whether a single rate was applied throughout the empire or whether the rate was allowed to vary between prefectures. Second, we cannot be sure, and in fact it seems unlikely, that the government adjusted the ratio in response to short-term fluctuations (in the market). Third, the only really firm pieces of evidence we seem to have are: (1) the ratio of 1:12 in 301 (since this is given in the Prices Edict), (2) the ratio in *CTh.* 13.2.1 of 397 of 1:14.4 since this concerns tax payments, (3) the ratio of 1:14.4 in *c*.423 (in *P. Oxy.* 3628 ff.), and finally (4) the Byzantine ratio of 1:18. The most we can say is that these seem to reflect a steady decline in the price of silver. The rates adopted in internal regulations (viz. *CTh.* 8.4.27, 19.6.422), which give a ratio of 1:18, seem more problematic as evidence, for why should the price schedules in *P. Oxy.* 3628 ff., which are clearly official records from the office of the provincial governor (of Arcadia) hold the price of silver steady at 5 solidi per lb. if the ratio in *CTh.* 8.4.27, of similar date, was universally applicable?[17] In short, the only reliable citations imply a gradual or steady shift in favour of gold from 1:12 in the Prices Edict to the 'Byzantine' ratio of 1:18 (not random, erratic fluctuations). But whether the evolution actually occurred in this form is quite uncertain.

Again, Callu (for instance) has repeatedly characterized the fourth-century system as a 'bimetallism'. However, it is worth noting that at no stage in the fourth century was the monetary system strictly bimetallic. One indication of this is that in the Oxyrhynchite price lists published as *P. Oxy.* 3773 the monthly schedules begin with the price of the solidus (*nomismation*), then state the price of uncoined silver (*asēmon*), expressing both in talents

[15] Malalas, *Chron.* 480c (*Ioannis Malalae Chronographia*, ed. L. Dindorf, Bonn, 1831; E. Jeffreys *et al.*, *The Chronicle of John Malalas: A Translation*, Melbourne, 1986, 285).

[16] *P. Oxy.* LI 3628.9n (p. 82).

[17] My dating of *P. Oxy.* 3628 ff. depends on the price of the solidus implied there, viz. 3,800–4,000 myriads. *P. Köln* III 151, a Cynopolite loan contract of July 423, involves a potential interest of 480 myriads per solidus per year. At the standard rate of 12 per cent, this would mean a solidus price of 4,000 myriads. At 12½ per cent, the other common rate, e.g. *CPR* VII 40 (492), *P. Flor.* III 300 (597), *P. Lond.* V 1737 (613), the price would be 3,840.

and denarii. Again, the solidus is treated as a commodity,[18] and silver merely as bullion.[19] Moreover, both things were true around the year 340, thus within roughly three decades of Constantine establishing the solidus *c.*311.

This leaves us with the problem of why a silver coinage existed at all. The only solution I can think of is that the state issued silver largely for military purposes, to supplement its disbursements of gold once the pressure for commutation began to succeed. In support of this one may note that the very large issues of *siliquae* from the mint of Trier after 367 mainly involve reverse types representing the emperor in military dress.[20] Also, the fact that 'After Constantius had control of the whole of the empire, his silver production expanded but only his vota siliquae were issued at a large number of mints'[21] may imply a deliberate policy to confine silver payments to bonuses. The *miliarensis* too was clearly conceived as a military coinage with its duality of weight standards allowing flexibility in the process of pay bargaining with the army. Neither of these coins (light/heavy miliarensis) was affected by the weight reductions which reduced the siliqua first late in the reign of Constantius and again, in the west, in the 380s from *c.*3 grams to *c.*1.6 grams. This shows that if there was a fixed value relationship between the siliqua and the miliarenses, as Bruun implies,[22] this had certainly disintegrated by the end of Constantius' reign. The miliarensis was clearly a substitute for gold, an attempt to ease the pressure on the gold reserves, and thus in some sense a submultiple of the solidus. The metrological sources imply that the military were paid in 'light' miliarenses: 'There is another follis consisting of the light (silver) coins (ἀργύρια) which are given to the soldiers.'[23]

[18] That is, a particular *money* is treated as having a commercial demand for it. This might fluctuate from day to day, cf. *P. Oxy.* XXXIV 2729 verso line 37, where the writer says, τὸ νομιζμάτιον σήμερον μυρ(ιάδων) ψλ'. In *P. Giss.* 47 = *WChr.* 326 (Hadrian) a second hand has added, 'As you know, in Coptos prices fluctuate from day to day (καθ' ἡμέραν διάφοροι γείνονται τιμαί)', with reference to the price of silver (*asēmon*).

[19] See C. E. King on late Roman silver hoards in Britain, 'The fact that precious metal in the form of coin, ingots, plate, or jewellry was often hoarded together suggests that silver coins were probably considered to be bullion in some sense', 'Late Roman Silver Hoards in Britain and the Problem of Clipped Siliquae', *The British Numismatic Journal* 51 (1981) 5–31, at 5. On the use (and abundance) of silver in the east see Maria Mundell Mango, *Artistic Patronage in the Roman Diocese of Oriens, 313–641 A.D.* (Oxford University D. Phil., 1984), ch. 3, II.

[20] C. E. King, *Roman Silver Coins*. 5: *Carausius to Romulus Augustus* (Seaby, London, 1987) 43.

[21] King, *Roman Silver Coins*, 22.

[22] Bruun, *RIC* 7.6 '3 miliarensia equalled 4 siliquae'.

[23] F. Hultsch, *Metrologicorum scriptorum reliquiae*, 2 vols. (Leipzig, 1864) 1.308.22 ff., ἔστι δὲ ἕτερος φόλλις συναγόμενος ἐξ ἀργυρίων λεπτῶν τῶν τοῖς στρατιώταις διδομένων, cf. 307.18, Μιλιαρίσιον, στρατιωτικὸν δῶρον.

This is confirmed by Zosimus who tells us that Julian gave or promised his men 130 *argyra nomismata* on the eve of the Persian campaign.[24] If these coins were light miliarenses,[25] then what Julian promised his troops was equal to just over 9 solidi. In the Byzantine sources published by Hultsch, 125 *lepta argyria* are equated with 9 solidi, 1 miliarensis, and 9 nummi.[26] This is because the equivalence adopted for this denomination is 1¾ carats of gold: 'Each one of these coins is equal to 1¾ carats'.[27] But if the light miliarensis = 1.728 carats of gold (=(24 × 72)/1000),[28] as it should, and is not rounded up to 1.75, as the writer has done, then 125 'light' miliarenses are exactly equal to 9 solidi (125 × 1.728 carats = 216 carats = 9 solidi). Of course, this was the cash value of the accession donative in 578, paid by that stage entirely in gold.[29] If Julian was simply promising a repeat of his own accessional donative paid as 5 solidi + 1 lb. of silver,[30] then in 363, 1 solidus would have been worth 12 light miliarenses: (5 × 12 =) 60 + (1 lb. =) 70 = 130. This implies a ratio of 1:12, the level surmised by Adelson for the closing years of Constantius' reign,[31] and reinforces the suggestion that the bimetallic ratio did not in fact fluctuate beyond certain major historical shifts. Finally, it is worth noting that by Justinian's reign the miliarensis was being used as a currency of wage payments for building workers[32] and that when John Moschus refers to the *hexagrams* minted by Heraclius these pieces are called 'large miliarenses'.[33] It is clear that 12 of these exchanged to the solidus because the ratio was now 1:18.[34]

[24] Zosimus, 3.13.3 (Paschoud, 2/1, 28), *ἀργυρῶν τε νομισμάτων τριάκοντα καὶ ἑκατὸν τῶν στρατιωτῶν ἕκαστον δόσει τιμήσας.*

[25] Light miliarenses were the only type that Julian minted, cf. Adelson, 'Silver Currency and Values', 3, except possibly at Arles, *RIC* 8.228, no. 312, which Kent says needs reconfirmation.

[26] Hultsch, *Metr. script. rel.* 1.309.5 f., *γινόμενα ἐν χαράγματι νομίσματα θ′, μιλιαρήσιον ἓν νούμμοι θ′.*

[27] Hultsch, *Metr. script. rel.* 1.309.1 f., *ἔχει δὲ ἕκαστον τῶν τοιούτων λεπτῶν ἀργυρίων κεράτιον ἓν ἥμισυ τέταρτον.*

[28] See Hultsch, *Metr. script. rel.* 1.307.20, *Μιλιαρίσιον, τὸ χιλιοστὸν τῆς τοῦ χρυσοῦ λίτρας.*

[29] M. Hendy, *Studies in the Byzantine Monetary Economy c.300–1450* (Cambridge, 1985) 481.

[30] Ammianus 20.4.18.

[31] Adelson, 'Silver Currency and Values', 13; also Pearce, *RIC* 9, p. xxviii.

[32] Anon., *Διήγησις περὶ τῆς οἰκοδομῆς τοῦ ναοῦ*, 9 (Preger, *Script. Orig. Const.*, 1.84, G. Dagron, *Constantinople imaginaire. Études sur le recueil des "Patria"* (Paris, 1984) 200).

[33] Moschus, *Pratum spirituale*, 184 (*PG* 87/3.3060), *ἓν μιλιαρίσιον μέγα*, cf. *Miracula S. Artemii*, 18 (Crisafulli and Nesbitt (eds.), *The Miracles of St. Artemios* (Leiden, etc., 1997) 120), *καὶ δοὺς τῷ σεκρεταρίῳ ἑξάγραμμα μιλιαρήσια ὀκτὼ.*

[34] Hultsch, *Metr. script. rel.* 1.309.4, *πρὸς τὸ νῦν κρατοῦν μιλιαρήσια κτλ.*

Gold and Bronze

The main issue posed by the repeated decline of the base-metal coinages is whether the process reflected here was endemic to the monetary system of the late empire or simply an avoidable product of government policies. Here the evidence of the papyri on the long-term movement of the gold/copper exchange-rate seems to be of considerable value. The papyri show a steady secular decline in the value of the base-metal currencies (in relation to the solidus), such that the correlation between date (where certain or probable dates are available, to within a year) and the price of the solidus yields an R^2 of over 0.95 (see Appendix 1, Table 1).[35] The clear implication of this is that the government was contending with forces beyond its control rather than wilfully or unconsciously 'causing' inflation. Thus one has to reverse Bagnall's picture, and see the state responding to forces beyond its control rather than the market reacting (passively but immediately) to arbitrary alterations in the fineness and/or weight of the subsidiary coinage.[36] This raises the issue of what those forces were. The most important change in the monetary system of the late empire was of course the introduction of a stable gold coinage and its progressive diffusion as a mass currency. If one visualizes this as an economic revolution which occurred over a century or more, then the analogy of similar revolutions in other epochs might provide a clue to the nature of what probably happened. A possible analogy is the shift in the monetary system of Egypt at the turn of the fourteenth century, when the disappearance of silver destroyed its position as the monetary standard and the *fals* re-emerged as Egypt's most widely used currency.[37] In the *Treatise on Famines* composed *c.*1405,[38] al-Maqrīzī claimed that the abundant circulation of *fulūs* (under al-Ẓāhir Barqūq) *destroyed* the value-relations between the metals and added to the general catastrophe.[39] Whatever the merits of this description, the point worth noting is

[35] The correlation is based on a subset of eighteen observations from a total of twenty-six listed in App. 1, Table 1, covering the period from 300 to 618, including eight with 'probable' dates. It would be better to exclude the latter, however. Basing the calculation on just the ten observations with secure dates yields a coefficient of 0.967! Accepting *c.*388 as the date of *CPR* V 26 (Skar Codex) would reduce the correlation by several points but Bagnall has in any case now opted for a date in the late 5th cent.

[36] Bagnall, *Currency and Inflation*, esp. 27–48.

[37] e.g. B. Shoshan, 'From Silver to Copper: Monetary Changes in Fifteenth Century Egypt', *Studia Islamica* 56 (1982) 97–116.

[38] See A. Allouche, *Mamluk Economics: A Study and Translation of al-Maqrīzī's Ighāthah* (University of Utah Press, 1994).

[39] Al-Maqrīzī, *Ighāthat al-umma*, 71 = Allouche, *Mamluk Economics*, 8, 71–2, superseding Wiet's translation in 'Le Traité des Famines de Maqrīzī', *JESHO* 5 (1962) 1–90, at 69–70.

Maqrīzī's suggestion that there was an intrinsic connection between the use of a metal as the monetary standard and its price relative to other metals.[40] Suchodolski has made a similar point about the silver monometallism of the eighth century when, despite the reduced availability of gold, it became even cheaper in the Carolingian period.[41] This relation seems to me transposable to the monetary events of the fourth century and to be the background reflected in the Anonymous' critique of fourth-century monetary policy. In the following section I shall try to restate the significance of this critique.

Money and Society: The General Background

A 'Fundamental Text'

As I suggested in the last chapter, Mickwitz's work was perhaps the first serious blow to the traditional historiography founded on the postulate of a late antique regression. What Mickwitz established was less the survival of money economy than its expansion and restructuring, in other words, a fundamentally new period in the monetary history of the empire. Though this 'revolution' is scarcely ever mentioned by our documentary sources (largely because it is presupposed by them), there is of course a famous passage in the Anonymous which attacks Constantine for monetary policies whose social consequences were, according to that writer, disastrous.[42] Mazzarino's dating of this work to the 350s strikes me as being most compatible with the extraordinary emphasis which its author ascribes to the quality of the gold coinage in circulation at the time of writing.[43] Such an emphasis would have seemed not a little misplaced once the solidi in circulation actually came to announce levels of purification of close to 100 per cent, with the letters OB, and so at any time after February 368. It follows that a Valentinianic date for the Anonymous would have to restrict itself to the earliest years of the reign, thus incurring the objection Mazzarino has raised to a date involving the joint reign of Valentinian I and Valens.[44] Of

[40] Esp. Allouche, *Mamluk Economics*, 80, Wiet, *JESHO*, 1962, 79.

[41] S. Suchodolski, 'Vom Gold zum Silber', *Lagom. Festschrift für Peter Berghaus zum 60 Geburtstag* (Munich, 1981) 97–104, esp. 102 f.

[42] Compare Mazzarino, *Aspetti sociali*, 110, 'egli invece si riferisce alle disastrose conseguenze del sistema monetario costantiniano per le classi inferiori'.

[43] Anon. *de rebus bellicis* 3 (E. A. Thompson, *A Roman Reformer and Inventor, being a new text of the treatise "De Rebus Bellicis" with a translation and introduction* (Oxford, 1952), 95).

[44] Mazzarino, *Aspetti sociali*, 78.

course, the most recent monograph puts the Anonymous in the fifth century.[45]

According to the Anonymous,

> It was in the age of Constantine that extravagant grants assigned gold instead of bronze (which earlier was considered of great value) to petty commercial transactions (*Constantini temporibus profusa largitio aurum pro aere, quod antea magni pretii habebatur, vilibus commerciis assignavit*); but the greed I speak of is thought to have arisen from the following causes. When the gold and silver and the huge quantity of precious stones which had been stored away in the temples long ago reached the public (*aurum argentumque et lapidum pretiosorum magna vis in templis reposita ad publicum pervenisset*), they enkindled all men's possessive and spendthrift instincts. And while the expenditure of bronze itself . . . seemed already vast and burdensome enough, yet from some kind of blind folly there ensued an even more extravagant passion for spending gold, which is considered more precious (*quod pretiosius habetur*). This store of gold meant that the houses of the powerful were crammed full and their splendour enhanced to the destruction of the poor (*Ex hac auri copia privatae potentium repletae domus, in perniciem pauperum clariores effectae, tenuioribus videlicet violentia oppressis*).[46]

The essential ideas contained here are as follows: first, Constantine overturned the monetary system of the empire first by flooding the market with gold (his 'profusa largitio'), then above all by eliminating any possible duplication of the measure of value by displacing the function of that measure to gold, with the general expression of commodity prices as gold prices (prices expressed in gold).[47] This is the specific point of saying—with a precision which is quite unusual for an ancient author—that Constantine's monetary policies involved 'assigning gold instead of bronze . . . to petty commercial transactions'.[48] Second, these enormous changes in the monetary economy of the fourth century formed the context for an accumulation of money-capital in the form of gold which in turn formed the basis, or was closely bound up with, a promotion of these *domus* into the clarissimate, the formation of a new aristocracy whose economic basis was gold and whose roots lay in the 'destruction of the poor'. Finally, these economic and social changes were accompanied by considerable violence against the masses—a process

[45] H. Brandt, *Zeitkritik in der Spätantike. Untersuchungen zu den Reformvorschlägen des Anonymus De rebus bellicis* (Munich, 1988).

[46] Anon. *de rebus bellicis* 2.1–2 (Thompson, 94, 110).

[47] Contrast the Prices Edict. At that time the denarius 'was clearly still regarded by the state as the basic measure of value', A. S. R. Bolin, *State and Currency in the Roman Empire to 300 A. D.* (Stockholm, 1958) 297.

[48] Since the Romans saw the essence of money in its *Formbestimmung* of 'standard of price' (*pretium*), this was tantamount to saying that Constantine made gold money instead of bronze.

of which there is scarcely any direct expression in the surviving late Roman sources.

In chapter four the author describes a system of provincial administration in terms which imply that late Roman fiscalism was a source of considerable profit to the governors. This critique already presupposes extensive commutation and the progress of fiscal practices which used commutation as the chief instrument of extortion. The 'commercialism' of the late Roman tax system is the crucial point in this passage and not simply the ritual moral jibe at the corruption of Roman administrators. Jones's verdict that 'The economic thought of this anonymous fourth-century author is crude. He appears to think that using a more precious metal for the currency makes things dearer' is way off the mark.[49] The Anonymous was not constructing a 'theory of inflation' but describing the evolution of monetary economy as he and his generation had witnessed and experienced it within their own lifetime. His remarks on the 'commercialism' of the tax system are borne out in a general way by Ammianus' complementary testimony that if 'Constantine was the first of all [the Emperors] to open the jaws of his favourites, . . . Constantius stuffed them with the marrow of the provinces'.[50] Ammianus saw Constantius' reign as a period of intensified bureaucratic enrichment, with much of the wealth drawn from the provinces. But his remarks are also borne out in a much more precise way by what one can discover of the actual functioning of provincial taxation from sources like *CJ* 10.27.2, which, though drafted under Anastasius, undoubtedly describes practices which had crystallized in a much earlier period, as certain constitutions in the Theodosian Code prove.[51] The idea of provincial governors behaving like merchants[52] is in fact an important clue to the increasing centrality of both money and prices to the nature of late Roman taxation.

In short, the Anonymous connects monetary circulation to the process of social mobility. His image of the late Roman state inject-

[49] A. H. M. Jones, 'Inflation under the Roman Empire', orig. *EcHR* 1953, repr. in *The Roman Economy: Studies in Ancient Economic and Administrative History*, ed. P. A. Brunt (Oxford, 1974) 187–227, at 206.

[50] Ammianus 16.8.12: note what looks like a remarkable appeal to documentary evidence for this assertion, 'Namque ut documenta liquida prodiderunt, proximorum fauces aperuit primus omnium Constantinus, sed eos medullis provinciarum saginavit Constantius'. The translation is Thompson's, *Roman Reformer*, 33.

[51] See pp. 53 ff., 57 ff. below.

[52] Anon. *de rebus bellicis* 4.1 (Thompson, *Roman Reformer*, 95): 'hi, despecta reverentia dignitatum, velut mercatores in provincias se missos existimant' (For these men, despising the respectable character of their office, think that they have been sent into the provinces as merchants, Thompson, 112).

ing too much gold into circulation seems to me the one that best captures the economic revolution of the late empire. The following sections are an attempt to draw on some of these ideas and develop them in some interconnected way, using both numismatic and documentary sources. The argument itself will shift increasingly from determinations connected with the state to those bound up with the market.

General Evolution

Though the Anonymous attributes the first large-scale emissions of gold to the reign of Constantine (*Constantini temporibus*), it would be wrong to suppose that the development of monetary economy following the disruption of the third century came about solely in the fourth or purely as a result of the 'Constantinian revolution'. Kent refers to the 'provision once more of a fairly abundant gold coinage' with reference to Diocletian[53] and Callu has described the years 286–311 as a period when the empire re-established a 'dense, stable and well organised' coinage in gold.[54] The Beaurains hoard and Mediterranean treasure prove that gold was available[55] and at least one of these finds is a strong indication that the Tetrarchs continued the late third century or Illyrian practice of paying the donatives of officers in gold.[56] Among the Egyptian hoards listed by Edde in 1905 is a find at Abukir said to consist of gold ingots and roughly 600 aurei, ranging from Severus Alexander to Constantine I but chiefly of the Tetrarchic period.[57] Certainly the hoard evidence carries no implication of a sudden upsurge under Constantine.[58] On the other hand, it is clear that the government struck increasingly large quantities of gold in the course of the fourth century. Furthermore, it struck substantially more gold in the latter part of the century than in the former, and it now seems possible to date the beginnings of this expansion to the final years of Constantius' reign.[59] Thus in terms of the volume of coinage

[53] Kent, 'Gold Coinage', 191.

[54] J. P. Callu, *La Politique monétaire des empereurs romains de 238 à 311* (Paris, 1969) 428.

[55] P. Bastien and C. Mezger, *Le Trésor de Beaurains (dit d'Arras)* (Wetteren, 1977), R. A. G. Carson, 'A Treasure of Aurei and Gold Multiples from the Mediterranean', in *Mélanges de numismatique, d'archéologie et d'histoire offerts à Jean Lafaurie* (Paris, 1980) 59–73.

[56] See P. Bastien, *Monnaie et "Donativa" au Bas-Empire* (Wetteren, 1988) 19, 30–1, 38.

[57] For references see Callu, *La Politique monétaire*, 414.

[58] Nor, of course, do the collections and sales catalogues, cf. Bastien, *Donativa*, 35.

[59] Analyses of the trace elements in a sample of specimens and the discovery that the platinum content shows a sudden increase after 346, rising from 45 ppm under

struck (in gold), the contrast between the reign of Constantine and the Tetrarchic period may have been less significant than that between Constantine and the reign of Constantius. Thereafter the 'total hoard statistic' suggests a continuous and steady progression for roughly a century, with a net increase of over 22 per cent (in average intensity) between periods 2 and 5.[60] If one assumes a constant rate of remelting from one period to the next and also assumes that the amount of money hoarded was in some sense proportional to the amount available for circulation (and thus to the aggregate money supply),[61] then, for a constant velocity of circulation, the evolution of the aggregate hoard between the main chronological periods should reflect the real movement of the supply of gold currency. On the other hand, these are merely 'simplifying assumptions' and may even be unsustainable methodologically, and the most one can say here is that the overall impression is one of sustained monetary expansion.

The forces behind this movement were doubtless complex and varied. An immediate one must have been the pressure of the late Roman bureaucracy, a group which Constantius more than any other late Roman emperor helped to crystallize.[62] Within this group power was rapidly shifting to the *militares*. As Ammianus intimated, the regime of Valentinian would be their golden age.[63] But Valentinian reflected pressures which had been active for well over a decade. Though Ammianus maintains that no senior officers were ever promoted to the clarissimate under Constantius, who in general curbed the aspirations of the *militares*,[64] one has evidence to show that at least a few became *clarissimi* in the last years of his reign. Thus the *duces Aegypti* Syrianus and Flavius Artemius are both called *clarissimi*, one by 356, the other by 360.[65] Again, the

Constantine to three times that level under Constantius to reach 400 ppm in the 5th cent., strongly suggest that a new source was being mined, thus expanding the supply of metal for an expansion in output, see J. P. Callu *et al.*, '"*Aureus obryziacus*"', in C. Morrisson *et al.* (eds.), *L'Or monnayé*. 1: *Purification et altérations de Rome à Byzance*, Cahiers Ernest-Babelon, 2 (Paris, 1985) 81–111, esp. 92 ff.

[60] This refers to the calculations in Table 3 of my thesis, 'Rural Communities', vol. 1.

[61] Since money supply = the size of the monetary stock × velocity of circulation.

[62] See C. Vogler, *Constance II et l'administration impériale* (Strasbourg, 1979) 232 ff.

[63] Ammianus 27.9.4.

[64] Ammianus 21.16.2: 'Nec sub eo dux quisquam cum clarissimatu provectus est. Erat enim (ut nos quoque meminimus) perfectissimi' (Under him no military commander was ever promoted to the rank of *clarissimus*. For, as far as I can recall, they were *perfectissimi*).

[65] See D. Hoffmann, *Das spätrömische Bewegungsheer und die Notitia Dignitatum*, 2 vols. (Düsseldorf, 1969–70) 1.314, B. Lorincz, 'Die *duces* des Provinz Valeria unter Valentinian I', *Alba Regia* 15 (1976) 99 ff.

military governor of Isauria was *clarissimus* by 359.[66] Another job to be upgraded in this way was that of the *comes largitionum*. He was *perfectissimus* in 345, *clarissimus* by 356.[67] Over the next three decades there was a veritable flood of promotions, with a reorganization of the grading pattern, creation of new grades, and constant upgrading.[68] The late Roman grading pattern was essentially due to Valentinian I, who seems both to have overhauled the existing structure of grades[69] and based the new policy on a systematic promotion of the imperial bureaucracy over the traditional 'senatorial' offices.[70] Mobility within the hierarchy entailed increases in pay which in turn prompted reform of the gold coinage and reorganization of the mint system. And both sets of changes implied a more liberal policy on commutation. With his usual lucidity, Ammianus noted these connections when he wrote that Valentinian was the first of the late Roman emperors to consolidate the social dominance of the *militares*[71] 'with inordinate increases in their gradation and pay' (*dignitates opesque eorum sublimius erigentem*).[72] Re-grading the *militares* was obviously part of the general overhaul of grading pattern which Valentinian is said to have carried out. Increasing their pay involved both conceding commutation on a wider scale[73] and linking the increased money payments to a purified gold coinage. These were movements which no subsequent regime would either want or be able to reverse.

Bargaining for Gold[74]

The great originality of Mickwitz lies in the fact that he was the first to draw attention to a form of social conflict peculiar to the late

[66] See Hoffmann, *SBND* 1.314, on Bassidius Lauricius, *Comes (et dux) et praeses Isauriae*.

[67] Compare *CTh.* 11.7.5 with 11.16.7.

[68] The best survey is still R. Guilland, 'Études sur l'histoire administrative de l'empire byzantin. Les titres nobiliaires de la haute époque (IVe–VIe siècles)', in *Mélanges G. Ostrogorsky*, 2 vols. (Belgrade, 1963) 1.117–33.

[69] *CTh.* 6.5.2 (384): 'Valentinianus genitor numinis nos(tri sin)gulis quibusque dignitatibus certum locum me(ritum)que praescribsit' (Valentinian, the ancestor of our Imperial divinity, prescribed a fixed rank and compensation for each separate dignity).

[70] e.g. *CTh.* 6.11.1 (372) states, 'Magistros scriniorum nostrorum praeferri volumus vicarianae potestati'. *CTh.* 6.9.1 (372) and 6.7.1 (372) comprise further examples.

[71] Ammianus 27.9.4: 'hunc imperatorem omnium primum in maius militares fastus ad damna rerum auxisse communium' (he was the first of all the emperors to increase the arrogance of the military, to the general detriment of society).

[72] Ibid. *Dignitates* were of course grades within the imperial hierarchy, though technically one referred to *gradus dignitatum*, as in *CTh.* 6.5.1, 8.1.10, etc.

[73] See K. L. Noethlichs, 'Spätantike Wirtschaftspolitik und *Adaeratio*', *Historia* 34 (1985) 102–16, esp. 107, who sees Valentinian reversing previous policy.

[74] S. J. B. Barnish, 'The Wealth of Iulianus Argentarius: Late Antique Banking and

empire, in the sense that no other period of Roman history reflects the opposition of the *militares* and the landed classes to the same degree. Of course, as I argued in the previous chapter, Mickwitz misinterpreted the interests of these groups in supposing that the latter wanted commutation, when it is quite clear both from the Code and from other sources that the fourth-century bureaucracy mounted continuous pressure for payment in money, and seems on the whole to have succeeded. In *CTh.* 7.4.1–31 it is possible to discern the main aspects of this struggle—the groups involved, the forms of bargaining used, and the government's responses. However, since the late Roman pay system is the presupposed framework of these rulings, perhaps it is worth saying something briefly about this.

Procopius' *Secret History*, ch. 24, contains some valuable passages on the system which regulated pay relationships in the Byzantine (and surely also the late Roman) bureaucracy. The backbone of the system was the late Roman grading pattern, with the bureaucracy classified into distinct pay scales and amounts of pay dependent on where jobs were classified (on their grade, i.e. *dignitas* or *βαθμός*)[75] as well as on a payment for seniority governed by some system of increments, if not the usual annual increments.[76] The pay packet consisted of a basic salary *evaluated in kind* and cash bonuses which again varied between grades.[77] Promotion was based strictly on seniority, though Justinian, according to Procopius, drastically

the Mediterranean Economy', *Byzantion* 55 (1985) 5–38, esp. 11, relates commutation to the division of the empire and the decline in the inflow of gold to the west, accepting Jones's assumption that the west adopted *adaeratio* 'more quickly than the wealthier east'. For M. F. Hendy, *The Economy, Fiscal Administration and Coinage of Byzantium* (Northampton, 1989), ch. 7, 36 the shift to cash payments occurred because these were 'much more convenient'. A. Cerati, *Caractère annonaire et assiette de l'impôt foncier au bas-empire* (Paris, 1975) 154, 169, likewise sees *adaeratio* as a matter of 'technical convenience'. The trouble with the latter view is that it ignores the whole group of constitutions which treat the problem precisely as a social one. My own interpretation differs from both the above in being more classical, so to speak (that is, closer to the way both Mickwitz and Mazzarino understood and debated the issue).

[75] *CTh.* 6.30.7 (384) states this explicitly: 'Annonas etiam iuxta definitum dignitatum modum volumus postulari nec amplius quicquam praesumi' (It is Our will also that their allowances of pay should be claimed by them in accordance with the established scale of ranks, and they shall not presume to demand more). Compare *CTh.* 7.4.1 (325), 'annonas suae congruas dignitati' (allowances commensurate with their grade); 7.4.32 (412), 'species . . . debitas dignitati'; 7.4.36 (424), 'annonas . . . quas pro dignitate sua consequuntur' (the allowances which they obtain in keeping with their rank); *CJ* 1.52 (439) 'pro annonis et capitu dignitati suae debitis'. Thus amounts of pay were clearly linked to job groups.

[76] On increments see Procopius, *HA* 24.2–4.

[77] See Gregory of Nazianzus, *Or.* 19.11 (*PG* 35.1056): *Τί λέγων ὀψώνιον; Τὸ βασιλικὸν σιτηρέσιον δηλονότι, καὶ τὰς ὑπαρχούσας ἐκ νόμου τοῖς ἀξιώμασι δωρεάς*. cf. *Or.* 4.82. Ammianus 30.8.8 calls the bonuses *supplementa*.

scaled down the rate of promotions by instructing the financial controller (λογοθέτης) not to fill vacancies.[78] Different jobs must have had different promotion ladders,[79] but even at the middle level of the bureaucracy employees due for promotion were feted by the emperor at a special banquet.[80] Finally, job changes which circumvented the prescribed channels of promotion were strongly resented because this sort of corruption (*usurpationis ambitio*) undermined the whole pattern of grading.[81] Since employees felt strongly about promotions,[82] they doubtless shared this attitude.

Commutation of pay came about through a concerted application of bargaining pressure by specific groups of the bureaucracy. *CTh.* 7.4.21 (396) accuses them of inflicting losses on people in the provinces, especially the *possessores*, by their deliberate failure to collect supplies: 'Si a militaribus provinciales quaelibet damna pertulerint ac non ipsas species, quae in provinciis a possessoribus congregantur, fuerint consecuti ...' (If the provincials should sustain any losses whatsoever at the hands of military officials, and the latter refuse to accept the supplies which are collected from the landholders ...). *CTh.* 7.4.20 has a similar context and is more explicit. This describes them as rejecting their pay in kind (*annonae*) in the post-harvest period to extort commutation later in the season at rates reflecting increasing scarcity in the market: 'Nulli militarium pro his annonis, quae in provinciis delegantur, repudiata ad tempus specierum copia et inopiae occasione captata pretia liceat postulare' (No military official shall be allowed to demand money in lieu of the allowances which are allocated to him in the provinces, if he has spurned those supplies at the proper time, due to their seasonal abundance, and tried to profit from a seasonal scarcity). It seems certain that both these rulings refer to the military side of the administration and especially to the various groups of military officers.[83] For these groups part of the attractiveness of commutation was the opportunity it afforded of speculative gains in local markets. This applied chiefly of course to foodgrains, whose prices fluctuated seasonally, between seasons and across districts.

[78] Procopius, *HA* 24.5 f.

[79] Jerome, *Contra Joannem Hierosolymitanum* 1.19 (*PL* 23.370) lists eight grades of junior officers before *tribunus*.

[80] Malalas, *Chron.* 474D (Dindorf; Jeffreys *et al.*, *Chronicle*, 275).

[81] *CTh.* 6.5.1 (383?) 'Nihil est tam iniuriosum in co(nser)vandis et custodiendis gradibus dignitatum quam usurpationis ambitio' (Nothing is more injurious to preserving and monitoring the system of classification of ranks than the drive to usurp a higher dignity). For the state it was essential that the grading system should retain its objectivity if only because the whole structure of pay relativities depended on it.

[82] 'dignitatum augmenta', Ammianus 20.8.8.

[83] This is clearly the sense of *militares*, as in Ammianus 21.16.3, 27.9.4, 16.8.13, etc.

But the assumption is that by this stage commutation rates were either based on or proportional to market prices.

Within the army the decisive role was played, clearly, by the senior officers.[84] *CTh.* 7.4.1 (325) deals specifically with the middle-grade commanders—'tribuni sive praepositi qui milites nostros curant', men like Flavius Abinnaeus, commander of the camp at Dionysias in the south-west of the Fayum. It seems that by the 320s they had started leaving supplies to rot in the warehouses so that the *procuratores* or *susceptores* or *praepositi pagorum et horrearum* would (have to) buy them. Constantine characterizes this as a strategy consciously intended to force the municipal functionaries to demand money instead of supplies from the taxpayers 'while the actual supplies are left there rotting and spoiled' (ut a provincialibus non annonas, sed pecunias postulent memorati ipsis etiam speciebus remanentibus vitiatis adque corruptis). Thus these sections of the bureaucracy were clearly involved in a type of bargaining intended to influence the form of payment. The reference to 'pecuniae' leaves it unclear in what coin they would actually have received pay commuted in this way. By the early fifth century, however, this was clearly gold.[85]

It seems likely that *CTh.* 7.4.1 is the background implied in *P. Abinn.* 26 = *P. Lond.* 237. This is a letter from an accountant to a local camp commander requesting him to make sure that the *annona* quotas, when collected from a certain village, would be locked up. It points out that the *actuarii* of the Upper Thebaid had got the military governor (*dux*) to lock up the year's supplies for inspection by an official. But the supplies in question involved only 'the wheat and barley not accepted' (*τὸν ἐν ἀθέτῳ σιτόκριθον,* ll. 23–4). The writer, himself an *actuarius*, does not explain why these quotas had 'not been accepted' but presumably this is because the reason was obvious both to him and to Abinnaeus, the commander at Dionysias. In view of *CTh.* 7.4.1 it seems likely that the 'rejection' of supplies in kind was at the instigation of Abinnaeus, since he was precisely the sort of military officer being blamed there. Since the two documents are separated by approximately twenty years, it is possible that in the meantime the government had reacted with a formal stipulation that accountants would be held responsible for the financial loss.

[84] Compare R. Grosse, *Römische Militärgeschichte von Gallienus bis zum Beginn d. byzantinischen Themenverfassung* (Berlin, 1920) 143 ff. (*Oberoffiziere*).

[85] *CTh.* 7.4.36 (424) refers to the same groups (*tribuni sive comites vel praepositi numerorum*) collecting their pay *in aere* (i.e. 'in money', cf. *Thes. Ling. Lat.* 1.1075, s.v. *aes*, III.2 for the sense of *aes* as money in general) but to the fringe benefits of the *duces sive tribuni* as *in auro*.

CTh. 7.4.1 poses the issue entirely in terms of cash payments versus payments in kind—'ut a provincialibus non annonas, sed pecunias postulent memorati' (The said officials are demanding from the provincials not payments in kind, but money). Commutation was desirable in its own terms. But 'taxationes pretiorum dispendiosae' in *CTh.* 11.2.4 shows that half the point of commutation lay in the rates which the bureaucracy could extract from one occasion to the next. Government responses fluctuated between outright opposition and regulated acceptance. Thus in 358 Constantius imposed an outright ban on encashment of the *sportulae* which the *duces* extracted from the commissary officers—'whether in base metal or in gold'—'so there should be no need for complaints about the enormity of the rates charged' (*super immensitate pretiorum*).[86] Yet by Julian's reign these perquisites were paid in money, for he is supposed to have prescribed a limit of fifty pounds of silver.[87] As commutation spread, government regulation involved either a fixed schedule of rates—*adaerationes statutae*,[88] *nummaria defixa pretia*[89]—or market-based rates of commutation. The existence of these two methods of regulation implies a third, unregulated situation in which officials and state employees could impose arbitrary rates on the taxpayers—through the authorities who dealt directly with the latter.[90] Thus there were three distinct sorts of *pretia* in the commercialized fiscalism of the late empire: official rates, market rates, and unofficial rates.[91] Várady has argued, 'The official prices were, of course, always lower than the market prices, for their main purpose was to set a limit on the money claims which were based on the high free market and speculation prices when . . . goods were scarce.'[92] This may or may not be true, but the obvious implication of accepting regulation at market prices is that the unofficial rates were considerably above average market levels.

Control over rates of commutation enabled the bureaucracy to convert the particular late Roman fusion of market and fiscal forces into a source of systematic profiteering, so that repeated

[86] *CTh.* 8.4.6 (358).

[87] *CTh.* 8.4.9.

[88] *CTh.* 7.4.30 (409), 'statutory rates of commutation'.

[89] *CTh.* 7.4.29 (407), 'fixed cash rates'.

[90] Cf. *CTh.* 7.4.22 (396) *pro arbitrio proprio*, with reference to the rates exacted.

[91] Schedule rates were determined by the *praefectura* or (less frequently) governed by a special statute. For the former cf. *P. Beatty Panop.* 2.230 f., esp. ὁπόσον ἡ θεῖα ὥρισεν διατύπωσις, *P. Lips.* 63.10 ff. (388), *CTh.* 7.4.22.1 (396), *CJ* 1.52 (439). For the latter cf. *CTh.* 7.4.22 which refers to a *generalis lex* of Valentinian I prescribing rates for the crack troops.

[92] L.Várady, 'Contributions to the Late Roman Military Economy and Agrarian Taxation', *AArchHung.* 14 (1962) 403–38, esp. 405.

contemporary references to *cupiditas*[93] imply not abstract moral judgements but a specific set of bargaining and fiscal practices which hastened the accumulation of gold in the bureaucratic class. Libanius attacked a *consularis* of Syria for shamelessly exploiting the *apodektai* over the rates (*timai*) officially allowed to governors in respect of their allowances of agricultural produce. This man both exercised his option of commuting and chose to enforce extortionate rates, forcing the local collectors to buy back supplies which were useless to them.[94] This is exactly analogous to the situation in *CTh.* 7.4.1 where the army officers are accused of forcing the various local authorities to 'buy' supplies which they themselves refused to accept. Thus if strategies of this sort reflected bargaining pressure with respect to the state (to influence the form of pay), they also embodied a degree of coercive bargaining with the municipal authorities deployed by the state, both because a commutation that was optional for one was obligatory for the other,[95] and in the sense that determination of the rate at which commutation occurred would have to be bargained with *them* if (or because) the prescribed rates were simply discarded as irrelevant. The passages cited earlier (*CTh.* 7.4.21, etc.) leave us in no doubt that the officials dominated this bargaining process and that the local aristocracies fiercely resented this.

That the *militares* were using essentially similar tactics to influence their form of pay in the reign of Arcadius[96] shows that the officers continued to fight for commutation as long as there was still official resistance to the latter. As Cerati has shown, the reign of Theodosius I began to bring about a fundamental shift in the structure of taxation, with government extracting more revenue in money form because a larger share of public revenue was now

[93] Ammianus 16.8.13, on the reign of Constantius, 'Sub hoc enim ordinum singulorum auctores infinita cupidine divitiarum arserunt' (For under him the leading representatives of the different orders raged with a boundless desire to amass wealth); Anon., *de rebus bellicis* 4.1 (Thompson, *Roman Reformer*, 95), 'Ad haec igitur incommoda . . . accedit etiam iudicum execranda cupiditas' (Now in addition to these injuries . . . comes the appalling greed of the provincial Governors, Thompson, 111); *CTh.* 7.4.32 (412), 'Nam cum adaerationis aestimatio prius per centum et viginti capita exactione solidi teneretur, per sexaginta recens redegit aviditas' (For whereas the rate of commutation was previously established at a solidus for every 120 *capita*, sheer greed has recently raised this to a solidus for every 60).

[94] Libanius, *Or.* 57.51 (Foerster, *Libanii opera*, 4.171 f.), cf. P. Petit, *Libanius et la vie municipale à Antioche au IV siècle après J.-C.* (Paris, 1955) 153.

[95] Compare *P. Reinach* 56.15 ff. where the writer says, 'We don't want (i.e. shouldn't touch) chaff. In case it isn't taken and we are forced to pay the commutation price (*ἀναγκασθῶμεν τὴν τιμὴν διαγράψαι*)', and the discussion in H. Brandt, 'P. Rein. I 56 (= W. Chrest. 419): Die *Διαδόται* und das Problem der Adäration', *ZPE* 68 (1987) 87 ff.

[96] Cf. *CTh.* 7.4.18 (393), 7.4.21 (396).

assessed in money.[97] The ensuing need to sustain the level of supplies in kind meant an increased use of *coemptiones*, but also renewed (but ultimately temporary) opposition to excessive *adaeratio*.[98] Thus by the end of the fourth century gold was being used (1) for the payment of state salaries and perquisites (due to commutation),[99] (2) for payment of a certain portion of the land tax, and (3) for the bulk purchase of agricultural commodities on a *coemptio* basis.[100]

Coemptiones

Legal texts of the fifth century reflect widespread commutation into cash of payments due in kind, especially in terms of the emoluments of officials.[101] By 423 even the lowest grades of the bureaucracy received their pay in money form, with conversion formulas linked to the model applied to ordinary soldiers.[102] But the fiscal and bargaining practices of the fourth century to some extent survived and continued to dominate relations between the bureaucracy and the landowners, so that in John Malalas' report of the Anastasian fiscal reforms (part of a general restructuring of imperial finances under Anastasius), the further extension of money payments was seen as a conscious attempt to undermine the whole system (i.e. existing practices) of the *annona militaris*. Malalas says, 'The most sacred emperor Anastasius imposed on all land-holders a tax to be paid in gold, based on acreage, *to prevent taxes in kind being demanded and used for their own purposes by the soldiers*.'[103] If this was an interpretation of the reform, the gist of it is abundantly

[97] Cerati, *Caractère annonaire et assiette de l'impôt foncier*, 71–85; linked at 355 to the stability of the solidus.

[98] For the latter cf. *CTh.* 11.2.4 (384), 7.4.18 (393).

[99] Compare esp. *CTh.* 8.4.17 (387 or 388) (cf. Mazzarino, *Aspetti sociali*, 198), commuted payments were paid in gold; even earlier, Ammianus 26.8.6, 'ut aurum susceptum stipendii nomine militibus per Orientem diffusis viritim tribueret', of the year 365. Jones's view that this reference to a gold *stipendium* and an earlier one in Ammianus 15.6.3, actually refer to 'delayed donatives', *LRE* 2.1259 n. 32, seems unlikely.

[100] *CTh.* 11.15.2 (384), *P. Mich.* 613 (415).

[101] E. Stein, *Histoire du Bas-Empire*. 1: *De l'État Romain à l'État Byzantin (284–476)*, ed. J.-R. Palanque (Paris, etc., 1959) 117.

[102] *CTh.* 7.4.35 (423), 'Annonas omnes, quae univ(er)sis officiis atque sacri palatii ministeriis et sacris scriniis ceterisque cunctarum adminiculis dignitatum adsolent delegari . . . ad similitudinem militum, quibus aerariae praebentur annonae, adaerari praecipimus' (We suggest that all allowances of pay which are customarily allocated to all the office staffs and ministries of the sacred Imperial palace and the sacred Imperial bureaus and to the various subaltern grades who service the higher dignities should be commuted on the formula applied to the soldiers, who receive their allowances in money).

[103] Malalas, *Chron.* 394B (Dindorf; Jeffreys *et al.*, *Chronicle* 221). J. Karayannopoulos, 'Die Chrysoteleia der Iuga', *BZ* 49 (1956) 72–84 offers a more restrictive interpretation of this passage, citing Evagrius, *HE* 3.42.

substantiated by *CJ* 10.27.2, a document of inestimable importance both for its description of the way the system worked and for its coinage references. (For a translation of the relevant portions of this constitution, see App. 2) Here the following points seem fairly clear. The system of *coemptiones* continued to be based on market prices, as in the reign of Theodosius I.[104] Anastasius states that if it became absolutely necessary for local landholders to provision the state, supplies should be 'bought at fair prices, namely those current in the district (*polis*) from which the goods are supplied'.[105] Such purchases would be credited to the taxpayers' account by way of the payments due from them in gold (*τὰ συντελούμενα παρ' αὐτῶν ἐν χρυσῷ δημόσια*), the sums imputed being based on the prevailing price levels (hence *ὑπολογιζέσθω δὲ τοῖς πιπράσκουσι τὰ τιμήματα τῶν εἰδῶν*). It is claimed that officials deliberately dissociate these phases of the transaction so that the prices eventually paid by them should be as low as possible, and that this is unfair.[106] Again, a conscious use of price fluctuations is implied, though now in a movement which reverses the one described in *CTh.* 7.4.20 roughly a century earlier.[107] Byzantine, like late Roman, fiscalism was closely bound up with market processes. Next Anastasius states that no landowner should be compelled to sell the whole of his output but only 'surplus' output (*τὰ ἐκπεριττεύοντα εἴδη*).[108] *Coemptio* (*synōnē*) should never be used except in absolute emergencies, and then in such a way that the gold paid by way of public purchase (*τὸ τῆς συνωνῆς χρυσίον*) should be deducted (*παρακατέχεσθαι*) from the landowner's money taxes in case the sums accruing to the state on this account sufficed to cover the value of such purchases.[109] In these cases the payments would be purely notional. Where this was not the case, and actual payment was involved, this should first be settled in full and in solidi of full weight (*ἐν εὐστάθμοις νομίσμασι*). Officials are expressly instructed not to palm off solidi which are *parastathma*. The difference in weight between the proper weight standard and the actual weight of light-weight solidi is called *parallēlon*,[110] which is a clue to the meaning of the term *parallēlismos* in the papyri, suggesting that the latter would have something

[104] See n. 100 above.

[105] *CJ* 10.27.2.1. The date is *c.*498, cf. Stein, *HBE* 2.202.

[106] *CJ* 10.27.2.2. The precise word used for a fall in prices or depressed market conditions is *euthēnia*, so this passage helps to clarify the sense in which this word is used in *P. Oxy.* XXVII 2479.24 ff., where an Apion *geōrgos* tells his employer that he and his children have nothing to eat because of a slump in prices, *προκειμένης τ[αύ]της [ἕνε]κα τῆς εὐθενίας*. Triantaphyllopoulos' explanation in '*Εὐθηνία* (P. Oxy. 2479)', *REG* 80 (1967) 353–62, makes no sense. For other references see p. 86 f. below.

[107] See p. 53 above.

[108] *CJ* 10.27.2.4 [109] *CJ* 10.27.2.5 [110] *CJ* 10.27.2.6

to do with the difference between weight standards.[111] *CJ* 10.27.2 is thus formal proof that a not inconsiderable portion of the gold currency in circulation *c*.498 was of substandard weight. The economic background of Anastasius' legislation is a money economy in which the functional dominance of gold combined with fiscal and purely economic factors to produce a high velocity of circulation (of gold).[112] Obviously this assumes that 'if a coinage became very worn, the implication is that it was handled a lot'.[113] Finally, clause eight states that when *coemptio* does occur, each landowner (*κτήτωρ*) should be liable in strict proportion to his acreage or total assessment (*πρὸς τὴν ἀναλογίαν τῶν ζευγῶν ἤτοι ζυγοκεφαλῶν*).[114] The term *ktētōr* which occurs twice in this law probably refers specifically to big landowners.[115]

In principle, then, *coemptiones* continued to be geared to market prices. In an economic sense, such transactions represented a huge *extension* of the market sector (whose existence they presupposed) though within the peculiarly late Roman structure of 'fiscalized commercialism', with fiscal and market forces interacting repeatedly, from the essential pressure that money taxes imposed on landowners to produce for the market to the different ways in which salaries, tax commutations, and state purchases tied in with market fluctuations. The classic sources of the sixth century show that these tendencies continued to operate. In a remarkable passage Lydus specifically mentions the pressure of money taxes in the early years of Justinian's reign, during John the Cappadocian's first prefecture, listing a whole range of exactions and referring to the 'merciless exaction of these taxes in gold (*ἐπὶ τοῦ νομίσματος*)'.[116] The finances of Aphrodito are proof of the evolution under Justinian, for the amount payable in gold increased by a factor of almost 3 between 525 and 567, to over a thousand solidi per year.[117] The sixth century

[111] This is already implied by the expression *παραλληλ(ισμὸς) ζυγ(ῶν)* in *P. Oxy*. 16 1918 verso 7; *LSJ* 1316, 'equating of payments' is hard to understand.

[112] See 'Weight Loss', p. 70ff. below.

[113] D. M. Metcalf, *Coinage in South-Eastern Europe, 820–1396* (London, 1979) 4.

[114] *CJ* 10.27.2.8.

[115] As it certainly does in Malalas, *Chron*. 444B–C (Dindorf), *χαρισάμενος . . . τοῖς κτήτορσιν ἀξίας ἰλλουστρίων*, referring to Justinian's favours to large landowners in the east. This supports Dölger's view, *BZ* 34 (1934) 371, that *coemptiones* affected chiefly the bigger landowners.

[116] John Lydus, *Mag*. 3.70. Bandy's translation 'in currency' is equally possible. John's assertion that the rate of rural–urban migration had increased sharply in the early part of Justinian's reign is fully borne out by *Nov. Just*. 80, Praef., dated 539, which complains of *geōrgoi* deserting their own districts to come to Constantinople.

[117] See R. Rémondon, '*P.Hamb*. 56 et *P.Lond*. 1419 (notes sur les finances d'Aphrodito du VIe siècle au VIIIe)', *CE* 40 (1965) 401–30 for our only detailed study of the evolution of money taxes, and cf. App. 1, Table 7.

saw an increasing monetization of the tax system, which in turn presupposes both that more gold was in circulation and that market production had expanded (or was expanding) to allow for increased revenues in gold. The significance of *coemptiones* is that, depending on the scale and frequency of such transactions, the state must have injected substantial sums of gold into the rural economy, making it possible for villages and large estates to use this coinage as the essential means of payment in smaller transactions such as labour hiring, land purchases, and so on. The prices paid in such purchases were a continuing source of grievance: payment at below market prices was a crushing blow to the majority of landlords, according to Procopius.[118] It is unlikely that the bigger sections of the aristocracy actually allowed this to happen. It is interesting, nonetheless, that the market remained the essential frame of reference for these transactions.

Civil Society

Gold became not only the dominant currency, in the sense that its use in coin or bullion accounted for by far the biggest share of monetary transactions in the economy as a whole,[119] but also a mass currency which permeated all levels of social life, as it continued to do in Egypt in the period covered by the Geniza records. 'The use of money', said John Chrysostom in 388, 'welds together our whole existence and forms the basis for all sorts of contracts, whether one has to buy something or sell something.'[120] Thus the dominance of money reflected an economy in which market relations were equally widespread. Now this was true not only of the great urban centres of the eastern Mediterranean, cities like Antioch where John preached, but of landlocked rural districts such as the countryside of eastern Cappadocia, where Basil saw landowners extracting

[118] Procopius, *HA* 23.11 (Haury and Wirth, 142), *τοὺς τὰ χωρία κεκτημένους*; 13, *τοῖς τῶν χωρίων κυρίοις*. In 23.11 *τιμημάτων καταβαλλομένων οὐχ ᾗπερ ἐφίησιν ὁ παρὼν τῇ χρείᾳ καιρὸς, κτλ.* clearly refers to the fixing of prices at levels below the market; the Loeb translation 'the deliveries being made' (271) is simply wrong.

[119] Compare D. M. Metcalf, 'The Mint of Thessalonica in the Early Byzantine Period', in *Villes et peuplement dans l'Illyricum protobyzantin* (Rome, 1984) 111–28, at 117, also 'The Minting of Gold Coinage in the Fifth and Sixth Centuries and the Gold Currency of Illyricum and Dalmatia', *SEBGC* 65–109, esp. 75, 'Gold was the major part of the money supply in terms of its book value'. Contrast J. F. Haldon, 'Some Considerations on Byzantine Society and Economy in the Seventh Century', *Byzantinische Forschungen* 10 (1985) 75–112, esp. 80 ff., who thinks that gold was restricted to a state circuit and the work of sustaining the huge volume of commercial transactions devolved largely on the 'bronze coinages'.

[120] John Chrysostom, *In principium Actorum apostolorum* 4.2 (*PG* 51.99), *Πάλιν τῶν ἀργυρίων ἡ χρῆσις πᾶσαν ἡμῶν συγκροτεῖ τὴν ζωὴν, καὶ συμβολαίων ἁπάντων ὑπόθεσις γίνεται, κἂν ἀγοράσαι τι, κἂν πωλῆσαι δέῃ, κτλ.*

revenues in gold from the sale of wheat, wine, and wool,[121] or the rugged towering mountains east of Anzetene where, later, John of Ephesus described a huge monastic vineyard selling wine to Cappadocian merchants 'who used to go out as far as Syria and buy wine'.[122] Monasteries and aristocrats were in the forefront of the revival of wine economy. Production for the market stimulated monetary circulation. The cash wages of grape-pickers employed by a large ecclesiastical complex in the uplands around Abu Mena were paid in solidi.[123] In his *Life of St Martin* Sulpicius Severus notes that most monasteries engaged in commodity relations; that Martin's own monastery near Tours did not do so was (evidently) exceptional.[124] The market was so pervasive that in Sulpicius' *Dialogues* Postumianus thought it was worth recounting the following story about a community which he came across some five miles inland from the Gulf of Sidra (between Cyrenaica and Egypt) soon after the year 400. 'By our inquiry into the customs of the inhabitants we learned one notable thing, they neither buy nor sell . . . As for gold and silver . . . they neither have them nor wish to. When I offered our priest ten gold pieces (*decem nummos aureos*)[125] he recoiled in horror, declaring in his profound wisdom that with gold one does not build up the Church but, rather, destroys it.'[126] Though such attitudes may have been widespread in monastic circles, they did not prevent either monasteries or the urban Church from amassing considerable sums of gold. In part this was the result of accumulation, of a conscious drive to amass a large sum of money, which characterized not only the trading classes and a section of the aristocracy but small-scale producers such as the weaver in Jerome's story.[127]

For Chrysostom gold was money *par excellence*. The *ergastēria* of the *trapezitai* formed focal points of the business life of Antioch around 388.[128] They were primarily bankers who became involved

[121] Basil, *Hom.VI de avaritia* 5 (*PG* 31.269), *Ὁ σῖτος χρυσός σοι γίνεται, ὁ οἶνος εἰς χρυσὸν μεταπήγνυται, τὰ ἔριά σοι ἀποχρυσοῦται.*

[122] John of Ephesus, *Lives* 8 (*PO* 17.129–30). The currency in which these purchases were settled was obviously gold, cf. 'forty or fifty denarii' on p. 130, and see Mundell Mango, *Artistic Patronage*, 66.

[123] See D. Wortmann, 'Griechische ostraka aus Abu Mena', *ZPE* 8 (1971) 41–69. The ostraca appear to date from the 7th cent.

[124] Sulpicius Severus, *Vita Mart.* 10 (*PL* 20.166), 'non emere aut vendere, ut plerisque monachis moris est, quidquam licebat'.

[125] Surely solidi; not 'ten pieces of silver', as in Peebles (n. 126).

[126] Sulpicius Severus, *Dialogues* 1.5 (*PL* 20.187), trans. B. M. Peebles, *The Fathers of the Church. A New Translation*, vol. 7 (1949) 167.

[127] He was a monk who accumulated 100 solidi without the knowledge or consent of his superiors, cf. Jerome, *Ep.* 22.33 (Labourt 1.149).

[128] John Chrysostom, *In princ. Act.* 4.2.

in money changing and the testing of coin as the circulation of gold increased. John refers to them rejecting solidi which were counterfeit or adulterated (Καθάπερ γὰρ οἱ τραπεζῖται τὸ μὲν κίβδηλον καὶ παράσημον ἐκβάλλουσι νόμισμα). In the late sixth century Gregory refers to the *nummularii* examining first the *qualitas* of the coin (he uses the Greek word for the solidus), then the *figura* (type), and finally the weight. Here 'qualitas' clearly refers to the alloy, since Gregory says that this is examined 'ne sub auri specie aes lateat'.[129] A passage in John Cassian which would have been published *c.*425 is even more systematic. Discussing the skills of the *trapezitai*, he distinguishes four possible ways in which a solidus might warrant grounds for rejection. Adulteration and forgery are obviously among them but solidi might vary in terms of the fineness of the gold and coins might be light weight.[130] *Trapezitai* might also be *argyropratai*.[131] That they were employed by the aristocracy as bankers is shown by the Apion archive.[132] That the *argyropratai* could also have associations with the big estates is proved by a passage in Malalas which refers to a certain Isaac who was *argyroprat*ē*s* (money-dealer) 'with (*kata*) the *patricius* Belisarius'.[133] In the west the *argentarii* were probably the élite group in the money market. Julianus who contributed 26,000 solidi towards the construction costs of S.Vitale in Ravenna is described by Agnellus as an 'argentarius'.[134] Finally, by the sixth century it was usual for official receipts to certify the weight-value of payments by an expression such as 'accurately measured by weight' (εὔσταθμα ζυγῷ).[135] These regular or routine functions were clearly handled by the *zygostatai*, or coin-weighers, whose closest western counterparts were probably the *collectarii*.[136] In *P. Laur.* III 110, dated 615, a 'public weigher' states in the *subscriptio*, πεποίημαι τὸ εὔστ(αθμον) τῶν νομ(ισμάτων) δεκ[α]πέντε κτλ. This meant not that he had tested each solidus

[129] Gregory, *Moralia in Job* 33.60 (*PL* 76.711D–712A).

[130] John Cassian, *Collationes* 1.20 (*SC* 42.101). The descriptions of these functions are as follows: 'probare quodnam sit aurum purissimum et ut vulgo dicitur obrizum quodve sit minus purgatione ignis excoctum . . . deinde ne quid illis a legitimo pondere deminutum sit censura trutinae diligenter inquirere'. On *obryzum* see Benveniste, *Rev. Phil.* 27 (1953) 123–6.

[131] John Moschus, *Pratum spirituale* 185 (*PG* 87/3.3061A), Grégoire, *Recueil des inscriptions grecques chrétiennes d'Asie Mineure* (Paris, 1922) 98 quater (p. 29).

[132] Compare also *P. Oxy.* LVIII 3935 (591) which involves a *trapezitēs* of the *endoxos oikos* of Flavius Strategius.

[133] John Malalas, *Chron.* 494D (Dindorf; Jeffreys *et al.*, *Chronicle* 302): '[Sergius] . . . made a deposition that Isakios, the money dealer, from the household of the patrician Belisarios, also knew about the plot'.

[134] Agnellus, *Lib. Pontificalis Ecclesiae Ravennatis* 57; 59 (pp. 318, 319).

[135] e.g., *P. Flor.* III 291 (6c.), *P. Herm.* 83 (6c.).

[136] In *P. Michael.* 35 Victor is both *collectarius* and *zygostatēs*.

for weight and fineness, and found all of them to be of the proper standard, but that he had determined the real value of the payment net of any depreciation due to wear. The *zygostatai* started as public functionaries but private estates must have employed them on a large scale.[137]

The proliferation of functions connected with the handling of money and their repeated occurrence in late antique sources are obvious reflections of a substantial growth in the supply of gold money. 'In terms of value monetary affairs were dominated by the gold currency.'[138] Vryonis refers to a 'money economy based on gold' which 'played an important part in the provincial life of the empire' from the seventh to the ninth centuries.[139] The starting point was Ostrogorsky's critique of Kazhdan, based on the general postulate that 'it is the gold coinage which was more important in the question of urban continuity and commercial activity'.[140] This is obviously correct. The late Roman and later the Byzantine state eventually lost interest in the copper coinage despite repeated attempts to produce a currency that was both stable and differentiated. On the other hand, as Ostrogorsky noted, 'gold issues not only did not diminish in the seventh century, but on the contrary increased significantly'.[141] This is borne out by the 'total hoard statistic' which shows a sharp increase in the number of hoarded solidi in the first half of the seventh century.[142] This seems to me to deal with Grierson's objection that Ostrogorsky's estimates were misleading since the collections are not a representative sample of the monetary mass.[143] In regions close to the heart of Byzantine power (viz. Turkey) most of the more substantial hoards (over 100 solidi) are both seventh-century deposits and consist chiefly of solidi struck in the course of that century.[144] Among

[137] e.g., *P. Oxy.* XXXVI 2780.22 (553), *zygostatēs* of the *patricia* Gabrielia.

[138] Metcalf, 'The Mint of Thessalonica', 117.

[139] S. Vryonis, 'An Attic Hoard of Byzantine Gold Coins (668–741) from the Thomas Whittemore Collection and the Numismatic Evidence for the Urban History of Byzantium', in *Mélanges Ostrogorsky*, 1.291–300, esp. 296, 298.

[140] Ibid. 292.

[141] G. Ostrogorsky, 'Byzantine Cities in the Early Middle Ages', *DOP* 13 (1959) 44–66, at 51.

[142] See n. 60 above.

[143] P. Grierson, 'Byzantine Coinage as Source Material', in J. M. Hussey, D. Obolensky, and S. Runciman (eds.), *Proceedings of the XIIIth International Congress of Byzantine Studies, Oxford 5–10 September, 1966* (London, 1967) 317–33, esp. 323–4, *DOC* 2/1.5–6, and most recently, 'Iconografia, circolazione monetaria e tesaurizzazione', in A. Guillou (ed.), *La Cultura bizantina. Oggetti e messaggio: moneta ed economia* (Rome, 1986) 29–57, at 38–9. Ostrogorsky's estimates were based on the gold pieces in London (Wroth), Leningrad (Tolstoy), and Washington (DOP).

[144] Compare Yildiz Palace 2, Chatalja, Aydin II, Yildiz Palace 1, and Istanbul in Table 4, last column.

Greek hoards the biggest attested so far, from Samos, consists almost entirely (97 per cent) of solidi of Phocas and Heraclius.[145] In Sicily the largest find of gold reported to date, that of Pantalica near Syracuse, consisted of up to 2,000 solidi of the seventh century.[146] From Africa one has the substantial hoard of solidi of Constantine IV.[147] Thus the monetary economy of the late empire survived well into the seventh century, in the sense that gold continued to circulate on a scale comparable with the earlier period.

The scattered textual references are concordant with this. Sbeitla's wealth in 647 consisted chiefly of gold.[148] In that year the Arabs are said to have extracted some 2–3 million solidi by way of an evacuation payment.[149] The aristocracy of the high steppe region came up with this astonishing sum of money doubtless to avoid further destruction of their olive plantations. The unwillingness to jeopardize those investments was a key factor in the collapse of the resistance to the Arabs.[150] In the sixth century John of Ephesus estimates the gold amassed by Khusro I at Dara in the general region of a million solidi.[151] Procopius cites Khusro's estimate of the monetary wealth of Edessa at 500 *centenaria*, that is, 3.6 million solidi.[152] This was clearly a minimum estimate since Khusro was offering the Edessenes a choice between that amount and the certainty of capture with the systematic plunder of as much gold and silver as he could find. The consistency between these estimates is remarkable and shows that the average commercial city of the central and eastern Mediterranean of the sixth to seventh centuries in terms of gold reserves alone would have had assets totalling several million solidi. One way of understanding this is to see the aristocracy and the trading classes accumulating wealth (in the precious metals) on the basis of a stock of solidi which had expanded

[145] M. Oeconomidès and P. Drossoyianni, 'A Hoard of Gold Byzantine Coins from Samos', *RN* 31, ser. 6 (1989) 145–82.

[146] P. Orsi, 'Byzantina Siciliae', *BZ* 19 (1910) 63–90, at 64f., and *Sicilia bizantina*, 2 vols. (Rome, 1942), 1.137.

[147] C. Morrisson, 'Un trésor de *solidi* de Constantin IV de Carthage', *RN* 22, ser. 6 (1980) 155–60, with 'Supplément au "trésor de Constantin IV"', *BSFN* 36 (1981) 92–4.

[148] 'Ubayd Allāh, *Récit de la conquête*, 4 (Lévi-Provencal, *Arabica* 1 (1954) p. 37).

[149] The sources are discussed by Slim, in R. Guéry, C. Morrisson, and H. Slim, *Recherches archéologiques franco-tunisiennes à Rougga. 3: Le trésor de monnaies d'or byzantines* (Rome, 1982) 76–94.

[150] See M. Talbi, 'Un nouveau fragment de l'histoire de l'occident musulman (62–196/682–812): l'Epopée d'al-Kāhina', *Cahiers de Tunisie* 19 (1971) 19–52, repr. in *Études d'histoire ifrīqiyenne et de civilisation musulmane medievale* (Tunis, 1982) 125–67.

[151] John of Ephesus, *Ecclesiastical History* 3.3.5 (pp. 383–4), Brooks, *CSCO* III, 3.220 ('centum vel ducenta centenaria'). John was careful about the way he phrased the estimate.

[152] Procopius, *De bello Pers.* 2.26.39 (Haury, 1.274), πεντακόσια κεντηνάρια χρυσοῦ.

progressively over the centuries. Certainly by the end of the sixth century there was a vast amount of gold in circulation in the eastern empire. John of Nikiu states that Maurice 'sold all the grain of Egypt and converted it into gold, and likewise the grain for Byzantium he sold for gold'.[153] Gascou sees *P. Oxy.* 1909 (a list of assessments arranged by the chief territories of the province of Arcadia) as a reflection of these measures. Here the Oxyrhynchite and the Cynopolite contribute a total of 59,500 solidi, Heracleopolis 57,500.[154] The *Διήγησις περὶ τῆς οἰκοδομῆς τοῦ ναοῦ* put the annual revenue extracted from Egypt (under Justinian) at over 2.5 million solidi[155] and the gross cash revenue or total assessment[156] of the empire at a thousand *centenaria* or 7.2 million solidi—figures which are wholly credible since the orders of magnitude are precisely what we should expect.[157] Assuming that the provincial aristocracy retained most of its cash flow, as the Apion accounts seem to indicate,[158] this implies a 'gross provincial product' of *at least* 20 million solidi.[159]

[153] John of Nikiu 95.21 (Charles 154), cf. Gascou, *Domaines* 11.

[154] *P. Oxy.* XVI 1909 (with *BL* 8.251 for the suggested date): Arcadia as a whole would have paid 195,000 solidi if the relative shares of the individual districts were still the same as in *P. Oxy.* LI 3636 from the 5th cent.

[155] *Diegesis*, *c.*25 (*Scriptores orig. Constantinopolitanarum*, fasc.1, 101–2, cf. G. Dagron, *Constantinople Imaginaire. Études sur le recueil des "Patria"* (Paris, 1984) 207). The early Arab administrations extracted 2–4 million dinars by way of *kharāj* and poll-tax, cf. al-Balādhurī in *Futūḥ al-buldān*, 216 (de Goeje), tr. P. K. Hitti, *The Origins of the Islamic State* (New York, 1916) 340. For corroborating evidence cf. M. A. H. el-Abbadi, 'Historians and the Papyri on the Finances of Egypt at the Arab Conquest', in *Proceedings of the XVIth International Congress of Papyrology, New York, 24–31 July 1980* (ASP 23, 1981) 509–16. Bagnall's estimation of the total tax yield of Egypt as roughly 1.6 million solidi, *TAPA* 115 (1985) 289–308, is based on a sown acreage figure of 6.7 million arouras, which may be too low (cf. *SB* 14.12208 = Bagnall and Worp, *ZPE* 37 (1980) 263–4, where the Oxyrhynchite's total sown acreage in the mid-4th cent. is 202,534 arouras). A government survey of 724/5 put the total *cultivable* area of Egypt at 30 million feddans, that is, about 191,000 km^2 or well over 40 million arouras, cf. al-Maqrīzī, *Description*, 283 and see H. Halm, *Ägypten nach den mamlukischen Lehensregistern. I Oberägypten und das Fayyūm* (Wiesbaden, 1979) 10.

[156] *Diegesis*, *c.*25, *πάκτα γὰρ ἐλάμβανε μέχρι χίλια κεντηνάρια*, that is, Justinian extracted a total revenue of 'up to 1,000 centenaria'.

[157] e.g. this estimate of the empire's total income (in gold revenues) would mean that the surplus accumulated by Anastasius in 518 was notionally equal to just over three years' receipts, which is entirely plausible in a reign of twenty-seven years.

[158] See App. 1, Table 2.

[159] Much more, of course, if the state absorbed less than a third of the total cash revenues of the aristocracy; cf. Jones, *The Roman Economy*, 83: 'The tax therefore comes to nearly one-third of the gross yield' (on the tax register of Antaeopolis).

Economic Aspects

Economic Relations: The Exchange-Rate between Gold and Copper

In *CPR* VIII 22, dated 314, the daily wages of casual labour vary from 400 to 650 drachmas.[160] Since the same account gives the price of wheat as 8,000 drachmas to the artaba,[161] an unskilled labourer would have had to work, say, for sixteen days to be able to purchase one artaba of wheat. The standard ration in Egypt was 12 artabas per adult (male?) per year, so at these prices roughly 6.2 months (192 days) of continuous employment would have provided for the annual grain requirements of one (adult) family member. The helper who earned 3 solidi per year in 588 working for an Oxyrhynchite goldsmith[162] was clearly better off even at his abysmal wages, for at the average (gold) price of wheat in the sixth century he would have been able to purchase close to 19 artabas for an equivalent period of employment. The difference lay, clearly, in the strength of one currency vis-à-vis the other. Insofar as Byzantine wage earners were paid mostly in gold (for jobs or types of employment which involved cash wages wholly or in part) this obviously secured a stable living standard as long as employers paid the same wages in money terms. (Heraclius, for example, is accused of having cut the wages of public employees.)[163] Casual labour was the crucial exception.[164] There is abundant evidence to show that the usual earnings of casual workers in urban employment (in the Byzantine period) was 1 keration per day even for strenuous jobs like construction and stone-cutting.[165] If received on a daily basis, this presumably would have been paid in folles or its submultiples. Thus, for strata of the wage-earning population without the skills or bargaining power to enforce payments in gold, the exchange-rate between gold and copper was of decisive importance. This is shown by the repeated references in Byzantine sources to popular reactions to policies which affected this exchange either by a wholesale restructuring of the copper coinage (as under Anastasius)[166] or by

[160] *CPR* VIII 22.67 f., 80 ff., various jobs at 400; 49, 59–64, at 500; 40 ff. at 650.

[161] *CPR* VIII 22.29.

[162] *P. Oxy.* LVIII 3933 (588).

[163] *Chronicon Paschale*, s.a. 615 (Dindorf 1.706), *Τούτῳ ἔτει γέγονεν ἀπο νόμου νόμισμα ἑξάγραμμον ἀργυροῦν, καὶ βασιλικαὶ ῥόγαι δι᾽ αὐτοῦ γεγόνασι καὶ κατὰ τὸ ἥμισυ τῆς ἀρχαιότητος*, referring to his creation of the hexagram (Dindorf, 1.706).

[164] e.g. *P. Strasb.* III 395 (5/6c.), *SB* I 4909 (Byz.): *ergatai* paid in myriads.

[165] Leontius, *Vie de Jean de Chypre dit l'Aumonier* 38 (Festugière 387), *ἡμέριον κεράτιν*, Nau, *Revue de l'orient chretien* 5 (1900) 256, *ἡμερούσιον ἑνὸς κερατίου*.

[166] Marcellinus Comes, *Chronicon*, s.a. 498.

successive and even attempted alterations in the ratio.[167] Malalas describes the groups which rioted against Justinian's attempted devaluation of the follis in 553 as *ptōchoi*. Clearly the word implies sections of the population dependent, at best, on casual employment.[168] Copper hoards show how desperately poor much of this population must have been if people actually felt it was worthwhile hoarding sums (in small change) whose book value in gold would not have equalled even a tenth of a solidus.[169] Since gold was the measure of value, and prices expressed in folles or submultiples of the follis would have fluctuated with changes in the exchange-value between gold and copper, the latter was clearly fundamental to employees' effort standards and to urban welfare. At 600 folles to the solidus (see Appendix 1, Table 3) a worker earning five folles a day[170] would have had to work four months to earn one solidus and would have earned the equivalent of only three solidi in the course of a year.[171] With an alteration in the rate, such as occurred throughout the early seventh century, such groups would have had to force employers to pay more or work longer hours or reduce consumption. It is possible that the notable lack of any mass resistance to the Arab invasions had as much to do with this profound monetary divide as with the sustained persecution of the Monophysites which simply drove a wedge between the state and the masses.

Table 3 tabulates the movement of the exchange-rate mostly

[167] John Malalas, *Chron.* 486c (Dindorf; Jeffreys *et al.*, *Chronicle* 293), *Μηνὶ μαρτίῳ ἰνδικτιῶνος α΄ ἐγένετο διαστροφὴ τοῦ κέρματος· καὶ ἐκ τῶν πτωχῶν στάσεως γενομένης καὶ θορύβου ἀνηνέχθη τῷ αὐτῷ βασιλεῖ· καὶ ἐκέλευσε τὴν κατάστασιν τοῦ κέρματος κρατῆσαι κατὰ τὸ ἀρχαῖον ἔθος.*

[168] e.g. John Moschus, *Pratum spirituale* 37 (*PG* 87/3.2888), where a bishop says, 'I am one of the *ptōchoi* of this city and since I don't have any means of subsistence I work at casual jobs (*ἐργασείας ποιῶ*).'

[169] e.g. Oikonomidès, *Archaiologika Analekta* 12 (1979) 63–71, Priolithos, *c.*584, cash value *c.*612 folles; Dengate, *Hesperia*, 50 (1981) 153 ff., Corinth, Gymnasium hoard 2, *c.*600, cash value 232 folles; Russell, *ANSMN* 28 (1983) 119–31, Anemurium, *c.*602, cash value 352 folles (on p. 131 Russell describes the cash value of the hoard as equal to one-sixth of a solidus, on Grierson's suggestion, but in 602 there were 600 folles in a solidus, so the hoard would have equalled only one-seventeenth of a solidus); Callot, *Report of the Department of Antiquities, Cyprus* (1985) 335–9, Constantia (Salamis), *c.*610–615, cash value 9 folles. In a higher bracket: G. E. Bates, *ANSMN* 14 (1968) 67–109, Coelesyria (vicinity of Baalbek, anc. Heliopolis), *c.*635, cash value 2,722 folles (not more than a third of a solidus); A. Spaer, *NC* 138 (1978) 66–70, Rafah in the Gaza Strip, 573/4, cash value 322 folles (close to half a solidus); finally, V. Athanassopoulou-Penna, *Archaiologike Ephemeris* (1979) 200–13, suburban Thebes, *c.*582/3, cash value *c.*164 folles (somewhat less than a solidus).

[170] Cf. John Moschus, *Pratum spirituale* 134 (*PG* 87/3.2997c), *Καὶ ὡς ἐλάμβανεν ἡμερούσιον φόλεις πέντε κτλ.*, rate of pay for manual labour in building a well (*lakkos*).

[171] These were low wages, for Leontius notes that an acquaintance paid one of his employees only 3 solidi a year 'although the man had a wife and two children', *Vie de Jean de Chypre*, Prol. 345.

on the basis of Hahn's hypotheses. Justin II broke sharply with Justinian's policy of attempting to preserve some sense of balance between the currencies. Now insofar as copper deteriorated against gold it follows that the essential division within the monetary system between its dominant denominations reinforced as much as it reflected the basic stratification of late antique society between a landed, bureaucratic and commercial aristocracy on one side and the mass of *humiliores* on the other. This in any case was strongly implied by the Anonymous when he wrote that the rise of a gold-dominated economy entailed the 'suppression of the poor'. Enforcing the relations of the monetary system presupposed considerable force, at least in the sense of large masses held down in mute subjection through the sheer power of the late Roman state. This is not a process one can glimpse in the sources, not because they lacked interest in such issues but because the overwhelming sense of power which defined late Roman society removed the possibilities of protest and forced large groups to internalize the violence inflicted on them.[172]

The antagonism of gold and copper caused as much resentment from the other side. It is of some interest that the money-changers (*ἀργυραμοιβοί*) were blamed for the devaluation of the solidus in 542, since this implies that commercial factors (or economic ones) were as important in determining fluctuations in the gold/copper exchange rate as political ones.[173] Hahn has reconstructed the evolution of the ratio for a period of well over a century.[174] These deductions are based largely on the metrology of the follis. In Egypt prices expressed in copper used a traditional unit of account based on the denarius, which was called the 'myriad' (i.e. 10,000 denarii). Now it is obvious that there would have had to be a fixed relationship between the follis and this unit of account. If there were a way of determining what this might be, one would have a further means of tracing the history of gold/copper relations using the abundant testimony of the papyri and thus supplementing (or improving) the series proposed by Hahn. I would like to suggest that a solution can be found which enables us to do this.

In work on the copper coinage of Thessaloniki Michael Metcalf has drawn attention to the fact that the denominational structure of the base metal currency was characterized by a certain localism.[175] This is evident in Egypt from the fact that the main denominations

[172] And of course re-externalize it in urban rioting, 'factionalism', pogroms, etc.

[173] Procopius, *HA* 25.11–12.

[174] Hahn, *MIB* 1.24–7, 2.15–16, 3.16, 39, 63–4.

[175] D. M. Metcalf, 'Folles and Fractional Copper Minted at Thessaloniki under Justin I', *JNG* 30 (1980) 19–27.

below the follis were the 12-, 6-, 3- and 1-nummia pieces. The Antinoe hoard buried early in the reign of Heraclius and till recently the only published from Egypt, consisted almost entirely of 12-nummia issues of the mint of Alexandria with a span of *c*.85 years or more (Justinian on).[176] These issues were produced in some quantity through most of the sixth century. (There were 31 pieces of Justinian, 12 of Justin II, 14 of Tiberius II, 19 of Maurice, and 8 of Heraclius.) More recently, Hahn has published another hoard, said to be from India but in any case formed in Egypt, which includes, besides eighty-three 12-nummia pieces (of Alexandria), three 6-nummia ones.[177] The great value of this find is that it is our first bit of numismatic evidence for the continued production of the 6-nummia piece between the reign of Justinian and Heraclius. Of the three specimens two are of Justinian and one of Maurice. Now it would have been immensely convenient if the Egyptian unit of account related in some way to this duodecimal denominational system. I believe there are good grounds for supposing that the myriad, a money of account, was in fact 'embodied' in the 6-nummia piece. (1) According to Hahn's reconstruction, in (or rather by) 570, 720 folles of a standard weight of 13.64 g. exchanged to the solidus at a gold/copper price of 30 lb.[178] In nummia this would yield 28,800 to the solidus, which would equal either 2,400 12-nummia coins or 4,800 6-nummia ones. Now in *P. Oxy*. 3804.271, which is dated 566, the exchange rate (in myriads) is 4,800 to the solidus. This suggests that fairly soon after Justin II came to power there was a rapid shift in favour of gold, and that the aristocracy at least, in its internal transactions, was exerting a downward pressure on the value of the follis. (2) For 616–18 Hahn gives the value of the follis in terms of gold as 1/1,080. That is, 1,080 folles of 9.10 g. exchanged to the solidus at 30 lb. per solidus. This would yield 43,200 nummia to the solidus equal to 7,200 6-nummia coins. In *P. Oxy*. 1917.59, dated 616/17,[179] the exchange rate is in fact 7,200 myriads to the solidus. Again, the equivalence is striking and suggests that at least from the reign of Justin II, if not earlier, the myriad was embodied in the 6-nummia piece. Finally, a further argument in favour of identifying the myriad with a 6-nummia coin is the fact that where one knows the rate of exchange of the solidus in terms of myriads every *fraction* employed yields a sum (in

[176] J. G. Milne, 'Report on the Coins Found at Antinoe in 1914', *NC* 7, ser. 6 (1947) 108–14, esp. 109 ff.

[177] W. R. O. Hahn, 'A Sixth-Century Hoard of Byzantine Small Change from Egypt, and its Contribution to the Classification of African Minimi', *NC* 140 (1980) 64–70.

[178] Hahn, *MIB* 2.15.

[179] See Rea, *P. Oxy*. LVIII 3958.26n (p. 114).

myriads) which is divisible by six. This is the case, for example, in the Apion account *P. Oxy.* 1917 just referred to. Here the fractions used include not only 1/2, 1/3, 1/4, 1/24 but also 1/10, 1/15, 1/20, 1/30, 1/40, 1/60, 1/100, 1/120, all of which break down into sums of myriads divisible by 6 (so that one would have needed 120, 80, 60, 40, 30, 20, 12 and 10 6-nummia pieces for these respectively). It seems likely that most of these amounts were circulated in purses. The follis itself exchanged against gold in sealed purses or bags on a weight basis.[180] This confirms Pottier's view of the Byzantine copper coinage as strictly non-fiduciary, which explains why the mints exercised such tight control over the weight standards of the follis and its fractions.[181] It also illustrates the continuity in monetary practice between the Byzantine and the Arab periods (in Egypt at any rate) when *fals* glass weights (that is, weights intended for the copper *fulūs*) were manufactured to what Miles has described as 'truly extraordinary' accuracy.[182] In the Byzantine period, however, follis weights were almost certainly called *keratia*, compare *P. Vindob.* G 25874 where a local manager complains to his employer that the villagers had been accusing him of deliberately using heavier weights for the solidi and tremisses and lighter ones for the *keratia*.[183] Finally, this papyrus proves that payments were made in gold coin. The implication of this is that ordinary villagers would have had to have ways of securing it either through commercial production or by wage employment.

Weight Loss

Julian's law addressed to the praetorian praefect Mamertinus *CTh.* 12.7.2 (23 Apr. 363) is reproduced in *CJ* 10.73.2 with the following summary: 'Quotiens de qualitate solidorum orta fuerit dubitatio, placet quem sermo Graecus appellat per singulas civitates constitutum zygostaten . . . contentionem dirimere' (It is a good idea for each district to have the kind of official described in Greek as a *zygostatēs* handling any disputes that may arise in future regarding the quality of solidi). *CTh.* 12.7.2 referred to buyers rejecting solidi

[180] See Metcalf, *NCirc.* 82 (1974) 14–15, summarizing Hahn's theory.

[181] See H. Pottier, *Analyse d'un trésor de monnaies en bronze enfoui au VIe siècle en Syrie byzantine* (Brussels, 1983), 224–5, for the relevant evidence.

[182] G. C. Miles, 'On the Varieties and Accuracy of Eighth-Century Arab Coin Weights', in M. Avi-Yonah *et al.* (eds.), *L. A. Mayer Memorial Volume (1895–1959)*. Eretz-Israel 7 (Jerusalem, 1964) 85. Miles likewise concludes that 'copper (or bronze) actually had a monetary value and the fals was not strictly a fiduciary or token coin' (p. 86).

[183] *SB* VI 9400. 3–7 (Fayum, 6c.): *ἔμαθον, ὡς οἱ ἀπὸ τῆς κώμης ἐλθόντες πρὸς τὴν σὴν θαυμασιότητα ἐμέμψαντό με ὡς βαρυτέρου ὄντος τοῦ ζυγίο[υ], ᾧ ὑποδέχομαι τὸ χρυσίον τῆς ἀπαιτήσεως καὶ τῶνδε κερατίων ἐλαφροτέρων ὄντω[ν].*

'as light weight or substandard' ('tamquam leves vel debiles nonnullis repudiantibus') but seemed to think that this was due to the coins being clipped. If one abstracts from this explanation, the ruling allows for two possibilities: either there was widespread adulteration of the coinage so that 'solidi adulterini' were fairly common, as *CTh.* 12.6.13 of 367 in fact implies when it claims that they were 'frequently' substituted by local collectors; or 'qualitas' refers primarily to the metrology of the coinage in circulation and the fact that worn solidi were already becoming a problem by the 360s.[184] Clearly, both factors must have been at work, but the balance of probability favours the second more than the first. Whatever the general implications of the argument that 'A characteristic of mid-fourth-century gold hoards is the relative scarcity of coins earlier than those of the reigning emperors',[185] we have the explicit testimony of *CJ* 11.11.1 (*c.*367) to show that weight loss was a problem, or at least perceived as one by the public at large by the 360s.[186] According to the manuscripts, the recipient of this law is a certain Germanus, praetorian prefect. Godefroy's suggestion that the recipient was Germanianus, *comes sacrarum largitionum*, would give us a date *c.*365–7.[187] So at least prior to the reform of 368 a lot of the gold in circulation must have consisted of solidi issued by Constantius. But no fewer than thirty-six hoards start with solidi of Valentinian or his brother as opposed to, say, sixteen for Constantius or twenty-three for Justinian. This implies that the reform itself involved an extensive removal and melting down of the older coinage. The next major references to a problem of weight loss are from the middle of the fifth century, and both from the west. The period between 363 and 445 must have seen an enormous expansion in the quantities of gold in circulation.[188] By 445 market rejection of worn solidi was again common.[189] Older solidi were

[184] In Gregory, *Moralia in Job* 33.60 (see n. 129) *qualitas* refers to the alloy.

[185] Kent, *RIC* 8.72.

[186] *CJ* 11.11.1, 'Solidos veterum principum veneratione formatos ita tradi ac suscipi ab ementibus et distrahentibus iubemus, ut etc.', which implies public disapproval of older solidi. In *RN* 14, ser. 6 (1972) 51 Bastien suggests that transactions in solidi had always involved some process of weighing.

[187] See *PLRE* 1.391, Germanianus 1; 367 if *CJ* 11.11.1, 10.72.5, and 11.7.2, were originally parts of the same law.

[188] e.g. C. Morrisson, 'La circulation de la monnaie d'or en Afrique à l'époque Vandale. Bilan des trouvailles locales', in H.Huvelin *et al.* (eds.), *Mélanges de numismatique offerts à Pierre Bastien* (Wetteren, 1987) 325–44, esp. 327 (Africa), 'le siècle "vandale" fournit en moyenne quatre fois plus de monnaies d'or que le précédent', Jones, *LRE* 1.445 (in general).

[189] *Nov. Val.* 16 (18.1.445), 'Frequens ad nos . . . querela pervenit ut in parentum nostrorum contumeliam insigniti solidi eorum nominibus ab omni emptore recusentur' (A frequent complaint . . . has come to us that in contemptuous disregard of Our ancestors, solidi stamped with their names are constantly refused by buyers).

only accepted at a discount. People seemed to feel that one should pay out more older solidi to obtain an equivalent value by weight.[190] Clearly, if weight loss was a sufficiently serious problem to call for legislation, the implication is that older solidi were usually in a worn state (contrary to Kent's assumption that 'The chance of any individual piece circulating for long was slight')[191] and that a not inconsiderable portion of the circulating gold currency consisted of such pieces (contrary to the view that older issues were usually scarce)[192]. *Nov. Val.* 16 refers explicitly to the coinage of Theodosius II and indirectly to that of Honorius.[193] Thirteen years later, in 458, *Nov. Maj.* 7 refers to the numerous losses inflicted on landowners by an exaction called *mutatura*.[194] This, too, may simply have been a general discount (or set of discounts) against older solidi, with government insisting, against its own officers, that the weight of a coin mattered more than its age or general appearance unless the gold could be shown to be of inferior alloy.[195] But the problem was endemic to the fifth century. Substantially the same position had to be taken by Gundobad in the lex Burgundionum.[196] By the end of the century, in the east at any rate, the government had come to recognize that solidi could in general be divided into coin of full weight and coin of less than full weight. The distinction appears clearly in *CJ* 10.27.2.6 (bef. 505) where Anastasius refers to these classes, contraposing *nomismata* described as *eustathma* to others called *parastathma*.[197] Since there is no evidence for official issues of light weight solidi before the reign of Justinian, the *nomismata parastathma* must be gold coins which had lost weight in circula-

[190] Note 'si quisquam vel . . . solidum aureum integri ponderis refutandum esse crediderit vel pretio minore taxaverit' (If anyone should think of refusing to accept a gold solidus of full weight or of valuing it at a lower price) in *Nov. Val.* 16, and compare the public's rejection of good Carolingian coin in S. Suchodolski, 'On the Rejection of Good Coin in Carolingian Europe', in C. N. L. Brooke *et al.* (eds.), *Studies in Numismatic Method presented to Philip Grierson* (Cambridge, 1983) 147–52, esp. 148; 'paying out more etc.' is an expression borrowed from Suchodolski.

[191] Kent, 'Gold Coinage', 197.

[192] e.g. G. Depeyrot, 'La durée d'utilisation des solidi romains', in P. Kos and Z. Demo (eds.), *Studia Numismatica Labacensia Alexandro Jeloc nik Oblata* (Ljubljana, 1988) 213 ff.

[193] 'Si quisquam vel domini patris mei Theodosii vel sacrarum necessitudinum nostrarum vel superiorum principum solidum aureum integri ponderis refutandum esse crediderit'.

[194] *Nov. Maj.* 7.14, 'nullus solidum integri ponderis calumniosae inprobationis obtentu recuset exactor' (No tax collector shall refuse a solidus of full weight on the fraudulent pretext that there is something wrong with it).

[195] Compare 'excepto eo Gallico cuius aurum minore aestimatione taxatur', and see H. L. Adelson, *Light Weight Solidi and Byzantine Trade during the Sixth and Seventh Centuries* (New York, 1957) 69.

[196] On this see S. Suchodolsky, 'Est-ce que les Burgondes ont été forcés d'accepter l'or au poids?', *NAC* 20 (1991) 247–51.

[197] See p. 58 f. above.

tion.[198] This is confirmed by an interesting will from one of the villages of the Oxyrhynchite, where *ὑπ(ὲρ) παρασταθμ(ίας) αὐτ(ῶν)* (sc. *νομισμάτων*) refers to extra payments to make up for deficiencies in weight. This document concerns solidi which had seen circulation in the rural areas, since they represent the savings of a former village headman. The weighted average weight loss on the solidi owned by him (3.79 per cent) is just under 1 carat (0.91 carat). Assuming that the coins in question had been struck to full weight, this implies an average weight, in grams, of 4.3752 g., which corresponds to the average weight of the *oldest* pieces in the Nikertai hoard (also rural)[199] and to 'very worn' in Carcassone's matrix of correlations between weight loss and preservation levels.[200]

The date assigned to *P. Oxy.* 132, late sixth or early seventh century, shows that the Byzantine gold currency continued to be characterized by a problem of weight loss. Of course, the best evidence of this is Justinian's explicit reference to such a problem in Edict 11 (559). Though the language of the Edict is fairly straightforward, interpretations have usually started from presuppositions of a more general nature, with sometimes bizarre consequences. Thus Diehl took the Edict to be referring to a special class of debased solidi which were struck at Alexandria, which one called *τὸ ἀπόλυτον χάραγμα,* and thought that 1⅛ lb. of this 'depreciated' coinage exchanged for a pound of pure gold.[201] Apart from the fact that the local mint authorities could scarcely have made decisions of this sort without the explicit approval of the *sacrae largitiones*, Diehl simply ignored the sense of the term *apolyton*, which clearly refers to loose coinage, pieces not circulating in sealed purses. West and Johnson took *ἀπόλυτον χάραγμα* to refer to copper pieces, which completely misconstrues the sense of the Edict, which is specifically about the gold coinage.[202] Vryonis translated *τὸ χαραττόμενον ἐκεῖσε*

[198] The other possibility is that these were clipped solidi but if so none or almost none have turned up in hoards.

[199] C. Morrisson, 'Le trésor byzantin de Nikertai', *RBN* 118 (1972) 29–91; J. Guey, 'Symétrie ou dissymétrie d'émission', in Ch. Carcassone and T. Hackens (eds.), *Statistics and Numismatics* (Strasbourg, 1981) (= *PACT* 5, 1981) 77–105, at 91–2. The group with the smallest deviation from this overall average (Heraclian solidi Type IIB, 616–25, median weight 4.37g., N = 75) had seen a mean circulation of *sixty* years.

[200] Ch. Carcassone, 'Asymétrie de frais: solidi "Scandinaves"', *BSFN* 31 (1976) 126–7. For the resolution in *P. Oxy.* 132.5, etc., cf. P. J. Sijpesteijn, 'Deux papyrus byzantins de la collection d'Amsterdam', *CE* 48 (1973) 121–31, at 129, based on *P. Amst.* Inv. 39, l. 12, *ὑπ(ὲρ) παρασταθμίας*.

[201] Ch. Diehl, 'Une crise monétaire au VIe siècle', *REG* 32 (1919) 158–66, esp. 159–60. Like Diehl, Stein, *HBE* 2.767–8, thought that Alexandria minted light-weight solidi.

[202] L. C. West and A. C. Johnson, *Currency in Roman and Byzantine Egypt* (Amsterdam, 1967) 190.

χρυσίον in the title of the Edict as 'the gold cut there' and argued that since Egypt did not mint gold the phrase referred to 'cut but unminted gold' which 'circulated in business transactions'.[203] Since Justinian expressly refers to wear on the coinage which the Alexandrians call 'loose', and this obviously implies the circulation of *coined* gold, Vryonis construes the expression παρέφθαρται[204] to mean 'altered' in the sense of debased—a surprising interpretation for a native speaker of modern Greek where worn coins are standardly described as *ephtharmena*.[205] Hendy offers two translations of τὸ χαραττόμενον ἐκεῖσε χρυσίον: 'coined gold in these regions'[206] and, more recently, 'the gold marked there'.[207] But χαραττόμενον in the sense of 'marked' cannot refer to the seal or stamp of the public assayer, as Hendy (ambiguously) and Delmaire (more consistently) seem to imply, for the Edict reserves the term *sphragisai* to describe this process. Delmaire's view that χάραγμα in the Edict does not signify coined money[208] is also manifestly wrong.[209] Hendy's assertion that Edict 11 is 'comprehensible only within the context of the production and circulation of a standard gold coinage dependent virtually entirely upon weight for its value [and] the problems inevitably consequent upon this'[210] is surely correct, but it contradicts the terms in which he criticizes Diehl, viz. for 'supposing that there were officially produced defective solidi in circulation, and *not seeing that the whole phenomenon was basically a matter of accountancy*'.[211] None of these scholars has paid sufficient attention to the contrast obviously intended between the interior (rural) districts of Egypt (called *to Aigypton*) and the great urban

[203] S. Vryonis Jr., 'Two Numismatic Items from the Thomas Whittemore Collection', *Byzantinische Forschungen* 3 (1968) (= *Polychordia. Festschrift Franz Dölger zum 75. Geburtstag*, ed. P. Wirth) 229–34, esp. 232–3.

[204] Edict 11.1 (*CIC* 3.778), κἂν εἰ παρὰ τοὺς ἐν μέσῳ παρέφθαρται χρόνους ἐν τῷ παρὰ Ἀλεξανδρεῦσιν ἀπολύτῳ καλουμένῳ χαράγματι (Even if, in the meantime, there should be some loss of weight in the coinage which the Alexandrians call 'loose').

[205] The final impression of bars (?) of 'cut but unminted gold' circulating in debased form is utterly incoherent!

[206] M. Hendy, *Coinage and Money in the Byzantine Empire 1081–1261* (Washington, DC, 1969) 304.

[207] Hendy, *Studies*, 345. Morrisson, 'Alterazioni e svalutazioni', in *La Cultura bizantina* (n. 143 above) 59–134, at 76, takes *ekeise* with *ginesthai* ('l'or frappé ait là-bas (en Egypte) la même valeur que celui de Constantinople'), which is surely correct.

[208] R. Delmaire, *Largesses sacrées et res privata. L'aerarium impérial et son administration du IVe au VIe siècle* (Rome, 1989) 261, 'Le mot χάραγμα ne signifie pas ici "monnaie", comme pensent Diehl et Stein, il indique toute chose scellé'.

[209] *Kharagma* was standardly used in this sense, e.g. Pseudo-Athanasius, *Quaestiones ad Antiochum ducem*, 112 (*PG* 28.665D), ἀντὶ τοῦ βασιλικοῦ χαράγματος.

[210] Hendy, *Studies*, 345–6.

[211] For West and Johnson, 'basically a matter of accountancy' meant that the (alleged) deduction from the value of each solidus had nothing to do with the actual weights of coins.

money-market of Alexandria.[212] Coinage which had seen considerable circulation in the rural areas and district capitals exchanged at a loss in Alexandria (the receiving centre)[213] simply because most of it comprised older solidi which circulated as loose coin (the Alexandrians called it *ἀπόλυτον χάραγμα*) and which had clearly lost weight to one degree or another. The Edict implies both a geographical contrast—between circulation areas—and a distinction between old and new coin analogous to the situation implied in *P. Cairo Zen.* 59021 many centuries earlier, in 258 BC, when Demetrius, director of the Alexandria mint, complained to Apollonius that the shortage of trained assayers was hampering the conversion of worn gold into new coin, for 'all the residents in the city find it difficult to make use of their worn gold (*τῷ ἀποτετριμμένῳ χρυσίῳ δυσχερῶς χρῶνται*). For none of them knows to what authority he can refer and on paying something extra receive in exchange either good gold (*καλὸν χρυσίον*) or silver';[214] possibly also to the practice described (and attacked) in *P. Beatty Panop.* 2.92 f. where the *trapezitai* were clearly imposing some sort of charge related to the difference between loose and sealed coin, since the payments are described as *ἐπὶ βαλλαντίων προφάσει* (l. 97), 'on the pretext of purses'; and analogous, again, to the established medieval practice of distinguishing between 'fresh' and 'old' coin.[215] Worn gold was nothing new in the monetary economy of Egypt. The passages just referred to create a strong presumption in favour of thinking that Egyptian bankers, especially those in Alexandria, usually discriminated against such coin with outright rejection or heavy discounts. Given the intrinsic relationship between the fineness of gold and its weight,[216] the discount imposed on 'loose' solidi could be called *obryza* (*ὑπὲρ ὀβρύζης*), though technically this term referred primarily to the purity of the gold.[217]

212 e.g., *P. Giss.* 40 ii 16 ff. (215) which refers to *Αἰ[γύπτι]οι πάντες οἵ εἰσιν ἐν Ἀλεξανδρείᾳ, καὶ μάλιστα ἄ[γ]ροικοι, οἵτινες πεφε[ύγασιν] ἀλ[λοθεν κτλ*; *Nov. Just.* 7.11 (Krueger, p. 61), *παρά τε Ἀλεξανδρεῦσι καὶ Αἰγυπτίοις*. Also see *P. Oxy.* I 144 (580), involving a discount of 6¼% on several hundred loose solidi which are described as *ἀπόλυτον Αἰγύπτιον χάραγμα* (and contrasted with a second payment *ἐν ὀβρύζῳ χαράγματι*).

213 e.g. *P. Oxy.* I 127 r where the Apions send 484 and 285 solidi to Alexandria, or *P. Oxy.* 1906 with amounts like 2,304, 2,158 solidi, etc.

214 *P. Cairo Zen.* 59021 = *Select Papyri* II 409.29 ff. (548 ff.). The most useful interpretations are Cl. Préaux, *L'Économie royale des Lagides* (Brussels, 1939) 271–3 (Préaux translates, 'où faire l'épreuve de leur teneur' and explains this as, 'à qui se référer sur la valeur des pièces usées') and Bogaert, *RBN* 122 (1976) 26.

215 S. D. Goitein, *A Mediterranean Society: The Jewish Communities of the Arab World as portrayed in the Documents of the Cairo Geniza.* 1: *Economic Foundations* (Berkeley and Los Angeles, 1967) 236–7.

216 Poirier, *Contribution à l'analyse de l'or antique*, esp. 157 ff. on the influence of alloy on weight.

217 Cassian, *Collationes* 1.20, 'probare quodnam sit aurum purissimum et ut vulgo

The Circulation of Gold from the Evidence of Hoards

It is sometimes argued that 'The gold coinage had an essentially military vocation.'[218] However, documentary evidence implies that the circulation of gold had an economic basis as much as a bureaucratic one. For example, we know from *CTh.* 11.15.2 (384) that payments in *coemptiones* occurred in gold. Peasants frequently resorted to cash loans in solidi.[219] Workers in regular private employment,[220] professionals,[221] public employees,[222] skilled labourers (clothworkers,[223] carpenters,[224] carpet weavers,[225] purple dyers,[226] stone masons,[227] irrigation workers,[228] etc.), even ordinary unskilled workmen[229] received wages partly or wholly in gold. As I noted earlier, casual labour was the crucial exception.[230] Gold was the currency of commercial transactions such as the cash advances which traders used to secure supplies of commodities like flax.[231] In fact, the expansion of contracts of advance sale in the sixth century is a remarkable index of gold liquidity and the flow of cash from urban to rural areas.[232] In these areas the sellers involved in such

dicitur obrizum', cf. Theodoret, *Is.* 13.12 (*PG* 81.328), ἄπυρον οὖν χρυσίον τὸ καὶ δίχα πυρὸς φαινόμενον δόκιμον . . . ὃ νῦν οἱ πολλοὶ εὔρυζον ὀνομάζουσι (as a definition).

[218] G. Depeyrot, *Le Bas-Empire romain. Économie et numismatique* (Paris, 1987) 37.

[219] e.g. Theodoret, *Ep.* 1.37 (*SC* 40.102), Moschus, *Pratum spirituale* 184 (*PG* 87/3.3056), *P. Oxy.* I 130, *SB* XVI 12538 (6/7c.), loan of four solidi to a *geōrgos*, also cf. *P. Strasb.* V 317 (530, *BL* 9.327) where a *geōrgos* (a rich peasant) *lends* eleven solidi.

[220] *P. Med.* I^2 48 (549, *BL* 7.103) = *SB* VI 9011.8 ff., 50 solidi over three years, *P. Köln* II 102 = *SB* XII 11239 (418), *SPP* XX 219 (604), *SB* I 4490 (641 or poss. 656, *BL* 8.309), but no cash in *CPR* II 152 = Till, 'Koptischen Arbeitsverträge', no.13, 285–6, and practically none in *P. Strasb.* I 40 (569). In *SB* I 4490.21 note Jördens' amendment, *ZPE* 64 (1986) 61, eliminating ἐκερματούμ(εν)α and the possible reference to payment in base metal coin.

[221] *P. Cairo Masp.* II 67151.288–289 (570), salary of an *archiatros*.

[222] *P. Iand.* 37 (5/6c.), *P. Oxy.* XXXVI 2780 (553), *P. Ross.-Georg.* III 47 (627/8 or 642/3, *BL* 8.291), John Lydus, *Mag.* 3.27.

[223] *P. Bod.* I 41 (604).

[224] *P. Coll. Youtie* II 95.12 (7c.).

[225] *P. Rein.* II 105 (432).

[226] *P. Grenf.* II 87 (602), *P. Herm.* 30 (551/2).

[227] *P. Oxy.* I 134 (569), *Vie de S.Syméon Stylite le Jeune*, 180 (Van den Ven, 1.159).

[228] *P. Vindob. Sal.* 9 (509), *PUG* 50, with H. C.Youtie, *ZPE* 23 (1976) 112, *MPER* 15.111 col. ii 16 (7c.), *SB* VI 9284 (553), *P. Grenf.* I 58 (*c.*561), *P. Mich. inv.* 502 = *ZPE* 79 (1989) 276 f. (6/7c.), *P. Flor.* I 70.8–9 (27.11.627, *BL* 8.125), *SPP* III 86 (593? cf. Palme, *CPR* XXIV, p. 149 n.32). 'Irrigation workers' includes employees hired chiefly for irrigation work, as in most of the contracts above.

[229] *P. Oxy.* LVIII 3933 (588), goldsmiths' helper.

[230] *P. Strasb.* V 395 (5/6c.), *SB* 1.4909 = *SPP* VIII 1070 (Byz.).

[231] *P. Oxy.* VIII 1130 (483 or 484); possibly more frequent later, cf. *KRU* 59 (8c.) = Till, 'Koptischen Arbeitsverträge', no. 42, p. 308, *CPR* II 91 = Till, 'Koptischen Arbeitsverträge', no. 45, p. 310.

[232] In my sample (N = 137), there are at least 55 contracts from the 6th cent.—more than any other period (40 per cent of the total). The 6th and 7th cents. together account

contracts were often people from the smaller settlements called *epoikia* (not even the villages). Considering the level of such transactions, it is striking that late Byzantine contracts drafted in Coptic should include sums such as 16, 36, and 48 solidi.[233] I have already argued that the distinctive feature of monetary circulation in late antiquity was the use of gold as a mass currency. Though this took time to develop, it had certainly started by the 380s (the reign of Theodosius).[234] Accounts like *P. Oxy.* 3416 verso (*c.*376?) show that by that stage Egyptian estates handled routine cash transactions in solidi.[235] In the 380s Syrian villages paid protection money in gold, otherwise in kind.[236] In view of all this documentary evidence it seems odd that the distribution of gold in hoards should reflect a geographical pattern of circulation where these circuits were simply ignored.[237] But a more systematic collection of the hoard material does imply a general consistency between numismatic and documentary sources.[238]

General Inferences from the Hoard Evidence

The circulation of gold occurred in at least the following forms:[239] (1) in the 'solidi streams' which materialized payments to foreign

for 62 per cent of all such contracts (and 77 per cent of the wine contracts!) in a sample period of six centuries (2nd to 7th). The evolution of such contracts seems in general to reflect the stability of the currency but within common monetary regimes the increasing pressure of money taxes.

233 *P. Flor.* XVIII 10 (=*P. Vat. Copt.* 5B) (7c.), *CPR* IV 48 = *PERF* 142 (7c.), *P. Flor.* XVIII 11 (=*P. Vat. Copt.* 5A) (6/7c.). All of these are likely to be fairly late. Cf. *P. Köln*, VII 322 (6/7c.), where a *geōrgos* borrows 50 solidi.

234 Cf. A. Piganiol, 'Le probème de l'or au IVe siècle', *Annales d'Histoire Sociale*, 1945 (=*Hommages à Marc Bloch*), 47–53, on the profusion of gold in his reign.

235 Cf. *SB* XX 15096, a sale of 30 arouras of irrigated land for 16 solidi, dated 363! Also *P. Vindob.* G 25871 = Hoogendijk, *Tyche* 10 (1995) 13f., a sale of 2⅛ arouras of arable for 5 solidi, dated 373.

236 Libanius, *Or.* 47.4, the cash payments included ἢ χρυσὸς ἢ χρυσίου τιμή, which L. Harmand, *Libanius. Discours sur les patronages* (1st edn.; Paris, 1955) 27 translates, 'en un poids d'or ou en une somme d'or'. The date is 386–92.

237 Depeyrot, *Le Bas-Empire romain*, 37, maintains that 'les études de répartition des monnaies d'or montrent leur concentration le long des zones des camps militaires'; contrast M. Vasić, 'Les découvertes de monnaies d'or dans la diocèse de Dacie du IVe au VIe siècle', in C. Brenot and X. Loriot (eds.), *L'Or monnayé 3. Trouvailles de monnaies d'or dans l'occident romain.* Cahiers Ernest-Babelon 4, 273–311, on the finds in Dacia, 'l'armée n'était pas la seule à disposer de monnaies d'or' (292).

238 See my paper 'The Circulation of Gold as an Index of Prosperity in the Central and Eastern Mediterranean in Late Antiquity', in C. E. King and D. Wigg (eds.), *Coin Finds and Coin Use in the Roman World. The Thirteenth Oxford Symposium on Coinage and Monetary History 25.–27.3.1993* (Berlin, 1996) 41–53, for an analysis based on 330 gold hoards of the period 300–700.

239 i.e. outside the big cities and towns which controlled the commercial life of the empire and which used gold as their staple currency.

mercenaries or allies;[240] (2) through the mobility of ruling-class personnel such as the officer whose savings ended up in the sands of Sidi-bu-Saïd;[241] (3) through the transport (under armed guard) of large quantities of coined gold from estates in the rural districts to urban centres such as Alexandria;[242] (4) through the countless fiscal and commercial transactions of rural economy where gold functioned as means of payment and medium of circulation; (5) through the mechanism of imperial gifts and donations and the frequent infusions of gold for disaster relief; (6) through the flow of coined or uncoined precious metal beyond the boundaries of the empire as capital accumulated in international trade of the sort witnessed by Egeria at Clysma (near Suez) in the 380s.[243] Geographical context or certain features of their composition may mean that it is possible to relate some hoards to one or more of these backgrounds. For example, Theodosius II's payments to the barbarians are reflected in numerous hoards from the regions west of the Carpathians and in the astonishing scale of some of these.[244] The composition of the hoard from the Casa delle Vestali makes it likely that it belonged to a highly placed official connected with the imperial court under Anthemius.[245] Again, it seems likely that the hoards from Arras

[240] See J. M. Fagerlie, *Late Roman and Byzantine Solidi Found in Sweden and Denmark* (New York, 1967).

[241] N. Dürr and P. Bastien, 'Trésor de solidi (353–388)', *SNR* 63 (1984) 205–40, esp. 215 f.

[242] e.g., *PSI* VIII 953.68, *P. Oxy*. 2243(a).92–3 (Apion revenues).

[243] Discussions of outflow concentrate overwhelmingly on payments to the barbarians, Persians, etc., but the real imponderable is the outflow due to trade with the East. The recent hoard from Akkialur in Karnataka, S. India (P. J. Turner, *Roman Coins from India* (London, 1989) 48), shows that the long-distance trade continued in the 6th cent.: among 43 solidi, the last coin or coins are of Justin I. That it continued in the late 6th cent. is indicated by the report in Antoninus of Placentia that Indian vessels docked at Akaba (Abela) loaded with various sorts of incense, and that Suez (Clysma) still functioned as a port for Indian ships (*Antonini Placentini Itinerarium Rec. Alt*. 40–1, in R. Weber, *Itineraria et alia geographica*. CC, ser. lat., 175–6, 2 vols. (Turnholt, 1965) 1.172, cf. A. A.Vasiliev, *Justin the First: an Introduction to the Epoch of Justinian the Great* (Cambridge, Mass., 1950) 364 f.). Now these relations must have continued over centuries, for when Egeria visited Clysma (in the 380s) what she saw suggests a high level of trading activity with India. A passage in her travel diary (which survives only in the excerpts of Peter Diaconus) tells us, 'Ships from India can dock only at this port, nowhere else in Roman territory. But the ships there are *numerous and massive* (*Naves autem ibi et multe et ingentes sunt*) because the port is famous for the Indian merchants who come there', *Appendix ii ad Itinerarium Egeriae*, in Weber, *Itineraria*, 101 (Y6), cf. J. Wilkinson, *Egeria's Travels* (London, 1971) 206. The best recent survey is M. M. Mango, 'Byzantine Maritime Trade with the East (4th–7th centuries)', *ARAM* 8 (1996) 139–63.

[244] e.g. A. Kiss, 'Die Goldfunde des Karpatenbeckens vom 5.–10. Jahrhundert', *AArchHung* 38 (1986) 105–45.

[245] L. Ungaro, 'Il ripostiglio della Casa delle Vestali, Roma 1899', *Bolletino di Numismatica* 4 (1985) 47–160.

(*c*.315) and Sidi-bu-Saïd (*c*.392) represented the emoluments of senior military officials (*militares*) of the sort who led and sustained the pressure for commutation throughout the fourth century.[246] A series of hoards stem from known military sites and the least this tells us is that payments in gold were already common by the middle decades of the fourth century (Sirmium, Borča, Ljubljana I).[247] It is not certain, however, that the frequency of hoards is a reliable clue or any sort of clue to the extent of monetary transactions (using gold) in different regions of circulation. Both the degree of liquidity and the velocity of circulation would have varied between these 'regions' of the circulation process, creating a complex monetary map that was both fragmented and unified. If, as Shetelig and Falk maintain with reference to Scandinavian hoards, 'the amount of gold acquired was quite out of proportion to the economic needs of Scandinavia',[248] one would expect a high frequency of hoards as well as a high ratio of hoarded to circulating solidi. By Fagerlie's definition of any find consisting of five or more solidi as a hoard, there are at least thirty hoards from Scandinavia. This compares with seventeen from Turkey, ten from Egypt, or twenty-one from North Africa. Yet no one would want to argue that Scandinavia was in any sense more advanced than the regional economies of the eastern Mediterranean or Africa. This feature of the hoard evidence is clear in another way. In the entire sample of 330 hoards there is only one substantial find of gold from a major urban centre in the eastern Mediterranean—the hoard from Chatby in Alexandria, deposited, as Grierson showed, early in 611.[249] Yet Alexandria must have been the biggest and most flourishing money market anywhere in the East! Again, a little over half the total number of pieces in this hoard consisted of fractions (mostly tremisses), which shows that the smaller denominations were probably far more frequent in actual circulation, especially in the great urban markets, than they tend to be in the hoard evidence. A similar process of reasoning can be applied to the circulation of gold in the countryside. With the

[246] Bastien, *Trésor de Beaurains*, esp. 200f., and Dürr and Bastien, *SNR* 63 (1984) esp. 215f. The date suggested for Sidi-bu-Saïd is John Kent's suggestion (communicated privately).

[247] M. Vasić and V. Popović, 'Un trésor de monnaies d'or de Sirmium', *MEFR(A)* 87 (1975) 425–43; G. Elmer, 'Ein Fund römischer Goldmünzen aus Borča', *Numismatische Zeitschrift* 63 (1930) 39–46; P. Kos, *FMR Slowenien*, 1.155/2, with P. Kos, *Monetary Circulation in the Southeastern Alpine Region c.300 B.C.–A.D. 1000* (Ljubljana, 1986) 157 (last coin dated 346/47).

[248] H. Shetelig and H. Falk, *Scandinavian Archaeology* (Oxford, 1937) 235.

[249] E. D. J. Dutilh, 'Une trouvaille de 191 monnaies d'or byzantines et de 1 pièce en argent', *RBN* 61 (1905) 155–64; P. Grierson, 'The Consular Coinage of "Heraclius" and the revolt against Phocas of 608–610', *NC* 10, ser. 6 (1950) 71–93, esp. 77.

possible exception of Aïn Meddah,[250] our only substantial find from a discernibly rural context is the hoard of 534 gold pieces from the monastery of Nikertai at the foot of the Ǧebel Zāwiye (in Syria). Theodoret describes Nikertai itself as a 'large and populated village (*kōmē*)' and puts the size of the monastery, in the fifth century, at 'over 400'.[251] Like Chatby, Nikertai has an extended age structure, roughly eighty years, which shows that hoards from purely civilian contexts are probably better clues to the age of the currency in circulation than the compact hoards of the fourth century found in military contexts. The implication is not that no hoarding occurred in the countryside—we know from the *Life of Theodore of Sykeon* that hoarding was widespread in the countryside of Galatia where Theodore, archimandrite of the monastery of Sykeon, spent most of his life.[252] What this analysis suggests, rather, is that the hoard evidence *cannot* be a reliable clue to the distribution of gold between the various sectors, circuits and monetary uses, and the general impression that the army monopolized circulation is therefore misleading.

On the other hand, the accumulation and concentration of hoards in specific geographical regions can provide illumination in more general ways. The Carpathian hoards (especially Bína and Szikáncs) abundantly confirm Ammianus' testimony that the Huns 'burned with a desire for gold'.[253] Likewise, the mainly seventh-century hoards from the south Russian steppe region show that this was probably true of other tribal confederacies.[254] Italian hoards of the fifth century (Parma, Gravisca, Comiso, Casa delle Vestali, Naples) create a distinct impression of the region's wealth in coined gold and the decline in the average size of Italian hoards between the fifth and the sixth centuries can perhaps be construed as a sign of monetary regression.[255] (But conversely, as I have just argued, an absence of

[250] Ninety-three solidi discovered 'dans les ruines d'une villa romaine du Bas-Empire', according to Salama, *BSAF*, 1959, 238.

[251] Theodoret, *Hist. Phil.* 3.4 (*SC* 234.252), κώμη γάρ τίς ἐστι μεγίστη καὶ πολυάνθρωπος, Νικέρτη δὲ ὄνομα ταύτῃ.

[252] *Vie de Théodore de Sykéon*, 43, 114, 116; these were clearly gold hoards, precisely the sort that have turned up in various parts of Turkey in more recent times. For the world described in the Life of Theodore, see now S. Mitchell, *Anatolia: Land, Men, and Gods in Asia Minor.* 2: *The Rise of the Church* (Oxford, 1993) 122–34.

[253] Ammianus, 31.2.11, 'auri cupidine immensa flagrantes' (burning with an immense desire for gold).

[254] See J. Smedley, 'Seventh-Century Byzantine Coins in Southern Russia and the Problem of Light Weight Solidi', *SEBGC* 111–30.

[255] Cf. S. Bourgey, 'L'évolution du monnayage d'or aux Ve et VIe siècles après J.-C.', in *Numismatics—Witness to History* (Wetteren, 1986) 65–71; she refers to 'une grande impression de richesse du pays en monnaies d'or' (at 66) and notes the subsequent decline.

hoards need not indicate that no gold was in circulation, the best case of this is Palestine.[256]) Hoard evidence proves that there was a large-scale circulation of gold in Sicily and North Africa in the seventh century.[257] Finally, the accumulation of hoards from seventh-century Syria reflects the continued circulation of Byzantine solidi in regions under Umayyad control and shows how both the velocity of circulation and life-span in circulation might compensate for a diminished or stagnating supply.[258]

Prolonged Circulation and an Increasing Average Scale of Accumulation

Age structures. The fourth, fifth, and sixth centuries brought about a cumulative increase in the stock of gold in circulation both because large quantities of gold were struck by various regimes from the fifth to the seventh centuries and because much of this gold stayed in circulation and in private hands. The latter part of this assertion conflicts with existing notions about the character of monetary circulation in the late empire. Thus John Kent argued that 'The chance of any individual piece circulating for long was slight. *If it escaped recoining, it must have gone quickly to ground*',[259] and Depeyrot has maintained that the bulk of the gold coinage in circulation was continually pulled in, melted down, and restruck, with the result that late Roman hoards contain few gold pieces older than a maximum of thirty years.[260] These ideas can be tested by examining the age structure of gold hoards, as Michael Metcalf has argued recently.[261] In tackling the postulate of rapid withdrawal it is sufficient, it seems to me, if even one or two hoards, especially bigger ones, reflect 'extended' age structures. In fact there are roughly twenty hoards of this type. For example, in the hoard from Comiso in Sicily (*c.*440) over 75 per cent had circulated for more than thirty years;[262] in the Naples hoard (*c.*480) 68 per cent were

[256] P. Grierson, 'The Monetary Reforms of Anastasius and their Economic Consequences', in A. Kindler (ed.), *The Patterns of Monetary Development in Phoenicia and Palestine in Antiquity* (Tel-Aviv, 1967) 283–302 , esp. 292, 297: 'few gold hoards . . . have come to light, though the literary evidence shows that plenty of gold was in circulation'.

[257] Cf. App. 1, Table 4, last column.

[258] See C. Morrisson, 'Le trésor byzantin de Nikertai', *RBN* 118 (1972) 29–91, esp. 58 f., cf. W. E. Metcalf, 'Three Byzantine Gold Hoards', *ANSMN* 25 (1980) 87–108, esp. the hoards from Daphne and Damascus.

[259] Kent, 'Gold Coinage', 197.

[260] Depeyrot, 'La durée d'utilisation des solidi romains', 216.

[261] D. M. Metcalf, 'The Minting of Gold Coinage', 70 f., reaching conclusions which are fully supported by the analysis below.

[262] F. Panvini Rosati, 'Ripostiglio di *aurei* tardo-imperiali a Comiso', *Atti della Accademia Nazionale dei Lincei. Rendiconti* 8, ser. 8 (1953) 422–40.

over twenty years old;[263] in the hoard from Chatby in Alexandria (611), 3 of the solidi, 29.6% of the semisses and 57.7 per cent of the tremisses (38 per cent in total) were over thirty years old;[264] 58–63 per cent of the solidi in the large deposits from Aïn Meddah and Djemila in Algeria (both *c*.495) were at least twenty years old.[265] It is possible that the composition of the currency varied from region to region and that generalizations are unsafe, one way or the other. But the postulate of rapid withdrawal certainly cannot be extended to either the fifth or the seventh centuries which (wherever hoard spans can be established with some precision) both show high average circulation periods, almost four times higher in the fifth century (compared to the fourth), two and a half times higher in the seventh (see Appendix 1, Table 5). Finally, one should note that the total hoard statistic provides only a minimum estimate of the proportion of older solidi in actual circulation. Regulations governing the public use and circulation of gold, in particular, *CJ* 11.11.1 (*c*.367) and *Nov.Val.* 16 (445), prove that the public discriminated between new and worn solidi and were generally only willing to accept the latter at a discount. But if there was a reluctance to accept the solidi of earlier emperors, this would also imply that *hoarders* discriminated against such pieces, thus reducing drastically the proportion of such coins in the total hoard as compared to their proportion in actual circulation.[266]

Hoard size by region. We can work on the assumption that though a hoard represents a sum of value removed from circulation, hoard size reflects the amount of money both potentially and actually available for circulation. This assumption can be applied in two ways. Geographically, variations in hoard size may be construed as reflecting actual differences in the scale of monetary accumulation in different parts of the Mediterranean and of the empire as a whole.[267] (Table 6 in Appendix 1 documents the scale of monetary activity in the central and eastern Mediterranean from the later fourth to the seventh centuries, a period from which there are roughly forty substantial deposits from this region.) Chronologically, one can isolate the bigger hoards and see whether there is a tendency for larger

[263] A. de B., 'Découverte de 255 sous d'or du bas-empire dans l'ancien royaume de Naples', *Annuaire de la Société Française de Numismatique*, 10 (1886) 139–40; F. Panvini Rosati, 'Osservazioni sulla circolazione in Italia nel V secolo d. C. di monete d'oro romane', *BollNum* 4 (1985) 7–14, at 8, no. 14.

[264] See n. 249 above.

[265] Morrisson, *Mélanges Bastien*, 336 f., Albertini, '[Note sur deux découvertes faites à Cuicul, auj. Djemila]', *BCTH* 1924, clix ff., at clxiii–clxiv.

[266] Compare Mommsen, *Geschichte des römischen Münzwesens*, 780 for this argument.

[267] See Banaji, 'Circulation of Gold', 46.

deposits to come from the later period and thus for an increasing average scale of accumulation.

In Table 4, eighty-two hoards with a minimum value of roughly one pound of gold (69 solidi) have been assigned to one of four centuries, according to the date of deposition, and to the relevant geographical group. This makes it possible to trace the chronological evolution of the bigger hoards by broad regional sectors. Of twenty (?) western hoards[268] (of 69 solidi or more) not one stems from the seventh century. The political disintegration of the western empire had obviously drastically altered its economic geography. In the west, the peak of gold circulation may even have been reached as early as the fifth century. In the central Mediterranean, fourteen deposits, about 54 per cent of the regional total, close in the sixth or seventh centuries, mostly (over 70 per cent) in the latter. But here the essential contribution is due to the Byzantine possessions in North Africa and Sicily. In eastern Europe over 70 per cent of the large hoards are from the sixth or seventh century. Finally, in the eastern Mediterranean close to 80 per cent of the bigger deposits are from the sixth or seventh century, again mainly from the seventh. In general, 34 per cent of all hoards of 69 solidi or more are from the seventh century. Of eastern hoards the proportion is as high as 60 per cent. Assuming that circulation was at least in some general sense proportional to survival, the numismatic evidence emphatically rules out any notion of monetary recession in the seventh century.[269] The circulation of gold may even have intensified[270] as the revenue system was almost totally monetized by the closing decades of the sixth century, preparing the way for the sort of situation that evolved about a century later when the Marwānids extracted an average of close to 4,000 (on average precisely 3,952) solidi a year from a village the size of Aphrodito.[271] By early Byzantine standards this was a colossal level of money payment, over ten times as much as the village contributed (in gold coin) *c*.525.[272] Numismatically there is strong evidence for the expansion of gold in the main provincial mints. Thus Morrisson has shown that at Carthage regular annual issues of gold began in the reign

[268] Again, 'Portugal' may or may not belong to this group.

[269] Compare Ostrogorsky, *DOP* 13 (1959), 50 ff., *pace* Grierson who characterizes the hypothesis of a greater circulation of gold in the seventh century as an 'illusion', *DOC* 2/1, p. 6. Cf. p. 63 above, at n. 143.

[270] Even Grierson, *DOC* 2/1, p. 10 agrees the solidus 'was minted in very great quantities throughout the century'.

[271] See the important article of L. Casson, 'Tax-Collection Problems in Early Arab Egypt', *TAPA* 69 (1938) 274–91.

[272] See App. 1, Table 7 for the evolution and other 7th-cent. examples.

of Justin II.[273] In Syria and Egypt, likewise, Justin II's reign was characterized by 'abundant local issues of solidi'.[274] Finally, if the money supply of Proconsularis is any indication, the bulk of the solidi in circulation by the seventh century comprised local issues. Thus the hoards from Bulla Reggia and Thuburbo Maius (Hr. Kasbah) consisted only of such issues and Morrisson has stated that among the 200 stray finds (of Byzantine solidi) 72 per cent are from the mint of Carthage.[275] The hoard from Bulla Reggia also shows, incidentally, that the lush villas of provincial small towns continued to be occupied till the Arab conquests and above all, as Quoniam noted in his publication of the hoard, that there was 'an abundance of gold in Africa in the Byzantine epoch'.[276]

The Centrality of Prices: The Marketed Surplus and the 'Wingate Effect'

What impact would late antique monetary expansion have had on the incomes of ordinary rural households? Late Roman sources depict large landowners as almost obsessed by the desire to dominate the storage of grain and wine. In Ammianus' description Symmachus' father was a 'paradigm of learning and moderation'. But these were personal qualities and it seemed insufficient not to mention the fact that his *domus* across the Tiber had been burned down because (it was alleged) he had said 'he would rather use his own wine for quenching lime-kilns than sell it at the price which the people hoped for'[277]—an incident emblematic of his social position as a large producer. In roughly the same period Ambrose claimed that big landlords were more excited by inflationary prices (*enormitate pretiorum*) than abundant harvests and that bad years were always more profitable.[278] John Chrysostom describes the aristocracy as 'possessing villages and estates and being more interested

[273] C. Morrisson, 'Carthage: The *Moneta Auri* under Justinian I and Justin II, 537–578', in *SEBGC* 41–64, at 62.

[274] C. Morrisson, *Catalogue des monnaies byzantines de la Bibliothèque Nationale*, 2 vols. (Paris, 1970) 1.126.

[275] C. Morrisson, in Guéry, Morrisson, and Slim, *Recherches archéologiques à Rougga*, 60 (Bulla Reggia and Thuburbo Maius), 62 (stray finds).

[276] P. Quoniam, 'Fouilles récentes à Bulla Regia (Tunisie)', *CRAI*, 1952, 460–72, esp. 472. Cf. Tusa's similar remarks on Sicily in 'La circolazione monetaria nella Sicilia bizantina ed il ripostiglio da Castellana (Palermo)', in *Byzantino-Sicula. Scritti di G. Agnello et al.* Istituto Siciliano di Studi Bizantini e Neoellenici. Quaderni 2 (Palermo, 1966) 104–10, at 107 (on the earlier hoard from Castellana).

[277] Ammianus 27.3.3–4 (with Rolfe's translation).

[278] Ambrose, *De Nab.* 35 (*PL* 14.741), 'Delectatur magis enormitate pretiorum quam abundantia copiarum'.

in the construction of bath complexes and the jacking up of prices (ὅπως τὰ τιμήματα ἐπιταθείη) and the furnishing of their villas and residences than anything with some sense in it'.[279] The fact is that rural incomes depended crucially on prices, and what all rural producers feared most were years of low prices.[280] What distinguished the aristocracy, high officials, and rich peasants from small producers was control over the outcomes of market transactions.[281] Wendy Olsen has argued (1) that the timing of grain sales and purchases is an important determinant of the real income of rural households, and (2) that 'differences in the ability to space out foodgrains transactions over the seasons lead to a division of rural households into distinct types'.[282] 'Poor farmers will sell at the post-harvest low price, since they need the cash immediately and they depend on wages for cash to buy grain later in the year.'[283] In the late empire the need for cash increased in direct proportion to the monetization of the tax system, so that 'intertemporal flexibility' was especially crucial to the ability of different groups to survive in the economic climate of the fourth and fifth centuries.

The 'Wingate effect' is my term for a model of how restricted intertemporal flexibility worked in a dynamic sense, that is, of how the market interacted with the transaction patterns of poorer households to exaggerate seasonality and reduce the value of their sales even further. It was first described in its complete form by George Wingate when he was Superintendent of the Revenue Survey and Assessment in the Southern Maratha Country of the Bombay Presidency in 1849. Wingate's experience as a revenue administrator was probably unparalleled and his ideas are thus exceptionally important. Commenting on the report of another official who noted that 'Prices . . . sometimes fall so low that a ryot [cultivator] . . . is compelled to dispose of his grain at an immense sacrifice', Wingate wrote:

> I think also that the great fluctuation of prices and their extreme depression in abundant seasons, which have borne so severely on the resources of the ryots, were the consequences of a heavy assessment, collected by quickly following instalments, even more than of a contracted market. The assessment was always too

[279] John Chrysostom, *In Acta Apost.*, *Homilia* 18.4 (*PG* 60.146).

[280] Compare J. Matthews, *The Roman Empire of Ammianus* (London, 1989) 410 ff. for Libanius' attitudes.

[281] I borrow this formulation from Wendy Olsen's thesis, see n. 282.

[282] W. K. Olsen, *Seasonality, Transaction Patterns and Real Incomes in Indian Village Foodgrains Markets* (Oxford University M. Phil., 1984) 42, 44.

[283] Olsen, *Seasonality*, 90. This depends on the crop, however, cf. Olsen, *'Distress Sales' and Exchange Relations in a Rural Area of Rayalaseema, Andhra Pradesh* (Oxford University D.Phil., 1991), for a more complex argument.

heavy to be defrayed in full, but in a good season the remissions given were of less amount and the demand on the ryot consequently greater than in less favourable years. He was, in consequence, obliged to bring forward to market a larger amount of produce than in ordinary seasons to meet this additional demand, and by thus forcing sales prices were lowered, and more & more produce had to be sold in order to raise the money he required to meet the extra demand made upon him by Government, until the market became so glutted and prices so ruinously low, that we can easily imagine a very abundant crop to have been a misfortune rather than an advantage.[284]

The Syriac Chronicle conventionally attributed to Dionysius of Tell-Maḥré contains vivid descriptions of the way this worked for the peasantry of Upper Mesopotamia in the eighth century.[285] In the Byzantine sources certainly the best description of the Wingate effect comes from an eighth-century Constantinopolitan chronicle which was used both by Theophanes and by Nikephoros in the *Breviarium*. In the latter's more detailed summary, in what seems to have been the year 766–7, Constantine V

proved to be a new Midas, who stored away all the gold. As a result, the taxed people, hardpressed as they were by the exaction of imposts, sold cheaply the fruit and produce of the earth, so that 60 modii of wheat and 70 of barley could be bought for 1 nomisma and many ⟨other goods⟩ were sold for very small sums. This was considered by the senseless as a sign of the earth's fertility and the abundance of commodities (*εὐφορία τε γῆς καὶ πραγμάτων εὐθηνία*), but by the wise as the result of oppression and avarice and as an inhuman sickness.[286]

Compared to these descriptions the late Roman/early Byzantine evidence is much less satisfactory but some evidence does exist. In *SB* XVI 12607, in the late second or early third century, the general manager of an estate told local managers that according to his information: 'The majority of those who are being dunned for taxes do not respond because of the cheapness of the crops (*διὰ τὴν τῶν γενῶν εὐωνίαν*). For he (the inspector) was saying that wheat was

[284] *Selections from the Bombay Government Records*, NS 117, Report on the Assessment of the Rahooree Talooka in the Ahmednuggur Collectorate, G. Wingate, Superintendent Revenue Survey and Assessment, Southern Maratha Country, to E. H. Townsend, Revenue Commissioner, Southern Division, 15 Dec. 1849, p. 50.

[285] See Claude Cahen, 'Fiscalité, propriété, antagonismes sociaux au Haute-Mésopotamie au temps des premiers ʿabbāsides d'après Denys de Telle-Maḥré', *Arabica* 1 (1954) 136–52.

[286] Nikephoros Patriarch of Constantinople, *Short History*, text, trans. and comm. by C. Mango. Corpus Fontium Historiae Byzantinae 13 (Dumbarton Oaks, Washington, 1990) 85.12 ff., p. 160. Cf. Theophanes, *Chron. AM* 6259 (C. Mango and R. Scott, *The Chronicle of Theophanes Confessor. Byzantine and Near Eastern History AD 284–813* (Oxford, 1997) 611) who says that Constantine 'stripped the peasantry naked through the exaction of taxes which forced them to sell the produce of God's earth at low prices (*εὐώνως*)'. For the common source, a 'chronicle composed towards the end of the reign of Constantine V', see Mango, *Short History*, 15.

going in your locality for 12 drachmas.'[287] In other words, wheat was the tax-paying crop, and the peasants in this locality refused to sell because the prices were too low. Centuries later, in *P. Hamb.* III 228 (6c.) an entire village was said to be refusing to pay the *dēmosion* as long as the landlord (*geouchos*) did not send the "monopolarius" to purchase their stocks of woad.[288] In the fifth century Theodoret alleged that a slump in prices owing to an abundant harvest (*euthēnia*) was even more of a hardship to rural producers than a year of crop failures.[289] In one of his letters he explained that in crises of this sort, when the flow of cash (gold) was restricted, peasants resorted to loans of 5, 10, or 20 solidi.[290] Finally, Table 7 (in Appendix 1) shows the gold payment levels of individual villages or districts in Egypt at various times from the sixth to the eighth centuries. The inference from this is that if villages were capable of paying sums like 350 to 1,000 solidi a year this was because a considerable proportion of the crop formed a marketed surplus. Table 7 implies extensive commercialization by the standards of most 'peasant economies' and the persistence of this sort of commercialism as late as the eighth century.

To sum up, the conception of late antiquity as a period of expanding natural economy is completely lacking in credibility. On the contrary, the fourth century saw a significant process of monetary expansion, triggered by Constantine's break with the orthodoxies of the past and the radical decision to shift to a gold-based monometallism. Silver was abandoned as the dominant metal for coining, and the base-metal coinages were re-articulated into a system dominated by gold. All of this, coupled with the state's unswerving commitment to maintain the purity of the gold coinage, formed an obvious basis for renewed economic expansion, and tied in with major social changes. I have also argued that the forces of monetary economy were, to a very great degree, spearheaded by the state, partly in response to massive pressures within its own ranks. By the end of the fifth century, the almost complete monetization of

[287] *SB* XVI 12607 = *P. Mich. inv.* 341 (2/3c.), H. C. Youtie, *ZPE* 36 (1979) 77ff. (prov. uncertain).

[288] Ibn Ḥauqal, *Kitāb Ṣūrat al-ʿarḍ*, tr. Kramers and Wiet, *Configuration de la terre*, 1.135–6 notes that under the ʿAbbasids collection of arrears depended on the flax harvest which took place in September–October.

[289] Theodoret, *De prov.* 7 (*PG* 83.677C), *τῶν καρπῶν γὰρ τοὺς ὠνητὰς περισκοπῶν οὐχ εὑρίσκει, καὶ γίνεται αὐτῷ τῆς εὐκαρπίας ἡ εὐθηνία μικρῷ τινι ἀφορητοτέρα.* Of course, landowners were equally worried about price falls, cf. Zeno of Verona, *Tractatus* 1.5, 'De avaritia', 4.14, 'Ingemescit praeterea, si annus est sterilis, multo magis, si fertilis fuerit'.

[290] Theodoret, *Ep.* 1.37 (see n. 219 above): *ἐν τοσαύτῃ σπάνει χρυσίου τῶν ὠνίων ἐρριμμένων.*

the revenue system would have presupposed (and further encouraged) a considerable production for the market at all levels, with, by now, a regular and large-scale circulation of gold in the countryside and considerable wear on the coinages used in trade. Since the late Roman monetary system was tendentially based on an acute polarization between currencies, once silver, or billon, and intermediate coinages collapsed or disappeared for long stretches, the 'retail trade' itself was simultaneously serviced by both gold and copper, though of course the areas where they overlapped, or allowed for mutual substitution, could not have been that large. In other words, even within the retail trade numerous payments had to be handled through gold. This, of course, is the point that scandalized the Anonymous, since he saw the solidus driving bronze out of circulation even in the sphere where it might have retained vitality as a subsidiary currency. But conversely, the bronze coinage would also have had to service fairly substantial payments, so that traders could not have afforded to take it but for its intrinsic worth.[291] The state was obviously aware of the unsatisfactory nature of this situation and responded, first by creating fractional pieces for the gold, and much later, under Anastasius, by revamping the whole base-metal coinage system and trying to produce a higher-value, 'full-value', and stable copper currency where the minimi would be reabsorbed as the lowest denomination in a hierarchy based on the follis. This system, which required careful regulation of the weights of the coins, succeeded for the greater part of the sixth century, a measure of its great achievement, till revaluation of the solidus led to its eventual collapse.[292]

[291] In the markets there was always a deep suspicion of token coinages above a certain extremely low threshold value (the lower the value of the individual denomination, the less it matters whether its current value retains its connection with intrinsic value), and therefore also considerable built-in resistance to the acceptance of such coins.

[292] There is an excellent discussion of the distinction between the 'main payments' and the 'retail trade' in David Buchanan, *Observations on the Subjects treated of in Dr Smith's Inquiry into the Nature and Causes of the Wealth of Nations* (Edinburgh, 1817, repr. New York, 1966) ch. 1, 'On the Principles of Metallic Currency', and the later chapter on 'Paper Currency'. Buchanan also makes the important point that 'The substitution of gold for silver in the main payments, must immediately occasion an excess of the latter currency, and consequently a fall in its value' (p. 9), a remark clearly applicable to the early 4th cent.

CHAPTER 4

Existing Accounts of the Byzantine Large Estate

Hardy and Byzantine 'Feudalism'

For Hardy the Byzantine large estate grew up in a context of major changes in the social and administrative system of the late empire. The large estate, fully formed by the end of the fifth century,[1] emerged through some process which enabled a bureaucratic élite, the officials who were 'among the most frequent patrons and founders of estates',[2] both to accumulate holdings and to assert new types of control over the population. 'We have no picture of how estates were built up after 415', Hardy wrote,[3] but it was clear, for him, that the rise of the new landed élite involved both their 'assumption, or usurpation, of government functions' and what he called 'the system of serfdom'.[4] The municipal aristocracy declined in importance,[5] the old nomes re-emerged as pagarchies,[6] and the new landed élite established wide-ranging fiscal autonomy through the autopract exemption of their own estates and pagarchic control over the taxation of the residual rural territories. Hardy maintains that 'the only reason why the subject of autopragia does not appear in the legislation of the sixth century is that the institution was a thoroughly recognized one'[7]—a conception which presupposes an almost total breakdown of provincial government in its primordial late Roman form. For Hardy *autopragia* is the crux of Byzantine provincial feudalism.

[1] Cf. Hardy, *Large Estates*, 24, 'When the curtain rises on the social history of Byzantine Egypt at the end of the century we find the large estates of the period in existence'.
[2] Ibid. 25.
[3] Ibid. 24, a statement still substantially true today.
[4] Ibid. 50 (from the chapter entitled 'Feudalism and Serfdom').
[5] Ibid. 22, 'the depression of the municipal aristocracy'.
[6] Ibid. 18, 'For purposes of local government the old nomes had, practically speaking, come into being again under the name of pagarchies'.
[7] Ibid. 54.

As for the estates themselves, the description is drawn largely from the Apion archive, ignoring both differences between landowners (scales of landownership) and alternative methods of management.[8] Thus Hardy says almost nothing about leasing, although curiously his account of the Apion estate seems to assume that it was organized on the basis of rents extracted from a peasantry which, while bound to the soil,[9] nonetheless leased its land from the proprietors. Hardy totally ignores the important differences between districts revealed by a closer study of the leases themselves, in particular by their distribution (why does Oxyrhynchus have almost no leases in the material surviving from the sixth and seventh centuries, which is otherwise fairly substantial?).

However, there are two features of his account which are worth emphasizing—the considerable importance which the Apions attached to the *management* of the estate—the managerial system and its specific levels—and the fact that the Apion estates (and by implication, presumably, most Byzantine large estates) showed no tendency to shut themselves off from monetary economy, that is, no particular inclination to *Naturalwirtschaft*. 'So far from any tendency to abandon the use of money, the Apion estate *seems definitely to have preferred to have its income in cash rather than in kind*.[10] Two of our accounts of pronoetae show an administration so arranged as to leave a large surplus in money and a small surplus in grain . . .'[11] Hardy is also correct in emphasizing the fluidity which characterized the recruitment of labour on the large estates[12] and in particular to state that 'the estate managers were apparently able to find workers as they needed them'[13]—a situation which should discourage us from supposing that the 'binding of the peasant to the soil'[14] was dictated essentially by the needs or requirements of estate agriculture (as opposed to, say, purely fiscal motives, which of course had as much to do with the state as with landowners). The practical needs of estate administration at all stages outweighed the aspects of dogmatism which may have characterized the intellectual

[8] Of course, Hardy is aware of the existence of 'smaller landlords', cf. *Large Estates*, 93.

[9] 'The fundamental fact about the condition of coloni was that they were bound to the soil' (ibid. 75).

[10] Contrast Vera's argument about the organization of large estates in late antiquity, *SRIT* 1.367–447—not supported by the papyrological evidence.

[11] Hardy, *Large Estates*, 100, with specific reference to *P. Oxy*. XVI 1911. 209, 1914. 5–7. Rouillard and Gascou enunciate similar views, cf. n. 23 and p. 96 below.

[12] Hardy, *Large Estates*, 122, and esp. 126, 'The whole system was apparently quite fluid'.

[13] Ibid. 126.

[14] Cf. 'The binding of the peasant to the soil was no novelty in Egypt' (ibid. 22).

make-up of large estate owners,[15] and flexibility in the use of labour was doubtless a reflection of the essential realism of any large enterprise faced with a labour demand schedule which was both complex and inherently fluid. Hardy claims that skilled workers or independent craftsmen were usually engaged by the job,[16] but even such a formula fails to underline the complexity which characterized Apion labour arrangements, for example, *P. Oxy.* LI 3641 is a lifelong contract with a millstone cutter who undertakes to service all the sectors of the estate which might require his services. Here, clearly, recruitment was not simply 'by the job'.

Given the nature of his account, it is doubtful if Hardy actually accomplished his stated aim of establishing a basis for 'a judgement as to the nature of [the] estates'.[17] Thus, no specific discussion can be found in *The Large Estates* of any of the three issues which are surely central to such a judgement. On the first issue, the nature of the relationship between the aristocracy and Byzantine fiscalism, he simply takes it for granted that the estates were autopract, and that autopragia was widespread if not universal by the sixth century. The weakening of central authority presupposed by this picture is of course far from evident, at least in the sixth century. In any case, Gascou's work, fundamental on this issue, has profoundly undermined the traditional conception of an aristocracy installing its own control systems in the wake of declining central authority. Second, Hardy leaves us with a strangely incongruous view of the Apion labour force, since the agricultural side is construed largely in terms of 'serfdom'[18] and the industrial occupations in terms of a free labour market.[19] Yet the postulate of a serf-like peasantry is clearly not derived from any actual analysis of the archive's documentation (e.g. there is no discussion of the term ἐναπόγραφος) so much as from the general preconception that 'The colonate was an accepted part of the social system of the sixth century.'[20] Finally, there is no conception in Hardy either of the peasantry or of the large estates as enterprises engaged in a market economy—although Hardy does explicitly dissociate himself from the Bücherian thesis of *Oikenwirtschaft*, and also assumes, naturally, that the estates participated in the market as *buyers* of commodities which their own product

[15] The passion for large vineyards is cited by Palladius as an example of such dogmatism, cf. *Opus agric.* 1.7.2, 'quod plerique fecerunt studendo famae tantum et latitudini pastinorum'.

[16] Hardy, *Large Estates*, 129.

[17] Ibid. 17.

[18] See n. 9 above and cf. *Large Estates*, 133, 'The serfs . . .'.

[19] Cf. ibid. 124, 'these building trade workers were generally independent craftsmen rather than estate employees'.

[20] Ibid. 75.

structure or production quotas failed to supply.[21] Thus despite its seminal role as the first systematic account of the 'large estate', Hardy's study remains insufficient in several important respects.

Rouillard

In the picture which Rouillard developed in the lectures published posthumously as *La vie rurale dans l'Empire byzantin*, the estates were seen as arising out of a process of centralization, their expansion rooted in the conflict between large property and the small peasant holding, the former succeeding at the expense of the latter.[22] This presupposes, of course, that before the main period of the late empire the Egyptian villages contained a considerable number of free peasants (in the sense of a group which owned its own means of production rather than one which was forced to survive largely through the leases it acquired on land owned by others). At any rate, the estates which grew up on this basis were flexible and highly organised enterprises which, in her view, were *'far from constituting* a closed economy'.[23] The estate extracted the bulk of its payments in kind,[24] while the level of such payments could (sometimes?) be determined by contract. The Apion estates were divided into a sector under direct management and lands which were leased out, so the Apion labour force comprised both tenants (*fermiers*), or permanent cultivators (*colons*), and free workers (*ouvriers agricoles, ouvriers salariés*).[25] The proprietors dealt not with individuals but with collectivities.[26] The tenants formed a unified economic community. Rural slavery was of no significance.[27] The same was not true, however, of hired labour. Estate administration was a major and highly structured affair, requiring a considerable staff with its own internal hierarchy.[28] However, owners did not abandon

[21] e.g. *Large Estates*, 126–7. Hardy is right to emphasize the open character of the estate economy, the fact that 'almost never, as far as we can tell, do they tend to be in any sense economically self-sufficient units' (p. 145).

[22] G. Rouillard, *La vie rurale dans l'Empire byzantin* (Paris, 1953) 15; on p. 14 she refers to 'une classe moyenne de paysans libres'.

[23] Ibid. 27, 'D'une façon générale, on ne saurait trop insister sur ce fait que le domaine *est loin de constituer dans son ensemble une économie fermée*', repeated on p. 47, 'le grand domaine ne constitue pas une économie fermée se suffisant à elle-même'; cf. Hardy, n. 21 above.

[24] Rouillard, *La vie rurale*, 26.

[25] Ibid. 26–8.

[26] Ibid. 28, 'C'est généralement, en effet, non pas avec des individus, mais avec des collectivités que le propriétaire est en rapport.'

[27] Ibid. 29.

[28] Ibid., 'Cette administration est une tâche assez lourde et fort complexe.'

administrative control of their estates entirely to their managers. They would often intervene directly.[29] The large estate regulated its work relationships by written agreements,[30] using the contract as a general means of control over obligations as well as assets. Rouillard accepts the traditional thesis of autopragia, so that the very biggest estates were self-regulating fiscal circumscriptions, the *πρόσωπα* of Edict 13.[31] Finally, she emphasizes an important fact about the social structure of Egypt in late antiquity—the existence of a stable and relatively prosperous middle class actively involved in agriculture both as lessors and as lessees.[32] In short, whatever their impact on the former peasantry, the growth of the large estates did not lead to any obvious 'polarization', with the crushing of the intermediate strata by some emerging wave of large-scale enterprise. The aristocracy was overwhelmingly powerful but not at the expense of the middle strata. Thus, below the aristocratic level we have to define the features of a large and stable group, the social basis of the occasional conflicts which erupted between the independent *kōmai* and pagarchic control. 'Typical of this rural bourgeoisie', writes Rouillard, 'whose representatives are both owners and lessees, is the famous advocate Dioscorus, the poet of Aphrodito.'[33] Since Rouillard states that Dioscorus 'appartient à une famille de cultivateurs', presumably the rural middle class she describes included a group with the features of a rich peasantry.

Gascou and the Model of 'Fiscal Participation'

In the general area of Byzantine papyrology Gascou's *Les grands domaines* is certainly the most important contribution to have appeared since *Byzantine Egypt: Economic Studies*. With the exception (mainly) of the Hermopolite archive published by Maehler (*BGU* XII) and new documents from the Apion archive and Oxyrhynchus in general, both use substantially the same sources. Yet Gascou was able to produce a profoundly significant reinterpretation of the material concerning large estates, and to do so, of course, with a conciseness and rigour which are not always evident in *Byzantine Egypt*. The crux of this reinterpretation concerns

[29] Ibid. 33, 'mais, en général, il semble que le grand propriétaire n'abandonne pas entièrement la gestion de ses biens à ses intendants. C'est lui qui donne parfois des ordres oralement ou par écrit.'

[30] Ibid. 38, with perhaps too much emphasis on the estates' 'méfiance contre les paysans'.

[31] Ibid. 31.

[32] Ibid. 49–50, calling it 'la classe moyenne des populations rurales'.

[33] Ibid. 50, where the group is called 'cette bourgeoisie rurale'.

the nature of the relationship between the state and the provincial aristocracy, which Gascou has construed in a precise and remarkably systematic form. However, before turning to the more general interpretation, it is worth noting the possible features of Gascou's analysis which seem to me to divorce the large estates too radically from the social as well as economic background presupposed in their real forms of existence (as opposed to their purely 'institutional' reality), and thus in some sense to *limit* his overall conception of the estates.

Building, clearly, on Rémondon's incisive assertion in his paper to the Thirteenth Congress (published posthumously) that 'the large estate is an economic enterprise. But it is also an institution',[34] Gascou is strangely indifferent to the economic realities of Egyptian agriculture. Almost at the outset of his analysis he notes (but does not explain) the indifference of Byzantine leases to flood variations, using Herrmann's sample, where 120 out of 156 Byzantine leases contain a fixed rent.[35] He also notes the high proportion of crop-sharing leases, 'forte proportion de "Teilpacht" ', but fails to suggest any link with the type of produce involved or to grasp their sudden frequency as a major symptom of the expansion of the wine economy. (In Herrmann, 36 out of 156 usable Byzantine leases are of this type: 23 per cent).[36] Absolutely correctly, Gascou notes that the majority of leases do not stem from the *oikoi*[37]—an observation of considerable importance and one which is scarcely compatible with the usual picture of the 'large estates'—but argues, nonetheless, that the latter leased their land on long-term, emphyteutic leases. For Gascou the ἀπότακτα or ἀπότακτοι φόροι of the Apion estate accounts are a reference specifically to leases of this sort.[38] Prima facie this sounds improbable since emphyteusis involved, for all practical purposes, abandonment of control over the property[39]

[34] R. Rémondon, '[Situation présente de la papyrologie byzantine]', *Akten des XIII. Internationalen Papyrologenkongresses, Marburg/Lahn, 2.–6. August 1971*, ed. E. Kießling and H.-A. Rupprecht (Munich, 1974) 367–72, esp. 372, 'Le domaine est une entreprise économique. Mais il est aussi une institution'; a contribution of supreme importance, like much of Rémondon's later work.

[35] Gascou, *Grands domaines*, 9 and n. 25.

[36] J. Herrmann, *Studien zur Bodenpacht im Recht der graeco-aegyptischen Papyri* (Munich, 1958) 274–87. In my own, updated, sample (182 5th- to 7th-cent. leases where the form of rent is determinable) the proportion is almost identical, 24.2 per cent (n = 44), but higher if we include mixed leases with a crop-sharing component (27.5 per cent, n = 50).

[37] Gascou, *Grands domaines*, 9, 'la plupart de ces *misthoseis* n'émanent pas des *oikoi* et ne caractérisent pas spécifiquement le régime agraire de ces établissements'.

[38] Gascou, *Grands domaines*, 9, 'leurs livres de comptes font plusieurs fois allusion à des *apotaktoi phoroi* ou *apotakta* (sans doute des "cens" emphytéotiques)'.

[39] As Gascou realizes, cf. *Grands domaines*, 32, 'Ce mode de location très proche de l'aliénation, selon Justinien,' and n. 192.

(control over the management of such properties lay with the 'lessee', hence the requirement that holders of such leases should be men of some capital[40]) and of course it is unlikely that the Apions would have wanted to relinquish control on such a systematic scale. (Estate accounts are full of references to payments denoted by the expression *ὑπὲρ ἀποτάκτου* or *ὑπὲρ ἀποτάκτου χωρίων*.[41]) More specifically, the only passage which seems to support Gascou's identification of *ἀπότακτον* with *ἐμφύτευμα* is *P. Cairo Masp.* III 67299. 39 f. (6c.), in an emphyteutic lease involving the monastery of St Phoebammon. But here *apotakton* is used in a more general sense to mean any type of fixed rent (the usual meaning of *apotakton*) and *emphyteuma* added to clarify the specific type involved. Moreover, if *apotakton* were simply equivalent to *emphyteuma*, as Gascou seems to want to suggest, it is hard to see how the term could apply to lease durations of, say, ten years or, in the majority of cases, far shorter periods. Again, the level of the Apion *hyper apotaktou* payments also implies that they were not emphyteutic rents since they are considerably higher than the usually low annual rents involved in emphyteusis[42] where the main payment was the lump-sum down payment purchasing the right to a perpetual lease and the major costs those of actual redevelopment (as opposed to leasing)—cf. *P. Oxy.* LV 3805, from the archive, where a payment of precisely this sort, far higher than any rents known to us (*c.*83 solidi), is called *emphytia,* that is, designated by a name which expressly indicates its emphyteutic nature.[43] (Thus we seem to revert to the dilemma that leasing was not an integral part of estate management on the largest estates—those of the *oikoi*—and yet the accounts refer to payments which imply some form of rent called or characterized as *apotakton.* Clearly, the solution must lie in an alternative view of the meaning of this term. Gascou, as we have just seen, equates it with *emphyteuma* on the strength of *P. Cairo Masp.* III 67299. For him the fixity implied here is one of stability over generations, so that

[40] Cf. *CJ* 1.2.24.5 (530), *Μόνοις εὐπόροις δεῖ τὰ ἐκκλησιαστικὰ ἐμφυτεύειν διὰ τὴν ἀποκατάστασιν τῆς ὄψεως*, about the immoveable property of the Church, cf. Gascou, *Grands domaines*, 27.

[41] For Gascou all the essential rent terminology seems to be reducible to emphyteusis! cf. *Grands domaines*, 7 f., '*Pakton*, *apotakton* et *kanon* semblent se rapporter spécifiquement au tribut ou "cens" emphytéotique et équivalent donc à *emphyteuma*', with his n. 16; repeated in n. 28.

[42] Thus *P. Cairo Masp.* III 67299, the lease cited by Gascou, has a rent of 1 sol. less 5 ker. per year, *BGU* IV 1020 (6/7c., Hermopolis) a rent of 3 sol., *CPR* IV 150 (7c., Hermopolis) a rent *(pakton)* of 1 sol., *P. Lond.* II 483 (615 or 616) a rent of 1⅔ sol., *P. Lond.* 1072b (6c., *BL* 9.138) 22½ keratia.

[43] The editor, John Rea, observes, 'If sol. 83 car. 8 represents an annual rent, the land must have been extensive' (*P. Oxy.* LV, p. 168), but it seems better to see the payment not as a rent but as the purchase price of the lease.

effectively the Apions were either uninterested in the issue of rents or abdicating control over the level of payments for reasons which are altogether unclear.[44])

Like Hardy, Gascou draws attention to the dominance of monetary economy and to the Apions' '*marked preference for gold*'.[45] However, the associated idea that the Romano-Byzantine state was content with a fixed level of public revenue is an odd one in view of Rémondon's demonstration that agrarian taxes increased sharply in the course of the sixth century.[46] Even more doubtful, indeed altogether untenable, is Gascou's interpretation of *phoros* as a term which no longer designates rent in the usual sense but something which he calls 'rent-tax'.[47] Now, the ambiguous nature of the 'rent-tax' can certainly be conceded for the lands of the imperial household (though this is hardly a peculiarity of the Byzantine world, since the same ambiguity may be said to exist wherever the state functions as landed proprietor). As Gascou says, it is more surprising to find such a confusion (between rent and public revenue) in the documents of the 'private' *oikoi* of Egypt.[48] But Gascou's arguments for his thesis are unconvincing. In *P. Oxy*. 2479 the use of the term συντελεῖν implies, for Gascou, a fiscal context,[49] while in *P. Oxy*. 130 the term τὰ δημόσια clearly indicates one.[50] But neither of these texts implies any reference to a separate payment of private estate rents, the only obligations involved are fiscal ones,[51] so it is not clear why these passages should be construed as supporting the notion of a 'rent-tax' or in what way they actually do so. (All they

[44] Cf. Gascou, *Grands domaines*, 9, esp. n. 29, and 10, with his reference to 'la stagnation relative du revenue'.

[45] Ibid. 10, 'préférence marquée pour l'or'.

[46] Rémondon, *CE* 40 (1965) 401–30.

[47] Gascou, *Grands domaines*, 12 ff.

[48] Ibid. 14, 'Mais il est plus surprenant de rencontrer cette confusion entre la rente et le revenue public dans les papiers d'*oikoi* "privés" égyptiens.'

[49] Gascou accepts Triantaphyllopoulos' interpretation of *euthēnia* as the 'annona', *Grands domaines*, 14. To me it seems more probable that the word has the same meaning here as it does in an important passage in Theodoret, *de prov*. 7 (*PG* 83.677c, cited Mickwitz, *Geld und Wirtschaft*, 157), of a price depression due to an abundant harvest. What Pieous is saying (quite correctly, of course) is that one's ability to pay depends at least partly on the level of market prices, cf. Claudian, *In Rufinum* 1.190–1, 'metuenda colonis fertilitas', and the more detailed discussion in Ch. 3.

[50] Gascou, *Grands domaines*, 66 n. 330, dates *P. Oxy*. I 130 to 548/9 on the basis of *P. Lond*. V 1708 (whose own date is conjectural), but since Flavius Apion II does not appear as a *patricius* in *P. Oxy*. I 133 (550) or *P. Lond*. III 776 (552), the twelfth indiction must refer to 563/4.

[51] The need to keep up with one's payments of the *kephalē* would be a sufficient explanation of these contexts, cf. *P. Lond*. V 1793.13 (471) for use of the term *dēmosia* in connection with the *kephalē*, and *P. Oxy*. XVIII 2195.34 (576/7) for the possibility that *syntelein*, when used on its own, probably referred to the poll tax (ὑπὲρ συντελ(είας) κεφαλῆς, from an Apion account).

do establish is that Apion employees had fiscal obligations, not that no other sort of obligation was involved in the payments extracted by the estate.) In *P. Oxy.* XXVII 2478 (595), the orchard is specifically described as 'belonging to the estate' (*γεουχικὸν πωμάριον* in l. 17), and one wonders why the *pōmaritēs* would be in any way responsible for the taxes on it. Here, surely, *φόρος* can only mean rent, as *τὰ ἐκφόρια* in l. 26 clearly does.[52] In *PSI* I 62 (612) *dēmosia* clearly refers to the employee's fiscal obligations (as in *P. Oxy.* 130), and there is no obvious reason to suppose that he was anything other than an estate labourer. Yet Gascou concludes, 'De ces formules strictement paralleles, on tire necessairement l'equation *phoros* ou *ekphorion* = *demosion*, rente = impôt'.[53] This will work as long as we ignore the distinction between estate residents or labourers whose only financial obligation involved fiscal payments, above all the poll tax, and the more substantial households who paid for the land they cultivated, through individual and collective payments, and also, presumably, paid taxes through the estate. Since it is essential to draw such a distinction, Gascou's deduction seems quite unwarranted.

In contrast to Rouillard's conception of a relatively diversified workforce, Gascou posits a more uniform one; for him the Apion employees were neither wage labourers nor slaves but 'locataires'.[54] With Eibach, correctly, he rejects the usual interpretation of the *enapographoi geōrgoi* as a semi-servile labour force. The conception he favours most is Seidl's view of the relation between landowners and *coloni* as one of 'droit public', i.e. landlords were not free to dispose of workforces as they liked. For the state the composition and level of rent were public matters, not private decisions.[55] Surely, the issue then becomes: how widely did such public control extend over the internal transactions of rural society? Were the mass of *geouchoi* subject to such a regime or only the very biggest owners who specifically undertook the sort of role described by Gascou, that is, on the descripton I shall propose later, assumed the function of the pagarchy? Since Gascou fails to draw this institution centrally into the argument, the attributes of the pagarch's role are converted into symptoms of a more general and less easily definable 'assimilation' between private and public. Thus Gascou wants to argue that the relation of the tenant (*tenancier*) to the *geouchos* was at some stage

[52] Preisigke, *WB* 1.461 cites no instance of *ekphorion* in the sense of 'taxes'.

[53] Gascou, *Grands domaines*, 14.

[54] Gascou, *Grands domaines*, 20, 'Les agents économiques le plus fréquemment attestés auprès des *oikoi* égyptiens ne sont ni des salariés ni des esclaves, mais des locataires, prestataires de *phoroi*'.

[55] Gascou, *Grands domaines*, 22–3.

'assimilated' to that of a taxpayer or other liturgical agent to his city and consequently estate rent necessarily assumed the function of a tax.[56] Egyptian peasants saw in the *geouchos* a tax-collector and administrator rather than a landowner. This explains why deeds of surety were commonly used as a means of control and discipline. In other words, it was entirely natural that these quintessentially fiscal instruments should be extended to cover relations between the estate and its *geōrgoi*. But Gascou, though he notes the 'astonishing parallel' between the Apion deeds of surety and *PSI* I 52 (617?) (which is addressed to a pagarch of Oxyrhynchus) and concludes, 'the authority of the *geouchos* over his coloni was *assimilated* to that of the municipal pagarch vis-à-vis his rural tax-payers' (emphasis mine), fails to draw the obvious conclusion that the resemblance was precisely there because it was by virtue of their pagarchic control over large parts of the Oxyrhynchite that the Apions could (or would expect to) extract undertakings of the kind embodied in the deeds of surety.

At any rate, Gascou's theory entails the more general characterization of the labour force of the large estates as a liturgical one (*une main-d'oeuvre liturgique*[57]), with the implied consequence that the relations of *Privatwirtschaft* had in some sense been largely superseded by the new arrangement between the state and the provincial aristocracy. He can thus claim, 'The key notions in the estate economy of Byzantine Egypt are "rent-tax" and "liturgical agricultural labour".'[58] That this was not so, that private landowners retained control over the economic organization of their estates despite the fiscal obligations they undertook, is proved by the freedom they retained in the actual operation of those estates and, in particular, by the survival and even extension of private leasing. Agricultural decision-making was fundamentally the *geouchoi*'s prerogative. They decided how their estates would be run, how much would be leased and on what terms, how much wine they would produce, etc. And Gascou himself admits that at an economic and social level the *geouchoi* of Byzantine Egypt enjoyed the main rights of private property.

Gascou's picture of the *geōrgoi* is a confused one. Behind the apparently liturgical subjection of the labour force lies a deeper social distinction—between an independent or 'rich' peasantry which could afford to lease the *chōria* with assured irrigation and stable

[56] Ibid. 23, esp. 'la rente domaniale revêt nécessairement la fonction de l'impôt puisque le rapport du tenancier à son *geouchos* est identifié à celui d'un contribuable ou d'un agent liturgique à sa cité'.

[57] Ibid. 27.

[58] Ibid. 28.

yields and the mass of *geōrgoi* who lacked such resources, and whose actual position vis-à-vis the estate was that of labourers,[59] as the first editors of *P. Oxy*. realized in retaining this term as the most appropriate one (in English) for *geōrgoi* in most passages. That these poorer households also engaged in leasing of some form is suggested by the collective payments which appear in the accounts—but unlike the individually listed rich cultivators—groups which elsewhere might have called themselves *leptoktētores*—their contracts were not individual leases but (presumably) collective ones. Moreover, for the estate these collective payments were not the main profit which it extracted from these groups, since their essential function was deployment in centralized estate production—a situation rarely evident in the archive but at least discernible in *P. Oxy*. XVI 1896 (577), where a group of local employees had failed to give the output which the Apions evidently required. In short, the real element of continuity between the *dēmosioi geōrgoi* of the Ptolemaic and early Roman periods and the *enapographoi geōrgoi* lay not in their juridical status (as Gascou suggests) but in their common landlessness, the fact that the bulk of the rural population depended in some form on the employment provided by the state or by private landowners, initially as 'lessees' and later, increasingly (once the very largest estates, the *oikoi*, came into being), as labourers incorporated into estates.

Finally, there is a curious omission at the heart of Gascou's analysis. The integration of the provincial aristocracy in the fiscal system is, of course, the crux of his conception of the nature of late imperial society in Egypt[60] (the sum total of obligations of a financial or liturgical nature was shared by the biggest *geouchoi* of each *polis* in ratios (*merides*) determined by some estimate of the revenue of different estates) and it can scarcely be doubted that the implied model (of a 'participant' aristocracy) is a more accurate reflection of the role of the large estates than the traditional picture of landowners exercising *patrocinium* or battling for *autopragia*. Discounting the obvious instances of an excessively rigid interpretation (notably, *apotakton*, *pronoētēs*, *apaitēsimon*, *meris*), Gascou has been able to show this through a careful and systematic analysis of the sources. However, even at this level, fundamental to his argument, it is essential to qualify his conception with some account of the *social* process at work behind the evolution of the pagarchy.

[59] Ibid. 27, refers to the 'aisance et l'honorabilité relative de ce milieu', with respect to the *geōrgoi*, ignoring the deep social divisions within this mass.

[60] This was first outlined by Rémondon in 'Les contradictions de la société égyptienne à l'époque byzantine', *JJP* 18 (1974) 17–32.

On the whole, Gascou tends to ignore this institution in *Domaines*, having dealt with it, presumably, in an earlier article (in *Byzantion* 42 (1972) 60 ff.). The qualification can be formulated in a more precise way. If, as Gascou himself argued, the pagarch's function was not a public office, and thus the pagarchs were not officials in the ordinary sense,[61] then the emergence and development of the pagarchy was surely an important reflection of the power of purely private 'civil society' over public functions which the late imperial state had always sought to control or exercise directly. The inner social tendency manifested in its development would express itself more or less forcefully depending on the control which government was able to impose and enforce over provincial taxation generally and the countryside in particular. Thus, Justinian sought to do precisely this in Edict 13 where the pagarchs, *politueomenoi* and *praktores* were isolated as the key groups on the operational side of the fiscal system.[62] He was also aware of the private power exercised by the pagarchs over rural taxation, and wished to assert imperial prerogative in the appointment and removal of holders of this position. Whatever the practical effects of such pronouncements, it is clear that with the decline of a strong central authority late Byzantine Egypt was being progressively abandoned to the unfettered domination of the local and provincial aristocracy more or less on the lines described by Gelzer.[63] In short, the model of provincial aristocratic participation in late imperial taxation has to be modified to allow for the workings of a more complex process where the arrangements desired by the state were not the sole determinants of social evolution, and the institutional landscape of Byzantine Egypt has to be supplemented by a social one where landholders represented the authority of the state not only through their collaboration with its requirements (the aspect stressed by Gascou) but in more private or autonomous forms which might conflict with those requirements.[64]

[61] J. Gascou, 'La détention collégiale de l'autorité pagarchique dans l'Égypte byzantine', *Byzantion* 42 (1972) 60–72, esp. 68 ff.; contrast M. Gelzer, *Studien zur byzantinischen Verwaltung Ägyptens* (Leipzig, 1909) 92, W. Liebeschuetz, 'The origin of the office of the pagarch', *BZ* 66 (1973) 38–46, at 38 ('the official known as the pagarch'), Palme, *Das Amt des ἀπαιτητής in Ägypten* (Vienna, 1989) 98 ('ranghohe Beamte').

[62] Edict 13, prol. (538/9), *οἱ παγάρχαι δὲ καὶ οἱ πολιτευόμενοι καὶ οἱ πράκτορες τῶν δημοσίων.*

[63] Gelzer, *Studien*, 35.

[64] Cf. the conflicts at Aphrodito.

CHAPTER 5

The Changing Balance of Rural Power

AD 200–400

The major conclusion of the analysis presented in this and the following chapter will be that in the eastern provinces the advent of the late empire revolutionized provincial landholding, signalling the rapid decline of the élites which had dominated urban and agrarian life for most of the earlier period, and the gradual emergence, especially in the course of the fifth century, of a new group of landowners whose social and professional roots were quite different from those of the municipal *geouchoi*. Thus I deal with the social changes which occurred in the Egyptian countryside between the third and the fifth centuries, and with the forms in which these changes crystallized in the 'classical' period of Byzantine Egypt, the sixth and seventh centuries. The distinction between 'types' and 'groups' which I start with is simply a way of trying to reintegrate the fragmentary information about individuals into some sense of the collective destinies which affected them at a historical level if not individually.

Landowners: Social Types and Social Groups

I shall define social 'groups' to mean clusters of individual landowners who share common social characteristics and thus reflect a unified social background, 'types' to mean particular individuals who illustrate most or even all of the features of that background with peculiar clarity. The 'type' individuals are by definition typical of their background, illustrations of the social groups which constituted their identity. I shall also assume that a 'unified social background' includes the property of a shared history, so that backgrounds in this sense cannot be transcendent with respect to historical periods, that is, we cannot have a landholder from the still undefined and rapidly changing world of the fourth century forming part of the same social background as one from the settled and very different world of the sixth.

The very nature of papyrological evidence (defined by high levels of contingency and considerable fragmentation) makes it improbable that we shall ever be able to discern more than a limited number of 'groups'. However, the search for such clusters is of some interest, as it forms our only concrete image of what the landowning class looked like in one period or another. The main 'groups' to emerge from a general scrutiny of the evidence (and the ones I shall mainly deal with, except for (9) below) are: (1) Alexandrian aristocrats of the third century, with holdings in the Fayum and Oxyrhynchite; (2) the military landholders of the Abinnaeus archive—in the Fayum in the 340s; (3) the family of Hyperechius, by far the wealthiest landowners in the Hermopolite élite of the first half of the fourth century; (4) the *eugenestatai* of Hermopolis in the fifth and sixth centuries, a 'no managers' group; (5) the *politeuomenoi* and middle-grade officials of Antaeopolis in the early sixth century; (6) the Antinoite bureaucrats of the 560s; (7) the powerful *stratēlatai* and pagarchs of the Fayum in the seventh century; (8) the rich peasantry of the sixth to seventh centuries; and finally, (9) the landed monasteries of the Byzantine period. A brief consideration of each of these groups should enable us both to trace the general process of evolution in the particular forms it assumed in reality and to gain a sense of the structure of rural society as a whole—the complexity of its divisions, initially in the form of the complex and changing character of its dominant strata. Finally, the methodological value of a 'group' should be obvious—it allows for a 'definition', in space and time, without which living communities become largely notional determinations (as in Rostovtzeff's account of the great conflict between urban and rural classes),[1] purely abstract or even largely conceptual shapes, because their 'reality' escapes us.

Alexandrians and Local Councillors

Alexandrians account for some 17 per cent of all 'selected' landholders (defined as those with a specific and usable social or professional designation) in the first/second centuries, 31 per cent in the third. It is possible that this result is simply a random one, but there are several reasons for rejecting this view and seeing the pattern as probably significant. First, the conception of the third century as the peak of Alexandrian involvement in the *chōra* goes well with

[1] Rostovtzeff, *SEHRE*, esp. 496–7, 503.

the trend elsewhere in the empire for an intensified aristocratic involvement in commercial agriculture—the most notable case of this being, of course, the investments by senatorial families in the African olive oil business.[2] Naturally, this assumes that Alexandrian involvement in the *chōra* was motivated primarily by commercial considerations of a similar sort. The increased frequency of wine in the documents of the third century, like its consistent association with the wealthiest landholders, is clearly symptomatic of this. Second, given the landholding traditions of Ptolemaic and early imperial Egypt, it required time for a landed aristocracy to emerge and consolidate, and the main part of the third century is precisely the period when we would expect its impact to be most in evidence, after the initial period of consolidation but before the local municipal élites established their own dominance at the district level (buying out Alexandrians, presumably), and certainly before the major changes which set in during the fourth century (when Alexandrians are almost invisible, down to 4.6 per cent of all 'selected' landholders).

The Alexandrian aristocracy of the Fayum is known to us largely through the Heroninus archive. Heroninus worked as *phrontistēs* for several local landholders, including Aurelius Appianus, whose wife Aurelia Demetria was the daughter of L. Septimius Aurelius Posidonius—perhaps Egypt's most obvious illustration of the group I have called the 'Severan élite'. By the reign of Severus he was already a former *hypomnēmatographos* of Alexandria, probably close to the end of his life since the payment in *BGU* VII 1617, dated to 227 by Lewis, refers to his heirs, the *κλη(ρονόμοι) Ποσιδωνίου ὑπο(μνηματογράφου)*.[3] We have no means of knowing whether Posidonius was one of the immediate coterie enriched by Septimius,[4] but we do know that the family's fortunes ended in a political disaster towards the end of the century, when their estates, now controlled by Antonius Philoxenus, husband of Aurelia

[2] The North African trade was dominated by large producers, see D. Manacorda, 'Prosopografia e anfore tripolitane: nuove osservazioni', in *PCAA* II 483–500; G. Di Vita-Evrard, 'Notes sur quelques timbres d'amphores de Tripolitaine', in S. Lancel (ed.), *Histoire et Archéologie de l'Afrique du Nord. IIe Colloque International (Grenoble, 5–9 Avril, 1983)* = *BCTH* 19B (1983) 147–59; D. J. Mattingly, 'The Olive Boom: Oil Surpluses, Wealth and Power in Roman Tripolitania', *Libyan Studies* 19 (1988) 21–41; J.-P. Laporte, 'Les amphores de Tubusuctu et l'huile de Maurétanie Césarienne', *BCTH* 1976–8, 131–57.

[3] *P. Mich.* XI 606.4–5 (224), *Αὐρελιου Ποσιδωνίου γενομένου ὑπομνηματογράφ(ου) τῆς λαμπροτάτης πόλεως τῶν Ἀλεξανδρέων* in a loan contract with one of his former slaves, *BGU* VII 1617.57–8 (Philadelphia, 227, for the date cf. *BL* 7.21); cf. *O. Mich.* 94 (after 197) for his full name; the date must be later than *P. Med.* I 63 = *SB* VI 8999 (3c.), since he is *ὑπομνηματογράφος* here.

[4] Cf. Pseudo-Aur. Victor, *Epitome de Caesaribus*, 20.5–6 (Pichlmayr 155).

Appiana Diodora alias Posidonia, were confiscated by the fisc.[5] The evolution of this family over three generations is thus an almost textbook case of the fortunes of the third-century landholding aristocracy, encompassed by the political upheavals of the middle empire but also pursued largely independently of that history in the more mundane business of organizing and running a large provincial estate.

That estate was equipped with an extensive managerial staff with a multiplicity of *phrontistai*, and evidently a conscious policy of having one manager at this level for each holding or location controlled by them. Thus in *P. Med.* I 63 (= *SB* VI 8999) (3c), a rent receipt, Posidonius is represented by a manager whose full designation is '*phrontistēs* of the village of Pelousion and the settlement called Cleopatra'.[6] In the case of Pelusium, which is described as a *kōmē*, the expression does not imply that Posidonius controlled the entire village as part of his estate. Heroninus is repeatedly described as φρ(οντιστὴς) Θεαδελφίας, and obviously there the family holdings were limited to only some part of the village lands. On the other hand, the *epoikion* 'named after Cleopatra' was a purely subaltern settlement, like the *ezba* of modern Egypt, its dependence on a private landlord embodied in its physical isolation from the other local communities. In *P. Laur.* I 11, an account dated 248 or 258, the manager is called φροντιστὴς ἐποικίου Ψέτ, which implies that each settlement of this sort would have had one *phrontistēs* as the 'manager' vested with general responsibility for its affairs and for the *ktēmata* in its vicinity.[7]

The marriage of Aurelia Appiana Diodora alias Posidonia to Antonius Philoxenus merged two streams of the Alexandrian aristocracy—the civilian, purely municipal side represented by her parents and her grandfather Posidonius, and the class of high imperial officials from which Philoxenus himself seems to have come, since the only epithet he bears is the quintessentially bureaucratic one *kratistos* and the only professional background attested

[5] This is now clear from *P. Prag.* I 117 (289/90), a rent receipt from the Arsinoite.

[6] Unusually, he bears the *tria nomina* L. Valerius Ammonius, *P. Med.* I 63.5 ff.; φροντιστὴς κώμης Πηλουσίου καὶ ἐποικίου Κλεοπάτρας καλουμένου (lines 7 ff.).

[7] Cf. *P. Prag.* I 107 (249–68), κτημάτων [τῆ]ς φροντίδος αὐτοῦ (ll. 6–7), about the wine estates in Heroninus' charge. But a *phrontistēs* could handle several villages, cf. *P. Strasb.* 459 (228), from the estate of Valerius Titanianus, who employed Valerius Hermias as φροντιστὴς κώμης Θεαδ[ελ]φ[ίας κ]αὶ ἄλλων κώμων (lines 7–9), these 'other villages' including Polydeukia. Pintaudi's translation of φροντιστὴς ἐποικίου Ψέτ as 'fattore di Pset' is also revealing since it seems to me to reflect the deeper levels of continuity in Mediterranean estate agriculture and management, since the Italian *fattore* was, like the *phrontistēs*, the agent who above all embodied the landowner's control over *production* on the Italian *fattorie*.

for him is the imperial procuratorship.[8] Thus the history of this family shows that among Alexandrian landowners at any rate the division between the municipal aristocracy and the imperial service élite was much less sharp than it was destined to become in the next century or so. Posidonius himself is not attested in any public office, as far as we know, and his son-in-law Appianus was likewise a purely 'municipal' aristocrat, addressed, for example, in *SB* VI 9408.1 (September 250) as *ἐξηγ(ητεύσας) βουλ(ευτῆς) τῆς λαμπροτάτης πόλεως τῶν Ἀλεξανδρέων*. On the other hand, a recent Prague papyrus refers to Philoxenus as the son of Alypius, whom Pintaudi has naturally identified as the landowner for whom Heroninus worked in the countryside around Theadelphia.[9] If this is true, then the daughter of Appianus and Aurelia Demetria married into a purely equestrian family whose influence was, apart from its agricultural assets, entirely rooted in the positions it occupied in official administration, since Alypius himself was a *κράτιστος δουκηνάριος*[10] and might be referred to, in the estate correspondence, simply as *ὁ κράτιστος*.[11]

The family of Valerius Titanianus is said by Gilliam to have 'maintained its equestrian status and its connections with the imperial administration over a period of fifty years, and presumably also managed to retain if not expand its property during these difficult decades'.[12] He was even more highly placed in the Alexandrian landed aristocracy than Alypius and is described (by Gilliam) as 'distinctly the highest known official . . . to be a member of the Museum', *praefectus vigilum* in 217 and *eminentissimus vir* (*ἐξοχώτατος* in a recently published inscription from a dedication to his son later redeployed in the baptistry of the church of the convent at Deir el Bayad).[13] A long account from one of his estates (near Theadelphia) shows that on large estates which retained a general

[8] For the references, see *Catalogue*, Fayum 3c. For *kratistos* cf. O. Hornickel, *Ehren- und Rangprädikate in den Papyrusurkunden. Ein Beitrag zum römischen und byzantinischen Titelwesen* (Gießen, 1930) 19ff.

[9] *P. Prag.* I 117 (n. 5 above).

[10] *SB* VI 9349.4–5 (3c., second half).

[11] e.g. in *P. Flor.* II 228.7–8, where he is called *τοῦ κρατίστου Ἀλυπίου*.

[12] J. F. G. Gilliam, 'Valerius Titanianus', *Mnemosyne*, 4th ser., 17 (1964) 293–9 (at 297), and 'An *ab epistulis Graecis* and *praefectus vigilum* from Egypt', in *Mélanges d'histoire ancienne offerts à William Seston* (Paris, 1974) 217–25 (on his career).

[13] See W. Van Rengen and G. Wagner, 'Une dédicace à Valerius Titanianus, fils du préfet des vigiles Valerius Titanianus', *CE* 59 (1984) 348–53, *Οὐαλερ(ίου) Τιτανιανοῦ τ[οῦ] ἐξοχωτάτου*. *Pace* J. D. Thomas, Valerius Titanianus who turns up in *P. Oxy.* 2107 (262) as a *vir egregius* (*kratistos*) is surely of the same family and probably the landowner's son (who was important enough for the dedication in *CE* 1984). The Coptic convent of Deir el Bayad is 115 km. south of Cairo.

manager (*epitropos*),[14] the *phrontistai* submitted their accounts to him and not directly to the employer (as Heroninus clearly did with Appianus and Aurelius Heraclides).[15] Thus *P. Mich.* IX 620 (239/240) is addressed to Valerius 'through' A. Arius, who moreover seems to have been a local councillor—an adequate reflection of the social gap which separated the true aristocracy based in Alexandria from the local élites for whom such a term is mostly an exaggeration. The account also reveals the dispersion of Valerius' holdings in the Fayum and the fact that landowners extracted at least some of their income from urban or, perhaps more accurately, non-agricultural rents, for lodgings described as *kellai* which were presumably single rooms. Finally, Shelton notes that 'The principal product of the estate as presented by these records was wine.'[16]

Wine is a consistent feature of the third-century Alexandrian-controlled estates. Valerius Titanianus was still investing in it in the 240s, towards the end of his life. It was clearly a major commodity on the Appianus estate, which comprised both artificially irrigated vineyards (*antletika ktēmata*) and 'vineyards in the plain' (*epipeda*) (i.e. based on natural irrigation).[17] It was produced on a massive scale by a certain Apollonius whose description as *axiologōtatos* shows him to be an Alexandrian.[18] Indeed, the distributions suggest that Alexandrians dominated the industry. Thus, of twenty-five Oxyrhynchite landholders involved in wine production (in the third century), no fewer than eleven are from the Alexandria-based aristocracy—a good 44 per cent. In the Fayum, of thirteen attested wine producers of that century, six are Alexandria-based—a slightly higher proportion. Of course, we have no obvious way of quantifying the level of investment over time, but impressionistically it seems certain that the latter increased substantially in the course of the third century. In *P. Oxy.* LI 3638, a sale contract dated 220, the wine estate is described in some detail. The contract involved

[14] Shelton, *P. Mich.* IX, p. 64 uses this term for the *phrontistai*, calling the *epitropos* 'agent'. But this seems to me to reverse matters somewhat.

[15] Cf. *P. Flor.* III 322 (258?) or *SB* VI 9408 (250–6), both to Appianus, *P. Lond.* III 1170 verso (258/9) to Heraclides.

[16] Shelton, *P. Mich.* IX, p. 66.

[17] *P. Flor.* II 148 recto (Jan. 266), see D. Rathbone, *Economic Rationalism and Rural Society in Third-Century A.D. Egypt* (Cambridge, 1991) 222, 248–50, contrast M. Schnebel, *Die Landwirtschaft im hellenistischen Ägypten* (Munich, 1925) 242, who sees the distinction as one between 'rai' and 'sharaqi' land.

[18] Cf. *P. Oxy.* XVII 2153 (3c), a wine account from which J. L. Rowlandson, *Landholding in the Oxyrhynchite nome 30 BC–c.300 AD* (Oxford D. Phil., 1983) 23 n. 1, infers a total wine area of over 100 arouras (given the production level of 5,464 *tetrachoa*). I suggest the owner Apollonius could have been Aurelius Apollonius alias Dionysius who is discussed by P. Pruneti, 'Aurelios Apollonios *alias* Dionysios, ginnasiarco ad Ossirinco', *YCS* 28 (1985) 277–81.

an *ampelikon ktēma* 'together with the date palms and plants and fruit trees and irrigation channels[19] and the *mēchanē* (*sāqiya*) lying over them and the farm building (*epoikion*) and treading-trough and vat and pressing machine and drying-ground and other appurtenances' (ll. 7 ff.). This estate was near the village of Sinaru in the lower toparchy. Sespha and Souis were likewise villages in the lower toparchy and the location of a substantial wine enterprise[20] whose ownership is uncertain but likely to have been part of the estate of Calpurnia Heraclia, daughter of Calpurnius Theon, who, like Valerius Titanianus, liked describing himself as ἀπὸ Μουσείου (former fellow of the Museum)[21] and whose own father, a former strategus and *archidikastēs* of Alexandria, described himself and his sons in a petition to Septimius and Caracalla as 'owning estates (*chōria*) in certain villages of the Oxyrhynchite' (note the clear implication that, normally, villages as such were not owned) and as 'utterly exhausted by the annual liturgies of the *fiscus*'—a policy which was simply undermining production, since it was forcing him to leave land uncultivated.[22]

The Sespha–Souis wine business gives us some insight into the forms of organization which owners adopted for large-scale ventures.[23] The owners of enterprises on this scale (the payroll refers to it as an *ousia*)[24] produced wine on a 'direct management' basis, i.e. seem consciously to have avoided leasing as a method of management. The reason, clearly, is that they could afford the costs of direct management in terms of supervisory personnel and wage bills to hired workmen. On this particular estate Nemesianus, a sort of general manager, had overall responsibility, with control over individual *ktēmata* deputed to local managers called either *pronoētai* or *phrontistai*—proof that these designations were simply alternative expressions for the middle management level where the real business of production would have to be handled from day to day. Each of these middle managers was responsible for specific 'sections' of the village—a fact which the employer seems to have wanted to

[19] The editor translates *hydreumata* (in l. 8) as 'wells' but they were the channels which enabled the water to reach the fields, hence the description of the *mechane* as ἐπικειμένη αὐτοῖς, and the fact that the word usually occurs in the plural, cf. nn. 30 and 32 below.

[20] See n. 23 below.

[21] He calls himself that in *P. Oxy.* L 3564.2 (235) and is correctly identified by Whitehorne (*P. Oxy.* L p. 162) as the father of Calpurnia Heraclia in *P. Oxy.* XLII 3047.2–3 (245).

[22] *P. Oxy.* IV 705 = *WChr.*153 (199/200), esp. ll. 69 ff.

[23] See S. A. Stephens, 'Nine Orders to Pay from Oxyrhynchus', *ZPE* 31 (1978) 145–60, republished as *P. Oxy.* XLIX 3513 ff.

[24] *P. Oxy.* XLIX 3521 (260).

emphasize, since their job designations specifically referred to the areas for which they were responsible. Thus one manager was called προνοητὴς βορίων μερῶν, another φροντιστὴς ἐνίων μερῶν Σούεως.[25] Below them, again, were the lower-level supervisory staff—as on the estates managed by Heroninus, though here called not *prostatēs ktēmatos* but *epistatēs ampelourgōn*.[26] Thus the organization of production presupposed at least three levels of management, with Nemesianus assuming formal responsibility for wage payments and the middle managers mediating his instructions at a level which implied direct contact with the workforce.

Nemesianus himself may well have been a *pragmateutēs*. At any rate, the only document which gives us an immediate grasp of the total personnel or labour force of a large estate of this size is *P. Oxy*. XLII 3048 from the archive of Calpurnia Heraclia. This text, dated 246, contains a proclamation of the *iuridicus* requiring all private landholders to declare their stocks of grain within twenty-four hours and the registration submitted on the following day by Calpurnia Heraclia. She declared over 5,000 artabas, most of this at Souis. It is clear that the *pragmateutai* were the chief managers at the local level, both because the stocks were under their formal control (and this implies that they were responsible for wage payments out of it) and because the various categories of the estate's personnel mentioned them first.[27] Thus an average large estate in the third-century Oxyrhynchite, owned by Alexandrians, would have comprised five fundamental groups of employees—all entitled to payments on a monthly basis (μηνιαῖαι συντάξεις)—πραγματευταί, φροντισταί, γεωργοί, παιδάρια, and a group called καταμήνιοι. It is worth noting that the *geōrgoi* were estate employees, not tenants, and that the term could contain the general sense of an 'estate labourer' already in the third century (see Appendix 1, Table 8). The *katamēnioi* may help to link the Nemesianus orders to pay to the archive of Calpurnia Heraclia or her descendants since they also turn up there,[28] while conversely those documents help to clarify the

[25] *P. Oxy*. XLIX 3515.2, 3516.2.

[26] *P. Oxy*. XLIX 3514.9–10, cf. *P. Ant*. III 189.10 (6/7c.) referring to a προεστὼς γεωρ(γῶν); for the Heroninus estates, cf. *SB* VI 9408(1).35, XVI 12382.7, etc.

[27] *P. Oxy*. XLII 3048.19–20 (246).

[28] See *P. Oxy*. XLIX 3518; otherwise the only occurrence of the term I am aware of (outside the Zenon archive) is *P. Oxy*. XVII 2155.8 (4c.). The *katamēnioi* were surely permanent employees of the estate whose wages were calculated on a monthly basis, like the monthly-rated staff of large modern companies, not temporary workers hired for a month, as J. Hengstl, *Private Arbeitsverhältnisse freier Arbeiter in den hellenistischen Papyri bei Diokletian* (Bonn,1972) 101 (followed by C. Orrieux, *Zénon de Caunos, parépidèmos, et le destin grec* (Paris, 1985) 213) supposes. Hengstl's argument that most employees received monthly wages ('die monatliche Entlohnung') ignores the

nature of this category of employees since the term is used to refer to what one might call service staff such as donkey drivers, teamsters, and settlement guards.

Another document from the archive of Calpurnia Heraclia, *P. Oxy.* XLII 3047, dated 245, shows that her estate in the villages of the eastern toparchy comprised at least some 1,700 arouras. The total estate was thus clearly massive, since Souis, where she kept most of her grain reserves, was in the lower toparchy. The declaration also shows that in some villages at least, up to a third of the total sown area might be under artificial irrigation. This implies a substantial investment in irrigation machinery, especially if we accept Ayrout's statement that 'about five feddans can be supplied by one wheel'.[29] The early spread of irrigation machinery on the private estates may well have been pioneered by the Alexandrian aristocracy. At least four other third-century Alexandrians are explicitly associated with equipment of this type. Thus *P. Flor.* I 16 (239), a lease addressed to Aurelia Demetria, *matrona stolata*, as she was usually called, involves one aroura of a vegetable garden 'including the well and *sāqiya*'. It is worth noting that the structure associated here with the *mēchanē* is designated by a term usually understood as a well (*phrear*), because it clearly suggests the sense in which we should understand the more common term *lakkos* (as opposed to the meaning usually ascribed to it, viz. cistern or tank).[30] In *P. Flor.* II

distinction between the frequency of wage payments and the basis on which wages are calculated.

[29] H. H. Ayrout, *The Egyptian Peasant*, tr. J. A. Williams (Boston, 1963) 44, followed by L. Ménassa and P. Laferrière, *La Sāqia. Technique et vocabulaire de la roue à eau égyptienne* (Cairo, 1974) 48; the feddan, of course, is slightly more than an acre while one aroura = 0.67 acres. Thus the *c.*307 (or 317) arouras under artificial irrigation at Thmoinepsobthis (*P. Oxy.* XLII 3047.17) would have required anywhere between 15 and 40 *mēchanai*, depending on the estimate we adopt for the amount of land efficiently irrigated by one *sāqiya*.

[30] Thus one 'dug' a *lakkos* (as one digs a well), e.g. Callinicos, *Vie d'Hypatios* 40.23 ff. (*SC* 177.238) (monks looking for water), *P. Oxy.* LV 3804.213, *τοῖς ποταμ(ίταις) ἀνορύξασι νέον λάκκον ἐν κτήμα(τι) Πακιὰκ*, *P. Lond.* II 483.43 (615 or 616), *λάκκους ἐνωρῦξαι* (in starting a vineyard). One referred to the *sāqiya* (*organon*) 'of' a *lakkos*, cf. *PSI* I 88, just as one described the main installation which went with a water wheel (*machina rotalis*) as a 'puteus' (well), cf. Sulpicius Severus, *Dialogues*, 1.13 (*PL* 20.192), in the Upper Thebaid, about 20 km. from the Nile, said to be of a depth of '1000 ft. or more' (!). H. Rabie, 'Some Technical Aspects of Agriculture in Medieval Egypt', in A. L. Udovitch (ed.), *The Islamic Middle East, 700–1900* (Princeton, 1981) 71: 'Nuwayrī, from the Mamluk period, states that wells were dug in the land . . . At the mouth of these wells, the sawāqī, made from acacia or other trees, were installed', and C. B. Klunzinger, *Upper Egypt, its People and its Products* (London, 1878), 136: 'The chief condition for the existence of such a wheel is a well that contains spring water all the year round.' Again, in the *Vie de S. Syméon Stylite le Jeune*, two *phreata* in 97.14 ff. (Van den Ven 1.75) are shortly afterwards referred to as *lakkoi* in 98.1 ff. Also, cf. the standard Byzantine formula *σὺν ἡμίσει μέρει λάκκου καὶ παντὸς αὐτοῦ δικαίου κτλ.* in *P. Coll. Youtie* II 90. 11 ff., *P. Ross.-Georg.* III 55, *SB* 12481.13 ff., with *P. Mich.* 274–5

152 Alypius refers to one or several *sāqiyas* as τὰ μηχανικά[31] τοῦ Πακι καὶ τῶν ἐνθάδε μερῶν, implying that the carpenter was being sent to make routine repairs. In *P. Oxy.* XXXIV 2723 L. Calpurnius Gaius buys a vineyard at Souis which includes ὑδρεύματα σὺν τῇ ἐπικειμένῃ τούτοις μηχανῇ, that is, irrigation channels[32] with the *saqiya* lying above them. For winemaking proper this estate included a στεμφυλουργικὸν ὄργανον or wine press. In *P. Oxy.* XLIX 3498 C. Julius Diogenes sells half of an arable estate with the corresponding share of the τροχὸς καὶ λάκκος καὶ μηχανή (line 11). This seems to imply a compartmented water-wheel driven by a *sāqiya* gear,[33] while *lakkos* must refer to the structure described by Ménassa and Laferrière in chapter one of *La Sāqia* (called 'Le puits'). Finally, the Julii Theones were another Alexandrian family whose estates contained *mēchanai*. However, it would be wrong to conclude that only Alexandrians could afford the costs of such equipment or that local landholders were unaware of the benefits of artificial irrigation, for the holdings of the prosperous (if less opulent) municipal élite were frequently equipped with similar devices.

The substantial estate which was divided equally between four siblings in the Hermopolite contract preserved in *P. Flor.* I 50 (268) included two *organa*—the standard term in the south for *sāqiyas*—as well as a structure called the ἀναβατικὸν ὕδρευμα which Oleson thinks refers to some form of pumping machinery. Claudius Eudaemon was a *bouleutēs Alexandreias*, his brother Claudius Theon a *tribunus*. The estate comprised well over 1,092 arouras in fourteen separate locations,[34] mostly substantial villages like Sinarchebis, Telbonthis, and Pesla, and in one village, Psobthonchenarsiesis, included a vineyard of 42 arouras which was divided into four equal shares. *P. Flor.* 50 is important in two

(46–7) ll. 5 ff., ἐν ἐς ἥμεσον μέρος φρέατος λίθινον (l. λιθίνου) κτλ., and *P. L. Bat.* XXV 21 (78 BC), τοῦ ἐπιβάλλοντος ε̄ μέρ(ους) ὑποδοχ(είου) καὶ κρή(νης) λιθίνης. Finally, cf. N. S. Hopkins, *Agrarian Transformation in Egypt* (Boulder, Colo., 1987) 98–9, for the importance of wells in Egypt, and Maspero, *P. Cairo Masp.* I 67097.2n (p. 141), 'Le *lakkos* n'est pas une mare: c'est un puits artificiel'.

31 For the expression, apparently a local one, cf. *P. Berl. Leihg.* I 23.11 ff. (252, Fayum).

32 For these cf. Ménassa and Laferrière, *Sāqia*, 48 f. on *gadwal* and *ganāya* = 'rigole d'écoulement principale' (see fig. 42); the published translation is fairly vague, 'irrigation works with the apparatus attached to them'.

33 Cf. *P. Ross.-Georg.* II 19 (Oxy., 141), *PSI* IX 1072 (276/77, *BL* 7.239), for the combination of *trochos* and *mēchanē*, with the comments in J. P. Oleson, *Greek and Roman Mechanical Water-Lifting Devices: The History of a Technology* (Toronto, Buffalo, London, 1984) 164 f., 167.

34 See the discussion in M. A. H. el-Abbadi, 'P.Flor.50: Reconsidered', *Proceedings of the XIVth International Congress of Papyrologists, Oxford, 24–31 July, 1974* (London, 1975) 91–6.

ways. It allows for a more or less precise reconstruction of the *scale* of a typical middle-sized property such as the more average sort of Alexandrian family probably controlled—a group not far removed from the more affluent local councillors such as the family of Hyperechius, whose estates—even larger—included some of the same locations (e.g. Sinarchebis, Pesla). Second, it reveals the important process which (even more than the factors usually evoked) would increasingly undermine the economic stability of the affluent landed élites of the middle empire and deprive them of the capacity to resist the entry of new groups of landholders—viz., the constant subdivision of the bigger properties among siblings by which middle-sized estates of a thousand or more arouras were falling to averages of a few hundred in the course of one or two generations.

Among private estates, the truly large ones, those called *ousiai*, were overwhelmingly Alexandrian-controlled. Thus of eight private *ousiai* of the third century, seven were owned by Alexandrians, one by Alypius, classified as a 'high official' and clearly from the same milieu, and none by any member of the gymnasial class who was not of Alexandrian descent.[35] This distribution surely cannot be accidental and is one reason why we should distinguish the aristocracy based in the great urban centres of the Mediterranean seaboard (Alexandria, Antioch, Carthage) from the less opulent and altogether less influential élites who controlled the town councils in cities which were inseparable from their rural background.

In the third century this local élite was still a solid, well-entrenched class, owners of substantial medium-sized properties (mostly 500–1,000 arouras) and active participants in the management of their estates. The fact that this group accounts for an overwhelming proportion of the lessors who turn up in the papyri is likely to create a misleading impression of absenteeism and lack of involvement in the business of farm management. But Egyptian leases above all show us why the usual distinction between entrepreneurs and absentees is too schematic and incapable of representing the more complex and nuanced relationships of Mediterranean agriculture (reflected, for example, in the sharecropping contracts

[35] Till Kaufmann's re-edition of *P. Oxy.* XII 1578 (*BASP* 3 (1965–6) 30–1), one might have thought of Claudia Isidora al. Apia as purely local (esp. in view of the title she bears in *SB* XVI 12235, cf. L. Casarico, 'Donne ginnasiarco', *ZPE* 48 (1982) 117–23) but the description of her as *axiologōtate* in l. 21 of that document (noted by Hornickel, *Rangprädikate*, 3) almost certainly shows that she was from an Alexandrian family (for the epithet see H. Geremek, 'P. Iandana 99: Italian Wines in Egypt', *JJP* 16–17 (1971) 159–71, at 162 f.). Thus the only *ousia* that might have been assigned to the gymnasial class turns out to be (yet again) Alexandrian-controlled.

of the Byzantine period or in the *contratti mezzadrili* of more recent times).[36] Thus Aurelia Sarapus, daughter of Theon, former exegetes of Oxyrhynchus, organized the cultivation of her small wine estate of 6 arouras on a pattern typical of wine producers from the third-century Oxyrhynchite. The contract, *P. Oxy.* XLVII 3354, is of the type usually called a 'vineyard lease', though strictly this is an inaccurate description since the peculiarity of such agreements was the fact that owners were 'leasing' not the land itself but the jobs connected with it, so that the lessees were as much workers as self-employing contractors. In any case, these leases, more like employment contracts, involve job descriptions of considerable precision. Sarapus (who is not approached through any manager) distinguishes no fewer than thirty-three separate tasks, and the 'lessees' propose an elaborate schedule of wage payments calculated as a total rate per aroura. Again, the contract refers to an *organon*, probably a *sāqiya*, and one of the lessees also agrees to sleep in the *epoikion* each night—this is translated as 'the farm building', though it could refer to a small settlement if Sarapus was a sufficiently wealthy landowner.

Another landowner who employed contracts of this type was Aurelia Diogenis also called Tourbiaina. Thus *PSI* XIII 1338 (299) is a so-called 'vineyard lease' where the wage formula again makes the amount of wages in some sense proportional to effort (the precise rate is 1,200 drachmas per aroura and since the contract is dated October 299, this can be directly compared with the price levels in the Prices Edict to form some idea of how much ordinary workmen were likely to make, in real terms, for work which involved both skill and considerable effort). The contract also shows that at this time Diogenis was expanding her production of wine (cf. ll. 5 ff.). Unlike Sarapus, however, Diogenis concluded agreements of this sort through her *pronoētēs*. A wine account, *PSI* I 83 (293) (added to her dossier by Vandoni)[37] shows that like many other employers, she paid her workers partly in 'sour' wine (ὄξος). In this account the estate (at Sennis) is regularly called a *ktēsis* (rather than a *ktēma*) and the main groups of workers involved in the disbursements are *potamitai* and *plintheutai*, both paid in ὄξος, unlike the builder in *P. Oxy.* 1569. Though the wife or daughter of a *clarissimus* and at least once called a *matrona stolata*, an indication, clearly, of aristocratic status,[38] Diogenis typified the group of owners

[36] e.g. G. Mori, 'La mezzadria in Toscana alla fine del XIX secolo', *Movimento operaio*, NS 7 (1955) 479–510, discussing sharecropping contracts which show tight control over labour.

[37] M. Vandoni, 'Note papirologiche', *RIL* 102 (1968) 439 f.

[38] *PSI* XIII 1338.2; for the title and a list, cf. B. Holtheide, 'Matrona stolata—femina stolata', *ZPE* 38 (1980) 127–34.

who were thoroughly involved in the running of their properties. Thus in *PSI* 472 (295) the *phrontistēs* Pangenous, in charge of the holding or estate (*ktēsis*) at Senepta, writes directly to her to effect a payment of wages to a group of *plintheutai*, and in *P. Oxy.* XII 1569 she instructs a manager to make sure that a builder is paid his allowance of wine, adding 'from whichever vat you prefer'. In *PSI* VI 712 (295) the workers involved in the production of bricks are simple *geōrgoi*, so brickmaking was presumably a seasonal activity which drew on the available reserves of labour during the slack periods.

This *personal* involvement of often substantial landowners in the day-to-day management of their own or others' estates is a remarkable feature of the attitudes and behaviour of the families who controlled the Egyptian countryside. The most striking example of a high-ranking landowner involved in agricultural management in a professional capacity is Alypius, whose correspondence with local managers fills a considerable part of the Heroninus archive.[39] Whatever the precise burden of his official duties in 268, when he was corresponding with Heronas, they were clearly not sufficiently compelling to undermine his active interest in farm management. Now if this argument is valid, it has one important implication. The need for a separate managerial staff was not primarily due to the influence of 'absenteeism' or therefore a reflection of any such tendency, but to the need which owners felt for an efficient organization of their estates and a carefully regulated control over disbursements in kind and money. Apart from his actual functional control over production, the *phrontistēs* or *pronoētēs* was mainly responsible for the drafting of accounts compiled, almost certainly, from daily ledgers or registers, since there would be no other way of retailing the more minute items of expenditure, of the number of workmen employed, and so on, than some record of this type.

Alypius was no exception. Hyperechius was the most substantial estate owner of the Hermopolite in the late third/early fourth centuries, yet the Archive of Apollonius shows him totally immersed in day-to-day management.[40] Apollonius was manager at Pesla—the term used for him is *paralemptēs*, 'receiver'—and again much of the archive consists of Hyperechius' instructions to him. In *CPR* VI 12

[39] See Rathbone, *Economic Rationalism and Rural Society in Third-Century A.D. Egypt*, 58 f., and cf. R. Pintaudi, 'Papiri fiorentini dell' archivio di Heronas', *ZPE* 20 (1976) 233–48, for his involvement with the estate at Thraso.

[40] See H. Harrauer, *Aus dem Archiv des Apollonios aus Pesla*, in H. Harrauer and S. M. E. van Lith (eds.), *Corpus Papyrorum Raineri Bd. VI* (Vienna, 1978) 51–102. *SB* XVIII 13309.11 = *P. Lond.* III 959 descr. (3.2.297) now shows that Hyperechius bore the title *axiologōtatos*.

(300/1) he deals with a wine payment to a builder—εἰς [λόγο]ν μισθῶν (showing that such labour was of course recruited, not retained)—specifying the rates at which the different sorts of wine should be priced, that is, imputing a cash value to the payment.[41] *CPR* VI 23 involves a complex schedule of payments but it is worth noting that here the imputation of cash values to wages in kind applies to wheat as well as to wine. In VI 31 he writes to Apollonius from Hermopolis to arrange for the transport of oxen and fodder for the threshing at Sinarchebis.[42] *CPR* VI 32 is a note telling Apollonius that he (Hyperechius) has arranged for the dispatch of 300 art. 'of the old barley' 'to the city' (which implies that he was then at Pesla). In VI 66 he adds a postscript asking for an estimate of the yield of the *lachanos*. All of these letters and notes were dictated by Hyperechius to a series of scribes, the owner himself usually writing the salutation in his own hand.

Hyperechius is thus an altogether remarkable figure—the owner of an estate of well over 5,000 arouras[43] who involved himself in the most ordinary aspects of farm management in a tradition more reminiscent of Cato than of Columella—of the paterfamilias whose personal intervention was still the basis of estate management even when much of the operational side was handled by a full-time manager or even managerial staff. Aelianus, who took over sole management of the estate by the 320s, was an active member of the council. In *P. Cairo Preis.* 4 (320) and 8 (321) he turns up as στρατηγὸς ἤτοι ἐξάκτωρ Ἑρμοπολείτου (with his full name Sostratus Aelianus) and was thus the leading official at district level.[44] The documents associated with him are largely orders to pay, showing how he, like most owners in this group and many in the aristocracy,[45] had a conscious policy of direct (personal) control over disbursements and cash flows. Finally, by the 350s, the date of *P.*

[41] The procedure seems to have been standard, cf. *CPR* VI 23 (303/4).

[42] Harrauer takes κυκλεύητ[ε in l. 11 to mean irrigation (turning the water-wheel) but the context implies a threshing operation. Κυκλεύειν could presumably refer to any job which involved the operation of guiding oxen around in a circle, including threshing, cf. Ayrout, *The Egyptian Peasant*, 51, on the *nurag*, 'The driver sits on the box and guides the buffalo in a circle over the ears, which are broken by the disks.'

[43] The calculation is minimalist, based on the assumption that the shares registered in the names of Heracleon and Ammonius in *P. Landlisten* II (*c.*1370 ar.) should be multiplied by 4 on the supposition that Hyperechius divided his estate equally between four sons. But at least Olympiodorus had a considerably larger amount of land, if we add up the totals in the names of Akylas and Pinution.

[44] The identity of Aelianus son of Hyperechius with the official Sostratus Aelianus is established by *CPR* VIII 23 (320), a wine lease addressed to [Σωστ]ράτῳ Αἰλιανῳ (l. 3) by lessees from Pesla. *P. Cairo Preis.* 4 and 8 have been republished as *CPR* XVII A 9b and 22 respectively.

[45] e.g. Sophia who is discussed later (ch. 6, esp. 141 f.), *SPP* VIII 1091 ff.

Landlisten, the average estate size in the family of Hyperechius had fallen to under 1,200 arouras, a drastic reduction and one that was destined to undermine the economic position of this 'aristocracy' in the next one or two generations.[46]

The Byzantine Middle Bureaucracy

In the third century, landholding members of the *boulē* total 74 (52 per cent of all selected landholders), in the fourth century 63 (44.5 per cent), in the fifth 9 (14 per cent) (this includes *politeuomenoi*). The decline of the gymnasial class and its weakened hold over the agriculture of the local districts is perhaps the most obvious change between the middle and late empire. The *bouleutai* simply do not figure as landholders of any significance in the Byzantine material, though a group of this sort continued to exist even as late as 581. The usual explanation which has been advanced for the decline of the curial class is the unrelenting pressure of late Roman taxation. However, by itself this is an insufficient explanation, since it ignores changes in the distribution of property, and thus the possibility, purely counterfactual, that the *bouleutai* might have increased their control over local resources to offset the increasing pressure of taxation. That they did not do so is due not directly to the fiscal machinery of the fourth century but to the important changes in the pattern of landownership which were beginning to emerge, in general in the period after the 360s, the decade to which, specifically, we can trace decisive advances in the consolidation of a 'social' bureaucracy whose agrarian influence is perhaps first discernible not in the Abinnaeus archive—Abinnaeus, we should note, does not figure explicitly as a major landholder and is never addressed as such—but in the important ruling, dated 360, which directly states that the peasantry of Aegyptus (the Delta region to the west of Damietta) was seeking protection with officials 'who are bolstered by high rank of various degrees, and even with Dukes'[47] (note, however, that no *estates* of such officials are referred to in this ruling). The next important clue is *CTh.* 1.14.1, dated 386, which refers directly to *militares possessores* in the Thebaid and Augustamnica

[46] See n. 43 above. The calculation (1,200 ar.) is based on the five clear cases of former Hyperechius holdings—those of Akylas/Olympiodorus, Dioscourides/Aelianus, Heracleon/Hyperechius, the descendants of Ammonius/Hyperechius and Pinution/Olympiodorus (*P. Landlisten* II 64 ff., 129 ff., 241 ff., 299, 408 ff.). If Helladius is included in the family of Hyperechius (cf. K. A. Worp, 'Unerwarteter Familienzuwachs?', *ZPE* 74 (1988) 252), the average falls even further, from *c.*1,192 ar. to *c.*1,092 ar., cf. *P. Landlisten* II 51 ff., 274 ff.

[47] *CTh.* 11.24.1 (360), to Helpidius PP: 'qui variis honoribus fulciuntur, ducum etiam . . .'.

(the eastern part of the Delta) who were clearly powerful landholders since the ruling was a concession to them, creating a special fiscal status which entitled only the *officium militare* to deal with their taxes.[48]

I have already argued that the regime of Valentinian and his brother played a decisive role in beginning to crystallize the new stratum which would progressively revolutionize the social physiognomy of the late empire.[49] At one level the bureaucracy (including the *militares*) were directly involved in the tax-collection process, and opportunities for fiscal speculation and profiteering were inherent in the workings of late Roman fiscalism.[50] But corruption (*pravitas, cupiditas, violentia*) cannot be the whole story, for it ignores the fact that the upper- and middle-grade officials received salaries which were substantial by the standards of the time and that these emoluments were increasingly being drawn in a coinage (gold) whose stability represented an immediate relative enrichment.[51] Thus the economic evolution of the curial class cannot be abstracted from the more total changes which were producing in the structure of civil society the indelible impression of the late empire.

A papyrological study of the pattern of landownership confirms the general impression of the legal texts that the late fourth century was a period of major structural change. *Circa* 350 the countryside of Hermopolis was still largely controlled by its municipal élite, with the family of Hyperechius retaining overall primacy, despite the increasing dissolution of their estate in the process of partitioned inheritance. Aurelia Charite, daughter of Amazonios, is registered with a total of 375 arouras but we know from the archive that her estate at some stage in the previous one or two decades had been around 500 arouras.[52] Amazonios/Euthalios who turns up in *P. Landlisten* II with *c*.630 arouras[53] may have been a relation of hers or related to the family of Hyperechius.[54] Two sons of a certain

[48] *CTh.* 1.14.1 (386), to Florentius praef(ectus) aug(ustalis), 'Si qui militares possessores in memoratis provinciis fuerint, hi in tantum per militare officium exigantur' (If there are landholders with a military background in the aforesaid provinces, their taxes shall be collected only by the army office staff).

[49] See Ch. 3, 49 ff.

[50] Cf. Mazzarino, *Aspetti sociali*, esp. 151 ff., 206 ff. For the position in the 5th cent. see the scathing picture outlined in *Nov. Maj.* 2.2 (458).

[51] This seems to me to be the essential idea behind Mazzarino's statement that 'the Constantinian revolution in the monetary system also allowed for a new hierarchical social order based on the high purchasing power of the new salaries paid in gold' (*Aspetti sociali*, 165), a fundamental remark.

[52] Cf. *P. Charite* 12 (*c*.320–50), 498 arouras in eleven pagi.

[53] *P. Landlisten* II 94 ff.

[54] In any case, he cannot be the *father* of Charite, as Sijpestein suggested, once we accept Bagnall's date for *P. Landlisten* II, *c*.340. He may well have been his grandson

Helladios account for 741 and 939 arouras respectively, and Worp now suggests that Helladios was probably yet another member of the family of Hypercchius (using *P. Lond.* III 930 descr.).[55] Though councillors' designations are consistently omitted in the land lists, it seems certain that the families which controlled the *boulē* also controlled the largest properties around Hermopolis *c.*350.

On the other hand, the social types characteristic of the new stratum of landowners—the groups classified in my thesis as 'middle bureaucracy' and 'high officials'—though emerging slowly, are still largely inconspicuous in the fourth-century material. Thus veterans, soldiers, middle military grades, and lower bureaucracy account for almost as many 'selected' landholders as the bouleutic class (58 compared with 63) but it is certain that their qualitative impact in terms of the size of resources controlled by them was minimal.[56] As for the 'middle bureaucracy' (in the strict sense) and 'high officials', the fourth-century papyri can show not a single notable example of either of these groups. There is thus a curious disproportion between the legal texts with their general implication that military landholders were gradually controlling increasing amounts of land (in the period 360–400) and the papyri which can show only six cases of landholders from the 'middle military grades' (4.4% of the total) for the fourth century. I take this to mean, in a more general sense, that the real processes which survive in the papyrological evidence were the more stable, deeply rooted, larger-scale processes (e.g. the dominance of groups like the *bouleutai* over several centuries) and that by and large the new imperial bureaucracy was, at a social level, a still largely embryonic group.

At any rate, the social differentiation which began to develop in the course of the fourth century between an old-style municipal élite and a new-style bureaucratic one found a precise and ineluctable expression. Keenan has drawn attention to the all-important social pattern which contraposed the Aurelii to the Flavii. According to him, 'the Aurelii of the later Roman Empire were civilians in the strict sense—craftsmen, merchants, labourers, farmers'. On the other hand, 'As in the fourth century . . . the most important

through a son called Euthalios, and thus a nephew of Charite, cf. *SPP* XX 85 recto 17 for a Euthalios son of Amazonios in an estate account relating to a fifteenth indiction. Alternatively, cf. Euthalios in *P. Lond.* III 930 descr. = Parássoglu, *Aegyptus* 67 (1987) 79 f., which Worp relates to the family of Hyperechius, see n. 55.

[55] Cf. Worp, *ZPE* 74 (1988) 252, for the *oikia* of Hyperechius in the West Citadel Quarter and the hypothesis that H. had eight children, seven sons and one daughter.

[56] The best proof of this is again the Hermopolite land registers which show a striking contrast in the average holding size of the two groups (councillors vs. bureaucracy).

civil and military officials in the Empire in the fifth and following centuries were Flavii.'[57] However, it is worth separating the 'professional' and the 'social' aspects here. The nomen Flavius, starting as the designation of a professional status (and, at a deeper level, of a mental attitude, of inflexible devotion to the late imperial state in the personified form of the emperor), became, through the actions and fortunes of the Flavii, the expression of a social one. As Mócsy says, 'Constantine wished, through the Flaviate, to create a new rank-class of loyal cadre.'[58] On the other hand, in Egypt (and probably elsewhere) the distinction between the Aurelii and the Flavii was soon emblematic of a social division (as Keenan shows), and to understand this, to see why this was so, we have to turn more directly to the impact of the bureaucracy on society as a whole. In other words, we cannot simply assume that bureaucrats would be socially dominant but have to explain how such dominance is likely to have been established. The appearance of Flavii among landowners of the fourth century is thus an important symptom of the more general social process by which a bureaucratic élite was consolidating its social dominance, displacing groups who, at least through their names, seemed increasingly to symbolize and stand for a declining social order which each successive regime of the fourth century drove deeper into the ground.[59]

I shall deal with the aristocracy of this new period separately in the sections which follow, and concentrate here on those groups, less powerful but certainly affluent, who in some sense retained elements of continuity with the local élites of the earlier empire and early fourth century, yet within a religious and social world with a more nuanced if exaggerated sense of hierarchy and a spiritual devotion which might lead even the more substantial proprietors among them to transfer whole estates to the church or to monasteries. Whereas the councillors remained by and large Aurelii, these

[57] J. G. Keenan, 'The Names Flavius and Aurelius as Status Designations in Later Roman Egypt', *ZPE* 11 (1973) 33–63, esp. 52, 56.

[58] A. Mócsy, 'Der Name Flavius als Rangbezeichnung in der Spätantike', *Akte des IV Int. Kongresses f. griechische u. lateinische Epigraphik Wien, 1962* (Vienna, 1964) 257–63, at 260.

[59] See F. Millar, 'Empire and City, Augustus to Julian: Obligations, Excuses and Status', *JRS* 73 (1983) 76–96, for the argument that it was the imperial state itself which created the division between office-holding landowners on the one hand and *curiales* on the other, by allowing bureaucratic status to confer immunity from city obligations. Millar describes the fourth-century shift to permanent exemption from the civic liturgies as a 'crucial one, with immense consequences'. For its impact on the local councils, cf. *CTh.* 12.1.27 (339), which shows the municipal aristocracy of Carthage buying its way into the higher dignities early in the reign of Constantius, at the cost of what it dubs a 'disgraceful squandering of family wealth', cited Millar, 93.

groups are all, without exception (though with some ambiguity in the case of women) Flavii.

Lowest among them, probably, were the landholders who inhabited the world of Flavius Abinnaeus in the villages around the camp at Dionysias (in the Fayum). They were mainly soldiers or retired army personnel who seem, from the complaints formulated by them, to form a minor rural middle class, resident in the villages, with holdings confined to a single village (the usual expression is *geouchōn/geouchousa en kōmē* etc.).[60] This group was especially numerous in the Fayum, where it began to own land from the late first/early second centuries. Though individual veterans might become substantial landholders and local employers (cf. especially L. Bellienus Gemellus whose estate covered several villages), or the mass of veterans and their families dominate entire villages (e.g. Karanis in the second century, with a special involvement in olive growing), in general they were distinguished from the other sections of the rural middle class by the fact that they managed their own holdings (there is no evidence that they retained managers) and from other groups of military personnel by the modest scale of those holdings. Aurelius Harpokration and his wife Thaesis had a total 'estate' of around 81 arouras in Philadelphia early in the fourth century and are classified as 'among the more important residents of their village'.[61] In terms of the Antinoite holding sizes in *P. Landlisten*, this would correspond to job groups of minor officials between the middle and lowest grades of the bureaucracy[62]—somewhat above the level of most *beneficiarii*. About Abinnaeus himself, we have no information that he was a substantial landholder, though that is entirely possible.

Thus the sort of *militaris possessor* for whom *CTh.* 1.14.1 was formulated lay at a higher level and since the legal process must reflect real developments it is curious that this group is so scarce in the papyri. The best example of it is probably Flavius Vitalianus whom Rémondon had no hesitation in classifying as a 'grand propriétaire foncier' by 378 when he turns up in *P. Grenf.* I 54 as 'landowner in the Arsinoite', an expression worth noting (and in obvious contrast to the formula found in *P. Abinnaeus*), and as subleasing

[60] Cf. *P. Abinn.* 45 (343), 47 (346), 49 (346), 51 (346), 57 (4c.), mostly from Theoxenis and the Fayum village Hermoupolis.

[61] Cf. R. S. Bagnall and K. A. Worp, 'The Fourth-Century Tax Roll in the Princeton Collection', *APF* 30 (1984) 53–82, at 58 (on *SB* V 7521, involving payments from 309/10 to 323/4).

[62] Cf. Jones, *LRE* 1.595, 'The standard of wealth of *cohortalini* naturally varied greatly according to the grade of the service which they occupied, and the importance of the province', and the examples at 596.

to another official part of a substantial holding which he had leased from Nonnus a *politeuomenos*.[63] (Again, the relationships revealed by this contract are highly significant.) In 359, about twenty years earlier, Vitalianus had been *biarchus* of a vexillation of *cataphractarii* and even at that stage was prosperous enough to purchase a slave for 18 solidi.[64] He also turns up in *P. Lond.* V 1656, whose date and provenance are both uncertain, but which is clearly a contract of advance sale for wine. Since Vitalianus is addressed simply as *geouchōn [ ]*, this document must date from roughly the same period as *P. Grenf.* 54, but we have no means of knowing whether he was then involved in a business transaction or simply purchasing for personal consumption.

Vitalianus reflects the slow emergence of a new bureaucratic élite with estates which covered *whole districts* in a tradition reminiscent of the wealthiest municipal families and Alexandrian aristocrats of the previous period. Again the legal texts imply that the accumulation of landed estates occurred steadily throughout the early part of the fifth century.[65] Yet the papyrological evidence for the estates of this emerging fifth-century aristocracy is, at the moment, weak. Maehler suggests that the Taurinus archive (which begins in 426) reflects an evolution of precisely this type, the progressive accumulation of land in the hands of a latifundist class, but this seems implausible since the family of Flavius Taurinus I, who began his career as a *stratiōtēs*,[66] was quintessentially from the middle levels of the provincial bureaucracy, non-commissioned officers and financial clerks who cannot be said to have started as 'Kleinbauern',[67] and certainly did not end (by 513, the terminal date of the archive) as latifundists, and who were, within the *Beamtenhierarchie*, never more exalted than *aidesimoi*.[68] Again, no member of this family ever employed a manager, or at least none is attested in the numerous contracts, a situation inconceivable with the true aristocracy. Thus we still lack any papyrological reflection of the powerful new groups of landholders whose *Grundherrschaften* destroyed the fiscal system

[63] *P. Grenf.* I 54 (378), addressed to *Φλαουίῳ Οὐιταλιανῷ γεουχοῦντι ἐν τῷ Ἀρσι(νοίτῃ)*, cf. R. Rémondon, *La Crise de l'empire romain de Marc-Aurèle à Anastase* (Paris, 1964) 303; with substantial corrections in *BL* 1.183. Contrast R. S. Bagnall, 'Military Officers as Landowners in Fourth-Century Egypt', *Chiron* 22 (1992) 47–54, at 48 f.

[64] *BGU* I 316 = *MChr.* 271 (359).

[65] *CTh.* 11.24.4 (399), 11.24.6 (415), esp. 'qui ex Caesarii et Attici consulatu [397] possessiones sub patrocinio possidere coeperunt'.

[66] Cf. *BGU* XII 2137 (prob. after 6.10.426, *BL* 9.30), *στρατιώτῃ [ἀπὸ νουμ]έρο[υ Μα]ύρων Λυκωνπόλεως* (ll. 3–4), then a *biarchus* by 430, in *BGU* XII 2138, cf. Maehler, *BGU* XII, xxiv–xxv for the essential career structures.

[67] Maehler, *BGU* XII, xxiv actually calls them *Kleinbauern*.

[68] Cf. Hornickel, *Rangprädikate*, 1 f., on *aedesimos*, the quintessentially middle bureaucratic epithet, but by now a hopelessly incomplete list.

of the fourth century, following the legal recognition accorded to them in *CTh.* 11.24.6 (415).[69]

But the world reflected in the archive of Taurinus I and his descendants does express important aspects of the fifth century evolution. The only landholders who figure in the archive are officials or state employees, or the women of their social milieu who called themselves *eugenestatai*. They were an affluent agrarian middle class with probably substantial sums of money tied up in loans through which they could establish control over small parcels of land such as the seven 'waterless' arouras which Aurelia Kyra alias Eustorgia *eugenestatē* leased out in two separate contracts, one dated 509, the other 510.[70] This plot or farm, located at Pselamynthis, had been mortgaged to her by a certain Archontia, also described as *eugenestatē*. Neither of these contracts makes any reference to the amount of the loan capital against which Kyra had acquired the use of these seven arouras. But *SB* XIV 11373, dated 513, involves Kyra in a third contract of the same type, and here she controls 9½ arouras with their quarter share of a *lakkos* or *sāqiya*, 'in lieu of interest' on a loan amounting to 37 solidi.[71] Since the rent charged was 81 keratia per year, Kyra was evidently content with a rate of interest of just over 9 per cent.

Aurelia Eucharistia daughter of Hermogenes illustrates the connection between the *eugenestatai* and the middle bureaucracy. Her brother Sarapodorus was a provincial staff officer of the *magister officiorum*, a 'magistrianus',[72] doubtless related in some way to Flavius Sarapodorus, *μαγιστριανὸς τῶν θείων ὀφφικίων*, who turns up in two contracts dated 439[73] (forty-four years before the first dateable document mentioning him in *BGU* XII).[74] In *SPP* XX 121 his predecessor seems to have bought a substantial farm or arable estate (*georgion*) at Thrake, paying one of the owners no less than 40 solidi for his parcel of 8 arouras and its associated share of the

[69] So M. Gelzer, *Studien zur byzantinischen Verwaltung Ägyptens* (Leipzig, 1909) 79. I have no doubt, however, that papyri will turn up to illustrate the important social changes of this period (390–415).

[70] *BGU* XII 2181 (509, *BL* 9.31), *SB* V 7519 = *P. Berl. Frisk* 5 (510).

[71] *SB* XIV 11373 (513), first published by G. Poethke, 'Bodenpachtvertrag aus Hermupolis (P. Berlin 11746)', in *Festschrift zum 150jährigen Bestehen des Berliner Ägyptischen Museums* (Berlin, 1974) 409–14.

[72] *BGU* XII 2169.10 (5c.), 2145 r 4, 2165.8, 2166.8, 2167.11.

[73] *CPR* VI 6 (439), *SPP* XX 121 (6.7.439), both by the same scribe and related to the same transaction. S. also figures in *SPP* XX 122 (prob. 439, *BL* 10.271), where his title is *magistrianus*, the other party is a *scholasticus*, and the witnesses include a *zōgraphos* and a *philosophos*.

[74] *BGU* XII 2156 (27.8.483) where he is called 'Aurelius' by association with Eucharistia. See B. Palme, 'Flavius Sarapodorus, ein *agens in rebus* aus Hermupolis', *APF* 40 (1994) 43–68 for recent discussion, and my note in App. 4.

sāqiya.[75] The fact that middle-grade officials had funds of this sort to invest in agricultural purchases is surely symptomatic of the successful fight which the bureaucracy had waged over the structuring of their pay—against the determination of successive emperors to hold down the cash component to a level which could ease the pressure on public spending in gold.

Like the bigger Hermopolite owners in *P. Landlisten* who inhabited the West Citadel Quarter,[76] their fifth-century successors controlled estates composed of arable farms, vineyards, or smaller parcels of land in or near a number of villages. The Taurinus family is associated with some eight locations,[77] Sarapodorus and his sister with at least five, Aurelia Kyra with three—and this on the basis of archives which clearly represent only a small fraction of the contracts and other papers of each of these families.

The notary who handled Aurelia Kyra's work also drafted documents for Flavia Aphthonia. She probably represented the most affluent stratum of the local landowning class (below the level of the provincial aristocracy). Like Kyra and Eucharistia, she was *eugenestatē* but unlike them she bore the nomen Flavia and her full honorific was *lamprotatē kai eugenestatē*. Again, it is curious that the lessees address her directly (and not through the mediation of a manager), a feature which seems in general to characterize the women landholders of Hermopolis (cf. Aurelia Charite). *SB* XIV 12050 (498) involves the lease of a massive *geōrgion* of 68 arouras (45½ acres) plus the vineyard associated with it (σὺν ἀμπελῶνι ἑτέρων ἀ[ρουρῶν]), so presumably at least 70 in total. Like most substantial farms this had a *lakkos* and undoubtedly this is why the lessees renounced the usual entitlement to a rebate in years of poor flood. The arable rent would be paid κατ' ἔτος ἔν τε συμβρόχῳ καὶ ἀβρόχῳ.[78] The terminology is clear-cut: the farm producing wheat is called a γεώργιον, the vineyard a χωρίον, and Aphthonia, like most wine producers, includes a work standard to ensure an appropriate rate of watering.

Finally, in *P. Vindob. Sal.* 9 (509), a contract covering part of a new plantation (*neophytion*), we can see how some of these owners

[75] This might look like an extraordinary price to pay for land but cf. *P. Cairo Masp.* III 67169 bis + II 67169 for an even higher land price at another Hermopolite village, Magdola Mire. Also cf. *SB* I 4661 a–b (Fayum), 4 solidi for 1 aroura. Clearly, these were the sort of *terrulae fertiles* which *CTh.* 11.24.6.1 refers to in AD 415, in a presumably unsuccessful attempt to discourage land transfers in the bigger villages.

[76] See A. K. Bowman, 'Landholding in the Hermopolite Nome in the Fourth Century A.D.', *JRS* 75 (1985) 137–63, for an analysis of these lists.

[77] See the discussion in Maehler, *BGU* XII, xxi–xxii.

[78] I suggest φόρο[ν] τῶν αὐτῶν ἀρουρῶν ἑξήκοντα ὀ[κτὼ ἀποτάκτου] κατ' ἔτος in ll. 10–11, cf. *SB* III 7167.9–10 (477, Hermopolis), *PSI* III 188.8–9 (540, Hermopolite).

(the lessor is again a *eugenestatē*) preferred to treat their 'lessees' as pure labourers rather than as sharecroppers, for in the draft which survives the usual formula for a division of the crop has been struck out (lines 9–10) and the lessee's wages determined as a lump-sum of 7 solidi (inserted above the cancelled phrase), the 'lease' looking as much like a work contract as possible. The implication is not that sharecroppers were not labourers but that they were a more independent type of labour.

One conclusion is worth emphasizing: the rural economy of the eastern provinces reflected the widespread influence of *Geldwirtschaft* by the main part of the fifth century. The transactions of urban-based landholders presupposed the framework of monetary economy and made extensive use of gold. Gold was used for the purchase of land, payment of rentals (when rents were in cash), wage payments, loans, contracts of advance sale, payment of fines, and clearly for the buying and selling of commodities from which money taxes would have to be paid. West and Johnson's assertion that 'By the end of the fifth century gold was the chief accounting medium of the country'[79] is abundantly confirmed by the papyrological evidence and in particular by the Taurinus archive which dates largely from the period before Anastasius' far-reaching fiscal reform (towards commutation) enormously accelerating the pace of monetization in the villages.

In terms of social structure, the Hermopolite villages of the fifth century must have had more than this affluent agrarian middle class (of bureaucratic origin) and the lessees who depended on them for regular employment. But there is no indication in the archive of any groupings between these strata, such as the more substantial peasant households of the sixth century. The municipal élite of the former period appears only in the dismal shape of a local councillor who is badly in debt to Flavius John I (then *scriniarius* in the military administration) with several land parcels mortgaged to the latter.[80] It is certain that the councils underwent a major process of restructuring and that the *politeuomenoi* of the Byzantine period were a more prosperous and thriving group than the surviving *bouleutai*, who obviously associated with them in some form.

At any rate, the sixth-century sources reflect a more complex social landscape. The quintessential agrarian middle class was still an affluent group of urban landlords, *politeuomenoi* and middle-level imperial bureaucrats who retained local managers and whose

[79] West and Johnson, *CRBE* 115.

[80] *BGU* XII 2150 (472), Phoibammon son of Athanasius, described as a *bouleutēs*, with Maehler's note to l. 7, ref. to *P. Berol.* 21836.

estates might even span several districts. Thus Flavius Cyrus, a *politeuomenos*, was represented by a manager called προνοητὴς τῶν Ἀνταιοπολιτικῶν πραγμάτων, with the clear implication that Cyrus had holdings outside the district of Antaeu. He turns up with five other landlords in a series of rent receipts discussed recently by Keenan.[81] All the Phthla landowners who dealt with Apollos, father of Dioscorus, were connected either with the municipal councils of the sixth century (they were *politeuomenoi*) or with the provincial middle levels of the imperial bureaucracy. Flavius Megas was a former *defensor* of Panopolis, whose local manager was called, unusually, a *phorologos*, 'rent accountant'.[82] His rank predicate was *lamprotatos*, the epithet most widely used for the middle bureaucracy of the sixth century.[83] Flavius Nemesianus was a *scholasticus*, Flavius Colluthus a *scriniarius* (based presumably in Antinoopolis).[84] Keenan brings up the Antinoite bureaucracy of the 560s and refers to all these individuals moving 'in the same social, political and economic circles'.[85]

Among non-institutional landholders (as opposed to the monasteries), the biggest accumulations in the cadastral list of Aphrodito belong to individuals representing this bureaucratic élite of the small towns. Eudoxia, the sister of a Count Theoteknos, had a local estate of *c.*50 arouras (in 8 separate parcels), the *exceptor* Triphiodorus must have had over 60 arouras (since he left his sons with about that much), a *scholasticus* Theodosius had accumulated over 66 (in 19 parcels).[86] Since these are estimates for the amount of land held by *ktētores* on the 'urban' tax account (ὑπὲρ ἀστικῶν ὀνομάτων)[87] and we have no idea how much they controlled on the village account, they are obviously minimum estimates. The only aristocrat who figures in the cadastral list is the *comes consistorii* Ammonius, and since some of his local estate accounts have survived, we know that he paid about 40 per cent of his taxes on the 'rural' account (ὑπὲρ τῆς κώμης).[88] This yields a coefficient which would put the total

[81] *P. Cairo Masp.* III 67327.5–6, discussed J. G. Keenan, 'Victor, son of Psaios, and Three Aphrodito Rent Receipts', *BASP* 20 (1983) 127–34, and, 'Notes on Absentee Landlordism at Aphrodito', *BASP* 22 (1985) 137–69, esp.147 ff.

[82] *P. Cairo Masp.* III 67327. 21–2.

[83] Cf. Hornickel, *Rangprädikate*, 22–7.

[84] Cf. J. G. Keenan, 'Aurelius Apollos and the Aphrodito Village Élite', in *Atti del XVII Congresso internazionale di papirologia (Napoli, 19–26 maggio, 1983)*, 3 vols. (Naples, 1984) 3.957–63, at 961.

[85] Keenan, 'Absentee landlordism', 150.

[86] *P. Freer Aphrod.*, *passim*.

[87] *P. Freer Aphrod.* 292, cf. 304, (ὑπὲρ) ἀστικ(ῶν) κτητόρ(ων).

[88] *P. Cairo Masp.* II 67139 fol. II verso 12 ff., fol. IV recto 5, taking 67.66 artabas (= 203 modii) as his village contribution out of a total payment of 166 art. (= 40.76 per cent).

Aphrodito properties of the more affluent middle bureaucracy, at least hypothetically, in the size range 80–110 arouras. But to know how much they controlled in the district or even the region as a whole we would have to have some conception of the structure of their estates, comparable to the information from Hermopolis *c*.350.

The middle bureaucracy, a group peculiar to the social and political development of the late empire, existed throughout Egypt (and the other eastern provinces), and its features were undoubtedly even better defined in the provincial capitals. In *P. Cairo Masp.* III 67312 (567) Flavius Theodore, *exceptor* in the *officium ducale* of the Thebaid and son of a former barrister at the provincial court, who was from Antinoe, where his father had practised, bequeathed all his landed possessions to the monastery of Apa Shenute (at Triphiou/Atripe, today Sohag, opposite Panopolis). This was evidently a substantial estate since his properties sprawled across the boundaries of three entire districts—the Hermopolite, the Antinoite, and the Panopolite. Theodore also manumitted his entire slave workforce, with a gratuity of 6 solidi to each. Among all the documents of the Byzantine period his will is perhaps the most striking expression of the mentality of the new upper classes and, by implication, of the ruling groups among them.

In *P. Cairo Masp.* II 67151 (*c*.545/46) Flavius Phoibammon, chief medical officer at Antinoe and the son of a former chief medical officer (*archiatros*), bequeathed one aroura of vineland to the monastery of Apa Jeremias[89] from the wine estates inherited from his father. The land was at Ibion Sesembythis in the Hermopolite and equipped with a full range of irrigation machinery, since the document refers both to *organa* and to *kykleuteria*. Phoibammon also wished to settle an outstanding debt of fifty solidi, a sum which he had borrowed from a *clarissimus* Flavius Christopher, son of Theodore, and wanted repaid from the sixty solidi still owing to him by way of his official salary. Finally, Christopher turns up in *P. Cairo Masp.* 67162 (568) as a *γεουχῶν*, a substantial landowner, based in the capital.

Next to the monasteries and the aristocracy, the urban-based agrarian middle class was the only group which could afford the investment costs of wine growing (cf. Columella, 'amplissimas impensas vineae poscunt'[90]). But unlike the aristocracy and like the

[89] Cf. P. E. Kahle, *Bala'izah: Coptic Texts from Deir el-Bala'izah in Upper Egypt*, 2 vols. (London, 1954) 1.23.

[90] *RR* 3.3.8, cf. A. C. Johnson and L. C. West, *Byzantine Egypt: Economic Studies* (Princeton, 1949; repr. Amsterdam, 1967) 55, for 'those who had the necessary capital to invest in the development of vineyards'.

smaller monasteries, they relied heavily on sharecropping. In *P. Hamb.* I 23 (569) Flavius Philippus, *exceptor* in the *officium ducale* and one of the many *geouchountes* who resided in the provincial capital, leases an ἀμπελικὸν χωρίον of four arouras, 'in full production' (ἔμφυτον), which had been walled off from surrounding properties (it was περιτετειχεισμένον) and was located, like most suburban vineyards, on the slightly higher ground normally inaccessible to the flood, described, locally, as *nēsos*.[91] Again, this small estate was superbly equipped, included an orchard and a vegetable garden and contained a 'fully equipped' *organon*—a *sāqiya*—misconstrued by Meyer, the editor, as a wine press.[92] For Philippus—who was directly approached by the lessees, *ampelourgoi* from Ibion Sesembythis (where Phoibammon owned his vineyards) but now residing in the capital—it was essential to ensure a certain quality of job performance—which he did by combining the 'incentive' effect of a crop-sharing arrangement with an explicit work standard (for watering, twice a month in winter, three times in summer) and a detailed task specification. No reference is made to any manager and the whole presupposition of contracts of this type is that the lessees are as interested as the owner in the best possible output. Like most leases signed with the landowning urban middle class, extra payments were involved—an extra 80 *kadoi* of wine, fifty of which were earmarked for other groups of employees required as helpers, ὑπὲρ παιδαρικῶν. Finally, Philippus thought it prudent to write in a penalty clause in case the *ampelourgoi* decided to move elsewhere before the expiry of the contract. This seems to have been regulated by a standard rate, at twelve solidi, so presumably *ampelourgoi* could earn at least as much as that for a year's work for one employer.[93]

The middle bureaucracy was thus the pure type of the urban-based agrarian middle class. Undoubtedly, these were the groups whom the pagarch Menas described as οἱ μεγάλοι κτήτορες τῆς πόλεως, 'the big landowners based in the city'.[94] But the description carries no obvious attribution of aristocratic status or influence. In fact, it would be quite wrong to suppose that this local élite of provincial small towns was even vaguely close to the levels of wealth and power peculiar to the Byzantine *aristocracy*. Thus no individual in this group is ever associated with an *ousia* (the only ones attested

[91] e.g. the 'island' of Panehēou in the Sahidic life of Shenute, which says, 'There was an island to the west of Panopolis over which Gesius the pagan had control'. (I owe the translation to Ariel Lopez).

[92] Meyer, *P. Hamb.* I, p. 93, 'vollständiger Kelterapparat', a common mistake.

[93] This was at least four times as much as the earnings of daily-rated unskilled employees living in the cities of the eastern Mediterranean some decades later.

[94] *P. Cairo Masp.* 67060 = *WChr.* 297.2.

for Aphrodito are controlled by two aristocrats—including Count Ammonius—and the monastery of Apa Sourous which had by far the most land in that village).[95] The truly impressive feature of the sixth century is thus the dominance of the aristocracy, the group I shall now turn to.

The Byzantine Aristocracy

Table 9*a* in Appendix 1 is a rough estimate of the weight of the aristocracy in the landholding structure of the sixth and seventh centuries. The Table counts families rather than individuals, and double-counts across districts, though not, obviously, within them. It also excludes institutional landholders, since there was no obvious way of including them in such a calculation. With these qualifications, in the sixth century as a whole, the aristocracy (large and medium) accounts for as much as 30 per cent of the total (64 out of a counted total of 210 landed families). On the other hand, for the *seventh* century, the proportion is as high as 56 per cent (58 out of 104 families). This is clearly not a reflection either of the actual frequency of such landholders or of the amounts of land they controlled relative to other groups, but it does seem to reflect the enormously reduced weight of the non-aristocratic classes in the agrarian structure of the seventh century. These smaller landholders turn up in considerable numbers in the seventh-century Hermopolite ledger published by Gascou, *P. Sorb.* II 69,[96] but the very arrangement of the codex also suggests that the larger landowners were a group apart.[97] Gascou treats the *clarissimi* of the seventh-century Hermopolite as a part of the aristocracy. By the seventh century, however, it was difficult to draw the line between the moderately affluent urban-based agrarian middle class and minor aristocratic families classed as *lamprotatoi*. The term *clarissimus* was now increasingly (though not exclusively) used for sections within the middle reaches of society, such as the landowner Flavius Theodore whose father Magistor was a *boēthos*, 'secretary', in the department of public finance in Hermopolis and *diastoleus* for the *meris* of Dioscorides, a typical middle-grade tax official, the sort who handled disbursements of pay to functionaries at a higher level.[98]

95 *P. Freer Aphrod.*, *passim*.

96 J. Gascou, *Un Codex fiscal hermopolite (P. Sorb. II 69)* (ASP 32; Atlanta, 1994) 60 ff. (henceforth *P. Sorb.* II 69).

97 Gascou, *P. Sorb.* II 69, pp. 38 f.

98 *P. Flor.* I 70 (627). The father Magistor is *clarissimus* in *P. Würz.*19.3 ff. (622, *BL* 8.513), for other references see *P. Laur.* III p. 89, and cf. *P. Laur.* III 110 (600, *BL* 8.167) for Magistor's payment to Duke Leon.

However, it seems fairly certain that in the seventh century several landowners, especially women, whose sole epithet is *lamprotatos* belonged to purely local aristocratic families, notably, a sizeable group of women in the Hermopolite tax register.[99]

The clear implication of these figures is that by the seventh century the aristocracy had enormously tightened its grip over landholding and (by implication) over society as a whole. It is a striking fact that the middle strata (*politeuomenoi*, *bouleutai*, middle and lower bureaucracy, etc.) have all but disappeared from the seventh-century landholding structure. Again, this could be an illusion peculiar to the survival pattern of our sources, but the increased weight of institutional landholders such as the Church and the monasteries (the only other groups of any significance) also suggests that the countryside of late Byzantine Egypt was now firmly under the control of the most powerful landholders (above all, the aristocracy).

The second major conclusion to emerge concerns the *character* of the landed aristocracy of the late empire—it was, overwhelmingly, and in striking contrast to its Alexandrian counterpart of the *Haut-Empire*, a class of high officials, office holders whose social honorifics were the epithets peculiar to the élite levels of the imperial administration. At a purely historical level, the crucial question this raises is whether the late empire saw established landowning families moving into imperial service or families essentially connected with imperial administration accumulating land to become powerful landed proprietors. It is my view that the second of these possible evolutions is a truer reflection of the process which actually occurred, for nothing in the evidence indicates, for the fourth and early fifth centuries, an established landed aristocracy other than the local district-level élites, and, as I have tried to show, this was a group in dramatic decline by the late fourth century, in Egypt at any rate, largely due to the unabated fragmentation of its properties. Evidence from elsewhere in the Mediterranean supports this general hypothesis. Thus Roques' recent work on Cyrenaica in the time of Bishop Synesius clearly shows both the clear-cut division between officials and councillors and the possible conflicts and tensions which could develop between them, largely due to the restless expansionism of the former.[100] Again, the world reflected in the speeches and letters of Libanius implies a clear duality between

[99] J. Gascou, 'Comptabilités fiscales hermopolites du début du VIIe siècle', *Tyche* 1 (1986) 97–117, and *P. Sorb.* II 69, Index IV, 281 f., s.v. λαμπροτατή, where I count eighteen or nineteen individuals.

[100] D. Roques, *Synésios de Cyrène et le Cyrénaïque du Bas-Empire* (Paris, 1987) 138 ff., 202 (for Artabazakos and Marcellinus).

the administrative élite and the middle-class landowners, and the mutual antagonism of these social forces.[101]

Thus it would be entirely appropriate to refer to the great estate owners of the eastern Mediterranean in late antiquity as a new aristocracy—a group distinguished from the local 'aristocracy' by the scale of its resources and by its roots in the political formation of the late empire, and from the Alexandrian aristocracy by its specific styles of management, a historical existence defined by deeper stability, and its more durable, almost "corporate" character.

Though the roots of this class lie in the political revolution of the late empire and the deep social changes which that brought about, chronologically the decisive break falls much later, in the main part of the fifth century. Thus if we survey the various districts individually, that is, those for which evidence survives, the Hermopolite, more firmly dominated by the smaller landowners, can show not a single aristocrat before the sixth century, the Fayum, where a severe crisis was producing profound changes in rural topography, has only Flavius Eustochius, a *comes domesticorum* and *principalis* of Arsinoe,[102] the Heracleopolite has Flavius Olympius, *vir clarissimus et spectabilis* and a *comes consistorii* by 475, but first attested as a landowner in 462 (following John Rea's proposal for *P. Vindob. Sijp.* 7, a deed of surety which involves the substitution of one worker for another in a *misthōsis* signed presumably with Olympius),[103] but no other fifth-century landholder of comparable status. Thus the only district where a fifth-century aristocracy is discernible in more than a purely fragmentary or episodic form is the Oxyrhynchite, and here the earliest period for which any member of this group is attested is certainly not earlier than the last years of the reign of Theodosius II, assuming that that is when the first Apion, Flavius Strategius, pursued the main part of his career to become *comes consistorii* and assume general responsibility for the

[101] J. H. W. G. Liebeschuetz, *Antioch: City and Imperial Administration in the later Roman Empire* (Oxford, 1972) 42, 48, 50 (for Thalassius I and Modestus).

[102] *SB* I 5273 (487), XVIII 13951 (487–91), but not identical with Fl. Eustochius son of Cyrillus in *SPP* XX 140 (533), since *SB* 5273 describes him as *endoxotatos*. The identification was proposed by Hardy, *Large Estates*, 42, but with some uncertainty: thus the 6th-cent. landowner 'is *probably* to be connected with the Fl. Eustochius who was civil governor of the district in 487' (my emphasis). R. Rémondon, 'L'Égypte au 5e siècle de notre ère: les sources papyrologiques et leurs problèmes', *Atti dell'XI Congresso Internazionale di Papirologia, Milano 2–8 Settembre 1965* (Milan, 1966) 135–48, at 142, calls him a 'grand propriétaire'. For the date of *SPP* XX 140, 18.4.533, cf. *BL* 7.263.

[103] See *Catalogue*, Heracleopolite 5c. Change 'Alypius' to 'Olympius' in Rémondon, *Atti dell'XI Congresso, 1965*, 144, and O. Montevecchi, *La papirologia* (Turin, 1973) 259, no. 77.

Oxyrhynchite estates of Aelia Eudocia (who died in October 460).[104] From the first half of the fifth century the only comparable figure is the *politeuomenos* who worked as general manager for the estates of Arcadia, daughter of the emperor Arcadius, in 440/1. He was the recipient of *P. Med.* I² 64 = *SB* 9503 (441), possibly the first papyrus ever to mention the *enapographoi geōrgoi* (the restoration seems plausible)[105] and certainly our first water-wheel receipt.[106] Otherwise, all other surviving exemplars of the fifth-century Oxyrhynchite aristocracy are either from the reign of Leo or later.

Thus Rémondon was surely justified in the supposition that 'C'est vers le milieu du 5e siècle en effet que prend corps la noblesse égyptienne, d'origine bureaucratique, et qui associe la puissance foncière aux hautes fonctions administratives.'[107] The characterization involved here is of course of fundamental importance, since it accurately describes the essential feature of the Byzantine aristocracy as a class which fused the power of high-ranking officials with the affluence of big landowners in a combination characteristic of the late empire. *This* aristocracy is chiefly a product of developments which occurred in the important middle decades of the fifth century, even if its presuppositions lie deeper, of course, in the whole evolution of the late empire. It was precisely in this period, 450–530, according to Jones, that the social distance between the *illustres* and the other grades was redefined and re-emphasised to confine senatorial control effectively to the former while '*spectabilis* and *clarissimus* became mere titles of honour'.[108] And just as the extension of the clarissimate had once signified the "democratization" of the upper classes, the renewed polarization of the fifth century now led to a general degradation of all titles of rank other

[104] Most recently, surely, *SB* XX 14091 = *P. Med. inv.* 71.86c (5c.). D. Hagedorn, *P. Heid.* IV, pp. 219–20, calculates that he would have been 60–70 years of age in 460, so it seems reasonable to suppose that his transition from a purely local landholder, described simply as a *politeuomenos*, *P. Oxy.* 3584, to an aristocrat, *comes consistorii* in *P. Oxy.* 3585, occurred when Theodosius II was still alive. Of course, if Strategius was the recipient of *P. Med.* I² 64 = *SB* VI 9503 (6.12.441, *BL* 7.103), we would have a precise *terminus post quem* for his promotion into the aristocracy.

[105] *P. Med.* I² 64.4–5 γεωργὸς [ἐναπόγραφος], but see Gonis, *P. Oxy.* LXVIII 4697.6-7n.

[106] Its historical significance can thus scarcely be exaggerated.

[107] Rémondon, *Atti dell'XI Congresso, 1965*, 145. So too Fikhman, who describes them as 'the new aristocracy which sprang essentially from military and bureaucratic circles', *JÖBG* 22 (1973) 18. Rémondon's inference that the Apion *oikos* was in operation by 457/8 ('Par exemple, nous savons par *P. Oxy.* 2039 que la maison des Apions est constituée vers les années 457/458', ibid.) is brilliantly confirmed by the appearance of the new Flavius Strategius. For the deduction (from *P. Oxy.* XVI 2039) see D. Bonneau, 'L'administration de l'irrigation dans les grands domaines en Égypte au VIe siècle de n.e.', in D. H. Samuel (ed.), *Proceedings of the Twelfth International Congress of Papyrology*. ASP 7 (Toronto, 1970) 45–62, at 56 n. 96.

[108] Jones, *LRE* 1.529.

than the few reserved specifically for the aristocracy[109]—*illustris*, *endoxotatos*,[110] and (for an élite group within this class, families at the very top) the newer titles *hyperphuestatos*[111] and *paneuphēmos*[112]—associated chiefly with the Apions and Flavius Strategius of the Fayum.

The structure of the aristocracy can thus be analysed by paying closer attention to the nuances of titulature. Indeed, this is the most reliable basis we have, immediately, for drawing distinctions within the aristocracy, between a higher and a lower group, and within the higher group between the real élite and others. Indications of a more purely economic order—those related to the size and organization of estates, the type of labour force deployed, and so on—correlate extremely well with the stratifications established on the basis of *Rangprädikate*.

Again, it is best to discuss the aristocracy of the Byzantine period as an ensemble of groups distinguished both by the scale of their resources and the organization of their estates and by the power and influence they wielded locally (in the district or the province as a whole). For reasons which are still largely obscure, such differences (between 'levels' of the aristocracy) were partly embodied in local ones, with some districts (notably the Oxyrhynchite) showing a greater predominance of the high aristocracy, others (notably the Hermopolite) left largely to the control of the smaller aristocrats (mostly 'Counts'), and yet others (chiefly the Fayum) displaying some combination of both these models without the exclusive predominance of either group, though with a clear tendency, as time wore on, for a more complete aristocratization to prevail even here. In concentrating on the Oxyrhynchite material, Hardy abstracted from these geographical differences and thus projected a picture of the Byzantine aristocracy which was both structurally simplified and geographically monotonous. Yet Hardy's account is still our only overall study of landownership in this period. In the chapter which follows I shall deal with the main groups of the aristocracy of the sixth and seventh centuries, following a brief discussion of some remaining exemplars of the fifth-century Oxyrhynchite aristocracy.

To conclude, I began by suggesting that for the purposes of agrarian

[109] The exception to this pattern is the group of titles reserved largely for the middle bureaucracy, esp. *eugenestatē*, *aidesimos*, and, to a lesser degree, *peribleptos*.

[110] For the distinction between these, see P. Koch, *Die byzantinischen Beamtentitel von 400 bis 700* (Jena, 1903) 42–3, 65.

[111] First attested in 489, in *P. Flor.* III 325 (for the date, 20 May 489, cf. Bagnall and Worp, *CSBE* 120).

[112] First attested in 497, in *P. Oxy.* XVI 1982.

history the best use we can make of the papyrological evidence, given the nature of this evidence, is to reconstruct the landed classes of the third to seventh centuries as an ensemble of 'groups' varying in their individual characteristics and strength. The chapter began by outlining nine groups of this sort, and then went on to a more detailed if symptomatic consideration of two important kinds of landowners typical of either side of the great watershed that destroyed the dominance of the earlier landed élites at some stage in the later fourth century. Till then the countryside had been firmly in the grip of families connected with the town councils, in Alexandria and the local districts, and it is difficult, in the Egyptian evidence at any rate, to posit any class resembling a powerful or unified aristocracy. However, from the middle decades of the fifth century, it is possible to discern the emergence of precisely such a class, suggesting a major cleavage in the agrarian structures and political forms of late antiquity. I have argued that the late imperial bureaucracy was the decisive crucible of this transformation, and that the change itself was closely bound up both with the expansion of monetary economy and with the widening gulf between the municipal classes and their imperial counterparts. The papyri show landowners emanating from all echelons of the bureaucracy, including advocates of the various provincial courts,[113] middle-grade employees of the provincial offices,[114] and of course holders of the highest dignities. The middle bureaucracy was a particularly striking expression of the affluent agrarian middle class of late antiquity, extensively involved in moneylending and commercial agriculture. The fifth century also saw the consolidation, throughout the eastern provinces, of a Byzantine 'new aristocracy', drawn from the aristocracy of office and actively involved in the management of their estates, which were extensively irrigated, directly managed, and founded on the control of private settlements. These landowners were a driving force in the incipient expansion of Byzantine viticulture (impossible without irrigation). They were also, by the main part of the fifth century, a largely hereditary group. As more papyrological evidence is published, the origins of this class will undoubtedly become much clearer to historians. The interesting recent case of Flavius Strategius I suggests that the Apions were

[113] *P. Oxy.* LXIII 4394 (494–500), for two examples (Flavius Olympiodorus and Flavius Maximinus, both with the designation *συνήγορος τοῦ Αὐγουσταλιανοῦ φόρου*), 4398 (553) (Flavius Dioscorus, *συνήγορος φόρου τῆς μεγίστης ἀγορᾶς τῆς τῶν ὑπερλάμπρων καὶ ἐξοχωτάτων ἐπάρχ(ων) κτλ.*).

[114] e.g. *exceptores* or speedwriters; John Lydus, *Mag.* 3.6 (Bandy 139), notes that the 'throng of speedwriters is large in fact beyond count, and had no small opportunities for the pursuit of profit (*καὶ οὐ μικρὰς ἐχούσης ἀφορμὰς ἐπὶ κέρδους ἐργασίας*)'.

one of the earliest families of the Byzantine new aristocracy, with an estate in the Oxyrhynchite by the 430s.[115] Yet the expansion of the Apion properties must have had much to do both with the fact that Strategius was entrusted with the management of the estates of Aelia Eudocia in the middle decades of the fifth century and may have been promoted into the highest aristocracy in recognition of those services, and, more interestingly, with the investments in land mortgages made by his descendants.[116] Finally, women were prominent in both classes, for example, Strategius' daughter, Flavia Isis, ran some part of the estate by the end of the 460s when Strategius himself was evidently deceased.

[115] See *P. Oxy.* LXIII 4389 (439), and John Rea's surmise there. Strategius is also found in *P. Oxy.* L 3584 (5c.), 3585–6 (both before Oct. 460), *P. Heid.* IV 331 (465), *P. Oxy.* LXIII 4390 (14.12.469), and see n. 104 above.
[116] *P. Oxy.* LXIII 4397. 48 ff. (545).

CHAPTER 6

A Late Antique Aristocracy

A New Aristocracy

While Flavius Strategius I is the first landowner from a discernibly Byzantine tradition (in Rémondon's sense of the aristocracy which he characterizes as 'les hauts fonctionnaires latifondiaires'[1]), other surviving exemplars of this group embody its essential features in an even purer form. But their connection with the Oxyrhynchite is worth emphasizing. With the appearance, in our evidence, of Strategius, Hardy's suggestion that Count John, *comes consistorii* and governor of Arcadia in 488, was the 'first Apion' must certainly be rejected.[2] Whatever his relation to the Apion family, he was not in the main line of descent which, as far as we can tell, must have passed directly from Strategius to Flavius Apion I, who was *Praefectus praetorio orientis* in 518. At any rate, the small archive of Count John[3] preserves his full title[4] and shows him to be an active participant in the running of his estate. The most illuminating agricultural document is *P. Oxy.* I 141, dated 503, where John ratifies a series of wine payments (through his wine manager Phoibammon) to various groups ('those from Sepho', 'those from Kesmouchis') including workers called χωρικοὶ ἐργάται. These were clearly agricultural labourers recruited on a purely casual basis. John's exalted position in the Byzantine bureaucracy had in no sense distanced him from the immediate life of his estate, any more than Hyperechius had been precluded from immediate involvement by the scale of his affluence. Flavia Kyria, who is described as both *lamprotatē* and *eugenestatē*,[5] would likewise intervene to sanction payments

[1] Rémondon, *Atti dell'XI Congresso*, 1965, 141.

[2] E. R. Hardy, 'The Egyptian Policy of Justinian', *DOP* 22 (1968) 21–41, at 29, *Large Estates*, 25.

[3] Noted by Montevecchi, *Papirologia*, 259, no. 78, to which add *P. Oxy.* I 155.

[4] *P. Oxy.* XVI 1877.11, ...] Apio Theodosius I[oha]nnes viri sp(ectabilis) com(es) sacri consist(orii) et praesis provinc(iae) Arc(a)d(iae).

[5] In *P. Oxy.* XXXIV 2724 (469).

(e.g. foodgrains to donkey drivers),[6] implying that the general field of expenditures was an area where local managers had minimum autonomy. The most important document associated with her is *P. Oxy.* XXXIV 2724, dated 469, the first of a long series of water-wheel receipts from the private estates. This is the document which contains our first clear papyrological reference to the *enapographoi geōrgoi*.[7] Like most big landowners, Kyria housed her labourers in the special settlements called *epoikia*, for the receipt was issued on behalf of *geōrgoi* 'from the *epoikion* of Chaira (which is part of) the estate of your Illustriousness'.[8] The characteristic Byzantine habit of referring to estate settlements (*epoikia*) as '(part of) your estate'[9] was a way of emphasizing the subordination of the peasantry to the new landowners. In the decades which followed, Byzantine owners would frequently refer to 'their' villages and 'their' *geōrgoi*—a tradition which is by no means equally discernible in earlier centuries.[10] What was new here was not the fact of domination but the fact that the aristocracy sought to emphasize that domination, to assert it in more open, formal ways, and to indoctrinate their own workforces in the passive submission of a language of dependence. Gascou has argued that much of this new power derived from the implicit adjustments of Byzantine fiscalism,[11] and this seems a more natural interpretation than the notion that villagers actually became more 'submissive and even servile'.[12]

P. Oxy. XVI 1899 is the second water-wheel receipt attested from the archives of a private estate. In the year it was drafted, 476,[13] the owner, Flavius Alexander, was a *μεγαλοπρεπέστατος καὶ ἐνδοξότατος στρατηγός*, the highest military official for the eastern command,[14] and of a status clearly more exalted than that of John, who governed Arcadia in the 480s.[15] In his case the labourers' settlement, *epoikion Piaa* (from the Coptic *Piah* for 'field') is actually referred to as *τοῦ αὐτοῦ ἐνδοξοτάτου ἀνδρὸς*, showing that, unlike villages, settlements

[6] See *P. Lond.* V 1798 (470), with Gascou, 'Notes critiques sur quelques papyrus des Ve et VIe siècles', *CE* 47 (1972) 243–53, esp. 248–50.

[7] But see n. 105 in the previous chapter.

[8] *P. Oxy.* XXXIV 2724.5–7, *ἀπὸ ἐποικίου Χαιρᾶ κτήματος τῆς σῆς θαυμασιότητος.*

[9] Not confined to water-wheel receipts, cf. *P. Oxy.* XLIX 3512, a contract of advance sale dated 492.

[10] See App. 1, Table 8.

[11] Gascou, *Grands domaines*, 52.

[12] de Ste. Croix, *Class Struggle*, 223, refers to 'the submissive and even servile attitude of the villagers', cf. 213, 'the abject villagers of Aphrodito . . . who grovelled before their local bigwigs', disputed by Keenan, *Atti del XVII Congresso* (1984) 962 f.

[13] Cf. *BL* 8. 250.

[14] Cf. *PLRE* 2.59 Alexander 2, *magister utriusque militiae*.

[15] He was *dux Aegyptiaci limitis et praefectus Augustalis* in 468, *CJ* 2.7.13, cf. *CJ* 1.57.1 (469).

of this sort were inseparable from the large, privately controlled properties.[16] The transaction was handled by a certain Flavius Joseph who was obviously a fairly senior manager, both because he was a Flavius (with the epithet *lamprotatos*, perhaps unusual for this period but a confirmation of Jones's theory that the tendential degradation of the lesser titles began some time after 450),[17] and because he was *dioikētēs* for the general's estates in the Oxyrhynchite as a whole—*διοικητὴς πραγμάτων τοῦ αὐτοῦ ἐνδοξοτάτου ἀνδρὸς διακειμένων κατὰ τὴν Ὀξυρυγχιτῶν* (ll. 5–6)—with the implication, of course, that the estates covered several districts. Thus everything in this document looks forward to the fully formed Byzantine aristocracy of the sixth century: Alexander's official standing, the form of the contract, and the manager's designation, since *dioikētai* were the functionaries most characteristic of the 'late Byzantine' system of estate management.

Fikhman has characterized *P. Oxy.* 2724 as a turning point in the history of Egyptian land relations.[18] After the slow incubation of the previous decades, owners like Flavia Kyria, Flavius Alexander, and Count Theodosius John represented the formation of a genuine *provincial* aristocracy. Arguably, this was the first time in the history of the empire that a class with precisely these characteristics was emerging. Jones refers to the evolution of a hereditary aristocracy by the second quarter of the fifth century.[19] This, at any rate, is entirely in keeping with the emergence, precisely in this period, of the new institutional reality of the *oikoi*. We know from *P. Oxy.* L 3583, dated 444, that the *clarissimus* Timagenes, who was still alive in 432 and responsible at that time for a substantial part or "share" (*meris*) of the Oxyrhynchite's taxes,[20] was dead by this year and that the function performed by him had now been incorporated into an *oikos* named after him.[21] In short, the *estate* became the centre of the

[16] Consequently, de Ste. Croix's statements in the paragraph starting 'The characteristic unit in which peasant life was organised was the village' (*Class Struggle*, 221) should be modified in at least two ways: first, by allowing for the existence of *numerous* smaller settlements of the *epoikion* type, secondly, by the qualification that landlords rarely controlled entire *kōmai* (in Egypt, at any rate).

[17] See p. 130f. above.

[18] I. F. Fikhman, 'Quelques données sur la genèse de la grande propriété foncière à Oxyrhynchus', in J. Bingen *et al.* (eds.), *Le Monde Grec. Hommages à Claire Préaux* (Brussels, 1975) 784–90, at 790, 'le premier texte du Ve siècle qu'on peut, typologiquement, ranger parmi les textes de l'époque postérieure se rapportant aux grands domaines privés'.

[19] Jones, *LRE*, 1.180, 'In the reigns of Arcadius and Theodosius II a hereditary aristocracy was beginning to form from the sons and grandsons of the new men who had risen to the top in the fourth century.'

[20] Cf. *PSI XVII Congr.* 29.3 (31 Aug. 432), which refers to *τῇ μερίδι λαμπροτάτου Τιμαγένους*, so, as Andorlini says (109), 'mentre questo era in vita'.

[21] *P. Oxy.* L 3583.3 (13 Nov. 444), *[μερί]δι τοῦ οἴκου τοῦ τῆς περιβλέπτου μνήμης Τιμαγένους*.

fiscal responsibilities assumed by Timagenes when he was alive, and though the basis of this move remains unclear it relates, undoubtedly, to his status as a landholder. The universalism of Byzantine society, the aspect in which it most resembled the late Roman state (and further developed the essential nature of that state), came to subordinate the individual landowner to the abstract but enduring reality of his/her estate. And conversely, the temporal continuity of estates acquired an abstract, almost transcendental expression in the reality of the *oikos*. The new corporatism welded persons and property, estate and family, into a single institutional reality more permanent than the actual or immediate line of successors (which might cease to exist) and more efficient than any immediate group of proprietors.

The Byzantine aristocracy was thus a permanent and stable group, its corporatism rooted in the whole tendency of late antique society, and related, more directly, to the scale of its resources. Thus the *oikos* of Flavius Apion I was in operation in at least two districts by the 490s, with the group of holdings in the Heracleopolite described, evidently, as an *ousia*.[22] His son Strategius, a *comes domesticorum* by 497,[23] was formally responsible for the Oxyrhynchite for most of the 490s.[24] In the Arsinoite Flavius Varius, also *comes domesticorum*, describes himself in a lease dated 504 as 'from Memphis, and landowner also in the Arsinoite'—with the implication, clearly, of multiple ownership.[25] The patrician Sophia turns up with an *endoxos oikos* in both the Arsinoite and Heracleopolis.[26] Flavia Christodote, daughter of a former patrician, described her estate as οὐσία κατὰ τὴν Ἀρκάδων, again with the implication of holdings throughout Arcadia.[27]

Christodote, who turns up in an affidavit dated 572 (or 573), was owed 61 lb. of gold and made it clear to the Alexandrian banker Flavius Eustathius (an *argyropratēs*) that she was willing to pursue the matter as far as Constantinople.[28] The amount, 4,392 solidi,

[22] *SPP* XX 129.2 (497), [παρὰ Αὐρηλίου Πτο]λεμαίου παραλή[μπ]του οὐσίας Ἀπίωνος τοῦ ἐνδοξ(οτάτου) καὶ ὑπερφυεστάτου ἀπὸ ὑπάτων, with *BL* 8.468.

[23] Cf. *P. Oxy.* XVI 1982.3–5 (497); contrast *P. Flor.* III 325 (20 May 489), assuming Hornickel, *Rangprädikate*, 11 n. 2 is correct in restoring [Φλ( ) Στρατηγίῳ τῷ].

[24] This follows from the conjunction of *P. Oxy.* XVI 1982 and *P. Flor.* 325, see n. 23.

[25] *P. Ross.-Georg.* III 32.3 (504), [ἀπὸ τῆς Μ]εμφιτων πολεως, γεουχοῦντι καὶ ἐπὶ τῆς Ἀρσινοειτῶν πόλεως.

[26] *SPP* VIII 1090–1097 (late 6c.), *P. Erl.* 67 (17 Sept. 591) with the corrections in *BL* 8.120.

[27] *PSI* I 76. 6 (572 or 573, *BL* 8.392), ἡ ὑπολειφθεῖσά μοι ἀκίνητος οὐσία κατὰ τὴν Ἀρκάδων (the landed estate bequeathed to me in the province of Arcadia).

[28] Cf. J. G. Keenan, 'From the Archive of Flavia Christodote: Observations on *PSI* I 76', *ZPE* 29 (1978) 191–209, re-editing *PSI* I 76, with a discussion. On the date see R. S. Bagnall and K. A. Worp, 'Chronological Notes on Byzantine Documents, II', *BASP*

was more than a fifth of the annual revenue, in solidi, which the Apions extracted from their Oxyrhynchite estates.[29] Sophia bore the epithet *hyperphuestatē*, while Christodote described herself as an *illustris*.[30] Closer attention to the titulature of the aristocracy shows that by the main part of the sixth century families at this level had evolved a clear-cut internal stratification—while most aristocrats described themselves as *illustres*, the leading families in each district distinguished themselves as a patrician élite. Of course, these titles could be found within the same family, for example, Christodote who was *illoustria* was the daughter of a former *patricius*. Within the top aristocracy the most usual epithets were *hyperphuestatos* (for males and females) and *paneuphēmos* (mostly for males), typical of the Apions. Finally, below both groups was a smaller aristocracy which consisted chiefly of the numerous Counts who were still essentially *megaloprepestatoi*. Thus the provincial society of the late antique period was doubly stratified, both in the sense that the aristocracy dominated the landowning class (and the rest of society) and because within the aristocracy, as the dominant landed group, the formal gradation of statuses implied both economic and bureaucratic differentiation.

It is also obvious that a group which believed so fiercely in the formal differentiation of statuses would hardly operate outside a carefully defined hierarchy of offices at the more local, district level. It seems likely that the functions or pseudo-functions which were most characteristic of provincial aristocratic life in the sixth and seventh centuries thus fell into a fixed order of promotions, a sort of provincial career structure, and that the titles which individual aristocrats bore at any given time merely reflected phases of a mobility cycle which bound the lowest or most junior levels of the aristocracy, who might be tribunes or counts, to the highest levels of the provincial administration. A careful study of the papyri should enable us to make sense of this promotion ladder and my remarks here are of a purely preliminary nature.

The career of Flavius Atias, one of the last Dukes to reflect the workings of a system of provincial administration whose basic features had been defined in the Byzantine period, shows at least three distinct stages of such a career at the upper level. Thus Atias was pagarch towards the end of 694—described simply as *σὺν θ(εῷ)*

16 (1979) 221–37, at 235 f. The money was owed to her by her brother Cometes through a contract in which Eustathius stood surety.

[29] *P. Oxy*. XVIII 2196 verso (*c*.586), 18,512 solidi.

[30] *P. Erl*. 67.5 (p. 74) (591, *BL* 7.47), *τοῦ ἐνδόξ(ου) [ο]ἴκου Σοφίας τῆς ὑπερφυεστάτης πατρικίας*, *PSI* I 76.2, *Φλ(αουΐα) Χριστοδότῃ σὺν θεῷ ἰλλουστρία*.

παγ(άρ)χ(ης) in *CPR* VIII 73, Duke by the middle of 698—with the epithet normal for this office, viz. *eukleestatos*[31]—and finally Duke of the combined provinces of Arcadia and the Thebaid by 699 when he figures in a work contract which I refer to later.[32] Thus here it seems certain that between the pagarch's function and the highest provincial office (that of Duke) the transition was immediate and no further stages of promotion are likely to have intervened. This is confirmed by the career of another Fayum aristocrat—not so far attested as a landowner—Flavius John who turns up in the recently published *CPR* XIV first as *illustris* and pagarch in XIV 1 (651?)[33] and then (surely the same person) as Duke of Arcadia in XIV 32 (655?).[34] At a lower level of the same administrative structure, it is clear that the *stratēlatai*—when designated only by this function—were inferior to the pagarchs. The Fayum Strategius (variously called pseudo-Strategius III and Strategius *paneuphēmos*) who is never addressed as *stratēlatēs*,[35] was both *patricius* and pagarch. On the other hand, Flavius Cyrillus, connected with his household in some capacity which is unclear,[36] is always only *stratēlatēs*. It seems fairly certain that the latter was a status inferior to the former, perhaps the level immediately preceding that of control over the pagarchy.[37]

Maspero identified the Byzantine *stratēlatai* with the tribunes or local garrison commanders, but this is almost certainly wrong.[38]

[31] *CPR* VIII 79.1 (*c*.697/8), *Φλ( ) Ἀτίας εὐκλε(έστατος) δοὺξ*, cf. VIII 74 dated 20 Aug. 698; 75 (*c*.698).

[32] *CPR* VIII 82.4 = *SB* VI 9460 (699/700), *Φλ(αουΐῳ) Ἀτίᾳ τῷ εὐκλεεστάτῳ δουκὶ Ἀρκαδίας καὶ Θηβαίδος*.

[33] *CPR* XIV 1.21–22, *εἰς Φλ(άουιον) Ἰώαν[νην] τὸν ἐνδοξ(ό)τ(ατον) ἰλλ(ούσ)τ(ριον) (καὶ) π(άγα)ρχ(ον)*.

[34] *CPR* XIV 32.5–6, *Φλ(αουΐῳ) Ἰωάννῃ τῷ ε[ὐκ]λεεστάτῳ δουκὶ ταύτης τῆς Ἀρκάδων ἐπαρχ[ία]ς*, cf. Fantoni, *CPR* XIV 1.6–7 n., 'after holding the office of pagarch, the natural promotion was to Duke of Arcadia'.

[35] So Fantoni, *CPR* XIV, pp. 44 f., correctly.

[36] *SPP* VIII 1072.1–2 (*c*.610, *BL* 8. 450) describes him as *στρατηλ[άτης] ἐνδόξου οἴκ(ου) Στρατηγίου*, implying that he exercised this function for the *oikos*. For other references to him see *Catalogue*, Fayum 7c.

[37] Fantoni's theory (in *CPR* XIV, p. 44, n. 4) that there were two Fl. Menases in the early 7th-cent. Fayum aristocracy (because one holds a single office, the other two) seems to me to be based on a simple misunderstanding of the aristocratic career structure. It seems more probable that all documents which refer to Menas simply as *stratēlatēs* stem from a period in his career when he had not yet progressed to the pagarchy. However, the same cannot be argued from the career of the Fayum pagarch Theodorakios, since Theodosakios in *BGU* I 3, dated 605, where he turns up as *stratelates* of Arsinoitonpolis (see W. Schubart, *Papyri Graecae Berolinenses* (Bonn, 1911) pl. 47 for a photograph) is a totally different person from the official who appears thirty-eight years later as *stratēlatēs kai pagarchos*, see *Catalogue*, Fayum 7c. Thus J. M. Diethart, *Prosopographia Arsinoitica I, s.VI–VIII* (Vienna, 1980) 5438 is surely wrong to include *BGU* I 3 in the archive of Theodorakios.

[38] J. Maspero, *L'Organisation militaire de l'Égypte byzantine* (Paris, 1912) 88–9;

Thus Flavia Theophania, who turns up in *CPR* X 127 (584) as *stratēlatissa*, was obviously not connected with any local garrison, and derived the title presumably from the fact that her husband, Strategius, had been a *stratēlatēs*.[39] Rémondon suggested, more plausibly, that the *stratēlatai* were imperial functionaries—with regular control over troops of *bucellarii*[40] once the order banning the retention of such armed squads had been lifted in a concession to the aristocracy which presumably had never ceased to maintain forces of this type and now—through the function of the *stratēlatēs*—merely formalized its control over them.[41] If this is true, it might help to explain the connection (synchronous or diachronic) between *stratēlatai* and pagarchs, since it is likely that control over *bucellarii* or equivalent forces was a formal prerequisite for the pagarchy or exercise of the pagarch's function.[42] In short, it seems plausible to conclude that the essential career structure of the Byzantine provincial aristocracy was defined by the three main offices or functions of *stratēlatēs*, pagarch and Duke, with possible combinations of an intermediate nature, notably the fact that most important pagarchs continued to retain the title *stratēlatēs*, though the Fayum Strategius seems to have wanted to be an exception in this respect.

I shall argue elsewhere that there seems to be no obvious distinction between the institution of the pagarchy and the granting of autopract status to the most powerful landholders, and that the institution itself is in fact likely to have emerged as the logical outcome of a situation where *autopragia* was threatening to undermine the fiscal efficiency of the state. For the moment, it is worth noting that Table 9*b* in Appendix 1 strongly supports the usual picture of the Byzantine pagarchs as essentially landowners,[43] e.g., of sixteen

against Maspero cf. Durliat's survey in 'Magister militum—*Stratelates* dans l'empire byzantin (VIe–VIIe siècles)', *BZ* 72 (1979) 306–20, esp. 318, on Egyptian *stratēlatai*, 'Ce sont le plus souvent des personnages considérables, membres des plus grandes familles d'Égypte . . .'.

39 So Worp in *CPR* X, pp. 151–2.

40 R. Rémondon, '[Situation présente de la papyrologie byzantine]', in *Akten des XIII. Int. Papyrologenkongresses*, at 369, 'des fonctionnaires impériaux, militaires, ou plus souvent civils, disposant régulièrement de troupes de bucellaires'; *P. Mon.* III 130 (7c.) (from the archive of Flavius Menas, cf. *Catalogue*, Fayum 7c.) confirms the link between *stratēlatai* and *bucellarii*, and does so in a context related, remarkably enough, to the collection of taxes or estate revenues.

41 For the ban, dated 476, cf. *CJ* 9.12.10, proof that paramilitary squads were common on the estates of the new aristocracy.

42 Thus Flavius Menas controlled *bucellarii* when he was *stratēlatēs*, prior to becoming pagarch (see n. 40), *pace* Fantoni, *CPR* XIV, p. 44 (n. 4), who wants to distinguish *two* 7th-cent. Fayum Menases, cf. n. 37.

43 See Gelzer, *Studien*, 97–8; L. Mitteis and U. Wilcken, *Grundzüge und Chrestomathie der Papyruskunde*, 2 vols. (Leipzig, 1912) 1.83 ('Pagarchen die meist selbst zu den grossten Grundbesitzern gehorten'); Rémondon, *P. Apoll.*, p. 104 ('le pagarque est

sixth-century pagarchs (counting Flavius Apion II's control of the office only once), twelve were aristocratic landowners! By the seventh century, roughly a quarter (26 per cent) of all ruling-class landowners[44] were pagarchs or associated with that function at some time in their career.

In the following sections I shall deal with the *geouchoi* as an ensemble of groups—the Fayum aristocracy of the later sixth century, the Oxyrhynchite landowners of the same period, the *stratēlatai* and pagarchs of the seventh-century Fayum, before and after the conquest, and finally the smaller aristocrats of late Byzantine Hermopolis.

The Top Aristocracy

The Fayum

The clear vertical stratification of the aristocracy makes it possible to discuss this group by looking at each stratum in turn. In the Fayum in the last century of Byzantine rule our chief exemplars of the high élite within the aristocracy are Sophia and Flavius Strategius or pseudo-Strategius III. They distinguish themselves from the rest of the Fayum aristocracy by the fact that they are the only cases we know of Fayum *patricii*. Sophia's Arsinoite estate which Rémondon has estimated at some 10,000 arouras[45] included villages in the area bordering Heracleopolis. Thus *SPP* VIII 1092, relating to a ninth indiction which is probably 590/1[46] (otherwise 575/6) is an order to pay, issued by Sophia, involving cash payments to two employees for the transport of bricks required for a προάστειον (suburban villa) near the *kōmē* Syrōn.[47] Sophia was clearly

généralement grand propriétaire'); Gascou, *Byzantion* 42 (1972) 69; Liebeschuetz, *JJP* 18 (1974) 163 ('A pagarch was often a local man, a big landowner'); Palme, *Das Amt des ἀπαιτητής in Ägypten*, 98 ('meist selbst Grundherren').

44 This group is defined as 'High officials' + 'Pagarchs' (not attested as 'High officials') + 'Counts' + '*Clarissimi*'.

45 Rémondon, *Akten des XIII Int.Papyrologenkongresses*, 368–9.

46 The date of *P. Erl.* 67, from the Heracleopolite (n. 26 above). *SPP* 1092 should be read with *BL* 9.341.

47 For the location see Ch. 7. *Proasteia* were suburban estates and not just villas, e.g. *P. Oxy.* XVI 1913 iii 34 refers to τοῖς ἀμ(πελουργοῖς) χωρ(ίου) προαστίου, and the *Miracula S. Demetrii* 246 (Lemerle 1.212) describes people desperately foraging in the *proasteia*, estates, outside Thessalonica. But *proasteia* were not simply suburban estates, they were estates with a substantial investment in semi-urban luxury (note esp. *P. Oxy.* 1925, cf. G. Husson, 'Recherches sur les sens du mot προάστιον dans le grec d'Égypte', *Recherches de Papyrologie* 4 (1967) 187–200, at 195, and J. J. Rossiter, 'Roman Villas of the Greek East and the Villa in Gregory of Nyssa, *Ep.* 20', *JRA* 2 (1989) 101–11), thus mainly associated with the wealthiest and most powerful sections of the aristocracy, cf.

also connected with the south-west Fayum, the area which was then called the Theodosiopolite, since the major payment associated with her involves *c.*112 solidi for the *embolē* of Theodosioupolis for a ninth indiction.[48] *SPP* VIII 1091 is addressed to a certain Theophania, which may link the archive of Sophia to that of the Fayum Strategii who were landowners in the Theodosiopolite and represented, in 584, not far from the date of Sophia's transactions, by a certain Flavia Theophania, wife of a deceased Strategius, described as *stratēlatissa.*[49] Whatever the precise relation of pseudo-Strategius III to these families, it is clear that they were the very social background from which he came.[50] Since there is no reference to him in *CPR* X 127 (584) whereas he is now attested as already ὑπερφυέστατος in 591 (in an Oxyrhynchite document),[51] it seems unlikely that he was a son of Theophania and Strategius. It is just possible that he was Sophia's son, but that would mean redating the orders to pay to 575 since her son, described as *endoxos*, was still a minor when she managed the estate on his behalf.[52] At any rate, with the archive of pseudo-Strategius III we reach the heart of aristocratic Egypt, the quintessential big landowner.

In an evolution roughly similar to the titles of Apion III but

P. Princ. III 158, etc. (Apions); *SPP* VIII 1092 (Sophia); *SPP* VIII 1139 (Stephanus); Palladius, *Dialogus de vita S. Ioannis* 8 (*PG* 47.28); Sozomen, 8.17.3 (Bidez 371) (Rufinus, cos. 392); *Vie anonyme d'Olympias* 5.32 (Malingrey 418) (Olympias); and G. Dagron, *Naissance d'une capitale: Constantinople et ses institutions de 330 à 451* (Paris, 1974) 185 for other references. Proximity to an urban centre is strongly implied in passages such as, *Miracula S. Demetrii* 123 (p. 131), 127 (p. 137), 246 (p. 212); Callinicos, *Vie d'Hypatios* 7.4; *P. Oxy.* 1925 verso, τοῦ προαστίο[υ] ἔξω τῆς Πύλ[ης]; and Theodoret, *Hist. Eccl.* 4.23 (*PG* 82.1185). From a reference in *P. Oxy.* 1925. 42, it seems that the Apion *proastion* outside Oxyrhynchus had a hippodrome adjoining it, cf. Rea, *P. Oxy.* 3941.19n (p. 76).

[48] The only specific trace of this may be the curious toponym منشاة بارض الصفاونه (*manshā bi ʿarḍ aṣ-ṣofāwīna*) which figures in the *Taʾrīkh al-Fayyūm* (p. 174). This was less than a kilometre from Abusir Difinnu (Bousiris), separated by a canal. *ʿArḍ* clearly has the meaning 'estate'.

[49] *CPR* X 127 (584), with *P. Oxy.* 3805.38n, and Papathomas, *Tyche* 10 (1995) 145f.

[50] Palme has argued recently that pseudo-Strategius III or 'Strategius Paneuphemos' married into the Apion family and was the husband of Flavia Praejecta and father of Flavius Apion III, see B. Palme, 'Flavius Strategius Paneuphemos und die Apionen', *ZSS* 115 (1998) 289–322. This hypothesis is based, crucially, on seeing *P. Oxy.* XVI 1829 verso as a conflated set of references both to him, on the one hand, and to the son of Flavius Apion II who was also called Strategius but who is otherwise among the least conspicuous members of that family.

[51] *P. Oxy.* LVIII 3935. 7 (591).

[52] In all the orders to pay from which she is known to us Sophia describes herself as acting for her son, who is called *endoxos*. A more likely candidate for her son is the *stratēlatēs* Theodosius, cf. the remarkably similar formats of *SPP* VIII 1091 (archive of Sophia) and 1111 (Theodosius), and see Gascou, *Bibliotheca Orientalis* 39 (1982) 105.

characterised by an obvious regional diversity,[53] Strategius' career shows four specific stages—*hyperphuestatos* in 591 (in the Oxyrhynchite),[54] then πανεύφημος καὶ ὑπερφυέστατος ὕπατος by 598 (still in the Oxyrhynchite where the same title is attested in 601),[55] then πανεύφημος πάγαρχος καὶ ὕπατος shortly afterwards, in 600 (in the Fayum where he was pagarch of the Arsinoite and Theodosiopolite)[56], and finally, for most of his attested life, *hyperphuestatos* or *paneuphēmos patricius*—by 604[57]—with or without the title *pagarchos*. The only deviations from this pattern are *SPP* VIII 1158 where he is Στρατήγιος σὺν ʽθ(εῷ)ʼ ἀπὸ ὑπάτων, and the Memphite flood report *P. Rain. Cent.*125 (*c.*605) in which he is addressed simply as *endoxotatos*. Thus it is clear that Strategius was in control of the Fayum pagarchy by *c.*600 and that he retained control of this crucial position in the terrible conflicts that devastated Egypt towards the end of that decade.[58] Of the three previous holders of a combined Arsinoite-Theodosiopolite pagarchy so far known to us, at least two were from the highest group in the aristocracy—Flavius Apion II who may have retained the function for several years since *BGU* I 305 (556) calls him ἐνδοξότατος στρατηλάτης πάγαρχος τῆς Ἀρσινοιτῶν καὶ Θεοδοσιουπολιτῶν (cf. *BL* 9.18), whereas he now turns up in *CPR* XIV 10 (date uncertain) with the distinctly more elevated title ὁ πανεύφημος ἀπὸ ὑπάτων πάγαρχος, etc.;[59] a certain Strategius who was an ἐνδοξότατος στρατηλάτης πάγαρχος of the combined territory with Flavius Christopher in 578 and who is unlikely to have been Strategius II of the Oxyrhynchite Apions since Christopher takes precedence over him but who may have been the husband of Flavia Theophania;[60] Christopher is unknown.

Strategius can be directly connected with at least nine locations. Seven of these occur in *SPP* X 1, which is a list of villages and their

[53] For the titles of pseudo-Strategius III, see App. 1, Table 10. For Apion III see John Rea, *P. Oxy.* LVIII 3939.4–5n.

[54] See n. 51.

[55] *P. Oxy.* LVIII 3936.6–7 (598), *P. Berol. inv.* 10526.9–11 (cf. G. Poethke, 'Empfangsbescheinigung für Weizen aus Oxyrhynchos: P. Berol. 10526', *JJP* 23 (1993) 133–7) (598), *P. Oxy.* XVI 1991.7–8 (18 Sept. 601), for the date cf. R. S. Bagnall and K. A. Worp, 'Christian Invocations in the Papyri', *CE* 56 (1981) 112–33, at 129.

[56] *P. Lond.* I 113.5(c) (p. 212) (600), with *BL* 1.237.

[57] Fantoni, *CPR* XIV, p. 42, no.7 would like to read τῷ πανευφήμῳ π[ατρικίῳ (καὶ)] παγάρχῳ in *SB* XVI 12701.5, dated 600, but he does not bear the title *patricius* in *P. Oxy.* XVI 1991 dated 601.

[58] See Z. Borkowski, *Alexandrie II. Inscriptions des factions à Alexandrie* (Warsaw, 1981) chs. 2–4.

[59] Unless of course this man is Fl. Apion III, a possibility which concords with his nomenclature in phase one, see Rea, *P. Oxy.* LVIII 3939.4–5 n.

[60] *CPR* XIV 11.5–7 (578). Of course, this implies that the husband of Theophania is again not likely to have been the Oxyrhynchite Strategius II, as Fantoni suggests, *CPR* XIV, p. 43, n. 1, followed by Palme, 'Strategius Paneuphemos und die Apionen'.

contributions (towards perquisites, *synētheiai*) 'given to the *oikos* of the deceased Strategius'.[61] The geography of these places will be discussed later. Phentemin and Psineuris were close to Arsinoitōnpolis, to the north-west. In the countryside near Ptolemais Hormou (El Lāhūn), Strategius is attested at Herakleōn where the estate (*ousia*) had several *mēchanai* (*sāqiyas*) and a group of employees called μηχανάρ(ιοι).[62] He was bound to have been a big landowner in the region of Memphis since he turns up as a *phrontistēs* (?) of the church of Memphis, like other *geouchoi* who assumed formal responsibility for the administration of church properties.[63] He certainly had land in the Oxyrhynchite, where he may well have been the premier aristocrat in 591 when Flavius Apion III was still *aphēlix*.[64] Finally, three of the toponyms in *SPP* X 1 (Bernikis, Karpe, and Ampeliou) recur in *SPP* X 78 (7c.), which is a wine account listing payments or production quotas from local Fayum villages. Wine growing was widespread throughout these sectors of the Fayum. Localities like Bēlou could be assessed for the substantial sum of 752 solidi, implying a huge production of wine and other cash crops.[65]

The archive of pseudo-Strategius III, potentially one of the most valuable, is also one of the least unified and most fragmented.[66] It is therefore difficult to form any conception of the organization of his estates in the Fayum. That the *dioikētai*, the characteristic Byzantine

[61] *SPP* X 1.1 f. (7c.) [*Γ*]ν`ῶ΄(σις) συνηθει`ῶ΄(ν) διδομ(ένων) εἰς τὸν οἶκο(ν) τοῦ ἐν ἁγί(οις) Στρατηγίου. The list goes: *Psineure(os), Ampeliou, B[er]nikido(s), Karpe, Phentemin, Psineure(os), Kainou, [ ]nol.*

[62] The verso of *SPP* VIII 1121 (7c.) has the tantalizingly incomplete specification,] (ὑπὲρ) ἀποτριβ(έντων?) διαφόρ(ων) μηχαν(ῶν) τῆς ο[ὐσίας? /] ἀποτριβ( ) μηχαναρ( ) χωρ(ίου) 'Ηρακλέ[ω]νος. John Rea has suggested (ὑπὲρ) ἀποτριβ(ῆς) διαφόρ(ων) μηχαν(ικῶν) τῆς ο[ὐσιάς /] with, possibly, μηχανικ(ῶν) instead of μηχαναρ( ) in l. 2.

[63] *P. Rain. Cent.* 125 (605, *BL* 8.287), from Memphis; the report has a blank space before [τῆς] ἁγία[ς ἐ]κκλ(ησίας) Μέμφ(εως) (ll. 1–2). John Rea, *P. Oxy.* LVIII 3933.12n (at 62–3) suggests we might read, [ἡ] ἁγία [ἐ]κκλ(ησία) Μέμφ(εως). For other examples of aristocrats managing church properties, cf. the *patricius* Senouthios, *SPP* III 271 B (*c.*642), with Gascou, *Domaines*, 79, and the *endoxotatos* Joannakios in *SB* XII 10805 (mid-7c.), with E. Wipszycka, 'Les factions du cirque et les biens ecclésiastiques dans un papyrus égyptien', *Byzantion* 39 (1969) 180–98, both described as *phrontistai* of the church of Hermopolis.

[64] *P. Oxy.* LVIII 3935.6–7, τοῦ ἐνδόξου οἴκου τοῦ ὑπερφυεστάτου Στρατηγίου, dated 6 Mar. 591, and *P. Berol. inv.* 10526 (see n. 55 above). Cf. R. Rémondon, 'Papyrologica', *CE* 41 (1966) 165–79, at 179.

[65] The figure occurs in *SPP* X 62.3 (7c.). Bēlou appears with Bernikis and Karpe in *SPP* X 78.4–7. For wine at Belou, apart from *SPP* X 78 (7c.), cf. *SPP* X 255, which starts ἀ[πὸ] ἀμπ(ελικοῦ) χωρ(ίου) Βηλο`υ΄, *SPP* X 290 (7/8c.), VIII 1328 (7c.). Also see App. 3 n. 32.

[66] Certain and probable documents are listed in App. 1, Table 10; see B. Palme, 'Die *domus gloriosa* des Flavius Strategius Paneuphemos', *Chiron* 27 (1997) 95–125, for unpublished material from the archive.

management level, were responsible for groups of locations is certain both from the Apion accounts and from the Fayum material in *SPP* X. I shall discuss the essential features of this managerial system elsewhere and only draw attention here to a remarkable document which in a rudimentary way reveals the basic organization which must have encompassed the estates of the top aristocracy. This is *SPP* X 138, dated to the seventh century, an account of payments in kind listed by groups of locations of no special or uniform size but defined, apparently, by the general contiguity of their locations. With one exception, all groups (six altogether) have a manager in charge of them, mostly *dioikētai*, each of whom was called 'Count so-and-so'. Since the amounts (expressed in artabas, of wheat presumably) are listed against his name rather than the name of the village, the implication is that it was his responsibility to distribute the burden between individual localities. The remarkable feature of this account is that the villages are specifically said to belong to an owner or official whose title shows him to be from the Fayum aristocracy. Thus the heading is + *γνῶσι(ς) κωμ(ῶν) το[ῦ μ]εγαλοπρε(πεστάτου)* [. . . . Since Flavius Strategius never bore this title which, among the aristocracy,[67] was usually borne either by pagarchs (when used alone; whether before or after the Arab conquest)[68] or by *stratēlatai* (when used with *endoxotatos*),[69] otherwise by the more numerous smaller aristocrats with the dignity of 'Count',[70] it seems probable that the owner of this massive Fayum estate was a powerful pagarch (note that the simple *stratēlatai* represented a lower rank), in the period following the demise of Strategius himself, or, conceivably, a high-ranking official whose titles included *stratēlatēs*. For the two decades following the death of Strategius,[71] the most likely candidates seem to me to be (1) Flavius Theodorakios, who was a *megaloprepestatos pagarchos* (of the Arsinoite) *c*.639/40 (the last thirteenth indiction before the

[67] That is, excluding the numerous administrative personnel to whom the term was applied.

[68] See *PSI* I 52.4 (Fl. Julianus, but read *τῷ μεγαλ(οπρεπεστάτῳ) παγάρχῃ*), *BGU* II 366.5 verso (Fl. John), *P. Lond.* I 113,10.5 (Fl. Theodorakios), *SB* VIII 9749.1 (Apa Cyrus), *BGU* I 304.1 (Fl. Christopher), BM 8903 (Liberius).

[69] e.g., *P. Lond.* V 1786.2–4 (*c*.610, *BL* 8.193), *τῷ μεγαλωπρεπεστάτῳ καὶ ἐνδοξωτάτῳ στρδηλάτου* (l. *στρατηλάτῃ*) *Κυρίλλῳ*, though for the 7th-cent. *stratēlatēs*, *endoxotatos* by itself was more usual.

[70] Cf. Hornickel, *Rangprädikate*, 29, 'Besonders gerne wird es [*megaloprepestatos*] zum Comes' Titel gestellt'; Fl. Demetrius/John in *SPP* XX 218 and *P. Laur.* II 26 (see p. 167 f. below) is a good example.

[71] As far as we know, he left no heirs. John Rea, *P. Oxy.* LVIII, p. 116 speculated that Strategius may have been eliminated by the Persians. Also see p. 256 below.

conquest)[72] and *stratēlatēs* and pagarch (of the Arsinoite) by 643, now with the label *endoxotatos*,[73] and (2) Flavius Theodosius, who was Duke of Arcadia in 636 and an *endoxotatos stratēlatēs* at some stage before that[74] and who turns up in *SPP* X 249 (633), a payments list with a remarkable similarity to *SPP* X 138,[75] with a total individual contribution (an actual payment since the account refers to a balance) of 4,000 artabas (of wheat, presumably) but here with the abbreviated title *ὁ στρα(τηλάτης)*, so in the 620s or early 630s. The fact that Theodorakios was actually called *megaloprepestatos* when he functioned as pagarch (during the notorious politico-financial autocracy of the Patriarch Cyrus)[76] may favour the first possibility.[77]

At any rate, the issue raised by *SPP* X 138 is the problem of the sense in which villages such as those listed there could be said to belong to (to be 'of') aristocrats like Theodorakios and Theodosius (if not actually one or the other). We have seen that the smaller settlements called *epoikia* were certainly owned by private landholders, both physically integrated into a single complex of landholding and subject to the control and supervision of the employer.[78] But the problem posed by the *kōmai* which are said to 'belong to' private landholders is of a different order, and more complex. First, did the higher aristocracy control such villages as pagarchs, that is, by virtue of a quasi-official function, or did they actually own such villages in the sense in which they owned most *epoikia* and certainly the *epoikia* named after them?[79] Second, did different large landowners operate in the same villages or was there a tendency to divide up stretches of rural territory between the major *oikoi* and lesser aristocrats and thus avoid the same villages?

The papyri rarely contain solutions to questions like these since the meaning of a document is scarcely ever self-evident, given that 'by itself the papyrological document is inert and isolated',

[72] *P. Lond.* I 113 (10). 5 (639–40) = *WChr.* 18; cf. Worp, 'Regnal Formulas of the Emperor Heraclius', *JJP* 23 (1993) 230 f.

[73] See *CPR* X, p.154 for the references and dates; cf. *Catalogue*, Fayum 7c.

[74] See *Catalogue*, Fayum 7c.

[75] For the date, 3 Jan. 633, see *BL* 9.343. It is worth noting that the dimensions of the two papyri as given by Wessely are almost identical.

[76] Cf. J. Gascou, 'De Byzance à l'Islam: les impôts en Égypte après la conquête arabe', *JESHO* 26 (1983) 97–109, esp. 98.

[77] Cf. *P. Lond.* I 113 (10) = *WChr.* 8 where he arranges for the mass purchase of provisions *κατὰ κέλευσιν τοῦ δεσπότου ἡμῶν Κύρου τοῦ ἁγιοτ[άτ]ου καὶ θεοτιμήτ[ου] πάπα*, (l.14), perhaps our only papyrological reference to Cyrus.

[78] Cf. the characteristic Oxyrhynchite formula, *epoikion X ktēma Y*, where *Y* refers to the owner (in the genitive).

[79] Cf. the *ἐποίκιον καλούμενον Στρ[ατηγί]ου* in *CPR* X 127.7–8, the epoikion Eustochiou in *SPP* XX 239.9 and *CPR* X 45.1, etc.

as Bataille put it,[80] and its gradual elucidation requires a complex labour of totalization. Thus in *SPP* X 154 individual *chōria* are grouped under *ousiai*, with the general implication that villages or locations were divided between distinct estates. Again, in *SPP* X 111 two groups of villagers write a joint letter to a *comes* who is addressed as ὁ δεσπότης ἡμῶν, the term usually reserved for landowners who exuded a clear sense of authority.[81] In neither case is it obvious that individual estates or owners had established monopolies in these villages. What does seem clear is that in the bigger villages the chance of such monopolistic domination declined in direct proportion to the size and independence of the village—thus in Aphrodito, which was a *metrōkōmia*, the agrarian structure was characterized by a great diversity of landowners with even the μεγάλοι κτήτορες τῆς πόλεως[82] failing to establish any obvious, discernibly overwhelming, dominance in the agrarian landscape, while even the single biggest landholder (on the urban account, at least), the monastery of Apa Sourous, controlled not more than about a fifth of the total area registered under that description.[83] *Epoikia* and *kōmai* were very different sorts of worlds and it is possible that in the latter medium-scale landowners were of considerably greater importance, though the basis of this judgement remains purely impressionistic. Thus Flavius Philoxenus son of Ision, a *clarissimus*, who is described specifically as a 'landowner in Oxyrhynchus and in the village of Spania'[84] (γεουχῶν ἐν τῇ λαμπρᾷ Ὀξυρυγχιτῶν πόλει καὶ ἐπὶ κώμης Σπανίας)[85] dominated a whole quarter of the village with his 'massive residence' (since a lessee actually refers to that section of Spania as ἄμφοδον τῆς μεγάλης οἰκείας τῆς ὑμῶν λαμπρότητος,[86] probably implying that the quarter was named after the house). Yet Philoxenus was definitely not an aristocrat: we know from *PSI* I 77 (551)[87] that his father Ision had been a priest in the church of Oxyrhynchus[88]—at best the sort of social milieu where we find the Byzantine middle bureaucracy (for example, Flavius Taurinus

[80] A. Bataille, *Les papyrus (Traité d'études byzantines II)* (Paris, 1955) 2, 'Par lui-même le document papyrologique est donc inerte et isolé'.

[81] *SPP* X 111 (5/6c., ed. pr.), a letter from οἱ ἀπὸ κώμης Ἰβίωνος (καὶ) Μαγδόλων.

[82] *P. Cairo Masp.* 67060 = *WChr.* 297.2, see p. 126 above.

[83] *P. Freer Aphrodito* proves this.

[84] Otherwise associated with the Apions, cf. *P. Oxy.* XVI 2034, *P. Oxy.* LV 3805.93, 101 and probably *P. Oxy.* XVI 2058, since only the Apions would have been powerful enough to impose individual fines on a whole village!

[85] *P. Bad.* 172.5–6 (547).

[86] *P. Bad.* 172.14–16; the actual reading is ἐπ' ἀμφόδου τῆς μεγάλης οἰκείας τῇ ὑμῶν λαμπρότητι.

[87] Cf. *BL* 7.232.

[88] *PSI* I 77.3–6. Note that *P. Bad.* 172 intr. (p. 12) is inaccurate in describing Philoxenus himself as the priest.

II actually became a priest following his official career).[89] Again, *P. Cairo Masp.* I 67002 ii 24 (567) refers to the *φανερὰ `οἰκήματα´ λαμπρὰ τῶν ἀρχαίων κτητόρων μεγάλων τῆς κώμης*, showing that the affluent middle group were conspicuous in the bigger villages like Aphrodito where they must have constructed substantial and impressive buildings, though they need not necessarily have resided in them all or even most of the time.[90]

However, what this establishes is only that large owners were more likely to dominate (own as well as control) smaller villages than large ones. It says nothing specifically about the nature of agrarian power in late Byzantine Egypt and, in particular, about the basis on which landowners like the *megaloprepestatos* of *SPP* X 138 could establish or build up minor agrarian empires staffed and run, clearly, by a considerable estate bureaucracy. It also fails to answer the question whether, in the Oxyrhynchite, the Apions could actually be said to have 'owned', say, two-fifths of the land in this district and Cynopolis, as Jones asserts.[91] Whatever its precise relation to the issue of ownership, it is certain that the institution of the pagarchy did not simply formalize the de facto control which the higher aristocracy had come to exercise over the tax system of the rural areas but actively encouraged that process of control in a peculiar fusion of private and official power. Of course, Gascou has construed this as implying a permanent obliteration of the distinction between the categories of 'rent' and 'tax' and their mutual sublation in something called a 'rent-tax'. I have adduced grounds for rejecting this view[92] and also noted that in *Grands domaines* at least Gascou curiously avoids any explicit discussion of the relationship between the pagarchy and his (and Rémondon's) view, an eminently acceptable one, of a collaborative (rather than recalcitrant, subversive, or rebellious) aristocracy.[93] Yet the whole terminology of fiscal shares is of course directly linked to the operation of the pagarchy as an institution which delegated fiscal authority to local landowners, as Gascou observed at length in his article in *Byzantion*, and it

[89] *SB* IV 7369 (512) with *BL* 7.193.

[90] Cf. Tate, 'Les campagnes de la Syrie du Nord', 63–77, on the domestic architecture of the villages of the limestone massif in northern Syria, the best analogy I can think of for the description in *P. Cairo Masp.*, loc. cit.

[91] Cf. Jones, *LRE* 2.780, 'In ... the combined territories of Oxyrhynchus and Cynopolis which totalled 280,000 *arurae*, the Apion family alone owned two-fifths', followed by W. Liebeschuetz, 'The Origin of the Office of the Pagarch', *BZ* 66 (1973) 38–46, at 44. Jones based the deduction on *P. Oxy.* XVI 1909 (cf. *LRE* 2.1320 n. 28). Contrast Gascou, *Domaines*, 46, against inferring estate sizes from fiscal shares, correctly.

[92] See Ch. 4.

[93] See Rémondon, 'Les contradictions de la société égyptienne à l'époque byzantine', the fundamental statement of the model of 'collaboration'.

seems only logical to make its evolution an essential feature of the theory first outlined by Rémondon (especially in 'Les contradictions de la société égyptienne') and then restated, with considerable rigour but not a little ambiguity, by Gascou. Finally, the fact that Strategius is associated with no official position other than that of pagarch is thus surely significant, an unmistakable expression of the centrality of this institution, above all others, to the agrarian power of the later Byzantine period.

The Oxyrhynchite

In the Oxyrhynchite the patriciate was, of course, largely a monopoly of the Apions. Here, as in the Fayum, the average aristocrat was an *illustris* or something lower. Outside the Apion circle, only two Oxyrhynchus-related *patricii* are known—one of them the father of Flavia Christodote[94] who was owed the substantial sum of 61 lb. of gold by her brother, secured for him by the Alexandrian banker Flavius Eustathius (who was only a *clarissimus*).[95] The brother Cometes turns up in *P. Oxy.* XVI 2020 (from the 580s) with a substantial payment of 1165 artabas of barley, among private landholders the fourth biggest in the list (7.4 per cent of the total).[96] In *P. Oxy.* 2040, cash contributions for the public bath, his cash payment is almost precisely half the level assigned to the Apion *oikos* and this time the second highest in the list (15 per cent of the total payment).[97] Thus by the 560s (the presumed date of *P. Oxy.* 2040)[98] Cometes had become the formal head of an *oikos* inherited, presumably, from the *patricius* John, since both payments are described as δ(ιὰ) τοῦ οἴκ(ου) τοῦ ἐνδοξ(οτάτου) Κομήτου. The world presupposed in *PSI* I 76, his sister's affidavit, is thus that of a provincial aristocracy which moved, financially if not physically, between the bankers of Alexandria and estates in the province of Arcadia, where the *oikos* figured among the leading *politeuomenoi* of Oxyrhynchus.

The Oxyrhynchite payments lists are an excellent synopsis of the aristocracy which ran a provincial town in the decades between 560 and the 580s. The leading families of *endoxotatoi* paid 40.9 per

[94] It is possible that he is the person referred to in *P. Oxy.* XVI 1913.28, τῶν ὀρνίθ(ων) τοῦ ἐνδοξ(οτάτου) ἰλλουστρ(ίου) Ἰωάννου.

[95] See p. 137–8 above.

[96] *P. Oxy.* XVI 2020.24. For the date cf. Gascou, *Domaines*, 48.

[97] *P. Oxy.* XVI 2040.8, 4 solidi 8 keratia; line 5 refers to the Apions, δ(ιὰ) τοῦ ἐνδόξου οἴκ(ου), paying 8 solidi 15 keratia. In terms of my later remarks (p. 155 f.) on the 'mathematics of fiscal shares' it is worth noting that the share of Cometes' *oikos* seems to have declined to precisely half its previous level.

[98] Cf. Gascou, *Byzantion* 42 (1972) 64.

cent of the amount required in *P. Oxy.* 2020,[99] the *domus divina*, the single biggest payer, another 22.2 per cent, so close to two-thirds of the total payment derived from the higher aristocracy and the estates of the imperial household. (Adding the church, the proportion rises to 73 per cent.) If this is any indication of the concentration of actual holdings, this was obviously quite considerable, reflecting substantial divisions not only between agrarian classes but within the aristocracy itself. On average, owners classified as *megaloprepestatoi* (a middle aristocracy) contributed less than one-third of the average payment of the *endoxotatoi* (27.4 per cent),[100] a remarkable expression of the logic of aristocratic accumulation, that is, the tendency for the aristocracy to apply to itself the norms it considered valid for society as a whole (stratification by status and the underlying economic differentiation).

It is perhaps some indication of the rate of survival of our sources that of the eight bigger aristocrats in *P. Oxy.* 2020 (those with payments of 350 artabas or more) at least two turn up in other sources (if we exclude the complementary list, *P. Oxy.* 2040). Thus Cometes is known from his sister's affidavit, though not from any document which emanates directly from his own archive, and Anastasia appears in roughly ten other documents. Anastasia is the second woman known to us to have exercised the pagarch's function, with the guarantor in *P. Oxy.* XLIV 3204 (588) describing his village as [πα]γαρχουμένης ὑπὸ τῆς ὑμῶν ἐνδοξότητος.[101] By the date of this document, 588, Anastasia was an *endoxotatē illoustria*.[102] If this signifies a *promotion* from her status as a *megaloprepestatē illoustria*,[103] then it may contain some meaning for the date of *P. Oxy.* 2020 where she is still described as *megalopre(pestatē)*. *PSI* VIII 956.20 refers to an *illustris* Menas who may have been her father and who was, conceivably, a pagarch of Oxyrhynchus.[104] Van Haelst asserts that Anastasia possessed 'vastes propriétés' in and around Oxyrhynchus[105] but this is true only in a general sense, since the

[99] *P. Oxy.* XVI 2020.17, 18, 24, 25: four *endoxotatoi* show a total contribution of *c.*6,416 artabas = 40.89 per cent of the total.

[100] *P. Oxy.* XVI 2020.19, 20, 22: an average payment of 439.25 artabas (n = 3) against 1,604 (n = 4, cf. n. 99).

[101] *P. Oxy.* XLIV 3204.12.

[102] See Gascou, *Domaines*, 77, for the restorations which link *P. Oxy.* 3204 to Flavia Anastasia, and cf. *SB* VI 9561 (590).

[103] Cf. *SB* VI 9368.1, Ἀναστασίας τῆς μεγαλοπρε(πεστάτης) ἰλλου(στρίας), with Bagnall, *P. Turner*, p. 195 n. 4 for the date as 577/8.

[104] So Gascou, *Byzantion* 42 (1972) 70f., n. 3. The date is 567/8. Anastasia is described as the daughter of τοῦ τῆς ἐν[δό]ξου μνή[μ]ης Μηνᾶ Εὐδαίμονος in *SB* 9561.7, with *BL* 10.201.

[105] J. Van Haelst, 'De nouvelles archives: Anastasia, propriétaire à Oxyrhynchus (II) Le P.Giss.Univ.Bibl.inv. 33', *CE* 34 (1959) 292–9, at 296. Part of Anastasia's estate lay

differential in payment levels implies that her total assets in land were less than 30 per cent of the estate values (or sizes) controlled by the bigger aristocracy, such as the families of Justus and Ptolemaeus which had dominated the pagarchy in the 560s.[106] Since even these *oikoi* were at best only half as big as the Apions,[107] the difference in scale between Anastasia and the Apions presumably deprives the term 'vastes propriétés' of much meaning.

P. Oxy. XVI 2026, sixth-century accounts of the *megaloprepestatē* Christodora of Cynopolis, reflects the domestic consumption levels of a middling aristocratic estate in the course of one year[108] and gives us a rough idea of the size of the permanent staff—including a 15 per cent surcharge, the estate consumed 4,849 artabas of wheat in the course of a fifteenth indiction. On the standard managerial ration applied on the Apion estates, 24 artabas of wheat per annum,[109] this implies a staff strength of just over 200 employees. Of course, most ordinary employees were paid much less than this,[110] so it seems feasible to treat this as a minimum estimate of the size of the permanent labour force. On the estate (*ousia*) of the *stratēlatēs* John, son of the aristocrat Euphemia (who probably figures in *P. Oxy.* 2040, as a *megaloprepestatē*[111]), the *epikeimenos* received an annual wheat allowance of 36 artabas—apart from his cash payment, his wine, his ration of barley, and the fringe payments which he extracted directly from the labour force.[112] That owners like John or the Apions usually signed annual contracts with managerial levels who were clearly vital to their production needs shows a certain striving for efficiency. John's estate was extensively equipped with *sāqiyas* since the plots or farms in each *ktēma* bore the general

in or near Maiuma, which was probably in the region south-east of Oxyrhynchus, cf. *SB* VI 9561.21. *Pace* Van Haelst who writes, 'il est difficile de localiser ce village ou lieu' (p. 297), I can see no obvious problems in localizing Maiuma if one accepts that *P. Oxy.* VI 999 descr. (616/17) implies the general proximity of the various localities mentioned as part of Stephen's *pronoēsia*; the list includes Maiuma and Pangouleiou; P. was near Seryphis, according to *P. Harr.* 137 (2c.), cf. S. Daris, 'Ricerche di papirologia documentaria', *Aegyptus* 56 (1976) 47–95, esp. 70 ff., and Seryphis close to Oxyrhynchus, cf. P. Pruneti, *I centri abitati dell' Ossirinchite: Repertorio toponomastico* (Florence, 1981), map (mod. Eshrūba a few kilometres south-east of El Bahnasā).

106 *P. Oxy.* XVI 2020.19 (payment level), 2040.9–13 (pagarchy, with each *oikos* controlling half).

107 Cf. *P. Oxy.* XVI 2040 for the differential.

108 The gross output level implies an arable area of roughly 3,000 arouras, which is substantial but certainly below the 'patrician' level.

109 See App. 1, Table 11.

110 e.g. *P. Princ.* II 96 (6c., Apion estate, a modal ration of 12 artabas of wheat for male *paidarioi*), *P. Oxy.* XVI 1911.156, LV 3804.238 (Apion, 16 artabas for camel drivers), *P. Amh.* II 155 (an average of 14 artabas for *geōrgoi* on a Hermopolite estate).

111 *P. Oxy.* XVI 2040.16.

112 *P. Oxy.* XIX 2239.16–20, see App. 1, Table 11.

description *mēchanai,* implying that they were artifically irrigated and that perennial irrigation could be presumed for most or all of these fields.[113] John's workforce were the '*geōrgoi* of your Excellency', 'his' *geōrgoi* in the sense of workers subject to his authority. The contract reflects a visible concern with improvements in cultivation and with the attitudes of the *geōrgoi* to the tasks defined for them, to what modern managerial theory calls the employee's 'commitment to work'.[114] Finally, Euphemia herself, unlike Anastasia, had been a landowner in several districts, hence *γεουχοῦσα καὶ ἐνταῦθα,*[115] and this description is repeated for John who is called *γεουχῶν καὶ ἐνταῦθα* in *P. Oxy.* 2239, though unfortunately not attested in any other document from the Oxyrhynchite or elsewhere.

Thus below the Apion level (the *élite* aristocracy) the Oxyrhynchite can show a substantial stratum of medium aristocrats, families like those of the *endoxotatoi* Ptolemaeus and Justus who exercised joint control of the pagarchy in the 560s, or the numerous women whose status fluctuated between *megaloprepestatē* and *endoxotatē*, independent heads of households such as Anastasia, Euphemia, Christodora, or the less well-known *megaloprepestatai* Athanasia and Maria,[116] and of course their descendants like the *stratēlatēs* John.

The Fayum, Seventh Century

It was noted earlier that the connection between large landowners and the pagarchy becomes even more obvious in the seventh century.[117] Taken by region, the association is closest in the Fayum, where 48 per cent of all high-ranking landowners were pagarchs in the later period.[118] The Fayum aristocracy assigned central importance to this institution, while, conversely, the inference that most pagarchs were in fact powerful large landowners seems a perfectly plausible one.[119] Moreover, there is no evidence that the conquest

[113] *P. Oxy.* XIX 2239.14, *ἐν ἑκάστῳ κτήματι [τῆ]ς αὐτῆς οὐσίας [σ]πεῖραι τὰς γεουχικὰς μηχανάς.*

[114] *P. Oxy.* XIX 2239.13–16, esp. *[πα]ρασκευάσαι τοὺς πάντας γεωργοὺς ὑμετέρας ἐνδοξ(ότητος) . . . ἑτοίμως ἔχε[ι]ν πᾶσαν σπουδὴν συνεισενεγκεῖν εἰς βελτίονα ὄψιν τὰ ὑμέτερα γεουχικὰ ἀγρ[οι]κικὰ πράγματα ἐντεθῆναι.*

[115] *P. Oxy.* VII 1038.9 (568), a nuance not noted by J. Van Haelst, 'De nouvelles archives: Anastasia, propriétaire d'Oxyrhynchus', *CE* 33 (1958) 237–42, at 239, comparing Anastasia to Euphemia. Change *τῇ ἐνδόξ(ῳ)* to *τῇ ἐνδοξ(οτάτῃ)* in l. 7.

[116] *P. Oxy.* XVI 2020.20, 22.

[117] See pp. 140 f. above.

[118] Of eleven 7th-cent. Fayum pagarchs, 1 was a *patricius*, 3 were *illustres*, 4 *endoxotatoi*, 1 *megaloprepestatos*, and the last in date (Flavius Atias) went on to become Duke of the combined 'Duchy' of Arcadia and the Thebaid.

[119] Cf. Wilcken, *Grundzüge*, 231, also 83.

undermined the control which the landed aristocracy had established over the pagarchy. Thus, of the nine known landed pagarchs of the seventh-century Fayum, six are actually from the period after the conquest.[120] Indeed, our only substantial seventh-century archive contains the official and private papers of a pagarch who administered the district around Apollōnos Anō (mod. Edfu) in the last quarter of the seventh century—Papas, whose father Liberius had likewise been pagarch, on a dynastic pattern which was common in the aristocracy of this period.[121] On the other hand, the conquest did bring one fundamental change: there is no trace in the papyri of the Umayyad period of the great *oikoi* which had embodied the élite of the Byzantine aristocracy and, in a sense, represented the climax of late antique social evolution. Thus the survival and continued workings of the classic institutions of Byzantine Egypt cannot be the sign of a simple continuity—major changes did occur, if only because the most powerful group of the Byzantine period had now completely disappeared, and it is likely that the pagarchy itself no longer had the same meaning for the big landowners as it had, clearly, in the final century before the conquest.

It has been traditional to emphasize the essential conservatism of the Arabs, given the survival of a Graeco-Christian élite whose titles were quintessentially Byzantine.[122] But this view ignores the reality

[120] Flavius John, Flavius Stephanus/Cyrus, Flavius Paul/Stephanus (his son), Flavius Petterios, Flavius Atias, and the *illustris* in *BGU* II 396 which is from the Arab period ('sicher aus arab. Zeit', *BL* 1. 44). For references see my *Catalogue*, Fayum 7c. *SB* XVIII 13898 (6/7c.), is probably from the archive of Flavius Stephanus; it is an order to pay issued by Damianus to the 'secretary at Paki'; for the conjunction of these names, cf. *SPP* VIII 1139, where Stephanus' estate cashier Damianus is asked to handle payments relating to work at the '*proastion* Paki'.

[121] R. Rémondon, *Papyrus grecs d'Apollônos Anô* (Cairo, 1953). Liberius appears in BM 8903, cf. Crum, *ZAS* 60 (1925) 106, J. Gascou and K. Worp, 'Problèmes de documentation Apollinopolite', *ZPE* 49 (1982) 83–95, at 84.

[122] Arab conservatism has been very much part of an orthodoxy among papyrologists familiar with the later material: cf. Bell, *P. Lond.* IV, p. xviii, id., 'The Administration of Egypt under the 'Umayyad Khalifs', *BZ* 28 (1928) 278–86, esp. 281, Rémondon, *P. Apoll.*, p. 118 ('nous ne pouvons que reprendre la conclusion de Wilcken: *autant que possible, les Arabes ont laissé subsister le système fiscal et administratif anterieur*, et, à l'échelon local, ils l'ont conservé à peu près integralement'). For specific institutional survivals cf. Rémondon, *P. Apoll.* 46 introd., on the *defensor civitatis*, *P. Apoll.* 47 introd., on the *boēthos tou logistēriou*, Gascou, *JESHO*, 1983, 100 ff., on the *dēmosion*, etc., *KRU* 10 (8 Dec. 722), the *Dux* was still called *eukleestatos* and functioned from Antinoopolis, *CPR* VIII 84.2 (7/8c.), referring to a *polit(euomenos)*, *P. Ross.-Georg.* III 23 (early 8c.), a *ripa(rios)*, *P. Apoll.* 31 (*c.*713?), a *bucellarius*. But note the innovations: first, if Gascou and Worp are correct in their suggestion that Jordanes presided over a unified territory combining the former provinces of Arcadia and the Thebaid (cf. *ZPE* 49 (1982) 90, 'C'est le premier cas net d'union administrative de ces deux provinces') then this radical change had already occurred by October 669, the date of *P. Merton* II 100; second, new titles (if not functions) like *symboulos* (*P. Apoll.* 2.4), *amiras pagarchias*

of the conquest. The disappearance of the *oikoi* signified not only a permanent weakening of the aristocracy but administrative changes which—through the introduction of an exceptionally centralized regime—deprived the surviving district élites of the sort of control which landowners had enjoyed in the classic era of the pagarchy. From an expression of aristocratic control the pagarchy became a merely administrative arrangement with a decisive reduction in the status and power of the pagarchs. The Duke Jordanes could threaten the pagarchs of the Thebaid with a fine of 1,000 solidi,[123] and the whole tone of Qurrah's correspondence with Basilius shows that pagarchs were mere functionaries subject to the harrassment of the higher state authorities.[124] By the latter part of the seventh century (certainly by 677)[125] the pagarchy was decisively territorialized, *παγαρχία* signifying a merely territorial unit whose boundaries coincided with the old nomes or Byzantine *poleis*.[126]

(*KRU* 70, dated 750) and *epik(eimenos) pagarch(ias)* (*SPP* III 260, etc., see n. 126); the last of these is already attested in *P. Ross.-Georg.* IV 1.20 (710); third, a completely new system of taxation, *pace* Bell, *BZ* 28 (1928) 281 ('In the taxation system the new government made even fewer changes'), cf. Gascou, *JESHO*, 1983, 101 f., on *diagraphon* in *SB* VIII 9756 (653). Finally, note the almost total disappearance of the old terminology (*geouchon*, *oikos*, etc.) by which the aristocracy had described itself.

[123] *P. Apoll.* 9 (incorporating *PSI* XII 1266, acquired Cairo 1938), cf. H. Bell, 'An Official Letter of the Arab Period', *JEA* 31 (1945) 75–84, a copy of a circular, *ἴσο(ν) σιγελλίου*, addressed to *τοῖς ἅπασι παγάρχ(οις) Θηβαΐδ(ος)* (B 5), esp. its threatened fine (l. 3). The date is 675/6 or 660/1, *BL* 8.10.

[124] e.g. *P. Lond.* IV 1338, cf. H. I. Bell, 'Translations of the Greek Aphrodito Papyri in the British Museum', *Der Islam* 2 (1911) 269 ff., 372 ff., 3 (1912) 132 ff., 369 ff., 4 (1913) 87 ff., and add H. Cadell, 'Nouveaux fragments de la correspondance de Ḳurrah ben Sharīk', *Récherches de Pap.* 4 (1967) 107–60 (= *SB* X 10453–60).

[125] Cf. W. F. G. J. Stoetzer and K. A. Worp, 'Zwei Steuerquittungen aus London und Wien', *Tyche* 1 (1986) 195–202, at 198–9, *P. Vindob.* G 39738 (= *PERF* 573), referring to the [*χωρίον*] *Ἀπίωνος παγαρχ(ίας) Ἡρακλε(οπολίτου)* (l. 10).

[126] Since the evidence for this has never been collected (much less discussed), cf. (from north to south): *SPP* X 297 ii 1 (7/8c.), *παγαρχ(ίας) Μέμφε(ως)*, *SPP* X 299 verso (7/8c.), *παγαρχ(ίας) Μέμφεως*, but not *SPP* VIII 960, *παίδ( ) οὐσί(ας) παργαρχ( ) Μεμφ( )*, cf. *BL* 7. 257, 9. 340 (→ *Πιναρχ(θ) μισθ(οῦ)*); *CPR* VIII 73.1–2 (694) (= *PERF* 586), *ἀπὸ χω(ρίου) Παντικ(οῦ) Ἀλλ[αγῆς] παγ(αρ)χ(ίας) Ἀρσινοΐτ(ου)*, *CPR* VIII 75.1 (*c*.698), *ἀπὸ χω(ρίου) Ἀνίνου παγαρχ(ίας) Ἀρσινοΐτο[υ]*, *SPP* VIII 1333.3 (prob. 751/52), *[ἐπικ]ειμ(ένου) π(αγαρ)χ(ίας) Ἀρ[σινοΐτου]*, cf. K. A. Worp, 'Studien zu spätgriechischen, koptischen und arabischen Papyri', *BSAC* 26 (1984) 99–107, esp. 103 ff., *SPP* III 260 (prob. 752/3), *ἐπικ(είμενος) παγαρχ(ίας) Ἀρσιν[ο]ΐτου*, *P. Vindob.* G 41268 (*c*.759–75), cf. *Archiv* 31 (1985) 17, *ἐπικ(ειμένῳ) π[αγ(αρ)]χ(ίας) [Ἀρσινοΐτου]*, *SPP* X 169.1 (762, cf. Worp, *BSAC* 1984, p.103 f.),] *ἐπικ(είμενος) παγαρχ(ίας) Ἀρσιν(οΐτου)*, P. Berol. 2966.9 (mid-8c.), cf. *Archiv* 31 (1985) 14, *ἐπικεί(μενος) π(αγαρ)χ(ίας) [Ἀρσινοΐτου* (?)], *SPP* X 175.2 (8c.), *ἐπι]κείμ(ενος) παγαρ[χ](ίας) Ἀρσινοΐτου* ; *SPP* VIII 1198.2 (25 Apr. 664 or 25 Apr. 679, Worp, *BL* 8.451), *ἀπὸ χ(ωρίου) Τεκμι παγ(αρχίας) Ἡρακλ(εοπολίτου)*, *P. Vindob.* G 39738 (677), see n. 125, *SPP* VIII 1191.2 (7c.), *παγαρχ(ίας) Ἡρακλε(οπολίτου)*, *SPP* X 217.1 (7/8c.), *ἀπὸ χ(ωρίου) Δάφν[ης] παγαρ[χίας Ἡρακλεοπολίτου]*, *SPP* XX 206. 2–3 (7c.), *ἀπὸ χ(ωρίου) Πεσεν παγ(αρ)χ(ίας) Ἡρακλ(εοπολίτου)*, and *ἀπὸ χ(ωρίου) Πακι παγ(αρ)χ(ίας) Ὀξυρυγχ(ίτου)*, *SB* XVIII 13870.1–2 (early 8c.), *ἀπὸ χ(ωρίου)*

This implied a permanent end to the system of self-allocation of quotas among the leading *oikoi* of each district, the peculiar expression, in Egypt, of the power which the provincial aristocracy had progressively conquered following its economic evolution in the late Roman period.

Fiscal documents such as *P. Oxy.* 127 recto (late 6c.) are strong grounds for believing that (prior to the conquest) the top aristocracy had allocated the fiscal burden in precise mathematical ratios, and that these shares were a convenient form in which each *oikos* grasped the precise extent of its obligations in a given indiction. Of course, there is much about this system that we simply do not know. For example, how were the shares determined? How often were they revised? Were shares divisible in the sense that parts or fractions could be assigned to other *oikoi*? What is certain is that the system was not peculiarly Oxyrhynchite and that it must have operated throughout Egypt. As Gascou has noted, one of the clearest proofs of this is *P. Ant.* II 110 (6c.), where the top aristocracy of Antinoopolis divided a certain payment 'according to the eight shares'.[127] Among the Fayum documents the *patricia* Sophia's reference to her 'one-fourth share' could perhaps be an allusion to this system, as Gascou suggests.[128] Otherwise *SPP* X 249 (633) is in my view the best expression of its workings. Since a substantial portion of the document is missing at the start, it is difficult to be precise about its nature and in particular about whether the payments listed in the previous columns and before col. 2 line 8 represented the contributions of a single estate (as the terminology—*dioikētēs*, *argentar(itēs)*[129]—implies). At any rate, if we concentrate on the contributions of the great aristocrats listed

Φιλονίκου παγαρχ(ίας) Ἡρακλε(οπολίτου); *P. Lond.* IV 1347.4–5 (710), *χωρί(ου) Μουναχθη παγαρχίας Ἀνταίο(υ) καὶ Ἀπολλωνος*, cf. *P. Lond.* IV 1435.8 (715/16), *P. Ross-Georg.* IV 25 (8c.?), [*χ(ωρίον) Μουναχθη παγ(αρχίας) Ἀν(ταίου) (καὶ) Ἀπ[ολλωνος*]; *P. Berl.* 10607 (early 8c.), cf. S. Timm, *Das christlich-koptische Ägypten in arabischer Zeit* (6 vols; Wiesbaden, 1984–92) 172, *τῷ ἐνδ/ ἀμίρα ἀπὸ παγαρχ/ Διοσπ(ό)λεως Λάτω(ν)* ; *KRU* 106 (735), **ⲉⲩⲕⲗ/ ⲁⲙⲓⲣⲁ ⲧⲏⲥ ⲡⲁⲅⲁⲣⲭⲓⲁⲥ ⲉⲣⲙⲟⲛⲑⲉⲟⲥ**, *KRU* 70 (750), **ⲉⲩⲕ ⲁⲙⲓⲣⲁ ⲡⲁⲅⲁⲣⲭⲓⲁⲥ ⲉⲣⲙⲟⲛⲑⲉⲟⲥ**; *P. Lond.* IV 1435.8 (715–16), *παγαρχ(ίας) Λάτω(ν)*. It is abundantly clear from this list that by the 8th cent. the old nomes had been transformed into pagarchies. The process began before April 677, the date of *P. Vindob.* G 39738. Finally, cf. *P. Lond.* IV, Index, 633 f. s.v. *παγαρχία*.

[127] *P. Ant.* II 110.1 (6c.), *Μερ(ισμὸς) χρυσ(οῦ) νομ(ισμάτων) κ̅δ̅ κατὰ τῶν ή/ μερί(δων), ὅυτως*.. cf. Gascou, *Domaines*, 47–8.

[128] *SPP* VIII 1091.8 ff., *κατὰ τὴν ἀνήκουσαν μοι μοῖραν ὑπερ ἐνάτης ἰνδ(*), referring to *εἰς τὸ δ''* (l. *τέταρτον*) (*καὶ*) *κδ''* (l. *εἰκοσιτέταρτον*) *μέρ(ος) τούτων* in l. 4, Gascou, *Domaines*, 45.

[129] *SPP* X 249 ii 1, *Paulou argentar(iou)* can also be read *Paulou argentar(itou)* following *CPR* XIV 41.7 (6/7c.) which is clearly from a large estate and refers to *Μηνᾶς ἀργενταρίτ(ης)*, 'cashier'.

in col. ii, ll. 8–12 and on the total payment registered in line 13 (calculating this as 20,963 artabas (received) + 1,237 artabas (owing) = 22,200 artabas) it is possible to discern a "mathematics" of fiscal allocations. The *stratēlatēs* Theodosius who turns up in *P. Prag.* I 64 (636) as the Duke of Arcadia and who was obviously a powerful individual, is here listed against a payment of 4,000 artabas, which is exactly 49 per cent of the total stated for the four great aristocrats, 8,163 artabas.[130] Thus Patricius, Cyrillus, and the heirs of Eustochius paid a total of 4,163 artabas.[131] If we isolate the 163 artabas as a 4 per cent surcharge on a total payment of 4,000 artabas, Theodosius' share works out to precisely 50 per cent (of the total for the four households). Of the remaining 50 per cent (with or without the surcharge, it makes no difference), the heirs of Eustochius contribute precisely 44.4 per cent (1,850 art.), Patricius contributes 33.3 per cent (1,388 art.), Cyrillus contributes 22.2 per cent (925 art.). The beauty of this allocation is immediately apparent and obviously reflects a very precise calculation of predetermined shares worked out in careful consideration of the resulting ratios between individual *oikoi*. Thus the Eustochius share is precisely twice the level of that paid by Cyrillus, and Patricius' share exactly half way between them, as if their shares had been added and then divided by two to determine the amount due from his *oikos*. Now if we calculate these payments against the computed total of 22,200 artabas, it is clear that the share of each *oikos* was in fact calculated as a determinate fraction of the total—the Eustochius heirs pay one-twelfth, Cyrillus pays one-twenty-fourth and Patricius one-sixteenth. In short, the top aristocracy of late Byzantine Egypt clearly functioned with an obvious sense of solidarity, bound by their fiscal obligations and binding themselves collectively to a system of shares whose precise internal distribution must have reflected the underlying distribution of economic power between the *oikoi*. *SPP* X 249 shows us that this system survived into the last years before the conquest and almost certainly disappeared with the sudden extinction of the *oikoi* themselves.

The families mentioned in *SPP* X 249 (633) were the last great representatives of the former Byzantine aristocracy. The conquest broke the backbone of the aristocracy, retaining the external attributes of Byzantine administration in a framework which massively altered its content. Centralization deprived the surviving élites of any power other than the purely administrative one of enforcing and realizing the innumerable demands (ἐπιστάλματα) formulated in

[130] *SPP* X 249 ii 8, 12. [131] *SPP* X 249 ii 9–11.

Fusṭāṭ. The pagarchs themselves were reduced to simple functionaries. Consequently, even if big landowners continued to exercise control over the office of the pagarch (in the period after 641), the framework within which that control operated was a completely different one.[132] The traditional association between landownership and pagarchic authority survived the conquest but was deprived of the peculiar significance which its emergence had heralded in the classic period of the Byzantine large estate.

One implication of these profound changes is an immensely reduced scale of individual landholdings. It is inconceivable that magnates like Flavius Theodosius or Strategius *paneuphēmos*, let alone the Apions, could have survived in Arab Egypt. It follows that the surviving aristocracy—*illustres* like Flavius Stephanus, who retained an *antigeouchos*, and pagarchs like Flavius Petterios—can no longer be conceived on purely Byzantine models since their official titles were, on the whole, similar to those of the former aristocracy while their economic power was undoubtedly much reduced.[133] This reduction in the scale of landownership coupled with the enormously increased pressure of money taxes may have led the more enterprising landholders to seek increases in productivity largely through further investments in irrigation. At any rate, it is a curious coincidence that our last precisely dated lease should also be the one to contain the *highest* money rent attested in our entire sample of surviving leases. In *SB* XVI 12481, dated 668, Petterios, addressed as ἐνδοξότατος πάγαρχος, leases an orchard of 1 aroura in the rich suburban countryside around Arsinoe for the astonishing rent (*dēmosion*) of 8⅔ solidi. It is unlikely that any *pōmaritēs* would have undertaken such a contract unless he hoped to be able to extract a gross output worth approximately twice that level to compensate for the effort of cultivating the orchard and to defray his other costs. This implies a very high level of productivity (a gross output worth at least 16 solidi per annum), and the solution must obviously lie in an incomparably higher intensity of cultivation, supported, of course, by the constant infusions of water.[134]

[132] Moreover, even if the office began to reacquire a certain prestige with the purely Arab pagarchs (cf. G. Poethke, 'Pagarchen im Papyrus Berolinensis 2966', *APF* 31 (1985) 13–15, at 14, 'Die Leitung einer Pagarchie galt als so bedeutend, daß diese Stelle ab Ende des 7. Jahrhunderts in steigendem Maße mit Arabern besetzt wurde'), the latter were primarily officials, not landowners.

[133] At the social level Petterios describes himself simply as *ktētōr*, cf. *SPP* VIII 1188, 1079, which is perhaps significant.

[134] Note the equipment available in this orchard—*πωμάριον σύμφυτ[ον σύν]δενδρον ὅσου ἐστὶν ἀρουρηδοῦ μετὰ καὶ τοῦ ἐν αὐτῷ ἡμίσεως μέρους λά[κκου καὶ] μηχανῆς καὶ μηχανοστασίου καὶ μηχ[αν]ικῶν ὀργάν[ων καὶ] τῶν δύο βοειδίων* (*SB* XVI 12481.13–16, dated 28 Nov. 668).

The only comparable document I have been been able to find is *P. Merton* I 49 (purchased at Edfu), which, significantly, also dates from the period after 641 and involves the extraordinary rent of 31¼ solidi for an eighth part of a *ktēma*. The editors conclude that the total holding 'must have been a very large estate'[135] but the implication is unnecessary, if I am correct in supposing that the more enterprising landholders were being forced to effect increases in productivity and that these would affect both the level of rents and land values.[136]

Finally, the relentless pressure for taxation in money would also mean that despite the commercial decline which is supposed to have occurred in the Mediterranean of the seventh century, Egyptian landowners and rural communities were undoubtedly forced to meet their monetary obligations through increased production for the market (or participation in it as wage labourers), on lines similar to those described by the Chronicle of Pseudo-Dionysius for Mesopotamia in the eighth century,[137] and thus that in the territories that fell to the Muslims commercialization, far from collapsing, was probably stronger than ever. But these were pressures already evident in the latter part of the sixth century when the reign of Maurice introduced a second (or third) great 'leap forward' in monetary taxation following Anastasius' commutation of the land tax late in the fifth century.[138]

In fact, the latter part of the sixth century is precisely when the export of Egyptian wine is first attested, in any significant way, in the ceramic evidence.[139] The important indication here is not the actual scale of exports (which may well have been low) but the fact that Egyptian landowners felt the need to raise the commer-

[135] *P. Merton* I, p. 153.

[136] *P. Flor.* XVIII 2 (7c.), of uncertain provenance but from the south (cf. ξυλικὸν ὄργανον in l. 1), involves 34.66 solidi as the purchase price of a farm fully equipped with the usual irrigation machinery—the biggest single payment recorded next to the 40 solidi which Sarapodorus had paid for 8 arouras early in the fifth century, see p. 121 f. at n. 75.

[137] See Cahen, *Arabica* 1 (1954) 136–52.

[138] The evidence is *P. Oxy.* XVI 1909 which Gascou, *Domaines*, 46 n. 267, dates to the reign of Maurice, citing John of Nikiu, 95.21, cf. *Domaines*, 11. The second great 'leap forward' may have been the reign of Justinian.

[139] Cf. Carthage Late Roman Amphora 7 (Riley LR 6), *Type B*, Riley, 'The Coarse Pottery from Berenice', in J. A. Lloyd (ed.), *Excavations at Sidi Khrebish Benghazi (Berenice)*, 3 vols. (Tripoli, n.d.) 2.91–467, at 224 f., Peacock and Williams, Class 52. C. Panella, 'Anfore', in L. Anselmino *et al.*, 'Cartagine', *SRIT* 3.163–95, at 178, dates the export of LR 7 to the Carthage market to the *end* of the 6th cent.; also cf. 270, 'A Cartagine le presenze piu rilevanti sembrano appartenere ai contesti della fine del VI-inizi del VII secolo (8% *ca* negli scavi americani)', and R. S. Valenzani, 'Anfore', in Anselmino *et al.*, 'Cartagine', *SRIT* 3.192, 'Da notare la comparsa della *Late Roman* 7 di produzione egiziana', about the late 6th/early 7th cent.

cialization process to this new level, beyond the huge Alexandria market.[140] This also implies, of course, that despite the massive political upheavals of the later sixth and early seventh centuries there was no perceptible decline in the commercial activity of Egyptian wine producers of the late Byzantine period and, if anything, an actual expansion.[141] In the Fayum almost every major rural site can be associated with wine production even and indeed especially in this late period. It is remarkable, however, that in the Fayum at least wine growing spread beyond the narrow circle of the aristocracy to include the most diverse strata of the local upper and middle classes. Aurelius Andreas, who like most Fayum landlords extracted a share of 75 per cent, was a *grammateus*,[142] Menas son of Pousi a *chartopratēs*,[143] Appa Cyrus son of Theodore an *ostiarius*,[144] Justus a notary and senior manager (*oikonomos*) for the church of the martyr Theodore.[145] There is no doubt, however, that the bulk of the activity was concentrated in the hands of the aristocracy, whether the producers were élite aristocrats like Flavius Strategius[146] or middling aristocrats like the pagarch Flavius Menas[147] or the smaller aristocracy of counts such as a certain Count Damianus who formulated the quantity of work assigned on an irrigation job in terms of the number of ζυγά.[148]

Around Antaeu and Hermopolis

One of the rare occurrences of a *patricius* outside the small circle of great *oikoi* which dominated the Fayum and the Oxyrhynchite

[140] Riley's LR 6 Type B 'is the dominant amphora of the late Roman levels from the Polish excavations at Alexandria', 'Coarse Pottery', 225. It also dominated the more local district markets, but 'is not well represented in other parts of the Mediterranean'.

[141] Cf. W. Kaegi, 'Egypt on the Eve of the Muslim Conquest', in C. F. Petry (ed.), *The Cambridge History of Egypt*. 1: *Islamic Egypt, 640–1517* (Cambridge, 1998) 34–61, referring to 'the vitality and volume of commerce in the 630s' (at 44).

[142] *P. Vindob. Inv* G 25652 = A. Jördens, 'Teilpachtverträge aus dem Arsinoites', *ZPE* 65 (1986) 107–22, at 108 f. (early 7c.).

[143] *BGU* I 319 (630–41, *BL* 8.23).

[144] *P. Ross.-Georg.* III 51 (630), for the date cf. *BL* 7.171.

[145] See *Catalogue*, Fayum 7c. Restore υἱῷ τοῦ [μα]καρίου [Νειλάμμ(ωνος) ἀπὸ τῆς αὐτῆς πόλεως] χ(αίρειν) in *P. Ross.-Georg.* III 55.7–8 (prob. 24 Apr. 630, *BL* 8.291), following *SB* I 4483.4 (621, *BL* 7.184). *SPP* III 164 refers to the church of *Saint* Theodore, so *[megal]ou* in *P. Ross.-Georg.* III 55 may not be the best restoration, *[hagi]ou* seems more natural. His connection with wine is established by *SB* I 4488 (635).

[146] *BGU* II 368 (615), receipt of a *kouphokeramourgos*. *SPP* X 78, a wine account arranged by *choria*, may come from the archive of Strategius.

[147] *SPP* XX 240 (622), cf. *BL* 7.264. Fantoni, *CPR* XIV, p. 42, calls this a contract of advance sale but neither the form nor the description on the verso (*apodeix(is) loi( )*...) support this.

[148] *SB* VI 9459 (7c.), with *CPR* X, p. 155 (read κόμες). The workload appears in ll. 14 ff.

is Flavius Athanasius. He was Duke of the Thebaid for a second year in 567 when he received a famous petition from the villagers of Aphrodito.[149] The fact that apart from his other titles he is also addressed as *ἐνδοξότατος στρατηλάτης* is of some significance, given that Athanasius also turns up in *P. Oxy*. XVI 1920 (563) in control of a substantial paramilitary contingent.[150] The connection between his title in *P. Cairo Masp*. I 67002 (567) and his role in *P. Oxy*. XVI 1920 seems to me to be strong support for Rémondon's view of the Byzantine *stratēlatai* as 'military, or more often civilian, imperial officials in regular control of troops of bucellarii'.[151] But again, as with the pagarchy, it is important to see this formalized control over paramilitary forces as the expression of a decisive shift in the balance of power between the state and the eastern aristocracy, the institutionalization, under aristocratic pressure, of a practice which had become regular on the new estates of the fifth century, certainly by 476 when the emperor Leo attempted to ban the retention of *bucellarii* by the big landowners.[152] Thus the usual definition of the issue of the *stratēlatai* in terms of whether the title implied an actual military command or was purely honorific is somewhat misleading, since the function was not a traditional military one but a recognition of the landowners' de facto control over armed forces and a formalization of that power despite the largely private ends for which landlords doubtless used and retained the services of such personnel. Durliat is correct in noting that the title is usually associated with the aristocracy,[153] but fails to establish the connection between them through the fact that the large estates had increasingly modified the composition of their personnel through the regular inclusion of armed guards who were indeed, in Fikhman's apt description, simply 'armed servants of the estate'.[154]

[149] *P. Cairo Masp*. I 67002 (567); cf. *PLRE* IIIA, pp.145 f., Athanasius 3, and N. Gonis, 'Six Notes on Documentary Papyri', *ZPE* 129 (2000) 179–81, at 180, for other references.

[150] *P. Oxy*. XVI 1920.1, + *Γνῶσις τοῦ δοθ(έντος) ἀναλώμ(ατος) τοὶς ἀνθρ(ώποις) τοῦ ὑπερφυεστ(άτου) πατρικίου Ἀθανασίου ἐλθ(οῦσιν) ἐνταῦθ(α) ἀπὸ Θηβαείδος*. For the date, cf. *BL* 10.145.

[151] Rémondon, *Akten des XIII Int.Papyrologenkongresses*, 369, and *JJP* 18 (1974) 27.

[152] *CJ* 9.12.10 (476), 'Omnibus per civitates et agros habendi bucellarios vel Isauros armatosque servos licentiam volumus esse praeclusam' (It is our desire that no one shall have the license to retain armed bands of *bucellari* or Isaurians or slaves on their estates or in the towns). Of course, the practice of retaining such forces continued and became quite traditional, cf. *Nov. Just*. 116 (542) for a later reaction.

[153] See n. 38 above.

[154] I. F. Fikhman, 'On the Structure of the Egyptian Large Estate in the Sixth Century', in *Proceedings of the Twelfth International Congress of Papyrology*, 127–32, at 129, also describing the *bucellarii* as 'military servants of a large estate'. O. Schmitt, 'Die Buccellarii. Eine Studie zum militärischen Gefolgschaftswesen in der Spätantike', *Tyche* 9 (1994) 147–74, esp. 167 ff., argues that landowners deployed such troops in a

The chief cause behind the paramilitarization of the estates was probably their increased exaction of revenue in the form of gold. To the extent that such a tendency reflected inherent features of the organization of the new estates, the retention of armed forces of a quasi-official character and the corresponding description of big landowners as *stratēlatai*—a practice which is attested till at least the third quarter of the seventh century[155]—were not incidental features of the Byzantine estate economy but intrinsic to its whole form of development.

P. Cairo Masp. I 67002 (567) is one of the clearest expressions of the internal divisions within the aristocracy between different groups of differing status. Thus Athanasius, as a *patricius*, represented the élite level, the absolute summit of the provincial aristocracy, those who, more obviously than the other groups in their class, connected the provinces to the imperial state and the aristocracy based in Constantinople. Below him was the *illustris* Serenus whom the villagers of Aphrodito were careful not to criticize despite a certain association with the pagarch Menas.[156] He appears repeatedly in the Aphrodito papyri, usually as the *ἐνδοξότατος ἰλλούστριος πάγαρχος τοῦ γ′ (τριτου) μέρους Ἀνταίου*, 'pagarch of the one-third share of Antaeu'.[157] *P. Ant.* III 206 refers to a *patricius* Athanasius and an *illustris* Serenus, obviously the same pair, with payments against each of them for a fourth indiction. Serenus' payment was small by comparison with Athanasius', 9 modii (?) compared to 84,[158] but it is best not to base economic deductions on isolated documents of this type.

One document in which Serenus appears several times is *P. Flor.* III 298. Fournet's dating of this to the late 550s now supersedes Rémondon's proposal for a date *c.*544/5[159] but it still helps to fix the date of the pagarchy of Serenus to a period much earlier than is usually supposed.[160] At this time his colleague in the pagarchy was

purely official capacity. However, it seems to me that the distinction was a largely formal one, as the references in *Nov. Just.* 30, c.5, 7, suggest.

155 Cf. Flavius Stephanus in *P. Ross.-Georg.* III 53 (673/4 or 674/5).

156 *P. Cairo Masp.* I 67002 ii 2–4; the date is 567.

157 *P. Flor.* III 298 14–15, 19–20, 25, etc. (*c.*560), *P. Cairo Masp.* III 67325 III verso 12. For the date of these documents, now see J.-L. Fournet, 'Le système des intermédiaires dans les reçus fiscaux byzantins et ses implications chronologiques sur le dossier de Dioscore d'Aphrodité', *APF* 46 (2000) 233–47, at 241ff.

158 *P. Ant.* III 206.10, 13–14 (7c., ed. pr.), an account on papyrus of good quality, receipts of a *catholicus* Theodore for Athanasius, *[ἐν]τάγι(ον) τ̀οῦ′ αὐτ̀οῦ′ (ὑπὲρ) τ̀οῦ′ πατρικίου Ἀθανασίου (ὑπὲρ) δ ἰνδ(ικτίονος) μό( ) πδ*, and for Serenus, *ἐντάγι(ον) τ̀οῦ′ αὐτ̀οῦ′ (ὑπὲρ) Σερήνὸυ′ ἰλλ(ουστρίου) καταβληθ(ὲν) δ(ιὰ) τ̀οῦ′ ἐνδοξ(οτάτου) ἰλλ(ουστρίου) (ὑπὲρ) δ ἰνδ(ικτίονος) μό( ) θ*. The resolution of *μο( )* remains uncertain.

159 Rémondon, in *Studi in onore di Edoardo Volterra*, 6 vols. (Milan, 1971) 5.769–81. Cornelius son of Philantinous also appears in *P. Flor.* III 297.231, dated 525/6 (*BL* 9.86), making Maspero's date for *P. Cairo Masp.* 67325 (see n. 160) impossible.

160 *P. Cairo Masp.* III 67325 is dated 'après 585', *P. Strasb.* 699 'fin du VI siecle'.

a certain John who controlled the remaining two-thirds, *πάγαρχος τοῦ (διμοίρου) μέρους Ἀνταίου*.[161] Since he held this office in the late 550s, he is unlikely to be the pagarch John who turns up in a receipt dated 589,[162] or the *κόμ(ες) (καὶ) ἐμ(βολάτωρ)* of a fodder account published recently by MacCoull.[163] Nor would he have been the *endoxotatos* Count John whose daughter possessed a vineyard just north of the monastery of Apa Victor in the 530s.[164] *This* John may well be John son of Cometas who figures in Justinian's *Edict* xiii.24 a few years later, and who was Duke of the Thebaid by 537 (see App. 4). If his daughter was Patricia, who turns up as pagarch with Julianus *c.*553[165]—acting through Flavius Menas her *dioikētēs* (note that the daughter of Count John employed a Flavius Menas as her *procurator*)[166]—then it is likely that she succeeded her father in that function on a pattern which tended to make the pagarchy hereditary, or, at any rate, to allow for a certain dynastic control. Her co-pagarch Flavius Julianus was a former governor (*ἀπὸ ἀρχόντων*),[167] at some stage, apparently, a prefect,[168] and evidently the first of such officials to initiate the protracted struggle to bring Aphrodito under pagarchic control.[169] He was blamed by the villagers for increasing the tax rates, doubling the assessment on arable (from 2 to 4 keratia per aroura).[170] He was one of the *μεγάλοι κτήτορες τῆς πόλεως*, owner of an estate (*ousia*) which paid at least part of its taxes (for the land at Aphrodito) *εἰς τὸ κωμητικόν*, that is, on the village account.[171] A

[161] *P. Cairo Masp.* III 67325 iii verso 10–12, *P. Flor.* III 298.4, 9–10, etc.

[162] *SB* VI 9144 ('589' in the ed.princ., but from the Arab period according to *BL* 8.340).

[163] Cf. P. Hyvernat inv. 372 = L. S. B. MacCoull, 'An Account of Fodder for Pack-Horses', *ZPE* 25 (1977) 155–8, dated 587.

[164] *P. Cairo Masp.* I 67104 (530). He could also have been the *megaloprepestatos komes* John who was asked to investigate the affairs of the monastery of Stratonikis (in *P. Fouad* I 87), cf. Gascou, 'P. Fouad 87: les monastères pachômiens et l'état byzantin', *BIFAO* 76 (1976) 157–84, at 177, n.1.

[165] *P. Lond.* V 1660.5–7 (*c.*553). In *P. Cairo Masp.* I 67104.2 I would propose [*Φλ(αουΐα) Πατρικί*]*α τῇ μεγαλοπρε*[*πεσ*]*τάτῃ θυγατρὶ το`ῦ´ μεγαλοπρ*[*ε*]*πεστάτο(υ) καὶ ἐν*[*δ*]*οξοτάτο(υ) κό*[*μι*]*τος Ἰωάννο(υ)*.

[166] Cf. *P. Cairo Masp.* I 67104.2–3.

[167] *P. Lond.* V 1661 (553), see n. 173. Presumably not the polyonymous Flavius Theodore Menas Julianus Jacob, *ὁ μεγαλοπρε(πέστατος) κόμε(ς) καὶ ἄρχ(ων) τῆς Θηβ(αίων) ἐπαρχείας τὸ δ´* who issued the order in *P. Cairo Masp.* I 67030 (cf. *BL* 10.33; prob. 531/2, Gascou's date in *BL* 9.41). Cf. *P. Cairo Masp.* III 67321 (A), prob. 533/4, where this official is called governor of the Thebaid 'for the sixth year' (*ἄρχων τῆς Θηβ(αίων) ἐπαρχ(είας) τὸ s''*)! In any case, Maspero's date for 67030 seems quite uncertain.

[168] *P. Cairo Masp.* I 67060 = *WChr.* 297.2, *τοῦ ἐνδ*[*οξ(οτάτου) ἀπὸ*] *ἐπαρχων Ἰουλιανου*, *P. Lond.* V 1674.13 (*c.*570), *Ἰουλιανοῦ τοῦ* [*ἀπ*]*ὸ ἐπάρχων καὶ* [*παγάρχου?*]. Possibly [*ἀπ*]*ὸ ἐπάρχων καὶ* [*ἀρχόντων*], cf. n. 173.

[169] *P. Cairo Masp.* I 67024 recto 30 ff. (*c.*551).

[170] *P. Lond.* V 1674 (*c.*570).

[171] *P. Cairo Masp.* 67060 = *WChr.* 297.2–3. It is not clear where Julianus actually

minor correction in *SB* XVI 12510 (551) shows that Julianus was an *illustris*,[172] on the same social level as Serenus who followed him in the pagarchy. In *P. Cairo Masp.* 67008.8 the official forwarding the petition to the *patricius* Athanasius is a certain *ἐνδοξότατος καὶ πανεύφημος στρατηλάτης* Flavius Julianus, so if this is the same person he was clearly on his way into the élite aristocracy from the middle ranks where, typically, he had spent most of his career.

The officiating pagarch Flavius Menas who worked with him (by delegation), on the other hand, was of distinctly lower rank, *lamprotatos*, conceivably the third and lowest level of the aristocracy (though still employed as a financial official (*scriniarius*) in the provincial bureaucracy) and the target of a fierce denunciation in *P. Cairo Masp.* 67002.[173] If he was really the *procurator* of the daughter of Count John, as I have suggested,[174] then it is easier to see why the villagers of Aphrodito, led by the local village élite, felt no compunction in mounting an attack on him. As manager of an aristocratic estate in the 530s his function was essentially similar to that of Apollos, father of Flavius Dioscorus, who worked as manager (*dioikētēs*) for Count Ammonius in 545.[175] Menas is thus a good example of the aggressive, power-seeking element, but he was not the only one. In a letter written from Constantinople to the Duke of the Thebaid (547–9) the *curator* of the *domus divina*, summarizing Aphrodito's grievances, claimed that (according to the village) a certain Theodosius, *megaloprepestatos*, had made off with the entire taxes of the eleventh indiction, 547–8.[176] It is not clear who this man was; he may have been a largish landowner with local possessions and sufficient authority to seem to have a pretext for the exaction of revenue—perhaps a pagarch from Antinoe, since a Flavius Theo[ ] appears in *P. Ant.* II 97 (6c.) discussing some issue related to 'the pagarchy managed by me' (*τῆς διοικουμένης παρ' ἐμοῦ παγαρχ[ίας]*).[177]

resided, since *ἡ πόλις* could refer to any of several locations from Antaeu or Antinoopolis to Alexandria.

[172] *SB* XVI 12510.4–5, *Ὁ ἐνδοξ(ότατος) πάγαρχος Ιουλιανὸς ἰλλουστρ(ίος)* (instead of *Ἰλλουστρ(ίου)*).

[173] *P. Lond.* V 1661.5–6 (553), *Φλ(αουΐοις) Ἰουλιανῷ τῷ μεγαλοπρεπεστάτῳ ἀπὸ ἀρχόντων καὶ Μηνᾷ λαμπροτάτῳ σκρινιαρίῳ καὶ παγάρχαις τῆς Ἀνταιοπολιτῶν*, *P. Cairo Masp.* I 67002.6 (567).

[174] See n. 165.

[175] *P. Ross.-Georg.* III 37 (545).

[176] Cf. R. G. Salomon, 'A Papyrus from Constantinople (Hamburg Inv.No.410)', *JEA* 34 (1948) 98–108, published as *SB* VI 9102 (547–9), a letter written in Constantinople, probably to the Duke of the Thebaid. Theodosius is also mentioned in *P. Cairo Masp.* I 67024.8 (*c.*551) and 67029 (548/9).

[177] Cf. *P. Ant.* II 96 which is from the same archive. Note also that an *endoxotatos* Theodosius turns up in *P. Flor.* III 377 (6c) as manager of several *ousiai* around Ptolemais. He appears to have been an official, not a private employee.

More typical of this stratum, the small aristocracy, were the numerous 'Counts' who dominated the countryside around Hermopolis in late antiquity. They occur throughout the codex edited by Gascou.[178] They were the backbone of the resident aristocracy, owners who clearly resided in the areas near their estates (something we can be much less certain about for the *illustres*). The *megaloprepestatos komes* Menas appears in a Coptic wage receipt of the seventh century.[179] He used hired labour for irrigation—like most owners—and paid for it in the usual gold coinage. In *CPR* IX 70 (7c.) a Count Menas collects various cash amounts owed to him from a series of villages which are described as 'yours'—*ἀπὸ διαφόρ(ων) ὑμῶν κωμ(ῶν)*.[180] All the sums listed are multiples of 3 and the total comes to 198 solidi, equivalent (roughly) to 2,500–3,000 artabas of wheat at the usual price levels. Menas was clearly a substantial landowner and the description of the villages (*kōmai*) as 'his' adds to that impression. Another late Hermopolite account in which the payments are generally multiples of 3 is *P. Amst.* I 85 (6/7c.); out of eleven payments listed, four are for 9 solidi, five for 12. This account is called 'List of landholders [. . .] of Tarruthis for the 8th indiction' (followed by names and payments in solidi)[181] and shows that *CPR* IX 70 could have involved aggregate amounts based on similar individual payments. A possible clue to the date and, indirectly, to the identity of Count Menas may be contained in *P. Ross.-Georg.* III 49. This is a sharecrop lease dated 604/5 and involves land at the village of Tertonkano. The location of the plot is specified in some detail and one of the defining boundaries involves the *γήδια* of the *megaloprepestatos komes* Menas.[182] Since Tertonkano is one of the villages in *CPR* IX 70[183] we are surely dealing with the same landowner in the two documents. Again, two of the locations in this list reappear in *SPP* XX 257,[184] which is a list of villages and cash payments relating to a certain Count Menas (presumably the same person).[185] The structure of the two lists is identical except that here the payments vary randomly (though the order of magnitude is the same) and are described as *(ὑπὲρ) προσθήκ(ης)*. In *CPR*

[178] Gascou, *P. Sorb.* II 69, Index IV, p. 281, s.v. *κόμης*, where one finds about twenty-three. See *Catalogue*, Hermopolite 7c. (Count Dorotheus, Count Hadrianus, Count Jacob, Count Menas, etc.).

[179] *CPR* IV 166 = *CPR* II 112 (7c.); Till, 'Koptischen Arbeitsverträge', pp. 314f., no. 51, dates this document to the 8th cent.

[180] *CPR* IX 70.2–3.

[181] *P. Amst.* I 85.2–3, *[Γ]νῶσις τῶν κτητόρ(ων)* [.. . ..] *Ταρρούθε(ως) η' ἰνδ(ικτίονος)*.

[182] *P. Ross.-Georg.* III 49.7.

[183] *CPR* IX 70.9.

[184] *SPP* XX 257.9 (Phomosis), 13 (Tertembythis).

[185] So Zereteli, *P. Ross.-Georg.* III 18.13n (p. 80).

IV 161, a copy of a contract of employment (σύμφωνον) drafted in Coptic, a *megaloprepestatos* Menas, son of Joannakios, hires a *paramonarios* for work of a general description on wages paid entirely in kind (there is no reference to a cash component) but with a total cash value of less than 3 solidi per year.[186] Again, this may be the same Menas—in which case apart from controlling villages throughout the district (cf. *SPP* XX 257), he was also a substantial employer of labour.

Menas was by no means unusual. In *P. Ant.* III 189 (6/7c.) a certain Count Callinicus issued a list of wanted persons 'from various villages of his'—ἀπὸ διαφ(όρων) κωμ(ῶν) αὐτοῦ. Again, the description of substantial villages like Sinkere and Phbu as αὐτοῦ reflects the sort of land relations which had become—or were becoming—characteristic of the Egyptian rural districts by the late sixth and early seventh centuries. The topography of these villages shows that they lay close to each other in the general region of Etlidem a few kilometres north of Ashmunein.[187] But given that these were *kōmai*, not *epoikia*, it would be wrong to conclude that Callinicus actually owned such villages as opposed to owning land in them or controlling them in some other way. A pagarch Flavius Callinicus turns up in a sixth-century receipt of uncertain provenance—possibly the same man—and this could indicate one of the possible meanings of describing villages as 'of' Count so-and-so.[188]

There is no evidence to suggest that the level of activity declined sharply in the seventh-century Hermopolite. The fiscal machinery was intact,[189] there was no obvious decline in the rate of leasing (even if the absolute number of leases falls with the general decline in the number of seventh-century papyri relative to sixth-century finds), landowners continued to invest in land (purchases,[190] plantations,[191] wells[192]), skilled workers were paid high rates of money

[186] *CPR* IV 161 = *CPR* II 153 (7c.); for relative pay see App. 1, Table 11.

[187] Cf. M. Drew-Bear, *Le Nome Hermopolite: Toponymes et sites* (ASP 21, 1979) 255.

[188] *P. Monac.* III 152.4 (6c.). Now see App. 4.

[189] Cf. *P. Sorb.* II 69 (618/19 or 633/4), with Gascou's lengthy introduction, as also his comments in *Tyche* 1 (1986) 97 ff.

[190] e.g., *P. Laur.* II 26 (7c.).

[191] Cf. M. Schnebel, 'An Agricultural Ledger in P. Bad. 95', *JEA* 14 (1928) 34–45, esp. 42, on *P. Bad.* 95 (7c.).

[192] e.g., *P. Lond.* II 483 (pp. 323 ff.) (5.8.616), esp. ll. 42 ff., πᾶσαν φιλοκαλείαν ἐν αὐταῖς (sc. ἀρούραις) ποιήσασθαι τὴν αὐτῷ δοκοῦσαν καὶ ἄμπελον ἐν αὐταῖς ἀνάξαι καὶ λάκκους ἐνωρῦξαι εἰ βουληθείη, referring to the rights of the lessee in an emphyteutic lease. The well-digging clause may have been standard in emphyteutic leases, cf. *P. Vindob.* G 29.386, line 19 (6/7c.) in P. J. Sijpesteijn and P. J. De Wit, 'Fragment einer spätbyzantinischen Emphyteusisurkunde', *Tyche* 7 (1992) 55–9, where a monastery leases out an *ousia*.

wages,[193] cash payments were widespread suggesting ready access to markets and a continuing demand for labour. In particular, we should note the widespread prevalence of money rents in the Coptic leases of the seventh and eighth centuries published in *CPR* II by J. Krall—no sign, at least, of the decline of monetary economy.[194] The ability of landowners to extract considerable sums in the prevalent gold coinage is strong proof of a continuing commercial vitality in the Hermopolite countryside. The estate in *P. Bad.* 95 yielded an annual average *net* cash income of *c*.97 solidi. Here was an extensively irrigated medium-sized estate collecting the greater part of its revenue in monetary payments chiefly from what looks like a substantial peasantry. Thus in Thelbonthis four *geōrgoi* connected with this estate paid an average of 17 solidi each,[195] which is certainly comparable with the bigger individual payments in the Apion accounts. Since we can rule out wage labour as the main source of cash earnings for households of this type, the clear presupposition is production for the market: money rents were only possible because villages like Thelbonthis could count on a regular market for their produce. In practice the estate granted rebates of 33 per cent *ὑπ(ὲρ) ἀβρόχ(ου)*—for years of poor flood—absorbing the losses due to fluctuations in output despite the description of rents as *τοῦ φόρου ἀποτ(άκτου)* (with the implication that these were rents which would not vary with the season).[196] For three of the four indictions covered by the account gross monetary receipts were stable at 222 solidi 16 keratia, though cash expenditure fluctuated slightly between *c*.104 and 123 solidi. At the prices used in the account itself the estate's cash ratio (proportion of monetary receipts to total including *imputed* cash income) was about 76.45 per cent.[197] Obviously the owners, whoever they were, had a strong preference for receipts in cash (almost a third of the wheat income was paid out in taxes, but less than ten per cent of the money they received). The other aspect

[193] *P. Flor.* I 70 (27 Nov. 627, Harrauer, *BL* 8.125).

[194] Note the predominance of cash rents in *APEL* II 77 ff. (pp. 29 ff.)—leases from the Islamic period.

[195] *P. Bad.* 95.505–8. For corrections, see F. Morelli, 'Note a P. Bad. IV 95', *ZPE* 122 (1998) 139–43. I am not convinced by Gascou's redating of this account to the 'early or middle sixth century' (*P. Sorb.* II 69, p. 39 and n. 163, accepted by Morelli, 'Note', at 139); as Table 1 shows, the solidus was still tariffed at 32,000 talents (= 4,800 myr.) as late as 614.

[196] Cf. *P. Bad.* 95.31, referring to a 'fixed' rent on which a rebate is granted in l. 506; for my interpretation of *apotaktos* in Byzantine leases, see *Rural Communities*, 1, app.1. *κούφ(ων) ἀβρόχ(ου)* in *P. Bad.* 95.360, etc., should read *κουφ(ισμοῦ) ἀβρόχ(ου)*, see Schnebel, 'Agricultural Ledger', 34 n. 3, and cf. *P. Oxy.* XVI 2038 i 1, *Λόγος*] *κουφισμ(οῦ) ἀβρόχ(ου)*.

[197] Schnebel, 'Agricultural Ledger', 36, including the estate's income in barley; see Table 2*b* (77.9% excluding barley).

is scale. The great patrician *oikoi* which dominated the districts further north were conspicuously absent from the Hermopolite. Here the dominant estates were middle-sized operations owned by a small to middling aristocracy, *illustres* and *clarissimi*, whose scales of ownership certainly failed to match the landed assets of the church of Hermopolis, which was the largest institutional taxpayer in Temseu Skordon, with a total assessment of *c*.74 solidi in this village alone.[198] Even within the aristocracy there was of course considerable economic stratification. Thus the estate's gross cash income of 222.66 solidi[199] compares with a gross cash income of 18,512 solidi from the Apions' Oxyrhynchite estate[200]—a differential of 1:83. Again, *P. Bad.* 95's average annual expenditure of wheat was *c*.662 artabas (about 41 solidi a year), whereas the estate of Christodora of Cynopolis registered an annual domestic consumption—ὑπ(ὲρ) [ἰ]διοτικ(ῶν) ἀναλ(ωμάτων)—of 4,217 artabas,[201] over six times as much. Thus the élite aristocracy was on the whole much less conspicuous in the late Byzantine Hermopolite, whose estates were chiefly in the hands of a small aristocracy, *illustres* like Count Hadrianus whose holdings were based largely in the villages around the city itself (the most distant of these, Thynis, was about a dozen kilometres from Ashmunein)[202] or the several *clarissimi*, especially women, who figure in the Hermopolite fiscal lists published by Gascou.[203]

Unlike the Oxyrhynchite aristocracy, these owners relied heavily on sharecropping. In *SPP* XX 218, one of our best preserved 'late Byzantine' leases, Flavius Demetrius, μεγαλοπρεπέστατος κόμες καὶ πολιτευόμενος, leased a vineyard of 3 arouras on this basis. His father too seems to have been a *megaloprepestatos*, possibly the governor and pagarch of Hermopolis who turns up in *P. Lond.* V 1753.[204] Demetrius is known from at least two other documents. *CPR* II 114 (7c.), a Coptic contract of surety where he acts as the representative of the *endoxotatos* Chris( ) (Christopher? Christodorus?), and in *P. Laur.* II 26 (7c.) as a witness in an ἐπίσταλμα τοῦ σωματισμοῦ

198 Cf. L. S. B. MacCoull, 'Money and People in the Late Antique Hermopolite: BM 1075 and Related Texts', *Tyche* 2 (1987) 99–105, esp. 102.

199 For the ninth to eleventh indictions, following a certain reorganization.

200 *P. Oxy*. XVIII 2196 verso, with Gascou, *CE* 1972, 246.

201 *P. Oxy*. XVI 2026.6.

202 Cf. *P. Lond.* V 1907 (Pselamynthis, Hermopolis, Adelphiou), *P. Lond.* V 1761.19 (Thynis), with Gascou, *P. Laur.* I/4(3).7n (*Tyche*, 1986, 113), and *PSI* VII 836 for his full title.

203 Gascou, *Tyche* 1 (1986) esp. no. 5 (pp. 108 ff.), no. 7, no. 8.

204 *SPP* XX 218.6–7, υἱῷ τοῦ τῆς μεγαλ[ο]πρεποῦς μνήμης Ἰωάννου λα(μπροτάτου), with *BL* 2/2.165, 7.264, emending λα( ) to π(αρα); cf. *P. Lond.* V 1753.1 (6/7c.), Φλ( ) Ἰωάννης σὺν θε(ῷ) ἄρχοντος (l. ἄρχων) κ(αὶ) πάγαρχ(ος) Ἑρμοπόλ(εως).

(application for transfer of taxes) in which a certain Count Theodore son of Clarus, a *ktētōr* (?) from Hermopolis, requests the formal transfer of taxes on some land he has bought at Metachraire.[205] Demetrius owned a *ktēma* called ⲡⲙⲁⲧⲓⲛⲡⲉϩⲣⲉ, 'the place where one dispenses medicine', according to Amelineau,[206] presumably a dispensary. This had a *sāqiya*, of course, as well as wine-press and was located near Thynis (Touna el-Gebel) within commuting distance of Hermopolis. In *SPP* XX 218 the lease is for three years and involves a work standard of five diggings per year. A feature of exceptional interest is the reference to keratia of 36 *folles* each—which, in purely numismatic terms, should make the thirteenth indiction of this contract 624/5, since the previous thirteenth indiction, 609/10, was a time when the value of gold in terms of copper involved an exchange of 25 *folles* to the keration.[207] It is also worth noting that unlike most crop-sharing leases for wine the contract says nothing about watering among the several tasks specified for the lessee.[208] The strong implication of this is that Demetrius probably recruited other employees to handle this job, signing a contract of the type preserved in *P. Flor.* I 70 (627). In this Flavius Theodorus, a *clarissimus*, hires a *geōrgos* from the epoikion called ⲡⲥⲁϩⲃⲟⲩ near Tertembythis,[209] one of the villages where the *megaloprepestatos* Menas controlled land. The use of paid labour for irrigation was widespread by this period, indicating both an increased demand for such labour and perhaps an increased supply of wage labour more generally. The occurrence of two Coptic place-names—presumably settlements in some proximity—is also interesting. Bilingualism was widespread in the Hermopolite countryside (and elsewhere).[210] Contracts could be drafted in Greek yet described, on the verso, in Coptic,[211] or the main body of the contract

[205] *P. Laur.* II 26.23–4, *Φλάουϊος Δημήτριος υἱὸς τοῦ τῆς μεγαλοπρ(επεστάτης) μνήμης Ἰωάννου ἀπὸ Ἑρμ(οῦ) π(όλεως)*. In l. 21 *[κτή]τ[ω]ρ ἀπὸ Ἑρμοῦ πόλ(εως)* is a possible restoration. *P. Laur.* II 26 is securely dated to the early part of the 7th cent. and rules out Carrié's numismatic speculations about the date of *SPP* XX 218 as quite unnecessary.

[206] Cf. Drew-Bear, *Le Nome Hermopolite*, 213–14.

[207] See C. Morrisson, 'Monnaie et prix à Byzance du Ve au VIIe siècle', in *HREB* 1. 239–60, at 248, table 2, relying partly on *P. Grenf.* II 87. The usual interpretation of the amount as 12 folles per keration (West and Johnson, etc., contrast Hahn who is baffled by it) rests on a confusion between the equivalence functions of *apo* and *eis*. If the 3 keratia had been *equal to* 36 folles, the scribe would clearly have written *eis pholleis triakonta hex* in *SPP* XX 218.29–30.

[208] Cf. esp. *SPP* XX 218.19–22.

[209] *P. Flor.* I 70.3–4, with Drew-Bear, *Le Nome Hermopolite*, 282.

[210] Cf. J. G. Keenan, 'On Languages and Literacy in Byzantine Aphrodito', in *Proceedings of the XVIIIth International Congress of Papyrology, Athens 25–31 May 1986*, ed. B. G. Mandilaras, 2 vols. (Athens, 1988) 2.161–7, esp. 161, 'even the Greek papyri leave small doubt about the Coptic basis of village life'.

[211] *P. Prag.* I 46 (522) from Antinoopolis.

might suddenly include some lines of Coptic.[212] Places could have one name in Greek and another, possibly different one, in Coptic. **ⲤⲈⲚⲀⲒϨⲞ** from which Menas recruited labour for irrigation was probably Sinape, since the place-name reappears in a Greek form on the verso.[213] Thus the local-cultural Coptic substrate becomes increasingly more apparent as the seventh century advances, especially in the more southern districts like the Hermopolite where landowners regularly gave their estates Coptic names (even when these owners belonged to the Greek-speaking aristocracy),[214] accepted wage receipts in Coptic, and now agreed to draft more formal documents such as deeds of surety in a language ordinary people were more familiar with.[215] Decades ago Bardy pointed out that by the start of the seventh century Coptic was dominant even in Alexandria,[216] so one can easily imagine the dominant linguistic situation in the rural areas of Egypt.

Theodore paid his employee the impressive wage of 6 solidi (on the Alexandrian standard),[217] a clear indication both of the widespread use of money in rural transactions and the considerable intensity of labour involved in keeping the estates of the aristocracy properly irrigated. The worker Isaac agreed he would return the advance if he showed any intention of abandoning the job before the expiry of his contract.[218] Like the Oxyrhynchite document *P. Oxy.* XVI 1909 (p. 65 above), the Hermopolite documentation of the middle and late Byzantine periods (*P. Flor.* I 70, *P. Bad.* 95, etc.) reflects a thoroughly monetized countryside and makes the subsequent evolution of taxes (under the Umayyads) less difficult to understand than it would otherwise be. Access to money and the circulation of commodities are the presuppositions of private

[212] Cf. *SB* VI 9146.18–19 (6/7c.), Heracleopolis: two lines of Coptic before a Greek *subscriptio*.

[213] See Drew-Bear, *Le Nome Hermopolite*, 337. For another example cf. *CPR* IV 86 = *CPR* II 10 (7c.) where Tbo-nalaali (ⲦⲂⲰ-ⲚⲀⲖⲀⲀⲖⲒ) in l. 2 = *ch(ōrion) Ampeliou* in l. 7.

[214] The *endoxotatos* Olybrius owned a *ktēma* called Thmoun Pamoun in the region around Ptolemais, cf. *P. Flor.* III 377.20. *P. Mich.* XIII 666 (6c.) refers to a *ktēma* called Prmres ('man from the south') near Aphrodito. Cf. the *χωρίον Πκαμε*, a vineyard or wine estate, in *SPP* XX 213 (end of 6c.), now assigned to the Hermopolite by Diethart, *Anagennesis* 4 (1986) 13 ff.

[215] Cf. *CPR* II 114 (7c.), which involves Count Demetrius.

[216] G. Bardy, *La Question des langues dans l'Église ancienne* (Paris, 1948) 50, citing Anastasius Sinaita, *Hodegos*.

[217] For other wage levels, cf. App. 1, Table 11.

[218] *P. Flor.* I 70.10 ff., *ἅπερ ὁμολογῶ παρασχεῖν ὑμῖν μέλλων ἀποστῆναι τῆς τούτων γεωργίας τοῦ κτήμ(α)τ(ος) ἐν χρυσῷ ὡς παρέλαβον παρ' ὑμῶν*. A similar formula has now turned up in *P. Mich. inv.* 502.5 f. (6/7c.) = T. Gagos, 'Three Short Byzantine Papyri from the Michigan Collection', *ZPE* 79 (1989) 271–80, esp. 276 ff., no. 3, *ἅπερ παρέξω σοὶ ἡνίκ[α] ἀποσταίη τῆς ἀρδείας τοῦ αὐτο`ῦ´ χωρίου ἀμπελικοῦ ἐν χρυσῷ χαρά[γματι] ὡς παρέλαβον*, proof that such workers were paid in gold coin.

lists like *CPR* IX 70 (7c.), estate accounts like *P. Bad.* 95 (7c.) and fiscal payments like the 354 solidi which the Hermopolite village of Temseu Skordon made for a tenth indiction in the sixth century[219] or the 292½ solidi paid by Sinarchebis (also in the Hermopolite) in roughly the same period.[220]

To sum up, the late antique eastern Mediterranean aristocracy was not a *Reichsaristokratie*, if by that we mean a mobile aristocratic élite lacking strong local roots. It resembles rather an ensemble of powerful regional groups with a strong sense of place. By contextualizing the aristocracy in this way, it is possible to pick up important differences in the degree of concentration of agrarian property in different localities. Thus the Oxyrhynchite had a considerable stratum of middling aristocrats and at least one extremely powerful 'super-rich' family of élite aristocrats. In the mid-sixth century it displays, in fact, a substantial concentration of holdings, with the *endoxotatoi*, the *domus divina*, and the Church accounting for close to 75 per cent of its fiscal burden. The Hermopolite, by contrast, was dominated by a smaller, more dispersed aristocracy of 'Counts', in less effective control of the independent villages. It is likely that most districts displayed varying combinations of these various strata, reflecting both the historical circumstances of aristocratic growth in different regions and the particular conditions within each locality. Second, it is also clear from the papyri that the seventh-century countryside was not in a state of obvious depression, even if it is certain that between them the Persian occupation and the Arab conquest destroyed the power of the aristocracy, leaving only a much debilitated and downsized landed élite. The widespread use of both paid labour and irrigation are especially striking.

[219] Cf. MacCoull, *Tyche* 2 (1987) 105.

[220] *P. Amst.* I 84 (6c.).

CHAPTER 7

Estates

The large rural properties of the Mediterranean evolved in a variety of distinctive cultural and ecological settings which exerted an obvious influence on their topographies and structural form. In abstraction from these settings, the term 'estate' conveys little beyond the rough impression of a large agricultural property. Even if we hold the factor of scale constant, the large properties of the Roman Mediterranean display irreducible diversity. To begin with, there was the vast conglomeration of oil-producing estates along the middle reaches of the Guadalquivir which François Jacques brilliantly linked to several generations of a senatorial family identified as *F( )*.[1] The core of this 'estate' is said to have coincided with a triangle of roughly 20 km². The constituent 'estates' here were called *fundi*, and it is not clear by what term one would have referred to the economic aggregation of all these units in the late second or third century. In roughly the same period, in the Antonine Itinerary, one encounters a series of substantial estates along the Libyan coast west of Lepcis, called *villae*.[2] One of these, the 'Casas villa Aniciorum', was probably a specialized oil-producing estate owned by the third-century Anicii.[3] Further east along the coast, in the direction of Lepcis, was the establishment called 'Minna villa Marsi', owned by the Servilii Marsi, who have been described as

[1] F. Jacques, 'Un exemple de concentration foncière en Bétique d'après le témoignage des timbres amphoriques d'une famille clarissime', *MEFR(A)* 102/2 (1990) 865–99, esp. 889 ff., also see B. Liou and A. Tchernia, 'L'interprétation des inscriptions sur les amphores Dressel 20', in *Epigrafia della produzione e della distribuzione. Actes de la VIIe Rencontre franco-italienne sur l'épigraphie du monde romain . . . Rome, 5–6 juin, 1992* (Rome, 1994) 133–56, at 149 ff.

[2] J. Kolendo, 'Les grands domaines en Tripolitaine d'après l'Itinéraire Antonin', in *Actes du IIIe Colloque sur l'histoire et l'archéologie d'Afrique du Nord* (Paris, 1986) 149–61.

[3] *Itin. Ant.* 61.2, see Ch. 1, n. 45. It has been argued recently that the 'Antonine Itinerary' was probably compiled in the second quarter of the 4th cent., though largely on the basis of 3rd-cent. sources, see P. Arnaud, 'L' *Itinéraire d'Antonin*: un témoin de la littérature itinéraire du Bas-Empire', *Geographia Antiqua* 2 (1993) 33–49, esp. 43 ff.

among the biggest olive-oil producers of the third century.[4] In the late fourth century, in the Grande Kabylie, and to its west, a single family of tribal chieftains controlled a vast network of *agadir*-type estates called *fundi*. Ammianus' description of the fundus Petrensis as built 'in the style of' or 'on the scale of' a city suggests estates controlled from mountain strongholds.[5] In the central Mediterranean, the *massa* emerged as a characteristic form of large agrarian property, especially in late antiquity. Sicilian evidence suggests that *massae* were geographically compact agglomerations of smaller *fundi*, often of substantial extent.[6] It is likely that *massae* were found chiefly in the plains of the Mediterranean.[7] By contrast, the estates of the Sasanian aristocracy in Iraq in the seventh century consisted of villages,[8] and that tradition continued to be the peculiar form of large landed property, certainly in Persia, down to the twentieth century.[9] In fact, 'village estates' were also characteristic of Egyptian landownership till recent times.[10] Thus the large estates of the Mediterranean displayed considerable structural and topographic diversity, conditioned by the slower and more ponderous determinisms of geography and culture.

The reference to 'village estates' is particularly interesting, since there *is* evidence of the subsumption of whole villages under private or imperial ownership. A constitution of 415 implies that individuals were able to establish possession even of the villages

[4] *Itin. Ant.* 63.1, and Di Vita-Evrard, 'Timbres d'amphores', 154, with the statement, 'Les Servilii seraient, dans les années 230, parmi les plus gros producteurs.'

[5] Ammianus 29.5.13, with *AE* 1901, 150 = *ILS* 9351 (M'lakou, in Kabylia), cf. G. Camps, 'Rex gentium maurorum et romanorum. Recherches sur les royaumes de Maurétanie des VIe et VIIe siècles', *AntAfr* 20 (1984) 183–218, Matthews, *Ammianus*, 369 ff.

[6] D. Adamesteanu, 'Due problemi topografici del retroterra gelese', *Rend. Acc. Naz. Lincei, Cl. Sc. Mor., St. e Filol.*, 8th ser., 10 (1955) esp. 205 ff. Note Cracco Ruggini's definition of the *massae* as 'aggregati di fondi contigui', 'La Sicilia tra Roma e Bisanzio', in R. Romeo, ed., *Storia della Sicilia*, 10 vols. (Naples, 1977–81) 3.12. A. Castagnetti, 'Le strutture fondiarie ed agrarie', in A. Carile (ed.), *Storia di Ravenna*. 2.1: *I Dall' età bizantina all' età ottoniana* (Comune di Ravenna, 1991) 55–72, esp. 62, notes that, unlike the Lombard *curtis*, the *massa* was not necessarily, or even generally, operated as a single integrated unit.

[7] Braudel, *The Mediterranean*, 1.60 ff., esp. 75–7.

[8] M. G. Morony, 'Landholding in Seventh-Century Iraq', in A. L. Udovitch (ed.), *The Islamic Middle East, 700–1900* (Princeton, 1981) 135–75.

[9] A. K. S. Lambton, *Landlord and Peasant in Persia* (Oxford, 1953). In the 6th cent., John of Ephesus, *Lives* 21 (*PO* 17.289) describes the estate of an Armenian satrap. This was an *ousia* which, apart from its beautiful buildings (*benyane*) and attractive watering places (*bet sheqya*), included villages or hamlets (*qurya*) connected by the solid roads (?) that were laid out between them. This is my interpretation of a difficult sentence referring to *platawaṭa* (*plṭwt'*), which Brooks translates as 'courts'. I am grateful to Sebastian Brock for help with the passage.

[10] G. Baer, *A History of Landownership in Modern Egypt 1800–1950* (Oxford, 1962).

described as *metrocomiae*.[11] Libanius, as we know, counterposed villages (*kōmai*) comprising numerous landholders to others controlled by a single landowner (*despotēs*).[12] One of the villages Theodoret writes about in the *Hist. Relig.* was owned by a *prōteuōn* of Antioch, Letoius, described as ὁ τῆς κώμης ἐκείνης δεσπότης. It seems likely that landowners like him controlled not one but several villages, for in the later fourth century Chrysostom would claim that there were 'many individuals who possess villages (*kōmai*) and *chōria*',[13] and Libanius declaim that some villages were the private possessions of the élite.[14] In the *Syriac Chronicle* Zachariah tells us that Anastasius bought a 'village which belonged to the Church',[15] and the *Life of Theodore of Sykeon* refers, as noted earlier, to 'villages belonging to the local Church', τῶν διαφερόντων χωρίων τῇ ἐκκλησίᾳ, whose management was subcontracted to urban notables.[16] Finally, there is the curious story in Procopius about a certain rhetor of Caesarea who purchased a 'coastal village' (κώμη ἐπιθαλασσία) for 21,600 solidi, which Justinian confiscated because he thought it was not appropriate for a simple rhetor to be the 'owner' (*kyrios*) of such a village.[17] In short, the ownership of villages was a possible form of landholding, which may or may not have been common in the eastern provinces.

Given all this evidence, it is surely surprising that till today the papyri contain not a single instance of the village-estate, though Egypt herself would see a considerable development of this kind of landed property in later centuries. It is as if villages (*kōmai*) were simply immune to ownership, and only open to domination in less direct forms. Large estates were invariably organized as physically discrete units centred on the settlements called *epoikia*. The discreteness of these units or land areas from the main village settlements is even emphasized in the Apion archive by the generic

[11] *CTh.* 11.24.6.1, 'nec quisquam eas vel aliquid in his possidere temptaverit' (Nor should anyone seek control of [these villages themselves] or of anything in them).

[12] Libanius, *Or.* 47.11; 4; in 11 note the expression τῶν ἐπιφανῶν εἰσιν αἱ κῶμαι (There are villages which belong to the élite).

[13] Chrysostom, *In Acta apostolorum homilia* 18.4 (*PG* 60.146), Πολλοὶ κώμας ἔχουσι καὶ χωρία.

[14] See n. 12.

[15] *The Syriac Chronicle known as that of Zachariah of Mitylene*, 165.

[16] *Vie de Théodore de Sykéon*, 75.19–20 (Festugière, 1.63). The villages of Galatia are invariably described as *chōria* in this 7th-cent. Life. In hagiography, the transition from κώμη to χωρίον seems to have occurred in the late 6th/early 7th cent. Thus in the early 7th-cent. Life of St Anastasius, Bethsaloe is called a *kōmē* once, otherwise and more frequently a *chōrion*, B. Flusin, *Saint Anastase le Perse et l'histoire de la Palestine au début du VIIe siècle*, 2 vols. (Paris, 1992) 1. 86, 77, 83. So too in the Life of the younger Symeon, cf. P. Van den Ven, *La Vie ancienne de S. Syméon Stylite le Jeune (521–592)* (Brussels, 1962–70).

[17] Procopius, *HA* 30.18–19.

description of the *epoikia* as ἐξωτικοὶ τόποι, that is, 'outlying' or 'peripheral' localities, with the implication that the co-ordinates of this system of rural topography were the villages themselves (someone looking for an *epoikion* would clearly do so by reference to the nearest village).[18] Thus the 'public' villages circumvented and deflected aristocratic dominance of the countryside, creating space for a more complex rural order which included a substantial agrarian 'middle class' of minor aristocrats, middle bureaucrats, professionals, traders, and the more wealthy peasant stratum. On the other hand, the spread of *epoikia*-type estates also symbolized the greater interest of the aristocracy in rural production and their ability to organize a system of direct management with the requisite amounts of labour and the required degree of subjection of these labour forces to supervision by the estate.

Estate 'Villages'

The general dichotomy and physical discreteness of village and *epoikion* achieves its clearest expression in the Oxyrhynchite material, which is of course dominated by the Apion archive. From this it is clear that the *epoikia* far outnumbered the independent villages and were almost never named after the latter. In the Fayum, by contrast, many *epoikia* bear the names of substantial villages, which must clearly have been in their immediate vicinity. This obfuscates the distinction between village and *epoikion*, and thus between the ownership of villages and the exploitation of *epoikia*. However, it seems certain that in the Fayum, as in the Oxyrhynchite, large estates were based on the exploitation of *epoikia*, even if many or most of them existed in some proximity to the main village centres, as their names indicate. The majority of these estates are simply toponyms. A few, however, are associated with a current owner. In 486, the *clarissimus* Flavius Julius owned the epoikion Sabina.[19] The epoikion Strategiou, owned by a branch of the Fayum Strategii, then headed by Flavia Theophania, was located in the Theodosiopolite.[20] Ampeliou and Psineuris were both part of the estate of pseudo-Strategius III.[21] Koueisan was part of the *ousia*

[18] *P. Oxy.* I 136.15–17 (583), XVIII 2196.5 (after 587?), XIX 2243.88 (590), VI 999 (616/17), XVIII 2204.4 ff. (6c.), with *BL* 8.255, XVI 2019.3–4 (6c.).

[19] *SB* I 4481 = XVIII 14001 (486).

[20] *CPR* X 127.7–8 (584); called *ch(ōrion) Stratēgiou* in *SPP* XX 229 ii 4.

[21] *SPP* X 1.3–4, *P. Lond.* I 113. 5 (c) 8–15 (= *BL* 1.237) (600) with *BL* 9.125, *SPP* X 114.

of the *stratēlatēs* Theodosius, who was Duke of Arcadia in 636.[22] Embolou and Pantikou belonged to the *ousia* of a landowner who was probably the pagarch Theodorakios.[23] An *ousia* is now attested at Melitōnos,[24] there was an *ousia* at Dikaiou owned by one of the great aristocratic families mentioned in *SPP* X 249,[25] Touroubestis and Syrōn were connected with aristocratic estates,[26] and the *chōrion* Phanamet turns up in the eighth century, it seems, as part of the *ousia* Pkōm.[27] *SPP* X 114 refers to the *epoikion* Psineuris as a property owned by pseudo-Strategius III,[28] thus strongly suggesting that all of the localities mentioned in *SPP* X 1 were in fact *epoikia* controlled by Strategius' Fayum estate. Though the Fayum evidence is much less coherent than that from the Oxyrhynchite, there is no reason to doubt that the large landowners of this district organized their estates on fundamentally similar lines. It is worth emphasizing, however, that the Fayum pattern was more complicated due to the demonstrable or implied replication of the names of existing villages, either obviously large and independent centres such as Sebennytos and Alabantis in the north, and Kerkeēsis in the south, or the more numerous and relatively more obscure locations which are known simply as *chōria* and which, it is safe to presume, were in fact villages of a possibly less substantial order. It is simplest to assume that where the papyri present estates (*ousiai*) which reportedly consist of localities which are either undescribed or described only as *chōria*, these localities were in fact *epoikia*, and that the Fayum *ousia* was an ensemble or system of *epoikia* such as one finds in the Apion archive.[29] The clearest instance of this is *SPP* X 154, which mentions two Fayum estates (*ousiai*) with a brief (but partial) inventory of the settlements that each comprised.[30] In other documents, the *ousia* itself is treated as a *chōrion*, a discrete,

[22] *P. Lond.* I 113.6 (c) (635), cf. *BGU* I 323.5.

[23] *SPP* X 154.7–8, restoring ἀπὸ τ(ῆς) οὐσί(ας) Θεοδω[ρακίου] in l. 6, cf. *PRG* III 50 (21 July 643, *BL* 8.291), which refers to the epoikion Pantikou in l. 6.

[24] *P. Prag.* II 179 iv 2–3 (6c.), διὰ τῶν εἴσων (l. ἴσων) ἐνταγίων σίτου οὐσία[ς] Μελίτωνος.

[25] *SPP* X 249 ii 2 (3 Jan. 633, *BL* 9.343), X 24.3, also n. 36 below.

[26] *SPP* X 251 B 2 (7c., *BL* 9.343) (reference to Šahrālānyōzān in l. A 9, B 10 suggests that the fifteenth indiction of this account was 626/7, cf. n. 105), *SPP* VIII 1092, with *BL* 9.341.

[27] *PRG* V 71 (8c.); Πκωμ appears in *SPP* XX 229 i 23 (7/8c.).

[28] *SPP* X 114.2–3, ἐν ἐποι[κίῳ] Ψινεύρεως διαφέρ(οντος) τοῦ [δ]εσπ(ότου) ἡ[μῶ]ν τοῦ πανευφ(ήμου) πατρικίου.

[29] The nuance is lost on Palme, 'Die *domus gloriosa* des Flavius Strategius Paneuphemos', 118f., who fails to see the significance of the distinction between *komai* and *epoikia*, and concludes, inevitably, that late antique estates of the kind owned by Strategius in the Fayum were simply collections of scattered land parcels.

[30] Discussed below; that neither estate was being inventoried in full is clear from the wording in ll. 2 and 6, 'from the estate . . .'.

topographically distinctive entity.[31] In short, the large estates of the eastern Mediterranean were neither 'village estates' nor mere assemblages of small scattered parcels[32] but agglomerations of compact settlements subject to a common management.

The upshot of this is that it is safer not to construe documents like *SPP* X 154 or the reference to localities like Syrōn and Herakleōn as 'of the *megalē ousia*' or 'of the *mikra ousia*'[33] as evidence of the evolution of estates composed of actual villages. Thus the *chōr(ion) Theaxenidos kōmēs* remained distinct from the *chōr(ion) Theaxenidos ousias*,[34] just as the village of Kerkeēsis was topographically distinct from the epoikion Kerkeēseos,[35] or the *ousia* Dikaiou different from the village of that name.[36] Papyrologically, then, one still lacks any specific evidence that landowners might have owned entire villages (*kōmai*), and the village estate of the Islamic period seems therefore to emerge from a historical vacuum. On the other hand, it is surely worth asking whether *epoikia*-type estates, or estate 'villages', in the Fayum showed signs of being grouped together or consolidated in the same geographical sector, that is, whether aristocratic owners clustered their settlements to achieve economies of scale or simply amassed property on a dispersed and even completely random basis. The basis for a response to this question must ultimately lie in a reconstructed topography of the Fayum countryside in late antiquity. Some of this topographic evidence is discussed in detail in Appendix 3 (together with the relevant references), and the following paragraphs, therefore, are simply a summary of the conclusions advanced there. Of course, it should be emphasized that the evidence is fragmentary and much of it uncertain, and the conclusions that follow are often tentative.

SPP X 154 (7 c.) groups a series of settlements under their *ousiai*. Of the three localities mentioned in ll. 3–5 (Eikosi, Eustochiou, and Paniskou), Eikosi is a fixed point of reference. Whatever its precise location, it was clearly not far from Magdōla = Medinet en-Nehas in the Gharaq basin,[37] north-west of Kerkeosiris, and

[31] *SPP* X 262.8 (7c.), *ἀπὸ χω(ρίου) Κερκεσούχω(ν) ὅρου(ς) οὐσία*, *SB* VI 9583 fr. 3 recto 17, *χωρ(ίον) Θεαξενί(δος) οὐσίας*, *P. Prag.* I 26 verso 4 (7c.), *χωρ(ίον) Θεοξενίδ(ος) οὐσί(ας)*.

[32] Such as the early imperial *ousiai*, e.g. *SB* X 10512 = *SB* XIV 11657 (Theadelphia, 139), which implies a model of highly fragmented estates.

[33] *SPP* X 149.5, 9.

[34] *SB* VI 9583 fr. 3 15, 17, *P. Prag.* I 26 verso, *SPP* X 131.3–4.

[35] *SB* VI 9583 fr. 3 7–8, *SPP* X 3 (7c.).

[36] Dikaiou appears as a *kōmē* in *SB* VI 9293 (573) and VIII 9777 (597). In *SB* 9583 fr. 5 l. 4 it should be possible to restore *χωρ(ίον) Δικαίο(υ) οὐσ]ία*, since l. 5 has *χωρ(ίον) Δικαίο(υ)*.

[37] *SB* I 5139 (6c.), *SPP* X 111, both linking Ibiōn to Magdōla; the former was Ibiōn Eikosipentarourōn = Eikosi for short.

sufficiently close to both Narmouthis and Tali for common administrative arrangements to prevail at various times. This suggests a location roughly equidistant between Medinet Madi (Narmouthis) and Talīt, somewhere in the central portion of the basin. In 487 it appears as a *kōmē*, related in some way to the aristocrat Flavius Eustochius.[38] The next locality, Eustochiou, is never described as a *kōmē*, and was probably, as the name suggests, a settlement founded by the Eustochii as part of their estate in the southern Fayum. (The sheer resilience of these families is obvious from the fact that the 'heirs of Eustochius' are still mentioned as late as 633.) Its associations with other place-names suggest a location outside the Gharaq basin, to the north, probably not far from Narmouthis (Medinet Madi). Finally, the third toponym of the *ousia*, Paniskou, was further east than either Eustochiou or Eikosi. In *SPP* X 281 Paniskou is wedged between Oxyrhyncha and Kerkesēphis (ll. 9–11), and payments for Oxyrhyncha and Paniskou seem to be made through the same individual. Oxyrhyncha was south of Eleusis (Itsa, Etsa?), and not far from Kerkeēsis which occupied a fairly central position in the Tutun basin.[39] The general impression, then, is one of some cohesion, with localities spread within a certain radius of the Gharaq basin. The second estate in *SPP* X 154 reflects similar cohesion. In this case there is less uncertainty, since two of the three locations are actually known. Piamouei survives as Biyahmu 7–8 kilometres north-east of Medinet el Fayyum, and about 10 kilometres west of Seila, and Pantikou was clearly medieval Bandīq near the Baḥr Seila. The location of Embolou is unknown. It appears next to Pantikou in two other documents, and may have been on one of the canals along the eastern edges of the Fayum.[40]

Another estate with a wider spread of settlements but a similar pattern of regional concentration was the estate of pseudo-Strategius III or that part of it which is listed in *SPP* X 1. Strategius himself was dead by this time and it is interesting that the estate (*oikos*) retained its identity regardless. *SPP* X 1 mentions seven locations: Psineuris, Ampeliou, Bernikidos, Karpe, Phentemin, Kainos, and [ ]nol. Of these the last is likely to have been Psinol, which has turned up in a recently published papyrus of the early sixth century as a *kōmē* in the Arsinoite (that is, not in the Theodosiopolite).[41] This fact is of some interest as it means

[38] *SB* I 5273.4–5; almost certainly from the same family which founded the epoikion Eustochiou.

[39] *P. Erasm.* I 2.7 ff. (Eleusis), *BGU* IV 1035 (Kerkeēsis).

[40] See esp. *SPP* X 246.1–6 where all the other localities lie in the eastern Fayum.

[41] *P. Dub.* 34.2 (511).

that, prima facie, Bernikidos is more likely to have been Berenikis Aigialou than the village in the Gharaq basin, Berenikis Thesmophorou, since none of the other sites are in the Theodosiopolite. Psinol's location can scarcely be conjectured, however. Phentemin's identification with Fidimīn has long been accepted, and it was therefore approximately 10 kilometres north-west of Arsinoitōnpolis. Kainos had a local fishing industry. It was presumably in the region of Lake Moeris and not far from Karanis. Ampeliou bore the Coptic name Tbōnalaali,[42] and Ṭebhār/Ṭubhār a few kilometres south of Abu Ginshu may well have been the site of Ampeliou. Karpe should surely be identified with Minya Karbīs in Nabulsi's description of the Fayum, to the south and east of Fidimīn and Sanhūr, a few kilometres north of Medinet el Fayyum. This leaves Psineuris. In the Fayum papyri, there are two toponyms with similar-sounding names, Psineuris and Psenyris. Psenyris shows particularly close links with Neiloupolis of the Fayum,[43] and was clearly on or near the site of the more substantial centre of Sinnūris, while Psineuris is likely to have been Sanhūr. Psineuris was thus a few kilometres north of Phentemin.

Of course, we simply do not know how many *more* settlements Strategius is likely to have controlled in this sector of the Fayum. On the other hand, we know that localities in other parts of the Fayum were included in the estate. One of these was Herakleōn, which it is tempting to identify with El Ḥaraga (med. Mūš al-Ḥaraga) 2 kilometres south-east of El Lāhūn.[44] In the late second century, Ptolemais Hormou (El Lāhūn), Syrōn kōmē, Kerkesoucha Orous, and epoikion Herakleōnos formed part of a single unit of rural administration, with its centre at Ptolemais Hormou. Syrōn was roughly a day's journey south of Ptolemais Hormou, on the Baḥr Yūsuf,[45] which would mean a location in the neighbourhood of Sidamant el Gebel. In *SPP* X 149, which clearly is also estate-related, Syrōn, Anōgēs, Herakleōn, and Skelous appear in obviously close association. Here, curiously, Syrōn is described as 'of the large estate', and Skelous and Herakleōn (in l. 9) as 'of the small estate'. Moreover, both Skelos and Herakleōn figure separately as well, in their determination as villages (as opposed to estate settlements), underlining the Fayum pattern of the replication of village names in estate settlements. The conjunction of Skelos and Herakleōn within the boundaries of a single estate which is described as 'small'

42 *CPR* IV 86 (7c.).
43 Esp. *P. Petaus* 40.20, but see App. 3 for other references.
44 *SPP* VIII 1121 (7c.).
45 *P. Lille* 1 ii 31 ff.

implies that Skelos, wherever it was, was obviously not far from Herakleōn.

Despite the dehydration of the villages on the northern fringe, and some contraction of settlement, the countryside along the canals of the eastern Fayum, including the Baḥr Yusuf and the sector south of El Lāhūn, shows no signs of crisis. The aristocracy amassed estates in this region. Piamouei,[46] Selē,[47] Embolou,[48] Pantikou,[49] Skelos,[50] Herakleōn,[51] Syrōn,[52] and Kerkesoucha Orous[53] are all directly associated with big estates (*ousiai*). For example, Syrōn was related in some form to the estate of the patricia Sophia, and so probably was Kainē in the Heracleopolite.[54] The sheer prosperity of some of these east Fayum towns can be gauged from Nabulsi's report in the thirteenth century that at one time Saila (Gk. Selē) had up to forty churches![55] Moreover, there are no signs of a shortage of labour. Wage labour was widespread, and the repeated reference in the Fayum wine leases to the evictability of the sharecropper[56] proves that landlords who employed this kind of contract, mostly the middling aristocracy and smaller owners, were not unduly worried about the availability of labour. Finally, most of these features are reflected in a Vienna papyrus which must be one of our last surviving Greek documents from the Fayum in the period following ʿAbd al-Malik's instruction formally converting the language of administration throughout Egypt to Arabic. This is a work contract dated 699/700, addressed to Flavius Atias, then Duke of the combined administration of Arcadia and the Thebaid, for work

[46] *SPP* X 148 (7c.), X 154.9 (7c.).

[47] *SPP* X 148.5.

[48] *SPP* X 154.7.

[49] *P. Ross.-Georg.* III 50 (21 July 643, *BL* 8.291), *SPP* X 154.8.

[50] *SPP* VIII 1150 (Byz.), X 149.9.

[51] *SPP* VIII 1121 (7c.).

[52] *SPP* VIII 1092 (6c.) with *BL* 9.341, *SPP* X 149.5.

[53] *SPP* X 262.8 (7c.).

[54] *P. Erl.* 67 (17 Sept. 591) with *BL* 7.47, 8.120. Kainē's identification with Qāi is rendered uncertain by F. Gomaà *et al.*, *Mittelägypten zwischen Samalūt und dem Gabal Abū Sīr: Beiträge zur historischen Topographie der pharaonischen Zeit* (Wiesbaden, 1991) 95. At any rate, Kainē was 'in the region of Qāi', *P. Oxy.* LXIII pp. 100 f. and in some proximity, therefore, to El Zerība, cf. p. 248 below.

[55] Al-Nābulusī, *Ta'rīkh al-Fayyūm wa-Bilādih*, 114 (= *Description du Faiyoum au VIIe siècle de l'hégire*, ed. B. Moritz) (Cairo, 1899); cf. G. Salmon, 'Répertoire géographique de la province du Fayyoûm d'après le *Kitâb Târîkh al-Fayyoûm* d'An-Nâboulsî', *BIFAO* 1 (1901) 29–77, at 45.

[56] *SB* I 4481 = XVIII 14001.21 (486), *SB* VIII 9778.15 ff. (6c.), *SB* VI 9294.21 ff. (6/7c., *BL* 8.343), I 4839 = XVIII 13999.3 (6/7c.), XVIII 13997.11 f. (early 7c.), I 4483.20 ff. (621), *P. Ross.-Georg.* III 51.22 ff. (630), *SB* XVI 12481.21 ff. (28 Nov. 668), and I 4495 (Byz.), all from the Fayum!

related to one of the jobs in a winery near Selē.[57] The interesting feature of this contract is that it refers to an estate (*ousia*) of the caliph himself, most probably in the vicinity of Saila where the worker came from.[58] The caliph's *ousia* in the eastern Fayyum had both vineyards and a wine factory, and presumably it continued to produce wine on a substantial scale. In short, *CPR* VIII 82 reflects the characteristic features of the earlier seventh-century aristocratic economy: the control of estates by high-ranking officials, in this case, indeed, the highest-ranking official for the region, acting on behalf of the caliph; the continuance of wine production in the eastern Fayyum; and the use of wage labour on the lands of the aristocracy.

The Organization of Labour

In her study of employment relations in the papyri, Andrea Jördens notes that the number of labour contracts (*Arbeitsverträge*) surviving from the Byzantine period (sixth and seventh centuries) far exceeds those of all earlier centuries put together.[59] One implication of this is that wage employment had expanded significantly by the Byzantine period. It is hard to see why this would be happening if there were a shortage of labour, as most historians have assumed.[60] It seems more likely that the increased supply of labour was due to demographic causes, and that this was true of most regions of the eastern Mediterranean. In his *Life* of Simeon the Mountaineer, John of Ephesus tells us that when Simeon came to a certain village in the region of Claudia, on the Euphrates, 'he was astonished that all the mountains were *so full of people* . . . There are there not only cattle-sheds such as some men make, but great houses and substantial dwellings'.[61] The village itself is described as a dispersed settlement, 'so extended (and so full of people) that other hamlets are settled from it within its boundaries'. John settled in the region of Claudia a short while after his exile of 537 and was there till 540, when he left for Constantinople.[62] He was therefore describing a

[57] *CPR* VIII 82, improving considerably on the ed. princeps in *SB* VI 9460, and dated 9 Aug. 699/700.

[58] The caliph ʿAbd al-Malik is referred to as *prōtosymboulos* (l. 5), cf. Theophanes *AM* 6171, referring to Muʿāwiya b. Abī Sufyān by the same term, on which see Mango and Scott, *The Chronicle of Theophanes Confessor,* 500 (*AM* 6171 n. 1).

[59] Jördens, *Vertragliche Regelungen von Arbeiten*, 148.

[60] e.g. Jones, *Later Roman Empire*, 2.817, 'Landlords seem to have been perennially short of tenants.'

[61] John of Ephesus, *Lives* 16 (*PO* 17.232–3).

[62] A. Palmer, *Monk and Mason on the Tigris Frontier: the Early History of Tur ʿAbdin* (Cambridge, 1990) 81.

situation that was true several and probably many years before the plague of 541. More important, the general impression from recent archaeological work is one of expanding settlement, related, almost certainly, to a demographic upsurge.[63]

An expanding supply of labour would naturally increase landowners' options with respect to the organization of labour. It would remove an important constraint on the expansion of large enterprises and facilitate direct management of production. For smaller landlords, it would expand the available pool of 'tenant' labour and allow for a greater flexibility in the integration of tenancy and wage labour. The extension of sharecropping would reflect precisely this, since the Byzantine sharecropper was effectively a labourer,[64] frequently subject to high rents and easily evictable.[65] Finally, the threat of eviction could act as a powerful means of restoring discipline among rural wage labourers, and contribute to maintaining high levels of productivity.

Now the fact that labour was freely available has an obvious bearing on the issue of how estates structured their organization of labour. Mickwitz argued, on the basis of Egyptian evidence, that 'Day labourers seem to have been employed on a progressively reduced scale, and their place was taken by farm-servants employed on a permanent basis (*fest angestellten Knechten*). This transformation was conditioned by the increasing size as well as number of estates, and its consequence was that wages in kind became considerably more important compared to earlier centuries.'[66] That such workers were probably also seen by Mickwitz as bound by a kind of 'serfdom'[67] is surely less significant than his assertion that permanent labour became more widespread in late antiquity, for the general implication is that aristocratic estates were subject to direct management, and that the peasantry employed on such estates was a largely proletarianized labour force. This is particularly clear in the occasional description of such peasants (resident employees) as *ergatai*, since *ergatēs* was standard terminology for the day labourer or casual worker, and served to emphasize the condition of wage labour and, indirectly, of landlessness. Thus, some Fayum estates of the seventh century or later described their permanent labourers

[63] See p. 20 above.

[64] S. Waszyński, *Die Bodenpacht: agrargeschichtliche Papyrusstudien* (Leipzig, 1905) 92, Jördens, *Vertragliche Regelungen*, 258.

[65] J. Banaji, 'Modernizing the Historiography of Rural Labour', in M. Bentley (ed.), *Companion to Historiography* (London, 1997) 88–102, at 95.

[66] Mickwitz, *Geld und Wirtschaft*, 142.

[67] Ibid. 179ff., where he espouses a view that was standard for the generation represented by Seeck and Stein.

as *ergatai*,[68] and in Novel 162 Justinian defined the *coloni* in general as 'residents of estates and field labourers',[69] suggesting both that resident labour was normal on the larger estates and that these rural workers were largely landless, as they were seen simply as labourers (*ergatai*). It is important to bear in mind, however, that these workers were generally described simply as *geōrgoi*, and that the rigid dichotomy that Philo had been able to draw between the *geōrgos* and the *ergatēs*[70] was much less true of the late antique period.

Resident labour was dominant on the large estates. This was certainly true of North Africa, where a Novel of Justin II assumes that rural workers were generally born on the estates they worked for.[71] It was surely true of church estates in the region of Apamea, for the managers of those estates sought to re-establish control over the progeny of women workers who had married employees of other estates.[72] It was true of Egypt where labourers (*geōrgoi*) residing on the Apion estate described themselves as settled there for generations ('since [the time of] their fathers and forefathers'),[73] and workers could be described as having fled from one estate to another.[74] It is also clear from the Egyptian evidence that many of these workers were housed in standard residential units in those parts of the *epoikia* which comprised the labourers' quarters.[75] Most workers (*geōrgoi*) lived here with their families,[76] and their labour was, in principle, tightly controlled.[77]

Apion managers received both cash wages and allowances in kind.[78] On the other hand, surviving accounts make no reference to the remuneration of permanent agricultural workers. The wage receipts show that a significant part of their earnings must have come from money wages (advanced in solidi), but there is also

[68] *P. Ross.-Georg.* V 71.1, *SPP* X 80.15.

[69] *Nov. Just.* 162.2 (539) (*Corpus Iuris Civilis* 3.748), τοὺς οἰκήτορας τῶν χωρίων καὶ τῶν ἀγρῶν ἐργάτας.

[70] Philo, *Peri geōrgias* 4–5 (Colson and Whitaker 3.109 ff.).

[71] Just. II, *Nov.* 6 (570) (*Jus Graecoromanum* 1.10).

[72] *Nov. Just.*, 156 (*Corpus Iuris Civilis* 3.733).

[73] *P. Oxy.* I 130.9, *PSI* I 58.7.

[74] Notably *P. Oxy.* XVI 2055.1, where *geōrgoi* of one *ktēma* were said to have fled to another belonging to the Domus Divina.

[75] See *P. Oxy.* XVI 1917.56 (*c.*616/17) for a reference to 'a hundred *kellia*' in the epoikion Noklē, and the suggestion in l. 98 that Ostrakinon had the same number of 'rooms'.

[76] e.g., *P. Oxy.* I 135.17, XLIV 3204.14 ff., XXVII 2479.11, 17, 25.

[77] *P. Oxy.* LVII 3914.5–6, XIX 2243(a).83, LV 3804.155–6, all suggesting that *ergodiōktai* were assigned to individual settlements or groups of them, so that no settlement was without a 'foreman'.

[78] *P. Oxy.* XVI 1913.40 (30 solidi, 90 artabas of wheat, and 90 artabas of barley for a fairly highly placed manager), 1911.152, 1912.130, see App. 1, Table 11.

evidence that various groups of employees received food rations. The Apion *paidaria* and their families received food allowances whose amount varied.[79] In *P. Amherst* II 155, similar rations are explicitly described as 'wages' and their recipients called *geōrgoi*.[80] On Strategius' Oxyrhynchite estate, workers were paid at least partly in wheat.[81] However, most of the surviving wage receipts relate to cash advances. It is possible that with the extension of wage labour in agriculture, the system of 'advancing' wages was extended from industrial workshops such as weaving shops to rural estates.[82] The Apions made extensive use of this system. Volume 58 of the Oxyrhynchite papyri contains a series of (fragmentary) receipts with the description *γρα(μματεῖον) προχρ(είας)*.[83] The *prochreia* was an advance of wages,[84] and the Apion receipts suggest that this was standardly made in the course of November when employees on cash wages received their first instalment of pay.[85] Fortunately, other Apion receipts contain more complete specimens of such cash advances.[86] These show that the disbursement of cash wages was widespread in the cultivation of irrigated plots, including orchards and vineyards. Thus in *P. Amherst* II 149 the recipient is a 'gardener', and in *P. Oxy.* I 206 (535) a *γεωργὸς μηχανῆς*. The allocation of labour took place through the assignment of individual

[79] *P. Princ.* II 96.1 ff. (see *P. Oxy.* LVIII 3960.28n), a wage account which starts *Βρέ(ουϊον) ὀψωνίων παιδαρ(ίων) Αἰγυπτ(ίων) καὶ γυναικ(ῶν) καὶ ἄλλ(ων) ἐπὶ τῆς ιε ἰνδ(ικτίονος)*, followed by allowances in wheat, mostly 12 artabas. The date is 551/2 or 566/7; cf. H. Harrauer and P. Sijpesteijn, 'P. Princ. II 96 und Schreibübungen', *ZPE* 64 (1986) 115 f.

[80] *P. Amh.* II 155.1, with the heading *Λόγ(ος) σίτου μισθοῦ τῶν γεωργ(ῶν) ἡμῶν σὺν θ(ε)ῷ ιβ ἰνδικ(τίονος)*, not from the Apion estate.

[81] *P. Berol. inv.* 10526 (28 Aug. 598) = Poethke, *JJP* 23 (1993) 133 ff., cf. *P. Oxy.* LVIII 3936 (5 May 598), also from Strategius' estate and the same location.

[82] e.g. *P. Oxy.* LXIII 4353 (304), *P. Rein.* II 105 (432), *P. Stras. inv. gr.* 1550 (Oxy., 5c.) = A. Malnati and A. F. Moretti, 'P. Stras. inv. gr. 1550: un contrat de *ΠΡΟΧΡΕΙΑ*', *ZPE* 113 (1996) 219 f., *P. Prag.* I 34 (Fayum, 6c.), all involving wage advances to weavers.

[83] *P. Oxy.* LVIII 3943–6, issued within three days of each other, between 15 and 18 Nov. 606.

[84] Cf. Jördens, *Vertragliche Regelungen*, 277 ff., and 'P. Prag. I 34: Ein Arbeitsvertrag', *ZPE* 75 (1988) 164–6. For *prochreia* clearly in the sense of a wage advance, cf. *SPP* III 56.4 (6c.).

[85] *P. Oxy.* XVI 1970.22 ff. (554), in which two water-wheel mechanics refer to the first instalment of their wages: *καὶ ὁμολογοῦμεν ταῦτα* (sc. 4 solidi) *ἀποδοῦναι τῇ ὑμῶν μεγαλοπρ(επείᾳ) . . . ἐν τῇ πρώτῃ δόσει τοῦ ἡμῶν [μι]σθ(οῦ) τοῦ ἐνδόξ(ου) οἴκου ἐν τῷ Ἁθὺρ μην[ί]*.

[86] *P. Oxy.* I 206 (535) = D. Montserrat, G. Fantoni, and P. Robinson, 'Varia descripta Oxyrhynchita', *BASP* 31 (1994) 11–80, at 70 f., *P. Iand.* 48 (582), *P. Oxy.* I 192 (600 or 615) = Montserrat, Fantoni, and Robinson, pp. 56 f., and *P. Amh.* II 149 (6/7c.). The tendency to describe such contracts as 'loans' is of course misleading.

workers to specific plots.[87] These assignments could change,[88] but of course one has no idea how frequently they did. The point to note is that the deployment of wage labour in this form would have given the employer considerable flexibility.

The contention that it would have been inefficient for estates to hire labour throughout the year and that consequently 'the bulk of the labour on the land through most of the year was not done by hired men'[89] ignores the fact that it was always possible for owners to structure the organization of labour to secure maximum flexibility. An Oxyrhynchite papyrus, *P. Washington University* II 102, suggests that in part the estate treated the *epoikia* as 'common labour pools'[90] by drawing on the labour contribution of individual settlements.[91] At a certain level, it made no difference to the estate administration which individuals were actually deployed. This is remarkably reminiscent of the organization of labour on some nineteenth-century *ezbas*.[92] In recent work Roger Owen and Alan Richards have reconstructed Egyptian estate organization in the period 1880–1914, when the expansion of large properties led to the rapid proliferation of *ezbas*, chiefly in Lower Egypt and due mainly to the cotton boom. 'The basis of the ezba system lay in the fact that its peasant inhabitants were given a dwelling place (or at least the materials to build one) and the lease of one or two feddans of land—at an equivalent of perhaps half the normal rent—in exchange for labor services. J. F. Nahas describes a system by which each peasant family was required to supply an agreed number of workers at a daily wage to be determined in advance.'[93] Owen calls such workers 'service tenants', and it is possible that the bulk of the

[87] This is clear from the expression γεωργὸς μηχανῆς which occurs throughout the axle account *P. Oxy.* XIX 2244 (bef. 565/6, *BL* 9.194). In *P. Oxy.* XVIII 2197 (*c.*567) the expression appears in a reversed form, viz., μηχανὴ γεωργοῦ or μηχανὴ ὑπὸ γεωργόν.

[88] John son of Paleus from the epoikion Leontos appears in both *P. Oxy.* I 206 (n. 86 above) and XIX 2244.34, at an interval of several years, but employed on different farms.

[89] R. S. Bagnall, *Egypt in Late Antiquity* (Princeton, 1993) 121.

[90] I borrow the expression from Nomaan Majid, 'Contractual Arrangements in Pakistani Agriculture: A Study of Share Tenancy in Sindh' (Oxford D.Phil., 1994).

[91] *P. Wash. Univ.* II 102 (5/6c.), called 'list of labourers', with the following title in the margin: † [γν]ῶσ(ις) ἐργ(ατῶν) ὀφειλ(όντων) ἀπελθ(εῖν) εἰ(ς) τὸ παρ( ) πρὸς κατασπορ(ὰν) τῆς γεουχ(ικῆς) αὐτουρ(γίας) ια ἰνδ(ικτίονος).

[92] See J. Banaji, 'Agrarian History and the Labour Organisation of Byzantine Large Estates', in A. K. Bowman and E. Rogan (eds.), *Agriculture in Egypt from Pharaonic to Modern Times*. Proceedings of the British Academy, 96 (Oxford, 1999) 193–216, for more discussion.

[93] E. R. J. Owen, 'The Development of Agricultural Production in Nineteenth-Century Egypt: Capitalism of What Type?', in A. L. Udovitch (ed.), *The Islamic Middle East, 700–1900* (Princeton, 1981) 521–46, esp. 524, A. Richards, 'Land and Labor on Egyptian Cotton Farms, 1882–1940', *Agricultural History* 52 (1978) 503–18, cf. J. F. Nahas, *Situation économique et sociale du fellah égyptien* (Paris, 1901) 140 ff.

permanent labourers who worked on Byzantine large estates were in fact 'service tenants'.[94] The formulas structuring the exchange of labour against land varied between estates,[95] and there was considerable fluidity about the arrangements between landowners and labourers.[96] The important conceptual point is that service tenancy (or 'labour tenancy') involved a complex and flexible integration of tenancy and wage labour. Among other things, this means that within the framework of large estates it was always possible to find a large number of peasants working as sharecroppers, with no suggestion either that these sharecroppers were independent tenants, i.e. not simple labourers, or that the estate was not run as a single unit.[97]

[94] In other words, it is possible that usufruct rights were the main feature of the *epoikion* as a system of labour organization. On Appianus' Fayum estate, a special class of workers were those described by Rathbone, *Economic Rationalism*, 159, 146, as 'tenants of estate accommodation with labour dues to discharge' or simply 'tenants with labour dues'. It is perhaps significant that these workers were called *epoikiōtai*, suggesting that the estates were designed to generate reserves of labour through the mechanism of labour tenancy. Another 3rd-cent. estate that used labour tenants was Valerius Titanianus' estate in the Fayum. Here '[m]ost persons renting rooms on the estate were obliged to provide 12 days of labor semi-annually' (Shelton, *P. Mich.* 620, introd. 65). The late antique evidence is less certain, however. *P. Michael.* 48 (572) shows that shepherds were recruited as labour tenants. On the Apion estate, fruit workers of the three orchards 'outside the Gate' in one account were paid 22½ artabas of wheat 'by way of compensation, in lieu of the three arouras sown by them', *ἀντὶ τῶν (ἀρουρῶν) γ τῶν σπειρομ(ένων) παρ' αὐτῶν λόγ(ῳ) παραμυθ(ίας)* (*P. Oxy.* XVI 1913.6–7). This strongly suggests that these employees normally received a small plot of land as part of their remuneration by the estate, perhaps 1 aroura for each orchard assigned to them, and that the payment in kind advanced on this occasion compensated for the transfer or reassignment of this land to some other use unrelated to employees' subsistence. Lines 67 ff. of the same account show that there was considerable flexibility about the type of adjustments the estate was willing, and able, to make in structuring its supplies of labour: here the expected (cash) receipts of a second indiction were carried forward to the third and treated as an advance payment of wages for work connected with the irrigation of orchards and gardens 'outside the Gate'. Again, in *P. Oxy.* 1917, a 7th-cent. account from the Heracleopolite part of the estate, the administration charged a rent of 2 artabas for standard units of accommodation called *kellia* (rooms). It is unlikely that the leasing of these units was what mainly interested the estate and much more probable that the rooms were occupied by unmarried wage-labourers whose rent was deducted from wages ('at source') and whose chief function was the provision of labour to the estate, perhaps on a seasonal basis (cf. the *epoikiōtai* on the Appianus estate).

[95] e.g. J. C. McCoan, *Egypt as it is* (London, Paris, and New York, n.d.) 183, Saleh Nour ed-Din, *Revue de l'Islam* 3 (1898) 5 f., Nahas, *Fellah égyptien*, 141, 143, Samir Saffa, *L'Égypte contemporaine* 40 (1949) 275 ff., at 409.

[96] Owen, *The Middle East in the World Economy*, 146, 230.

[97] Thus in *SB* 9293 (28 June 573, cf. *BL* 8.343), a sharecropper agreed to work for a certain landowner and be remunerated 'on the same pattern as the *geōrgoi* of your brother the *clarissimus* [....]' (*δέξασθαί με παρὰ σοῦ τὸν γεωργικόν μου [μισθὸν* or *μέρος καθ' ὁ]μοιότητα τῶν γεωργῶν τοῦ σοῦ [ἀδελφοῦ].ου τοῦ λαμπροτάτου*), with the correction in Jördens, *Vertragliche Regelungen*, 267 n. 25. This suggests the deployment of sharecroppers on standardized terms, implying the sort of retention of control suggested above.

Of course, the service tenants, if that is what they were, were simply the core of a larger and more diversified labour force that included many other groups: skilled and less-skilled employees attached to other occupations/jobs on the estate (water-wheel mechanics,[98] carpenters,[99] millstone-cutters,[100] iron smiths,[101] potters,[102] weavers,[103] bakery workers[104]), purely casual labourers,[105] other kinds of workers recruited for specific tasks,[106] the domestic and administrative staff who were probably known by the term *paidaria*,[107] and so on. These workers were employed on a range of contracts,[108] and this reinforces the impression that the large estates were aware of the need for flexibility and far from schematic in their deployment of labour.

The other antithesis that might usefully be discarded is the inexorable opposition between bureaucracy and economic efficiency. The elaborate administrative bureaucracies that were characteristic of Russian estates of the eighteenth century[109] were replicated to an even higher degree in the organization of the *oikoi*. Bureaucratiza-

[98] *P. Oxy*. XVI 1970.14, μηχανουργοὶ τοῦ αὐτοῦ ἐνδόξ(ου) οἴκου, XXVII 2480.45, τοῖς τεκτόσ(ιν) μηχανουργ(οῖς), LV 3805.106, τοῖς τέκτ(οσι) μηχανουργ(οῖς), also presumably the ὀργανάρ(ιος) on the large southern estate in *CPR* XIV 41.5 (translated 'waterwork-engineer').

[99] *P. Oxy*. XXVII 2480.96, τοῖς τεκτόσ(ι) τοῦ ἐνδόξ(ου) οἴκου, *P. Coll. Youtie* II 95.12 (Fayum, 7c.), with Reekmans' note, 'Patouos must have been a permanent worker of the estate's staff'.

[100] *P. Oxy*. LI 3641 (544).

[101] *SB* XVIII 12943.1 (Fayum, 6c.), σιδηροχαλκεύς τῆς μεγάλης ἐκκλησίας, *P. Oxy*. XXVII 2480.24, τοῖς χαλκεῦσ(ι) τῶν κτημ(άτων).

[102] *BGU* II 368 (Fayum, 615), estate of Strategius, pay receipt of a *kouphokeramourgos*.

[103] *SB* XIV 12195.10–12 (Fayum, 608), [λίνυ]φος Κυρίλ[λου τοῦ] ἐνδοξοτάτου στρατηλ(άτου).

[104] *PSI* VIII 956.38, τοῖς ἐργάτ(αις) τοῦ ἀρτοκοπ(ίου).

[105] *P. Oxy*. I 141.5, τοῖς χωρικ(οῖς) ἐργάτ(αις), *SPP* X 251 B 4 (Fayum, 7c., *BL* 9.343), *SPP* III 86 (623?), *P. Hamb*. III 216.2–3 (Oxy., 586), *PSI* III 200 (Oxy., 592). The fifteenth indiction of *SPP* X 251 was 626/7, since the account, clearly from a very substantial estate, makes several references to Šahrālānyōzān, indicating that the Fayum was then under Persian occupation.

[106] e.g. *P. Oxy*. I 134 (569), stonemason's contract, reading κεφαλ(αιωτής) in l. 15.

[107] Cf. *CPR* XIV 41 (6/7c.) which refers to the staff of a large estate by the generic description τῶν ὀντῶν παιδαρ(ίων) ἐν Θηβ(αΐδι) (ll. 1–2). Also in *P. Princ*. II 96 (n. 79 above), where most employees of this description are *meizoteroi* or ex-*meizoteroi* or their relations, *P. Oxy*. LVIII 3960.28, *P. Bad*. 97.5, τοῖς παιδαρ(ίοις) τοῦ οἴκου, *P. Herm*. 84, *SPP* XX 222 with *BL* 1.421. 'Helpers' may be a more nuanced translation than either Wilcken's 'Knaben' (*P. Würz*. 14.16n) or Rathbone's 'servant' (*Economic Rationalism*, 91), and may help to resolve the dilemma of whether such employees were invariably young (like the Mexican *muchachos*) or invariably free (cf. Rea, *P. Oxy*. 3960.28n).

[108] The Apions wanted lifelong control over skills which may have been in short supply, cf. *P. Oxy*. 3641, whereas most administrators were retained on one-year contracts.

[109] See P. Kolchin, *Unfree Labor: American Slavery and Russian Serfdom* (Cambridge, Mass., 1987) 58–62, 68, 99.

tion contributed to efficiency by allowing for more stringent administrative control,[110] tighter financial monitoring, and larger scales of operation. Indeed, it is difficult to imagine the Byzantine large estate *without* the bureaucratic form that enabled it to function as a stable and coherent entity. There was considerable specialization. The precise hierarchies are far from clear, however. Above a huge army of subordinate staff were supervisors,[111] stewards,[112] secretaries, stenographers and other clerical staff,[113] senior administrators (*dioikētai*), coin-weighers,[114] bankers,[115] treasurers,[116] storekeepers,[117] rent-collectors,[118] armed personnel, etc. The διοικηταί were the hallmark of the new managerial hierarchies which emerged in the course of the fifth century, though there is a confusing elasticity in the use of estate terminology. *Dioikētēs* functioned as a generic term for the main groups of managers,[119] and even the steward might be described as a *dioikētēs*.[120] On the other hand, *dioikētai* were peculiar to the administration of large estates and not found on smaller-sized properties, and the term was applied chiefly to the senior administrators whose circumscriptions (διοίκησις) involved both settlements and villages.[121] Thus the village headmen (*meizones*) and village secretaries (*boēthoi*) were probably directly responsible to these administrators, insofar as the jurisdiction of estates extended over villages. It is not certain that the larger estates imposed a single system of classification on estate managers throughout the various districts. The Fayum aristocrats described their

[110] e.g. *P. Oxy*. XVI 1830, careful monitoring of flood levels on the Apion estate.

[111] The *ergodiōktai*, see n. 77 above.

[112] *P. Oxy* XVI 1916, 2031, 2032, and 2034 suggest that each settlement (*epoikion*) had one steward (*pronoētēs*).

[113] *Chartularioi*, secretaries, and *notarioi*, stenos: some of these would have worked in the estate office, the χαρτουλάριον, which is mentioned in *P. Oxy*. LVIII 3960.26 (621) and LV 3804.239 (566), τῶν διφθερ(ῶν) καὶ τῶν λόγων καὶ ἄλλ(ων) τοῦ γεουχικ(οῦ) χαρτουλαρίου, 'the ledgers and the accounts and other (papers) of the landlord's office'.

[114] *P. Oxy*. XXXVI 2780.21 f. (553, estate of Flavia Gabrielia).

[115] *CPR* V 18 (538?), Πέτρῳ τῷ θαυμα(σιωτάτῳ) τραπεζ(ίτῃ) τῶν ὑπὸ τὴν Ἡρακλέους κτημά(των) διαφερό(ντων) τῷ θειοτά(τῳ) οἴκῳ, *P. Oxy*. XVI 1970.7 (554), *SB* VI 9153.7–8 (596) with the corrections in *BL* 8.340, *P. Oxy*. LVIII 3935.6–7 (591), *P. Erl*. 73.10–11 (pp. 81 f.) (604), *P. Vars*. 31 (609).

[116] *MPER* XV 111 III 54 (6/7c.), *SPP* VIII 1111 (633).

[117] *SPP* VIII 1247.2, κελλ(αρίτης?) οὐσί(ας) Κυρίλλ(ου), X 251 B 7, τοῦ κελλαρ(ίτου) τοῦ οἴκου, *P. Oxy*. VIII 1131 (Bagnall, *CE* 66 (1991) 289), οἰνοχει(ριστῇ) [τοῦ ἐνδό]ξ(ου) [οἴ]κου.

[118] *P. Oxy*. VII 1038.13 (568), LVIII 3958 (614).

[119] *P. Oxy*. 3641.18, διὰ τῶν αὐτῆς (sc. ὑμετέρας ὑπερφυείας) διοικητῶν. Secretaries were regularly described as *dioikētai*.

[120] *P. Oxy*. XVIII 2196.4, δι' ἐμοῦ Σερήνου διο[ι]κ(ητοῦ) καὶ προ(νοητοῦ) Ματρεῦ κτλ.

[121] See *P. Oxy*. VIII 1147 especially; cf. *P. Oxy*. 1913.64, 2031, 1908.10–11, XVIII 2197 verso 172, all referring to 'Counts'.

highest ranking administrators as *megaloprepestatoi*.[122] On the Apion estates, *lamprotatos* was the highest epithet conceded to the *dioikētēs*.[123] Other Oxyrhychite aristocrats described their *dioikētai* as *peribleptoi*.[124] It is possible that practice varied between estates. Several and probably most large estates maintained *epikeimenoi*.[125] They bore a special relation to the organization of labour, and may have been similar to the 'field boss' on the North Peruvian plantations, in the sense that the supervisory personnel answered directly to them.[126] Above this whole hierarchy was the *antigeouchos*, the landlord's direct representative, who also has a counterpart in the "representante" on the better organized South American haciendas.[127]

To sum up, estates which were organized around settlements seem to have proliferated by some stage in the fifth century. These were privately owned settlements built to house permanent workers on a pattern familiar from the Egyptian *ezbas* of the late nineteenth century, and, like the *ezbas*, they were usually located in the open countryside away from the villages. The workers residing in these 'estate villages' were largely landless and attracted to the estate by the prospect of stable long-term employment. The ancient economy had always depended to some degree on reserves of free labour, as the following chapter argues, but the considerable expansion of *epoikion*-type estates from the fifth century onwards suggests that rural wage labourers became more common in that period. With his usual perspicacity, Mickwitz noted that the later evidence contains fewer references to the use of casual labourers. This comports with a situation where the bigger estates sought to 'internalize' employment, with as much control over the labour market as they could

[122] *P. Erl.* 67.4–5 (Sophia), *BGU* I 323.4–5 (Theodosius), *P. Oxy*. LVIII 3936.9–10 (Strategius), *P. Berol. inv.* 10526.13–15 (Strategius).

[123] *P. Oxy*. LVIII 3954.8–9. The *meizoteros* Theodore was also *lamprotatos*, *P. Oxy*. XVI 1857 verso.

[124] *P. Oxy*. VII 1038.11–12 (Flavia Euphemia), *SB* VI 9561.11–13 (Flavia Anastasia), *P. Oxy*. XIX 2239.5–6 (Flavius John), also on Strategius' Oxyrhynchite estate, *P. Oxy*. XVI 1991.10–12.

[125] e.g. *SB* I 5270 (610), *Τῷ θα[υ]μ[ασ(ιωτάτῳ)] Κοσμᾷ ἐπικειμένῳ οὐσί[α]ς Στρατηγίου*. The best document is *P. Oxy*. 2239, discussed at p. 151–2. *P. Oxy*. LV 3805.34 shows that villages contributed to the perquisites of the *epikeimenos*. In *P. Oxy*. XVI 2051.45 the proper expansion is obviously ἐπικ(ειμένῳ), cf. *P. Oxy*. 3805.34, 35, 118 for the abbreviation.

[126] M. J. Gonzales, *Plantation Agriculture and Social Control in Northern Peru, 1875–1933* (University of Texas Press, 1985) 75 f.

[127] L. Maltby, 'Colonos on Hacienda Picotani', in B. S. Orlove and G. Custred (eds.), *Land and Power in Latin America: Agrarian Economies and Social Processes in the Andes* (New York, 1980) 101.

have. The large estates also developed elaborate hierarchies to ensure the vertical co-ordination needed to bind clusters of settlements into coherently functioning networks, and landowners clearly sought to minimize agency problems by retaining their crucial managers on short-term contracts, as the Apions did. However, the kind of estate known to us from the Egyptian evidence was only one in a gallery of various types of estates; the countryside comprised other estate structures and forms of estate organization, and much more work is needed before we can have a more balanced picture of the large rural establishments of late antiquity.

CHAPTER 8

Wage Labour and the Peasantry

The Peasantry of the Byzantine Period

Geōrgoi regularly described themselves as '*geōrgoi* of such and such owner', as in *P. Köln* III 152 (477?) where John son of Apphu called himself γεωργὸς τῆς ἁγίας ἐκκλησίας ἀπὸ κώμης Ψενύρεως in an advance sale of fodder,[1] or in *P. Berl. Zilliacus* 8 (663) where Sarapion son of Victor signed a good conduct bond with Peter, bishop of Arsinoe, calling himself ὑμέ(τερος) γεωργὸς κώμης Καμίνων κτλ.[2] The implication is that such 'peasants' worked as regular employees of the owner rather than tenants bound by short-term contracts.[3] *SPP* X 128 (Fayum, 7c.) refers to the *ampelourgoi* of the *clarissimus* Apphous, again with the implication that these were workers normally employed in this owner's vineyards at Ampeliou.[4] In the third century, *P. Oxy.* XLII 3048 had included *geōrgoi* among the groups of employees who were paid a regular monthly wage on the estate of Calpurnia Heraclia—alongside *paidaria* and *katamēnioi*.[5] Doubtless these peasants would have been known locally as *geōrgoi* 'of' Calpurnia Heraclia. Numerous examples suggest that *geōrgoi* were often simply resident employees of an estate rather than lessees working on short-term contracts and moving between estates, and rather than discuss these individually I have brought the main evidence together in Appendix 1, Table 8.

Geōrgoi also regularly engaged in wage labour. On the Abu Mena estate, which was probably controlled by the church, the labour force which handled the vintage included a group called γεωργοὶ τρυγῶντες.[6] Since grape-picking was a seasonal activity these

[1] *P. Köln* III 152.7–8 (477?).

[2] *P. Berl. Zill.* 8.7 (663).

[3] Thus it is possible that the γεωργοί who were distinguished from the μισθωταί in *SPP* XX 151.30–1 were regular estate employees as opposed to lessees. *P. Amst.* I 78.2 (5c.), οἱ ἀμπελουργ(οὶ) τοῦ κτή(μα)τ(ος) is more ambiguous.

[4] *SPP* X 128.1–2 (7c.), τοὺς ἀμπελουργοὺς τοῦ λαμπροτάτου κυροῦ Απφουα.

[5] See p. 108 above.

[6] See Wortmann, *ZPE* 8 (1971) pp. 43 f., nos. 3 and 7.

peasants need not have been permanent employees of the estate but farmers engaged in seasonal labour. Brick-making was another seasonal occupation which *geōrgoi* depended on for regular cash earnings.[7] *Geōrgoi* also appear frequently as hired workers employed by various sections of the aristocracy on irrigation work.[8] Such workers were normally paid wage advances and there is no implication in any of the receipts that their employers looked on these as anything other than a straight advance of wages. The standard formula that the worker would 'return' the amount advanced applied just in case he abandoned his contract before its date of expiry.[9] On the other hand, it is not clear from these contracts whether such *geōrgoi* were either barred or discouraged from working for other employers during the period of the agreement, and the reason why landowners felt it was necessary to bind workers through a clause of this type may well have been their accepted and commonly presumed mobility between several jobs (different estates) in the course of the year. All contracts of this type involved money wages (calculated and probably also paid in solidi), so that the spread of peasant wage labour on the farms and estates with stable yields was inseparable from the more general involvement of such estate owners in production for the market and money economy.[10]

The *geōrgoi* who turn up in Aphrodito leases as workers employed by *lessees* leasing irrigated farms on a crop-sharing basis were almost certainly agricultural labourers, not subtenants. *P. Cairo Masp.* I 67095.19 (548) shows that "geōrgos" by itself could be used to refer to a person who was actually a *γεωργὸς μίσθιος* or hired agricultural worker (cf. ll. 7 and 19). Here Dioscorus apparently forced such a 'peasant' to accept a wage reduction of 10 artabas of wheat. In *P. Apoll.* 75 the *μισθίοι γεωργοί* turn up as a distinct occupational group, presumably full-time agricultural workers and apparently one of several professional corporations.[11] On the other hand, the *geōrgoi* who were paid various amounts of wheat as wages in *P. Amh.*

[7] Cf. *PSI* VI 712 (295), two *geōrgoi* paid wages of 8,000 drachmas each for a total production of 40,000 bricks.

[8] *SB* VI 9284 (553), *P. Iand.* 48 (582), *SPP* III 86 (593?), *P. Flor.* I 70 (627), etc. On the Apion estates irrigation work seems to have been regularly handled through wage advances, cf. *P. Oxy.* XVI 1913.67 f., *τοῖς ἀπὸ Φατεμῆντ(ος) καὶ Ἀκτουαρίου κτλ. . . . λόγ(ῳ) προχρείας διὰ τὸ αὐτοῖς* (l. *αὐτοὺς*) *ἀρδεῦσαι εἰς τὰ πωμάρια καὶ εἰς τὰ κηπία ἔξω τῆς πύλ(ης) νο(μ) η π(α.) μ.*

[9] Cf. *SB* VI 9284.11–12, *P. Amh.* II 149.14–16 (6c.), *P. Flor.* I 70.10, *P. Lond.* III 1037.10 ff. (6c.), though here l. 8 refers to the advance, inaccurately, as *κεφάλαιον*.

[10] Note the special association of such contracts with wine, e.g. *P. Lond.* III 1037 (pp. 275–6), *SB* VI 9459, *SPP* III 86.

[11] So Rémondon, *P. Apoll.* 75.12n (p. 155). In *P. Apoll.* 98 part of a disbursement of barley is described as (*ὑπὲρ*) *μισθ(οῦ) γεωργῶ(ν)* and referred, perhaps, to the wages of such workers.

II 155 (5c.), which is called *Λόγ(ος) σίτου μισθοῦ τῶν γεωργ(ῶν) ἡμῶν σὺν θ(ε)ῷ ιβ ἰνδικ(τίονος)*, were probably permanent farm servants connected to an estate near Hermopolis. In short, there is considerable evidence to suggest that *geōrgoi* both engaged in paid labour and constituted regular estate employees in the Byzantine period, and thus that the term *geōrgos* lacked any specific connotation of independence. It is even possible that the majority of *geōrgoi* were actually landless.

However, the Byzantine peasantry was a deeply differentiated group, and it would be wrong to ignore the existence, in the sixth century, of a considerable class of 'substantial peasants'. *Nov. Just.* 128, c.14 (545) clearly implies that the majority of the *geōrgoi* who were registered with the estates were landless cultivators—they would not normally be expected to possess any land liable to taxes.[12] A Novel of Justin II contraposes the *geōrgoi* to the *ktēmenoi*, again with the probable implication that most of the former were landless.[13] On the other hand, it is clear that the Apion estates comprised a group of substantial peasants (*geōrgoi*). Averaging the larger individual payments in five Apion accounts shows that households of this sort paid 95½ artabas of wheat (N = 26) and 8½ solidi in cash (N = 25)[14]—a total contribution roughly equivalent to 200 artabas of wheat. If *P. Oxy.* XVIII 2195.37 can be construed as implying that the Apions regarded 7 artabas *or* ½ solidus as a standard rate for the *mēchanai* or irrigated acreage, these would be households renting substantial irrigated farms of *c.*30 arouras,[15] at least partly for market production, which was the most likely source of the cash earnings from which money rents could be paid. It follows that the peasantry of the sixth century was clearly a differentiated group and it makes no sense to advance general propositions about them which ignore these important differences. In the fourth century Sakaon son of Satabous had been the pure type of this 'campagnard

[12] *Nov. Just.* 128.14, *ἀλλὰ καὶ εἰ συμβαίη γεωργούς τινι προσήκοντας ἢ ἐναπογράφους ἰδίαν ἔχειν κτῆσιν, ἐκείνους ὑπὲρ αὐτῆς τὰς δημοσίας εἰσπράττεσθαι συντελείας, τοῦ δεσπότου αὐτῶν μηδεμίαν ὄχλησιν ὑπὲρ αὐτῶν ὑπομένοντος.* Clearly the nuance is, 'even if *geōrgoi* belonging to or registered with (some landowner) should happen to have farms of their own . . .'.

[13] Just. II, *Nov.* 1 (Zacharia von Lingenthal, *Novellae et aureae bullae imperatorum post Justinianum*, p. 2), so too *Nov. Just.* 17.14 (535).

[14] See p. 166 above for the rich peasants of Thelbonthis (in the Hermopolite). Fifteen solidi was a large sum for an ordinary *geōrgos*, cf. *P. Oxy.* I 130.12 (563/4?), *καὶ χρυσίον οὐκ ὀλίγον ἐδανισάμην νο(μίσματα) ιε.*

[15] If 95½ artabas is converted at 14 art./sol., the rate implied in *P. Oxy.* 2195.37, and added to the average cash payment of 8½ solidi, the total cash amount of 15⅓ solidi paid by the 'average' big peasant implies an irrigated holding of 30.6 arouras (if the rent is ½ solidus per aroura).

relativement riche' or 'gros paysan'.[16] The officials who drafted the local village accounts and presumably his lessors such as the *clarissima* Rufina daughter of Rufus, whose husband Claudius Lambadius sat in the *boulē* of Alexandria (so that she herself may have been from an Alexandrian family) called Sakaon a *geōrgos*.[17] In *P. Thead.* 17, re-edited by John Rea as *P. Turner* 44, he and two other villagers of Theadelphia represented the *koinon* of the village in 331/2, at a time, apparently, when the gross cropped area had shrunk, drastically, to a mere five hundred arouras and most of the taxable population had fled to other locations (including private estates). Sakaon may have controlled some 10 per cent of the village land which was liable for taxes on the rural account.[18] In the petition just referred to he and his two colleagues described themselves as ἄνθρωποι μέτριοι.[19] This was not mere rhetoric but a more or less precise description of the social standing of *geōrgoi* like Sakaon. In 309/10, some twenty years earlier, Aurelius Isidorus had described himself in precisely the same way, as 'in every way a man of small means (μέτριος παντελῶς)' and as one of the *metrioi*.[20] Some twelve years before that, Isidorus was usually addressed as *geōrgos*,[21] just as his father Ptolemaeus had been.[22] At this time *P. Cairo Isid.* 5 (299) shows the total area of his landed property to have been *c.*54 arouras, not inconsiderable. In 310 when he composed the petitions in which he insistently classified himself as *metrios*, he owned (was liable to taxes for) no less than 140 arouras.[23] Thus we have a precise indication of how far up the landed hierarchy the terms *geōrgos* and *metrios* could actually stretch—even if we suppose, with the editors, that Isidorus came by most of the extra land (almost 86 arouras) not through acquisition but by inheritance ('perhaps from his mother').[24] In fact, an index of how much Isidorus owned in 310 is valuable in another way—from *P. Cairo Isid.* 6 (300–5) we know

[16] P. Jouguet, *Papyrus de Théadelphie* (Paris, 1911) 32, A. Déléage, *La Capitation du Bas-Empire* (Macon,1945) 117. For Sakaon's archive see G. M. Parássoglu, *The Archive of Aurelius Sakaon: Papers of an Egyptian Farmer in the Last Century of Theadelphia.* Papyrologische Texte und Abhandlungen 23 (Bonn, 1978).

[17] *P. Strasb.* I 45.17. For Rufina, see *Catalogue*, Fayum 4c.

[18] Cf. *P. Thead.* 30 where he contributes 43½ artabas out of a total of 421, in an account entitled Εἴσπραξις σίτου κώμης Θεαδελφίας ὑπὲρ ι ἰνδι(κτίωνος) κωμητὸν κτλ.

[19] *P. Turner* 44.15.

[20] *P. Cairo Isid.* 68.6–7 (309/10), cf. *P. Cairo Isid.* 69.25ff. (310).

[21] Cf. *P. Cairo Isid.* 111.4 (298), Αὐρη[λίῳ] Ἰσιδ[ώ]ρῳ γεωργῷ.

[22] *P. Cairo Isid.* 109.3, [Αὐ]ρη(λίῳ) Πτολεμαίῳ γεωργῷ.

[23] *P. Cairo Isid.* 69.17f., cf. *P. Cairo Isid.*, p. 7.

[24] *P. Cairo Isid.*, pp. 7f. Note that the early 2nd-cent. Hermopolite family of Sarapion/Eutychides are sometimes described as *geōrgoi*, yet their holdings are put at *c.*230 arouras by J. Schwartz, 'La terre d'Égypte au temps de Trajan et d'Hadrien (Archives de Sarapion)', *CE* 34 (1959) 342–56, at 350.

that the size of the larger holdings in the village area of Karanis (as opposed to its *horiodeiktia* or wider circumscription) was in the general size range 46–103 arouras.[25] Thus Isidorus' accumulation of land between 299 and 310 would have made him *one of the biggest village landholders* (if not the biggest) among the 150 odd landed proprietors—local and metropolitan—presumed for Karanis in 309.[26]

Villagers like Sakaon and Isidorus represented a stratum which clearly survived the fiscal pressures of the fourth and fifth centuries to re-emerge in the heyday of Byzantine Egypt as households firmly in control of the village, community leaders (at the local level) and the counterparts of what the *geouchoi* were for the imperial state in areas where the estates acquired (or assumed) responsibility for their own taxes. The village 'community' was essentially an expression of their social and fiscal solidarity, on the one hand against pagarchs who sought to break their dominance and incorporate the village (*kōmē*) into their own semi-private control, on the other, against the mass of the poorer village population which they controlled or even had conflicts with.[27] By now, between the rich peasant (the Byzantine successor of the *geōrgos* Sakaon who had represented the *koinon* of his village) and the κτήτωρ or middling landowner there were largely imperceptible gradations, since the village oligarchy[28] came to describe themselves no longer mainly as *geōrgoi* but in terms of the corporate identity they acquired, as *prōtokōmētai* (village leaders) and *syntelestai,* the people on whose collaboration the efficient functioning of the fiscal machinery chiefly depended. The *prōtokōmētai* were certainly in existence by the early fifth century though our first traces of them appear not in the papyri but in hagiography.[29] Aurelius Apollos, father of Dioscorus, was of course the pure type of this village oligarch, described in the middle of the sixth century by his son as (at one time) 'the premier local landholder and the one who collected the taxes for the entire village'.[30] Apollos is never called a *geōrgos* but his social roots lay

[25] Cf. *P. Cairo Isid.*, p. 58.

[26] *P. Cairo Isid.*, p. 77. The introduction to *P. Cairo Isid.* 9 is a strong argument for the strength of the rich peasantry in the agrarian structure of the early fourth century, esp. p. 79.

[27] See *P. Cairo Masp.* I 67087 (543) with the commentary in J. G. Keenan, 'Village Shepherds and Social Tension in Byzantine Egypt', *YClS* 28 (1985) 245–59, esp. 250 ff.

[28] This term was used by Irfan Habib to describe equivalent groups in the 'village communities' of Mughal India (in the first of his Radhakrishnan Memorial Lectures at Oxford in June 1991).

[29] The earliest reference I have found is *Historia Monachorum in Aegypto*, 14.10, which concerns the year 394.

[30] *P. Cairo Masp.* 67024.1–3, an imperial rescript addressed to the Duke of the Thebaid which starts by informing us that Dioscorus had described his father as [τὸ]ν

deep within the peasantry with whom he shared both cultural[31] and economic characteristics.[32] The lesser *geōrgoi* who depended on leasing were more like workers seeking jobs in a sort of labour market (their labour was being recruited by landlords through the mediation of 'tenancy' contracts). But the leases which Apollos and other village oligarchs took had a completely different meaning and clearly involved the employment of others (again *geōrgoi*) to work the land. For these prosperous households the monasteries were an important source of leasing and the leases simply a mechanism to enable better-off peasants to produce on a larger scale, e.g., by extending activity into physically contiguous farms (*ktēmata*) owned by others. Phoibammon son of Triadelphus signed leases of this sort with several monasteries[33] and with the church of Antaeu.[34] Apollos father of Dioscorus had a similar sort of arrangement with the monastery of Zmin, named after a village opposite Panopolis, on the left bank of the Nile.[35] His brother Besarion leased land from the Holy New Church of Aphrodito, which he then sublet (on shares) but on one occasion cultivated directly in partnership with a local *geōrgos*.[36] *P. Freer Aphrodito* contains the strange but recurrent expression ἀπὸ ἐκβ(ολῆς) which the translation renders by 'par suite d'expulsion'. But it seems more natural to interpret the phrase as meaning 'following the expiry of the lease held by'. If this is right, this survey of *c.*525 shows that there was considerable turnover in the rentals market of a substantial village like Aphrodito early in the sixth century. But the sort of lease arrangements which the village oligarchs signed with churches and monasteries may have had a certain stability (whatever the duration of the contracts themselves). Thus Apollos is thought to have taken over Besarion's arrangements with the Holy New Church.[37] Receipts issued by the latter refer to an *organon* or irrigated farm south of the village,[38] yet much of the

ἐν αὐτῇ (sc. Aphrodito) κε[κτημ]ένον (l. –μένων) πρῶτον γενόμενο[ν], καὶ τὰς ὑπὲρ τοῦ παντὸς χωρίο(υ) συντελείας ἀναλεγόμενον.

[31] His grandfather had the purely Coptic name Psimanobet, cf. *P. Ross.-Georg.* III 36.3–4 (537) and the reff. in the note there. Note the Syriac-speaking *prōtokōmētēs* in Leontius, *Vie de Syméon le Fou*, 156D (Festugière, 90), referring to Justinian's time.

[32] Thus Apollos like Sakaon was both lessor and lessee.

[33] *P. Ross.-Georg.* III 48, *P. Mich.* XIII 667, *PSI* IV 284.

[34] *P. Flor.* III 289. In *P. Mich.* XIII 667 the *ktēma* of the monastery of Apa Sourous lies directly west of his own *ktēma* called τῶν βαφέων.

[35] *P. Lond.* V 1690 (527), cf. *P. Cairo Masp.* II 67170.5–8 for the location.

[36] *P. Lond.* V 1694, *P. Lond.* V 1705, cf. the discussion in Keenan, *BASP* 22 (1985) 162.

[37] So Keenan, *BASP* 22 (1985) 165.

[38] e.g. *P. Cairo Masp.* III 67307.4, cf. G. Malz, 'The Papyri of Dioscorus: Publications and Emendations', in *Studi in onore di Aristide Calderini e Roberto Paribeni*, 2 vols. (Milan, 1956) 2.345–56, at 353 ff., τ]ο(ῦ) ὑπό σε τῆς ἁγίας ἐκκλησίας ὀργάνο(υ).

land which Apollos leased *out* was described as 'waterless'.[39] Leases and sales embodied a rational economic strategy by which the better-off peasants altered the average productivity of their operational area (as opposed to the owned area) by leasing out or selling off the waterless arouras and leasing in (and presumably buying) the high-yielding irrigated farms. Thus the *klēros* which contained the farm leased by Besarion included some waterless land which belonged to the family, and in *P. Lond.* V 1686 (565) Dioscorus sold this to the monastery of Zmin which seemed to want to exploit its own holdings in the area.[40] At the other end of the village, in the 'northern plain', Dioscorus was lessee of an *organon* belonging to the monastery of Apa Sourous.[41]

This entire group constituted the élite of local rural society (as opposed to the μεγάλοι κτήτορες τῆς πόλεως).[42] In *P. Mich.* XIII 667 Phoibammon son of Triadelphus calls himself *ktētōr* but for most of his later life he seems to have preferred the description *syntelestēs*, to emphasize not only the fact of his owning land but the more significant aspect, surely, of his control over the village community.[43] For the last few years of his life Apollos would likewise call himself *syntelestēs*.[44] Dioscorus was the local success story, since he had moved from the largely Coptic and purely agricultural world of his family[45] to the ambiguous Hellenism of the provincial middle class, as he reminded fellow villagers with the name 'Flavius'. The daughters of *syntelestai* could be *eugenestatai* in a style otherwise peculiar to the urban middle bureaucracy.[46] But in describing this stratum as stable and even prosperous it is essential to emphasize the relativity of all our judgements. Keenan has characterized the particular mentality as 'capitalistic', but this process of accumulation was only gradual and confined, overwhelmingly, to the economic and cultural boundaries of the village. Indeed, Egyptian rural society had always contained a strongly acquisitive element, manifested in the high proportion of loans which involved mortgages on agricultural land

[39] *PSI* VIII 931.12 ff. (524), *P. Ross.-Georg.* III 36.12 ff. (537), *P. Flor.* III 282 (520), *P. Cairo Masp.* III 67301.15 (531).

[40] *P. Lond.* V 1686.12 ff. The location of the plot is described as ἐν τῷ μεγάλῳ γεωργίῳ τοῦ αὐτο(ῦ) εὐαγοῦς μοναστηρίο(υ) Ζμινος.

[41] *P. Cairo Masp.* I 67087 (543).

[42] See p. 126 above.

[43] A. Laniado, '*ΣΥΝΤΕΛΕΣΤΗΣ*. Notes sur un terme surinterprété', *JJP* 26 (1996) 23–51, shows that *syntelestēs* was simply the Greek translation of *collator* (taxpayer), and frequently equivalent to *ktētōr*. Keenan's suggestion that one progressed from the title *syntelestēs* to that of *ktētōr* seems improbable.

[44] His death is dated to 546/7 by Rémondon, *Studi Volterra* 5.774–5.

[45] For the linguistic background at Aphrodito, see Keenan, 'On Languages and Literacy in Byzantine Aphrodito' (referring, at 161, to the 'Coptic basis of village life').

[46] See Sibyl and Herais, *Catalogue*, Aphrodito 6c.

or other assets. Nor did local economic power protect the village élite from the depredations or violence of pagarchs determined to reduce their independence. So in emphasizing the divisions *within* rural society it would be wrong to ignore its peculiar unity, the fact that in the end it was the village community which stood out against the background of a world controlled from the cities and dominated by urban classes.

Rural Labour Markets

Existing notions about labour in late antiquity suffer not only from the state of our evidence but from the idea, once dominant, that the 'declining' phase of the Roman empire was characterized by a generalized transition from slavery to the 'colonate'. However, these formulas are on the whole useless as ways of trying to understand problems of labour use, estate organization, and the structure of the labour force. In the rest of this chapter I shall develop (as briefly as I can) an alternative approach to the problem of labour.

To begin with, it is worth distinguishing (1) the forms in which employers *recruited* labour from (2) the methods of *control* which they used to regulate either the long-term *supply* of labour or the day-to-day *performance* of jobs. The whole science of agrarian management was essentially about the latter not the former (that is, it took the labour market as given), and it is hazardous to base deductions about the structure of the labour force (which reflects the first of those levels) on sources concerned primarily with farm management, as so many scholars have done.[47] We simply cannot use the agricultural writers (or the jurists) as a substitute for the sort of 'labour enquiry' which the ancient world either failed to produce or never transmitted to us. In this respect the papyri are a far better clue to how employers used labour, at least in the limited regions and areas of production which mainly figure in these

[47] e.g. V. I. Kuziščin, 'Le caractère de la main-d'oeuvre dans un domaine du IVe siècle d'après l traité de Palladius', in I. Bieżuńska-Malowist and J. Kolendo (eds.), *Actes du colloque sur l'esclavage, Nieborów 1975* (Warsaw, 1979) 239–55, who concludes from the fact that Palladius is writing for big landowners, 'Cette main-d'oeuvre est servile, comme du temps de Columelle' (242). (Contrast W. Kaltenstadler's radically opposite conclusion in 'Betriebsorganisation und betriebswirtschaftliche Fragen im *Opus Agriculturae* von Palladius', in H. Kalcyk, B. Gullath, and A. Graeber (eds.), *Studien zur alten Geschichte Siegfried Lauffer ... dargebracht*, 2 vols. (Rome, 1986) 2.501–57, esp. 550 and n. 164.) Rathbone, *Economic Rationalism and Rural Society*, is a brilliant reversal of this method—the study of a single estate and its deployment patterns, without the usual obsession to come up with a general characterization of the structure of the labour force.

documents (that is, a handful of districts among well over seventy, and chiefly agriculture).

My notion of a labour market is constituted at the first level rather than the second. One can speak of a 'labour market' wherever labour was recruited through contracts, regardless of the nature of those contracts or the terms and conditions of employment embodied in or entailed by them, and thus of the coercion and domination of labour which such agreements may have represented.[48] That much of this labour worked under conditions which, though contractual, involved considerable harshness on the part of employers is undeniable. Thus a famous passage in John Chrysostom refers to Syrian landowners 'overworking' their *geōrgoi* and treating them worse than animals.[49] Shenute refers to employers deliberately withholding payment of wages to force workers to return to work the following year.[50] But these types of coercion are true of labour markets throughout the world and are scarcely a distinguishing characteristic either of the Roman world or of the late Roman period. In the following I shall attempt a 'conceptual' division of the rural labour market as I see it, showing how contracts which are usually seen in isolation can be integrated into a consistent network of economic relationships.

The complexity of labour market relationships may in general be due to two sorts of complication. Thus in the ancient world the 'opacity' of the labour market was shaped firstly by deployment practices which made it traditional for landowners to *combine* categories of labour which are normally regarded as historically specific and even antithetical, e.g. slaves and hired labourers, as in the type of countryside the Elder Cato had envisaged; secondly, by the diversity of contractual forms in which the same economic transaction might be expressed and effected. For example, the sale of labour power could be "mediated" (1) as a contract of employment which might or might not involve an advance payment of wages (it generally did, and this was invariably called *prochreia*);[51]

[48] Hengstl, *Private Arbeitsverhältnisse freier Arbeiter*, 27, correctly notes that the *paramonē* employee was always a free person.

[49] John Chrysostom, *Hom. in Matth.* 61 (cited again later).

[50] *Sinuthi Opera III*, 19 (*CSCO*² IV, ed. Wiesmann, p. 34) ('Nisi mihi proximo operaberis anno, mercedem huius anni tibi non dabo praeteriti'), cf. W. J. Leipoldt, *Schenute von Atripe und die Entstehung des national ägyptischen Christentums*. TU 10 (Leipzig, 1903) 168.

[51] e.g. *P. Strasb.* I 40 (569), *SB* XVI 12868 (592/3), both called μισθωτικὴ ὁμολογία, the first with a domestic servant, the second with a bath attendant; *SPP* XX 219 (604), called μισθωτικ(όν), with a *stablitēs*; especially common in the 7th cent., cf. *P. Vindob.* G 36435.15–18 (7 Sept. 638) = E. Jonker, R. Risselada, and A. M. Tromp, 'Drei Wiener Papyri', *ZPE* 50 (1983) 127–32, at 130ff., no. 3, where the employee says, ὁμολ[ογῶ

(2) as a type of lease in which the worker appears as a lessee who undertakes to 'lease' a series of operations, the tasks involved in them being the specific object of the lease (here the usual formula was *ἐπιδεχόμεθα μισθώσασθαι τὰ ἔργα*, as in the so-called vineyard leases);[52] (3) as advance payment of rent, that is, a *μισθαποχή* contract where the lessor is in fact a worker;[53] (4) as a consumption loan, a form in which the advance payment of wages is simply mystified to strengthen the employer's control over the employee (the employer becomes a 'creditor' but his essential interest is the exaction of labour);[54] (5) as the price paid in advance for the product of labour, that is, as a contract of advance sale where the owner of money appears to buy not labour itself but its product (the 'advance system');[55] (6) in the form of sharecropping, where the employee appears to pay his employer a 'rent' in the form of a share of the crop, whereas actually his own share is a form of incentive wages and the whole relation akin to piecework.[56] In the papyri arable leases, wine, flax, industrial and service occupations, and seasonal work (harvests, embankments, etc.) emerge as the chief sectors of the labour market. A large proportion of arable leases were concluded for the duration of a single year.[57] Insofar as the *geōrgoi* recruited through such leases were usually landless, these agreements were their major source of livelihood. The distinction between such leases and the crop-sharing agreements concluded for wine lay not in the economic nature of the transaction but in the nature of the contract

ἑκουσίᾳ] γνώμῃ μεμισθ[ωκέναι ἐμαυτὸν τῇ ὑμ[ετέρᾳ λαμπρότητι] ἐπὶ ἐνιαυτὸν ἕν[α], in a contract called a *ὁμολ(ογία) π[α]ραμ[ονῆ]ς*, *SB* I 4490 (7c.), with the same expression in ll. 8–9, *CPR* VIII 82 (699/700) (superseding *SB* VI 9460), the work contract with Fl. Atias, Duke of Arcadia and the Thebaid, cited in the previous chapter.

[52] e.g. *P. Oxy.* XLVIII 3354 (257), cf. Jördens, *Vertragliche Regelungen von Arbeiten*, ch. 4.

[53] Cf. *Inv. OL* 1988.25 (wooden board) (Oxy. 475), published J. Shelton, 'A Fifth-Century Contract on Wood in the Archaeological Institute at Trier', *ZPE* 78 (1989) 143–6, at 145, with his n. 4 at 144.

[54] e.g. Crum, *Varia Coptica* 29 = W. C. Till, *Die koptischen Rechtsurkunden aus Theben* (Vienna, 1964) 239–40 (flax), E. Stefanski and M. Lichtheim, *Coptic Ostraca from Medinet Habu* (Chicago, 1952), no. 61 (flax), both with strong loan terminology; contrast *KRU* 57 = Till, 'Koptischen Arbeitsverträge', no. 43, p. 309 (irrigation and farm labour), *CPR* II 112 = Till, 'Koptischen Arbeitsverträge', no. 51, p. 314 ff. (irrigation), both 8th cent. and wage advances not described as loans; and cf. Jördens, *Vertragliche Regelungen von Arbeiten*, ch. 7.

[55] Probably more frequent in the medieval period, cf. Y. Rāġib, *Marchands d'étoffes du Fayyoum au IIIe/IXe siècle d'après leurs archives (actes et lettres). Les actes des Banu 'Abd al-Mu'min* (Cairo, 1982) 6 ff., nos. ii–ix.

[56] Cf. Jördens, *Vertragliche Regelungen von Arbeiten*, ch. 5, and see n. 59 below. 'Akin to piecework' is based on J. Martinez-Alier, *Labourers and Landowners in Southern Spain* (London, 1971) 131, 279, 283.

[57] See App. 1, Table 12 (where arable leases are the majority).

and chiefly of course the type of payment involved. I have argued elsewhere that in most agrarian contexts sharecroppers are simply hired labourers who receive their wages as a share of the crop.[58] In using sharecroppers landlords behave more like employers than like rentiers. Papyri of the Byzantine period show this especially well, for lessees usually refer to their share of the crop as 'the half share we receive for the work we do', that is, as a form of wages, while the employers themselves place considerable emphasis on work obligations. The same analysis was presented by Waszyński in 1905[59] and by Gerstinger and Hengstl more recently.[60] Flax involved the hiring of peasant labour through advances which some employers treated as if they were loans.[61] Industrial and service occupations were based on standard employment contracts, with or without the traditional *paramonē* terminology, which now simply expressed the nature of the employment as non-casual.[62]

These divisions within the labour market reflected a more general feature of the behaviour of employers which I have described as *deployment practices*. Agrarian employers in particular engage in a type of decision-making which could perhaps be called a "logic of deployment". The chief result of this is that in agriculture the *use* of labour is characterized by more diversity than in other types of production, e.g. the composition of contracts will vary both within districts (between crops) and between districts (due to 'differences in the extent and regularity of labour demand'[63]). To take an example from the papyri, the spread of sharecropping in Egyptian agriculture was largely due to its association with the wine industry. Wine was invariably sharecropped, by contrast with most other crops and certainly the food crops where fixed payments (in kind)

[58] J. Banaji, 'Historical Arguments for a Logic of Deployment in "precapitalist" Agriculture', *Journal of Historical Sociology* 5 (1992) 379 ff., esp. 385–6.

[59] Waszyński, *Die Bodenpacht*, 157, arguing (from share levels), 'Demnach sind auch diese byzantinischen γεωργοί keine Pächter mehr, sondern Arbeiter, die einen Vertrag über Dienstverding eingehen. Um also diese Verträge richtig zu beurteilen, müssen wir bei der Verteilung des Ertrages nicht die dem Verpächter zufallende Quote as Pachtrente, sondern den dem γεωργός zufallenden Bruchteil als Dienstlohn im Auge behalten.' Weber's own characterization of the Byzantine sharecropper as a labourer paid in kind was clearly influenced by Waszyński, see 'Agrarverhältnisse', 184 f.

[60] H. Gerstinger, 'Gräko-ägyptische Landpachtverträge byzantinischer Zeit aus der Sammlung "Papyrus Erzherzog Rainer" in Wien', *WS* 69 (1956) *(= Festschrift Lesky)* 237–55, esp. 247, Hengstl, *Private Arbeitsverhältnisse*, 75.

[61] *CPR* II 91 = Till, 'Koptischen Arbeitsverträge', no. 45, p. 310, W. E. Crum and H. G. Evelyn White, *The Monastery of Epiphanius at Thebes*, 2 parts (New York, 1926) ii 85 (pp. 173–4).

[62] e.g. *P. Grenf.* II 87 (602) which involves piece-rates.

[63] H. P. Binswanger and M. R. Rosenzweig, *Contractual Arrangements, Employment and Wages in Rural Labor Markets in Asia* (New Haven, 1984) 153.

were the preferred formula.[64] Given this highly distinctive pattern of labour use, it is obvious that some set of considerations induced landowners to adopt specific sorts of contractual arrangements for different crops or types of operation. That a logic of deployment was even consciously at work in Roman agriculture is shown by various passages in the Roman agricultural writers, notably one in which Varro specifically recommends the use of casual labour for labour-intensive operations and hazardous jobs.[65]

Now this way of conceptualizing the use of labour in agriculture has an interesting implication. Once we construe patterns of labour use in terms of a logic of deployment, it is unnecessary to have to suppose that the agricultural institutions of the empire rested predominantly on a specific type of labour force or category of labour. The failure to recognise this, or the search for a dominant type of labour institution in systems shaped by a logic of deployment, explains why historians necessarily come up with conflicting accounts of whether slave labour was or was not important in the Mediterranean as a whole, when and how rapidly it declined, and so on.[66] But it also accounts for the deep resistance among most ancient historians to the idea that wage labour may have been far more important to the ancient economy than they would like to suppose. As I noted in the previous chapter, Jördens has pointed out that the number of labour contracts (*Arbeitsverträge*) surviving from the Byzantine period far exceeds those of all earlier centuries put together.[67] If this is not a pure accident it must mean that wage employment had expanded significantly by the Byzantine period. But the presupposition here is not only processes which could have accounted for an increased supply of labour on the market[68] but the whole background of the 'ancient economy' which had always depended on substantial inputs of casual labour for a wide range of activities. Paid labour was used

[64] G. Perusini, *Vita di popolo in Friuli, patti agrari e consuetudini tradizionali* (Florence, 1961) 15, notes an identical pattern in leases from medieval Friuli: in mixed leases 'i cereali sono sempre pagati in quantità fisse; il vino, invece, è a metà'.

[65] Varro, *RR* 1.17.2–3.

[66] Jones's assertion that in the late Roman period 'there is no evidence for the extensive use of slave labour except in Italy and Spain' (*LRE* 2.794) depends on what counts as 'no evidence'. Presumably the Numidian *mancipia rustica* in *CTh.* 10.8.4 (353, cf. Seeck, *Regesten der Kaiser und Päpste*, 199) were slaves; Ferrand in his Life of Fulgentius refers to the latter 'controlling his slaves (*servos*) with a mixture of compassion and strictness', *Vie de Fulgence* 1; the aristocrat Fl. Monaxius (cos. ord. 419) owned slaves, Callinicos, *Vie d'Hypatios* 21 (*SC* 177); *P. Apoll.* 51.5 (Edfu, early 8th cent.) refers to *τὰ χριστιανὰ ἀνδρ[άπο]δα τοῦ μακ(αρίου) Ιουστίνου*, cf. L. S. B. MacCoull, 'The Coptic Papyri from Apollonos Anô', in *Proceedings of the XVIIIth International Congress of Papyrology*, 2.141–60, at 143–4.

[67] Jördens, *Verträgliche Regelungen von Arbeiten*, 148.

[68] See the section on the 'Wingate Effect' in Ch. 3.

in a whole series of operations and types of employment such as public works,[69] cargo handling,[70] iron ore mining,[71] press operating,[72] crop watching,[73] grape picking,[74] the maintenance and repair of channels and embankments,[75] harvesting of flax.[76] It was used extensively in viticulture. Irrigation likewise was conducted largely with the help of hired labour.[77] Large quantities were needed for the olive harvest.[78] Whatever the general impression of scholars regarding the significance of paid employment in 'pre-capitalist' periods, wherever one has coherent pieces of evidence such as estate accounts the use of hired labour emerges in its true proportions. For example, in his recent study of a section of the Appianus estate in the Fayum, Rathbone has pointed out that even in quiet periods like December 'hired outside labour still made up almost a third of the total labour input on the *phrontis*'.[79] Overall, for seven different months on the *phrontides* of Euhemeria and Theadelphia, his calculations in table eleven show a casual labour strength of over 60 per cent. This is a huge proportion. W. S. Bagnall's work on the mainly second-century Laches archive established a similar impression of heavy use of hired labour.[80] Again, the Memphite estate in *BGU* I 14 (255) made extensive use of hired workers, recruited

[69] P. A. Brunt, 'Free Labour and Public Works at Rome', *JRS* 70 (1980) 81–101, esp. 84, 'free labour was extensively employed on public works at Rome' and the inference from Varro 1.17.3 that 'by the same token urban employers may have preferred to hire workers for dangerous operations, e.g. in building' (93 n. 65).

[70] Brunt, 'Free Labour and Public Works', 92.

[71] P. Ørsted, *Roman Imperial Economy and Romanization*, tr. D. Gress-Wright (Copenhagen, 1985) 237. In the gold mines as well, cf. Calderini, *Studi Romani* 2 (1954) 650f.

[72] *P. Fayum* 91 (99), contract for labour in an oil press.

[73] Augustine, *Ep*. 46.1 (*CSEL* 33/1, pp. 123f.), Publicola to Augustine, in 398, using tribal labour 'ad servandas fruges'.

[74] Wortmann, *ZPE* 8 (1971) 41–69.

[75] W. S. Bagnall, *The Archive of Laches: Prosperous Farmers of the Fayum in the Second Century* (Duke University Ph.D., 1974), 44.

[76] *SB* XX 14299 i 19f. (4c.), *μισθοῦ ἐκτινάξε* (l. *ἐκτινάξαι*) *τὰ σί[π]πια τοῦ κενδηναρίου ἑνὸς* (*τάλαντον*) *α*, superseding *SB* VI 9024.19–20.

[77] Usually paid in cash (solidi), see p. 76 n. 228.

[78] Cato, *De agricult*. 144. Cf. J. Poncet, *La Colonisation et l'agriculture européennes en Tunisie depuis 1881. Étude de géographie historique et économique* (Paris and The Hague, 1961) 459ff. E. Tengström, *Donatisten und Katholiken. Soziale, wirtschaftliche und politische Aspekte einer nordafrikanischen Kirchenspaltung* (Göteborg, 1964) 51ff. argued that the Circumcellions handled the olive harvests, cf. R. Lorenz, 'Circumcelliones—cotopitae—cutzupitani', *Zeitschrift für Kirchengeschichte* 82 (1971) 54–9, supporting this with an interpretation of Isidore, *Etym*. 8.5.53, 'Circumcelliones dicti eo, quod agrestes sint, quos Cotopitas vocant' (They are called Circumcellions because they are the kind of rural workers referred to as 'Cotopitae').

[79] Rathbone, *Economic Rationalism and Rural Society*, 152.

[80] Bagnall, *The Archive of Laches*, 169, 'For the daily chores on the estates, the overseers relied heavily on hired labour.'

partly through contractors and with a considerable wage differential between *potamitai* and *ergatai*, unskilled workmen.[81]

A widespread 'structural' dependence on hired labour is also implied by the frequent references in agricultural writings to labour cost considerations. The Elder Pliny's aphorism that there were certain harvests which landowners would be better advised to ignore if they computed the cost of labour is well known.[82] This corresponds perfectly to the distinction between 'dispensable' and 'indispensable' tasks which Martinez-Alier attributes to Andalusian landowners worried by the level of labour costs.[83] That a similar process of reasoning occurred in the Roman countryside is certain: gleaning, clearing stony ground, manual stripping of olive trees, the thoroughness or frequency of mowing, trenching, hoeing, etc. were all 'dispensable' tasks in Martinez-Alier's sense.[84] The vintage was clearly 'indispensable' since Columella says that badly planned vineyards simply forced their owners to hire a considerable mass of labour 'regardless of the cost'.[85]

The labour market in the localized sense of a place where the hiring of labour occurred appears only rarely in ancient sources. Optatus in a famous passage refers to the *nundinae* where gangs of Circumcellions would usually hang out.[86] This implies that landowners sent their agents to these markets to recruit casual labourers. In Matthew 20 the owner 'left early in the morning to hire casual workers' for the day's work.[87] Again this shows that employers sought workers rather than workers wandering about between employers looking for work.[88] But this would probably have varied

[81] Cf. *BGU* I 14 cols. iii–iv for the differential (4 drachmas as opposed to 9).

[82] Pliny, *NH* 18.7.38, 'domino aliquas messes colligere non expedit si conputetur inpendium operae' (There are some crops which it does not pay the landowner to harvest if the cost of labour is calculated).

[83] Martinez-Alier, *Labourers and Landowners in Southern Spain*, ch. 2, esp. 56–75.

[84] Varro, *RR* 1.53, Columella, *RR* 2.2.12, Pliny, *NH* 15.3.11 (on harvesting olives, 'tertia est culpa in parsimonia, quoniam propter inpendium decerpendi expectatur ut decidant olivae' (A third mistake is to be concerned solely with costs, in the sense that people wait for the olives to fall to avoid the costs of hand-picking); cf. Martinez-Alier, *Labourers and Landowners*, 72, 'The main reason for choosing a method of harvesting is the situation in the labour market'), 18.67.261, Columella, *RR* 4.5, 3.13.4–5.

[85] Columella, *RR* 3.21.9–10, 'quantocumque pretio'.

[86] Optatus, 3.4 (*CSEL* 26, ed. Ziwsa, 82), Taurinus orders an armed force to scour the markets (*nundinae*) where 'the madness of the Circumcellions was wont to rove', and the earlier reference (at 81), to the bishop of Bagai sending heralds through the local markets (*per omnes nundinas*) to rally the Circumcellion militants, cf. Mark Edwards, tr., *Optatus: Against the Donatists* (Liverpool, 1997) 68–9.

[87] Matthew 20:1, ... ἀνθρώπῳ οἰκοδεσπότῃ ὅστις ἐξῆλθεν ἅμα πρωὶ μισθώσασθαι ἐργάτας εἰς τὸν ἀμπελῶνα αὐτοῦ (a landowner who left at the crack of dawn to hire casual labourers for his vineyard).

[88] Cf. J. Drèze and A. Mukherjee, 'Labour Contracts in Rural India: Theories and Evidence', *Proceedings of the Eighth World Congress of the IEA, Delhi, India.* 3:

between regions and even localities.[89] One has the impression, at any rate, that in antiquity the casual labour market was a highly organized affair and that landowners could generally expect to find labour when they needed it. This is particularly true if one includes seasonal work under casual labour. The majority of these workers would undoubtedly have come in gangs represented either by a head labourer[90] or by a labour contractor.[91] Dealing with contractors was probably more convenient for employers[92] and part of the resentment aroused by the Circumcellions may have stemmed from their more independent relationship with landowners or their more egalitarian organization as work groups. Augustine implies that their gang leaders (*principes*) shared their militancy. This was partly directed against debt contracts which Optatus describes as *debitorum chirographa*.[93] It seems likely that these were bonds which employers used to tie labour down or strengthen their own control over its exertion—a common feature of rural labour markets. The rejection of such agreements was part of the attempt to preserve one's mobility. In a passage from John Chrysostom's *Homilies on Matthew* which is often cited, it is difficult to figure out what the actual relations were, but it seems clear (1) that wine was the main crop, and (2) that if the *geōrgoi* employed in these vineyards were sharecroppers, they were generally deprived of their shares through debt relations. But since Chrysostom refers to the owners 'throwing a bit of cash their way' (*καὶ ὀλίγον αὐτοῖς ὑπὲρ τούτου προσριπτοῦντες ἀργύριον*), it is possible that they simply hired labour, advancing wages and treating the cash advances as 'loans'.[94] In either case debt

Manpower and Transfers (IEA, 1989) 246, 'Search on the casual labour market is carried out by employers who usually "call" labourers on the evening preceding the execution of the work', and at 249: 'Most village studies confirm that search on the labour market is typically carried out by employers.'

[89] The monks who supplied some of the harvest labour in Egypt obviously went *to* employers, cf. John Moschus, *Pratum spirituale* 183 (*PG* 87/3.3056), *ἐν μιᾷ οὖν ἀπῆλθεν θερίσαι μετὰ καὶ ἄλλων μοναχῶν. Τοῦτο δὲ ἔθος ἐστὶ ἐπὶ τοῖς Σκητιώταις ἀπέρχεσθαι εἰς τὰ κτήματα καὶ θερίζειν.*

[90] Cf. *P. Oxy*. I 134.15–16 (but a permanent work group).

[91] Suetonius, *Vesp*. 1.4. The *demessor* in *CIL* 8.11824 (*ILS* 7457) could have been either. References to the Circumcellions consistently portray them as gangs, cf. *GCC*, 3.978 (*PL* 11.1420), 'Hii autem qui in praediis suis circumcellionum turbas se habere cognoscunt', from the *Edictum cognitoris*; August. *Ep*. 23.7 (*CSEL* 34/1.71), 'terror congregatorum Circumcellionum'; Possidius, *Vita Aug*. 10.1, 'erant in ingenti numero et turbis per omnes pene Africanas regiones constituti', and refer to their 'principes' or gang leaders, August. *Contra litt. Pet*. 14.33 (*Oeuvres* 30.256) 'principes circumcellionum', August. *Contra epist. Parmen*. 1.11.18 (*Oeuvres* 28.254), 'circumcellionum mancipes'.

[92] e.g. Cato seems to have dealt only with contractors.

[93] Optatus 3.4 (p. 82), cf. August. *Ep*. 185.4.15 (*CSEL* 57.137).

[94] John Chrysostom, *In Matth*. 61 (*PG* 58.591–2).

contracts seem to play a decisive role in the exposition.[95] Moneylending was of course widespread in antiquity, but the renewed importance of the problem in the late antique period should in part be construed within the framework of relationships between employers and employees rather than some traditional 'peasant' indebtedness. Debt was the essential means by which employers enforced control over the supply of labour, fragmenting the solidarity of workers and 'personalizing' relations between owners and employees.[96] The implication of this is not that labour was scarce but that workers were usually reluctant to stay with one employer for too long.[97] However, the *paramonē* no longer survived as an independent contract but largely as terminology intended to emphasize the period of employment in contracts for periods of up to or beyond one year.[98] The tendency to treat wage advances as loans was no longer a special feature of any special class of contracts but a *general* characteristic of the labour market, much as in Third World countries till recently, reflecting (probably) a high instability of labour, with workers frequently deserting jobs.

Rural contracts such as leases were certainly less coercive, for landowners usually thought it was sufficient to include a caveat against premature termination on the lessee's part. It is very probable that this was because, here, as opposed to most types of urban employment, employers actually wanted the flexibility of hiring new labour. Thus the labour market was characterized by a whole spectrum of relationships which, while presuming the freedom of the worker in a social and legal sense, were defined by widely

[95] Cf. Rostovtzeff, *SEHRE* 2.661 n. 23, 'the most powerful weapon of the rich being loans at high interest'. Of course, Rostovtzeff probably thought these really were loans.

[96] Cf. Sheila Bhalla, 'New Relations of Production in Haryana Agriculture', *Economic and Political Weekly* xi, 27 March (1976) A23–A30, at A28, on the function of rural labour indebtedness in contemporary India: 'to re-assert the atomistic character (from the labourer's side) of the hiring process, to institutionalise and strengthen the personal obligations of the individual labourer'.

[97] Cf. John Moschus' report of a *misthios* who had served on his employer's estate (*ktēma*) for fifteen years, with the latter simply refusing to pay his wages, *νύκτα καὶ ἡμέραν ἐργαζόμενος, καὶ μισθὸν οὐκ ἀνέχεταί μοι παρασχεῖν, ἀλλὰ κατ' ἐνιαυτὸν θλίβει με οὐ μετρίως*, Moschus, *Pratum Spirituale* 154 (*PG* 87/3.3021–3). He was clearly a 'bonded labourer'.

[98] *SB* XII 11239 = *P. Köln* II 102 (418) is a good example. Here the employee acknowledged an advance payment (*prochreia*) of 2 solidi on the condition that he would 'serve continuously' with the creditor (*ἐπὶ τῷ με πα[ρ]αμένειν παρὰ σοὶ*, l.8) but in ll. 9–10 the contract gives him the freedom to terminate employment as long as he is able to pay back the advance (*καὶ ὁπότ[αν βο]υληθῶ ἀν[αχω]ρεῖν ἀπὸ σοῦ . . . ἐπάναγ[κέ]ς με π[α]ρ[α]σχεῖν σοι ἄ[ν]ευ διαφόρου τὰ προκείμενα τοῦ χρυσοῦ νομισμάτια [δ]ύο*). B. Adams, *Paramoné und verwandte Texte. Studien zum Dienstvertrag im Rechte der Papyri* (Berlin, 1964) 74 ff., is lucid on the role of 'loan' terminology in *paramonē* contracts of the later period.

differing degrees of coercion, independence, and bargaining strength. Since the short-term leases which lessees bid for were as much a form in which landowners recruited labour[99] the whole short-term lease market as it operated in Egypt was in fact a sector of the rural labour market in my sense. The analogy between leases and labour contracts is emphasized by their similar durations. If one accepts the usual analysis of indefinite lease durations as an expression of employer control in the lease market,[100] then there is no contradiction between the frequency of such durations in the Byzantine period and the continued importance of one-year contracts—under *both* arrangements employers were simply maximizing their freedom to recruit new labourers if they felt dissatisfied with existing ones.[101] But this analysis implies that there was clearly no shortage of labour (in Egypt at least) if landlords could enforce durations of these types, that is, contracts where a high turnover of labour was was taken for granted. George Tate's work on the limestone massif has drawn attention to a considerable demographic upsurge which he dates to the fourth century to *c*.550.[102] There the pressure of this cyclical upsurge assumed the form of a large-scale colonization of the jebels, with growing and expansive settlements creating a remarkably affluent rural world of solidly built homes and numerous village churches. In Egypt the scope for this sort of expansion was clearly limited and investments probably took a more aristocratic form. The 'opposition' between town and country existed within the countryside in the relations between the *oikoi* and the *geōrgoi* and consequently their integration was also much deeper. The spread of indefinite durations may thus be an expression not of labour shortage but its opposite, a surplus peasant population willing to take leases on landowners' terms.

The Spread of Permanent Labour

One implication of the existence of large reserves of labour in the eastern Mediterranean countryside is that the development of the

[99] One indication of this is the controls which landlords imposed on methods of cultivation and the corresponding acknowledgement by lessees of these requirements, as in the formula *καὶ ἐπιτελέσω τὰ καθήκοντα ἔργα ὅσα καθήκει*, cf. D. Hennig, 'Die Arbeitsverpflichtungen der Pächter in Landpachtverträgen aus dem Faijum', *ZPE* 9 (1972) 111–31, and *Rural Communities*, vol. 1, table 21, for the use of work standards.

[100] Waszyński, *Die Bodenpacht*, 92; Herrmann, *Studien zur Bodenpacht im Recht der graeco-aegyptischen Papyri*, 92, on the *ἐφ' ὅσον χρόνον βούλει* formula.

[101] See App. 1, Table 12.

[102] Tate, 'Les campagnes de la Syrie du Nord', 74–5 (based on the number of rooms in the villages surveyed by him).

so-called 'colonate' cannot be explained by recourse to a *shortage* of labour. Of course, there is a minor orthodoxy which now argues that the colonate itself is, to a large degree, an invention of historiography. The obvious drawback of this position is that it simply fails to come to terms with the massive edifice of legislation, with its numerous references to *coloni* and their subordination to landowners who are generally described as *despotai* or *domini*. The challenge for the historiography of the late empire, surely, is to elucidate these new legal forms by searching for their basis in the very nature of late Roman society.[103]

Nov. Just. 157 (542), addressed to Lazarus, *comes Orientis*, contains a fascinating reference to *coloni* 'belonging to their masters by law'.[104] It seems to me that the basis of these rights of control could only have been the private power of employers over workers, whatever the personal status of those workers. The fundamental fact about the legal position of the *colonus* is that he or she was *iuris alieni*. Thus the expression *colonus iuris alieni* is used by Constantine in *CTh.* 5.17.1 (332), the famous law commanding slave-like treatment for runaway *coloni*,[105] and also appears in *CTh.* 5.17.2 of 386.[106] The *interpretatio* to *CTh.* 5.18.1 of 419 describes the *mulier originaria* in the text of the law as *mulier alieni iuris*. Now, from a famous passage in the Digest it is clear that persons described as *iuris alieni* were (in the classical law of persons) *personae quae alieno iuri subiectae sunt*,[107] 'persons subject to the legal control of others'.

[103] The following paragraphs draw on my paper 'Lavoratori liberi e residenza coatta: il colonato romano in prospettiva storica', in E. Lo Cascio (ed.), *Terre, proprietari e contadini dell'impero romano. Dall' affitto agrario al colonato tardoantico* (Rome, 1997) 253–80.

[104] *Nov. Just.* 157.1 (*CIC* 3.734), τοὺς γεωργούς ὅσοιπερ αὐτοῖς (sc. οἱ τὰ χωρία κεκτημένοι) κατὰ τόν νόμον προσήκουσιν, with which compare Tiberius II's Novel on the Domus Divina, which speaks of τινὰς γεωργοὺς ὑπὸ τὴν ἑτέρων τυγχάνοντας νομήν, '[who are] under the possession of others', see M. Kaplan, 'Nouvelle de Tibère II sur les "maisons divines"', *Travaux et Mémoires* 8 (1981) 237–45, at 237 ff.

[105] *CTh.* 5.17.1, 'Apud quemcumque colonus iuris alieni fuerit inventus, is non solum eundem origini suae restituat, verum super eodem capitationem temporis agnoscat. Ipsos etiam colonos, qui fugam meditantur, in servilem condicionem ferro ligari conveniet, ut officia, quae liberis congruunt, merito servilis condemnationis conpellantur inplere' (Not only will any individual in whose possession a labourer belonging to another is found restore the said labourer to his estate of birth, but he shall also assume liability for the man's head tax for the period he was with him. Furthermore, workers who contemplate flight should be bound in chains and treated on a par with slaves, so that they may be compelled to perform the tasks befitting free persons by virtue of their condemnation to slave-like status). Cf. U. Hildesheim, *Personalaspekte der frühbyzantinischen Steuerordnung* (Pfaffenweiler, 1988) 198 f., 302 n. 153, advancing a similar argument but restricting *ius* to its jurisdictional sense.

[106] *CTh.* 5.17.2, 'Quisquis colonum iuris alieni aut sollicitatione susceperit aut occultatione celaverit etc.' (If anyone receives a labourer belonging to another, through solicitation, or harbours him by concealment, etc.).

[107] D.1.1.6.1 (Gaius) (Watson, 1.17–18), 'De iure personarum alia divisio sequitur,

Moreover, the same passage shows that subjection to the *ius* of another was construed as being *in aliena potestate* and that the substantive sense of such subordination was given by the notion of *potestas*. Thus, to be *iuris alieni* involved a primary classical-law jurisdictional meaning which might be summed up or described roughly as 'household dependence'.[108] This is not all, however. In an important article from the 1950s Steinwenter showed that the vulgar or post-classical notion of *ius* acquired a proprietary sense, as in the expressions *casa iuris sui*, *villa iuris nostri*, and so on,[109] and it is certain that this stronger, proprietary, meaning was also being advanced when persons were later described as *iuris alieni*, or as *coloni iuris privati*,[110] or when the children of freeborn women who married *coloni* or slaves were ordered to remain 'in eorum iure et dominio apud quos creati sunt vel creantur',[111] or *originarii* and slaves who had joined the church were commanded 'ad dominorum iura redeant'.[112] In each of these passages (*coloni iuris alieni*, etc.) the word *ius* included an unmistakable sense of labour as property, of the 'master's authority as a kind of property that the master held in the worker's labor'.[113] The constitution which shows this most clearly, however, is *CTh.* 5.18.1 of 419, dealing with *coloni originales vel inquilini* who had left their estates and been absent for substan-

quod quaedam personae sui iuris sunt, quaedam alieno iuri subiectae sunt. Videamus itaque de his, quae alieno iuri subiectae sunt . . . dispiciamus itaque de his, quae in aliena potestate sunt. Igitur in potestate sunt servi dominorum' ('There follows another division within the law of persons: some persons are *sui juris*, others are within the jurisdiction of someone else. Let us, therefore, see who are subject to another's jurisdiction . . . So let us take a view of those who are in another person's *potestas*. Slaves, then, are in the *potestas* of their master').

[108] Cf. R. J. Steinfeld, *The Invention of Free Labor: The Employment Relation in English and American Law and Culture, 1350–1870* (The University of North Carolina Press, 1991) 55 ff.

[109] A. Steinwenter, 'Ueber einige Bedeutungen von "Ius" in den nachklassischen Quellen', *Iura* 4 (1953) 124–48; most clearly in *Epitome Gai* 2.1.1, 'Nostri iuris sunt, quae in proprietate nostra esse noscuntur, divini iuris sunt ecclesiae, id est templa Dei, vel ea patrimonia ac substantiae, quae ad ecclesiastica iura pertinent.'

[110] *Nov. Val.* 27.6 (449), 'lege divi parentis nostri Honorii de colonis utriusque sexus iuris privati' (the law of our divine ancestor Honorius regarding labourers of either sex who are in the private jurisdiction of their employers).

[111] *Nov. Val.* 31.6 (451), 'Filii earum, si denuntiatio non praecessit, in eorum iure et dominio, apud quos creati sunt vel creantur, colonario nomine perseverent' (Assuming a formal notification did not precede their birth, the children of such women shall be known by the designation of 'coloni' and remain in the ownership and control of the persons on whose property they have been born or may be born).

[112] *Nov. Val.* 35.6 (452), 'Originarii vero vel servi, qui iugum natalium declinantes ad ecclesiasticum se ordinem transtulerunt, exceptis episcopis et presbyteris ad dominorum iura redeant' (Unless they actually become bishops and priests, any slaves or labourers who are bound to estates by birth who evade the bondage of their birth status and secure a transfer to the ecclesiastical order, shall return to the jurisdiction of their masters).

[113] Steinfeld, *The Invention of Free Labor*, 66.

tial periods of time, for this law clearly implies that such cases were likely to generate disputes between landowners over the ownership (*proprietas*) of labourers.[114] It would be pointless to ask whether such proprietary notions extended to the person of the *colonus* or simply to his labour, for undoubtedly both conceptions were prevalent, the stronger one among landowners, who, as slaveholders, were scarcely inclined to discriminate between ordinary resident labourers (*coloni*) and the average slave.[115] The crucial point is that such notions operated with respect to free labour.

To emphasize the *colonus'* legal subordination to an employer as the crucial aspect of his/her *condicio* or legal status circumvents the problem of whether the colonate involved the evolution of a special 'personenrechtliche Status', and makes perfect sense of Justinian's question, 'Is there any perceptible difference between slaves and *adscripticii*, when both groups are placed in the power of their masters, and these can manumit slaves along with their savings as well as evict the *adscripticius* from their control, his subsistence plot and all?'[116] It was their common subjection to the landowner's *potestas* that made *coloni* 'like' slaves. However, such subjection was grounded, in their case, not in slavery but in wage labour, and compatible with a legal and ideological tradition that had always assimilated wage labourers to slaves.[117] This also implies of course

[114] *CTh.* 5.18.1 (419), 'Si quis colonus originalis vel inquilinus ante hos triginta annos de possessione discessit neque ad solum genitale silentii continuatione repetitus est, omnis ab ipso vel a quo forte possidetur calumnia penitus excludatur . . . Quod si forte ipse, de cuius proprietate certatur, fatali sorte consumptus est, eius posteritatem agrorum iuri cum omni peculio atque mercedibus, velut eo superstite qui decessit, celeri iubemus executione revocari' (If labourers bound to estates by birth or those assuming such status later left the estate thirty years ago and were not brought back to the soil of their birth because no mention was made of the issue, every unfounded action against them or the persons who may now own them shall, without exception, be excluded . . . On the other hand, if the person whose ownership is in dispute should happen to have been destroyed by the lot of fate, we command, with immediate effect, that his offspring shall be recalled to the *ius agrorum* together with their savings and wages as if the deceased parent were still alive). Cf. Max Kaser, *Römische Privatrecht*, 2 vols. (2nd edn. Munich, 1971–5) 2.147 n. 40 ('stehen die Kolonen in der *proprietas* ihres Herrn').

[115] Cf. Augustine, *Ep.* 24*.1 (*Lettres 1*–29**, *Oeuvres de Saint Augustin*, 46B) (Études Augustiniennes, 1987), 'utrum liceat possessori servos facere colonos vel filios colonorum suorum' (whether it is legal for a landowner to transform his labourers or his labourers' sons into slaves), and the prohibition in *CTh.* 5.6.3 (409) forbidding landlords from turning the workers assigned to them into slaves.

[116] *CJ* 11.48.21.1 (530), with the expression 'adscripticium cum terra suo dominio expellere'; for *dominium* cf. Augustine, *de civitate Dei*, 10.1 (*CC* 47.272), 'non sicut appellantur coloni, qui condicionem debent genitali solo, propter agriculturam sub dominio possessorum' (The word 'colonists' is here used not as it is applied to those who are bound by birth to cultivate their native soil under the lordship of its owners, Dyson, *Augustine: The City of God against the Pagans*, Cambridge, 1998, 391, though *dominium* is better translated 'control' or 'ownership').

[117] Francesco M. De Robertis, *I rapporti di lavoro nel diritto romano* (Milan, 1946)

that the *coloni* were simply not ordinary tenants in the classical law sense, since, in law at least, the tenant was 'not subject to the landlord's control'.[118] Thus the whole argument requires a much less clichéd and more nuanced idea of labour relationships on the large aristocratic estates which controlled the bulk of this sort of labour. Neither slaves nor tenants, then, but a form of wage labour subject to intense landlord controls.

Nov. Just. 162, c.2 (539) implies that such resident labourers were usually natives of the estates where they resided (οἷα ἐκεῖσε γεννηθέντας). Of course, the strongest indication that birth on an estate automatically qualified workers as 'tied' *coloni* is terminology itself, for during most of the late fourth and first half of the fifth century *coloni* were usually referred to as *originarii*, and it is certain, as De Martino has suggested,[119] that in the mid-fifth century the chancery still used 'originarius', so that *enapographos*, when it first appeared, was a rendering of *originarius*, and *adscripticius* was eventually established through the diffusion of the Greek term.[120] The most direct textual reference to rural workers being born in the estate settlements called *vici* is Novel 6 of Justin II from 570, responding to pressures from the aristocracy of 'Africana provincia'.[121] Thus in economic terms these were estates that depended

esp. 130 ff., id., *Lavoro e lavoratori nel mondo romano* (Bari, 1963) 143–81, id., '"Locatio operarum" e "status" del lavoratore', *SDHI* 27 (1961) 19–45. D. Nörr, 'Zur sozialen und rechtlichen Bewertung der freien Arbeit in Rom', *ZSS* 82 (1965) 67 ff., is not totally convincing—he is unable to explain Paulus, *Sent.* 2.18.1 (esp. 103), and underestimates the prevalence of hired labour, restricting it to seasonal tasks (90 ff., 100, 'Freie Landarbeiter sind in der Regel Saisonarbeiter'). There is some discussion of the passage in C. Möller, *Freiheit und Schutz im Arbeitsrecht. Das Fortwirken des römischen Rechts in der Rechtsprechung des Reichsgerichts* (Göttingen, 1990) 22 ff.

[118] B. Frier, *Landlords and Tenants in Imperial Rome* (Princeton, 1980) 178, about Gaius, 4.153, 'Possidere autem videmur non solum, si ipsi possideamus, sed etiam si nostro nomine aliquis in possessione sit, licet is nostro iuri subiectus non sit, qualis est colonus et inquilinus' (We seem to have possession not only when we ourselves hold but also when someone holds for us, even if he is not in our power, such as an agricultural or urban tenant), with M. I. Finley, 'Private Farm Tenancy in Italy before Diocletian', in M. I. Finley (ed.), *Studies in Roman Property* (Cambridge, 1976) 115.

[119] F. De Martino, 'Il colonato fra economia e diritto', in A. Schiavone (ed.), *Storia di Roma*. 3/1 (Turin, 1993) 789–822, at 797.

[120] Indeed, the earliest appearance of *enapographos may* be *P. Med.* I² 64, dated 6 Dec. 441, cf. *BL* 7.103 and Gonis, *P. Oxy.* LXVIII, p. 158–9. *Originarius* itself had been preceded by *originalis*, which was first used of rural workers on imperial estates (cf. P. Rosafio, 'Coloni imperiali e coloni privati nella legislazione del quarto secolo', *Atti dell' Accademia Romanistica Costantiniana: X Convegno Internazionale* (Naples, 1995), 457), showing that the model which influenced the organization of labour on aristocratic estates was frequently an imperial one.

[121] Just. II, *Nov.* 6.1 (570) (*Jus Graecoromanum*², ed. C. E. Zachariae von Lingenthal, J. Zepos, and P. Zepos, 1.10 f.), 'Unde sancimus, in Africana provincia filios ex libera matre et adscriptitio patre productos liberos quidem esse et res proprias habere, in ordine tamen colonorum esse, et non posse eos dimittere praedia, in quibus nati sunt, et excolere

on a core of permanent workers, of whom a considerable number were native to the estate. These workers, certainly, were included on its tax lists, on the understanding that owners were 'responsible for the collection of tribute as villages had been before'.[122] This system, diversely described as *ius census*,[123] *ius colonatus*,[124] *ius agrorum*,[125] and so on, thus gave the colonate a markedly fiscal aspect, which became progressively weaker over the centuries. For the state it was essential to have a reliable estimate of the taxable labour capacity of estates, and landowners were thus required to maintain a list of all regular labourers who counted for taxation purposes. It is certain that this model was first evolved for rural slaves and later extended to permanent farm labourers recruited by estates as resident workers.[126] Thus such workers were usually referred to as *censibus adscripti*,[127] and later, when the term *enapographos* became established in the east, as *adscripticii*. The evidence certainly suggests

aliena, sed vicos ipsos, in quibus orti sunt, cum libertate colere' (We therefore decree that in the province of Africa the children of an *adscripticius* and a free woman are certainly free and enjoy the rights of property, but belong to the class of *coloni* and cannot abandon the estates in which they were born, to cultivate the fields of other owners, but should engage in agricultural work in their native settlements, as free persons).

[122] J. D. Riley, 'Landlords, Laborers, and Royal Government: The Administration of Labor in Tlaxcala, 1680–1750', in E. C. Frost, M. C. Meyer, and J. Z. Vázquez (eds.), *El trabajo y los trabajadores en la historia de México* (Mexico, 1979) 222, describing the homologous situation of the *gañanes*.

[123] *CTh.* 5.6.3 (409), 'nullique liceat velut donatos eos a iure census [in s]ervitutem trahere urbanisve obsequiis addicere' (No one is entitled to draw such persons away from the *ius census* into slavery or to assign them to various jobs in the cities).

[124] *CTh.* 5.6.3, 'Ideoque damus omnibus copiam ex praedicto ge[ner]e hominum agros proprios frequentandi, ita ut omnes [scia]nt susceptos non alio iure quam colonatus apud se futu[ros]' (Therefore, all owners now have the opportunity to staff their own estates with persons of the aforesaid race, on the understanding that they will be with them strictly in terms of the *ius colonatus*). *Nov. Just.* app. 9 (558) (*CIC* 3.803), 'Cognitum nobis est quod quidam in provincia Africana non adtendentes iussiones nostras, quas pro repetitione fecimus rusticorum, calumniam exercere non cessant, repetentes colonos vel rusticos vel filios eorum, qui ex propriis rebus ante adventum felicissimi exercitus exisse monstrantur; sed et clericos in officiis ecclesiasticis constitutos ex iure colonatus sollicitare non cessant' (It has come to our knowledge that certain persons in the province of Africa, failing to heed the instructions we issued regarding the reclaiming of rural labourers, continue to act on false pretences by seeking to reclaim farm labourers or their sons who can be shown to have left of their own resources before the advent of our most fortunate army; indeed, they even continue to harass clerics engaged in ecclesiastical duties on the grounds that they possess a *ius colonatus*).

[125] *CTh.* 5.18.1 (see n. 114), 10.20.10 = *CJ* 11.8.7 (380), 'iuri agrorum debitas personas'.

[126] The evidence for this is *CTh.* 11.3.2 (327), concerning sales involving *mancipia adscribta censibus*, 'slaves assigned to the taxrolls' (Pharr) or 'slaves registered in the census' (Jones), cf. Jones, *LRE* 2.795, and D. Eibach, *Untersuchungen zum spätantiken Kolonat in der kaiserlichen Gesetzgebung* (Cologne, 1977) 135.

[127] The expression was still used in 434, cf. *CTh.* 5.3.1. Otherwise in *CJ* 11.50.2 (396), *CTh.* 5.6.3 (409), with variants in *CTh.* 11.1.14 = *CJ* 11.48.4 (371), *CTh.* 11.1.26 (399), and 11.24.6.3 (415).

that the legal rights of employers (*domini*) were a consistent concern of the state,[128] that the subordination of *coloni* was increasingly conceptualized as subjection to a *ius privatum*,[129] and that the only significant restriction on the aristocracy's control over labour was that, technically, *coloni adscripticii* were not their property but the property of the estate.[130] Finally, both *CJ* 11.53.1 (371) and 11.52.1 (392–5) establish a clear distinction between the colonate (as this had come to be understood by the late fourth century) and the fiscal subjection of rural workers, showing that the *ius colonatus* or *ius colonarium*[131] or *nexus colonarius*[132] had an independent basis in law, irrespective of the method of assessing the taxable value of estates.

[128] e.g. *Fr. Vat.* 34 (313) (*FIRA* 2.469), 'Etiamnunc, si a suis parentibus certo pretio comparasti, ius dominii possidere te existimamus' (in a rescript of Constantine); *CJ* 11.51.1 (386), 'Cum per alias provincias, quae subiacent nostrae serenitatis imperio, lex a maioribus constituta colonos quodam aeternitatis iure detineat . . . neque id Palaestinae provinciae possessoribus suffragetur, sancimus, ut etiam per Palaestinas nullus omnino colonorum suo iure velut vagus ac liber exsultet, sed exemplo aliarum provinciarum ita domino fundi teneatur, ut sine poena suscipientis non possit abscedere' (Since in all other provinces subject to the reign of Our serenity, the law established by Our forebears detains farm labourers by a sort of right of permanent detention . . . but similar support is not extended to the landowners of the province of Palestine, we decree that in Palestine too none of the *coloni* may exult in their own rights, as if they were free individuals with the freedom to roam, but, following the example of the other provinces, let them be bound to the owners of estates so that they cannot leave without punishment visiting those who receive them) (with Lo Cascio, *Athenaeum* 57 (1979) 499), and nn. 111 and 112 above. Also see the excellent paper by Michel Humbert, 'Enfants à louer ou à vendre: Augustin et l'autorité parentale (*Ep.*10* et 24*)', in *Les lettres de Saint Augustin découvertes par Johannes Divjak: communications présentées au colloque des 20 et 21 septembre 1982* (Paris, 1983) 189–203.

[129] *Nov. Val.* 27.6 (449), 'lege divi parentis nostri Honorii de colonis utriusque sexus iuris privati', about *originarii* and their children.

[130] See Riley, 'Landlords, Laborers, and Royal Government', 229, for an interesting parallel ('A suit in 1742 makes it clear that the courts considered [*gañanes*] the property of an estate, not of the owner').

[131] *Nov. Val.* 31.1 (451), Gregory, *Ep.* 4.21 (Norberg, *CC Ser. latina* 140.239) (594).

[132] *Nov. Val.* 31.6 (451).

CHAPTER 9

Conclusion

It has been a major argument of this book that the emergence of gold as a stable high-value coinage revolutionized the economic conditions of the late empire. In gold the aristocracy rediscovered a powerful medium of accumulation, and the state a medium of taxation that would progressively displace taxes in kind as the dominant form of public revenue. The dogma of late antique isolationism, deeply rooted in the first generation of scholars who turned in a serious way to issues of economic history, was first seriously assaulted by Mickwitz in the early 1930s. However, even Mickwitz would see the late Roman state as a bastion of 'natural economy', and end his thesis with the strange dualism of a vibrant set of monetary relations in the private sector coupled with a large area of public finance that was impervious to monetary economy. Mickwitz made assumptions about the aspirations of the late imperial bureaucracy that were peculiarly defensive and excessively influenced by the historical experience of Sweden in the eighteenth century. According to him, the powerful new groups which governed the late empire resisted monetization and drove a whole sector of the economy inexorably in the direction of payments in kind. This, as Mazzarino showed, misconstrued the interests of the new governing class in a fundamental way. It failed to see that with the emergence of the gold coinage as a stable repository of value, the options before the official classes were less narrowly defined, and resolved, indeed, in favour of gold. Because of these pressures, experienced as a kind of counterfinality, the state came to exert a powerful influence on the monetary economy of the whole period, driving it forward to what were clearly historically unprecedented levels of monetization and monetary expansion, in keeping, arguably, with trends elsewhere in the world at the time. Moreover, as the harbinger of an expanding monetary sector, the state gave a powerful impetus to the general forces of economic expansion, boosting trade and encouraging a framework within which the 'business economy' of the Mediterranean both revived and prospered. That these economic trends were repeatedly intersected by the deepening political fragmentation of the Mediterranean is of course true, but not, in the final instance, of crucial importance, at least for the continued economic vitality of the eastern empire.

Within the general framework defined by this new period of monetary expansion, three features are especially striking. The first is the remarkable prosperity of the late Roman countryside. Where rural areas had suffered desolation in the early empire, they were now reoccupied and more densely settled, as in Greece.[1] Elsewhere, cultivation extended beyond the more fertile plains to marginal sectors such as the limestone hills east of Antioch[2] or the desert lands south and west of Nessana.[3] Where the possibilities of this kind of expansion were limited, as they were in Egypt, large estates emerged as a major source of investment in perennial irrigation, and the irrigated sector with stable yields must have expanded considerably. In the Fayum a dense network of estates covered much of the countryside that was still habitable after the progressive silting up of the canal by which the Nile water entered the depression and the further lowering of the lake produced a contraction of settlement to the west and north of the region.[4] In Lower Egypt a fifth-century ecclesiastical historian described Mareotis as typified by 'numerous and densely populated villages with their many resplendent churches'.[5] But we know from other evidence that these villages coexisted with substantial rural properties such as the wine estates in the area around Abu Mina[6] and valuable orchards owned by officials residing in Alexandria.[7] In Africa the transcripts of the Conference of Carthage in 411 convey a strong sense of countrysides carpeted by estates which were subjected to fierce rivalries between competing churches. In short, the resilience of the late antique rural areas is a fascinating and undeniable feature of large parts of the Mediterranean world, and one obvious implication of this boom is

[1] So S. Alcock, *Graecia Capta: The Landscapes of Ancient Greece* (Cambridge, 1993).

[2] C. Foss, 'Syria in Transition, AD 550–750: An Archaeological Approach', *DOP* 51 (1997) 189–269, at 201.

[3] P. Mayerson, 'The desert of Southern Palestine according to Byzantine Sources', *Proceedings of the American Philosophical Society* 107 (1963) 160 ff.

[4] See John Ball, *Contributions to the Geography of Egypt* (Cairo, 1939) esp. 219, and his discussion of Nabulsi, 219 ff.

[5] Socrates, *Hist. Eccl.* 1.27.13: *Μαρεώτης χώρα τῆς Ἀλεξανδρείας ἐστίν. κῶμαι δέ εἰσιν ἐν αὐτῇ πολλαὶ σφόδρα καὶ πολυάνθρωποι καὶ ἐν αὐταῖς ἐκκλησίαι πολλαὶ καὶ λαμπραί.*

[6] J.-Y. Empereur, 'La production viticole dans l'Égypte ptolémaique et romaine', in M.-C. Amouretti *et al.*, *La Production du vin et de l'huile en Mediterranée*. BCH Suppl. 26 (École Française d'Athènes, 1993) 39–47; also the ecclesiastical estate in Wortmann, 'Griechische ostraka aus Abu Mena'.

[7] See n. 40 below.

that the demographic pattern was more complex and differentiated than any sweeping notions of a generalized decline. It is now likely that for *most* of late antiquity population was on an upward climb, and that the dominant agrarian classes were able to draw on a "surplus" rural population, much as the English estates would do in the thirteenth century.[8]

Having said this, it would be useful to add two important qualifications to this picture. First, the changes in settlement patterns which emerged at some stage in the late antique expansion were far from uniform and may even have diverged sharply. The 'explosive' growth of settlement in the rural hinterlands of the East Mediterranean[9] was certainly not matched by any analogous process in either Italy or Spain. Some of the Italian evidence, for example, suggests a clear pattern of the restructuring of rural sites in the late antique period, with a reduction in site densities, accompanied, frequently, by the emergence of substantially larger establishments.[10] This is in contrast to the increasing density of rural sites in the Palestinian countryside and the fact that there 'the size of smaller towns also grew markedly in Late Antiquity'.[11] Whether these contrasting patterns of settlement change were in turn linked (or primarily linked) to fundamentally distinct underlying patterns of demographic growth is a moot point. The Italian story is one of demographic contraction, though Wickham notes, 'Every region, every city, had its own cycles of depression and revival, independent of the political and economic crisis of the western empire as a whole.'[12] Second, a more prosperous countryside was not necessarily one with less inequality. Indeed, all the evidence suggests that the rural society of the sixth century was more, not less, differentiated than that, say, of the third. In some areas the peasantry was clearly deeply stratified, with a handful of well-to-do households, village leaders, distinguished from a conspicuously larger mass of landless tenants and labourers. This was particularly true of Egypt. Elsewhere it may well have retained both a greater sense of cohesion and some sense of the kind of fierce egalitarianism displayed by the more substantial rural households of north-west Galatia. In

[8] G. Duby, *Rural Economy and Country Life in the Medieval West* (1968) 262–4.

[9] Alan Walmsley, 'Byzantine Palestine and Arabia: urban prosperity in Late Antiquity', in N. Christie and S. T. Loseby (eds.), *Towns in Transition: Urban Evolution in Late Antiquity and the Early Middle Ages* (Aldershot, 1996) 126–58, at 150.

[10] See G. Volpe, *Contadini, pastori e mercanti nell' Apulia tardoantica* (Bari, 1996) 206 ff.

[11] Walmsley, 'Byzantine Palestine', 150.

[12] Chris Wickham, 'Considerazioni conclusive', in R. Francovich ad G. Noyé (eds.), *La storia dell' Alto Medioevo italiano (VI–X secolo) alla luce dell' archeologia* (Florence, 1994) 741–59, at 743.

either event, it is unlikely that these differences either overrode the identity of late antique rural societies as, typically, hierarchical agrarian communities,[13] or did much to undermine their actual cohesion as social entities. Differences in the structure and levels of prosperity of the peasantry may well have served to differentiate different regions and topographical sectors of the late antique countryside, but they made no visible contribution to the disintegration of the communities themselves, which remained stable and relatively coherent features of the countryside everywhere.

Commutation had a major impact on the rhythms of monetary expansion, suggesting that there were two important processes running hand in hand. As taxes were commuted to cash, the countryside was more deeply integrated into commercial exchanges. In Chapter 3 I suggested that this process was fairly advanced by the sixth century, and would have represented a major transformation of the economy. On the other hand, much of the pressure for commutation stemmed from powerful groups within the bureaucracy, for whom the payment of salaries in gold had the crucial advantage of yielding 'liquid assets which could be used for all kinds of investment and especially speculation in land'.[14] The papyri contain numerous examples of members of the military and bureaucratic hierarchies buying into the assets of existing land-controllers and themselves coming to control substantial amounts of land at various times in the later fourth and fifth centuries. In addition to which, of course, there was widespread and systematic bureaucratic profiteering, involving the kinds of speculation and rent-seeking that were repeatedly denounced in contemporary sources.[15] As large sums of gold were accumulated through these various mechanisms in a late Roman equivalent of 'primitive accumulation' that appeared to contemporaries as the unbridled dominance of public officials, a new aristocracy emerged out of the expanded governing class of the fourth century, no longer merely an 'aristocracy of office', though it was always that as well, but an economically powerful and socially dominant group of businesslike landowners who dominated their respective regions. Unlike the west, where a small élite of the old

[13] For a general argument, see Victor V. Magagna, *Communities of Grain: Rural Rebellion in Comparative Perspective* (Ithaca, NY, and London, 1991).

[14] Rosemary Morris, 'The Powerful and the Poor in Tenth-Century Byzantium: Law and Reality', *Past and Present* 73 (1976) 3–27, at 15, on the *dynatoi* of the later Byzantine world.

[15] See p. 48 above for 4th-cent. views, and Salvian, *Gub. Dei*, esp. 5.17 (*SC* 220, ed. Lagarrigue, p. 324); 5.25 (p. 330). I do not subscribe to the view that the prevalence of these forms of corruption meant that late Roman society suffered from a permanent crisis of the efficacy of law, see Jill Harries, *Law and Empire in Late Antiquity* (Cambridge, 1999) for a rebuttal of this cliché.

senatorial families was hemmed in by deepening fragmentation[16] or displaced by the advance of a new local 'landed aristocracy of military officers',[17] the eastern provinces knew no juxtaposition of this sort, and the emergent aristocracies of (mainly) the fifth century were both more recent than the 'old' senatorial families of the western empire, and more precocious than the landholding military officers of sixth-century Italy. Indeed, it is difficult to speak of a 'crisis of the old ruling class'[18] in the case of the East Mediterranean, where the native municipal élites were simply no match for the powerful new elements who invaded the landholding structure and became the ruling class. In short, the late imperial state nurtured a new ruling class, much as the Stalinist regimes sought to do in parts of Europe in the twentieth century (but there unsuccessfully), and this process is particularly evident in the eastern provinces.

Finally, the expansion of wage labour is certainly one of the most interesting features of late antiquity. The wage form covered a wide range of occupations, and wage labour was structured in diverse, flexible ways (as labour tenancy, sharecropping, service contracts, the contracting of specific jobs, etc.). Moreover, the demand for wage labour in this broader, flexibly structured sense, derived to a great degree from the aristocracy. Thus late antiquity throws up a social formation combining aristocratic dominance with free labour on a model that conforms to none of the historical stereotypes distinguishing the classical from the medieval and modern worlds (aristocrats + slaves, aristocrats + serfs, capitalists + wage-labourers). These of course have always been extremely general formulations that seek to sum up the economic structure of different historical periods in terms of an essential or uniquely pervasive set of relations. But hired labourers were used on an extensive scale by the English estates of the thirteenth century;[19] slaves were used by agrarian capitalists down to the late nineteenth century;[20] and serfs, like slaves, could also be deployed in industrial production.[21] These disjunctures complicate the issue of a scholarly understanding of the possible sophistication of ancient economic behaviour, because they rule out the simplistic idea that the dynamic which drives an economic system is given primarily in terms of the organization

[16] For the general picture, see C. Wickham, 'Early Medieval Archaeology in Italy: The Last Twenty Years', *Archeologia Medievale* 26 (1999) 7–20.

[17] Brown, *Gentlemen and Officers*, x, 13 f., and *passim*.

[18] Ibid. ch. 2.

[19] G. Duby, *Rural Economy and Country Life*, 262 f.

[20] Laird W. Bergad, *Cuban Rural Society in the Nineteenth Century* (Princeton, 1990).

[21] Jerome Blum, *Lord and Peasant in Russia from the Ninth to the Nineteenth Century* (New York, 1968) ch. 16, cf. R. S. Starobin, *Industrial Slavery in the Old South* (New York, 1970).

of labour, i.e. that the 'forms of exploitation' of labour determine the 'relations of production', and to form some assessment of the nature of aristocratic activity the issue of the nature of the labour force is thus largely irrelevant.[22] The bureaucratization of the aristocratic large estates was a sign of their 'rationalization', their rational control as business enterprises, entities not fundamentally different from the South Italian *latifondi* studied by Petrusewicz and Arlacchi,[23] or the Andalusian estates of the seventeenth century.[24] The ideal of self-sufficiency which characterized these various kinds of estates did *not* imply isolationism or natural economy.[25]

Despite the prevailing minimalist views of the ancient economy, it is clear that enterprises were run only if they were profitable, which is not to say that all owners or businesslike entities strove to expand profitability from year to year in the way modern capitalist firms do as a condition of their survival. Flax,[26] fish,[27] silk,[28] olive-oil,[29] glass factories,[30] potteries,[31] brickyards,[32] metal-shops, dye-

[22] Therefore I disagree quite substantially with Haldon's characterization of the late antique aristocracy as a feudal class, J. F. Haldon, *Byzantium in the Seventh Century* (Cambridge, 1997).

[23] Marta Petrusewicz, *Latifundium: Moral Economy and Material Life in a European Periphery*, tr. J. C. Greene (Ann Arbor, 1996), P. Arlacchi, *Mafia, Peasants and Great Estates: Society in Traditional Calabria*, tr. J. Steinberg (Cambridge, 1983).

[24] Antonio Miguel Bernal, *Economía e historia de los latifundios* (Madrid, 1988).

[25] See Petrusewicz, *Latifundium*, 132, for this crucial point. E. Stein, *Geschichte des spätrömischen Reiches*, 1 (Vienna, 1928) 26–7, and A. Piganiol, *L'empire chrétien (325–395)* (Paris, 1972; orig. 1947) 308, conflate the two ideas (self-sufficiency/isolationism) and are misleading.

[26] The evidence is dispersed and chiefly papyrological, e.g. *CPR* IV 48 (Nov. 625), where 36 solidi were invested in acquiring close to 50,000 lb. of flax. The producing centre, Pousire, was surely the Busir which figures as a major flax-producing centre in the business papers of Ibn 'Awkal, Udovitch, 'International Trade and the Medieval Egyptian Countryside'.

[27] R. Étienne, Y. Makaroun, and F. Mayet, *Un grand complex industriel à Tróia (Portugal)* (Paris, 1994), J.M. Nolla-Brufau, 'Excavaciones recientes en la Ciudadela de Roses. El edificio bajo-imperial', in T. F. C. Blagg *et al.*, *Papers in Iberian Archaeology* (BAR Int. Series, 193/2, 1984) 430–50.

[28] Oikonomidès, 'Silk Trade', on the *kommerkiarioi.*

[29] D. J. Mattingly, 'The Olive Boom: Oil Surpluses, Wealth and Power in Roman Tripolitania', *LS* 19 (1988) 21–41 and, 'Megalithic Madness and Measurement. Or how Many Olives Could an Olive Press Press?', *Oxford Journal of Archaeology* 7 (1988) 177–95, and the massive estate in J.-P. Brun, 'La *Villa* gallo-romaine de Saint-Michel à la Garde (Var). Un domaine oléicole au Haut-Empire', *Gallia* 46 (1989) 103–62.

[30] G. D. Weinberg, *Excavations at Jalame: Site of a Glass Factory in Late Roman Palestine* (Columbia, 1988).

[31] M. Ponsich, *Implantation rurale antique sur le Bas-Guadalquivir*, vol. 1 (Madrid and Paris, 1974) esp. 145 ff. (El Tejillo); F. Mayet, *Les Céramiques sigillées hispaniques. Contribution à l'histoire économique de la Péninsule Ibérique sous l'empire romain* (Paris, 1984).

[32] Margareta Steinby, 'L'organizzazione produttiva dei laterizi: un modello interpretativo per l'*instrumentum* in genere?' in W. V. Harris (ed.), *The Inscribed Economy: Production and Distribution in the Roman Empire in the light of instrumentum domesticum* (Ann Arbor, 1993) 139–43.

works, moneylending, banking,[33] maritime commerce,[34] the grain trade,[35] fruit production, and the wine industry[36] were all sectors which saw a substantial investment of private capital based on the individual pursuit of profit. Late Romans were familiar with the idea that the value of estates depended on their active exploitation,[37] and the countryside clearly absorbed a great deal of investment, starting (or re-starting) in the fourth century. The estate of the aristocrat and general Heraclian disappointed expectations in being valued at only 2,000 lb. of gold, apart from an equivalent sum in cash on hand![38] Vineyards demanded substantial capital expenditures,[39] orchards near Alexandria were hugely expensive and presumably in considerable demand,[40] and large sums of money went into the rebuilding and expansion of villas in the late antique period,[41] the engrossment of land,[42] the acquisition of large properties that

[33] Edward E. Cohen, *Athenian Economy and Society: A Banking Perspective* (Princeton, 1992), the best study. (The attack on Cohen in Makoto Itoh and Costas Lapavitsas, *The Political Economy of Money and Finance* (Macmillan, 1999) 75, is not based on any grasp of the evidence.) On the significance of *P. Cairo Masp*. II 67126 (541) for a history of late antique banking (a loan is raised in Constantinople for repayment in Alexandria), see G. Mickwitz, 'Die Organisationsformen zweier byzantinischer Gewerbe im X. Jahrhundert', *BZ* 36 (1936) 63–4.

[34] U. von Lübtow, 'Catos Seedarlehen', in H. Hübner *et al.* (eds.), *Festschrift für Erwin Seidl zum 70 Geburtstag* (Cologne, 1975) 103–17.

[35] M. W. Frederiksen, 'Puteoli e il commercio del grano in epoca Romana', *Puteoli* 4–5 (1980–1) 5–27; Lellia Cracco Ruggini, *Economia e società nell' "Italia annonaria". Rapporti fra agricoltura e commercio dal IV al VI secolo d.C.* (Milan, 1961) *passim*.

[36] A. Aymard, 'Les capitalistes romains et la viticulture italienne', *Annales ESC* 2 (1947) 257–65; N. Purcell, 'Wine and Wealth in Ancient Italy', *JRS* 75 (1985) 1–19; E. Kislinger, 'Zum Weinhandel in frühbyzantinischer Zeit', *Tyche* 14 (1999) 141–56. Also P. Heine, *Weinstudien. Untersuchungen zu Anbau, Produktion und Konsum des Weins im arabisch-islamischen Mittelalter* (Wiesbaden, 1982).

[37] Ambrose, *Tob.* 6.23 (Giacchero, 101), 'de fructibus emptae possessionis pretium multiplicabis, debitum reddes' (by extracting an output from the acquired property, you will multiply its value and repay your debt), cf. Varro, *RR* 1.4.2, investments in the ordered planting of fruit and olive trees are said to make the farm 'more saleable' and to 'add to the value (*pretium*) of the estate'.

[38] Olympiodorus, 23 (Blockley 2.186), cf. Jones, *LRE* 1.423, 'the entire estate of Heraclian, which amounted to 2000 lb. gold in cash and lands of equal value'.

[39] Columella, *RR* 3.3.8, 'amplissimas impensas vineae poscant'.

[40] *P. Oxy*. LXIII 4394 (494–500), involving two orchards near Lake Marea (*c*.45 km. from Alexandria) valued at 675 solidi!

[41] e.g. G. Volpe, *Contadini, pastori e mercanti nell' Apulia tardoantica* (Bari, 1996) 160 ff., 197 ff., 206 ff.; Castellana and McConnell, 'Rural settlement', (Phase IV-A); A. M. Small and J. Freed, 'S. Giovanni di Ruoti (Basilicata). Il contesto della villa tardoromana', in *SRIT* 3.97–126. Cf. P. de Palol, 'Romanos en la Meseta: el Bajo Imperio y la aristocracía agrícola', in *Segovia: Symposium de arqueología romana* (Barcelona, 1977) 297–308.

[42] e.g. *P. Oxy*. LXIII 4397.53–68 (545), the *comes sacrarum largitionum* Flavius Strategius, father of Apion II, took possession of the whole estate of a certain Diogenes 'by right of the mortgages embodied in his loan contracts' with the latter. Cf. the much earlier ref. to the emperor Pertinax 'extending his own holdings by foreclosing mortgages', SHA, *Pert.* 3.4.

could be exploited on a commercial basis,[43] as well as a thriving Mediterranean commerce.[44]

To distinguish precisely these forms of profit-oriented activity from modern capitalism, Sombart proposed the more general category 'business economy' (*Erwerbswirtschaft*).[45] Mayet characterizes the overall organization of the Spanish fine-ware industry in terms of the operations of 'commercial capitalism', meaning by this the decisive role of merchant capital in the organization of production.[46] Much of the business activity that characterized the great commercial centres of the central and eastern Mediterranean could probably be subsumed under one or other of these categories.[47] In other words, we have to visualize bankers, shipowners, local traders, and wealthy mercantile houses operating within integrated networks of business that connected them to each other and to production and exchange in the urban and rural areas. These relations are largely invisible in our sources, beyond a singular attestation of the huge profits made by the Alexandrian bankers on currency transactions,[48] or a handful of documents reflecting the downstream activities of Alexandrian dealers in wine, flax, etc.[49] There is almost no papyrological evidence from Alexandria itself, and nothing remotely comparable to the substantial business archive found in the Cairo Geniza records. But an argument from silence would be

[43] Cf. the *arcarius* John, *vir clarissimus*, who was willing to advance 10,000 solidi to secure the lease on estates of the *patrimonium* in Apulia, Cassiodorus, *Var.* 5.7.

[44] Cf. Procopius' ref. to the 'numerous' eastern merchants resident at Carthage, *BV* 1.20.5 f. In the 4th cent., Batnae (in western Mesopotamia) was described by Ammianus as 'packed with wealthy merchants' (Amm. 14.3.2: 'refertum mercatoribus opulentis'), and several cities of the Near East were thought to be characterized by their savvy businessmen and 'scorching' pace of business, *Expositio totius mundi et gentium*, 22 (*SC* 124. 156), 24 (p. 158), 29 (p. 162).

[45] W. Sombart, 'Die gewerbliche Arbeit und ihre Organisation', *Archiv für soziale Gesetzgebung u. Statistik* 14 (1899), 1–52, 310–405, esp. 368 ff., arguing that it made no difference to businesses in this broader sense whether they exploited slaves, serfs, or hired workers (at 398).

[46] Mayet, *Les Céramiques sigillées hispaniques*, esp. 218.

[47] This is the sense in which Rostovtzeff himself understood capitalism 'in its wider meaning', as 'the economic form which aims at profit, not at consumption', adding, 'Naturally, modern capitalism is of a wholly different kind, and in the typical forms it manifests today unknown to the ancient world', *SEHRE* 2.543 n. 1.

[48] Banaji, 'Discounts, Weight Standards, and the Exchange-Rate between Gold and Copper', *Atti dell' Accademia Romanistica Costantiniana. XII convegno int. in onore di Manlio Sargenti* (Naples, 1998) 183–202, esp. 193–5 (on Edict 11). The bankers of Constantinople were powerful enough to influence the regulations relating to their business, see Franca La Rosa, 'La pressione degli *argentarii* e la riforma giustinianea del *constitutum debiti*', in *Nozione formazione e interpretazione del diritto dall' età romana alle esperienze moderne. Ricerche dedicate al Professore Filippo Gallo*, 4 vols. (Naples, 1997) 1.445–51.

[49] *CPR* X 39 (443), an Alexandrian spice trader places a substantial order for wine jars; *P. Oxy.* VIII 1130 (*c*.483), an Alexandrian merchant advances 10 solidi for flax.

absurd. The issue, at any rate, is not whether the large estates of late antiquity were governed by use-value and comprised forms of a 'closed household economy', but rather how far the aristocracy's involvement in the Roman monetary economy assumed a capitalist character in displaying the features that contemporaries associated with the purely capitalist behaviour of moneylenders.[50] Whatever the answer to this question, it is clear that we cannot conceive of the aristocracy of the period as a class of 'sybaritic oligarchs' riding out the storm of some late antique recession in the hermetic fastness of isolationist estates.[51]

Max Weber's dogma of a late antique isolationism is in fact the least tenable of the various propositions historians have advanced about late antiquity. It was widely accepted until Mickwitz put paid to the idea with his book about the monetary vibrancy of the fourth century. Weber's ideas have had a pervasive influence on the historiography of the late empire, though, reinforcing minimalist stereotypes of the ancient economy, and of late antiquity in particular, as somehow impervious to the sway of market relations. That modern capitalism would transform those relations in ways that were unimaginable to antiquity has misled historians into supposing that capitalism was not something the ancient world could ever have known in any fundamental sense. Misconceiving the issue as one of why modern capitalism did not develop in the ancient world, Weber himself adduced a plethora of possible reasons, which ranged from the impediments inherent in the use of slave labour to the bureaucratic stifling of entrepreneurial incentives characteristic, allegedly, of late antique society.[52] However, Weber realized that Bücher's picture was untenable in crucial ways, and that his ideas were overdrawn and not easily applicable to the actual writing of history.[53]

[50] Greg. Nyss. *Contra usurarios* 16 (*PG* 46.437B), Ambrose, *Tob.* 5.16 (Giacchero 95).

[51] Anderson's unequivocal vision in *Passages from Antiquity to Feudalism*, esp. 92–103.

[52] The final statement may have been Weber, *Wirtschaftsgeschichte. Abriß der universalen Sozial- und Wirtschaftsgeschichte* (Berlin, 1958), 287 f., lectures delivered in 1919/20.

[53] Beyond these general contestations, one should also note that the orthodoxy of technological stagnation will look increasingly less credible in future, cf. K. Greene, 'Technological Innovation and Economic Progress in the Ancient World: M. I. Finley reconsidered', *EcHR* 53 (2000) 29–59 (general); O. Wikander, *Exploitation of Water-Power or Technological Stagnation?* (Lund, 1984) and A. Wilson, 'Machines, Power and the Ancient Economy', *JRS* 92 (2002) 1–32 (water mills, water-powered saws); R. Frankel, 'Presses for Oil and Wine in the Southern Levant in the Byzantine Period', *DOP* 51 (1997) 73–84 (screw presses); Raepsaet, 'Prémices de la mécanisation agricole' (harvest machines, etc.). R. H. Rodgers, '¿Yuniyus o Columela en la España medieval?', *al-Andalus* 43 (1978) 163–72 shows that the "Yūniyūs" cited by the Andalusian agronomists Ibn Ḥajjāj al-Ishbīlī and Ibn al-'Awwām was the late (?) fourth-century writer Vindanius Anatolius of Beirut, author of the *Synagōgē geōrgikōn epitēdeumatōn* (Photius, *cod.* 163, ed. Henry, t. 2, p. 134). Thus agronomy was another field where late antique intellectual culture progressed beyond the imitation of classical models.

APPENDIX 1

Tables 1–12

Table 1: *The gold/copper exchange rate, 300–618 (the price of the solidus in terms of 'myriads of denarii')*

Source	Date	Value
1. *P. Beatty Panop.* 2, 215ff.	26 Feb. 300	0.083
2. *P. Oxy.* XVII 2106	*c.*304–6?	0.139
3. *P. Heid.* IV 323C	310	0.208
4. *P. Ryl.* IV 616 ii	*c.*312?	0.153
5. *P. Oxy.* XLIII 3121	*c.*316–18	0.600
6. *CPR* VIII 27	324?	0.351
7. *P. Oxy.* XII 1430.17	324	0.435
8. *P. Vindob.* G 13187	?	2.625?
9. *SB* XVI 12825	330–7	15.00
10. *SB* XIV 11593.39	?	27.50
11. *P. Oxy.* LIV 3773	*c.*340?	35.00–36.50
12. *P. Ryl.* IV 657 verso[a]	?	38.00
13. *P. Oxy.* XXXIV 2729	*c.*350?	730.00
14. *P. Oxy.* XX 2267.11–13	?	457.00
15. *P. Oxy.* LI 3624	359	1360.00
16. *P. Oxy.* XLVIII 3426	?	2250.00
17. *P. Oxy.* IX 1223	?	2020.00
18. *P. Oxy.* XLVIII 3429	?	3245.00
19. *PSI* VIII 959.13	?[b]	3750.00
20. *P. Oxy.* LI 3628–3636	*c.*423?	3900.00–4000.00
21. *CPR* V 26 (Skar Codex)	?[c]	4200.00
22. *P. Oxy.* XIV 1729	?	4713.33
23. *P. Oxy.* XVI 1911.208	557	5169.20
24. *P. Oxy.* 2195.48, 141–4	562/3[d]	4965.00–5008.00
25. *P. Oxy.* LV 3804.271	566	4800.00
26. *P. Oxy.* LVIII 3958.26	614	4800.00
27. *P. Oxy.* XVI 1917.59	616/17[e]	7200.00
28. *P. Oxy.* XVI 1904.3	618	7680.00

Notes:

[a] D. Hagedorn, *ZPE* 79 (1989) 251 f.

[b] R. S. Bagnall and P. J. Sijpestein, *ZPE* 24 (1977) 111–24 suggest *c*.385–8, but this depends on their date for *CPR* V 26 (see n. c).

[c] Bagnall and Sijpestein (see n. b) suggest any time between 373 and 388, which seems far too early to me (given the value of the solidus). Since then, however, Bagnall has argued for a date in the mid- to late 5th cent., see *ZPE* 69 (1987) 248.

[d] Gascou dates this account to 576/7, but see Table 2, n. f.

[e] For the date cf. Rea, *P. Oxy*. LVIII, p. 114.

Table 2: *Production levels and cash ratios in the estate economy of Byzantine Egypt*

Reference	Wheat		Cash		
	receipts[a]	expenditure	receipts[b]	expenditure	balance
(a) The Apions					
P. Oxy. XVI 1911 (556/7)	1535.25[c]	1514.50	647.125	140.042	507.5[d]
[Cash dominant. Converting wheat at 12 art./sol. (cf. *P. Oxy*. 2023),[e] the wheat receipts = 127.94 solidi. *Cash ratio = 83.49%* of total, cf. *P. Oxy*. 3804 (a decade later).]					
P. Oxy. LV 3804 (566)	1535.25	1535.25	647.125	167.33	480.50
[*Cash ratio = 83.49%*, cf. *P. Oxy*. XVI 1911 above.]					
P. Oxy. XVI 1914 (557)	1342	1330.75	284.50	46.5	238.00
[*Cash ratio = 71.78%*]					
P. Oxy. XVI 1912 (bef. 565/6)	3941.25	(3518)			
[Taxes (for the *embolē*) = 2025.25, so *embolē = 51.38%*]					
P. Oxy. 2195 (576/7?)[f]	4286.25	4086.50	314.33	87.8	226.83
[*Cash ratio = 46.81%*]					
P. Oxy. 2196 (586?)	1201	(lost)	239.5	(lost)	
[*Cash ratio = 70.53%*, cf. *P. Oxy*. XVI 1914]					
P. Oxy. 2196 verso (*c*.586)			18,512		
P. Oxy. 1918 verso (540/1)			20,010.62	6917.00 (= taxes)	13,092.8
[*Fiscal ratio = 34.6%*]					
P. Oxy. XVI 1906 ii, 14–21 (6/7c.)	98,321	79,069 (*= embolē*)			
[*Fiscal ratio = 80.4%*]					

Table 2 (*cont.*)

Reference	Wheat		Cash		
	receipts[a]	expenditure	receipts[b]	expenditure	balance
P. Oxy. XVI 1907 (7c.?) (poss. Apion)		25,372.5 (= *embolē*)		2297.44 (*chrysika*)	
[Possibly from an estate controlled by some other *oikos*; dated to the reign of Tiberius II by Johnson and West, *Byzantine Egypt*, 287. *Normal cash ratio = 43.86%*]					
(b) The Middle Aristocracy					
P. Cairo Masp. II 67139 (6c.)	1006	873			
[From a *logos embolēs*; the *embolē* = 166 art., so the *fiscal ratio = 16.5%*]					
P. Ant. III 190 (6/7c.)	583	409?			
[*Embolē* = 208 art., *fiscal ratio = 35.67%*]					
P. Bad. 95 (7c.)[g]	1010.66	743.00	175.25	107.36	
	1002.33	580.00	222.66	123.16	
	1010.66	468.00	222.66	103.93	
	1010.66	857.66	222.66	121.14	

Cash ratio = 77.9% at a commutation rate of 16 art./sol. (the one used in the account, i.e. 1½ carats per artaba). Converting the wheat amounts to cash at this rate, the *fiscal burden = 13.5%* of the gross revenue (cash + kind). However, the burden varies according to the form of payment, so that wheat taxes work out to 28.39% of receipts, money taxes to 9.30%.

Notes:

[a] In artabas; fractions of less than a quarter are usually ignored.

[b] In solidi.

[c] 1535½ in l. 207, but cf. Rea, *P. Oxy.* LV 3804.272 n.

[d] Or 503.125 net of the rebate in line 210.

[e] I use this as the standard rate of commutation throughout, when imputing a cash value to gross wheat receipts.

[f] The account relates to a tenth indiction and has been dated to 576/7, but if Strategius II (who appears in l. 108) was dead by 565/6, as John Rea argues (*P. Oxy.* LV, p. 97), we are dealing presumably with the previous tenth indiction.

[g] Following Schnebel, *JEA* 14 (1928) 43–4.

Table 3: *The gold/copper exchange rate: Hahn's reconstructions and papyrological supplements*

Period	No. of folles per solidus	Follis weight standard (g.)	Metallic ratio (lb. copper/solidus)
498–512	360	9.10	
512–38	360	18.19	20
538–42	210	24.95	16?[a]
542–50	180	21.83	12

Table 3 (*cont.*)

Period	No. of folles per solidus	Follis weight standard (g.)	Metallic ratio (lb. copper/solidus)
550–65	216	18.19	12
565	525	15.59	25
569	675?[b]		
570	720	13.64	30
579	432	18.19	24
580–7	576	13.64	24
587–?	600[c]	13.64	25
614	720		
616–17	1080	9.10	30
618	1152		
621	960[d]		
624/5	864[e]		

Notes:

[a] Pottier, *Analyse d'un trésor de monnaies en bronze enfoui au VIe siècle en Syrie byzantine*, 228, argues that the price was 15 lb.

[b] *P. Cairo Masp.* III 67309.40 (569) involves an interest (on part of the capital) of 300 T per solidus per month. This works out to 45 myriads per month or 540 myriads per year. Assuming a rate of interest of 12%, this implies a solidus worth 4,500 myriads. If my theory about the myriad is correct, this should give us an exchange rate of 675 folles. However, one should note that the Apions were already using an exchange rate of 720 folles (= 4,800 myriads) by 566, cf. *P. Oxy*. LV 3804.271 (566).

[c] *P. Mich* XV 740 (6c.) involves an exchange rate of 4,000 myriads to the solidus, which is 600 folles, so should probably be dated around this period.

[d] In *P. Oxy*. XVI 1921, dated 621 (see *P. Oxy*. LVIII 3958.26n, p. 115), 3 carats seem to be equivalent to 120 folles.

[e] See p. 168 above for my argument about the date of *SPP* XX 218. Here each carat is explicitly said to consist of (be equivalent to) 36 folles. It seems that Gascou has found the same rate of exchange in *P. Vindob*. G 41049.

Table 4: *The bigger hoards by region and date of deposition*[a]

Fourth century	Fifth century	Sixth century	Seventh century
Western	*Western*	*Western*	*Western*
Beaurains	Beja	Hyères	(none)
Ahn-Machtum I	Hautot-sur-Mer	Gourdon	*E. Europe*
Ohimbra	Dortmund	Viviers	Chibati
'Portugal'	Menzelen	Bresin	Firtosch
E. Europe	Xanten	Botes	Szegedin
(None)	Klein-Tromp	Biesenbrow	Maistrov Island
Central Mediterranean	Combertault	*E. Europe*	Pereshchepino
Central Italy	Vedrin	Razgrad	Varna
Partinico	Aby	Kleinschelken	
Sidi-bu-Saïd	Tournai	Hadji Sinanlar	
		Sekulitsa	
		Sadovetz D	

Table 4 (*cont.*)

Fourth century	Fifth century	Sixth century	Seventh century
E. Mediterranean	*E. Europe*	*Central Mediterranean*	*Central Mediterranean*
Abukir	Szikáncs	Crotone	Hammam Darradji
Egypt	Bína	Gernetto	La Goulette
	Roublevka	El Djem I	Henchir Kasbah
4th-c. hoards: 9	Donji Lapac	Monte Judica	Racalmuto
% of total: 10.97	*Central Mediterranean*	*E. Mediterranean*	Rougga
	Rome (Tiber)	Peloponnese	Lacco Ameno
	Parma	Thessaloniki	Pantalica
	Gravisca	Akkar	Milazzo
	Cherchel	Hama	'Constantine IV'
	Comiso		Mazara
	Casa delle Vestali	6th-c. hoards: 19	*E. Mediterranean*
	Naples	% of total: 23.17	Samos
	Cagliari		Asklepieion
	Djemila		Yildiz Palace II
	Aïn Meddah		Chatalja
	E. Mediterranean		Aydin II
	al-Madhāriba		Yildiz Palace I
	Dikla		Istanbul
			Chatby
	5th-c. hoards: 26		Jordan
	% of total: 31.71		Bat Galim
			Nikertai
			Khirbet Marus
			7th-c. hoards: 28
			% of total: 34.15

[a] 'Bigger hoards' are defined as those with a minimum value of 69 solidi.

Table 5: *Hoard spans and period of deposition*[a]

Fourth century	Fifth century	Sixth century	Seventh century
Beaurains 30	Chécy 4	Castellana 95	Çorum 35
Borča 9	Wiesbaden-Kastel 44	Grabovnik 27	Chibati 35
Sirmium 20	Groß-Bodungen 61	Monte Judica 45	Aydin II 37
Helleville 18	Dortmund 76		Hammam Darradji 29
Ljubljana I 15	Xanten 64	*Mean = 55.66*	La Goulette 32
Water Newton 20	al-Madhāriba 103	*Median = 45*	Hr. Kasbah 20
Ljubljana II 10	Szikáncs 31		North Africa II 20
Duisburg Großenbaum 16	Combertault 53		Hr. Sidi Amor Bouhadjla 31
Gudme 18			

Table 5 (*cont.*)

Fourth century	Fifth century	Seventh century
Qom al Kabir 13	Zeccone 49	Carthage (*c.*1945) 65
Karanis 14	Djemila 85	Palmyra 43[b]
Ellerbeck 20		Nablus 61
Konz 4	*Mean = 57.00 (excl. Chécy = 62.89)*	Nikertai 81
Poitou 24	*Median = 57*	Reḥob 60
Sidi bu Saïd 39		
Iatrus-Krivina 20		*Mean = 42.23*
Jerez de la Frontera 3		*Median = 35*
Mean = 17.23 (excl. Beaurains = 16.44)		
Median = 18		

Notes:

[a] Figures indicate the age structure or span of the hoard (in years). Within each period hoards have been arranged in chronological order.

[b] For Palmyra, Nablus, and Reḥob (Beisān), see Morrisson, in *Archéologie et histoire de la Syrie*, 2.198.

Table 6: *The scale of monetary circulation in late antiquity: amounts of gold in the documentary sources*

Description	Amount	Source
Treasury surplus left by Anastasius, 518	320,000 lb. (*c.*23 m. solidi)	Procopius, *HA* 19.7, Stein, *HBE* 2.193
Construction cost of St Sophia	3,200 centenaria	*Diegesis*, c.25 (Dagron, *Const.Imag.* 207)
Iluk's calculation of the general level of payments to barbarians in 422–602	17,455,968 solidi	Iluk, *Münstersche Beiträge z. antiken Handelsgeschichte*, 4/1 (1985) 79–102
Gross revenue or assessment of the empire under Justinian	1,000 centenaria (7.20 m. solidi)	*Diegesis*, c.25 (Dagron, *Const.Imag.* 207)
Tribute paid to the Avars over close to seven decades	6 m. solidi	Metcalf, *SEBGC* 68 n. 16, ref. to Kovačević
Cost of Leo's Vandal campaign	65,000 lb. (4.68 m. solidi)	Stein, *HBE* 1.359 (higher)
Khusro's estimate of Edessa's monetary wealth	50,000 lb. (3.60 m. solidi)	Procopius, *BP* 2.26.39 (Haury 1.274)
Revenue of Egypt in 969	3.4 m. dinars (3.14 m. solidi)	Ashtor, *Histoire des prix*, 116 f.

Table 6 (*cont.*)

Description	Amount	Source
Revenue of Egypt in the early Umayyad period	2–4 m. dinars (solidi must be meant)	Al-Balādhurī, *Futūḥ al-buldān*, in Hitti, *Origins*, 340
Revenue (πάκτον) extracted from Egypt under Justinian	365 centenaria (2.628 m. solidi)	*Diegesis*, c.25 (Dagron, *Const.Imag.* 207)
Sufetula's payment to the Arabs in 647	200,000 lb. (1.44 m. solidi)	Ibn Khayyāt in Slim, *Trésor de Rougga*, 81 (lowest estimate)
Gold amassed by Khusro Anōsharwān at Dara	100–200 centenaria (720,000–1.44 m. solidi)	John of Ephesus, *Eccl.Hist.* 3.6.5 (Payne Smith 383–4).
Olympias' assets in gold	100 centenaria (720,000 solidi)	*V.Sanctae Olympiadis* 5
Assets of the Church of Alexandria, early 7th c.	80 centenaria (576,000 solidi)	*Vie de Jean de Chypre* 57 (ed. Festugière, p. 404)
Tiberius Constantine's consular issue of 578/9	7,200 lb. (518,400 solidi)	John of Ephesus, *Eccl.Hist.* 3.3.14 (Payne Smith 189 f.)
Justinian's consular *largitio* of 521	288,000 solidi	Marcellinus Comes, *Chronicon*, s.a. 521
Cash revenues of the top aristocracy, early 5th c.	40 centenaria (288,000 solidi)	Olympiodorus, fr. 44
Money amassed by Justinian's almoner, Theodoulos	24–30 centenaria (172,800–216,000 solidi)	John of Ephesus, *Eccl.Hist.* 3.2.28 (Payne Smith 138)
Cash holdings of Heraclian's estate, early 5th c.	20 centenaria (144,000 solidi)	Olympiodorus, fr. 23 (*FHG* 4.62)
Annual income of Pinianus	120,000 solidi	Piganiol, *Hommages Bloch*, 50
Senatorial payment towards Valentinian II's *decennalia*	1600 lb. (115,200 solidi)	Bastien, *Donativa*, 22
Annual taxes of Mauretania Sitifensis in 445	40,000 solidi	*Nov.Val.* 13.5
Earthquake relief for Antioch, 526/7	5 centenaria (36,000 solidi)	Malalas, *Chronographia* 422 (Jeffreys, *Chronicle*, 242)
Cash revenue of the Ravenna Church estates in Sicily, late 7th c.	31,000 solidi	Agnellus, *Lib.Pont.Eccl. Rav.* 111 (*Script.Rerum Lang.* 350)
Tribute paid to Caucasian tribes in 555	28,800 solidi	Agathias 4.20
Banker's contribution towards construction cost of S.Vitale in Ravenna	26,000 solidi	Agnellus, *Lib.Pont.Eccl. Rav.* 59 (*Script.Rerum Lang.* 318), cf. Barnish, *Byzantion*, 1985

Table 6 (*cont.*)

Description	Amount	Source
Aristocrat's contribution for part of church, 449/50	3 centenaria (21,600 solidi)	*Patr.Const.* III 30 (*Script.Orig.Const.* 2.225)
Gross cash receipts from various Apion villages	18,512 solidi	*P. Oxy.* XVIII 2196 verso, with Gascou, *CE*, 1972, p. 246
Eudoxia's gift for construction of the church at Gaza, 402	2 centenaria (14,400 solidi)	*Vie de Porphyre* 53
Fine imposed on the merchants of Milan, 386	200 lb. (14,400 solidi)	Ambrose, *Ep.* 76 (20).6 (*CSEL* 82.111)
Cash holdings of an Armenian landed family	5,000 solidi	John of Ephesus, *Lives* 11 (*PO* 17.160)
Aristocrat's loan to her brother, *c.*574	61 lb. (4,392 solidi)	*PSI* I 76, cf. Keenan, *ZPE* 29 (1978) 192 ff.
Cash value of Porphyry's share of the family estate	3,000 solidi	*Vie de Porphyre* 6
Anastasius' gift to Sabas in 511/12	2,000 solidi	*Leben des Sabas*, p. 143.10, p. 146.21 (ed. Schwartz)
Assets of an impoverished aristocrat	564 solidi	Malalas, *Chron.* 439c (Jeffreys, *Chronicle*, 255)
Construction cost of Church of Mary in Pinara	400 solidi	*V.Nicolai Sionitai*, 69 (Anrich, *Hagios Nikolaos*, 50)
Assets of a former village headman (ἀπὸ μειζόνων)	360 solidi	*P. Oxy.* I 132 (late 6/early 7c.)
Purchase price of a hostel complex, 485	200 solidi	*Leben des Kyriakos*, p. 226.15 (ed. Schwartz)
Purchase price of *kellia* required for a hostel complex	170 solidi	*Leben des Sabas*, p. 116.18
Funds accumulated by a monk	100 solidi	Jerome, *Ep.* 22.33
Peasant loan for the purchase of livestock, mid-6th c.	15 solidi	*P. Oxy.* I 130 (563/4)
Stonecutter's wages or savings	12 solidi	*Vie de S. Symeon le Jeune*, 180
Civil servants' annual pay	9 solidi	Ostrogorsky, *BZ* 1932, p. 301
Annual allowance of monks	6 solidi	Theodosius, *de situ terrae sanctae*, 20 (*CSEL* 39.146)
'Low' annual wages	3 solidi	*Vie de Jean de Chypre*, Prol.
Helper's wages in 588	3 solidi	*P. Oxy.* LVIII 3933 (588)
Annual ration for refugee nuns	1.92 solidi	Jones, *LRE* 1.447

Table 7: *Monetary economy in the countryside: annual gold payments of individual villages, landowners, or districts*

Village/District	Payment (solidi)[a]	Source
Aphrodito, 525	352¼	*P. Flor.* 297 iv verso
Domus divina in Heracleopolis, 538?	374½	*CPR* V 18
Temseu Skordon, 516–46	354	BM 1075, cf. MacCoull, *Tyche* 2 (1987) 105
Tokois North, 12th ind.	263¾	*SB* XX 14580.1 (5/6c.)
Tokois North, 13th ind.	235¼	*SB* XX 14580.2 (5/6c.)
Sinarchebis, 6c.	292½	*P. Amst.* 84
Aphrodito, *c.*567	1,017	*P. Cairo Masp.* 67002
Oxyrhynchus and Cynopolis, late 6c.	24,500 59,500 (incl. commutation)	*P. Oxy.* XVI 1909
Heirs of Apphous/ Epimachus, 617	290	*P. Oxy.* VI 999
Tekmi, 664 or 679	193	*SPP* VIII 1198 (Date *BL* 8.451)
Thallou, 7c., first half	250	*CPR* IX 76 i 5
Monastery of Abba Horos, 7c.	265	*P. Lond.* III 1097b = *SB* XXVI 16665.8
Chor(ion) Theoxenid(os) ousi(as), 7c.	*c.*440	*P. Prag.* I 26.4 verso
Belou, 7c.	752	*SPP* X 62.3
Aphrodito, 642/3 or 657/8	1,241	*P. Hamb.* 56, see Rémondon, *CE* 40 (1965) 401ff.
Aphrodito, 732/3	1,786 (assessment) 1,338.8 (payment)	*P. Lond.* IV 1416 (date *BL* 8.190)
Aphrodito, 698/9–721/2	3,952 (average paid) 6,951⅔ (assessment)	*P. Lond.* IV 1412–1413, see Casson, *TAPA*, 1938, p. 274–91
Thmoiamounis, 7/8c.	364	*SPP* X 208
35 Fayum monasteries, 731–68	500 dinars	*PO* 5.94, cf. Abbott, *The Monasteries of the Fayyūm*, 52

[a] Unless stated otherwise.

Table 8: *The γεωργοί as estate labourers*

Reference	Owner	Description
P. Mich. VI 423–424.13 (197/200)	Gemellus Horion, *geouchōn* in Karanis	τὸν γεωργόν μου
P. Oxy. XLII 3048. 19 f. (246)	Calpurnia Heraclia, from the Alexandrian aristocracy	μηνιαῖαι συντάξεις πραγματευταῖς τε καὶ φροντισταῖς καὶ γεωργοῖς
P. Oxy. XII 1424 (*c.*318)	Ammonius, *centurio princeps*	γεωργός μου
P. Charite 26 = *SPP* XX 89.3–4 (341)	Aurelia Charite, daughter of a local councillor	οἱ γεωργοὶ ἐσοῦ τῆς Σενοάβεως τῶν ἀρουρῶν
P. Med. I^2 64 = *SB* VI 9503.4 (440/1)	Oxyrhynchite estate of the *Domus Divina*	τῆς αὐτῆς θειοτάτης οἰκίας γεωργὸς [ἐναπόγραφος ?]
P. Köln III 152. 7–8 (477)	Church	γεωργὸς τῆς αὐτῆς ἁγίας ἐκκλησίας ἀπὸ κώμης Ψενύρεως
SB XVIII 14001 (486)	Flavius Julius, *clarissimus*	ἀμπελουργος τῆς [σῆς λαμπρότητος]
P. Amh. II 155. 1 (5c.)	??	Λόγ(ος) σίτου μισθοῦ τῶν γεωργ(ῶν) ἡμῶν
P. Prag. I 45.7 f. (521–2)	Monastery of the Northern Hill (north of Antinoopolis)	ἀμπελουργοῦ τῆς ὑμῶν εὐλαβείας
SB V 8029 (538)	A. Phoibammon, *boēthos*, 'secretary'	τῶν ὑμετέρων αὐτ[όθι γεωργῶν καὶ] ἀμπελουργῶν (l. 12), τῶν γεωρ[γῶν] καὶ ἀμπελουργῶν αὐτοῦ (sc. τῆς αὐτου λαμπρό-τητος) (l. 17)
P. Vatic. Aphrod. 25 B 4 (6c.)	Phoibammon and Colluthus, substantial-looking landholders	τῶν γεωργῶν ἡμῶν ἀμφοτέρων
P. Oxy. XVI 1915.18 (556/7)	Apion estate	τοῖς ἑξῆς γεωρ(γοῖς) τοῦ ἐνδόξ(ου) οἴκ(ου)
SB VI 9293.18 f. (572) with Jördens, *P. Heid.* V, p. 267 n. 25	*clarissimus* and son of a *megaloprepestatos*	[καθ' ὁ]μοιότητα τῶν γεωργῶν τοῦ σου [ἀδελφοῦ] .ου τοῦ λαμπροτάτου
P. Oxy. 2239.13 (598)	Flavius John, *endoxotatos stratēlatēs*	τοὺς πάντας γεωργοὺς τῆς ὑμετέρας ἐνδοξ(ότητος)
BGU I 255 (15 May 599)	large landowner of Memphis	[πω]μαρίτης τῆς ὑμῶν [ἐνδ]οξ(ότητος)
PSI VII 823 verso (7c.)	Theodorakios, *endoxotatos*	τὸν γεωργὸν τοῦ σὺν ὑμῖν δεσπότο(υ) μο(υ) . . . το(ῦ) ἐνδοξο(τάτου) Θεοδωρακίο(υ)
P. Lond. III 1075 (p. 281 f.) (7c.)	Bishop?	Ἰωσηφ[ιος ὁ] ὑμετερος γεωργός (l. 7), οἱ γεωργοὶ ὑμῶν (l. 14)

Table 8 (*cont.*)

Reference	Owner	Description
P. Apoll. 98.38 (late 7/early 8c.)	Papas, pagarch of Edfu	(ὑπὲρ) μισθ(οῦ) γεωργῶ(ν)
P. Apoll. 42 (703–15?)	Pesynthius, friend of Papas	τῶν ὄντων μου ἐγγὺς ὑμῶν τε[σσάρων γεωρ]γῶν (l. 7), κἀγὼ δὲ ἔχω ἐγγὺς ὑμῶν τέσσαρας γεωργ[οὺς] (l. 6)

Table 9*a*: *The weight of the aristocracy among non-institutional landholders, sixth and seventh centuries*

District	Higher aristocracy	*Clarissimi*	'Counts' with no further indication	Other middle-class landholders
Sixth c.				
Fayum	12	2	1	11
Heracleopolite	2		1	4
Oxyrhynchite	23	5	1	12
Antinoopolis	11	8		4
Hermopolite	5	4	1	25
Aphrodito	10	8	5	51
South	1	1		2
Total sixth c.	64	28	9	109
Seventh c.				
Fayum	23	2	1	4
Heracleopolite	7	1		
Oxyrhynchite	4			
Hermopolite	21	18	3	17
South	3			
Total seventh c.	58	21	4	21

Table 9*b*: *Pagarchs among the higher aristocracy*

District	(1) Pagarchs (no.)	(2) Aristocrats in (1) (no.)
Sixth c.		
Fayum	3	3
Oxyrhynchite	4	4
Antinoopolis	2	0
Aphrodito	8	6
Total sixth c.	17	13
Seventh c.		
Fayum	11	10
Heracleopolite	4	2
Oxyrhynchite	2	1
Hermopolite	3	2
South	2	0
Total seventh c.	22	15

Table 10: *The archive of Flavius Strategius (Strategius "paneuphēmos")*[a]

Document	Type	Date	Strategius' title
P. Oxy. LVIII 3935	Fragment of contract	6 Mar. 591	τραπεζίτῃ τοῦ ἐνδοξοῦ οἴκου τοῦ ὑπερφυεστάτου Στρατηγίου
P. Oxy. LVIII 3936	Priest's receipt for salary	5 May 598	πανεύφημος καὶ ὑπερφυέστατος ὑπάτος
P. Berol. inv. 10526 = *JJP* 23 (1993) 133 ff.	Receipt	28 Aug. 598	πανεύφημος καὶ ὑπερφυέστατος ὑπάτος
P. Oxy. LXVI 4535	Acknowledge-ment of debt	600	πανεύφημος ὑπάτος
SB XVI 12701 (= SB I 4858) + 4718 + 4671 = Palme, *ZPE* 117 (1997) 175 ff.	Contract	2 June 600	πανεύφημος ὑπ[άτος καὶ] πάγαρχος
P. Lond. I 113.5 (c) + *BL* 1.237	Surety	8 Aug. 600	πανεύφημος πάγα(ρχος) [καὶ ὑπάτ]ος , cf. Worp, *ZPE* 56 (1984) 113
P. Oxy. XVI 1991	Receipt/ irrigation machinery	18 Sept. 601 (*BL* 8.252)	πανεύφημος καὶ ὑπερφυέστατος ὑπάτος
P. Vindob. G 28737	Surety	bef. 602	πα[νεύφημος]
P. Vindob. G 21026 + 21037		603	πανεύφημος ὑπάτος
P. Erl. 73		29 Mar. 604	πανεύφημος πατρίκιος
P. Bod. I 53	Agreement	16 Sept. 605	πανεύφημος πατρίκιος πάγαρχος
SPP III 66		604–9	
CPR XIV 9	Start of document	607	[πα]τρίκιος πάγαρχος
SB I 5266, with Palme, *Aegyptus* 76 (1996) 93–9	Settlement	8 Aug. 608	πανεύφημος
P. Vars. 31	Receipt	609	
P. Vindob. G 21350	Surety	8 Jan. 610	εὐκλεέστατος πατρίκιος πάγαρχος
SPP XX 209 = *SB* I 5270	Receipt	27 Feb. 610	οὐσίας Στρατηγίου τοῦ πανε[υφ]ήμου πατρικίου
SPP VIII 1072		610? (*BL* 8.450)	Flavius Cyrillus = στρατηλ[άτης] ἐνδόξου οἴκου Στρατηγίου
P. Vindob. G 20535		4 Sept. 611	ὑπερφυέστατος καὶ πανεύφημος

Table 10 (*cont.*)

Document	Type	Date	Strategius' title
CPR X 131		5 Feb. 612	
BGU II 368	Pay receipt	25 June 615	πανεύφημος πατρίκιος
SB I 5271	Settlement	10 Dec. 615	ὑπερφυέστατος πατρίκιος
P. Vindob. G 43308		616	
SB I 4815 verso, with *BL* 8.315		'Byz.'	
SB I 5253		'Byz.'	πανεύφημος π[ατρίκιος] πάγαρχος
SB I 4781		'Byz.'	
SPP X 114		6/7c.	πανεύφημος πατρίκιος
P. Rain. Cent. 119		611?	ὑπερφυέστατος [ ]
SPP X 1	List of *synētheiai*	After 617?	τοῦ ἐν ἁγί(οις) Στρατηγίου
SPP VIII 1158		12 Dec. 602	ἀπὸ ὑπάτων
SPP X 259		early 7c.	τοῦ ἐνδόξου οἴκο(υ) τοῦ δεσπότου ἡμῶν τοῦ θεο-φυλάκτου πατρικίου
Uncertain; probably or possibly related to the archive			
P. Oxy. XVI 1829 verso[b]	Deeds confirming the Apions' control of the pagarchy	*c.*577–83	ἐνδοξότατος καὶ ὑπερφυέστατος καὶ πανεύφημος
SPP X 138	List of estate villages	7c.	μεγαλοπρεπέστατος [ ]
SPP VIII 1121		7c.	οὐσί(ας) τῆς ἐν ἁγί(οις) ἡμ[ῶν..]
SPP XX 229 = *SPP* X 239	Alphabetical list of villages	7/8c. (ed. pr.)	
SPP XX 278		6/7c. (ed. pr.)	εἰς τὸ κτίσμα τοῦ οἴκου τοῦ [πα]νευφ(ήμου) πατρικ(ίου)
SPP VIII 1132		6c. (ed. pr.)	
SPP VIII 1228		7c.	

[a] Unpublished material is cited from B. Palme, 'Die *domus gloriosa* des Flavius Strategius Paneuphemos', *Chiron* 27 (1997) 119 ff.

[b] See Palme, 'Flavius Strategius Paneuphemos und die Apionen', *ZSS* 115 (1998) esp. 308 ff.

Table 11*a*: *Occupational wage levels in papyri of the Byzantine period: benchmark jobs*

Source	Occupation	Annual pay (solidi)[a]	Description
Rouillard, *ACEB* 40	Dux et augustalis	2,880 (= 40 lb. gold)	
P. Oxy. XVI 1913.40	Apion top manager	44.42* (30)[b]	ὑπὲρ ὀψωνίου
P. Oxy. LV 3805.34 (566 or later)	ἐπικείμενος (Apion) (production manager)	24.958	ὑ(πὲρ) συνηθ(είας)
Lydus, *De Mag.* 3.27 (early 6c.)	senior χαρτουλάριος (secretary)	24	
P. Oxy. XVI 1911.152 (556/7)	χαρτουλάριος (Apion)	21.917* (15.66)	ὑπὲρ λόγ(ου) ὀψωνίου
SPP VIII 970 (5c.?)	notarius (secretary)	15.833	ὑπὲρ μισθ(οῦ)
SB XII 11076 (6c.)	ἀρχίφρουρος (chief guard)	7.917	ὑ(πὲρ) μισθοῦ
P. Oxy. XVI 2045 (612)	σπαθάριος σύμμαχος (estate paramilitary)	4	(ὑπὲρ) μηνιαί(ου)
P. Oxy. LVIII 3933 (588)	ἐργάτης τῶν χρυσοχόων (goldsmiths' helper)	3[c]	λόγῳ μισθοῦ μου τοῦ παντὸς ἐνιαυτοῦ
P. Iand. 37 (5/6c.)	ῥιπάριος (police officer)	3[d]	
P. Oxy. LVII 3914 (519)	ἐργοδιώκτης (supervisor)	2	τοὺς μισθοὺς τοὺς ἡμετέρους
SB XX 14400 = *P. Lond.* III 1027 descr. (6/7c.)	σύμμαχος	2.25	(ὑπὲρ) μισθοῦ
P. Oxy. XVIII 2195.128 (576/7), XIX 2243(a).83 (590)	ἐργοδιώκτης (Apion)	1.708	ὑ(πὲρ) μισθο(ῦ)
P. Bad. 95.125 (7c.)	τυμπανιστὴς τῶν χωρίων (worker on sāqiya?)	0.33	ὑπ(ὲρ) μισθ(οῦ)
		Annual pay (artabas)[e]	
P. Prag. I 72 (7c.)	notarius (secretary)	180 *krithē*	λό(γῳ) δόσ(εως)
P. Oxy. XVI 1913.54 f.	scholasticus (legal adviser)	100	λόγ(ῳ) φιλοτιμ(ίας)
P. Oxy. XVIII 2195.192 (576/7), XIX 2243(a).81 (590)	προνοητής (middle manager)	24	λόγῳ ὀψωνίου

Table 11*a* (*cont.*)

Source	Occupation	Annual pay (artabas)[e]	Description
SPP VIII 1079 (7c.)	καμηλίτης (camel driver)	24	(ὑπὲρ) μισθ(οῦ)
PSI III 217 (4/5c.)	καψάριος (bath attendant)	16	ὑπὲρ συντάξεως ὀψωνίου
CPR IV 161 (7c.)	παραμονάριος (resident employee)	24½[f]	
P. Amh. II 155 (5c.)	γεωργός (peasant labourer)	16[g]	Λόγ(ος) σίτου μισθοῦ τῶν γεωργ(ῶν) ἡμῶν
P. Princ. II 96 (566/7)	παιδάριον (estate employee)	12 (males)[h] 6 (females)	Βρέ(ουιον) ὀψωνίων παιδαρ(ίων) Αἰγυπτ(ίων) καὶ γυναικ(ῶν)
CPR X 1 (608?)	παιδ(ια?) παραμένοντες (regular estate staff)	12	
P. Oxy. VI 994 (499)	μονάζων (monk)	12	λόγ(ῳ) ὀψωνίου κατὰ συνήθ(ειαν)
P. Bad. IV 95.285, cf. Morelli, *ZPE* 122 (1998) 143	παῖς (unskilled labourer)	10 + 5 *krithē*	ὑπ(ὲρ) ὀψωνίο(υ)

Table 11*b*: *Occupational wage levels in papyri of the Byzantine period: benchmark jobs*

Source	Occupation	Cash component (solidi)	Kind component (artabas, etc.)[i]	Total cash equivalent (solidi)[j]
P. Oxy. XVI 1913.40	Apion top manager	30	90 + 90 *krithē*	44.42
P. Oxy. XVI 1911.152 (557)	chartularius (Apion)	15.66	75	21.91
P. Oxy. XVIII 2239 (598)	ἐπικείμενος	6[k]	36 + 24 *krithē* + 80 wine	13.05–14.16[l]
P. Oxy. XVI 1912. 130, LV 3804. 154 (566)	προνοητής (Apion)	1.792	24	3.79
P. Oxy. XVI 1911.156 (557), *P. Oxy.* LV 3804.238 (566)	καμηλάριος (camel driver)	1.34	16	2.66[m]

Table 11*b* (*cont.*)

Source	Occupation	Cash component (solidi)	Kind component (artabas, etc.)[i]	Total cash equivalent (solidi)[j]
CPR IV 160 (7c.)	παραμονάριος	0.625	12 + 6 *krithē* + 24 wine + 12 oil	3.386–3.716
P. Strasb. I 40 (569)	familiarius (domestic servant of servile status)	0.792[n]	10 + 4 *krithē* 24 wine + 12 oil	3.232–3.565
SB I 4490 (7c.)	παραμονάριος	0.958[o]	9	1.708

Notes:

[a] 'Minus carats' expressions are construed as actual deductions of value except where a standard (*zygos*) is referred to.

[b] Actual cash component in brackets; * = total cash equivalent of a wage expressed partly in cash, partly in kind, commuting wheat payments at 12 artabas to the solidus, barley at 13.

[c] 3 solidi on the private standard.

[d] 3 solidi less 13½ carats on the private standard.

[e] 1 artaba = *c*.40 litres. Always *sitos*, unless otherwise.

[f] Including 8 artabas of *krithē*.

[g] Average; maximum = 24 artabas.

[h] Modal value.

[i] *Sitos* unless otherwise; wine payments in *knidia*, oil in *sextarii*.

[j] Converting wheat at 12 artabas to the solidus, barley at 13 artabas, wine at 18–24 *knidia* per solidus, oil at 40 *xestai* to the solidus.

[k] 6 solidi less 27 carats on the private standard.

[l] Depending on the wine price we choose.

[m] At the notional wheat price of 12 art/sol., an excellent case of a salary paid half in cash, half in kind.

[n] Actually a clothing allowance.

[o] 1 solidus of 23 carats.

Table 12: *Lease durations by half-century*

	Number of leases with discernible durations				
Period	1 year	2–4 years	5–9 years	over 10 years	indefinite
Early 3rd (n = 41)	19	19	3	0	0
Late 3rd (n = 32)	16	15	1	0	0
Early 4th (n = 50)	37	11	2	0	0
Late 4th (n = 21)	16	4	0	0	1
Early 5th (n = 5)	2	2	0	0	1
Late 5th (n = 21)	6	4	4	1	6

Table 12 (*cont.*)

	Number of leases with discernible durations				
Period	1 year	2–4 years	5–9 years	over 10 years	indefinite
Early 6th (n = 54)	17	16	13	3	5
Late 6th (n = 32)	3	10	6	1	12
Early 7th (n = 13)	3	5	0	1	4
Late 7th (n = 2)	0	0	0	0	2

APPENDIX 2

CJ X. 27.2.1–9: A Translation

Those who reside in the individual districts (πόλεις) or own land in them must not be coerced into supplying either the capital or districts other than their own. 1. However, if some unavoidable circumstance should make this necessary, goods should be sold at fair prices or the ruling market price in the district in question, and their transport should be the responsibility of those who require them. 2. The prices paid for these goods should be credited to the sellers' account, against those of their taxes which are normally paid in cash. It is also unfair that people should be asked to supply goods immediately but have the prices which are paid for them credited after a period of time, thus causing a glut in the market (*ὅυτως εὐθηνίας γενομένης*). 3. The *clarissimus* governor of each province will be held personally responsible for making sure that the prices offered are properly adjusted against the tax accounts and the goods themselves dispatched before the prescribed deadlines. 4. Furthermore, no one should be compelled to dispose of all of their stocks, which includes what they need for their own consumption, but only their surplus produce. For it is quite wrong to deprive people of their household requirements in order to supply these to others. Anyone who breaks the law or allows it to be broken will be subject to a fine of 100 lb. of gold and run the risk of being stripped of their rank and existing position. 5. No official must ever order a state purchase (*συνωνή*) from landowners except in the greatest emergency, and when that does happen, it should happen in strict accordance with the divine regulation (*κέλευσις*), namely, on the understanding that the cash payments due by way of the purchase are deducted from the tax liabilities which landowners are required to pay in gold, assuming those liabilities suffice to cover the purchase. 6. However, if the persons from whom a public purchase is required have no outstanding liabilities by way of money taxes (*δημόσια*), or have liabilities equal to less than the payments due to them, they should first receive the gold in solidi of full weight (*ἐν νομίσμασιν εὐστάθμοις πρότερον τὸ χρυσίον λαμβανέτωσαν*) and should be asked to supply goods only on that basis, and absolutely no one should have the temerity either to palm off solidi of less than full weight (*παράσταθμα δοῦναι τὰ νομίσματα*) or to make less than full payment of the amount of gold due or cause a financial loss to taxpayers in any other way, or otherwise the persons violating these conditions will have to reimburse as much as four times the whole difference in coin-weights (*παντὸς τοῦ παραλλήλου*) or of the financial loss caused or of the shortfall in payment. 7. If any official dares to order a state purchase illegally or conduct the operation itself in an unlawful manner, he shall be fined an extra 50 lb. of gold and be removed from his existing job and grade, and be subject to even worse punishment. 8. Whenever the imposition of a public levy proceeds in comport with the divine regulation, landowners should be liable to the levy in strict proportion to the acreage of their holdings or the combined fiscal value of their estates (*πρὸς τὴν ἀναλογίαν τῶν ζευγῶν ἤτοι ζυγοκεφαλῶν*). 9. Any official who uses the public purchase system as a pretext for enforcing disproportionately high demands on taxpayers,[1] will be liable to a fine of 50 lb. of gold and be removed from his position and rank, and may expect even worse punishment. 10. These regulations are being issued for all regions with the exception of the diocese of Thrace...

[1] Reading *συντελεστῶν* with Heimbach.

APPENDIX 3

The Relative Cohesion of Large Estates: Notes on the Topography of the Fayum in the Sixth and Seventh Centuries

SPP X 154 has a date in the seventh century and was transcribed by Wessely as follows:

Φιλοξέ(νου)
ἀπὸ ˋτ(ῆς)ˊ] ο[ὐ]σί(ας) τˋοῦˊ Θεο[
χˋωˊ (ρίον) Εὐστοχίου
χˋωˊ (ρίον) Εἴκοσι
χˋωˊ (ρίον) Πανίσκου

ἀπὸ τ(ῆς) οὐσί(ας) Θεοδώ[ρου
χˋωˊ (ρίον) Εμβόλου
χˋωˊ (ρίον) Παντικου
χˋωˊ (ρίον) Πιαμουε[ι

Of the three localities mentioned in lines 3–5, Eikosi is a fixed point of reference. Whatever its precise location, it was clearly not far from Magdōla = Medinet en-Nehas in the Gharaq basin,[1] north-west of Kerkeosiris and sufficiently close to both Narmouthis and Tali for common administrative arrangements to prevail at various times.[2] This suggests a location roughly equidistant between Medinet Madi (Narmouthis) and Talīt, at the centre of the basin. In *P. Ross.-Georg.* V 73, Eikosi appears with the Coptic name *tahanshute*, written in Arabic

[1] 'Eikosi' was short for Ibiōn Eikosipentarourōn. Ibiōn was probably adjacent to Magdōla and both were in the Theodosiopolite, cf. *SB* 5139 (6c.), κώμης Ἰβιῶνος καὶ Μαγδόλου τοῦ Θεοδοσιουπολίτου νομοῦ, and *SPP* X 111, a letter addressed to their landlord by οἱ ἀπὸ κώμης Ιβιῶνος (καὶ) Μαγδόλων. Magdōla is discussed by E. Bernand, *Recueil des inscriptions grecques du Fayoum*. 3: *La "méris" de Polémôn* (Institute Français d'Archéologie Orientale du Caire, Bibliotheque d'Étude, 80; Cairo, 1981), 29 ff.

[2] D. J. Crawford, *Kerkeosiris. An Egyptian Village in the Ptolemaic Period* (Cambridge, 1971) 48, *SB* XII 11164 (189/90), *P. Flor.* I 35 (167), *BGU* I 91 (170/1), *P. Tebt.* II 495 (2c.), and D. Rathbone's map in 'Towards a Historical Topography of the Fayum', in D. M. Bailey (ed.), *Archaeological Research in Roman Egypt* (JRA, Supplementary series, 19) (Ann Arbor, 1996) 50–6, fig. 1.

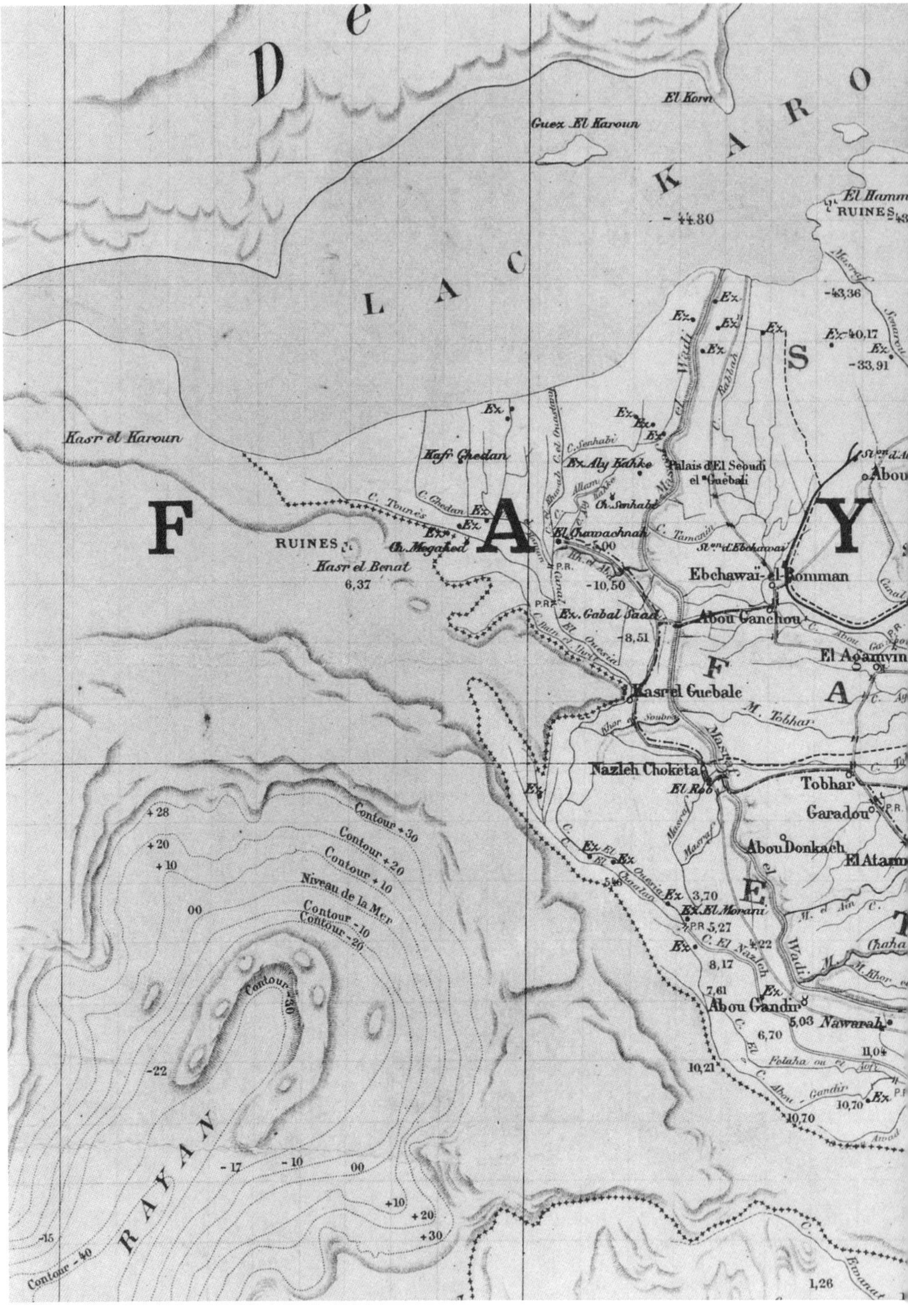

The Fayyum in the 1890s. Commission des Domaines de l'État Égyptien, *Carte de la Basse-Égypte et de la province du Fayoum* (Cairo, 1897) (Scale 1: 200,000). Key: *Ez* = ezba.

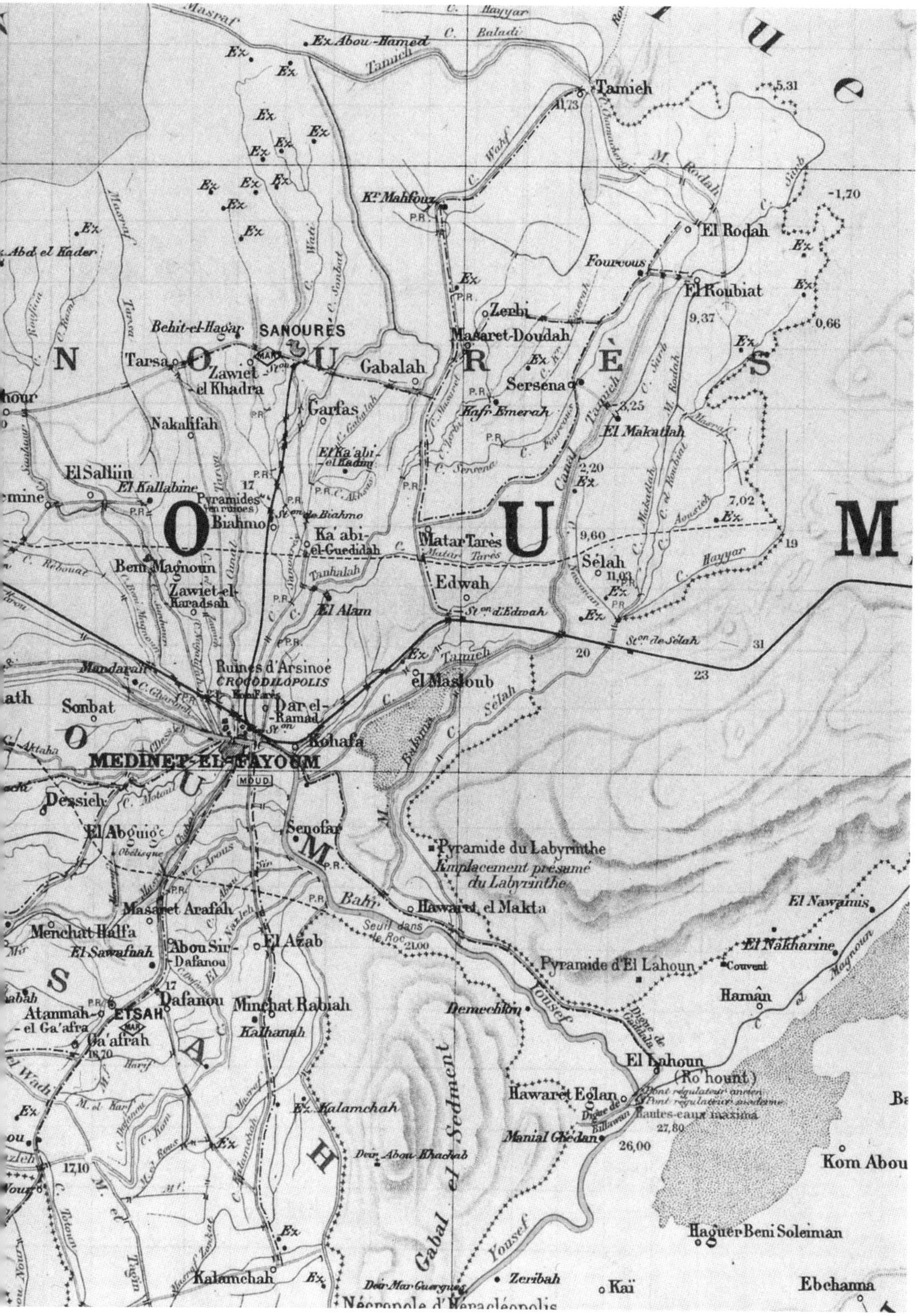
Ex Abou-Hamed
Tamieh
El Rodah
Fourcous
El Roubiat
Kr. Mahfouz
Zerbi
Masaret-Doudah
Sersena
Kafr Emerah
El Makatlah
Behit-el-Hagar
SANOURES
Tarsa
Zawiet el Khadra
Gabalah
Garfas
Nakalifah
El Salliin
El Kallabine
Pyramides (en ruines)
Biahmo
Ka'abi-el-Guedidah
Matar Tarès
Edwah
Sélah
Beni Magnoun
Zawiet-el-Karadsah
El Alam
St.on d'Edwah
St.on de Sélah
Mandarah
Ruines d'Arsinoë
CROCODILOPOLIS
el Masloub
Sonbat
Dar el-Ramad
Kohafa
MEDINET-EL-FAYOUM
MOUD
Dessieh
El Abguig
Obélisque
Senofar
Pyramide du Labyrinthe
Emplacement présumé du Labyrinthe
Masaret Arafah
Bahr
Hawaret el Makta
El Nawamis
Menchat Halfa
El Sawafnah
Abou Sir-Dafanou
El Azab
Seuil dans le Roc
El Nakharine
Couvent
Pyramide d'El Lahoun
Dafanou
Atammah-el Ga'afra
ETSAH
Ga'afrah
Minchat Rabiah
Kalhanah
Demechkin
Haman
Yousef
El Lahoun (Ro'hount)
Hawaret Eglan
Pont régulateur ancien
Pont régulateur moderne
Hautes-eaux maxima
Manial Ghedan
Kalamchah
Deir Abou Khachab
Gabal el Sedment
Kom Abou
Haguer Beni Soleiman
Kalamchah
Deir Mar Guergues
Zeribah
Kaï
Ebchama
Nécropole d'Héracléopolis
N O U R È S
O U M
O U M
S A H
M

(طهنشى).[3] In 487 it appears as a *kōmē*, related in some way to the aristocrat Flavius Eustochius.[4] The same document shows that Eikosi, and, by implication, all the Gharaq localities were part of the Theodosiopolite nome. This creates a presumption that ἀπὸ `τ(ῆς)´] ο[ὐ]σί(ας) τ`οῦ´ Θεο[δοσιουπολίτου νομοῦ is a possible restoration in l. 2. Eustochiou is never described as a *kōmē*, and was probably, as the name suggests, a settlement founded by the Eustochii as part of their estate in the southern Fayum. It is an *epoikion* in *CPR* X 45, from which we gather that its resident population numbered roughly one hundred and fifty. It turns up again as epoik(ion) Eustochi(ou) in *SPP* XX 239, where it is mentioned between Ōk( ) and Kyras Marias (ll. 8–10).[5] Ōk( ) was almost certainly Ōkeōs, which is mentioned in an important seventh-century list with Beki, Theaxenis, and Etēr.[6] Etēr turns up with Kyras Marias, Narmouthis, and Kieratou in *SB* 5339 ii,[7] while Beki, Etēr, and Theaxenis are mentioned, in that order, just before Narmouthis, Perkethaut, and Eustochiou in *SPP* X 147 ii.[8] Kieratou is also mentioned in *SPP* XX 239, one place away from Kyras Marias and two from Eustochiou. Thus, what seems clear from the emerging topographic cluster is a location outside the Gharaq basin, to the north, probably not far from Narmouthis (Medinet Madi). Wessely identified Perkethaut as Barağṭūṭ on the Baḥr Tanabṭawīya,[9] half-way between Garadū (anc. Kieratou)[10] and the Gharaq basin, and it is possible that Eustochiou lay somewhere in its vicinity. Finally, the third toponym of the *ousia*, Paniskou, can likewise be inserted into a topographic cluster. This was further east than either Eustochiou or Eikosi. In *SPP* X 281 Paniskou is wedged between Oxyrhyncha and Kerkesēphis (ll. 9–11), and payments for Oxyrhyncha and Paniskou seem to be made through the same individual.[11] A Ptolemaic papyrus informs us that someone travelling from Oxyrhyncha to Crocodilopolis would have passed through Eleusis.[12] Oxyrhyncha was thus south of Eleusis (Itsa, Etsa?).[13] It was also not far

[3] See *P. Ross.-Georg.* V 73.1n (p. 225).

[4] *SB* I 5273.4–5.

[5] The sequence is Ōk( ), epoikion Eustochiou, Kyras Marias, ousia Psinteo, Kieratou, epoikion Atammōnos (*SPP* XX 239.8–13). With the last of these, cf. El Atamnah wa el Mazara a few kilometres south-east of Garadū (see n. 10).

[6] *SB* 9583 fr. 3 ll. 13–16, with the sequence Beki, Ōkeōs, Theaxenidos kōmē, Etēr.

[7] *SB* 5339 ii 24–7.

[8] *SPP* X 147 ii 1–6, with Beki, Etēr, Theaxenis, Narmouthis, Perkethaut, Eustochiou.

[9] K. Wessely, *Topographie des Faijûm (Arsinoites Nomus) in griechischer Zeit*. Denkschriften der kaiserl. Akad. d. Wissenschaften in Wien, Phil.-Hist. Klass., 50 (Vienna, 1904) 22.

[10] Both Wessely (*Topographie des Faijûm*, 21) and M. Ramzī, (*al-Qāmūs al-g uğrāfī lil-bilād al-miṣrīyah*, 6 vols. (Cairo, 1953–68) 2(3).84, and 'Rectifications à l'ouvrage d'É. Amélineau "Géographie de l'Égypte à l'époque copte"', in *Mélanges Maspero III Orient islamique* (Paris, 1940) 273–321, at 290) have suggested that Kieratou was Garadū (جرجر) in markaz Itsā. The Arabic name had evolved by the early 8th century, when جرىوا/جراىوا appears in the Fayum marshland survey published by Karabacek, 'Der Papyrusfund von el-Faijûm', *Denkschriften Akad. Wien, phil.-hist. Kl.* 33 (1883) 207 ff., at 215 ff. (= *PERF* 597, dated 724/5).

[11] *SPP* X 281.9–10.

[12] *P. Erasm.* I 2.7 ff.

[13] Cf. Rathbone, 'Historical Topography', 55–6, for a plausible location.

from Kerkeēsis, since *BGU* IV 1035 refers to a conflict between the two villages.[14] In *SB* 9583, the important seventh-century list, Kerkeēsis appears with Paniskou, confirming these correlations.[15] Kerkeēsis occupied a fairly central position in the Tutun basin, with marshland stretching north towards Tebetnu and south towards Tebtynis.[16] It occurs repeatedly with Kerkesēphis.[17] Kerkesēphis was adjacent to Samaria,[18] which was close to Tristomos at the Fayum exit of the Baḥr Yūsuf,[19] and both Kerkeēsis and Kerkesēphis turn up in several documents with Kaminoi.[20] If the latter was medieval Qambašā at the eastern end of the basin[21] (this is simply a hypothesis), we would have to look for both villages towards the north-east end of the basin, north of Qalamsha. In that case, Paniskou would have to be found at some point close to all these villages, possibly closest to Oxyrhyncha.

The general impression, then, is one of some cohesion, with localities spread within a certain radius of the Gharaq basin. The second estate in *SPP* X 154 reflects similar cohesion. In this case there is less uncertainty, since two of the three locations are actually known. Piamouei survives as Biyahmū 7–8 kilometres north-east of Medinet el Fayyum, and about 10 kilometres west of Seila, and Pantikou was clearly medieval Bandīq near the Baḥr Seila.[22] The location of Embolou is unknown. It appears next to Pantikou in two other documents. One of these, *SPP* X 246, repeats the sequence of *SPP* X 154.7–9 in an expanded series which includes Kerkesoucha, Selē, and Syrōn.[23] All but one of these were villages along the eastern edges of the Fayum, with Kerkesoucha in the region of Karanis,[24] and Syrōn on the Baḥr Yūsuf south of El Lāhūn.[25] Thus one has to look for Embolou somewhere along this eastern extremity. It is vaguely possible

[14] *BGU* IV 1035.

[15] *SB* 9583 fr. 3 7–9.

[16] *P. Col.* X 256.5 (137), Daris, 'Toponimi della Meris di Polemone', *Aegyptus* 64 (1984) 101–20, at 104, Rathbone, 'Historical Topography', 55. Daris thinks that Kerkeēsis was closer to Tebetnu than to Tebtynis.

[17] *P. Tebt.* II 400 xiv 4–5 (1c.), a list with strong cohesion, *SB* XIV 11430 (86), esp. l. 16, *phore(tron) Kerkeseo(s) kai Kerkesepheo(s)*, *SB* VI 9313 (166), *P. Fam. Tebt.* 12 (112), *P. Strasb.* 607 (2c.).

[18] *BGU* I 94 (289), 'Kerkesephis also called Samaria', see B. Krämer, *Das Vertragsregister von Theogenis (P.Vindob. G 40618)* (Vienna, 1991) 100.

[19] *P. Lond.* III 1219 (196), *P. Mich.* 245.19 (47), *P. IFAO* III 42.14–15, and see D. Bonneau, 'La terre "arrosée par le Nil": *Neilobrochos*', *BASP* 16 (1979) 13–24, at 21, and *Le Régime administratif de l'eau du Nil dans l'Égypte grecque, romaine et byzantine* (Leiden, New York, and London, 1993) 71–2.

[20] *P. Berl. Leih.* II 26.8 ff. (167–8), which suggests that Kerkesephis was not far from Kaminoi, *P. IFAO* III 42.11–12. For Kaminoi's connection with Tristomos, cf. *P. Tebt.* II 400 xiv 6–7, *SPP* X 262.10–11, and *SB* XVI 12726 ii 3 with Bonneau, *Régime administratif de l'eau du Nil*, 71 n. 600.

[21] See H. Halm, *Ägypten nach den mamlukischen Lehensregistern. I Oberägypten und das Fayyūm* (Wiesbaden, 1979), Fayyum map, 19-20.

[22] Daris, *Dizionario*, 4(1).45, 'presso Sela, la medievale Bandiq'. Wessely's map shows Pantikou south of Seila, contrast Halm, *Ägypten*, Fayyum map, 20.

[23] *SPP* X 246 (7c.), with the sequence Embolou, Pankti (= Pantikou), Piamouei, Kerkesoucha, Selē, S[yr]ōn (in ll. 1–6).

[24] *P. Merton* II 88 xviii 5, and H. C. Youtie, *Scriptiunculae Posteriores*, 2 vols. (Bonn, 1981) 1.353, 'very near Karanis'.

[25] See below.

that the name of Embolou has survived in the modern Arabic toponym بحر بلاما which recurs as the 'Bahar Bela Ma' on Jacotin's Napoleonic map and as 'Balama' on the map constructed by the Commission des domaines d'Égypte *c.*1897,[26] and that Embolou itself lay somewhere in the vicinity of modern Demu east of Medinet el Fayyum.

Another estate with a wider spread of settlements but a similar pattern of regional concentration was the estate of pseudo-Strategius III or that part of it which is listed in *SPP* X 1. Strategius himself was dead by this time and it is interesting that the estate (*oikos*) retained its identity regardless.[27] *SPP* X 1 mentions seven locations: Psineuris, Ampeliou, Bernikidos, Karpe, Phentemin, Kainos, and [ ]nol. Of these the last is likely to have been Psinol, which has turned up in a recently published papyrus of the early sixth century as a *kōmē* in the Arsinoite (that is, not in the Theodosiopolite).[28] This fact is of some interest as it means that, prima facie, Bernikidos is more likely to have been Berenikis Aigialou than the village in the Gharaq basin, Berenikis Thesmophorou, since none of the other sites are in the Theodosiopolite. Psinol's location can scarcely be conjectured. Phentemin's identification with Fidimīn has long been accepted, and is in fact proved by the fascinating bilingual list in *P. Ross.-Georg.* V 73 (8c.), where χωρ/ Φεντε/ is rendered as فدمين in l.8. Thus Phentemin was approximately 10 kilometres north-west of Arsinoitōnpolis. Kainos had a local fishing industry.[29] It was presumably in the region of Lake Moeris and not far from Karanis.[30] At the opposite, south-western end of the lake was Berenikis Aigialou, evidently in the vicinity of Euhemeria (Qaṣr el Banāt), which must by this stage have disappeared.[31] 'Berenikidos' reappears with Karpe and a cluster of other west Fayum villages in *SPP* X 78.[32] One of these was Ampeliou. Ampeliou bore the Coptic name Tbōnalaali,[33] and is associated, in this form, with 'Pkalankeh' in two (Coptic) papyri.[34] Kosack's historical maps identify Pkalankeh with Qalamša near or possibly identical with Abu Ginshu (med. Babīg Anšū) just south of Ibshawai (ancient Pisai).[35] In that case, Ṭebhār/Ṭubhār a few kilometres south of Abu Ginshu may have been the site of Ampeliou, and medieval Babīg Anšū the site of Alexandrou Nēsos.[36] Karpe should surely

[26] *Carte topographique de l'Égypte et de plusieurs parties des pays limitrophes . . . construite par M. Jacotin*, flle 19 (Faïoûm), Commission des Domaines de l'État Égyptien, *Carte de la Basse-Égypte et de la province de Fayoum* (Cairo, 1897). Cf. 'Khōr bilā Mā'' on Halm's map, that is, 'waterless bay'.

[27] *SPP* X 1.1 (see Ch. 6, n. 61).

[28] *P. Dub.* 34.2 (511).

[29] *P. Ross.-Georg.* III 53 (673/4 or 674/5).

[30] *P. Mich.* XII 648.9–10 (4c.). It reappears with Phentemin in *SPP* VIII 1331 (7c.).

[31] *P. Flor.* II 126. 9n, 'prossima ad Euhemeria'.

[32] *SPP* X 78.4 ff. (7c.), including Pa[trēs], Bēlou, and Pisai. With Bēlou cf. Balāla (بلالة) in the *Taʾrīkh al-Fayyūm*, 64.

[33] *CPR* IV 86 (7c.).

[34] *CPR* IV 86, 81 (7c.).

[35] W. Kosack, *Historisches Kartenwerk Ägyptens: altägyptische Fundstellen, mittelalterliches arabisches Ägypten* . . . 2 vols. (Bonn, 1971).

[36] Alexandrou Nēsos was close to Theadelphia, cf. *SB* XVI 13001.11, but also not far from Ampeliou, *SPP* X 78.12–13, 193.1–2. In *SB* 5336.6 [Ἀμπελι]ο(υ) is probable, following *Alexand(rou)* in l. 5.

be identified with Minya Karbīs in Nabulsi's description of the Fayyum, to the south and east of Fidimīn and Sanhūr, not far from Medinet el Fayyum.[37] The general configuration of this complex of villages is arguably best represented in *SPP* X 90, where the sequence seems to run from north to south, starting with Phanamet and Kna in the immediate vicinity of Lake Moeris. Kna was clearly Aqnā, which turns up in an interesting Arabic lease of the early ninth century.[38] It is coupled with Phanamet in two other documents, including the important 'village inventory', *SPP* X 138.[39] Phanamet was probably further east along the shore of Birkat Qārūn, in the area to the north of Psineuris = Sanhūr.[40] Kna/Aqnā lay on the western edge of the Fayum, close to the lake, north-west of Pisai,[41] and Patrēs (which concludes the sequence in *SPP* X 90 recto) was probably medieval Badrīs further east and/or south along the Baḥr Tanbaṭwīya.[42] This leaves Psineuris, which is less problematic. In the Fayum papyri, there are two toponyms with similar-sounding names, Psineuris and Psenyris. Grenfell and Hunt seemed to think they were the same, and identified both with Sennoures/Sinnūris about seven miles from Arsinoe (directly north of Biyahmu).[43] Wessely, by contrast, drew a distinction between them, correctly, but identified Psineuris as Sinnūris and Psenyris as Sanhūr north of Fidimīn.[44] The reverse is true.[45] Psenyris was clearly on or near the site of the more substantial centre of Sinnūris, and Psineuris is likely to have been Sanhūr. Psenyris shows a strong connection with villages in the east and north-east,[46] and particularly close links with Neiloupolis of the

[37] Al-Nābulusī, *Taʾrīkh al-Fayyūm wa-Bilādih*, 146; shown as Akhṣaṣ Abī ʿUṣayya on Halm's map.

[38] Y. Rāġib. 'Contrat d'affermage d'un pressoir à huile en 205/821', *Studia Iranica* 11 (1982) 293–9, esp. 296. *SPP* X 90.2–7 (8c.?) shows the following sequence: Phanamet, Kna, Tassat, Pisai, Karpe, Patrēs. With Tassat compare Dasūda in *PERF* 597 (n. 10 above).

[39] *SPP* X 138.18–19, also *CPR* IV 18 (8c.). Lake Moeris was also called the 'lake (*buḥayrat*) of Aqnā and Tanhamat', Ibn Ḥauqal, *Ṣūrat al-ʿarḍ*, cited in Rāġib, 'Contrat d'affermage', 296 n. 16.

[40] For the conjunction of Phanamet and Psineuris, cf. *SPP* X 254.4–5, 268.5–6, 138.19–20.

[41] For the location, see Ali Shafei, 'Fayoum Irrigation as Described by Nabulsi in 1245 AD with a Description of the Present System of Irrigation and a Note on Lake Moeris', *Bulletin de la Société Royale de Géographie d'Égypte* 20 (1940) 283–327, Map I. Cf. *P. Tebt.* II, p. 385, 'not far from Ibshwai', and Halm's conjectural location, *Ägypten*, Fayyum map, 19.

[42] Patrēs appears with Karpe in *SB* 5339.17–18, with Ampeliou in *SB* 5338.1–2, and with Tassat in *SB* XVIII 13264.5–6 (7c.) and *SPP* X 97.1–2. For Badrīs, cf. al-Nābulusī, *Taʾrīkh al-Fayyūm*, 17, mentioned (with Aqnā, Baraġṭūṭ, etc.) as one of the ruined localities on the canal.

[43] Grenfell and Hunt, *P. Tebt.* II, p. 411, *P. Grenf.* II 61.8n. Timm, *CKAAZ*, 4. 2034, is inclined to endorse their position.

[44] Wessely, *Topographie*, 167, 12.

[45] So too E. Amélineau, *La Géographie de l'Égypte à l'époque copte* (Paris, 1893) 379–80, and Ramzī, *al-Qāmūs*, 2(3).113, and, more tentatively, map B V 21 in the *Tübinger Atlas des Vorderen Orients*.

[46] e.g. *P. Tebt.* I 24 iv 80ff., *SB* XII 11147.3–5, *BGU* XIII 2281 (189/90), *P. Petaus* 40.18–22 (late 2c.), *P. Strasb.* 608.17 (2c.), *SPP* X 147.7–8 (7c.), *P. Merton* II 100 (669),

Fayum,[47] which Bonneau has identified as Tell el Rusās at the northeastern tip of Birkat Qārūn.[48] The papyrological topography of Psineuris, on the other hand, has no such eastern orientation, and Psineuris itself appears twice with Phentemin (Fidimīn just south of Sanhūr) and once with Philoxenou, which was probably Abuksa south-west of Sanhūr.[49]

Of course, we simply do not know how many more settlements Strategius is likely to have controlled in this sector of the Fayum. On the other hand, we know that localities in other parts of the Fayum were included in the estate. One of these was Herakleōn, which it is tempting to identify with El Ḥaraga (med. Mūš al-Ḥaraga) 2 kilometres south-east of El Lāhūn.[50] The crucial piece of evidence for the location of Herakleōn is a Cologne papyrus published as *P. Petaus* 84. This shows that in the late second century, Ptolemais Hormou (El Lāhūn), Syrōn kōme, Kerkesoucha Orous, and epoikion Herakleōnos formed part of a single unit of rural administration, with its centre at Ptolemais Hormou, and that certain village liturgies were rotated between the villages of this common area of administration.[51] Thus Syrōn, Herakleōn, and Kerkesoucha Orous were all in the region or locality of Ptolemais Hormou. Moreover, Syrōn was roughly a day's journey south of Ptolemais Hormou, on the Baḥr Yūsuf,[52] which would mean a location in the neighbourhood of Sidamant el Gebel.[53] Fayum maps do in fact show a village by the name of El Zerība at this point on the canal (just north of Sidamant el Gebel),[54] and it seems plausible to identify this as the approximate site of Syrōn kōmē. Deir Mar Girgis (دير مار جرجس) a kilometre north of Sidamant el Gebel could then have been at least the approximate location of Kerkesoucha Orous,[55] the importance

with Stratōnos in the last three; Stratōnos was probably close to Karanis, cf. *SB* XII 11011.21–23 (2c.), *BGU* III 835 (216/17), *P. Mich.* XII 642 iii 61, 67 (1c.).

[47] *BGU* II 538 (100), *P. Vindob. Tandem* 15 ii 49–50, and *P. Petaus* 40.20, where Psenyris is paired with Neiloupolis, as Hephaistias is with Bakchias (l. 10) and Stratōnos with Sebennytos (l. 22). Sebennytos may have been El Zerbi (med. az-Zarbī). It was close to Ptolemais Nea, which is probably the Ptolemais identified, in *P. Ross.-Georg.* V 73.17, with medieval Dhāt aṣ-Ṣafā (ذات الصفا), shown as practically adjacent to az-Zarbī on Halm's Fayyum map.

[48] D. Bonneau, 'Niloupolis du Fayoum', *Actes du XVe Congrès International de Papyrologie, Bruxelles-Louvain, 29 août–3 septembre 1977*, 4 vols. (Brussels, 1979), 4. 258–73. Sinnūris, likewise, was within walking distance of the lake, which was 'on the West-side', F. Vansleb, *The Present State of Egypt or, A New Relation of a late Voyage into that Kingdom performed in the years 1672 and 1673* (London, 1678) 161.

[49] *SPP* X 268.3, 5, 15.7–8, and Ramzī, 'Rectifications', 305.

[50] *SPP* VIII 1121 (7c.).

[51] See Ursula Hagedorn's excellent discussion of the topography of the archive in *Das Archiv des Petaus* (Cologne, 1969) 22 ff.

[52] *P. Lille* 1 ii 31 ff. shows this, cf. Hagedorn, *Das Archiv des Petaus*, 27.

[53] *BGU* VI 1282 shows that Syron was not far from Neiloupolis = Dalāṣ.

[54] 'Zaribéh' on Jacotin's map, 'Zeribah' on the 1897 map (n. 26), and 'El Zerîba' on the Survey Department, Egypt, 1923, map of the Fayum (sheet 3-E).

[55] Deir Mar Girgis is shown on the most detailed maps of the Fayum. It appears as 'Deir Mar Guergues' on the 1897 map. The French transcribes an Arabic 'Girgis', corresponding to a place-name starting with Κερκε = Dem. grg/Coptic gōrg. On the latter see Hagedorn, *Das Archiv des Petaus*, 26–7, and W. Habermann, 'Kerkeosiris/Kerkeusiris im Arsinoites', *CE* 67 (1992) 101–111, at 110 n. 24.

of the latter being that it connected the main part of the Fayum to the Baḥr Yūsuf by a major desert communication track now called the 'Darb Sidmant el-Gabal'.[56] These reconstructions are obviously tentative, but they help to tie up some of the later topographic material, a lot of this from the now almost non-existent archives of aristocratic estates in this region. Thus Herakleōn and Skelous or 'To Skelos' both appear in the archive of Sambas, which is clearly from a very large estate.[57] Skelous and Heracleōn reappear, in approximate conjunction, in the important seventh-century topographic list in *SB* 9583, which also mentions Anōgēs and Tmouei.[58] 'Anō gēs' turns up with Skelou (*sic*) in *P. Vindob. Tandem* 17, where the other toponyms include Kerkesoucha, Syrōn, and Thmoioubestis,[59] and with 'Ptolemaidos' and Tmouei in *SPP* XX 271. Finally, in *SPP* X 149, which clearly is also estate-related, Syrōn, Anōgēs, Herakleōn, and Skelous appear in obviously close association. Here, curiously, Syrōn is described as 'of the large estate', and Skelous and Herakleōn (in l. 9) as 'of the small estate'. Moreover, both Skelos and Herakleōn figure separately as well, in their determination as villages (as opposed to estate settlements).[60] The conjunction of Skelos and Herakleōn within the boundaries of a single estate which is described as 'small' implies that Skelos, wherever it was, was obviously not far from Herakleōn. In a sixth century hay account published by Reekmans, To Skelos turns up as the headquarters of another estate with holdings at Tali, Bousiris, and Mouchis.[61] Bousiris in this context was Abusir Difinnu (med. Abū Sīr Dafadnū) about 2 kilometres from Tebetnu/Dafadnu,[62] and Mouchis Dumūšiya not far

[56] This is shown on the El-Nuweira map (1:25000, sheet 71/800), part of the 1:25000 series of Fayyum published by the General Egyptian Organization for Surveys, from the 1920s. (I am grateful to Alan Bowman for the chance to consult these.) The permeability of the Gebel at this point is unambiguously suggested by Kerkesoucha Orous's repeated association with south Fayum locations in the region of Tebtynis, and particularly with the latter, e.g. *PSI* VIII 909.26 (44), *SB* XVIII 13793.36 (101), *P. Hamb.* I 62 (123), *SB* VI 9491, *SB* XII 11047, *P. Giss. Univ.* VI 49, *P. Tebt.* 298 I 43 ff., and *P.Bad.* 29.10–11 (443). As Hagedorn notes, there was another Kerkesoucha Orous further north, in the region of Karanis.

[57] The archive is discussed by F. Mitthof and A. Papathomas, 'Das Archiv des ἐλαιουργός Sambas: Unterhaltszahlungen in Öl an die Bediensteten eines Gutes (Arsinoites; 6. Jh. n. Chr.)', *ZPE* 103 (1994) 53–84, esp. 64.

[58] *SB* 9583 fr. 1 11 ff., with the sequence *Σκέλους*, *Μῶντι*, *Ἡρακλέων(ος)*, *Οὐὼ βορ(ρινῆς)*, *Ἀνωγῆς*, *Ἀρ[ι]δέ(ου)* and *Τμουεί*.

[59] *P. Vindob. Tandem* 17 (6/7c.), transcribing *ἄνω γῆς* in ll. 3–4. Cf. Rea, *P. Oxy.* LI, p. 99 'In Egyptian topography *ἄνω* means "southern" . . .'. For Thmoioubestis, in the Heracleopolite, and often associated with Bousiris = Abū Ṣīr al-Malaq, cf. M. R. Falivene, *The Herakleopolite Nome: A Catalogue of the Toponyms with Introduction and Commentary*. ASP 37 (Atlanta, Georgia, 1998) 81 f.

[60] *SPP* X 149.5 ff., with the sequence *Σύρων μεγάλης οὐσιάς*, *Ἀνωγῆς*, *Ἡρακλέωνος κώμης*, *Ἀπανωκα[ι]ου σὺν Λευκ(ογίῳ)*, *Σκέλους (καὶ) Ἡρακλέωνος μικρ[ᾶς] οὐ[σίας]*, *Σκέλους*. Leukogion was the 'southern port of the Fayum'. It 'lay on the Nile in the Heracleopolite nome', *P. Cair. Isid.* 47.39n (p. 217).

[61] T. Reekmans, *A Sixth Century Account of Hay (P. Iand. inv. 653)* (Brussels, 1962), republished as *SB* VIII 9920.

[62] Wessely, *Topographie*, 21. Bousiris and Tebetnu appear in repeated conjunction in the archive of Paul son of Menas, *P. Med. inv.* 73.15 (6c.) = C. Salvaterra, 'Due nuove

from the latter.[63] Thus Skelos looked both ways, towards Herakleon (and the east) and towards the region around Tebetnu, and a location in the corridor would seem to fit the facts best. To Skelos may have got its name from the ancient embankment at the entrance to the Hawara channel near Lāhūn,[64] and may have been (at/near the site of) Dimašqīn al-Baṣal/ Demishqin a few kilometres north-west of El Ḥaraga in the Lāhūn pass.

ricevute di età bizantina a Paolo, figlio di Menas', *Aegyptus* 69 (1989) 48, *P. Med. inv.* 73.20 = *Aegyptus* 1989, 50f., *P. Worp* 1 = K. A. Worp, 'The Milano Tax-Receipts of Paulus Son of Menas: An Addendum', *Aegyptus* 67 (1987) 99f. = *SB* XVIII 13152 (6c.).

[63] *P. Flor.* III 317 (210) suggests that Mouchis was close to Bousiris. It was also close to Eleusis, cf. *P. Col.* II 1 recto 4 i 2–3 (155), and Daris, *Dizionario*, 3/1, p. 301 ('il villaggio ha legami particolari con Eleusis'), thus supporting the presumption that Eleusis occupied a site close to modern Etsa barely 2 km. from Difinnu. The Heracleopolite Mouchis has been identified with Dimšuwīya (= Dumūšiya) east of Ihnāsiyā al-Madīna (anc. Heracleopolis), cf. Gomàa *et al.*, *Mittelägypten zwischen Samalut und dem Gabal Abū Sīr*, 94.

[64] Cf. Bonneau, *Régime administratif de l'eau du Nil*, 17, 38, for possible senses of *skelos*.

APPENDIX 4

A Brief Update on the Aristocracy

Aurelia Charite: Worp publishes 8 documents from the archive of (probably) her mother Aurelia Demetria also called Ammonia, *P. Harrauer* 38–45; the latter was clearly a substantial landowner, cf. Hagedorn and Worp, *ZPE* 135 (2001) 157ff., publishing a lease dated 332, where she rents out a farm of over 50 arouras.

Taurinus archive: new material in *BGU* XVII, ed. Poethke (but with Gascou's corrections in *CE* 77 (2002) 326ff.), where documents from the archive (2675–2677, 2680–2681) range from Sept. 481 to Aug. 510, and in *BGU* XIX, ed. Maehler (eight documents, several fragmentary and only one precisely dated); P. Berol. 21836 cited at p.123, n.80 is now published as 2816, showing that the *bouleutēs* Phoibammon had mortgaged several plots or farms to John son of Taurinos I. Also see the discussion of this archive at http://lhpc.arts.kuleuven.ac.be/archives/texts/259.pdf

Flavius Sarapodorus: It is worth emphasizing that the four clearly dated papyri that mention Eucharistia in *BGU* XII are *all* late, from 483 to 498. This makes it unlikely that the three tax receipts that also mention her (now *SB* XXII 15317–19) date from the 440s, as Palme, *AFP* 40 (1994) 56ff. suggested. Two or even three indiction cycles later would yield a more likely date, esp. if we identify the notary Sarapion who drafted *BGU* XII 2165 with the homonym associated with documents dated to 481 and 485. The advantage of locating all of Eucharistia's papers late is that it is then possible to argue that the archive of the older Sarapodorus, who never gives us the name of his father and is never described as the son of Hermogenes, may well extend to 451 (i.e. include *CPR* IX 40 as well as the remaining tax receipts), which would explain why we have an 'Aurelius', a different and younger Sarapodorus, being addressed in 483 (jointly with his sister Eucharistia). It is possible that the earlier Sarapodorus was the grandfather of the later one.

5th cent. Strategius: His name is restored in *P. Oxy.* LXX 4780 (457?), from the estate of Aelia Eudocia, wife of Theodosius II, and the second in a long series of waterwheel receipts; almost certainly *not* the deceased *clarissimus* whose descendants turn up with other shipowners in *P. Oxy.* LXVIII 4685 from the early fifth century.

Flavia Kyria: Gonis, *Tyche* 17 (2002) pp.86–8.

Flavius Olympius: Palme in *Festschrift Ekkehard Weber* (see 'Further bibliography'), 461–76; the latest accretion is a lease dated 464 or 479 where the lessee describes himself as 'your lessee' (*misthōtes hymeteros*) and structures at least some of the terms of the lease *kath'homoitēta tōn allōn misthō[tōn]* (l.13; *tōn allōn s[o]u misthōtōn* in l.11); but Palme notes that *misthōtai* were generally substantial tenants; Gonis, *APF* 51 (2005) 90–2; possibly in *P. Rain. Unterricht* 63.33 (*c*.420), which refers to an Olympius *politeuomenos Herakleou(s)*.

Count John: Gonis, *P. Oxy*. LXVIII, pp.154ff., suggesting we distinguish (1) a *vir spectabilis* John who turns up in *P. Oxy*. 4696 (484) as *comes consistorii, politeuomenos* and son of Timagenes 'of splendid memory' (*lampras mnēmēs*); his sons—Fl. Phoebammon and Fl. Samuel— appear in *P. Oxy*. 4697 (Dec. 489) and *P. Oxy*. 4701 (505?), where Ph. is *comes domesticorum* and his brother S. *comes consistorii* and both are *politeuomenoi*; he may have been the *praeses Arcadiae* Apio Theodosius Johannes who turns up in *P. Oxy*. XVI 1877 but was in any case dead by Dec. 489; (2) the better- known Count John, who is associated with a series of 'orders to pay', most recently *P. Oxy*. 4699 (504), addressed to the 'wine steward Phoebammon'. D. Hagedorn and B. Kramer, *APF* 50 (2004) pp.161ff. publish new orders to pay, dated 472–76, issued (apparently written) by a Count John who may be different from both the above or possibly the same as (1). The disbursements are chiefly in solidi. With the *vir spectabilis* now seen to be the son of the *clarissimus* Timagenes (Andorlini, *PSI XVII Cong*. 29, p.109 n. 4), we have three generations of a relatively wealthy Oxyrhynchite family, straddling the greater part of the fifth century, 432 to 505 (?).

Aurelia Kyra al. Eustorgia: *BGU* XVII 2683 (513) = *SB* XIV 11373, *BGU* XIX 2808 (528), extending the span of her archive to 58 years!

Flavius Eulogius and family: Hickey and Keenan, *Analecta Papyrologica* 8–9 (1996–97) 209–18 (with corrections in *P. Bingen* 129 n.1; also *CE* 79 (2004) 241ff.), and Gonis, *P. Oxy*. LXVIII 4686 (440) and 4693–4 (both 466), leases from the archive of a family of civil servants who had reached aristocratic status by mid sixth century, if Fl. Serenus son of Martyrius (in *P. Oxy*. I 140 (26.iv.550)) is from this family. Even otherwise, the span of this dossier is some eight decades, 440 to 518 (*PSI* V 466).

Apions: Now see Mazza, *L'archivio degli Apioni*, and Sarris, *Economy and Society in the Age of Justinian*, esp. chs. 1–5, though the stemmas are obsolete. One of the earliest references to the *oikos* of the Apions, *SB* VI 9152 (492), has been republished as *P. Eirene* II 12 by Harrauer, with the integration of two new fragments, cf. *Eirene* 40 (2004) 101ff.; Gonis, *ZPE* 146 (2004) pp. 175–8, suggesting that Apion I may have been the son-in-law rather than son of the mid-fifth-cent. Flavius Strategius and married to the latter's daughter Flavia Isis. Strategius II (previously 'I'): Gonis, *Tyche* 17 (2002) pp. 89 f., revising *P. Mich.* XV 737 (bef. 497), which shows that estates retained their corporate identity long after the demise of their founders; *P. Oxy.* LXVII 4614 (late 5th c.); 4615 (505) expands the small number of leases from the Apion archive and is the first papyrus to refer to his father Apion I's prefecture of the east (*apo eparchōn*); 4616 (525) where the *geōrgos [tēs hymōn endoxo]tētos* is, interestingly, *not* described as "enapographos", as Gonis notes. Gonis has published a large clutch of documents in *P. Oxy.* LXX, viz. 4780–4802, mostly waterwheel receipts. Two of these show that Apion II was still alive (or thought to be alive) in late March 578. *P. Oxy.* 4789 involves a *pōmaritēs tou endoxou oikou*; as Gonis notes, 'The expression indicates a regular paid employee of the estate', 4789.12–13n. It is obvious that the Apions had a *huge* payroll. Being a "registered" employee of the estate did not stop one from having a job in the administration of the estate. In 4794 an *enapographos geōrgos* describes himself as a 'former headman' (*apo meizonōn*), meaning village headman. Even more interesting, two documents involve women workers from the estate, Aurelia Tarilla in 4797 (583) and Aurelia Therme in 4801 (617). Like their male counterparts, women employees were also described as *enapographoi geōrgoi* and also actively involved in production. Tarilla refers to the irrigated farm in her charge (*hyp' eme*). On Praejecta, see Beaucamp, *Revue des Études Byzantines* 59 (2001) pp.171ff. On Praejecta's newly discovered husband, see below under 'Strategius *paneuphemos*'. *P. Oxy.* LXVI 4536 (612?) suggests that theft was common in the villages (*kōmai*) under Apion control; Hickey, *ZPE* 146 (2004) 165–6 publishes a small fragment that suggests that the *pronoētai* may have dispatched their monies to the *zygostatai* who then forwarded the collections to the estate banker.

Flavius Athanasius: Now see Fournet, *Hellénisme dans l'Égypt du VIe siècle*, t.1, pp. 330–1, showing that *P. Cair. Masp.* I 67002 refers to the second *year* of Athanasius' office as Duke (that is, 566/67) and that the conventional reading of this to mean that he was duke for a second time is wrong.

Count Callinicus: See Fournet, *Hellénisme dans l'Égypt du VIe siècle*, t.1, pp.326ff., esp. 335, n.546, identifying the 'Count' in *P. Ant.* III 189 (p. 165 above) with the Duke who succeeded Athanasius' successor John son of Sarapammon. C. was the recipient of several of Dioscorus' poems. His brothers also occupied senior positions, Fournet, *BIFAO* 93 (1993) 223–35, underlining the tight control ('monopoly') that individual families exerted over the leading jobs in provincial government.

Flavius Julianus: he was pagarch before Serenus, not after, as I implied earlier, following Rémondon's date for *P. Flor.* III 298 and *P. Cair. Masp.* 67325: Fournet, *APF* 46 (2000) pp. 241ff. shows convincingly that these receipts must date to the 550s, not, as Rémondon finally argued, the early 540s. Serenus was pagarch from at least 556/7 to 559/60.

Flavia Christodote: a fragment of what looks like a third copy or perhaps draft of her famous affidavit has now been published as *P. Thomas* 29 by Hickey and Keenan; they suggest that her creditors may have gone on to seize part of the estate formally associated with her brother Cometes.

Flavia Maria: she is new, '*paneuphemos patricia*, daughter of John of well-famed memory, former *patricius* himself' in *P. Oxy*. LXIX 4754 (572). It is fascinating to see the Oxyrhynchite material still adding to the prosopography of late sixth-century landed families! What the new papyrus means is a proliferation of sixth-century aristocratic Johns to seven. It may be useful to map them out here in rough chronological order: (1) the *endoxotatos comes* John who turns up in *P.Cair. Masp*. 67104 (530) and who was probably father of Patricia, pagarch *c*.553; (2) the *endoxotatos* John son of Cometas who turns up in Just., *Edict* xiii.24 as Duke of the Thebaid in the late 530s; if he was the *paneuphēmos stratēlates* in *P. Cair. Masp*. I 67123.2, so Gascou, *Travaux et Mémoires* 12 (1994) 328 n.27, he was already duke by the end of October 537; (3) John son of Sarapammon who was duke after Athanasius, in 568, cf. Fournet, *Hellénisme*, t. 1, pp.333–6, t. 2, p. 524ff., 531; (4) the former *patricius* John who was father of Christodote and Cometes, dead by 573; (5) the former *patricius* John who was father of the *paneuphēmos* Maria in 572, also deceased by then; (6) the *hyperphuestatos patricius* John on whom devolved one of the eight fiscal shares of Antinoopolis at some indeterminate date in the sixth century, *P. Ant*. II 110.5; and (7) the *endoxotatos stratēlates* John who was Euphemia's son and heir, see below. (The list ignores another *stratēlates* John who is mentioned in *P. Grenf*. I 67 as the father of one Flavius Theodore *illustris*, since the date is uncertain.) In the commentary to *P. Oxy*. 4754 (p. 206) Gonis suggests that (4) and (5) may have been the same, in other words, that Christodote and Maria were sisters. If so, their father must have divided his estate three ways, since *PSI* I 76, Christodote's draft affidavit, certainly implies that the *ousia* she owned was bequeathed to her by her father (*hē hypoleiphtheisa moi akinētos ousia kata tēn Arkadōn*) and both Maria and Cometes appear as owners of independent estates. Beaucamp, *Le Statut de la femme à Byzance*, vol. 2, p. 446 suggests that (4) and (2) may have been the same. Again, given the dates, (1) and (2) seem a more probable identity and would account for Patricia holding the pagarchy some two decades later. (I doubt if Fournet, t. 2 p. 634, can be right in identifying the recipient of 35 with the *endoxotate* Patricia in *P. Lond*. V 1660.) Depending on the likely date of *P. Ant*. II 110, I think we can at best reduce the above list to 5 but probably no fewer than that.

Flavia Anastasia: Hickey, *APF* 49 (2003) pp. 199ff., surety dated 591, calling A. 'the most glorious *illoustria*, daughter of Menas son of Eudaemon of glorious memory' (*endoxou mnēmēs*); *P. Oxy*. LXIX 4756–4758, all deeds of surety, only one precisely dated; A. is now seen to have had several *dioikētai* working for her; note the description of the estate's employees as *hoi autē* (sc. Anastasia) *prosēkontes* in 4757.3 (590); *SB* XXII 15723 (late 6th c.), where one of those employees was a *chartoularios* called Anastasius.

Flavius John: *P. Oxy.* LXIX 4755 (586) is now a second surviving document from the papers of the *stratēlates* John, son of Euphemia, cf. p. 152 above.

Flavius George: *SB* VI 9587 has been re-edited as *P. Harrauer* 59 and dated to 604; the appearance of a *bouleutēs* in the early seventh century only emphasizes the marginality of this group in later late antiquity.

Flavius Strategius *paneuphemos*: new documents include *P. Oxy.* LXVI 4535 (600); here Strategius' general administrator (*dioikētēs*) Flavius Apollos, who is attested elsewhere (see p.183 n.81) turns out to be a *comes consistorii*, himself a high-ranking aristocrat, a tantalizing hint of the networks through which aristocratic properties were managed and controlled; also *CPR* XXIV 24 and 26–29, ranging in date from 582–602 to *c.*616, with the *epoikion* Psineuris turning up (again!) in 28. These are published by Palme with copious commentary, but the prosopography argued for 25 is undermined by the discovery that Apion III's mother Praejecta was married to a Strategius who was dead by 607 and so cannot have been Strategius *paneuphemos*. P. Vindob. G 13381 + 22003, dated April 607, refers to Apion III as the son of Strategius 'of well-famed memory' and of Praejecta. (My thanks to Bernhard Palme for sharing his transcription of the new papyrus!) It is this Strategius, not the Fayum *patricius*, who figures in *CPR* XXIV 25, since the missing greater part of line 6 clearly implies that he was a close relation of Apion II. On the other hand, the only document in Table 10 that I would re-assign to him is the first one listed there, *P. Oxy.* LVIII 3935 (591). The other Oxyrhynchite documents listed in the archive of the Fayum Strategius are almost certainly *not* papers involving the husband of Praejecta, since Apion III took over sole responsibility for the management of the Apion properties from as early as March 593 (*P. Oxy.* XVIII 2202) and it would be extraordinary if both father and son ran the estate at the same time, one directly and the other through an executive called Apollos! P. Vindob. G 25886 = *P. L. Bat.* XXX 2 is assigned to the archive of Strategius by Hoogendijk in *The Two Faces of Graeco-Roman Egypt* (Leiden, etc., 1998) 21ff., but the document is undated and there were, conceivably, more Fayyūm *patricii* than just the famous Strategius.

Flavius Cyrus, son of Victor: not from the aristocracy but a good example of the enterprising middle classes who ran workshops on a commercial basis; the best contract from his small archive is *P. Grenf.* II 87 (602) = *Sel. Pap.* I 23, a piece-rate contract with a group of dyers, but he now turns up in *P. Bodl.* I 41 (604) hiring a skilled worker (*cheiristēs*) for work in his *ergastērion*. Cyrus describes himself in all three documents as 'priest and master flax-spinner' (*authentēs stippourgos*).

Flavius Menas: *CPR* XIX 32 (29.12.622) is now a new edition of *SPP* XX 240; add *CPR* XXIV 30 (27.4.622), and *SB* XXIV 16287 = *SB* I 4805 (*c*.622, cf. Bagnall and Worp, *Chronological Systems*, 298). The fact that he was pagarch in 622 shows that the Fayyūm Strategius, *if* he survived, had been stripped of this position by then.

Flavius Theodorakios: now also in *CPR* XXII 4 (mid 7th c.); *CPR* XXIV 32 (651); certainly our best example of an aristocrat who managed to survive the turbulent years of the Arab conquest of Egypt and retain power! He first appears in 629, the son of a scholasticus but in possession of a large estate (*ousia*), *CPR* VII 51, with Palme, *CPR* XXIV, p. 198. Ten years later and for about a decade after that he was pagarch of a reorganized Fayyūm pagarchy, *endoxotatos stratelates kai pagarchos* in 643 and *illustris kai pagarchos* in 651. Thus Th. reflects a layer of the aristocracy that emerged in the aftermath of Shahrvaraz's withdrawal from Egypt, that worked for the restored imperial administration in the 630s, and that went over to the Arabs during or shortly after the conquest.

APPENDIX 5

Chris Wickham and the End of Late Antiquity

Chris Wickham's recent book *Framing the Early Middle Ages* is a superb account of the transition from late antiquity to the early middle ages, which successfully integrates a vast amount of literature into a coherent narrative of how political fragmentation or, more precisely, distinct waves of such fragmentation in the fifth, sixth, and seventh centuries respectively, translated into a deepening economic recession that climaxed in the latter part of the seventh century with the rapid dissolution of Mediterranean-wide exchange. In the model Wickham constructs the key variable is tax. Taxation fed into the existence of a strong central authority such as the late Empire, generated spin offs in terms of the integration of markets across a wider range of territories, and bolstered the aristocracy through the sheer scale of political and economic integration that went with it. Moreover, at each of these levels, the decline of taxation meant deepening fragmentation and more localized, vulnerable elites, aristocracies hung out to dry, each effect reinforcing the other. Insofar as all of this came to a head in the latter part of the seventh century, Pirenne was right to see that period, and not the fifth, as the major watershed, but not for the reason he postulated, namely, the Arab invasions and their impact on Mediterranean unity. Indeed, one of the most attractive features of Wickham's book is his refusal to dramatize the conventional ruptures of political history. The Lombards invaded an Italy that was half-devastated by the Gothic war and in demographic decline.[1] They cannot be blamed for its continuing involution. The Arab invasions of 632–45 swept through countrysides that were densely inhabited and did little to disrupt the normal course of their lives.[2] The strong industrial and commercial expansion of the Umayyad period would be hard to reconcile with dramatic economic dislocation in the mid seventh century.[3] Thus, political events are part of a more complicated causal

[1] Neil Christie, *The Lombards* (Oxford, etc., 1995) 69–73.

[2] Alan Walmsley, 'Pella/Fiḥl after the Islamic Conquest (AD 635–*c*.900): A Convergence of Literary and Archaeological Evidence', *Mediterranean Archaeology* 1 (1988) 142–59.

[3] This was already seen by Ehrenkreutz in a prescient paper, 'Another Orientalist's Remarks Concerning the Pirenne Thesis', *JESHO* 15 (1972) 94–104, repr. in A. S. Ehrenkreutz, *Monetary Change and Economic History in the Medieval Muslim World*, ed. J. L. Bacharach (Variorum, 1992) ch. 3.

machinery, not miraculous interventions, and the reader of Wickham comes away with an indelible sense of just how complex the "crisis" of the fifth to seventh centuries was.

But crisis there was, more profound in some regions than in others, and it is in constructing its mechanism that Wickham stakes a claim to advancing a substantive argument about late antiquity. As I indicated, the model builds on the role ascribed to taxation in producing a tendential integration of the economy as a whole, across the various regions encompassed by the empire. This thesis sometimes takes a strong form, namely, Wickham seems to argue that economic life, notably trade, was driven by fiscal networks.[4] There are two ways of understanding this. In the first place, it could mean that the demands of taxation were so intense that taxpayers had little choice but to produce more and to sell more of what they produced to meet government's requirements. This is the standard 'forced commercialization' model one associates with Keith Hopkins. Alternatively, it could mean that the complex infrastructures created for the movement of fiscal goods supplied a strong incentive to traders to build wider-ranging commercial links matching the scale of the fiscal system. These formulations are not incompatible, but it is clear that in Wickham the balance of emphasis lies with the second. One way of expressing this would be to say that late Roman taxation reduced transaction costs for private traders, and that much Mediterranean-wide trade was driven by the incentive this created.

The proposition is certainly coherent, but is it true? Let me put it this way. If it *were* true, how would we account for comparable levels of Mediterranean exchange in the late Republic and early Empire?[5] Why is it that the vigour of their commercial networks was so much less dependent on or bound up with an overpowering fiscality? Had something changed to make those dynamisms less functional in late antiquity? The conventional response, of course, is that the late Roman state was hostile to private

[4] e.g. Wickham, 'The Mediterranean around 800: On the Brink of the Second Trade Cycle', *DOP* 58 (2004) 161–74, at 172: 'driven by fiscal networks'.

[5] The bibliography is vast, e.g. Michel Christol, 'Marchands gaulois et grand commerce de l'huile de Bétique dans l'Occident romain', in Lucien Rivet and Martine Sciallano (eds.), *Vivre, produire et échanger: reflets méditerranéens. Mélanges offerts à Bernard Liou* (Montagnac, 2002) 325–34, Francis Tassaux, 'Laecanii. Recherches sur une famille sénatoriale d'Istrie', *MEFRA* 94 (1982) 227–69, Giuseppe Camodeca, '[Puteoli]: La società et le attività produttive', in Fausto Zevi (ed.), *Puteoli* (Naples, 1993) 31–50. André Tchernia, 'L'arrivée de l'huile de Bétique sur le *limes* germanique: Wierschowski contre Remesal', in Rivet and Sciallano, *Mélanges à Bernard Liou*, 319–24, is a fascinating discussion of an issue that is also central to Wickham's model and suggests one of the ways in which the state and private capital could complement each other. Robert Étienne and Françoise Mayet, *L'Huile hispanique* (Paris, 2004), is an excellent synthesis of one of the most thoroughly researched areas, and part 6 of the paper by Feliciano Serrao, 'Il modello di costituzione. Forme giuridiche, caratteri politici, aspetti economico-sociali', in Aldo Schiavone (ed.), *Storia di Roma, 2/2* (Turin, 1991) 29–71, suggests that the business aristocracy (*equites*) and the consolidation of their interests was a key social base in the regime created by Augustus. As an indication of scale, note the colossal fine Caesar imposed on Lepcis (it isn't clear which one), 3 million lbs of olive-oil per year (*B. Afr.* 97.3)!

enterprise and sought to dominate as much of the economy as it could, crowding out the private sector. That image of a monopolizing Behemoth, nurtured in the shadow of Stalinism, is not popular today, nor would Wickham subscribe to its credibility. He argues the opposite, namely, that the strength of the late Roman aristocracy was, in some basic way, proportional to the coherence of the state. 'The senatorial elites were profoundly dependent on the survival of the empire', as Wickham states (p.161). But if this was a partnership where each side needed and supported the other, why would the economically active elites, whether from the aristocracy or elsewhere, have lacked either the drive or the resources to sustain economic networks that could of course build on but also operate largely outside the framework of the fiscal state? Indeed, Wickham seriously underestimates the economic sophistication of late Roman elites and the traditions of business they inherited from their past.[6] This is because the textual evidence is underexploited (often dismissed as rhetoric) or just not cited, but crucially, perhaps, because he brings a medievalist's understanding of the aristocracy to the late antique world, narrowing the range of options from which aristocrats drew their wealth (the aristocracy was never a purely agrarian class) and ignoring the centrality of money to the economic structures of the late Empire. The enormous wealth of the late Roman aristocracy that impresses Wickham so much was *primarily* a product of Constantine's reorganization of the monetary system, as Santo Mazzarino never tired of emphasizing.[7] But in Wickham we tend to revert to an image of the late Empire where this seminal insight, the characterization of its "style", is lost.

Some of the most interesting argumentation in the book revolves around two major themes. The first is the general weakening and impoverishment of the aristocracy that was bound up with the fragmentation of the late Empire. The second is his characterization of the countryside of the western provinces and the thesis that there, in the West, the village was a creation of the early middle ages. In other words, only the Greek-speaking parts of the Roman empire knew village life in any identifiable sense. The dissolution of Roman power in the West threw up radically different trajectories: in Britain, a dramatic collapse in the fifth century, with the wholesale disappearance of the aristocracy, followed by a gradual recomposition of aristocratic power that is again visible in the eighth and ninth centuries; in the Frankish territories north of the Loire, the evolution of a powerful class of aristocrats, described in one passage as *potentes qui per diversa possident*,[8] already by the main part of the sixth century; while Italy saw a rapid loss of economic coherence in the sixth century and an aristocracy destroyed by war and fragmentation. (Tom Brown suggested

[6] e.g. Firmicus Maternus, *Mathesis*, 3.10.1 (Monat, t. 2, p.101), *magnorum aut potentium virorum . . . scribas, rationibus, mensis, apothecis negotiationibusque praepositos*, which should be read with the seminal reconstruction of Roman limited liability in A. Di Porto, *Impresa collettiva e schiavo "manager" in Roma antica (II sec. a.c.–II sec. d.c.)* (Milan, 1984).

[7] e.g. Mazzarino, *Storia sociale del vescovo Ambrogio* (Rome, 1989) ch. 2, esp. 27.

[8] *Pactus legis Salicae*, ii, 88 cited Heike Grahn-Hoek, *Die fränkische Oberschicht im 6. Jahrhundert* (Sigmaringen, 1976) 56.

that the senatorial survivors 'either moved East attracted by office and the flourishing Latin community still in Constantinople, or to Sicily, where an ossified senatorial rump can be traced throughout the seventh century'.[9]) Three models, therefore, three forms of discontinuity, and no discernible synchronism— with the rapid breakdown of Roman traditions of private landholding in Britain, the relatively rapid emergence of a new kind of aristocracy in Francia, and a permanent, even traumatic disruption of the senatorial elites that had survived into the sixth century under the Ostrogoths. Disappearance, mutation, decline/diaspora: to which we can add—survival, the remarkable continuity exemplified by the families who continued to control much of southern Gaul through the turbulent decades of the fifth and sixth centuries, a purely Roman (or 'Gallo-Roman') aristocracy or *Geburtsadel* with roots in the late Empire. But even this was a continuity that concealed a massive reorganization of the countryside in the fifth century, when the larger rural establishments became epicentres of a huge demographic regroupment, with widespread rural abandonment of smaller sites and the survival and stability of the largest ones.[10] Nor was their tenacity sempiternal. As Stroheker suggested, Gregory of Tours was the last great representative of these 'senators', since even they were destined to be absorbed into the wider circles of the Frankish aristocracy in the seventh century.[11]

Wickham maps this landscape of breakdown and mutation with exceptional finesse, demonstrating its essential complexity and the almost Althusserian sense of differential temporality that runs through the whole book. The "crisis" of the Roman empire has never been described with more verve or intricacy (not since Gibbon!). If Gaul under the Merovingians is our best example of the fusion of late Antiquity into the early middle ages (the absorption of an essentially late Roman society into a 'medieval' one), Italy before and after the Lombards is the most dramatic illustration of their *tension.* Wickham's account is strongly influenced by the medieval historian Delogu's image of Italy's regionalization, both cultural and economic, as the hallmark of the great watershed of the sixth and seventh centuries.[12] A degraded urban fabric, demographic decline, and the dissolution of ancient landscapes had little to do, directly, with the Lombards and the violence associated with their conquest. They were expressions of a deeper, slower-moving crisis, with its roots in the fifth century, a 'substantial economic and cultural impoverishment of Roman society' that was less

[9] T. S. Brown, 'The Aristocracy of Ravenna from Justinian to Charlemagne', *XXXIII Corso di Cultura sull'Arte Ravennate e Bizantina, Ravenna, 15/22 marzo 1986* (Ravenna, 1986) 135–49, at 137.

[10] See Stéphane Mauné, *Les campagnes de la cité de Béziers dans l'Antiquité* (Montagnac, 1998) 120ff. (with profuse thanks to Peter Brown for the reference).

[11] Karl Friedrich Stroheker, *Germanentum und Spätantike* (Zurich and Stuttgart, 1965) 205.

[12] Paolo Delogu, 'La fine del mondo antico e l'inizio del medioevo: nuovi dati per un vecchio problema', in Riccardo Francovich and Ghislaine Noyé (eds.), *La Storia dell' Alto Medioevo italiano (VI–X secolo) alla luce dell' archeologia* (Florence, 1994) 7–29, esp. 16.

evident in the countryside, initially, than in the cities.[13] A prolonged deflation, then, that weakened Italian links to Mediterranean markets, accentuating local heterogeneity and the kind of economic regionalism that would characterize Italy for the next thirteen centuries. And while the Lombards mainly aggravated these trends (did not *cause* them), they did create a divided Italy, adding political fragmentation to the general decline. This picture Wickham broadly accepts, with less of its catastrophism (Delogu's catalogue of disasters includes climate change, a substantially wetter climate in the sixth and seventh centuries that produced increased flooding; there is certainly evidence for this) and more certainty as to its causes. Whereas Delogu sees the contracting ceramic networks of the sixth century and even earlier reflecting a progressive depopulation of the countryside (a decline in *demand*),[14] which seems logical, Wickham has repeatedly argued that the evaporation of African fine ware exports began crucially with the breakdown of fiscal networks. Vandal control of Africa had a fatal long-term impact on Mediterranean exchange because it removed the subsidy that made a wider scale of commercial exports profitable (pp.710ff.). Yet, depending on how the chronology plays out, it may be that a fiscal narrative lacks the kind of elasticity one needs to explain a much slower, protracted movement. And the fact that Justinian relied on merchants, private entities, in the south of Italy to handle the fiscal exaction of grain, as Theoderic had done,[15] shows both the enormous resilience of commercial networks (Italian ones in this case; they had survived the Gothic war!) and the complex ways in which the two systems could interlock, with a *reversal* of the hierarchy posited by Wickham.

That all of this transformed the countrysides of Western Europe is undeniable, and again the chief certainty is how uneven the process was. Villas disappeared, sooner and more rapidly in the North (Britain, northern Gaul), within a broad span that runs from 350 to 700. Wickham is emphatic: the disappearance of villas is not a 'marker of economic and political crisis' (p. 481). But clearly in one sense it was. The monumental villas of the fourth century were one of the ways in which the consolidated imperial aristocracy of the period acquired a consciousness of itself and spoke the language of class. The crisis of *that* aristocracy, which is such a large part of Wickham's argument, must surely have reflected itself at this level as well. It is inconceivable that the quintessential aristocracy of the late Empire, the *potentiores*, would simply have switched lifestyles, abandoning standard forms of residence. As that aristocracy disintegrated, which it did at different times in different places, so did their network of villas. As Sartre might have put it, the villa *was* the aristocracy. (Obviously, one implication of this is the need for a clear distinction between the villas themselves and the sites they once occupied; crudely put, between physical and functional continuity.)

[13] Delogu, 'Longobardi e romani: altre congetture', in Stefano Gasparri and Paolo Cammarosano (eds.), *Langobardia* (Udine, 1990) 111–67, esp. 145ff. [14] Ibid. 152–3.

[15] Ruggini, *Economia e società*, 215, 219, Volpe, *Contadini, pastori e mercanti*, 336, 420, citing *Const. Pragm. ad Vig.*, 26.

Wickham's suggestion that the landscapes of the Roman west were invariably dominated by estates and that villages 'were secondary to estate organization, where they existed at all' (p. 514) overstates the case. Except for a passing reference to the *castellum* of Fussala, he ignores *castella* completely. Yet, there is the Elder Pliny's categorical statement that the bulk of the North African population resided in *castella*,[16] and of course Strabo's *Geography* is full of references to villages (*komai*, though usually expressed adverbially) in what seems to have been a still largely tribal West. Unless the expansion of estates (the *saltus privati* of Agennius Urbicus)[17] led to a widespread reduction of these forms of settlement and subsumption of the peasantry residing in them, it seems more credible to assume that a substantial part of the rural population continued to inhabit agglomerations of this kind. This is not to deny that dispersion was more characteristic of the western countryside than of the East, but it *is* an invitation to look at the issue of settlement with all the available sources in mind and not just what the archaeology can (and can't) tell us.[18]

This leaves one issue wide open, at least half so—where did the new landed elites live in the sixth and seventh centuries? Again, as with everything else in the West, the answer may be an amalgam. Wickham suggests that the relatively wealthy Merovingian aristocracy was firmly embedded in the countryside. It must have some significance, then, that despite the endemic political warfare of the sixth century, Merovingian estates stayed largely unfortified.[19] In Italy, the upper classes, Lombards included, remained overwhelmingly urban. The Spanish evidence is uncertain, since, as Chavarría notes, 'The massive accumulation of *fundi* in the hands of the Church and of the new barbarian elites could have unleashed the abandonment of many rural structures on the part of the new owners and their re-occupation by peasant communities . . . However, we still have to ask where the great landowners of the sixth and seventh centuries lived, since down to today and with the exception of a handful of buildings . . . not a single rural residence has been documented past the early sixth century that preserves a level remotely comparable to that of the fourth and fifth century villas.'[20] She suggests that part of the newer elite may have relocated to the more substantial hilltop settlements. Whatever the true

[16] See p. 7 above.

[17] *De controversiis agrorum*, ed. and tr. B. Campbell, *The Writings of the Roman Land Surveyors* (London, 2000) p. 20 line 3.

[18] See Kim Bowes and A. Gutteridge, 'Rethinking the Later Roman Landscape', *JRA* 18 (2005) 405–13 for the suggestion that the expansion of Christianity into the countryside encouraged new forms of agglomeration.

[19] Ross Samson, *J. of Medieval History* 13 (1987) 287–315, esp. 296ff. A passage in Gregory of Tours suggests that the Merovingian aristocracy could head for the town in times of serious war, cf. Peter Brown's preface to Kathleen Mitchell and Ian Wood, *The World of Gregory of Tours* (Leiden, 2002) 1–28, at 11, citing Gregory, *LH* 6.41, where Chilperic orders his counts and dukes to repair the city walls and to take shelter in them, while promising them compensation for any damage done to their estates.

[20] Alexandra Chavarría Arnau, 'Considerazioni sulla fine delle ville in Occidente', *ArchMed* 31 (2004) 7–19, at 17.

situation, it is clear that the pattern was vastly more heterogeneous than in the East.

The East was dominated by an 'essentially urban ruling class' (p. 462), an important clue to its unbroken urban vitality. The absolutely crucial difference, and no reader of Wickham's book can fail to notice this, is the contrasting demographic histories of the two halves of the empire, especially in late antiquity when western demographic decline (with parts of Italy and Spain losing up to half their population) was matched, in the East, by strong demographic resilience into the seventh century, and almost certainly later as well. Wickham, refreshingly, doesn't endorse Hugh Kennedy's arguments about a late sixth-century urban recession in the Levant (see p. 624), which, paradoxically, projects a kind of Orientalism back into late antiquity (the myth of the disordered 'Muslim' city, except that now it is late antique!). That view has recently been hammered in different ways by Jodi Magness and Rebecca Foote in some superlative work.[21] Wickham's own strong regional focus enables him to bring nuance into this picture as well, but in general the rapid economic recovery from the political dislocations of the early seventh century is what is truly remarkable about the East Mediterranean in this period. The densely inhabited countrysides of the East, coupled with the strong industrial and commercial expansion that has now been documented archaeologically for the late seventh and early eighth centuries,[22] are extraordinary features of this *late* late antiquity and even prompt Wickham to view the Levant as an exception to his fiscal model. 'The wealth of the countryside . . . was an essential support to the coherence of these [city-level economic] infrastructures. Urban and rural prosperity clearly went hand in hand in this region. All these features continued into the Umayyad period, even though most cities lost their fiscal centrality . . . We must conclude that the lasting strength of urban civilization was not, in this corner of the Mediterranean, dependent on the survival of the political and fiscal structures of the Roman empire' (p. 625). What this indicates is a set of 'wider economic relationships than just the state infrastructure' (p. 713).

Which ones? If there was a different model at work here, one driven by a different set of forces, then it certainly fails to emerge with the kind of clarity and emphasis that Wickham confers on his fiscal narrative. The Frankish North and the Tyrrhenian coastlands emerge as further exceptions to the fiscal model in the sense that relatively wealthy aristocracies had either stabilized (Francia) or survived (southern Italy) there and the scale of aristocratic wealth could actually 'compensate for the end of the fiscal system' (p. 804). Here we move to a demand-driven model that

[21] Jodi Magness, *The Archaeology of the Early Islamic Settlement in Palestine* (Winona Lake, Ind., 2003) ch. 9, Rebecca M. Foote, 'Commerce, Industrial Expansion, and Orthogonal Planning: Mutually Compatible Terms in Settlements of Bilad al-Sham during the Umayyad Period', *Mediterranean Archaeology* 13 (2000) 25–38.

[22] Alan Walmsley, 'Production, Exchange and Regional Trade in the Islamic East Mediterranean: Old Structures, New Systems?', in Inge Lyse Hansen and Chris Wickham (eds.), *The Long Eighth Century* (Leiden, etc., 2000) 265–343.

is closer to mainstream economic history, and we have three major and significant parts of the post-Roman world which seem to fit this kind of model better.

What is missing from Wickham's book is any sense of how such an economy might have worked. To begin with, he hugely underestimates the extent of monetization within the tax system. 'It was in general unlikely that most taxation was moved between regions in the form of money in our period, for the mechanisms by which gold would come back from (say) Constantinople to Egypt on a sufficiently regular basis *for the same money to be paid again* are impossible to imagine' (p. 768, emphasis mine). What Wickham means by this is that it is impossible to *believe* that the late empire could have had levels of commercial activity sufficiently high to sustain the widespread and regular exaction of money taxes from a largely peasant population. But all this boils down to is incredulousness, *a priori* one might add, about the successful operation of a monetized tax system in a largely agrarian economy such as most scholars imagine the late empire to have been. I find the reasoning odd. If Wickham is asking for examples of centralized imperial states that have successfully run monetized tax systems off the backs of a largely rural population, one could refer to the kind of fiscal and monetary integration that J. F. Richards describes, with a wealth of detail, in his brilliant papers on Mughal state finance and on the integration of Khandesh into the Mughal fiscal structure and monetary economy.[23] There is an important sense in which the Mughal revenue system was history's last exemplar of a strictly *late antique* tradition that was inherited and passed on by the Caliphate and its successor regimes. 'The flow of produce forced from the countryside by the imperial tax demand worked its way up through the system of markets in return for the cash needed to pay the revenue. At every level, graindealers/ moneylenders moved commodities toward the cities and cash back to the villages.'[24] That late antique and early medieval historians do not have the same kind of documentation to be able to describe the workings of this system in its primordially late antique form is a mere accident. But there is still sufficient evidence to indicate that it existed and that it worked. There is the extraordinary time series that Lionel Casson published decades ago, showing the phenomenal levels of monetary demand the Marwānids imposed on the district of Aphrodito at the end of the seventh century and into the 720s—a formal assessment of close to 7,000 solidi a year.[25] That actual collections ran at some 60 per cent of that only goes to underline the realism of those figures. There is al-Ṭabarī's precise report, part of which is also found in Ibn Khurradādhbih, that in the eighteenth year of his reign (607/8) Khusro II managed to collect 420 million drahms by way of taxes,

[23] J. F. Richards, 'Mughal State Finance and the Premodern World Economy', *Comparative Studies in Society and History* 23 (1981) 285–308, and 'Official Revenues and Money Flows in a Mughal Province', in J. F. Richards (ed.), *The Imperial Monetary System of Mughal India* (New Delhi, 1987) 193–231; both in *Power, Administration and Finance in Mughal India* (Aldershot, 1993) chs. 5 and 11 respectively.

[24] Richards, 'Mughal State Finance', 299.

[25] Casson, *TAPA* 69 (1938) 274–91.

and that the level of reserves in his treasury stood at 800 million drahms in 602.[26] There is Procopius' report that Anastasius left a treasury surplus of 23 million solidi, and Priscus' statement that the emperor Leo spent 130,000 lbs of gold on his useless expedition against the Vandals (over 9 million solidi!) and still managed to leave a surplus in the treasury.[27] All the examples just cited contribute to the distinct impression of a late antique (and not just late Roman) model that implies large amounts of money in circulation, and, at times, substantial liquid reserves. *The scale of the currency was clearly many times that of the actual collections or the reserves in the treasury*. In short, it is quite implausible to suppose that the money exacted by way of taxes accounted for all or almost all of the money in circulation, as the passage cited from Wickham seems to imply. Money is simply a form of value, and the amount of value in circulation a reflection of the wealth generated in society. There is absolutely no reason to think that the same stream of values was being recycled through the economy, unless we believe that late antiquity was a period of complete stagnation!

There is far too much about the seventh century that economic historians still have to sort out. If Wickham's hypothesis of a rapid and permanent dissolution of the Mediterranean commercial network at the end of the century seems plausible for the moment, given the way the ceramic evidence is being constructed and read, we still lack a clear picture of the broader economic forces at work, especially in the latter part of this period. Pirenne was probably right in emphasizing the continued vitality of commercial exchanges across the Mediterranean on the eve of Islam's expansion,[28] but certainly wrong to conclude that the 'Arabs' disrupted that by destroying the economic unity of the sea. On the contrary, the Umayyads were strongly committed to free trade and had no interest in undermining economic contacts that could only benefit their own mercantile elites.[29] And because Pirenne linked the continued circulation of gold in the western Mediterranean to the persistence of trade, he also believed that 'there was a very considerable stock of gold in the West'.[30] This was an exaggeration, as we now know, since in fact the whole of the late sixth and seventh centuries saw the West suffer from an increasing dearth of gold, so that the solidus 'gradually ceased to circulate in the west'.[31] The monetary fragmentation of the empire

[26] See my paper 'Precious Metal Coinages and Monetary Expansion in Late Antiquity', in F. De Romanis and S. Sorda (eds.), *Dal "Denarius" al "Dinar". L'Oriente e la moneta romana* (Rome, 2006) 265–303, esp. 274ff. The drahm contained *c*.4.17g of silver of very high fineness.

[27] Priscus, fr. 53,3 (Blockley, 2.363), 'They say that he [Leo] spent 130,000 lbs of gold to no avail', and Malchus, fr. 7 (Blockley, 2.412ff.) for the surplus that Zeno dissipated.

[28] S. T. Loseby, 'Marseille and the Pirenne Thesis, I: Gregory of Tours, the Merovingian Kings and "Un grand port"', in Richard Hodges and William Bowden (eds.), *The Sixth Century: Production, Distribution and Demand* (Leiden, etc., 1998) 203–29.

[29] Cf. Ehrenkreutz, 'Remarks', 97.

[30] Henri Pirenne, *Mohammed and Charlemagne* (New York, 1958) 111, and cf. 'Gold must have been pouring into the country [Gaul]. What brought it? Obviously commerce' at 113.

[31] Peter Spufford, *Money and its Use in Medieval Europe* (Cambridge, 1988) 19. But

following its demise in the West and the gradual but inexorable depletion of the stocks of gold available there must have had a considerable impact on the distribution and density of exchanges. At the very least it would have led to a relocation of capital to other markets, especially if international networks were dominated by traders from the East ('Syri'). The key surprise in the western Mediterranean is the continued existence of preferential markets with strong North African links down to the absolute end of the seventh century.[32] Perhaps because of its seeming centrality to late Roman taxation and the role tax plays in his argument, Wickham is keen to emphasize the vulnerability of Africa, which he believes was 'worse hit by the breakdown of the Mediterranean world system than any other region' (p. 643). But this is in manifest dissonance with the evidence of two of the best excavated West Mediterranean sites, both of which—the Bourse (Marseille) and the Crypta Balbi (Rome)—show the continued and massive preponderance of Tunisian amphorae in late ceramic assemblages of the sixth and/or very late seventh centuries.[33] Wickham overdoes the 'economic involution' of Tunisia in ways that make this late vitality harder to understand.[34]

In the Byzantine controlled parts of the East, it is the late seventh century that sees a progressive depletion of the currency,[35] suggesting *both* a severe deflation within the imperial heartland, reflected in a sharply reduced level of monetary activity, hence reduced demand for goods, and a massive strain on the state's financial reserves, with rapid depletion of the stocks of gold available for coining. It may be that government now had to *pay* for the goods it had once exacted, that this happened through the normal channels of trade, and that the result was an accelerated drain of gold to the caliphate.[36] The hoard from Rougga, where some 70 per cent of

cf. Caesarius, *Serm.*, 154.2, which shows that solidi of some kind still circulated in Provence in the sixth century; see W. E. Klingshirn, *Caesarius of Arles* (Cambridge, 1994) 205–6.

[32] Lucia Saguì, 'Il deposito della Crypta Balbi', in Saguì, ed., *Ceramica in Italia: VI–VII secolo* (Florence, 1998) 325.

[33] Marseille is discussed by Simon Loseby in two excellent papers, 'Marseille and the Pirenne Thesis, I', and the sequel to that, 'Marseille and the Pirenne Thesis, II: "Ville morte"', in Hansen and Wickham (eds.), *The Long Eighth Century*, 167–93; for the Crypta Balbi, see esp. Saguì, 'Roma, i centri privilegiati e la lunga durata della tarda antichità. Dati archeologici dal deposito di VII secolo nell'esedra della Crypta Balbi', *ArchMed* 29 (2002) 7–42.

[34] e.g. 'the evidence from sites like the Michigan ecclesiastical complex tends to suggest that the city [Carthage] was densely inhabited during the second half of the seventh century', J. H. Humphrey, 'Vandal and Byzantine Carthage: Some New Archaeological Evidence', in J. G. Pedly (ed.), *New Light on Ancient Carthage* (Ann Arbor, 1980) 85–120, at 116, or, 'there was still considerable wealth in Carthage in the late 7th c.', Simon Ellis, in J. H. Humphrey (ed.), *Excavations at Carthage 1976 conducted by the University of Michigan*, vol. 3 (Ann Arbor, 1977) 41–64, at 64, conclusions that are hard to reconcile with Wickham's more sombre perspective.

[35] D. M. Metcalf, 'Monetary Recession in the Middle Byzantine Period: the Numismatic Evidence', *NC* 161 (2001) 111–55.

[36] Cf. ibid. 150: 'Gold stocks, which represented the empire's cumulative balance of payments, would seem to have been draining eastwards . . .', but not, surely, to 'supply the Caliphate's currency of dinars'.

268 solidi are from the mint of Constantinople (*c*.647) and the apocryphal story in ʿUbayd Allāh that when the forces of ʿAbd Allāh b. Saʿd b. Abī Sarḥ asked the landowners of Sufetula where they got all their gold from, they replied 'By selling olive-oil'[37] both suggest that this pattern may have been true of Africa as well, and long before the final victory of the Arabs there. That the loss of the richest provinces cut off substantial *money* flows and precipitated a major crisis is clear. That both Africa and Egypt, for example, retained substantial amounts of gold in the seventh century is shown by the enormous sums offered to buy off the first Arab contingents and secure their withdrawal, *c*.640 in Egypt and 647 in Tunisia. When Heraclius heard that Cyrus made the offer, he was furious.[38] Wickham notes that the East Mediterranean exchange network continued to run even after the Arab conquests (pp. 716–17), but then concludes, bizarrely, that this network may have been 'more closely linked to taxation than that in the West' (p. 718). If the latter were true, the former wouldn't be, nor would the fact that although Heraclius lost control of most of the East by 610–20, trade continued at some level. The 'pull' of the fiscal narrative distorts the interpretation of phenomena even when these are reasonably clear. Another example of this: Wickham believes that of all the former provinces of the Roman empire Egypt demonstrates the greatest continuity through the final crisis of the seventh century; it is, as he says, the 'model for continuity across the early middle ages'. This strongly continuitist reading of the Egyptian evidence means that he tends to downplay aristocratic discontinuity, even suggesting at one point that if the former aristocracy lost much of its wealth, it did so 'probably slowly' (p. 253). Now of course it is true that the Arab conquest did not result in mass confiscations of land in Egypt,[39] but an aristocracy losing its wealth *slowly* is scarcely the picture one sees in the papyri, and also misses the point that the elite group had effectively been eliminated by the Sasanians two decades before the Arabs completed the job. Flavius Apion III, the last Apion known to us, was almost certainly killed by the Persians. He was alive in the first week of July 619, dead by early January 620. And the Fayyūm Strategius, *if* he survived, was stripped of the pagarchy and almost certainly of his estates as well. And there must have been many other families who do not appear in the papyri who could have met a similar fate. Certainly, the single most persuasive image of *rupture* rather than continuity is Ibn ʿAbd al-Ḥakam's report, which there is no reason to disbelieve, that some thirty thousand individuals from the wealthiest families loaded themselves and their possessions onto 'huge ships' (*al-marākib al-kibār*) and fled from Alexandria on the eve of the Conquest.[40] Finally, whether and how far an

[37] See Lévi-Provençal, *Arabica* 1 (1954) 17–49, at 37.

[38] Andrew Palmer, *The Seventh Century in the West-Syrian Chronicles* (Liverpool, 1993) 158: ʿAmr b. al- ʿĀṣ offered 200,000 solidi and Cyrus' dismissal.

[39] Petra Sijpesteijn, 'New Rule over Old Structures: Egypt after the Muslim Conquest', forthcoming in Harriet Crawford (ed.), *Regime Change in the Ancient Near East* (Oxford, 2007).

[40] Ibn ʿAbd al-Ḥakam, *Futūḥ Miṣr wa-akhbāruhā*, ed. Torrey, 82; cf. Omar Toussoun, *Bulletin de la Société Archéologique d'Alexandrie* 20 (1924) 213–39, at 231.

Arab aristocracy emerged to fill the vacuum will depend on a closer reading of the Arabic sources. For example, we know from al-Ya'qūbī's short treatise *Mushākalat al-nās li-zamānihim* that "'Amr b. al-'Āṣ built his house in Egypt and chose estates for himself there',[41] just as the high-ranking Sasanian official known as Šahrālānyōzān had done in the 620s.[42] Note also that the *ashrāf* of Damascus took over the residences abandoned by the former aristocracy ('twelve patricians'), who decided, eventually, to flee.[43]

Wickham's general argument that in the West a 'phase' of aristocratic retreat was followed by one of reassertion is unexceptionable, though of course there was no continuity whatsoever between the two phases (the late Roman aristocracy had simply disappeared). The notion that medieval estates replicated earlier forms of organization derived from late antiquity is most improbable, and Wickham disposes of it with finality. The *curtis* was imported into Italy by the Franks, and a fully formed *curtis* system was still not found in the Lombard period, despite increasing concentration of land.[44] Thus Wickham is surely right to posit a 'systemic break' between Roman and medieval labour patterns (p. 263). Certainly, corvées as the key instrument of organization of peasant labour are *not* important before the eighth century. There is no continuity at this level either. The middle ages were characterized by new forms of subjection of the peasantry bound up with the development of the manor or *sistema curtense*, starting with the intensely aristocratic region around Paris. It was the expansion of markets that 'encouraged the crystallization of demesnes', Wickham argues (p. 290), in a clear gesture to recent historiography, which 'lays considerable stress on exchange as an underpinning of the manor' (p. 291). The expanding economic conjuncture of the later eighth century re-stimulated forms of direct management, on an economic pattern (of the rapid subordination of labour, its intensified control) common to the most diverse historical periods. Pasquali's work on northern Italy suggests that the sections of the peasantry who were worst affected by the corvées were those who were least well endowed with land, many of them of servile origin.[45] In any case, just as the landscapes of the medieval world evolved in complex and uneven ways, so did its relations of production, and Wickham's pages on the bipartite estates and the intensification of labour connected with them (pp. 280–301) are among the most lucid in his book. All told, *Framing the Early Middle Ages* will remain a major breakthrough in historiography.

[41] William G. Millward, 'The Adaptation of Men to their Time: An Historical Essay by al-Ya'qūbī', *JAOS* 84 (1964) 329–44, at 336, where the same is said of Maslama b. Mukhallid and 'Uqba b. 'Āmir al-Juhanī, Mu'āwaiya's governors in Egypt. 'Amr came from a landed family: for his background and other estates, see Lecker, *BSOAS* 52 (1989) 24–37.

[42] *SPP* X 251 (626/7).

[43] Ibn 'Asākir, *Ta'rīkh madīnat Dimashq*, vol. 2, pt. 1, p. 126–7 (ed. al-Munajjid), cited Nancy Khalek, *From Byzantium to Early Islam: Studies on Damascus in the Umayyad Era* (Diss. Princeton, 2006) 56.

[44] Bruno Andreolli and Massimo Montanari, *L'azienda curtense in Italia. Proprietà della terra e lavoro contadino nei secoli VIII–XI* (Bologna, 1983) 40, 47.

[45] Gianfranco Pasquali, 'La corvée nei polittici italiani dell'alto Medioevo', in V. Fumagalli (ed.), *Le prestazioni d'opera nelle campagne italiane del Medioevo* (Bologna, 1987) 107–28, at 122.

GLOSSARY

actuarius record keeper, accountant
adaeratio commutation of taxes or salaries assessed in kind into money
agadir fortified granary (Moroccan); 'The word *agadir* probably goes back to Phoenician *gadir* = Hebrew *gādēr* "wall"', *EI*² (1960) 1.244
ampelourgos (Gk. ἀμπελουργός) vine dresser
anhydros (Gk. ἄνυδρος) 'waterless', lacking the equipment for irrigation (*P. Ross.-Georg.* III 36.14n)
annona the grain supply exacted by way of taxes; (pl.) the annual allowances of troops and officials
antigeouchos (Gk. ἀντιγεοῦχος) landlord's representative, cf. the South American *representante*
apolyton kharagma (Gk. ἀπόλυτον χάραγμα) loose coin, not circulating in sealed bags or purses
argentarius professional banker
argenteus the name commonly applied to the Roman silver coin minted by Diocletian, struck on a standard of 96 to the Roman lb.; no longer used in the late fourth century, when 'siliqua' emerged as a generic name for the silver coinage
argyropratēs (Gk. ἀργυροπράτης) banker, money changer; orig. silversmith
aroura Egyptian measure of land, = 0.68 acre
artaba unit of dry measure, usually *c.*39.3 litres
asēmon (Gk. ἄσημον) uncoined silver
aureus usual term for the Roman gold coin before Constantine's introduction of the solidus; under Diocletian the a. was struck at a standard of 60 to the pound and sometimes marked by the Greek numeral *Σ*
autopragia a fiscal privilege conceded to powerful landowners and major villages of handling their own tax collections; first attested in the reign of the emperor Leo, cf. *P. Cairo Masp.* 67019 verso 3 ff., and clearly formalizing the actual usurpation of these functions, *CTh.* 11.22.4 (409)
biarchus junior military grade
bimetallism 'Under a bimetallic standard, each of two precious metals, gold and silver, serves as legal tender, and the two metals are kept by the mint in a fixed proportion', M. D. Bordo, *The Gold Standard and Related Regimes: Collected Essays* (Cambridge, 1999) 158–9
boulē (Gk. βουλή) town council
bouleutēs (Gk. βουλευτής) councillor, member of the *boulē*

bucellarius armed private retainers employed by the aristocracy, privately hired soldiers, but cf. Schmitt, *Tyche* 9 (1994) 147 ff.

casae lit. huts; by extension, a settlement of agricultural labourers, cf. Lancel, *Actes de la Conférence de Carthage*, 1.138, comparing them with the *mechtas* of the more recent period

castellum rural settlement, esp. hilltop villages (*villages pitonniers, villages perchés*) of the type called *qal'a* (lit. fortress), once common throughout North Africa; cf. Louis, *Tunisie du Sud*

centēnarion (Gk. κεντηνάριον) 100 lb. weight of gold; Cathy King suggests that it may refer specifically to bullion, possibly in the form of ingots. Cf. Dagron and Morrison, *RN* 17, ser. 6 (1975) 145–62

chōra (Gk. χώρα) countryside, rural districts

chōrion (Gk. χωρίον) farm, estate; in the papyri—vineyard or other sort of plantation (e.g. dates), village; which of these senses is meant is usually obvious from the context

chryshypodektēs (Gk. χρυσυποδέκτης) 'receiver or collector of taxes in gold', *LSJ*, cashier

Circumcellions 'free agricultural workers who went from estate to estate offering their labour', Warmington, *The North African Provinces from Diocletian to the Vandals* (Cambridge, 1954) 87

clarissimus (Gk. λαμπρότατος) the quintessential honorific of the senatorial aristocracy, later devalued and confined to the lowest rung of senators

coemptio compulsory purchase/levy/requisition, usually of foodstuffs

collectarius money changer, banker, cf. Hultsch, *Metrol. script. rel.* 1.307

comes (Gk. κόμης) term employed for officials of different ranks, 'Count'

comes consistorii member of the Emperor's inner council

comes sacrarum largitionum the highest official in charge of public finance

despotēs (Gk. δεσπότης) master, owner, usually of large landowners

dignitas (Gk. ἀξίωμα) rank or grade in the hierarchy of imperial offices, a dignity

dioikētēs (Gk. διοικητής) (Byz.) senior manager or administrator of an estate; not before the fifth century

domus divina estates and palaces at the disposal of the emperor or of members of the imperial household

dux commander, general, military governor

embolē (Gk. ἐμβολή) the land tax, as distinct from the *chrysika dēmosia* or money taxes, but often and in the later period increasingly subject to commutation

enapographos (Gk. ἐναπόγραφος) (sc. γεωργός, etc.) registered (on the owner's tax rolls) and thus 'bound' to the estate

endoxotatos (Gk. ἐνδοξότατος) 'most glorious', usually of the more powerful *illustres*, and often combined with other exalted predicates

epikeimenos (Gk. ἐπικείμενος) (Byz.) field boss
epoikion (Gk. ἐποίκιον) estate settlement where the employees resided; also quarter (of a village, town, etc.)
ergastērion (Gk. ἐργαστήριον) workshop or industrial establishment
ergatēs (Gk. ἐργάτης) casual labourer, helper; sometimes, more generally, wage-worker
eugenestatē (Gk. εὐγενεστάτη) 'most noble', the standard epithet for women of the more affluent local families (e.g. the layer described above as 'middle bureaucracy'), esp. women with landed possessions of their own
eukleestatos (Gk. εὐκλεέστατος) 'most well famed'
euthēnia (Gk. εὐθηνία) prosperity, abundance; from which, by extrapolation, a slump in prices
exceptor copyist, speedwriter
ezba 'an agricultural settlement on a large estate in which the peasant population was given a small piece of land in exchange for labour service', Owen, 'The Development of Agricultural Production in 19th-c. Egypt', 523; 'It constitutes a hamlet for the workers which is the estate owner's property', Ayrout, *The Egyptian Peasant*, 18
fals (pl. fulūs) a generic name for the copper coinage of Islamic Egypt
feddan measure of area, about one acre
follis commonly used to describe the reform argentiferous bronze coin of Diocletian introduced *c.*295; later, after Anastasius, the largest copper denomination, equal to 40 nummi
fundus (small or midsize) estate, farm
geōrgos (Gk. γεωργός) peasant, farm labourer; also used of landless workers
geouchōn (Gk. γεουχῶν) large landowner, generally used of the more powerful, aristocratic owners
geouchos (Gk. γεοῦχος) landowner
hyperphuestatos (Gk. ὑπερφυέστατος) 'most extraordinary', honorific reserved for the élite aristocracy, such as the Apions
illustris (Gk. ἰλλούστριος) 'illustrious', in the sixth century the *haute noblesse* of the Empire, the dominant social group, more exalted than the *spectabiles* and *clarissimi*; title characteristic of the élite levels of the late Roman bureaucracy
keration (Gk. κεράτιον) carat, = 1/1728 of a Roman pound, or 0.19 g.; as a monetary value, equal to 1/24 of the solidus; in the papyri, also used of the weights used to measure coinage
ksar (pl. ksour) castle, palace; also (among the Berbers) fortified granary (synonymous with *gasr*, *gelāa*, *agadir*, etc.)
ktēma (Gk. κτῆμα) holding; vineyard
ktētōr (Gk. κτήτωρ) landowner
lakkos (Gk. λάκκος) well (cf. *P. Cairo Masp.* 67097.2n); also water-wheel, sāqiya, or the reservoir attached to one, Bonneau, *Le Régime administratif de l'eau du Nil*, 55, 56, 60

mapalia the portable huts used by nomads and transhumants in the ancient Maghreb, hence nomadic settlements or settlements of migrant workers; cf. the Moroccan *nouala*, J. Despois and R. Raynal, *Géographie de l'Afrique du Nord-Ouest* (Paris, 1967) 282

massa a large or very large estate comprising a number of distinct properties

matrona stolata title used for 'landowning ladies of equestrian wealth', Rathbone, *Economic Rationalism*, 48

mēchanē (Gk. μηχανή) water-wheel, sāqiya, or the farm irrigated by one

megaloprepestatos (Gk. μεγαλοπρεπέστατος) 'most magnificent', epithet/title used initially of high officials such as provincial governors and counts of the first rank; by the seventh century it had probably lost its aristocratic connotation

meizoteros (Gk. μειζότερος) (Byz.) an estate official of more exalted rank than the mass of *dioikētai*, cf. *BGU* II 368 (615)

miliarensis/miliarēsion (Gk. μιλιαρίσιον) a multiple of the *siliqua*, struck to two standards, a heavy denomination at 60 to the lb., and a light one at 72; Byzantine name for the hexagram in the seventh century

militaris military official

nomisma (Gk. νόμισμα) coin; usually the solidus

nummus/noummion (Gk. νουμμίον) generic name for the bronze coinage of the fourth century, applied later to the smallest copper denomination; the form νοῦμμος is not attested in Daris, *Il lessico latino nel greco d'Egitto* (Barcelona, 1991)[2] 76, after the fourth century

nundinae periodic markets

Oikenwirtschaft 'household economy', an expression used by the followers of Rodbertus and Bücher to demarcate a form of economy that was (allegedly) widespread in the ancient world

oikos (Gk. οἶκος) lit. 'household', usually of the big aristocratic families and their estates, hence 'house' in the sense of 'house of the Apions'; cf. Cohen, *Athenian Economy and Society*, 84ff. for its complex classical meaning

opsōnion (Gk. ὀψώνιον) wages of regular employees, in kind, cash, or both

organon (Gk. ὄργανον) water-wheel (usually in the Egyptian districts south of Oxyrhynchus)

ostiarius church janitor, cf. Sophocles, *Greek Lexicon of the Roman-Byzantine Periods*, 587, s.v. θυρωρός

ousia (Gk. οὐσία) estate (in the legal sense of a whole ensemble of landed or other possessions)

pagarch (Gk. πάγαρχος, παγάρχης) an official responsible for collecting taxes from villages and other rural localities; the position was usually occupied by the most powerful landowners

paidarion (Gk. παιδάριον) servant, helper, estate employee (cf. *CPR* XIV 41, 6–7c.); it is unlikely that all of these would have been slaves, and more likely that most of them were not

paneuphēmos (Gk. πανεύφημος) 'most renowned', honorific peculiar to the élite aristocracy; rarely used of women, but applied to Leontia, mother of Apion II, in *P. Oxy.* 4397.120

parallēlismos (Gk. παραλληλισμός) an operation involving adjustments between different weight standards for coins

paramonē (Gk. παραμονή) an employment contract originally resembling a form of debt bondage, later standard terminology for service contracts of about a year or more; *paramenontes* (in *CPR* X 1, etc.) clearly has the sense of 'resident'

parastathmon (Gk. παράσταθμον) (sc. νόμισμα) below full or standard weight (of coins)

patricius (Gk. πατρίκιος) initially (under Constantine) a special status conceded to a small circle of powerful individuals who were personally close to the emperor; later (in the fifth century) a title extended to the most powerful personnages in the imperial hierarchy, and later still (in the sixth century) a dignity distinctive of the leading *illustres* or élite aristocracy

perfectissimus (Gk. διασημότατος) originally a rank/title of the more important equestrians in public service, later extended to cover a wide range of middling functionaries

phrontistēs (Gk. φροντιστής) middle-level manager, similar to the *pronoētēs*; in the Byz. period a designation for the aristocratic managers of Church properties, equivalent to Lat. *curator*

plintheutēs (Gk. πλινθευτής) brickmaker

politeuomenos (Gk. πολιτευόμενος) probably the leading group within the town councils and in that sense not just equivalent to *bouleutēs*, as argued recently by Laniado, '*Βουλευταί* et *πολιτευόμενοι*', *CE* 72 (1997) 130–44

pōmaritēs (Gk. πωμαρίτης) peasant-gardener

possessor landowner

potamitēs (Gk. ποταμίτης) canal worker

pragmateutēs (Gk. πραγματευτής) merchant, businessman, business manager (on an estate)

pretium price; rate of commutation

proastion (Gk. προάστιον) 'grand suburban residence' (Rea, *P. Oxy.* LVIII, p. 75), suburban estate, cf. Ch. 6, n. 47 above; pl. *proastia* could refer to the suburban countryside surrounding a city, as in the Fayum papyri

prochreia (Gk. προχρεία) any sort of cash advance, esp. an advance of wages

procurator in an agricultural context, general administrator (of an estate); farm manager; more exalted than the *vilicus* or bailiff, cf. Aubert, *Business Managers*, 141 ff.

pronoētēs (Gk. προνοητής) the managerial designation most commonly associated with the day-to-day administration of estates or farms, cf. the Mexican *mayordomos*

pyrgos (Gk. πύργος) lit. 'tower'; also the term for a widespread form of rural establishment with architectural features which may have been designed to accommodate olive presses

sāqiya (Gk. μηχανή) water-wheel. Cf. H. Villiers Stuart, *Egypt after the War, being the Narrative of a Tour of Inspection* (London, 1883) 334f. 'each wheel would double the production of about 10 acres, and would repay the prime cost in the first year'

scholasticus (Gk. σχολαστικός) advocate, legal officer

scriniarius accountant

siliqua 'the normal silver piece struck for currency in the later fourth and most of the fifth centuries', Kent, *RIC* 10, 16

solidus the dominant gold denomination of the late empire, introduced in 310 or 311, on a standard of 72 to the Roman lb. and a theoretical weight of 4.50 g.

stratēlatēs (Gk. στρατηλάτης, Lat. magister militum) 'commander in chief', 'general', a title often applied to the dukes or military governors, e.g., Gascou, *Tyche* 9 (1994) 19–22 (Duke of Egypt), but also applicable to other senior officials, as an honorary title

susceptor person assigned responsibility for collecting taxes

trapezitēs (Gk. τραπεζίτης) money changer, banker, estate cashier

turris villa with towers; esp. common in North Africa

villa estate or the residential complex/buildings linked to one

zygon (Gk. ζυγόν) = σταθμός, weight, weight-standard (esp. for coins); there was considerable variation in these between localities

zygostatēs (Gk. ζυγοστάτης) coin-weigher, official weigher (when publicly appointed). There would have been several of them in the larger urban centres, cf. Rea, *P. Oxy.* LXIII 4395.26–7n

BIBLIOGRAPHY

EL ABBADI, M. A. H., 'P.Flor.50: Reconsidered', *Proceedings of the XIVth International Congress of Papyrologists, Oxford, 24–31 July, 1974* (London, 1975) 91–6.

—— 'Historians and the Papyri on the Finances of Egypt at the Arab Conquest', *Proceedings of the Sixteenth International Congress of Papyrology, New York, 24–31 July 1980* (ASP 23, 1981) 509–16.

ABBOTT, N., *The Monasteries of the Fayyūm* (new edn.; Chicago, 1972).

ADAMESTEANU, D., 'Due problemi topografici del retroterra gelese', *Rend. Acc. Naz. Lincei, Cl. Sc. Mor., St. e Filol.*, 8th ser., 10 (1955), 203–10.

ADAMS, B., *Paramoné und verwandte Texte. Studien zum Dienstvertrag im Rechte der Papyri* (Neue Kölner Rechtswissenschaftliche Abhandlungen, Heft 35) (Berlin, 1964).

ADELSON, H. A., 'Silver Currency and Values in the Early Byzantine Empire', in H. Ingholt (ed.), *Centennial Publication of the American Numismatic Society* (New York, 1958) 1–26.

ALCOCK, S., *Graecia Capta: The Landscapes of Roman Greece* (Cambridge, 1993).

ALFÖLDY, G., 'Eine Proskriptionsliste in der Historia Augusta', *Bonner Historia-Augusta Colloquium 1964/65* (Bonn, 1966) 257 ff.

—— 'Septimius Severus und der Senat', *BJ* 168 (1968) 112–60.

—— 'Herkunft und Laufbahn des Clodius Albinus in der Historia Augusta', *BHAC* 1966/7 (Bonn, 1968) 19 ff.

ALLOUCHE, A., *Mamluk Economics: A Study and Translation of al-Maqrīzī's Ighāthah* (University of Utah Press, 1994).

AMANDRY, M., *et al.*, 'L'affinage des métaux monnayés au Bas-Empire: les réformes valentiniennes de 364–368', *NAC* 11 (1982) 279–95.

ANDERSON, P., *Passages from Antiquity to Feudalism* (London, 1974).

ANSELMINO, L., BOUCHENAKI, M., *et al.*, *Il Castellum del Nador: Storia di una fattoria tra Tipasa e Caesarea (I–VI sec. d.C.)*. Monografie di Archeologia Libyca, 23 (Rome, 1989).

AUBERT, J.-J., *Business Managers in Ancient Rome: A Social and Economic Study of Institores 200 BC–AD 250*. Columbia Studies in the Classical Tradition, 21 (Leiden, etc., 1994).

AUFHAUSER, R. K., 'Slavery and Scientific Management', *JEconomic History* 33 (1973) 811–24.

AVI-YONAH, M., 'The Economics of Byzantine Palestine', *Israel Exploration Journal* 8 (1958) 39–51.

AYMARD, A., 'Les capitalistes romains et la viticulture italienne', *Annales ESC* 2 (1947) 257–65.

Ayrout, H. H., *The Egyptian Peasant*, tr. J. A. Williams (Boston, 1963).

Baer, G., *A History of Landownership in Modern Egypt 1800–1950* (Oxford, 1962).

Bagnall, R. S., 'Agricultural Productivity and Taxation in Later Roman Egypt', *TAPA* 115 (1985) 289–308.

—— *Currency and Inflation in Fourth Century Egypt*. BASP Supplements No. 5 (ASP, The Scholar's Press, 1985).

—— *Egypt in Late Antiquity* (Princeton, 1993).

—— and Worp, K. A., 'Grain Land in the Oxyrhynchite Nome', *ZPE* 37 (1980) 263–4.

Bagnall, W. S., *The Archive of Laches: Prosperous Farmers of the Fayum in the Second Century* (Duke University Ph.D., 1974).

Al-Bakrī, *Description de l'Afrique septentrionale par Abou-Obeïd-el-Bekri*, tr. Mac Guckin de Slane, ed., rev., and corr. (Paris, 1965).

Ballet, P., and Von der Way, T., 'Exploration archéologique de Bouto et de sa région (époques romaine et byzantine)', *MDAIK* 49 (1993) 1–22.

Balty, J. Ch., 'Notes sur l'habitat romain, byzantin et arabe d'Apamée: rapport de synthèse', *Actes du III Colloque Apamée de Syrie* (Brussels, 1984) 471–503.

—— 'Apamée au VIe siècle. Témoignages archéologiques de la richesse d'une ville', *HREB* 79–96.

Banaji, J., *Rural Communities in the Late Empire AD 300–700: Economic and Monetary Aspects*, 2 vols. (Oxford University D.Phil., 1992).

—— 'The Circulation of Gold as an Index of Prosperity in the Central and Eastern Mediterranean in Late Antiquity', in Cathy E. King and David G.Wigg (eds.), *Coin Finds and Coin Use in the Roman World. The Thirteenth Oxford Symposium on Coinage and Monetary History 25.–27.3.1993*. SFMA 10 (Berlin, 1996) 41–53.

—— 'Modernizing the Historiography of Rural Labour: An Unwritten Agenda', in Michael Bentley (ed.), *Companion to Historiography* (Routledge, 1997) 88–102.

—— 'Lavoratori liberi e residenza coatta: il colonato romano in prospettiva storica', in E. Lo Cascio (ed.), *Terre, proprietari e contadini dell' impero romano* (Rome, 1997) 253–80.

—— 'Discounts, Weight Standards and the Exchange-Rate between Gold and Copper', *Atti dell' Accademia Romanistica Costantiniana. XII convegno int. in onore di Manlio Sargenti* (Naples, 1998) 183–202.

—— 'Agrarian History and the Labour Organisation of Byzantine Large Estates', in Bowman and Rogan (eds.), *Agriculture in Egypt from Pharaonic to Modern Times*. Proceedings of the British Academy, 96 (Oxford, 1999), 193–216.

Bardy, G., *La Question des langues dans l'église ancienne*, 1 (Paris, 1948).

Barns, J. W. B., 'Loan of Money with Hypotheke: P. Cairo Maspero 67023 + P. Fitzhugh', in A. E. Hanson (ed.), *Collectanea Papyrologica. Texts published in honor of H. C. Youtie*, 2 vols. (Bonn, 1976) ii.589–94.

BASTIEN, P., *Monnaie et "Donativa" au Bas-Empire.* Numismatique Romaine, 17 (Wetteren, 1988).

—— and METZGER, C., *Le Trésor de Beaurains (dit d'Arras)* (Wetteren, 1977).

BELL, H. I., 'The Administration of Egypt under the 'Umayyad Khalifs', *BZ* 28 (1929) 278–86.

—— 'An Official Letter of the Arab Period', *JEA* 31 (1945) 75–84.

BENSEDDIK, N., 'La ferme Romanette, Aïn Benia, Aïn Bent Soltane: fortins ou fermes fortifiés?', *Roman Frontier Studies 1979 . . . 12th Int.Congress of Roman Frontier Studies.* BAR International Series 71/3 (Oxford, 1980) iii. 977–98.

BINTLIFF, J., 'The Roman Countryside in Central Greece: Observations and Theories from the Boeotia Survey (1978–1987)', in Graeme Barker and John Lloyd (eds.), *Roman Landscapes: Archaeological Survey in the Mediterranean Region* (London, 1991) 122–32.

BIRÓ, M., 'Roman Villas in Pannonia', *Acta Archaeologica* 26 (1974) 23–57.

BOGAERT, R., 'Geld (Geldwirtschaft)', *Reallexicon für Antike und Christ.* 9 (1975) 797–907.

BONNEAU, D., 'L'administration de l'irrigation dans les grands domaines en Égypte au VIe siècle de n.e.', in D. H. Samuel (ed.), *Proceedings of the Twelfth International Congress of Papyrology.* ASP 7 (Toronto, 1970) 45–62.

—— *Le Fisc et le Nil. Incidences des irrégularités de la crue du Nil sur la fiscalité foncière dans l'Égypte grecque et romaine* (Paris, 1972).

—— *Le Régime administratif de l'eau du Nil dans l'Égypte grecque, romaine et byzantine.* Probleme der Ägyptologie, 8 (Leiden, etc., 1993).

BORKOWSKI, Z., *Alexandrie II. Inscriptions des factions à Alexandrie* (Warsaw, 1981).

BOUCHENAKI, M., and FÉVRIER, P.A., 'Un castellum de la région de Tipasa de Juba à Septime Sévère', *BAA* 7 (1977–9) 193–215.

BOWERSOCK, G. W., BROWN, P., and GRABAR, O., *Late Antiquity: A Guide to the Postclassical World* (Cambridge, Mass., and London, 1999).

BOWMAN, A. K., 'Landholding in the Hermopolite Nome in the Fourth Century A.D.', *JRS* 75 (1985) 137–63.

—— and ROGAN, E., (eds.), *Agriculture in Egypt from Pharaonic to Modern Times.* Proceedings of the British Academy, 96 (Oxford, 1999).

BRANDT, H., *Zeitkritik in der Spätantike. Untersuchungen zu den Reformvorschlägen des Anonymus De rebus bellicis* (Munich, 1988).

BRAUDEL, F., *The Mediterranean and the Mediterranean World in the Age of Philip II,* 2 vols., tr. Sian Reynolds (Fontana/Collins, 1975).

BROISE, H., and THÉBERT, Y., *Recherches archéologiques franco-tunisiennes à Bulla Regia. 2: Les architectures. 1 Les thermes memmiens.* Collection de l'École Française de Rome, 28/2 (Rome, 1993).

BROWN, P., 'The Later Roman Empire', *EcHR*, 2nd ser. 20 (1967) 327–43 (review of Jones, *LRE*).

BROWN, T. S., *Gentlemen and Officers. Imperial Administration and Aristo-*

cratic Power in Byzantine Italy A.D.554–800 (The British School at Rome, 1984).

Brunt, P. A., 'Free Labour and Public Works at Rome', *JRS* 70 (1980) 81–101.

Bücher, K., *Die Entstehung der Volkswirtschaft. Vorträge und Versuche* (4th edn.; Tübingen, 1904), 3rd. edn. tr. S. M. Wickett, *Industrial Evolution* (London, 1901).

Cadell, H., 'Nouveaux fragments de la correspondance de Ḳurrah ben Sharīk', *Recherches de Papyrologie*, 4 (1967) 107–60.

Cahen, Cl., 'Fiscalité, propriété, antagonismes sociaux au Haute-Mésopotamie au temps des premiers 'abbāsides d'après Denys de Telle-Maḥré', *Arabica* 1 (1954) 136–52.

Camps, G., 'De Masuna à Koceila. Les destinées de la Maurétanie aux VIe et VIIe siècles', *Histoire et Archéologie de l'Afrique du Nord. IIe Colloque Internationale . . . BCTH* 19B (1983) 307–25.

—— 'Rex gentium maurorum et romanorum. Recherches sur les royaumes de Maurétanie des VIe et VIIe siècles', *AntAfr* 20 (1984) 183–218.

Camps-Fabrer, H., 'Une nouvelle huilerie romaine dans la région de Périgotville', *Libyca (Archéologie-Épigraphie)* 5 (1957) 43–7.

Capogrossi Colognesi, L., *Economie antiche e capitalismo moderno. La sfida di Max Weber* (Rome and Bari, 1990).

Carandini, A., 'Columella's Vineyard and the Rationality of the Roman Economy', *Opus* 2 (1983) 177–204.

Carrié, J.-M., 'Un roman des origines: les généalogies du "colonat du Bas-Empire"', *Opus* 2 (1983) 205–51.

Casson, L., 'Tax-Collection Problems in Early Arab Egypt', *TAPA* 69 (1938) 274–91.

Castellana, G., and McConnell, B. E., 'A Rural Settlement of Imperial Roman and Byzantine Date in Contrada Saraceno near Agrigento, Sicily', *American J. of Archaeology* 94 (1990) 25–44.

Catani, E., 'I frantoi della fattoria bizantina di El-Beida', *QAL* 8 (1976) 435–48.

—— 'Lucerne fittili dalla fattoria bizantina di Siret el Giamel in Cirenaica: tipologia ed inquadramento cronologico', *L'Africa romana* 6/2 (1988) 459–74.

Cerati, A., *Caractère annonaire et assiette de l'impôt foncier au bas-empire.* Bibliothèque d'histoire du droit et droit romaine, 20 (Paris, 1975).

Chabot, J.-B., *Chronique de Denys de Tell-Maḥré. Quatrième partie.* Bibliothèque de l'École des Hautes Études, Sc.phil. et hist. 112 (Paris, 1895).

Chadwick, H., 'New Letters of St. Augustine', *JThS* 34 (1983) 425–52.

Christol, M., 'À propos des Anicii: le troisième siècle', *MEFR(A)* 98/1 (1986) 141–64.

Claridge, A., 'Il vicus di epoca imperiale nella tenuta presidenziale di Castelporziano . . .', in *Castelporziano I. Campagna di scavo e restauro 1984* (Soprintendenza Archeologica di Ostia, 1985) 71–8.

—— 'Il vicus di epoca imperiale: indagini archeologiche nel 1985 e 1986',

Castelporziano II. Campagna di scavo e restauro 1985–1986 (Rome, 1988) 61–73.

CORBIER, M., 'Les familles clarissimes d'Afrique proconsulaire (I–III siècle)', *EOS* ii. 685–754.

COURCELLE, P., 'Une seconde campagne de fouilles à Ksar-el-Kelb', *MEFR(A)* 53 (1936) 166–97.

CRAWFORD, D. J., *Kerkeosiris: An Egyptian Village in the Ptolemaic Period* (Cambridge, 1971).

CRAWFORD, M., 'Finance, Coinage and Money from the Severans to Constantine', *ANRW* 2.2 (1975) 560–93.

DAGRON, G., *Constantinople Imaginaire. Études sur le recueil des "Patria"* (Paris, 1984).

D'ANGELA, C., and VOLPE, G., 'Insediamenti e cimiteri rurali tra tardoantico e altomedioevo nella Puglia centro-settentrionale: alcuni esempi', *MEFR(M)* 103 (1991) 785–826.

DASZEWSKI, W. A., *et al.*, 'Excavations at Marina el-Alamein 1987–1988', *MDAIK* 46 (1990) 15–51.

DAUPHIN, C., *La Palestine byzantine: Peuplement et populations*, 3 vols. (BAR International Series 726, 1998).

DELMAIRE, R., *Largesses sacrées et res privata. L'aerarium impérial et son administration du IVe au VIe siècle* (Rome, 1989).

DEMANDT, A., 'Der spätrömische Militarädel', *Chiron* 10 (1980) 609–36.

DE MARTINO, F., 'Il colonato fra economia e diritto', in A. Schiavone (ed.), *Storia di Roma. III, 1* (Turin, 1993) 789–822.

DENTZER, J. M., and ORTHMANN, W. (eds.), *Archéologie et histoire de la Syrie. 2: La Syrie de l'époque achéménide à l'avènement de l'Islam.* Schriften zur vorderasiatischen Archäologie, 1 (Saarbrücken, 1989).

DEPEYROT, G., *Le Bas-Empire Romain. Économie et numismatique* (Paris, 1987).

—— 'La durée d'utilisation des solidi romains', in P. Kos and Z. Demo (eds.), *Studia Numismatica Labacensia Alexandro Jeloc nik Oblata* (Ljubljana, 1988).

DERDA, T., *Deir el-Naqlun: The Greek Papyri (P.Naqlun I)* (Warsaw, 1995).

DESPOIS, J., 'Essai sur l'habitat rural du Sahel tunisien', *Annales de Géographie* 40 (1931) 259–74.

—— 'Les greniers fortifiés de l'Afrique du Nord', *Cahiers de Tunisie* 1 (1953) 38–60.

DI VITA-EVRARD, G., 'Note sur quelques timbres d'amphores de Tripolitaine', in S. Lancel (ed.), *Histoire et Archéologie de l'Afrique du Nord. IIe Colloque International (Grenoble, 5–9 Avril, 1983) = BCTH* 19B (1983) 147–59.

DIEHL, Ch., 'Une crise monétaire au VIe siècle', *REG* 32 (1919) 158–66.

DIETHART, J. M., *Prosopographia Arsinoitica*, 1 (Vienna, 1980).

DIETZ, K., *Senatus contra principem. Untersuchungen zur senatorischen Opposition gegen Kaiser Maximinus Thrax* (Munich, 1980).

Divjak, J. (ed.), *Oeuvres de Saint Augustin 46B: Lettres 1*–29*. Nouvelle édition* (Paris, Études Augustiniennes, 1987).

Dobrowolski, J., 'The Monastic Complex of Naqlun—Topography of the Site', in P. O. Scholz, *et al.* (eds.), *Orbis Aethiopicus: Studia in honorem Stanislaus Chajnaki* (Albstadt, 1992) 309 ff.

Donau (Cpt.), Le Boeuf (Cpt.), *et al.*, 'Notes et documents sur les voies stratégiques et sur l'occupation militaire du Sud Tunisien à l'époque romaine . . .', *BCTH*, 1903, 272–409.

Dopsch, A., *Naturalwirtschaft und Geldwirtschaft in der Weltgeschichte* (Vienna, 1930).

Drew-Bear, M., *Le Nome Hermopolite: Toponymes et Sites* (ASP 21) (The Scholar's Press, 1979).

Dürr, N., and Bastien, P., 'Trésor de solidi (353–388)', *SNR* 63 (1984) 205–40, pls. 31–9.

Egloff, M., *Kellia: La poterie copte. Quatres siècles d'artisanat et d'échanges en Basse-Égypte* (2 vols; Geneva, 1977).

Eibach, D., *Untersuchungen zum spätantiken Kolonat in der kaiserlichen Gesetzgebung unter besonderer Berücksichtigung der Terminologie* (Diss. Köln, 1977).

Empereur, J.-Y. (ed.), *Commerce et artisanat dans l'Alexandrie hellénistique et romaine.* BCH Supplément 33 (École Française d'Athènes, 1998).

—— and Picon, M., 'Les régions de production d'amphores impériales en Méditerranée orientale', in *ARHE*, 223–48.

Fagerlie, J. M., *Late Roman and Byzantine Solidi Found in Sweden and Denmark.* Numismatic Notes and Monographs No. 157 (ANS, New York, 1967).

El-Fakharani, F., 'Recent Excavations at Marea in Egypt', in *Das römisch-byzantinische Ägypten. Akten des internationalen Symposions 26.–30. September 1978 in Trier* (Aegyptiaca Treverensia Bd.2) (Mainz am Rhein, 1983) 175–86.

Faublée-Urbain, M., 'Magasins collectifs de l'oued el Abiod (Aurès)', *Journal de la Société des Africanistes* 21 (1951) 139–50.

Fikhman, I. F., 'On the Structure of the Egyptian Large Estate in the Sixth Century', in D. H. Samuel (ed.), *Proceedings of the Twelfth International Congress of Papyrology.* ASP 7 (Toronto, 1970) 127–32.

—— 'Quelques considérations sur les données sociales et économiques des papyrus d'Oxyrhynchus d'époque byzantine', *JÖBG* 22 (1973) 16–21.

—— 'Quelques données sur la genèse de la grande propriété foncière à Oxyrhynchus', in J. Bingen *et al.* (eds.), *Le Monde Grec. Hommages à Claire Préaux* (Brussels, 1975) 784–90.

—— 'Le codex fiscal *P. Sorb.* II 69', *CE* 72 (1997) 161–8.

Foss, C., 'Syria in Transition, AD 550–750: An Archaeological Approach', *DOP* 51 (1997) 189–269.

Frankel, R., 'Presses for Oil and Wine in the Southern Levant in the Byzantine Period', *DOP* 51 (1997) 73–84.

FREDERIKSEN, M. W., 'Theory, Evidence and the Ancient Economy', *JRS* 65 (1975) 164–71.

FULFORD, M. G., 'The Long Distance Trade and Communications of Carthage *c.*A.D.400 to *c.*A.D.650', in M. G. Fulford and D. P. S. Peacock, *Excavations at Carthage: The British Mission. i/2: The Avenue du Président Habib Bourguiba Salammbo: The Pottery and Other Ceramic Objects from the Site* (The British Academy, 1984) 255–62.

GASCOU, J., 'La détention collégiale de l'autorité pagarchique dans l'Égypte byzantine', *Byzantion* 42 (1972) 60–72.

—— 'De Byzance à l'Islam: les impôts en Égypte après la conquête arabe', *JESHO* 26 (1983) 97–109.

—— 'Les grands domaines, la cité et l'état en Égypte byzantine', *Travaux et Mémoires* 9 (1985) 1–90.

—— 'Comptabilités fiscales hermopolites du début du VIIe siècle', *Tyche* 1 (1986) 97–117.

—— *Un Codex fiscal hermopolite (P.Sorb. II 69)* (ASP 32) (Atlanta, 1994).

—— and WORP, K., 'Problèmes de documentation Apollinopolite', *ZPE* 49 (1982) 83–95.

—— and MACCOULL, L., 'Le cadastre d'Aphroditô', *Travaux et Mémoires* 10 (1987) 103–58.

GELZER, M., *Studien zur byzantinischen Verwaltung Ägyptens* (Leipzig, 1909).

GERSTINGER, H., 'Gräko-ägyptische Landpachtverträge byzantinischer Zeit aus der Sammlung "Papyrus Erzherzog Rainer" in Wien', *WS* 69 (1956) (= *Festschrift Lesky*) 237–55.

GIARDINA, A., and GRELLE, F., 'La tavola di Trinitapoli: Una nuova costituzione di Valentiniano I', *MEFR(A)* 95 (1983) 249–303.

GOITEIN, S. D., *A Mediterranean Society: The Jewish Communities of the Arab World as Portrayed in the Documents of the Cairo Geniza. 1: Economic Foundations* (Berkeley and Los Angeles, 1967).

GONZALES, M. J., *Plantation Agriculture and Social Control in Northern Peru, 1875–1933* (University of Texas Press, 1985).

GORGES, J.-G., *Les Villas hispano-romaines. Inventaire et problématiques archéologiques* (Paris, 1979).

GREENE, J. A., 'Une reconnaissance archéologique dans l'arrière-pays de la Carthage antique', in A. Ennabli (ed.), *Pour sauver Carthage. Exploration et conservation de la cité punique, romaine et byzantine* (Paris and Tunis, 1992) 195–7.

GREENE, K., 'Technological Innovation and Economic Progress in the Ancient World: M. I. Finley Reconsidered', *EcHR* 53 (2000) 29–59.

GRIERSON, P., 'The Monetary Reforms of 'Abd al-Malik. Their Metrological Basis and their Financial Repercussions', *JESHO* 3 (1960) 241–64.

—— 'Byzantine Coinage as Source Material', in *Proceedings of the XIIIth International Congress of Byzantine Studies, Oxford 5–10 September, 1966* (London, 1967) 317–33.

—— 'The Monetary Reforms of Anastasius and their Economic

Consequences', in A. Kindler (ed.), *The Patterns of Monetary Development in Phoenicia and Palestine in Antiquity. International Numismatic Convention, Jerusalem, 27–31 December, 1963. Proceedings* (Tel-Aviv, 1967) 283–302.

GRIMAL, P., 'Les maisons à tour hellénistiques et romaines', *MEFR* 56 (1939) 28–59.

GROHMANN, A., 'Der Beamtenstab der arabischen Finanzverwaltung in Ägypten in früharabischer Zeit', *Studien zur Papyrologie und antiken Wirtschaftsgeschichte Fr.Oertel ... gewidmet* (Bonn, 1964) 120–34.

GSELL, S., *Les Monuments antiques de l'Algérie*, 2 vols. (Paris, 1901).

—— 'Observations géographiques sur la révolte de Firmus', *Recueil des Notices et Mémoires de la Société Archéologique de Constantine* 36 (1903) 21–46.

GUÉRY, R., MORRISSON, C., and SLIM, H., *Recherches archéologiques franco-tunisiennes à Rougga. 3: Le trésor de monnaies d'or byzantines.* Collection de l'École Française de Rome, 60 (Rome, 1982).

GUILLAND, R., 'Études sur l'histoire administrative de l'empire byzantin. Les titres nobiliaires de la Haute Époque (IVe–VIe siècles)', in *Mélanges Georges Ostrogorsky*. Recueil des travaux de l'Institut d'Études byzantines 8, 2 vols. (Belgrade, 1963) i.117–33.

—— *Titres et fonctions de l'Empire byzantin* (London, 1976).

GUMMERUS, H., *Der römische Gutsbetrieb als wirtschaftlicher Organismus nach den Werken des Cato, Varro und Columella.* Beiträge zur alten Geschichte Bd. 5 (Leipzig, 1906).

HALM, H., *Ägypten nach den mamlukischen Lehensregistern. I Oberägypten und das Fayyūm* (Wiesbaden, 1979).

HAYES, J. W., *Excavations at Saraçhane in Istanbul. II The Pottery* (Princeton, 1992).

IBN ḤAUQAL, *Configuration de la terre (Kitāb Ṣūrat al-'arḍ)*, tr. J. H. Kramers and G. Wiet, 2 vols. (Beirut and Paris, 1964).

HEIL, W., *Der konstantinische Patriziat* (Basel and Stuttgart, 1966).

HENDY, M., *Studies in the Byzantine Monetary Economy c.300–1450* (Cambridge, 1985).

HENGSTL, J., *Private Arbeitsverhältnisse freier Arbeiter in den hellenistischen Papyri bei Diokletian* (Bonn, 1972).

HENNIG, D., 'Die Arbeitsverpflichtungen der Pächter in Landpachtverträgen aus dem Faijum', *ZPE* 9 (1972) 111–31.

HERRMANN, J., *Studien zur Bodenpacht im Recht der graeco-aegyptischen Papyri* (Munich, 1958).

HILTON-SIMPSON, M. W., 'The Influence of its Geography on the People of the Aures Massif, Algeria', *The Geographical Journal* 59 (1922) 19–36.

HIRSCHFELD, Y., 'Ancient Wine Presses in the Park of Aijalon', *IEJ* 33 (1983) 207–18.

—— 'Farms and Villages in Byzantine Palestine', *DOP* 51 (1997) 533–71.

—— and BIRGER-CALDERON, R., 'Early Roman and Byzantine Estates near Caesarea', *IEJ* 41 (1991) 81–111.

Horden, P., and Purcell, N., *The Corrupting Sea: A Study of Mediterranean History* (Blackwell, 2000).
Hornickel, O., *Ehren- und Rangprädikate in den Papyrusurkunden. Ein Beitrag zum römischen und byzantinischen Titelwesen* (Gießen, 1930).
Husson, G., 'Recherches sur les sens du mot *ΠΡΟΑΣΤΙΟΝ* dans le grec d'Égypte', *Recherches de Papyrologie* 4 (1967) 187–200.
Al-Idrīsī, *Description de l'Afrique et de l'Espagne par Edrîsî. Texte arabe publiée pour la première fois . . . avec une traduction, des notes et un glossaire*, ed. R. Dozy and M. J. de Goeje (Leiden, 1866).
Iluk, J., 'The Export of Gold from the Roman Empire to Barbarian Countries from the Fourth to the Sixth Centuries', *Münstersche Beitrage zur antiken Handelsgeschichte*, 4/1 (1985) 79–102.
Israel, Y., 'Ashqelon', *Excavations and Surveys in Israel* 13 (1995) 100–5.
Jacques, F., 'Un exemple de concentration foncière en Bétique d'après le témoignage des timbres amphoriques d'une famille clarissime', *MEFRA* 102/2 (1990) 865–99.
Jacques-Meunié, J., *Greniers citadelles au Maroc*, 2 vols. (Paris, 1951).
Jameson, M. H., Runnels, C. N., and Andel, T. H. van, *A Greek Countryside: The Southern Argolid from Prehistory to the Present Day* (Stanford, Calif., 1994).
Johnson, A. C., and West, L. C., *Byzantine Egypt: Economic Studies* (Princeton, 1949; repr. Amsterdam, 1967).
Johnson, B. L., and Stager, L. E., 'Ashkelon: Wine Emporium of the Holy Land', in S. Gitin (ed.), *Recent Excavations in Israel* (Boston, 1995) 95 ff.
Jones, R. F. J., 'The End of the Roman Countryside in the Iberian peninsula', in R. F. J. Jones, J. H. F. Bloemers, S. L. Dyson, and M. Biddle (eds.), *First Millennium Papers. Western Europe in the First Millennium AD*. BAR International Series 401 (Oxford, 1988) 159–73.
Jones, R. F. J., Keay, S. J., *et al.*, 'The Late Roman Villa of Vilauba and its Context. A First Report on Field-Work and Excavation in Catalunya, North-East Spain, 1978–81', *The Antiquaries Journal* 62 (1982) 245–82.
Jördens, A., 'Arbeitsverträge in der Sammlung des Louvre', *ZPE* 64 (1986) 59–71.
—— 'Teilpachtverträge aus dem Arsinoites', *ZPE* 65 (1986) 107–22.
—— '*Μίσθωσις τῶν ἔργων*. Ein neuer Vertragstyp', in *Proceedings of the XIXth International Congress of Papyrology*, Cairo 2–9 Sept., 1989, 2 vols. (Cairo, 1989) 259–70.
—— *Vertragliche Regelungen von Arbeiten im späten griechischsprachigen Ägypten* (= P.Heid.V) (Heidelberg, 1990).
Kaltenstadler, W., *Arbeitsorganisation und Führungssystem bei den römischen Agrarschriftstellern (Cato, Varro, Columella)*. Quellen und Forschungen zur Agrargeschichte, 30 (Stuttgart, New York, 1978).
—— 'Betriebsorganisation und betriebswirtschaftliche Fragen im Opus Agriculturae von Palladius', in H. Kalcyk, B. Gullath, and A. Graeber (eds.) *Studien zur alten Geschichte Siegfried Lauffer . . . dargebracht*, (Rome, 1986) ii.501–57.

KAPLAN, M., 'Nouvelle de Tibère II sur les "maisons divines"', *Travaux et Mémoires* 8 (1981) 237–45.

—— *Les Hommes et la terre à Byzance du VIe au XIe siècle. Propriété et exploitation du sol.* Byzantina Sorbonensia, 10 (Paris, 1992).

KARAYANNOPOULOS, J., 'Die Chrysoteleia der Iuga', *BZ* 49 (1956) 72–84.

KEENAN, J. G., 'The Names Flavius and Aurelius as Status Designations in Later Roman Egypt. IV. Selected Topics', *ZPE* 13 (1974) 283–304.

—— 'The Provincial Administration of Egyptian Arcadia', *Museum Philologum Londiniense 2*, ed. G. Giangrande (Uithoorn, 1977) 193–202.

—— 'The Case of Flavia Christodote. Observations on *PSI* 76', *ZPE* 29 (1978) 191–209.

—— 'From the Archive of Flavius Eulogius and his Descendants', *ZPE* 34 (1979) 133–8.

—— 'Village and Polis in Byzantine Egypt', in *Proceedings of the Sixteenth International Congress of Papyrology* (Chicago, 1981), 479–85.

—— 'Aurelius Phoibammon, Son of Triadelphus: A Byzantine Land Entrepreneur', *BASP* 17 (1980) 145–54.

—— 'Victor, Son of Psaios, and Three Aphrodito Rent Receipts', *BASP* 20 (1983) 127–34.

—— 'Aurelius Apollos and the Aphrodito Village Élite', in *Atti del XVII Congresso internazionale di papirologia (Napoli, 19–26 maggio, 1983)* (Naples, 1984) 3.957–63.

—— 'The Aphrodito Papyri and Village Life in Byzantine Egypt', *BSAC* 26 (1984) 51–63.

—— 'Village Shepherds and Social Tension in Byzantine Egypt', *YClS* 28 (1985) 245–59.

—— 'Notes on Absentee Landlordism at Aphrodito', *BASP* 22 (1985) 137–69.

—— 'On Languages and Literacy in Byzantine Aphrodito', in *Proceedings of the XVIIIth International Congress of Papyrology, Athens, 25–31 May, 1986* (Athens, 1988) 2.161–7.

KENT, J. P. C., *The Office of the Comes Sacrarum Largitionum,* London University Ph.D. thesis, 1951.

—— 'Gold Coinage in the Later Roman Empire', in R. A. G. Carson and C. H. V. Sutherland (eds.), *Essays in Roman Coinage Presented to Harold Mattingly* (Oxford, 1956) 190–204.

—— *The Roman Imperial Coinage* 8: *The Family of Constantine I A.D.337–364* (London, 1981).

—— *The Divided Empire and the Fall of the Western Parts AD 395–491.* RIC 10 (London, 1994).

KING, C. E., 'Late Roman Silver Hoards in Britain and the Problem of Clipped Siliquae', *The British Numismatic Journal* 51 (1981) 5–31.

—— *Roman Silver Coins.* 5: *Carausius to Romulus Augustus* (London, 1987).

—— 'The Fourth Century Coinage', in *L'"Inflazione" nel quarto secolo d.C. Atti dell'incontro di studio, Roma 1988.* Istituto Italiano di Numismatica, Studi e Materiali 3 (Rome, 1993) 1–87.

KING, G. R. D., 'Settlement Patterns in Islamic Jordan: The Umayyads and their Use of the Land', in *Studies in the History and Archaeology of Jordan*, 4 (Amman, 1992) 369–75.

——LENZEN, C. J., *et al.*, 'Survey of Byzantine and Islamic Sites in Jordan. Third Season Preliminary Report (1982). The Southern Ghōr', *ADAJ* 31 (1987) 439–59.

————and ROLLEFSON, G. O., 'Survey of Byzantine and Islamic Sites in Jordan. Second Season Report, 1981', *ADAJ* 27 (1983) 385–433.

KISS, A., 'Die Goldfunde des Karpatenbeckens vom 5.–10. Jahrhundert', *AArchHung* 38 (1986) 105–45.

KOCH, P., *Die byzantinischen Beamtentitel* (Jena, 1903).

KOLCHIN, P., *Unfree Labor: American Slavery and Russian Serfdom* (Cambridge, Mass., 1987).

KOLENDO, J., 'Les grands domaines en Tripolitaine d'après l'Itinéraire Antonin', in *Actes du IIIe Colloque sur l'histoire et l'archéologie d'Afrique du Nord* (Paris, 1986) 149–61.

KRAUSE, J.-G., *Spätantike Patronatsformen im Westen des römischen Reiches* (Munich, 1987).

KUZIŠČIN, V. I., 'Le caractère de la main-d'oeuvre dans un domaine du IVe siècle d'après le traité de Palladius', in I. Bieżuńska-Malowist and J. Kolendo (eds.), *Actes du colloque sur l'esclavage, Nieborów . . . 1975* (Warsaw, 1979) 239–55.

LAMBTON, A. K. S., *Landlord and Peasant in Persia* (Oxford, 1953).

LANCEL, S., 'L'affaire d'Antoninus de Fussala: pays, choses et gens de la Numidie d'Hippone saisis dans la durée d'une procédure d'enquête épiscopale (Ep.20*)', in *Les Lettres de Saint Augustin découvertes par Johannes Divjak: Communications présentées au colloque du 20 et 21 septembre 1982*. Études Augustiniennes (Paris, 1983) 267–85.

LAPORTE, J.-P., 'Les amphores de Tubusuctu et l'huile de Maurétanie Césarienne', *BCTH* 1976–8, 131–57.

LARTIGUE, R. de, *Monographie de l'Aurès* (Constantine, 1904); excellent photographs.

LEIPOLDT, J., 'Berichte Schenutes über Einfälle der Nubier in Ägypten', *Zeitschrift für Ägyptische Sprache und Altertumskunde* 40/2 (1902/3) 126–40.

LÉVI-PROVENÇAL, E., 'Un nouveau récit de la conquête de l'Afrique du Nord par les Arabes', *Arabica* 1 (1954) 17–49.

LEWICKI, T., and KOTULA, T., 'Un témoignage d'Al-Bakrī et le problème de la ratio privata sévérienne en Tripolitaine', *Ant. Afric.* 22 (1986) 255–71.

LIEBESCHUETZ, W., 'The Pagarch: City and Imperial Administration in Byzantine Egypt', *JJP* 18 (1974) 163–8.

LIOU, B., and TCHERNIA, A., 'L'interprétation des inscriptions sur les amphores Dressel 20', in *Epigrafia della produzione e della distribuzione. Actes de la VIIe Rencontre franco-italienne sur l'épigraphie du monde romain . . . Rome, 5–6 juin, 1992*. Collection de l'École Française de Rome 193 (Rome, 1994) 133–56.

LLOYD, J., 'Forms of Rural Settlement in the Early Roman Empire', in Graeme Barker and John Lloyd (eds.), *Roman Landscapes: Archaeological Survey in the Mediterranean Region*. Archaeological Monographs of the British School at Rome, 2 (London, 1991) 233 ff.

LO CASCIO, E., 'Appunti su Weber "teorico" dell'economia greco-romana', *Fenomenologia e società* 5 (1982) 123–44.

——'Teoria e politica monetaria a Roma tra III e IV d.C.', *SRIT* i. 535–57, 779–801.

——'Weber e il "capitalismo antico"', in M. Losito and P. Schiera (eds.), *Max Weber e le scienze sociali del suo tempo* (Bologna, 1988) 401–21.

——'Prezzo dell'oro e prezzi delle merci', in *L'"Inflazione" nel quarto secolo d.C. Atti dell'incontro di studio, Roma 1988* (Rome, 1993) 155–88.

——'Aspetti della politica monetaria nel IV secolo', *Atti dell'Accademia Romanistica Costantiniana, X Convegno Internazionale* (Naples, 1995) 481–502.

——(ed.), *Terre, proprietari e contadini dell'impero romano. Dall' affitto agrario al colonato tardoantico* (Rome, 1997).

LOMBARD, M., *Études d'économie médiévale. I: Monnaie et histoire d'Alexandre à Mahomet* (Paris, 1971).

LOPUSZAŃSKI, G., 'La transformation du corps des officiers supérieurs dans l'armée romaine du 1e au 3e siècle après J.-C.', *MEFR* 55 (1938) 131–83.

LORENZ, R., 'Circumcelliones—cotopitae—cutzupitani', *Zeitschrift für Kirchengeschichte* 82 (1971) 54–9.

LORINCZ, B., 'Die duces des Provinz Valeria unter Valentinian I (364–375)', *Alba Regia* 15 (1976) 99–105.

LOUIS, A., *Tunisie du Sud: Ksars et villages de crêtes* (Paris, 1975).

LOVE, J., *Antiquity and Capitalism: Max Weber and the Sociological Foundations of Roman Civilization* (London and New York, 1991).

LUZZATTO, M. J., 'P. Vat. gr. 52: trasporto di vino dall'Egitto a Costantinopoli nel VII sec. D.C.', *ZPE* 114 (1996) 153 ff.

MACADAM, H. I., 'Settlements and Settlement Patterns in Northern and Central Transjordania, ca. 550–ca. 750', in G. R. D. King and Averil Cameron (eds.), *The Byzantine and Early Islamic Near East II Land Use and Settlement Patterns* (Princeton, 1994) 49–93.

MCCOAN, J. C., *Egypt as it is* (London, Paris, New York, n.d.).

MACCOULL, L., 'Notes on the Social Structure of Late Antique Aphrodito', *BSAC* 26 (1984) 65–77.

——'Money and People in the Late Antique Hermopolite. BM 1075 and Related Texts', *Tyche* 2 (1987) 99–105.

MAEHLER, H., *Papyri aus Hermupolis (BGU XII)* (Berlin, 1974).

MAIER, J.-L., *Le Dossier du Donatisme*. 1: *Des origines à la mort de Constance II (303–361)*. Texte und Untersuchungen 134 (Berlin, 1987).

MALTBY, L., 'Colonos on Hacienda Picotani', in B. S. Orlove and G. Custred, (eds.), *Land and Power in Latin America: Agrarian Economies and Social Processes in the Andes* (New York, 1980) 99 ff.

MANACORDA, D., 'Testimonianze sulla produzione e il consumo dell'olio tripolitano nel III secolo', *Dialoghi di Archeologia* 9–10 (1976–7) 542–601.

—— 'Prosopografia e anfore tripolitane: nuove osservazioni', in *PCAA II*, 483–500.

MANGO, C., 'Isaurian Builders', in P. Wirth (ed.), *Polychronion: Festschrift Franz Dölger* (Heidelberg, 1966) 358–65.

AL-MAQRĪZĪ, *Livre d'Admonitions et de l'observation pour l'histoire des quartiers et des monuments ou Description historique et topographique de l'Égypte*, tr. in four parts, in *Mémoires publiés par les membres de la mission archéol. française du Caire* (Cairo, 1895–1920).

—— 'Le Traité des Famines de Maqrīzī', tr. G.Wiet, *JESHO* 5 (1962) 1–90.

MARTINEZ-ALIER, J., *Labourers and Landowners in Southern Spain*. St. Antony's Publications No. 4 (London, 1971).

MATTHEWS, J., *Western Aristocracies and Imperial Court A.D.364–425* (Oxford, 1975).

—— *The Roman Empire of Ammianus* (London, 1989).

MATTINGLY, D. J., 'The Olive Boom: Oil Surpluses, Wealth and Power in Roman Tripolitania', *Libyan Studies* 19 (1988) 21–41.

—— 'Megalithic Madness and Measurement: Or how Many Olives Could an Olive Press Press?', *Oxford Journal of Archaeology* 7 (1988) 177–95.

—— 'Maximum Figures and Maximizing Strategies of Oil Production? Further Thoughts on the Processing Capacity of Roman Olive Presses', in M.-C. Amouretti *et al.*, *La Production du vin et de l' huile en Méditerranée*. BCH Supplément 26 (École Française d'Athènes, 1993) 483–98.

—— 'First Fruit? The Olive in the Roman World', in G. Shipley and J. Salmon (eds.), *Human Landscapes in Classical Antiquity: Environment and Culture* (London and New York, 1996) 213–53.

MAYERSON, P., 'The Desert of Southern Palestine according to Byzantine Sources', *Proceedings of the American Philosophical Society* 107 (1963) 160 ff.

—— 'Some Observations on the Negev Archaeological Survey', *IEJ* 46 (1996) 100–7.

MAYET, F., *Les Céramiques sigillées hispaniques. Contribution à l'histoire économique de la Péninsule Ibérique sous l'empire romain* (Paris, 1984).

MAZZA, R., 'Ricerche sul pagarca nell'Egitto tardoantico e bizantino', *Aegyptus* 75 (1995) 169–242.

—— 'P. Oxy. XVI 1911 e i conti annuali dei *pronoetai*', *ZPE* 122 (1998) 161–72.

MAZZARINO, S., *Aspetti sociali del quarto secolo. Richerche di storia tardo-romana* (Rome, 1951).

—— *La fine del mondo antico* (Milan, 1959).

—— *L'impero romano*, 3 vols. (2nd edn.; Rome and Bari, 1976).

MÉNASSA, L., and LAFERRIÈRE, P., *La Sāqia. Technique et vocabulaire de la roue à eau égyptienne*. IFAO, Bibliothèque d'Étude 67 (Cairo, 1974).

METCALF, D. M., 'New Light on the Byzantine Coinage System', *NCirc* 82 (1974) 14–15.

METCALF, D. M., 'The Mint of Thessalonica in the Early Byzantine Period', in *Villes et peuplement dans l'Illyricum protobyzantin*. Coll.de l'École Française de Rome, 77 (Rome, 1984) 111–28.
—— 'The Minting of Gold Coinage in the Fifth and Sixth Centuries and the Gold Currency of Illyricum and Dalmatia', *SEBGC* 65–109.
METCALF, W. E., 'Three Seventh-Century Byzantine Gold Hoards', *ANSMN* 25 (1980) 87–108.
MEUNIER, J., 'L'huilerie romaine de Kherbet Agoub, Périgotville', *Bull. Soc. Hist. Géogr. Sétif* 2 (1941) 35–55 (not seen by me).
MEYER, E., 'Die wirtschaftliche Entwicklung des Altertums', *Jahrbüchern für Nationalökonomie und Statistik IX*, repr. in *Kleine Schriften*, 1[2] (Halle, 1924) 79–168.
MICKWITZ, G., 'Inflation', *Pauly-Wissowa*, Suppl.VI (1935) 127–33.
MILES, G. C., 'On the Varieties and Accuracy of Eighth Century Arab Coin Weights', in M.Avi-Yonah *et al.* (eds.), *L. A. Mayer Memorial Volume (1895–1959)*. Eretz-Israel 7 (Jerusalem, 1964).
MILLAR, F., 'Local Cultures in the Roman Empire: Libyan, Punic and Latin in Roman Africa', *JRS* 58 (1968) 126–34.
—— 'The World of the *Golden Ass*', *JRS* 71 (1981) 63–75.
—— 'Empire and City, Augustus to Julian: Obligations, Excuses and Status', *JRS* 73 (1983) 76–96.
—— *The Roman Near East 31 BC–AD 337* (Cambridge, Mass., and London, 1993).
MITCHELL, S., *Anatolia: Land, Men, and Gods in Asia Minor*. 2: *The Rise of the Church* (Oxford, 1993).
MITTHOF, F., and PAPATHOMAS, A., 'Das Archiv des ἐλαιουργός Sambas', *ZPE* 103 (1994) 53 ff.
MÓCSY, A., 'Der Name Flavius als Rangbezeichnung in der Spätantike', *Akte des IV. Int.Kongresses für griechische und lateinische Epigraphik Wien, 1962* (Vienna, 1964) 257–63.
MOMIGLIANO, A., 'Max Weber and Eduard Meyer: Apropos of City and Country in Antiquity', in *Sesto Contributo alla Storia degli Studi Classici e del Mondo Antico*, 2 vols. (Rome, 1980) 1.285–93.
—— 'After Gibbon's *Decline and Fall*', in *Sesto Contributo*, 1.265–84.
MONNERET DE VILLARD, U., 'La fondazione del Deyr el-Abiad', *Aegyptus* 4 (1923) 156–62.
MONTAGNE, R., *Villages et Kasbas Berbères. Tableau de la vie sociale des Berbères sédentaires dans le sud du Maroc* (Paris, 1930).
MONTEVECCHI, O., *I contratti di lavoro e di servizio nell' Egitto greco, romano e bizantino* (Milan, 1950).
MONTSERRAT, D., FANTONI, G., and ROBINSON, P., 'Varia descripta Oxyrhynchita', *BASP* 31 (1994) 11–80.
MORELLI, F., 'Note a P. Bad. IV 95', *ZPE* 122 (1998) 139–43.
MORI, G., 'La mezzadria in Toscana alla fine del XIX secolo', *Movimento operaio* NS 7 (1955) 479–510.
MORONY, M. G., 'Landholding in Seventh-Century Iraq', in A. L. Udovitch

(ed.), *The Islamic Middle East, 700–1900* (Princeton, 1981) 135–75.

MORRIS, R., 'The Powerful and the Poor in Tenth-Century Byzantium: Law and Reality', *Past and Present* 73 (1976) 3–27.

MORRISSON, C., 'Le trésor byzantin de Nikertai', *RBN* 118 (1972) 29–91.

—— 'La circulation de la monnaie d'or en Afrique à l'époque Vandale. Bilan des trouvailles locales', in H. Huvelin, *et al.* (eds.), *Mélanges de numismatique offerts à Pierre Bastien* (Wetteren, 1987) 325–44.

—— 'Carthage: The Moneta Auri under Justinian I and Justin II, 537–578', *SEBGC* 41–64.

—— 'La monnaie en Syrie byzantine', in J.-M. Dentzer and W. Orthmann (eds.), *Archéologie et histoire de la Syrie. 2: La Syrie de l'époque achéménide à l'avènement de l' Islam*. Schriften zur Vorderasiatischen Archäologie, 1 (Saarbrücken, 1989) 191–204.

—— BRENOT, Cl., *et al.*, *L'Or monnayé. 1: Purification et altérations de Rome à Byzance*. Cahiers Ernest-Babelon 2 (Paris, 1985).

MOSSER, S., *A Bibliography of Byzantine Coin Hoards*. Numismatic Notes and Monographs 67 (New York, 1935).

MUNDELL MANGO, M. C., 'Artistic Patronage in the Roman Diocese of Oriens, 313–641 A.D.' (Oxford University D.Phil., 1984).

—— 'The Origins of the Syrian Ecclesiastical Silver Treasures of the Sixth–Seventh Centuries', in N. Duval and F. Baratte (eds.), *Argenterie romaine et byzantine. Actes de la Table Ronde, Paris 11–13 octobre 1983* (Paris, 1988) 163–84.

AL-NĀBULUSĪ, *Ta'rīkh al-Fayyūm wa-bilādihi* (= B. Moritz, *Description du Faiyoum au VIIme siècle de l'hégire*). Publications de la bibliothèque Khédivale, 11 (Cairo, 1899).

NAHAS, J. F., *Situation économique et sociale du fellah égyptien* (Paris, 1901).

NAUMANN, R., and NAUMANN, F., *Der Rundbau in Aezani, mit dem Preisedikt des Diokletian und das Gebäude mit dem Edikt in Stratonikeia*. Istanbuler Mitteilungen, 10 (Tübingen, 1973).

NEURATH, O., *Antike Wirtschaftsgeschichte* (2nd edn., Leipzig and Berlin, 1918).

NOETHLICHS, K. L., 'Spätantike Wirtschaftspolitik und Adaeratio', *Historia* 34 (1985) 102–16.

NOLLA-BRUFAU, J. M., 'Excavaciones recientes en la Ciudadela de Roses. El edificio bajo-imperial', in T. F. C. Blagg *et al.* (eds.), *Papers in Iberian Archaeology* (BAR International Series, 193/2, 1984) 430–50.

NOLLE, J., *"Nundinas instituere et habere". Epigraphischen Zeugnisse zur Einrichtung und Gestaltung von ländlichen Märkten in Afrika und in der Provinz Asia*. Subsidia Epigraphica 9 (Hildesheim, 1982).

OECONOMIDES-CARAMESSINI, M., and TOURATSOGLOU, J., 'The 1948 Thessaloniki Hoard of Sixth Century Byzantine Gold Coins: A Contribution to the Study of the Mint of Thessaloniki', *NAC* 8 (1979) 289–312.

OECONOMIDÈS, M., and DROSSOYIANNI, P., 'A Hoard of Gold Byzantine Coins from Samos', *RN* 31, ser. 6 (1989) 145–82.

OIKONOMIDÈS, N., 'Silk Trade and Production in Byzantium from the Sixth to the Ninth Century: The Seals of Kommerkiarioi', *DOP* 40 (1986) 33–53.

OLESON, J. P., *Greek and Roman Mechanical Water-Lifting Devices: The History of a Technology* (Toronto, Buffalo, and London, 1984).

OLSEN, W. K., *Seasonality, Transaction Patterns and Real Incomes in Indian Village Foodgrains Markets* (Oxford University M.Phil.,1984).

—— *'Distress Sales' and Exchange Relations in a Rural Area of Rayalaseema, Andhra Pradesh* (Oxford University D.Phil., 1991).

OSTROGORSKY, G., 'Byzantine Cities in the Early Middle Ages', *DOP* 13 (1959) 44–66.

—— *History of the Byzantine State*, tr. Joan Hussey (Oxford, 1968).

OVERBECK, M., *Untersuchungen zum afrikanischen Senatsadel in der Spätantike* (Kallmünz, 1973).

OWEN, R., *The Middle East in the World Economy 1800–1914* (London, 1981).

—— 'The Development of Agricultural Production in Nineteenth-Century Egypt: Capitalism of what Type?', in A. L. Udovitch (ed.), *The Islamic Middle East, 700–1900* (Princeton, 1981) 521–46.

PALME, B., *Das Amt des ἀπαιτητής in Ägypten* (Vienna, 1989).

—— 'Flavius Sarapodorus, *ein agens in rebus* aus Hermupolis', *AfPap*. 40 (1994) 43–68.

—— 'Die *domus gloriosa* des Flavius Strategius Paneuphemos', *Chiron* 27 (1997) 95–125.

—— 'Flavius Strategius und die Apionen', *ZSS* 115 (1998) 289–322.

PALMER, A., *Monk and Mason on the Tigris Frontier: The Early History of Tur 'Abdin* (Cambridge, 1990).

PALOL, P. de, 'Romanos en la Meseta: el Bajo Imperio y la aristocracía agrícola', in *Segovia. Symposium de arqueología romana* (Barcelona, 1977) 297–308.

PANCIERA, S., 'Ancora sulla famiglia senatoria "africana" degli Aradii', *Africa Romana* 4/2 (1986) 547–72.

PANELLA, C., 'Appunti su un gruppo di anfore della prima, media e tarda età imperiale', *Ostia III = Studi Miscellanei* 21 (2) (1973) 460 ff.

—— 'Le anfore tardoantiche: centri di produzione e mercati preferenziali', *SRIT* ii. 251–72.

—— 'Gli scambi nel Mediterraneo occidentale dal IV al VII secolo dal punto di vista di alcune "merci"', *HREB* 129–41.

PEACOCK, D. P. S., and WILLIAMS, D. F., *Amphorae and the Roman Economy: An Introductory Guide* (London and New York, 1986).

—— BEJAOUI, F., and BELAZREG, N., 'Roman Amphora Production in the Sahel Region of Tunisia', in *ARHE* 179–222.

PERICAUD (Lte.), and GAUCKLER, P., 'La turris Maniliorum Arelliorum dans le massif des Matmata', *BCTH* 1905, 259–69.

PFLAUM, H.-G., 'Deux familles sénatoriales des IIe et IIIe siècles', *Journal des Savants*, 1962, 108–22.

PICARD, G.-Ch., 'Deux sénateurs romains inconnus', *Karthago* 4 (1953) 121–35.

PICCIRILLO, M., 'Rural Settlements in Byzantine Jordan', in A. Hadidi (ed.), *Studies in the History and Archaeology of Jordan*, 2 (Department of Antiquities, Amman, 1985) 257–61.

PIGANIOL, A., 'Le problème de l'or au IVe siècle', *Annales d' histoire sociale* 1945 (= *Hommages à Marc Bloch*) 47–53.

——'La crise sociale du Bas-Empire', *Journal des Savants* 1955, 5–15 (review of Mazzarino).

PINTAUDI, R., 'Papiri fiorentini dell'archivio di Heronas', *ZPE* 20 (1976) 233–48.

PLAYFAIR, R. L., *Travels in the Footsteps of Bruce in Algeria and Tunis* (London, 1877).

POINSSOT, L., 'Note concernant Castella (Qasṭîlîa)', *BCTH* 1938–40, 415–19.

POIRIER, J., *Contribution à l'analyse de l'or antique. Application aux monnayages du monde méditerranéen du IIe au XIV siècle* (Thèse de doctorat d'état, l'Université d'Orléans, 1983).

PONCET, J., *La Colonisation et l'agriculture européennes en Tunisie depuis 1881. Étude de géographie historique et économique* (Paris and The Hague, 1961).

PONI, C., *Gli aratri e l'economia agraria nel bolognese dal XVII al XIX secolo* (Bologna, 1963).

PONSICH, M., *Implantation rurale antique sur le Bas-Guadalquivir*, 4 vols. (Madrid and Paris, 1974–91).

POTTIER, H., *Analyse d'un trésor de monnaies en bronze enfoui au VIe siècle en Syrie byzantine* (Brussels, 1983).

PRÉAUX, Cl., 'La fin de l'Antiquité en Égypte', *CE* 24 (1949) 123–32.

PURCELL, N., 'Wine and Wealth in Ancient Italy', *JRS* 75 (1985) 1–19.

RAEPSAET, G., 'Les prémices de la mécanisation agricole entre Seine et Rhin de l'antiquité au 13e siècle', *Annales ESC* 50 (1995) 911–42.

RĀĠIB, Y., 'Contrat d'affermage d'un pressoir à huile en 205/821', *Studia Iranica* 11 (1982) 293–9.

——*Marchands d'étoffes du Fayyoum au IIIe/IXe siècle d'après leurs archives (actes et lettres): Les Actes des Banū ʿAbd al-Mu'min* (Cairo, 1982).

RAMZĪ, M., *al-Qāmūs al-ǧuġrāfī li-l-bilād al-miṣrīyah*, 6 vols. (Cairo, 1953–68).

RATHBONE, D., *Economic Rationalism and Rural Society in Third-Century A.D. Egypt: The Heroninos Archive and the Appianus Estate* (Cambridge, 1991).

REEKMANS, T., *A Sixth Century Account of Hay (P. Iand. inv. 653)* (Brussels, 1962).

REMESAL RODRÍGUEZ, J., 'L'economía oleícola bética: nuevas formas de análisis', *Archivio Español de Arqueología* 50–1 (1978) 87–142; tr. as 'Die Ölwirtschaft in der Provinz Baetica: Neue Former der Analyse', *Saalburg Jb* 38 (1982) 30 ff.

Remesal Rodríguez, J., 'Reflejos económicos y sociales en la producción de ánforas olearias béticas (Dressel-20)', in J. M. Blázquez Martínez (ed.), *Produccion y comercio del Aceite en la Antigüedad. Prímer Congreso Internacional* (Madrid, 1980) 131–53.

——'Transformaciones en la exportación del aceite bético a mediades del siglo III d.C.' in *PCAA II*, 115–31.

Rémondon, R., *Papyrus grecs d'Apollônos Anô* (Documents de fouilles de l'Institut Français d'Archéologie Orientale du Caire, 19) (Cairo, 1953).

——'P. Hamb. 56 et P. Lond. 1419 (notes sur les finances d'Aphroditô du VIe siècle au VIIIe)', *CE* 40 (1965) 401–30.

——'L'Égypte au 5e siècle de notre ère: les sources papyrologiques et leurs problèmes', *Atti dell'XI Congresso Internazionale di Papirologia, Milano 2–8 Settembre 1965* (Milan, 1966) 135–48.

——'Les contradictions de la société égyptienne à l'époque byzantine', *JJP* 18 (1974) 17–32.

Richards, A., 'Land and Labor on Egyptian Cotton Farms, 1882–1940', *Agricultural History* 52 (1978) 503–18.

Ricotti, E. Salza Prina, 'Le ville maritime di Silin (Leptis Magna)', *RPARA* 43 (1970–1) 135–63.

Riley, J. A., 'The Coarse Pottery from Berenice', in J. A. Lloyd (ed.), *Excavations at Sidi Khrebish Benghazi (Berenice)*, 2 (Supplements to Libya Antiqua—V—vol. 2) (Tripoli, n.d.) 91–467.

Rodriguez Almeida, E., 'Vicissitudini nella gestione del commercio dell'olio betico da Vespasiano a Severo Alessandro', in J. H. D'Arms and E. C. Kopff (eds.), *The Seaborne Commerce of Ancient Rome*. Memoirs of the American Academy in Rome, 36 (Rome, 1980).

Rodziewicz, M., 'Alexandria and District of Mareotis', *Graeco-Arabica* 2 (1983) 199–211.

——'Classification of Wineries from Mareotis', in J.-Y. Empereur (ed.), *Commerce et artisanat dans l'Alexandrie hellénistique et romaine*. BCH Suppl. 33 (École Française d'Athènes, 1988) 27–35.

Rogers, G. B., 'Analyse statistique de deux trésors de monnaies romaines en or', *Gallia* 33 (1975) 257–65.

Roll, I., and Ayalon, E., 'Two Large Wine Presses in the Red Soil Regions of Israel', *Palestine Exploration Quarterly* 113 (1981) 111–25.

Rouillard, G., *La vie rurale dans l'Empire byzantin* (Paris, 1953).

Rowlandson, J. L., 'P. Oxy. XLII 3047, VII 1044, and the Land Tax in Kind', *ZPE* 67 (1987) 283–91.

——*Landowners and Tenants in Roman Egypt: The Social Relations of Agriculture in the Oxyrhynchite Nome* (Oxford, 1996).

Ruschenbusch, E., 'Diokletians Währungsreform vom 1.9.301', *ZPE* 26 (1977) 193–210.

Ste. Croix, G. E. M. de, *The Class Struggle in the Ancient Greek World* (London, 1981).

Salmon, G., 'Répertoire géographique de la province du Fayyoûm d'après le *Kitâb Târîkh al-Fayyoûm* d'An-Nâboulsî', *BIFAO* 1 (1901) 29–77.

SALOMON, R. G., 'A Papyrus from Constantinople (Hamburg Inv.No. 410)', *JEA* 34 (1948) 98–108.

SARADI, H., 'Privatization and Subdivision of Urban Properties in the Early Byzantine Centuries: Social and Cultural Implications', *BASP* 35 (1998) 17–43.

SARNOWSKI, T., *Les Représentations de villas sur les mosaïques africaines tardives* (Warsaw, 1978).

SARTRE, M., *Bostra. Des origines à l'Islam.* IFAPO, Bibliothèque archéologique et historique, 117 (Paris, 1985).

—— 'Le peuplement et le développement du Hawran antique à la lumière des inscriptions grecques et latines', in J.-M. Dentzer (ed.), *Hauran I. Recherches archéologiques sur la Syrie du Sud à l'époque hellénistique et romaine. Première partie.* Institut Français d'Arch.du Proche Orient. Bibliothèque arch. et hist. 124 (Paris, 1985) 189–202.

SATO, T., *State and Rural Society in Medieval Islam. Sultans, Muqt's and Fallahun* (Leiden, etc., 1997).

SAUMAGNE, Ch., 'Ouvriers agricoles ou rôdeurs de celliers? Les circoncellions d'Afrique', *Annales d'Histoire Économique et Sociale* 6 (1934) 351–64.

SAUNERON, S., *Villes et légendes d'Égypte.* IFAO (2nd edn., Cairo, 1983).

SCHEIDEL, W., 'Zur Lohnarbeit bei Columella', *Tyche* 4 (1989) 139–46.

—— 'Grain Cultivation in the Villa Economy of Roman Italy', in J. Carlsen (ed.), *Land Use in the Roman Empire* (Rome, 1994) 159 ff.

SCHIØLER, T., *Roman and Islamic Water-Lifting Wheels* (Odense, 1973).

SCHMITT, O., 'Die Buccellarii. Eine Studie zum militärischen Gefolgschaftswesen in der Spätantike', *Tyche* 9 (1994) 147–74.

SCHNEBEL, M., *Die Landwirtschaft im hellenistischen Ägypten* (Munich, 1925).

—— 'An Agricultural Ledger in P. Bad. 95', *JEA* 14 (1928) 34–45.

SCHWARTZ, J., 'La terre d'Égypte au temps de Trajan et d'Hadrien (Archives de Sarapion)', *CE* 34 (1959) 342–56.

SHAW, B. D., 'Under Russian eyes', *JRS* 82 (1992) 216–28.

SHETELIG, H., and FALK, H., *Scandinavian Archaeology* (Oxford, 1937).

SHOSHAN, B., 'From Silver to Copper: Monetary Changes in Fifteenth Century Egypt', *Studia Islamica* 56 (1982) 97–116.

SIJPESTEIJN, P. J., 'Der Pagarch Petterios', *JÖBG* 30 (1981) 57–61.

SLIM, H., 'Le trésor de Rougga et l'expédition musulmane en Ifrikiya', in R. Guéry, C. Morrisson, and H. Slim, *Rougga III: Le trésor de monnaies d'or byzantines.* Collection de l'École Française de Rome, 60 (Rome, 1982).

SMALL, A. M., and FREED, J., 'S. Giovanni di Ruoti (Basilicata). Il contesto della villa tardo-romana', in *SRIT* 3.97–126.

SODINI, J.-P., 'Les églises de Syrie du Nord', in J.-M. Dentzer and W. Orthmann (eds.), *Archéologie et Histoire de la Syrie. 2: La Syrie de l'époque achéménide à l'avènement de l'Islam.* Schriften der vorderasiatischen Archäologie, 1 (Saarbrücken, 1989) 347–72.

Sodini, J.-P., 'La contribution de l'archéologie à la connaissance du monde byzantin (IVe–VIIe siècles)', *DOP* 47 (1993) 139–84.

—— and Tate, G., 'Maisons d'époque romaine et byzantine (IIe–VIe siècles) du Massif Calcaire de Syrie du Nord. Étude typologique', *Actes du IIIe Colloque Apamée de Syrie* (Brussels, 1984) 377–429 + pls.

Spurr, M. S., *Arable Cultivation in Roman Italy c.200 BC– c.AD 100*. JRS Monographs No. 3 (London, 1986).

Steinby, M., 'I senatori e l'industria laterizia urbana', *EOS* i. 227–37.

Stephens, S. A., 'Nine Orders to Pay from Oxyrhynchus', *ZPE* 31 (1978) 145–60.

Stoetzer, W. F. G. J., and Worp, K. A., 'Zwei Steuerquittungen aus London und Wien', *Tyche* 1 (1986) 195–202.

Suchodolski, S., 'Vom Gold zum Silber', *Lagom. Festschrift fur Peter Berghaus zum 60 Geburtstag* . . . (Munich, 1981) 97–104.

Talbi, M., 'Un nouveau fragment de l'histoire de l'occident musulman (62–196/682–812): l'Epopée d'al-Kāhina', *Cahiers de Tunisie* 19 (1971) 19–52, repr. in *Études d'histoire ifrīqiyenne et de civilisation musulmane médiévale* (Tunis, 1982) 125–67.

Tate, G., 'La Syrie à l'époque byzantine: Essai de synthèse', in J. M. Dentzer and W. Orthmann (eds.), *Archéologie et Histoire de la Syrie*. 2: *La Syrie de l'époque achéménide à l'avènement de l'Islam*. Schriften der vorderasiatischen Archäologie, 1 (Saarbrücken, 1989) 97–116.

—— 'Les campagnes de la Syrie du Nord à l'époque proto-byzantine', *HREB* 63–77.

—— *Les Campagnes de la Syrie du Nord du IIe au VIIe siècle. Un exemple d'expansion démographique et économique à la fin de l'antiquité*, vol. 1. IFAPO, Bibliothèque archéologique et historique, 133 (Paris, 1992).

Tchalenko, G., *Villages antiques de la Syrie du Nord. Le Massif de Bélus à l'époque romaine*. Institut Français d'Archéologie de Beyrouth, Bibliothèque . . . 50, 3 vols. (Paris, 1953–8).

Tengström, E., *Donatisten und Katholiken. Soziale, wirtschaftliche und politische Aspekte einer nordafrikanischen Kirchenspaltung* (Göteborg, 1964).

Thompson, E. A., *A Roman Reformer and Inventor, being a new text of the treatise "De Rebus Bellicis" with a translation and introduction* (Oxford, 1952).

Torelli, M., 'Per una storia della classe dirigente di Leptis Magna', *RAL* 28 (1973) 377–410.

Trousset, P., 'Les bornes du Bled Segui. Nouveaux aperçus sur la centuriation romaine du Sud Tunisien', *AntAfr* 12 (1978) 125–77.

—— 'Thiges et la Civitas Tigensium', in *L'Afrique dans l'Occident romain (Ier siècle av.J.C.—IVe siècle ap.J.C.). Actes du colloque organisé par l'École française de Rome sous la patronage de l'Institut National d'Arch. et d'Art de Tunis (Rome, 3–5 dec., 1987)*. Collection de l'École Française de Rome, 134 (Rome, 1990) 143–67.

Udovitch, A. L., 'International Trade and the Medieval Egyptian Countryside', in A. K. Bowman and E. Rogan, *Agriculture in Egypt from Pharaonic to Modern Times*. Proceedings of the British Academy, 96 (Oxford, 1999), 267–85.

VAN HAELST, J., 'De nouvelles archives: Anastasia, propriétaire d'Oxyrhynchus', *CE* 33 (1958) 237–42.

—— 'De nouvelles archives: Anastasia, propriétaire à Oxyrhynchus (II). Le P.Giss.Univ.Bibl.inv.33', *CE* 34 (1959) 292–9.

VÁRADY, L., 'Contributions to the Late Roman Military Economy and Agrarian Taxation', *AArchHung* 14 (1962) 403–38.

VASIĆ, M., and POPOVIĆ, V.,'Un trésor de monnaies d'or de Sirmium', *MEFR(A)* 87 (1975) 425–43.

VASILIEV, A. A., *Justin the First: An Introduction to the Epoch of Justinian the Great* (Cambridge, 1950).

VERA, D., 'Forme e funzioni della rendita fondiaria nella tarda antichità', *SRIT* 1. 367–447.

VELKOV, V., 'Les campagnes et la population rurale en Thrace au IVe–VIe siècle', *Byzantino Bulgarica* 1 (1962) 31–66.

VILLENEUVE, F., 'L'économie rurale et la vie des campagnes dans le Hauran antique (Ier siècle av.J.-C.–VIIe siècle ap.J.-C.). Une approche', in J. M. Dentzer (ed.), *Hauran I. Recherches archéologiques sur la Syrie à l'époque hellénistique et romaine. Première partie*. Institut Français d'Archéologie du Proche Orient, Bibliothéque arch. et hist., 124 (Paris, 1985), 63–136.

VOGLER, C., *Constance II et l'administration impériale* (Strasbourg, 1979).

VOLPE, G., *Contadini, pastori e mercanti nell' Apulia tardoantica* (Bari, 1996).

VRYONIS, Sp., 'An Attic Hoard of Byzantine Gold Coins (668–741) from the Thomas Whittemore Collection and the Numismatic Evidence for the Urban History of Byzantium', in *Mélanges Georges Ostrogorsky* (Belgrad, 1963) 1.291–300.

WARD-PERKINS, J. B., LITTLE, J. H., and MATTINGLY, D. J., 'Town Houses at Ptolemais, Cyrenaica: A Summary Report of Survey and Excavation Work in 1971, 1978–1979', *Libyan Studies* 17 (1986) 109–53.

WASZYŃSKI, S., *Die Bodenpacht: agrargeschichtliche Papyrusstudien* (Leipzig, 1905).

WEBER, M., 'Agrarverhältnisse im Altertum', repr. in *Gesammelte Aufsätze*, 1–288.

—— *Wirtschaftsgeschichte. Abriß der universalen Sozial- und Wirtschaftsgeschichte*, ed., J. F. Winckelmann (3rd edn., Berlin, 1958).

—— *Economy and Society: An Outline of Interpretive Sociology*, ed. G. Roth and C. Wittich, 2 vols. (Calif., 1978).

—— *Die römische Agrargeschichte in ihrer Bedeutung für das Staats- und Privatrecht*, ed. J. Deininger. Max Weber Gesamtausgabe, 2 (orig. 1891; Tübingen, 1986).

WEST, L. C., and JOHNSON, A. C., *Currency in Roman and Byzantine Egypt* (Amsterdam, 1967).

WICKHAM, C., 'Considerazioni conclusive', in R. Francovich and G. Noyé (eds.), *La storia dell' alto medioevo italiano (VI–X secolo) alla luce dell' archeologia* (Florence, 1994) 741–59.

——'Early Medieval Archaeology in Italy: The Last Twenty Years', *Archeologia Medievale* 26 (1999) 7–20.

WILCKEN, U., *Griechische Ostraka aus Aegypten und Nubien*, 2 vols. (Leipzig, 1899).

WIPSZYCKA, E., *Les Ressources et les activités économiques des églises en Égypte du IVe au VIIIe siècle*. Papyrologia bruxellensia 10 (Brussels, 1972).

WORP, K., 'Flavius Strategius: some notes', *ZPE* 56 (1984) 113–16.

——'Studien zu spätgriechischen, koptischen und arabischen Papyri', *BSAC* 26 (1984) 99–107.

WORTMANN, D., 'Griechische ostraka aus Abu Mena', *ZPE* 8 (1971) 41–69.

YOUTIE, H. C., 'P.Mich.inv.335 verso. A Summary Register of Wheat Land', *ZPE* 32 (1978) 237–40.

ZEVI, F., and TCHERNIA, A., 'Amphores de Byzacène au Bas-Empire', *AntAfr* 3 (1969) 173-214.

FURTHER BIBLIOGRAPHY

Azzarello, G., 'P. Oxy. XVI 2039 e la nascita della *domus gloriosa* degli Apioni', *ZPE* 155 (2006) 207–28.

Bagnall, R. S. (ed.), *Egypt in the Byzantine World, 300–700* (Cambridge, 2007).

—— and Worp, K. A., *Chronological Systems of Byzantine Egypt*, 2nd edn. (Leiden and Boston, Mass., 2004).

Balmelle, C., *Les Demeures aristocratiques d'Aquitaine: Société et culture de l'Antiquité tardive dans le Sud-Ouest de la Gaule* (Bordeaux and Paris, 2001).

Banaji, J., 'State and Aristocracy in the Economic Evolution of the Late Empire', in E. Lo Cascio and D. Rathbone (eds.), *Production and Public Powers in Classical Antiquity*. Cambridge Philological Society, Suppl. vol. 26 (Cambridge, 2000) 92–99.

—— 'Precious Metal Coinages and Monetary Expansion in Late Antiquity', in F. De Romanis and S. Sorda (eds.), *Dal* Denarius *al* Dinar: *l'Oriente et la moneta romana*. Istituto Italiano di Numismatica, Studi e Materiali 12 (Rome, 2006) 265–303.

—— 'Mickwitz's Modernism: The Writings of 1932–36', in M. Kajava (ed.), *Gunnar Mickwitz nella storiografia europea tra le due guerre*. Acta Instituti Romani Finlandiae, vol. 34 (Rome, 2007) 11–22.

—— 'The Identity of Šahrālānyōzān in the Greek and Middle Persian Papyri from Egypt', in P. Sijpesteijn (ed.), *Documents and the History of the Medieval Islamic World* (Leiden, etc., 2008).

Bijovsky, G., 'A Hoard of Byzantine Solidi from Bet She'an in the Umayyad period', *RN* 158 (2002) 161–227.

Bland, R. 'The Changing Patterns of Hoards of Precious-Metal Coins in the Late Empire', *AnTard* 5 (1997) 29–55.

Bonifay, M., 'La fin du grand commerce méditerranéen en royaume franc? Le témoignage de la céramique', *Dossiers d'Archeologie*, n° 256 (2000) 36–9.

—— *Études sur la céramique romaine tardive d'Afrique*. BAR International Series 1301 (Oxford, 2004).

Bowden, W., Lavan, L., and Machado, C., *Recent Research on the Late Antique Countryside* (Leiden, 2003).

Bowes, K., ' "Une Coterie Espagnole Pieuse": Christian Archaeology and Christian Communities in Fourth- and Fifth-Century Hispania', in K. Bowes and M. Kulikowski (eds.), *Hispania in Late Antiquity: Current Perspectives*. The Medieval and Early Modern Iberian World 24 (Leiden and Boston, 2005) 189–258.

Bowes, K., and Gutteridge, A., 'Rethinking the Later Roman Landscape', *JRA* 18 (2005) 405–13.

Brown, P., *Poverty and Leadership in the Later Roman Empire* (Hanover, New Hampshire, 2002).

—— *The Rise of Western Christendom: Triumph and Diversity 200–1000 A.D.*, second edition (Blackwell, 2002).

Campbell, B., *The Writings of the Roman Land Surveyors: Introduction, Text, Translation and Commentary*. Journal of Roman Studies Monograph 9 (London, 2000).

Chavarría Arnau, A., 'Interpreting the Transformation of Late Roman Villas: The Case of *Hispania*', in N. Christie (ed.), *Landscapes of Change: Rural Evolutions in Late Antiquity and the Early Middle Ages* (Aldershot, 2004) 67–102.

—— 'Villas in Hispania during the Fourth and Fifth Centuries', in Bowes and Kulikowski (eds.), *Hispania in Late Antiquity*, 519–52.

Christol, M., 'Marchands gaulois et grand commerce de l'huile de Bétique dans l'Occident romain. Quelques données provenant des amphores', in Rivet and Sciallano, *Vivre, produire et échanger*, 325–34.

Crone, P., 'Kavād's Heresy and Mazdak's Revolt', *Iran* 29 (1991) 21–42, repr. in P. Crone, *From Kavād to al-Ghazālī. Religion, Law and Political Thought in the Near East, c.600–c.1100* (Aldershot, 2005).

De Robertis, F. M., 'Il tramonto delle corporazioni da Teodosio II a Giustiniano', *Orpheus* 2 (1955) 45–54.

Delogu, P., 'Longobardi e romani: altre congetture', in S. Gasparri and P. Cammarosano (eds.), *Langobardia* (Udine, 1990) 111–67.

—— 'La fine del mondo antico e l'inizio del medioevo', in R. Francovich and G. Noyé (eds.), *La storia dell' Alto Medioevo italiano (VI–X secolo) alla luce dell' archeologia* (Florence, 1994) 7–29.

—— 'Alle origini della "tesi Pirenne"', *Bullettino dell'Istituto Storico Italiano per il Medio Evo* 100 (1995–1996) 297–325.

Depeyrot, G., 'Economy and Society', in N. Lenski (ed.), *The Cambridge Companion to the Age of Constantine* (Cambridge, 2006) 226–52.

Drexhage, H.-J., Konen, H., and Ruffing, K., 'Die Wirtschaft der römischen Kaiserzeit in der modernen Deutung: Einige Überlegungen', in K. Strobel (ed.), *Die Ökonomie des Imperium Romanum. Strukturen, Modelle und Wertungen im Spannungsfeld von Modernismus und Neoprimitivismus*. Pharos Bd. xvii. (St Katharinen, 2002) 1–66.

Étienne, R., and Mayet, F., *L'Huile hispanique*. Trois Clés de l'Économie de l'Hispanie Romaine, 3 (Paris, 2004).

Foote, R., 'Commerce, Industrial Expansion, and Orthogonal Planning: Mutually Compatible Terms in Settlements of Bilad al-Sham during the Umayyad Period', *Mediterranean Archaeology* 13 (2000) 25–38.

Foraboschi, D., 'Moneta ed economia nel tardo-antico', *RIN* 100 (1999) 173–99.

Fournet, J.-L., *Hellénisme dans l'Égypte du VIe siècle. La bibliothèque et l'oeuvre de Dioscore d'Aphrodité*, 2 vols. MIFAO 115 (Cairo, 1999).

—— 'Le Système des intermédiaires dans les reçus fiscaux byzantins et ses implications chronologiques sur le dossier de Dioscore d'Aphrodité', *APF* 46 (2000) 233–46.

FULGHUM, M. M., and HEINTZ, F., 'A Hoard of Early Byzantine Glass Weights from Sardis', *AJN* 10 (1998) 105–20.

GASCOU, J., 'Les Pétitions privées', in D. Feissel and J. Gascou (eds.), *La Pétition à Byzance*. Centre de Recherche d'Histoire et Civilisation de Byzance, Monographies 14 (Paris, 2004) 93–103.

GIARDINA, A., 'Esplosione di tardoantico', *Studi Storici* 40 (1999) 157–80.

—— 'Tardoantico: Appunti sul dibattito attuale', *Studi Storici* 45 (2004) 41–6.

—— 'Mazzarino e Rostovtzeff', in A. Marcone (ed.), *Rostovtzeff e l'Italia*. Incontri Perugini di Storia della Storiografia Antica e sul Mondo Antico 9 (Naples, 1999) 115–29.

GONIS, N., 'Studies on the Aristocracy of Late Antique Oxyrhynchus', *Tyche* 17 (2002) 85–97.

GUTSFELD, A., 'Zur Wirtschaftsmentalität nichtsenatorischer provinzialer Oberschichten: Aemilia Pudentilla und ihre Verwandten', *Klio* 74 (1992) 250–68.

HALDON, J. F., 'The Resources of Late Antiquity', in C. Robinson (ed.), *New Cambridge History of Islam. Vol. 1: The Formation of the Islamic World, Sixth to Eleventh Century* (Cambridge, 2008).

HARL, K. W., *Coinage in the Roman Economy, 300 B.C. to A.D. 700* (Baltimore, 1996).

HARRIS, W. V., 'A Revisionist View of Roman Money', *JRS* 96 (2006) 1–24.

HECK, G., 'Gold Mining in Arabia and the Rise of the Islamic State', *JESHO* 42 (1999) 364–95.

HICKEY, T., 'Aristocratic Landholding and the Economy of Byzantine Egypt', in R. S. Bagnall (ed.), *Egypt in the Byzantine World* (Cambridge, 2007).

HORSNÆS, H. W., 'New Gold Hoards from Bornholm with Rare Types of Valentinian III *solidi*', *RN* 158 (2002) 131–8.

IVANIŠEVIĆ, V., and KONDIJANOV, J., 'Le trésor de Sekulica', RN^6 34 (1992) 77–99.

KEENAN, J. G., 'Egypt', in A. Cameron, B. Ward-Perkins, and M. Whitby (eds.), *The Cambridge Ancient History. Vol. XIV: Late Antiquity: Empire and Successors, A.D. 425-600* (Cambridge, 2000) 612–37.

KELLY, C., *Ruling the Later Roman Empire* (Cambridge, Mass., 2004).

KHALEK, N. A., *From Byzantium to Early Islam: Studies on Damascus in the Umayyad Era* (Diss. Princeton University, 2006).

KINGSLEY, S., and DECKER, M. (eds.), *Economy and Exchange in the East Mediterranean during Late Antiquity* (Oxford, 2001).

KOLESNIKOV, A., 'The Quantity of Silver Coinage and Levels of Revenues in Late Sasanian Iran', in R. Gyselen and M. Szuppe (eds.), *Matériaux pour l'histoire économique du monde iranien*. Studia Iranica 21 (Paris, 1999) 123–30.

LANIADO, A., *Recherches sur les notables municipaux dans l'Empire protobyzantin*. Centre de Recherche d'Histoire et Civilisation de Byzance, Monographies 13 (Paris, 2002).

LECKER, M., 'The Estates of ʿAmr b. al-ʿĀṣ in Palestine: Notes on a New Negev Arabic Inscription', *BSOAS* 52 (1989) 24–37.

LEFORT, J., MORRISSON, C., and SODINI, J.-P. (eds.), *Les Villages dans l'Empire byzantin (IVᵉ–XVᵉ siècle)* (Paris, 2005).

LIGHTFOOT, C. S., 'Byzantine Anatolia: Reassessing the Numismatic Evidence', *RN* 158 (2002) 229–39.

LOSEBY, S. T., 'The Mediterranean Economy', in P. Fouracre (ed.), *The New Cambridge Medieval History. Vol. I: c.500–c.700* (Cambridge, 2005) 605–38.

MCCORMICK, M., 'Bateaux de vie, bateaux de mort. Maladie, commerce, transports annonaires et le passage économique du Bas-Empire au Moyen Âge', in *Morfologie sociali e culturali in Europa fra tarda antichità e alto medioevo*. Settimane di Studio del Centro Italiano di Studi sull' Alto Medioevo 45, 2 vols. (Spoleto, 1998) i. 35–118.

—— *Origins of the European Economy: Communications and Commerce, A.D. 300–900* (Cambridge, 2001).

MACCOULL, L., 'P. Lond. Copt. I 1077: Taxes in Money in Seventh-Century Egypt', *Orientalia Christiana Periodica* 67 (2001) 385–436.

MAGNESS, J., *The Archaeology of the Early Islamic Settlement in Palestine* (Winona Lake, Ind., 2003).

MARRA, R., *Capitalismo e anticapitalismo in Max Weber. Storia di Roma e sociologia del diritto nella genesi dell'opera weberiana* (Bologna, 2002).

MAUNÉ, S., *Les Campagnes de la cité de Beziérs dans l'Antiquité (partie nord-orientale) (IIe s. av. J.-C. – VIe s. ap. J.-C.)*. Archéologie et histoire romaine 1 (Montagnac, 1998).

MAZZA, R., *L'archivio degli Apioni. Terra, lavoro e proprietà nell'Egitto tardoantico* (Bari, 2001).

—— 'Donne, terra e amministrazione nell'Egitto bizantino', in H. Melaerts and L. Mooren (eds.), *Le Rôle et le Statut de la Femme en Égypte hellénistique, romaine et byzantine* (Paris, etc., 2002) 193–208.

METCALF, D. M., 'Monetary Recession in the Middle Byzantine Period: The Numismatic Evidence', *NC* 161 (2001) 111–55.

METLICH, M., 'Ein Komplex Alexandriner 12 Nummi des 6. Jahrhunderts n.Chr.', *NZ* 108/109 (2001) 53–9.

MITCHELL, S., *A History of the Later Roman Empire, AD 284-641: The Transformation of the Ancient World* (Oxford, 2007).

MÖLLER, C., 'Die *mercennarii* in der römischen Arbeitswelt', *ZSS, Rom. Abt.*, 110 (1993) 296–330.

MORONY, M., 'Economic Boundaries? Late Antiquity and Early Islam', *JESHO* 47 (2004) 166–94.

MORRISSON, C. (ed.), *Le Monde byzantin, t.1. L'Empire romain d'Orient 330–641* (Paris, 2004).

NOESKE, H.-C., *Münzfunde aus Ägypten,1. Die Münzfunde des ägyptischen Pilgerzentrums Abu Mina und die Vergleichsfunde aus den Dioecesen Aegyptus und Oriens vom 4.–8. Jhr. N.Chr.*, 3 vols. SFA 12 (Mann, 2000).

OUZOULIAS, P., and VAN OSSEL, P., 'Dynamiques du peuplement et formes de l'habitat tardif: le cas de l'Île-de-France', in P. Ouzoulias *et al.*, *Les Campagnes de la Gaule à la fin de l'Antiquité.* Actes du Colloque Montpellier, 11–14 mars 1998 (Antibes, 2001) 147–72.

PALME, B., *Dokumente zu Verwaltung und Militär aus dem spätantiken Ägypten* (= CPR XXIV) (Vienna, 2002).

—— 'Flavius Olympius, der "kaiserliche Hofrat"', in F. Beutler and W. Hameter (eds.), *"Eine ganz normale Inschrift" . . . und Ähnliches zum Geburstag von Ekkehard Weber* (Vienna, 2005) 461–76.

PHILLIPS, M., 'Currency in Seventh-Century Syria as a Historical Source', *BMGS* 28 (2004) 13–31.

POETHKE, G., *Griechische Papyrusurkunden spätrömischer und byzantinischer Zeit aus Hermupolis Magna* (= BGU XVII). APF Beiheft 7 (Leipzig, 2001).

POLLARD, N., 'The Chronology and Economic Condition of Late Roman Karanis: An Archaeological Reassessment', *Journal of the American Research Center in Egypt* 35 (1998) 147–62.

RIVET, L., and SCIALLANO, M., *Vivre, produire et échanger: reflets méditerranéens. Mélanges offerts à Bernard Liou.* Archéologie et histoire romaine 8 (Montagnac, 2002).

ROSAFIO, P., *Studi sul colonato* (Bari, 2002).

RUGGINI, L., *Economia e società nell'"Italia annonaria": Rapporti fra agricoltura e commercio dal IV al VI secolo d.C.*, 2nd rev. edn. (Bari, 1995).

SAGUÌ, L., 'Roma, i centri privilegiati e la lunga durata della tarda antichità. Dati archeologici dal deposito di VII secolo nell' esedra della Crypta Balbi', *Archeologia Medievale* 29 (2002) 7–42.

SARRIS, P., 'The Origins of the Manorial Economy: New Insights from Late Antiquity', *EHR* 119 (2004) 279–311.

—— *Economy and Society in the Age of Justinian* (Cambridge, 2006).

SCHILBACH, E., 'Glasgewichte für follis-prägungen aus der Zeit des Kaisers Justinos II', *BZ* 98 (2005) 495–501.

SERRAO, F., *Impresa e responsabilità a Roma nell'età commerciale. Forme giuridiche di un economia-mondo* (Pisa, 1989).

SHAW, B. D., 'Who were the Circumcellions?', in A. H. Merrills (ed.), *Vandals, Romans and Berbers: New Perspectives on Late Roman North Africa* (Aldershot, 2004) 227–58.

SIJPESTEIJN, P., 'The Arab Conquest of Egypt and the Beginning of Muslim Rule', in R. S. Bagnall (ed.), *Egypt in the Byzantine World* (Cambridge, 2007).

VERA, D., 'I silenzi di Palladio e l'Italia: Osservazioni sull'ultimo agronomo romano', *Antiquité Tardive* 7 (1999) 283–97.

—— '*Massa fundorum.* Forme della grande proprietà e poteri della città in Italia fra Costantino e Gregorio Magno', *MEFRA* 111 (1999) 991–1025.

WALMSLEY, A., 'Production, Exchange and Regional Trade in the Islamic East Mediterranean: Old Structures, New Systems?', in I. L. Hansen and C. Wickham (eds.), *The Long Eighth Century*. The Transformation of the Roman World, Vol. XI (Leiden, etc., 2000) 265–343.

WARD-PERKINS, B., 'Continuitists, Catastrophists, and the Towns of Post-Roman Northern Italy', *PBSR* 65 (1997) 157–76.

WHITTAKER, C. R., and GARNSEY, P., 'Rural Life in the Later Roman Empire', in A. Cameron and P. Garnsey (eds.), *The Cambridge Ancient History. Vol. XIII: The Late Empire, A.D. 337–425* (Cambridge, 1998) 277–311.

WICKHAM, C., 'Un pas vers le Moyen Âge? Permanences et mutations', in P. Ouzoulias *et al.*, *Les Campagnes de la Gaule à la fin de l'Antiquité*, 555–67.

WICKHAM, C., *Framing the Early Middle Ages: Europe and the Mediterranean 400–800* (Oxford, 2005).

WILSON, A., 'Machines, Power and the Ancient Economy', *JRS* 92 (2002) 1–32.

—— 'Cyrenaica and the Late Antique Economy', *Ancient West and East* 3/1 (2004) 143–54.

ZUCKERMAN, C., *Du village à l'Empire: Autour du Registre fiscal d'Aphroditô (525/526)*. Centre de Recherche d'Histoire et Civilisation de Byzance, Monographies 16 (Paris, 2004).

INDEX

With Pike and Musket

By the same author:

PRACTICAL WARGAMING

C. F. WESENCRAFT

WITH PIKE AND MUSKET

The Elmfield Press

Photographs by Mr V. Rooker of Morpeth

The author wishes to thank the Curator of the John George Joicey Museum, Newcastle upon Tyne, for allowing him to photograph armour and weapons

ISBN 0 7057 0059 3

A Morley Book published 1975 by
The Elmfield Press, Elmfield Road, Morley
Yorkshire LS27 oNN in association
with Shire Publications Ltd., Princes Risborough, Bucks

Designed by Bernard Crossland Associates

Printed in Great Britain by
Hazell Watson & Viney Ltd,
Aylesbury, Bucks

Contents

List of plates

Between pages 56 and 57

1 | *Introduction*

This book deals with the art and science of wargaming.

A wargame is a contest between two sides, either with a single player controlling both armies, or, with one player on each side (or even a number of players competing as two teams). It is a test of skill, linked to the element of chance, played using readily understandable rules in a known period of history.

H. G. Wells's claim that wargaming is 'Chess with a thousand pieces' is, therefore, correct only in outline. For chess is a mathematician's attempt to reduce warfare to a table-top exercise whilst wargaming as described in this book deals with the historian's interpretation.

In chess the battle is fought over a flat featureless landscape, void of trees and houses, rivers and hills; in short, an impossibly barren plain, equal in length and depth. At the beginning of the game, the opposing armies, one the mirror image of the other, entirely filling their respective baselines, glare at one another across a maze of alternating coloured squares. Even the pieces are stylized. Each king is accompanied by his queen, who proves to be the most active and vicious fighter on the field. The church is well represented, as are the nobility. Mobile towers guard the flanks. The rank and file are massed in the foreground, ready to bear the brunt of the assault and counter-attack, never prepared to retreat.

Being stylized, not a weapon is to be seen. The battle is set within the shades of history, at any imaginary date. Firepower is ignored. The attacker always destroys his victim. The battle is always fought with the same single objective: the elimination of the enemy king.

The modern wargamer has attempted to break away entirely from the rigid unreality of chess and to create a new approach to the table game. He is first and foremost an amateur military historian. With the history of warfare covering the existence of organized man, the wargamer must limit himself to one short period during any single game. Within his chosen era he will be able to study the type of weapons that were available to the warriors then living, and how these weapons were adapted to their requirements. The weapons governed the formations, thus men with missiles tended to be less densely grouped than those armed solely with the weapons of the mêlée.

Having divided the types of troops by arms, the wargamer now delves into the details of dress of the contestants. The model soldiers are bought direct from the mould and so require painting to as accurate a degree as desired in order to distinguish them both from their neighbours and their enemies.

The squared chess-board is put away and replaced by a table top of any size and proportion. Ideally it should be about twice as long as it is wide, the larger the better, with the limitation being the fact that one must be able to reach all the troops placed upon its surface. The empty table top must now be embellished with hills and valleys, rivers and woods, roads, villages, hedges, and walls.

A variety of possibilities emerge when it comes to designing scenery. Some wargamers go so far as to build a permanent landscape suitable for a single battle, as detailed as any used as background material by model railway enthusiasts. Others prefer to make 2- or 3-ft (600- or 900-mm) squares of built-up sections of landscape which may be fitted together to form many different battlefields. Some players go in for a very much simplified method of creating hills, using shaped blocks of foam rubber, 1½-in (40-mm) thick, painted green and placed directly on to the green table top. These may not look very natural, but they are easily stored and being flat-topped, the model soldiers are capable of standing upon them. Perhaps the most natural-looking, yet easily made and stored scenery is created by placing books on the table in the position of the desired hills and then laying cardboard slopes over them. When all is ready, a green cloth is draped over the table and the field is awaiting its woods, etc.

We now have our armies and our battlefields; we require the rules of play. These must express the capabilities and limitations of the weapons and the men of the age. They must be both playable and understandable by all the players. So often, in an enthusiasm for realism, the extreme detail makes the game virtually impossible to play. The secret of rule-writing lies in the ability to be able to take a detail of movement, fire effect, etc., study it, stretch it to its ultimate in an effort to cover all possibilities and then to *simplify* it until a playable rule emerges. So often this simplification is ignored.

The period chosen for study in this book is that covered by the use of the firelock musket. Even in the reign of Henry VIII, the bow and arrow as the main infantry missile weapon was in decline, thanks to the lack of practice among the yeomen. A new type of weapon was beginning to appear: the hand gun. At first a mere trickle (it would never catch on, of course), gradually it gained in popularity as the years went by and as soldiers returned from the continent, singing its praises. It was fairly cheap to produce, it made a great deal of noise, frightening those who had never met it. It was the perfect mate for the then king of the infantry weapons, the pike. It was lower down the social scale, of course. The higher born and bigger men trailed the pike, their lesser brethren shouldered the musket.

The English had never been great cavalrymen in comparison with their enemies and sometimes allies in Europe. In most of the great battles since the development of the longbow they had preferred to fight on foot. Only when fighting against less rich nations such as the Scots and the Irish did they attempt to use their cavalry arm. When they did they so often found that their horses were too heavy for the type of country in which they found themselves fighting.

Nor did the English possess the vast hordes of men that were so common on foreign fields. Many a fight was fought in Britain and given the name of 'battle', between armies whose combined strength hardly equalled more than one or two Swiss or German *tercios* when the pike was at its zenith. These forests of pike, flaunting dozens of gay banners, were protected by smaller blocks of missile men, operating either between the pike squares or even being attached to them in front or on their flanks. Various nations tried different methods of combining the fire-power with the mêlée power. The British watched and noted. Expeditions were sent to assist allies, their leaders learning their trade under the smoke of the guns. Some, like Sir Philip Sidney, died. Others returned and were sent to practice their newly learned skills upon the Irish.

As it is the weapon that governs the battle formation, we will commence by examining each instrument in turn in an effort to discover its strengths and weaknesses. We will see how their uses changed in the hands of various captains. We will consider the formations themselves and translate them into wargame terms, so arriving at the numbers and types required for fighting various battles over a hundred years and more of British history.

Having armed the reader with a working knowledge of the weapons and their uses, the next section of the book presents suggested rules of play which will enable the table-top general to manoeuvre and fight in the manner of Charles I, Rupert, Essex, Cromwell, and the rest.

The final section of the book is devoted to allowing the reader the opportunity of coming to grips with many of the military problems that faced these men. Twenty-seven battles have been chosen from the period and a brief description of each action is given. The reader is then told the number and types of troops actually engaged in each battle. These numbers are translated into wargame figures, so giving the players their number of pieces. A wargame map shows the starting lines of the opposing forces and the number of units on either side. The reader is now fully equipped. Let the battle commence.

2 *The weapons*

Before one is able to produce a set of rules governing the use of weapons on the wargame table, it is essential to examine the variety of types of weapon in use during the period in question, to study their reliability, their range and accuracy, if they are missile weapons, and their effect upon tactics. One should understand the reasons for their invention and be able to trace their development, how and why they replaced existing weapons and why they themselves were made redundant.

Throughout our chosen period, the main weapons in use were the bow, the cannon, the musket, the pike, the halberd, the sword, and the lance. The first three were missile weapons, the rest were used in the close-quarter mêlée. We will examine each in turn.

The bow

Falkirk, Halidon Hill, Crècy, Poitiers, Shrewsbury, Agincourt: a string of English battles linked by the whisper of the grey goose feather. Success piled upon success. Armour improved, yet still the arrow reigned supreme. Down through the bloody Wars of the Roses—Towton, Tewkesbury, Bosworth—on to Flodden. Then suddenly the clouds of smoke drifting over the field of Pinkie, masking a mixture of bullets and arrows; the musket had arrived!

Surely this noisy, inaccurate, and most unreliable weapon, only capable of being fired about once every three minutes (providing the weather was good) would never take the place of the Queen of Death, the longbow. This longbow was its equal in range, was far more accurate, and in the hands of a trained man was capable of firing six aimed arrows in a minute. And yet it is difficult to realize that by the end of the sixteenth century the English had virtually dispensed with the bow in favour of the new mechanical contrivance. Why?

To achieve perfection with the longbow, constant practice was necessary and this discipline had been sadly neglected. After Flodden, Britain enjoyed comparative peace, there being no major battles on English soil between 1513 and 1640, when the Scots attacked across the ford at Newburn on Tyne. English soldiers enlisted in foreign armies in order to gain experience of war. On the continent, the longbow had never been a popular weapon, so here the musket rapidly came into prominence. It became the fashionable weapon and the fashion crossed the Channel in the hands of returning soldiers. The trained bands were armed with them. The bow might be good enough for an Irish peasant, but real soldiers carried muskets!

The cannon

The first gun appeared in Europe round about 1300 and was used to fire arrows! At first sight this may appear extraordinary to us, but upon deeper reflection, the arrow would have been the obvious missile for our ancestors to have fired. After all, the Romans had fired large arrows in their day and the arrow was the weapon of the light infantry. So what would be more natural. However, within a very few years, ball shot, cast in metal or hewn from stone, superseded the arrow.

In 1346, Edward III used cannon at the seige of Calais. By the turn of the thirteenth century cannon were common on most battlefields, growing in size as well as numbers. The noise and smoke must have been spectacular, even if the effect was negligible. The barrel was a mere unrifled tube into which was placed an ill-fitting projectile. Thus the gun was hopelessly inaccurate, prone to misfire, often self-destructive and devoid of any method of recoil, so making every shot a ranging shot. As its weight increased and its mobility decreased, its usefulness once the battle proper had commenced, declined.

Tactics became stereotyped. Both sides would drag their guns into position, within range of one another, artillery units facing artillery units. The inevitable result was an artillery duel, which was often the signal that the battle was under way.

When the guns tired, the infantry would pass them by as they advanced into mêlée. With the artillery occupying the centre of the field, the flanks were protected by the cavalry.

The rate of fire was a pitiable four to six shots an hour. The military mind soon realized that what was also needed were smaller guns, capable of advancing with the infantry. So the field gun proper was born. It was Gustavus Adolphus who first realized how best to use this new weapon, attaching a pair to each of his blocks of infantry.

By the beginning of the English Civil War, field commanders had a choice of a dozen different types of cannon. Their ranges varied according to their size, but solid shot could be hurled up to 2,500 yd (2,300 m). However, in practice, artillery normally opened up at a range of about 400 yd (360 m).

The rate of fire was, to our minds, lamentably slow. The piece was fired by applying a lighted torch to a small hole situated towards the rear top of the barrel. This ignited the powder in the barrel, causing an explosion and this in turn hurled the ball down the barrel in the general direction of the enemy. Having fired, it was then necessary to clean out the barrel in order to remove the remains of the burnt powder. Fresh powder was then poured into the barrel and rammed down. The missile was then inserted and wadding rammed home, both to stop the ball rolling out and also to ensure a compact mass within the tube. The touch-hole was then recharged with powder, the gun was once again aimed and elevated as required and the piece was then once more ready to be fired. As the smaller guns were manned by a crew of two and even the larger ones by a crew of only three, it is hardly surprising that the rate of fire was so low.

The musket

We have seen how the cannon was used on the battlefield. A heavy, clumsy weapon, with little mobility. The tactician dreamed of the day when a smaller version could be handled by the individual infantryman. Within a few years of the cannon appearing we find a short-barrelled hand gun being tried out. It soon became apparent that the longer the barrel, the more accurate the shot and the recognizable musket shape developed, with a wooden stock in which rested a metal barrel. Of course, all guns were muzzle-loading; powder being poured down the tube and rammed home, followed by the shot and a plug. The weapon was fired in exactly the same manner as the cannon, using a burning ember or hot coal. As burning embers were not available just anywhere, it followed that movement was restricted. Also, both hands were required just to fire the gun, so a rest was essential to take its weight. The eyes of the firer were focused on the touch-hole. Actually aiming the gun was a matter of chance. Misfires averaged as high as four shots in ten! If it rained, the gunner may as well have gone home.

The problem was always one of how to improve this new military toy. The first break came with the invention of the slow-burning wick. This enabled the firer to move about, no longer having to remain near a fire. Next, the wick was clamped to the gun, so freeing one of the firers' hands. About 1520, the wheel-lock was invented. This was based upon the idea of making a spark by flint action, thus eliminating the necessity of always being dependant upon the lighted wick. With the invention of the wheel-lock it was possible to arm the cavalry with the short-barrelled pistol. This had the effect of changing cavalry tactics, cavalry becoming so dependant upon the pistol that they appeared to forget about the fact that they were capable of using the shock tactics of the charge.

The wheel-lock was a more expensive weapon to produce than the matchlock, so, throughout our period, its use was limited. Artillery guards were issued with wheel-lock muskets, it being considered that it was not a good thing for fire to be kept in the vicinity of gunpowder.

And what of the ranges of the musket and the pistol? The maximum range of any weapon is irrelevant. Man is capable of running a sub-four-minute mile, but this does not mean that the average man is so able. Similarly, it may be of academic interest to know that a musket was capable of hurling a ball over 400 yd (360 m). What is of greater interest is the fact that the enemy had to advance to within 80–100 yd (730–100 m) before the firer had any real chance of scoring a hit. (We have already noted that the artillery, although being capable of firing a shot well over 2,000 yd [1,800 m], normally opened up at a range of 400 yd [360 m].) So we have established that in practice there existed a ratio of four to one between the artillery piece and the musket.

The pistol was a much less accurate weapon and was always fired at point-blank range and never more than 40 yd (36 m) away from its target.

How reliable was the firearm and how accurate was it? First of all, there was no guarantee that the brute would perform. The percentage of misfires was always great and increased during rain and with every salvo fired. As the musket was not rifled, the ball tended to lack direction, making it virtually impossible to aim at any individual enemy. Only by aiming at a mass of men did the firer stand a fair chance of scoring his hit.

The bayonet had not yet been invented. If the musketeer was unfortunate enough to become involved in a mêlée he had the choice of either using the musket as a club or abandoning it altogether and fighting with his sword.

The pike

It is the Greeks who are credited with having first perfected the use of the pike as a military weapon. In essence, the pike is an elongated spear, varying in length from about 9 ft (3 m) to around 18 ft (5 m) according to the practice of the day. It was tipped by a steel point. Such a weapon required the use of both hands to wield. The pikeman of the Middle Ages, was clad in as much armour as he could carry, owing to the fact that it was impossible for him to be protected by a shield. During the period under study in this book, body armour was gradually abandoned by the pikemen.

The pike was never used as a throwing spear. Used singly, it was a particularly useless type of weapon as it was too slow and heavy to manoeuvre, but used in conjunction with many others, it provided the infantry with a defensive hedge, through which cavalry or other infantry could not pass. The effectiveness of the hedge was dependent upon its depth, the pikes of the second, third, etc., ranks protruding past the men who formed the front rank. So we arrive at the fact that this solid phalanx formation was the most suitable disposition for pikemen. The normal depth of a phalanx was at least six ranks deep.

Like all weapons, the pike had its limitations. As long as the formation was stationary or advancing slowly over open, even ground, with its flanks covered by other units, it was indestructable except by gunfire. However, once the formation was disrupted or broken by enemy trenches, gorse bushes, trees, etc., it became extremely vulnerable. Also, unless the phalanx formed a square or circle, with its pikes pointing in all directions, should a flank or its rear be attacked, the unit was powerless to offer any kind of resistance. Finally, the fact that pikemen had no firearms meant that unless the unit was able to close with the enemy in a mêlée, it could not inflict a single casualty. To remedy this last point, archers and musketeers were often attached to pike units. These men would shelter under the safety of the pikes whilst reloading or during cavalry attacks. Gradually, as the efficiency of the musket increased, the necessity for the pike declined, resulting in the number of musketeers per unit being increased. By the middle of the English Civil War the proportion of musketeers to pikemen was two to one.

The halberd

The halberd was designed as a dual purpose weapon, an attempt to combine the stabbing quality of the pike with the cutting action of the axe. It was, in fact, an axe-head mounted on a long pole which ended with a steel point. As a stabbing weapon it proved to be a relative failure, being much shorter than the standard pike and by its very design, too heavy at the head to be held in the traditional pike receiving position. However, as a cutting weapon, it was without equal.

Held with both hands, it required a reasonable area in which to operate, for the action was a swinging one. It was the ideal weapon for opening up lanes among the enemy pike, once they had become entangled and so halted in the mêlée.

Various designs were tried out, some having the added refinement of a hook situated to the rear of the blade. With this hook enemy cavalry were grappled and then torn from their horses, to be slaughtered by sword or dagger as they lay on the ground.

It was never the custom to form entire units of halberdiers, but rather to attach a few to each pike formation. These men were normally formed up around the units' standard as a bodyguard, filtering forward past the pikemen as and when their services were required. During Elizabeth's Irish wars, the halberdiers were still to be found in small numbers but as the ratio of pike to musket declined, so the usefulness of the weapon waned. Only the Irish, and the Scots with their Lochaber axes, were still using them during and after the two English Civil Wars of the Cromwellian period.

The lance

The lance was purely a cavalry weapon, designed to give the rider a reach advantage over enemy infantry or cavalry. It was, in fact, the cavalry's pike.

When man first rode horses in battle, he was armed either with a sword or a throwing spear. He rode bareback. Controversy rages as to whether a rider without the advantage of stirrups would have been capable of using a lance. We need not concern ourselves with this argument. Sufficient to say that during the Middle Ages, the heavy cavalry were usually armed with stout lances. As the use of body armour declined, so the weight of the lance was reduced. By Elizabethan times, only the Scottish light cavalry were equipped with the lance. It all but disappeared from the military scene, only to be revived during the Napoleonic wars (except in the British Army). Following the fall of Napoleon, even the British adopted the weapon and it became a universal cavalry tool until the machine-gun of the First World War removed the cavalry themselves from most battlefields.

As with the pike, it was the normal custom to equip entire regiments of cavalry with the lance, although there were instances when only the front rank would be armed with the lance, the following ranks being armed with swords, for like the pike, the lance lost much of its value once the mêlée settled into a stalemate.

The sword

Of all the weapons man has invented, the sword was probably the one most universally used during our period. Whatever other principal weapon the soldier carried, be it pike, musket, lance, etc., he usually had this extra blade hanging at his side, his second line of defence. In many instances, of course, this may have been his principal weapon. Entire units were primarily swordsmen.

Historically, the sword had proved itself to be a battle-winner. The Roman Empire had been carved out by the *gladius*, a short stabbing sword. The very power of the famous Swiss pikes had finally been broken by Spanish troops armed with sword and buckler (a small shield, with which the thrust of the pike was parried as the Spaniard closed for the kill). The sword had always been the main cavalry weapon, the rider preferring the long, heavy, and often curved variety, relying upon the cutting edge of the weapon rather than its point. To the Highland Scot, the claymore, a two-edged broadsword fitted his temperament perfectly. It was a close-quarter weapon and the Scot was never one to stand in well-disciplined lines, engaging in distant fire-fights, but rather he sought every opportunity to engage his foe in a mêlée.

The sword issued to the rank and file during the English Civil War was of poor quality, costing 4*s* 6*d* each, liable to break easily. Metal scabbards blunted its cutting edge and frequent misuse off the battlefield rendered it fairly useless. Little wonder that the musketeer, when his back was to the wall, preferred to use his musket as a club, rather than trust his life to such a weapon.

3 | *Historical organization*

THE ORGANIZATION OF AN ELIZABETHAN ARMY

Dead man's pay! It sounds like something out of *Treasure Island*. It was, in fact, a legalized method of subsidizing the pay of a company commander. A company, in theory, consisted of 100 men—half as large as a European army company of the day. The words 'in theory' are important, for in practice a full-strength company of infantry was made up of 94 or 95 men, the remaining 5 or 6 men did not actually exist. Their pay was drawn by the company commander and went straight into his pocket. Naturally, some were not satisfied with these 'perks' and by failing to report the odd casualty or deserter they further enriched themselves with these men's dues. Why the legitimate pay for the captain was not increased and the number of men brought up to full strength can only be surmised.

The dead man's pay system explains why, when reading about the composition of companies from actual records, the numbers never actually total to 100. For instance, one such record shows a company strength as 50 pike, 12 heavy muskets and 36 calivers, a total of 96; another shows 24 pikemen, 30 heavy muskets, and 40 calivers, 94 all told; while a third has 24 pike, only 20 heavy muskets, and as many as 50 calivers, again adding up to 94. These discrepancies were not caused by enemy action, but were part of the system.

The number of men have been detailed in the paragraph above in an attempt to prove to the reader two basic facts that should be borne in mind when one is considering the composition of an infantry company during Elizabeth's reign. First, it will be noticed that a company was not only made up of either pike or shot, but in practice both arms were included, so giving the unit an offensive and a defensive role. Secondly, there was no set pattern as to the balance of numbers of pike to shot. In the first instance quoted they were even numbers, while in the other two cases the shot outnumbered the pike by over two to one. This two-to-one proportion gradually became the norm, but it is one of the interests of the wargamer that he is able to experiment and change these proportions at his pleasure until he has achieved the balance that best suits his play.

It had become the practice, again adopted from the continent, of banding together a number of these companies, so forming an infantry regiment. No set number of companies to a regiment was laid down, they varied from between four and six: 800 to 1,200 men. They were commanded by the senior company commander, known as a colonel (from the Italian word 'colonello' 'a little column', and so the commander of a column).

Although most of the men were armed with either pike or shot—and in the earlier years of the reign, shot included the bow and arrows—some men were specialists with other weapons. It has long been the custom to surround the company standard with warriors armed with halberds or pole-axes. Theirs was a dual role. Apart from the already mentioned defensive one, the halberdier was also expected to wade into the enemy pikemen once their pikes had become wedged and useless during an abortive push of the pike.

When one thinks of a typical Scottish clansman, the mind's eye sees a kilted warrior armed with a sword and buckler. A romantic notion, no doubt, but it should be remembered that it was not only the Highlander who carried such weapons. On the continent the Spanish had discovered that they could defeat the mighty Swiss pike phalanxes by the use of the sword and buckler, dodging under the 18-ft (5-m) poles and slaughtering the now defenceless opponent.

All infantry, be they shot or pike, carried a side-arm such as a sword or a dagger with which they would defend themselves in close-quarter work if all else failed.

Before attempting to suggest different wargame groupings of Elizabethan infantry it will pay to take a quick glance at the different types of troops that were available to her field commanders. These fall into four categories.

The first, naturally, was the regular soldier filling the ranks of the standing army, a type of home-guard militia. In theory, at least, these men already had some kind of training, often gained in the ranks of a foreign prince's army on the continent. They had been expected to drill regularly, practising the complicated manoeuvres that their weapons dictated. These men formed the cadre of the army. They were not formed into special superior groups on the battlefield (as Napoleon was to do in later years with his Old Guard), but were scattered throughout the different companies, giving them a backbone.

To this first group should be added the volunteers, the enthusiastic amateurs. They had a thousand reasons for joining the army, but mainly they were escaping from poor local conditions or looking for what they hoped would provide a regular source of food and income. Some were seeking adventure. Patriotism would appear to come far down the list.

The main mass of the army consisted of conscripts, pressed men with little stomach for the job. As most were destined to be shipped to Ireland as part of an army of occupation with the task of attempting to subdue an enemy fighting a guerilla war, with death from disease or the shot in the back their ultimate fate, their reluctance to join the colours was understandable.

Finally there were the loyal Irish. Loyal, that is, to their own chiefs. Many were called Irish although they were in fact Scots who had come to Ireland for the fighting season, hoping to take home loot as well as pay at the end of their stay. They were known as Gallowglasses and were completely unreliable. At first they were formed into separate units so that they would not contaminate existing companies, but later they were used to fill in the gaps in the ranks of these units as the wars flowed on.

Taken over-all then, the quality of the English infantryman serving in Ireland under Elizabeth's generals was second-rate. Not that the opposition was much better, but at least it had the added incentive that they were defending their homeland.

However, let us finish examining the English before we turn to look at their enemies.

The cavalry was divided into groups of about fifty men per unit, which we will refer to as a squadron. These squadrons do not appear to have been formed into regiments, rather to have operated as individual units. Only light cavalry was used in Ireland.

The rider's principal weapon was either the lance or the sword. He also carred firearms, either a brace of pistols or a petronel. He was trained in the two basic methods of cavalry attack. When he came face to face with the foe he could either charge home into a mêlée or he could engage the enemy from a short distance with his shot, wheeling away to reload and returning to fire again into the thinning ranks. This, at least, was the theory. However, theory and practice rarely coincided in Ireland for the enemy rarely accepted the challenge of the open battlefield. English saddles were more often emptied by the silent arrow fired from ambush, with the enemy simply melting away before retaliation was possible.

As to the proportion of cavalry to infantry, the English commander could look upon himself as very fortunate if he could field more than one-tenth of his force as cavalry. Obviously, with such limited resources, pursuit of a beaten enemy was out of the question and so the fruits of any victory could not be properly harvested.

Yet if he thought himself deplete of cavalry, his lack of artillery was even more so. The shocking condition of the Irish roads, if they existed at all, was such that the movement of guns to support the field force was so limited as to be more of a hindrance than a help. On occasion the fleet could assist by transporting guns from one port to another, but once there, there they usually stayed. It is interesting to observe that in one of the major defeats suffered by the English, that of the Yellow Ford, part of the blame for the disaster was heaped upon the artillery, in that the army became over-extended in trying to move a number of guns, the biggest of which collapsed in the middle of the ford itself, causing an obstruction and so actually aiding the enemy instead of injuring him.

The guns themselves were smooth-bored, inaccurate weapons, manned by only two or three men. They were pulled by either horses or oxen. They had an effective range of about 400 yd (360 m) but rarely had the opportunity of exploiting it. There was no laid-down method of deploying them in action. Sometimes they would be grouped in twos and threes, sometimes used singly.

This then was the type of army that found itself constantly engaged under the command of a series of general officers, each one arriving with the Queen's commission, failing and being replaced, until eventually Mountjoy was appointed viceroy near the end of the reign and the Irish were brought temporarily to heel.

THE ORGANIZATION OF AN IRISH ARMY

The forces that opposed Elizabeth in Ireland were of a very different calibre from her mainly conscript army. Where the English relied upon the press gang to fill its ranks, the Irish placed their faith in the power of gold.

So we find that it was a mercenary army of foreign troops, supported by the semi-trained bands of Irish peasants that took to the hills to combat the oppressors. There was a sprinkling of Spaniards in the ranks of their instructors, for the Spain of Philip II and the England of Elizabeth I remained in a state of war, often unofficial, as long as both monarchs lived. Just as French officers were sent to assist James IV of Scotland in his disastrous campaign in Northumberland in 1513, so were Spanish troops to be found marching under the banner of Tyrone at the end of the sixteenth century.

Of course, the main source of supply of mercenaries was Scotland. Unfortunately, this was also the same mercenary supply of the English. Thus, in theory, Scot fought Scot. In practice, with both fighting purely for money, the Scot would change side to join the highest bidder; and this generally meant they joined the rebels, as the English called their enemy.

It was never the intention of the Irish to arm themselves to fight pitched battles, but rather for the dash of hit and run tactics. This is not to say that they were lacking in courage. Their method of fighting was adapted to the type of country in which they were engaged. Being lighter-armed, they were able to move with greater speed than their opponents. If the fight was going well they would stand their ground, but if at any time the English began to gain an advantage then they would fade from the scene, prepared to take up the struggle the next day if the advantage now lay with them.

So there developed within their army three distinct types of troops, the hired mercenary—the heavy infantryman of the corps; the Irish kerne—the light infantry; and finally the light cavalryman. The Irish did not bother bringing any artillery into the field; which is not to say that they didn't have any artillery. They had, but it was used against forts and ports, or in prepared defensive positions and not risked in the open country. Speed was the key to the Irish success, guns only slowed down their movement.

Let us look a little more closely at these three types of warrior. First of all, the mercenary. In the early years of the rebellion he probably wielded an axe and was dressed in body armour, as was the fashion in Europe. But as the campaigns wore on the armour was abandoned in favour of lighter leather jerkins and the axe replaced by the pike. In battle, the mercenaries would either fight as separate stands of pike or would be supported by Irish 'shot'.

Next we will turn to the Irish peasant. He was dressed as was any peasant of his day throughout the continent; in what he could make or steal. Fleet of foot and used to the country, his speed was his greatest asset. He was armed with a sword, a dagger, a short bow, or a musket; in fact, whatever was handed down to him by his father or taken from the dead—friend or foe. Whilst the mercenary fought in dressed ranks, the kerne were formed more into a group than what may be termed a company.

And finally, the so-called cavalry. They were of little use as a fighting force. They were armed with spears, not lances, and protected by mail. They were usually used as scouts for the main army.

So there they stand, a hired killer, an armed peasant, and a man on a hack. Yet not only were they able to defy everything sent against them, they were able to defeat them in detail. Speed, local knowledge, morale, money, and guts.

ARMY ORGANIZATION IN 1642

The Normans, after their successful conquest of England, planted a nobility across the country. Each lord, earl, knight, etc., was expected to be able to produce a certain number of men and horses according to his station and this method of recruitment in time of war survived down the centuries with few alterations. However, the civil Wars of the Roses took a terrible toll of the nobility and the system had to be amended. The large landowners still contributed private armies, but now counties were expected to levy and to train troops. So a home guard of trained bands came into existence. Unfortunately, training was very lax, with the exception of London. (This was to have a marked effect when London rose against the King in 1642, so forming a nucleus of 6,000 men in the ranks of his enemies.) One of the casualties of this slackness was the long-bow, which had become obsolete through lack of practice, so by the outbreak of the war, infantry either 'trailed the pike' or 'shouldered the musket'.

Thus, when the great Civil War broke out in England, neither side was able to field an experienced army. Some counties sided with the King, some with Parliament, their trained bands and more important, their weapons, being made available to their selected leaders. Even the loyalty of the nobility was divided, although as may be expected, more elected to join their sovereign than to fight against him. (This latter fact had the effect of giving Charles an advantage in the numbers and the quality of horsemen at the beginning of the war.) Both sides received a sprinkling of men returning from foreign service, filled with the latest ideas on warfare as they had experienced it on the continent.

Unfortunately, most counties were reluctant to allow the troops that they looked upon as their defenders to wander too far from their own borders. This had the effect that neither side was able to concentrate a single, overwhelming force with which to crush the enemy, but rather each found it had inherited a number of small, independent commands. The result of this was that most of the battles of the Civil War were on a small scale and even victory only produced limited gains.

An infantry regiment on either side was supposed to be made

up of 1,200 or 1,300 men, although this was rarely the case in practice. The proportion of musketeers to pikemen was rising to about two to one, although in the Royalist armies, certainly at the outbreak of the war, it stood even for each weapon. The regiment itself was subdivided into a number of companies, whose numbers and strength also varied as the regiment's total strength fell short of the maximum.

On the field, regiments formed in line, usually six deep, but on occasion they might adopt a three-deep formation if scarcity of numbers or the width of the terrain demanded.

In theory, a cavalry regiment totalled about 400–500 men, but again in practice it was probably only half that number. All, with the exception of the Scots who carried lances, were armed with swords and pistols and were usually protected by cuirasses. A few regiments wore full armour, but this practice was abandoned before the end of the war.

Like the infantry, the cavalry fought in solid block formations, three and sometimes six deep. As it was virtually impossible to charge home against pikemen, it became the normal practice rather to approach to within pistol range and then to fire into the massed ranks of the enemy. However, as the numbers of pikemen were reduced in ratio to musketeers, so the cavalry rediscovered the charge. Rupert was a great exponent of this latter method of fighting and thus we find that the Royalist horse learned to charge home, whilst the Parliamentarian cavalry preferred the use of the pistol. The charge formation was three deep, the pistol disposition being six deep (this allowed time for each rank to fire and then wheel away to the rear to reload). Even cavalry being charged rarely counter-attacked, relying upon their pistols to discourage the enemy.

In battle, the infantry usually were formed in the centre, opposite the enemy infantry, the cavalry forming the two wings. The guns were run out in front of the infantry. Thus four distinct actions were fought. First, the guns bombarded each other, then the two wings would clash, and finally the infantry met. Often each action was unaided by any other supporting one, even victorious troops often preferring to chase their own particular foe from the field instead of going to the assistance of another section.

If there was any organization in the artillery, I have failed to discover it. Each army appeared to be grateful for any pieces they could lay their hands on. Thus, many types of cannon were often present on the field, simply grouped together in no apparent manner. One thing was certain: the King was always short of artillery.

THE NEW MODEL ARMY: ITS ORGANIZATION

If either side was to win the war, it was obvious that the stalemate of small, meaningless victories must be ended. One side was going to have to put into the field a force capable of inflicting overwhelming defeats, which could then be followed up before the opponent had time to reorganize. A new type of army was required, built upon a new model, prepared to go anywhere, highly trained, well-armed, and well-led. The summer was the time for fighting, therefore the winter must be used for training.

After much debate, Parliament took the decision that would end the war. Sir Thomas Fairfax was appointed to command in the January of 1645. By April, he had completed his organization. By May, the army was ready to be put to the test.

On paper the New Model Army was to consist of twelve regiments of foot, each being 1,200 strong, each regiment being divided into ten companies, 200 men in the colonel's company, 160 in the lieutenant-colonel's company, 140 in the major's, and 100 in each of the seven captain's commands. The ten regiments of the cavalry were each to be 600 strong, being composed of six squadrons of 100 each. Finally, the single regiment of dragoons was to be 1,000 strong. The men were to be drawn from the ranks of the old armies of Waller, Essex, and Manchester. The artillery was also to be reorganized, but no records remain as to how. It can only be surmised that the number of guns were to be increased.

It is one thing to agree about the size and shape of a force: it is another to implement it. When the New Model Army moved out of its training area to join battle at Naseby, it was still between 3,000 and 4,000 men under strength. Fairfax was its commander-in-chief; Cromwell was the lieutenant-general, commanding all cavalry units; the major-general, commanding all the infantry units was Skippon. Thomas Hammond was created lieutenant-general of Ordnance.

Apart from actually reorganizing their force, the New Model Army was trained differently. The musket was shortened and so lightened, therefore the musket rest was dispensed with. The six-deep formation became standard in defence, three deep in offence. Instead of one rank firing, then the second, then the third, the entire three ranks were taught to fire at once, one kneeling, one stooping, and one standing up straight.

It was in the reorganization of the cavalry that we note the greatest changes. The Royalists had usually enjoyed superiority in the number of horsemen. Now all this was to be changed. Almost a third of the army was in the saddle and the size of each cavalry unit was raised by 50 per cent, to 600 riders. The armour-clad horsemen were gone, only the dragoons and the swordsmen remained. The successes of Rupert's charges had been noted. Cromwell's cavalry learned to charge, sword in hand. Pistols were only drawn and used if the mêlée became static.

4 | *Preparation*

THE BATTLEFIELD

When H. G. Wells was playing his wargames, no area was considered to be too large, owing to the fact he allowed his toy cannon to dominate the game, actually firing small missiles from them. The floor area of a large room or even his garden lawn provided the base over which his armies would manoeuvre.

Unfortunately, model soldiers are not really designed to withstand the rigours of the weather and their activities are completely curtailed by the approach of darkness. Nor are adult humans designed for crawling around wooden floors on their knees for hours on end. The result is that miniature battles are invariably played indoors and on a table top.

The very size of the table is, of course, never fully satisfactory. It is possible to fight a battle on a card-table 2 ft (600 mm) square. Immediately the forces are set out facing one another, there will be a natural desire by both commanders to outflank the opponent. If this is to be made possible the area must be extended on either wing. The next battle will be laid out using two card-tables standing together, with the players facing each other across the long baselines.

With a table width of only 2 ft (600 mm), the range of firing is extremely limited and there is no room for manoeuvring behind the lines, no area into which to retreat to regroup. So a greater depth is required! The square is re-created and a greater width is then called for, and so on.

There is, in fact, no ideal size for a table, simply the larger the better with the obvious limitation that if it is too large it will be impossible to stretch across its surface in order to move the figures. It is therefore suggested that an area of about 4×8 ft (1·2×2·4 m) should be the aim. (As this is a standard sheet size in the building industry, this is a further attraction for these measurements for anyone contemplating making their own wargames table.) A table-tennis board makes an excellent base on which to fight a wargame, both from the point of size and colour.

The twenty-seven battlefields described in this book are all designed with an area of 4×8 ft (1·2×2·4 mm) in mind.

No battle is ever fought over a completely featureless surface. A quick glance at our battle maps will reveal differences from one another in many details, some being extremely simple in layout, with the odd road, hedges, or occasional hill forming the main feature, in some the river may dominate, whilst in others numerous woods allow for ambush. In the most complex, the entire terrain is alive with obstacles. Just how are these features to be represented?

Hills

Take a look at any relief map. Here can be seen contours indicating height differentials. According to the scale of the map, these rises may be every 50 or 100 ft (15 or 30 m). Now examine a single hill. It will be made up of a number of concentric lines. Let us assume that there are three of these lines. They will each enclose an area, the largest designating the foothills, the next will represent the upper slopes and the third (being the smallest) indicating the peak. It is possible to emulate the map by cutting out three such shapes, using 1½-in (40-mm) foam rubber sheets. By piling one upon the other, a hill is created. From a wargaming point of view this is a very satisfactory hill. Its flat surfaces are excellent for standing figures upon, the actual area of the hill is clearly defined and figures standing behind the hill are hidden from sight and safe from fire. Steep slopes are indicated by the closeness of the contours (any such lines being within 1 in [25 mm] of another).

The main objection to the above method of making hills is an aesthetic one—hills do not look like a series of terraces. Overcoming this objection is quite simple. Obtain a number of sheets of cardboard from a good art dealer. A hillside is formed by placing some books on the table in the appropriate position and to the required height. Score the cardboard with a Stanley knife and bend it, laying part on the books and allowing the rest to overhang on to the table, so forming a slope. Repeat until all the desired hills are completed, then cover the entire table with a green woollen blanket. Experiment with the cardboard, cutting to shape to obtain the rounded hilltops. This method is ideal for creating battlefields where the action is to be fought over a mountain pass or across a valley floor. Providing the figures are mounted on stands and the slopes are not too severe, no difficulties will be experienced when units are ordered to scale the hills. Another advantage lies in the fact that the crest of the hill is easily defined. Troops standing 3 in (75 mm) back from this crest can claim cover from troops in the valley below.

Woods

Single trees should never be used on a wargames table. A wood is a group of trees standing in a definite area. As such, it is this area that must be defined upon the ground by a piece of cloth cut to shape, upon which are stood a number of model trees. By adopting this practice it is at once obvious to all when a unit enters or leaves the wood.

Villages

As with woods, so villages should have a clearly defined boundary. Each model house will represent perhaps ten or twenty actual buildings. Units sheltering within the bounds of the village will be subject to all the cover a village would naturally afford. Thus a village may be represented by an area of cloth on which will stand two or three model houses.

Farms

A farm is best represented by a single house and an area enclosed by either model walls or hedges, with a gap in the latter to allow for access.

Hedges and walls

Although these can be made, they are available for purchase at most model shops. Hedges are normally available in 3-in (75-mm) lengths, walls being in either 3-in or 6-in (75- or 150-

mm) sections. These are ideal as they allow for great variety in positioning. The use of even a few of these pieces helps to bring a battlefield 'alive'.

Roads

Roads should also be made in sections, preferably about 1½–2 in (40–75 mm) wide and in varying lengths. If the bare table is to be used as a base, it is suggested that thin plywood or hardboard strips will make adequate roads, but if a cloth is thrown over the area, then strips of felt make perfectly good roads. Where a road crosses a river, model bridges are used. Fords should have their dimensions clearly marked.

Rivers

Rivers may be constructed in a similar manner to roads, using blue lino tiles or felt, cut into lengths.

Swamps and lakes

These are clearly defined, suitably coloured areas of material which are laid upon the battlefield in the appropriate positions.

All the above are easily storable items of equipment. However, many wargamers prefer to go much further, constructing more permanent areas of landscape, with rivers and roads gouged out of solid chipboard and moulded valleys and hills. A variation of battlefields is achieved by constructing such areas of scenery in sections, 2 or 3 ft (600 or 900 mm) square. By setting them out in a different order, so the field of battle will be varied. A hill will dominate the centre of the board in one engagement, it will be relegated to a corner of the field in another.

Care must be taken to ensure that roads and rivers leave these sections at a centre of a baseline, otherwise they will not connect one with another. Houses, woods, etc., may be placed anywhere as desired, so adding to the variety of the scene. The main drawback to this permanent type of scenery is one of storage.

THE FIGURES

Figures suitable for using in table-top battles of the period described in this book are available from a number of manufacturers and no doubt by the time this book goes to press others will have joined their ranks.

Miniature Figurines, of 28–32 Northern Road, Southampton, produce a very comprehensive range of 25-mm figures and have recently started manufacturing 15-mm figures. All the photographs in this book are of this company's 25-mm range.

Frank Hinchliffe has also entered the field of 25-mm figures. His firm, Hinchliffe Models Ltd, of Meltham, Huddersfield, is rapidly expanding their range.

Warrior Metal Miniatures, 23 Grove Road, Leighton Buzzard, Beds, are a third company producing the 25-mm range.

Greenwood and Ball of 61 Westbury Street, Thornaby on Tees also produce a small but excellent range of 25-mm figures.

At a slightly smaller scale, 20 mm, comes Phoenix Model Developments, The Square, Eagle Barton, Northampton.

In the 15-mm group is another company, that of Peter Laing, 11 Bounds Oak Way, Southborough, Tunbridge Wells, Kent.

For the wargamer who cannot afford to buy metal figures, there are the Airfix plastic figures, obtainable from most toyshops. Airfix do not sell a pike and musket range, but armies can be easily converted from some of their existing kits. For example, artillery: use the American Civil War Confederate box. Musketeers: American Civil War Confederate Infantry. Pikemen: the Romans. Heavy cavalry: Sheriff of Nottingham. Other cavalry: French cuirassiers.

Stands

When fighting in this period, it is not really practical to group the figures together on to multiple stands. As regiments usually consisted of men armed with a variety of weapons, it is better that each figure should be mounted on a separate base of its own, an infantryman on a stand measuring $\frac{3}{4} \times \frac{3}{4}$ in (20×20 mm), a cavalryman on one $\frac{3}{4} \times 1\frac{1}{4}$ in (20×40 mm). These bases are easily made by cutting them from green 9×9-in (230×230-mm) lino tiles (not vinyl). A single tile will provide 100 infantry or 50 cavalry bases, at a cost of about 5p per tile. (The normal stand of the figure is usually too small to enable the figure to stand on a slope. By mounting the figure as suggested, this not only enables it to stand up on fairly steep slopes, but it also ensures that each figure will occupy a definite area, so aiding regimental dressing. There is nothing more off-putting to the eye than a heap of figures, bunched together as if in a rugger scrum and yet hoping against hope that they look like an army unit.)

Regimental organization

INFANTRY

Every infantry unit must be led by an officer. This figure will carry the unit's standard. The exception to this practice will be archer units and dragoons, neither of whom will display a standard. Any number of figures will form a unit, the minimum number being four. A unit which is reduced to under four will be considered too weak to perform on its own and will either seek to join another friendly unit, or, if none is available, it will surrender if in a mêlée or retreat from the field if free to do so.

CAVALRY

Cavalry units were usually smaller than infantry units. Each should be led by a standard-bearing officer. There should never be fewer than three cavalrymen to a unit. A unit reduced to two must seek to join another cavalry unit, or leave the field. (It will surrender if in a mêlée.)

DRAGOONS

It is essential that these figures are able to dismount. If the horse and rider are moulded as one, spare dragoons on foot will be required for all but the single figure which will remain mounted holding the horses as his colleagues fight on foot. A dragoon regiment normally consisted of about 1,000 men. Being more independent in action than infantry, they are only forced to leave the field through lack of numbers when they reach a minimum of three figures.

ARTILLERY

Two gunner figures will man a light piece, three a heavy one. Each figure represents an actual gun, the model gun itself merely indicating whether the battery is a light or heavy one. A single horse is required by each battery to enable the piece to move.

STAFF OFFICER

This will be a single figure, who is normally mounted.

5 | *The weather*

Most games are played to well-established, never varying rules. These rules are never questioned and so original ideas from the players are never required. This has the obvious advantage that when people meet to play, they are able to proceed without any undue delay. It also produces a certain dullness, which may account for the fact that many people find board games in general boring.

In wargaming, the participants are encouraged to think. Not only about weapons and troop formations, but also about the very rules themselves. The result is that rules are constantly being up-graded. Sometimes they become too complex and die. One reads an article and an idea is born. One kicks it about, tries to put it down on paper and eventually when next one meets the friendly enemy across the table-top one suggests that the idea be tried out. Usually it fails, but never quite. Two minds are at work on it. Modifications are tried. It is better, but rarely is it perfect.

A few years ago I had such an idea. It concerned the weather. During my early days as a wargamer it never entered my head that weather could play any part in a game. Yet the more history I read, the more it became apparent that rain, fog, and snow affected quite a number of battles. Rules were obviously needed to cover weather.

The first thought that came to mind was that a simple die throw at the beginning of the game would suffice. If a 6 was thrown, weather would play a part in the game. Otherwise forget it. This was not very satisfactory as it did not allow for rain falling after the battle had commenced. So the think tank came up with the bright idea that a die be thrown before every game move, a 6 again indicating weather. This appeared to fit the bill and it was adopted.

Unfortunately, what kind of weather had been ignored. We could soon put that right. Simply throw a second die if the first had fallen as a 6. A 1 would indicate snow, a 2 fog, and so on. The disastrous result of this idea was that in one move it could be fine, in the next snowing, in the next fine, in the next foggy. . . . Useless! What was needed was some kind of weather gauge, a barometer which would record gradual changes in the weather. Armed with such an instrument, one could even forecast the weather. As the glass fell, one could expect rain and with it a decrease in the efficiency of muskets. Guns would bog down and become immobile.

The end result was the weather gauge as shown on p. 31. It is divided into six parts, each indicating different weather conditions. For ease of reading, each part is painted a distinctive colour. Grey indicates fog, light blue, light rain; dark blue, heavy rain; black; storm; cream, fair weather. Each section is numbered, the numbers running from 2 to 12. These are the numbers it is possible to throw when using two dice. It will be noted that from 4 to 9 inclusive are all within the cream (fair) band. As the greater number of throws will fall within this area, it follows that most battles will start with dry weather.

Before the start of the first game move, one of the players from each side will each throw a single die. The scores are totalled and this will indicate the weather conditions at the start of the battle. From then on, only a single die is thrown each game move. This will be thrown by the player commanding the side who is going to move first in that particular move. A throw of a 3 or 4, will indicate that there is no change in the weather for that game move. A throw of a 1 or a 2 and the barometer indicator will move one point towards the two, a throw of a 5 or a 6 and it will move one point towards the twelve.

Example. At the beginning of the game each player throws a single die. One scores a 3 and the other a 6. Total 9. The barometer is set at nine. (Fair weather, but storm clouds can be seen gathering on the horizon.) At the start of the next game move, one of the players will throw a die. Should he throw a 1 or a 2, it will be appreciated that the clouds are moving away, as the indicator moves to eight. But should he throw a 5 or a 6, then light rain starts to fall, bringing with it certain reductions in the effectiveness of the muskets. These are detailed below.

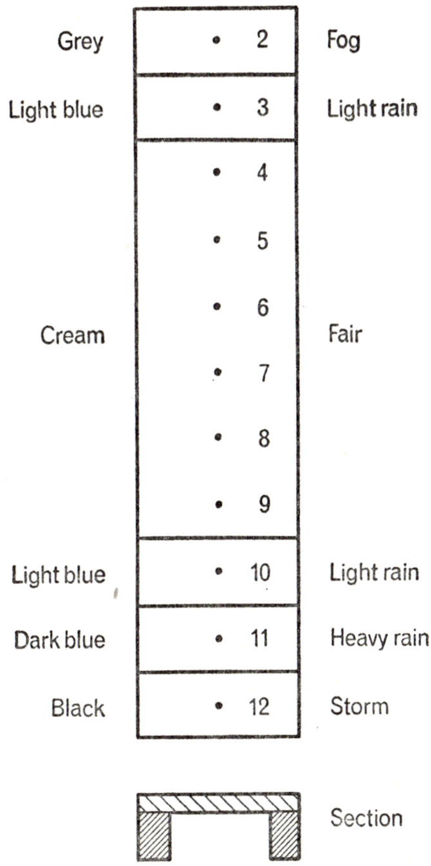

The weather barometer

The effect of weather upon a battle

Fair — Normal movement and fire.

Light rain — Normal movement. All unit efficiency ratings for firing of muskets or pistols reduced by 1 point (units thus having no points may not fire).

Heavy rain	Movement reduced by 25 per cent. Artillery off roads by 50 per cent. Infantry efficiency rating for firing reduced by a further point.
Storm	Movement reduced by 50 per cent. Artillery off roads may not move. Cavalry may not charge, musket may not fire.
Fog	Visibility 6 in (150 mm). All movement reduced by 50 per cent. No cavalry charges. Dice for every unit. 1, 2, 3, may not move. No firing unless enemy are within sight.

Construction of the weather gauge

Take a piece of plywood about 1 in (25 mm) wide and 6-8 in (150–200 mm) long. With a drill make eleven holes down the centre of the lath, ensuring that they are evenly spaced. Paint the surface as indicated in the diagram above. When dry, the gauge should be mounted on supports placed along its length. A single peg which will fit the hole size completes the gauge.

6 *The game move*

Wargamers are divided into two distinct camps when it comes to the game move. One group favours the simultaneous move, the other the alternative move.

In the simultaneous game move, both sides examine the position of all the units under their command and those of the enemy and then they write down on their order pads the moves they intend to make for each of their regiments, guns, etc. When both sides have completed their writing, the pieces are moved according to the orders. Advocates of this method claim that this is a more natural method of movement as this is what happens in life: both sides moving at once.

In reality, this is rarely the case. For so often in a battle neither side wishes to move. At the start of any engagement, both sides race for certain key positions, form their desired battle lines and then examine the enemy positions. The weaker army will more often than not prepare for a defensive battle only being prepared to move as a counter-stroke to the enemy's ploys. The stronger, realizing its opponents tactics, usually complies, building up an overwhelming assault force ready to strike against a limited front, whilst still engaging the enemy along the rest of his line. Should the forces be evenly balanced it is even less likely that both will be prepared to throw away their advantages by movement. Caution will dictate their moves. Thus it can be seen that if reality is the objective, it is the alternative move, attack and counter-attack, and not the simultaneous move, that will achieve it.

I have always found that the simultaneous move leads to argument, general confusion, and even cheating. No-one will ever admit to the cheating, of course, but argument and confusion are the very things that writing down the orders is supposed to eliminate. The claim is that if the movement of every unit is written down, there can be no argument. And this, in theory, must appear to be so. Yet in practice it does not work. For example, the commander of unit *A* decides to move against unit *B* to engage in a mêlée with him. He writes down mêlée unit *B*. But the commander of unit *B* has meanwhile written down, Move to position *X*, which will result in a move to his flank. Now the argument starts. As it is impossible to move all of one's units at once, we will assume that the commander of unit *A* moves his unit into a mêlée with *B*, only to be told that unit *B* isn't actually there, but over to its left, 12 in (300 mm) away. The commander of unit *A* quickly glances at the position of other units on the table. If unit *B* is isolated, he claims in a loud voice that his unit would have moved to its flank as it advanced, so ending up still engaged in a mêlée with unit *B*. But if unit *B*'s move had taken it into a group of other friendly units, then the commander of unit *A* either remains very silent, quietly agreeing that the mêlée would never have taken place or he produces an alternative move which he has also written down. Some wargamers actually do write down orders such as, 'Mêlée unit *B* unless it moves away, in which case stand still!' I ask you! Can you imagine Rupert, at the head of his cavalry, drawing his sword and shouting, 'Follow me—unless the enemy moves, in which case, stand still!' In other words, the advantage of the alternative move.

As to the actual cheating, this comes in the moving of the pieces and is possible in two ways. With both sides moving at the same time, one will inevitably move quicker than the other. The slower player has the advantage of seeing where the other has moved to and can then place his forces in such a manner as to gain an advantage—they are placed 1 in (25 mm) short or to the left of his intended position, his experienced eye telling him he is out of range of the overwhelming enemy fire, or, by moving one unit 1 in (25 mm) to its left and another 1 in (25 mm) to its right, a nasty gap may be filled. The opponent can never challenge this cheating, as the order 'advance towards wood *Y*' is clearly written, and yet. . . . The outcome of a battle often hangs upon a single unit succeeding in its task. If there is an argument about the movement of that unit, the loser of the game *feels* cheated, He cannot prove it, but it remains in the mind. The simultaneous move loses friends!

So we must turn to the alternative move game and look for its weaknesses. It is no longer necessary to write down orders, for only one side is going to move its pieces. This alone is going to save time when playing—and quite a considerable time at that. If five minutes is allowed for the writing down of orders, then a full hour is lost in a twelve-move game in the writing alone. As a twelve-move game may take about four hours to play, this is a phenomenal proportion to waste!

A complete move in an alternative move game is as follows. Side *A* will move all the units it wishes to, side *B* remaining stationary. Both sides now exchange musket-fire, fight out their mêlées and test the morale of units suffering casualties. Side *B* now moves his forces and the fighting is repeated. Thus we have had move and counter-move, so completing one full game move.

Opponents of this method claim that it is reducing the game to a chess-like format. But this need not be the case. In chess the moves are strictly alternate: white, black, white, black. In wargaming a simple throw of a die can destroy the sequence, as follows. Both sides throw, the higher moving first: resulting in side *A* moving, followed by side *B*. After *B* has completed his move and all fighting has ceased, both sides will throw again. If *B* is the higher, then *B* will move before *A*, so giving a sequence of *A*, *B*, *B*, *A*. With a light cavalry move of 24 in (600 mm), it is possible that between *A*'s first move and his second, *B*'s light cavalry could have moved up to 48 in (1·2 m) (56 in [1·4 m] if they have charged home). Thus a much more fluid and challenging game is achieved. A bold commander will be prepared to gamble upon the dice giving him the advantage of the double move, the timid will throw it away.

The main objection to the alternative move game is that one unit is always stationary when attacked, whereas in reality the defending unit may sometimes also be advancing when the mêlée occurs. To overcome this objection, one need only introduce a simple morale throw to test the reaction of a unit being attacked. This unit can only do one of three things. It can stand still and receive the charge; it can counter-attack; it can move away. A morale test will decide its reaction. If the morale is good the commander can order a counter-charge or stand as he thinks fit. (Obviously, a unit defending a strong position is not going to counter-attack.) If the morale throw indicates 'stand', the unit must accept the charge. If the test decides that the unit will either fall back or run, then so be it. It is so simple. No arguments. No cheating. No ill-will.

As I like fighting my friends, I will continue to use the alternative move game.

7 | *Movement*

In the main, the wargame table is a flat area over which blocks of troops manoeuvre. Therefore the distances moved by the various types of formation must first be considered in relation to each other as if they were marching over a flat, featureless plain. Once these basics have been established, then terrain may be introduced, increasing or decreasing movement.

Let us begin with the infantry, who usually formed the majority arm on the battlefield. In the period we are discussing, all the foot, irrespective of the different types of weapons they may be carrying, were regimented into block formations which varied in strength from 100 or 200 to over 1,000. (In this book we are not concerned with the massive *tercios* of 2,000 or 3,000 that were common on the continent.) This block could either advance in line, usually three or six rows deep, presenting a wide front to the enemy, or it could adopt a column, which in practice was nearly square-shaped. (This column block formation should not be confused with the column of march adopted by units on roads, which move at a much quicker pace.)

If we establish a game move distance of 12 in (300 mm) for the slowest-moving infantryman, then all other units will be scaled against it. Obviously, the slowest troops will be those who carry the greatest weight of equipment and these were the pikemen. Therefore, pikemen advancing in block formation over flat terrain will move at 12 in (300 mm) per game move.

Having agreed upon the move distance of the pikemen, let us now examine the basic move of the lighter-armed musketeers. Pure musketeer units were rare as they lacked the defensive protection of the pike, but such a unit will be allowed to move at a rate of 16 in (400 mm) per game move. Naturally, it follows that a mixed unit containing both musketeers and pikemen will be restricted to the speed of the slower pikemen.

The lightest of all infantry were those armed with either the sword and buckler or the bow and arrows. These will be given a game move of 20 in (500 mm), irrespective of formation.

So far we have only allowed our infantry formations to advance. But let us suppose that they have been ordered to fall back, still facing the enemy. This is an order that can only be given to men 'in line'. A column being ordered to fall back would be obliged either to about turn and march away, so ending with its back to the enemy, or, if the space was available, to wheel about, again finishing with its rear to the enemy. The line will fall back at half its normal advance speed. In other words, the pikemen will fall back 6 in (150 mm) in a game move; musketeers 8 in (200 mm), sword and buckler units 10 in (250 mm).

We have mentioned the about turn order. This also will cost a unit 50 per cent of its game move.

Throughout the game, units often wish to change formation for any number of reasons. The column wishes to convert to line or vice versa. Again, this will cost the unit half its game move. Thus a unit of pikemen wishing to change from line into column and advance during the same game move will be able to adopt the new formation and move 6 in (150 mm) (measured from the original position of the standard bearer of the unit).

Finally we must consider what happens when a unit runs. This may either be towards the enemy, when it is referred to as a charge, or away from him, when it is a route. Any shaped unit may perform either of these acts, adding 50 per cent to the unit's basic move. Thus a sword and buckler unit falling upon an enemy unit at the charge may move a maximum of 30 in (750 mm). Similarly, the same unit running away would cover 30 in (750 mm), losing nothing for the fact that it turns about. (This is because it is not attempting to retain its tight formation and dressing in flight.) There is, however, a difference in the actual execution of the route and the charge. Pikemen and musketeers never charge towards an enemy.

Sword and buckler and light cavalry are the only units eligible to charge. They may do so during their game move providing such an action results in a mêlée.

During the route, the unit is moved the full distance in one single action. In the charge, however, the unit is first moved its normal move distance, when it halts and receives any fire that the enemy may be able to hurl at it. It will check its morale and then complete the move distance providing its morale is still good (on occasion, a unit will be entitled to make a double game move, in which case the above procedure will again be followed).

So much for the basic infantry moves. We must now take a look at basic cavalry movement. There are three types of cavalry, so we will examine each in turn.

We will start with the heavy cavalry, horses carrying men mainly encased in armour, men carrying swords and what may best be described as long pistols. Such troops were reluctant to charge home, preferring to approach the enemy at the trot, halt and fire, then wheel away to reload. Speed was not of any great importance. Such cavalry will be given a maximum game move of 20 in (500 mm), irrespective of type of formation. However, any change of formation will cost the unit 50 per cent of its move.

Next, we have the dragoons. Any old hack was considered good enough for a dragoon to ride. (A dragoon's horse could be purchased for as little as £4, compared with about £10 for other cavalry horses.) The horse was used purely as a method of conveyance, moving the rider from *A* to *B*. Having arrived at his destination, the dragoon would dismount and prepare to fight on foot (one-tenth of the force was required to stay with the horses). So, taking into account the poor quality of the mount, the dragoon will have a game move of 20 in (500 mm), 4 in (100 mm) will be deducted from the move to account for the mounting or dismounting. On foot, the dragoon will move at the speed of a musketeer.

Finally, we have the light cavalry horse. This constituted the majority of the cavalry. Such a rider may either charge home or approach, halt, and fire. Normal movement will be the walk or the trot, having a move of 20 in (500 mm), in column of twos increasing in action to 24 in (600 mm) in line or the full charge (in line) of 36 in (900 mm).

All pieces of artillery will be pulled on to the field by horses. The basic move for light artillery in this limbered-up condition will be 16 in (400 mm), so enabling it to keep pace with most of the infantry. In order to bring the gun into action it is necessary to unlimber. This action will cost the gun-team 4 in (100 mm). To limber-up again also takes 4 in (100 mm) off the move. Thus a light gun will only be able to move 12 in (300 mm) during the move that it first comes into action. One already in action and wishing to advance and fire will have a maximum move of 8 in (200 mm) (16 [400], less 4 [100] to limber-up, and 4 [100] to unlimber).

Heavy artillery have a maximum move of 12 in (300 mm) with a penalty of 6 in (150 mm) for each stage of limbering. From this it can be seen that it is impossible for a heavy gun to limber-up, move, and unlimber all in one game move.

So far, only the maximum movements of all three arms crossing flat, firm ground have been detailed. However, very little of the world's land mass can be said to fit this description. Even if one started from such a position, one would very soon be faced with a variety of natural and man-made features. Before long a hill will block the way or a wood; there would be a river to ford; a group of buildings with their ancillary walls and hedges appear; roads to speed the traveller, swamps and lakes to impede him. How will these features affect movement on the wargames table? Rules must be set down to cover all these eventualities.

Hills

On so many wargame tables, the battles appear to be taking place over mountainous areas, with troops struggling up precipitous slopes that only a trained mountaineer would attempt. In reality, the actual crossing over a steep hill in a battle is a rarity. So often the wargamer, wishing to re-fight an actual battle, will obtain a map of the territory, his eye will pick out a contour line and immediately convert it into a hill. Recently I visited the battlefield of Blenheim. My map indicated that the village stood on a hill. I knew this because a contour line ran across before the area marked with houses. In actual fact, the ground is as flat as a pancake, the rise from the trickle that masquerades under the name of river, the Nebel, cannot be more than a few feet, enough to require a line on the map, but so insignificant a slope as to be indistinguishable to the eye. Such a rise would have no effect upon the speed of any advance.

Hills, therefore, must be treated under three categories; the insurmountable, the steep, and the gentle.

1. The insurmountable. Cliffs will be indicated as such and it will be agreed before the commencement of the game that such a feature is impassable to all units.

2. The steep slope. As with insurmountable cliff, so the area of the steep slope must be agreed before the game commences. All units attempting to climb a steep slope will lose 50 per cent of their speed for the part of the game move they are actually on the up slope.

3. The gentle slope. Gentle slopes will be scaled with no penalty to a unit's movement entitlement.

Woods

Woods should be treated as two distinct types: those that are too dense to allow any formed movement and those that will merely slow down movement, yet still provide cover for the troops either hidden behind them or passing through them. Before the game it is essential to agree upon which type of wood is represented.

1. Dense wood. Artillery are not allowed to pass through dense woods, although they may shelter within their outskirts. All other units will lose 50 per cent of their game move distance.

2. Open woods. All units may pass through open woods, artillery losing 50 per cent of their game move, all other units sacrificing 25 per cent.

Villages

Villages must be considered in two ways as far as movement is concerned. Units simply moving along a road which passes through a village must be in column and will gain the normal 25 per cent road bonus, the fact that they are in the village is irrelevant. However, a village may also be looked upon as a collection of intersecting walls. When street-fighting is introduced, speed is greatly reduced. Units engaged in street-fighting will lose 50 per cent of their game move.

Hedges

Hedges are planted by man to enclose an area, making it impossible for animals to pass from one area to another. Artillery may only move through a hedge after a gap has been cut in it. This will take a full game move by the gunners who may not fire whilst engaged in the operation. Cavalry and infantry may push their way through a hedge at a cost of 3 in (75 mm) from their game move.

Walls

Walls play a similar role to hedges in that they enclose areas. Being much more substantial, they are more difficult to cross. For the artillery there is no question of it crossing a wall. Cavalry and infantry will lose 6 in (105 mm) from their game move when they make the attempt.

Roads

Roads are laid to assist movement. Being comparatively narrow, all units using them must be formed in column. Artillery moving along them should be limbered-up.

Units on roads may not pass through slower-moving units, but they may pass by leaving the road, so losing their road movement bonus for the distance they are off the road.

Units moving on a road will add 25 per cent bonus to their basic move for as long as they are on the road.

Rivers

Rivers are natural barriers to all units. This is not to say that they are impassable, although many wargamers treat them so, allowing troops to cross them only at fords and by bridges. Other rules simply deduct 50 per cent from the game move of any unit attempting to cross, completely ignoring the mystery of any river: its unknown depth and speed. My solution to the problem is to introduce a chance card in the form of a playing card, placed face down on the river. In a section agreed upon as a ford, this card will be drawn from cards numbered 2 to 5. Other sections of the river will each have cards numbered from

6 to the Jack. Only when a unit reaches a river bank may the card be turned (seen by the advancing side alone). The number will indicate the number of inches to be deducted from the unit as it attempts to cross. A Jack means that that section is too deep and the current is too fast to allow any unit to pass across. Any unit which starts to cross a river without an adequate number of inches of movement, will halt in the river, completing the move during the following game move. No unit may fire while standing in a river.

Swamps

Artillery are not allowed to move into swamps. Any guns forced into such an area will sink in the morass and be removed from the board. Other arms may cross swamps at 25 per cent speed.

Lakes

Artillery are not allowed to enter lakes. Any guns being forced into a lake will be lost. Other units may move at 25 per cent speed. Every man will be diced for every move he remains in the lake, any throwing 1 will drown.

Falling back

When a unit is ordered or is forced to fall back, it does so at half its normal speed and with its face towards the enemy. The unit will remain a single force. It will retreat in the direction of its choice. Should the unit be forced to fall back as a result of a bad morale throw, this movement will constitute its next game move. It will be free to move as desired during the following game move.

Running away

Should a unit run away it will do so at a speed of 50 per cent above its normal advancing movement. It will remain as a single entity. To indicate that this is a panic move and therefore one that has not been previously thought out, a die will be thrown to ascertain the direction of the flight, the unit having about-turned.

5 or 6 The unit will move directly to its rear.
1 or 2 The unit will move along a line 45° to its left.
3 or 4 The unit will move along a line 45° to its right.

This movement will constitute its next game move. Before moving again, it will be necessary to carry out a reaction test. Should the unit fail to stand, ie carry on falling back or running, it will be removed from the field, indicating that the unit has split up during the rout and is incapable of reuniting.

Any unit that a running or falling back force collides into must immediately carry out a reaction test of its own. Providing this unit stands, the retreating unit will be allowed to pass through it without hindrance.

Any unit reaching the edge of the board while running or falling back will halt, even if it has movement in hand. During its next game move it will endeavour to remain on the board by carrying out a reaction test. Any unit chasing an enemy from the board may attempt to return at the same point by throwing a 5 or 6. Thus a unit may never return or may be able to do so after one or two game moves.

Flank attack

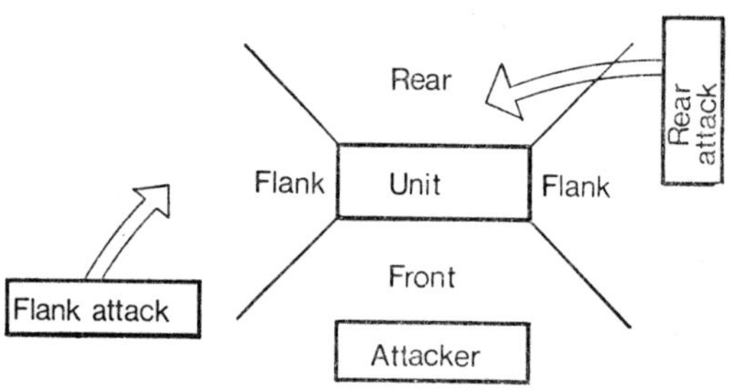

When a unit is engaged, either by fire or in a mêlée, it has the right to turn towards the attacker, providing it is not already running away. Thus a flank attack is normally only delivered by a second unit, as shown in the accompanying diagram. When such an attack is achieved, the casualties caused by the flanking unit are removed before the results of the frontal fight are calculated.

Rear attack

A rear attack may be launched under similar conditions to the flank attack, that is, the defending unit is already engaged by another unit to its front when the secondary attack is launched.

To achieve the movement to the rear, the attacking unit must start from a point within the area marked flank in the diagram, have enough room to complete the manoeuvre without being shot at in the flank themselves as they close.

A rear attack may also be launched against a unit already running.

8 | *The unit efficiency rating*

Let a unit commander assemble his men for action and lead them on to the battlefield. He may not be prepared outwardly to admit it, but in the pit of his stomach he will probably know exactly how they may be expected to perform. He knows how well or badly they have been drilled in the use of their weapons, how quickly they can change formation as the action demands. He knows when they last ate, when they last slept, and how far and how fast they have marched to the field. He knows if and when they were last paid or worse, perhaps they have been existing on promises. At his back he can hear their muttered grumbles, he can smell their fear. And being human himself he is caught up in the general feeling within the unit, be it one of determination or abject terror. His outward calmness will have a limited effect, but will it be enough?

Of course, none of these feelings are visible to the opponent unit assembled a few hundred yards away. The enemy captain is able to count the heads and note the variety of weapon. He can number their pike, assess their probable fire-power, the depth of their formation, and so calculate his chances of attack or defence. What he cannot tell is how the enemy will react to a well-aimed salvo of musket-fire. He cannot tell if he is opposed by a mass of raw recruits with just that stiffening of veterans or a battle-seasoned unit that will laugh at his clumsy manoeuvres before counter-attacking with devastating results.

So we are faced with the naked truth, the fact that until each commander puts his force to the test he has only a slight idea as to the final outcome. Cold steel and tearing shot are only partial battle-winners. The key to victory is morale. Morale. A movable factor, varying as the battle ebbs and flows, as casualties mount, as the enemy breaks and runs, as the company standard bearer is cut down and his beloved ensign carried away in triumph by his killer.

How can this morale factor be transferred to the table top? Surely a force of say fifteen 25-mm metal figures will not be expected to have a will of their own? Surely if a player decides to attack an enemy unit with his pride and joy bluecoats, it must happen. In chess, should a player decide to take one piece with another, then it must happen. Yet this is one of the fascinations of wargaming. The metal figures themselves begin to take over. The player finds himself still in over-all control, planning his general moves and hoping that the troops will react as he desires, but lacking the ability to control in detail.

What is required is a number—a secret number—relating to each individual unit, indicating the unit's pre-battle efficiency rating. This number will be recorded against the unit's name on the battle record chart. As the game progresses, the number will increase or decrease according to the unit's fortunes. If certain units are to be looked upon as being highly experienced, then they can expect to enter the game with a higher number than other similarly armed units. Again, a small force with a high efficiency rating will stand a good chance of overthrowing a larger but less efficient one.

This pre-battle efficiency, or morale, factor will be arrived at by the throw of a single die for each unit in the army. The throw of the die will be set against the simple table below, so giving the unit's *efficiency rating*. This number should be recorded in pencil, not in ink, as it may alter during the game, on the battle record chart.

PRE-BATTLE EFFICIENCY (MORALE) TABLE

	Die thrown			
Die throw for élite units		1, 2	3, 4, 5	6
Die throw for others	1	2, 3, 4	5, 6	
Unit's efficiency rating	1	2	3	4

This efficiency rating will govern all the actions taken by the unit, whether it be firing, engaging in a mêlée, or testing its morale for any reason. It may only be permanently increased if the unit is directly responsible for an enemy unit running away (increase 1 point). If more than one unit in a single game move was involved, the point is not awarded.

The unit's efficiency rating will be *permanently* reduced by 1 point under the following conditions:

1. If the unit runs away.

2. If the unit is reduced to 50 per cent of its original strength.

The unit's efficiency rating may be *temporarily* reduced by 1 point under the following conditions:

1. The unit is attacked in the flank.

2. The unit is attacked in the rear.

3. The unit is engaged either by fire or in a mêlée when crossing a river or fighting *in* a wood or *in* a village (not on their perimeters).

The unit's efficiency rating will be *temporarily* increased by 1 point under the following conditions:

1. The unit is under cover.

2. The unit is in a better position in a mêlée (top of a hill, defending a wall, etc.).

3. The unit is led by a staff officer.

Important note. Irrespective of all additions or subtractions, a unit's maximum efficiency rating is 4, its minimum is 1.

The efficiency rating of artillery units is dealt with under the chapter on artillery.

Control

Any unit being given an order to move will test its reaction to the command in the following manner:

1. Consult its current efficiency rating.

2. Throw a single die.

3. Add together the score of (1) and (2).

4. Consult the reaction table below.

REACTION TABLE

5 or over	Obey the order
4	Stand
3	Fall back
2	Run

Exceptions

1. A unit with a staff officer attached to it will obey without a reaction test.

2. A unit ordered into a mêlée will carry out a special reaction test (see p. 44).

3. Entry on to the board. All units all allowed to enter the field without being subject to the above test.

9 | *Personalities*

THE ROLE OF THE STAFF OFFICER

The over-all tactics of a battle are decided by the commanding officer, often in consultation with his staff officers. It is the role of these gentlemen throughout the course of the action to ensure that the proposed plans are carried out. They will also be expected to use their own initiative in any crisis that may arise, leading units into the attack, organizing them in the defence. Let us see how this role will be translated on to the wargames table.

Movement

Staff officers are normally mounted. They will move at the speed of light cavalry, a maximum of 36 in (900 mm). They may only command one unit at any one time. They may order a unit to carry out a certain course of action and then move to another unit during a game move. The first unit will obey the command, but the second unit will not be influenced until the following game move. Any unit under the command of a staff officer will automatically obey any movement orders without reference to a die throw.

Fighting

A staff officer is armed with a pistol (which has a firing range of 3 in [75 mm]) and a sword. His superior training in swordsmanship is reflected in the fact that his mêlée points value is half a point greater than that of an ordinary sword-bearing cavalryman. In a mêlée or a fire-fight, the staff officer will take his place in the line according to his own choosing. He is as liable as any other figure to become a casualty.

Casualty
Should a unit with which the staff officer is serving run or surrender, then he will be carried along with the others.

Efficiency factor
A staff officer adds 1 point to the efficiency of any unit to which he attaches himself (maximum of any unit will still not exceed 4). When he leaves the unit he carries this point with him.

THE ROLE OF THE STANDARD BEARER

In these rules, the standard bearer and all the officers of a unit have been collected together into one figure. He is the natural rallying point of any unit. The following rules will govern his behaviour on the field.

Movement
When the unit is advancing in column, the standard bearer will be situated half-way down the column. This has the advantage that should the column be ambushed and the leading files decimated, the standard bearer will not be among the first to fall. Also, when the column is ordered to form line, the standard bearer will find himself in the centre of the unit.

Fighting
A standard bearer has no fire-power. In a mêlée he will be given the same value as a pikeman.

When a unit is moving into the attack, the standard bearer must be in the front rank. When the unit is stationary, the standard bearer may be placed in the rear rank.

Casualties
The standard bearer must take his chance along with the other figures in the unit when casualties are being inflicted upon it. Should he fall, however, and the unit is not dislodged from its position, another figure (a pikeman if the unit possesses one) will be removed in his stead at the end of the game move and

the standard bearer will be reinstated, signifying that another officer has taken over the flag. Should the unit be forced back whilst the standard bearer is still down, then the standard will be deemed captured.

Efficiency factor

At any time that the standard bearer is not standing and with the unit, the efficiency factor of that unit will be temporarily down by 1 point (minimum unit factor is never reduced to less than 1, of course). Thus the loss of the standard by capture will automatically decrease the unit's efficiency factor by 1 point. Captured standards are immediately sent to the rear (removed from the table).

10 | *Firing*

THE SEQUENCE OF FIRE

Our wargame is based upon an alternative move system. This means that one army will be entitled to move all or any of its units, while the other side remains stationary. All firing, engaging in a mêlée, and checking of unit's efficiency are carried out before the opposing force is able to reply, moving, firing, engaging in a mêlée. Thus every unit that carries fire-arms is entitled to fire twice during a game move, once in the first half of the move and once in the second. With so many units involved, it is necessary to lay down an order of firing, not only as an aid to remembering to fire all one's pieces, but also to allow units that have not moved during the game move to have an advantage over those that did.

For simplicity's sake it is easier to separate the artillery fire completely from the infantry fire. We will therefore adopt the following order of fire.

1. Artillery

(*a*) Fire all non-moving guns. (A gun that merely selects a new target, but does not actually move from the spot is included in this category.) Firing is simultaneous by both armies. Casualties are removed when this firing is completed.

(*b*) Fire all guns that have moved and are still entitled to fire—namely, those light guns that are unlimbered and within range of the enemy. Firing is simultaneous by both armies. Casualties are removed when this firing is completed.

This completes the artillery fire.

2. Infantry and cavalry

(*a*) All infantry and cavalry units that have not moved during that section of the game move fire. Casualties are removed.

(*b*) All infantry and cavalry units that have moved during that section of the game move fire.

This completes the infantry and cavalry fire in the first part of the game move. After the mêlée and efficiency checks, the other side repeats the above two sections. It should be emphasized that units moving into a mêlée will not fire.

ARTILLERY

The methods of deploying artillery on seventeenth-century battlefields has been discussed elsewhere in this book. In the sections dealing with unit organization, it was decided to limit the number of types of guns available to the table-top general to two, a heavy field gun, which we will refer to as the saker and a light field gun, which will be known as a drake. (Purists have the choice of up to about a dozen types of gun and may wish to use other names.)

The heavy gun is manned by three gunners and so will represent a battery of three pieces, whilst the drake has a complement of two gunners, so representing two guns. Whenever the artillery is to fire, simply count the number of figures manning the pieces to obtain the number of guns available. When a hit is scored upon a gun, the gunner is removed to indicate the fact. Only when there are no gunners left is the model field piece removed from the table. In some wargame rules, infantry are allowed to be drafted into the ranks of the men serving the guns. As a retired artillery officer, I have always opposed this type of rule and under these rules with the gunner figures representing guns, such swapping about is impossible.

Artillery fire

Let us assume that the guns have been ordered to fire. The target has been selected and is found to be within range. The would-be firer declares his target and the number of guns he will fire at it. (The arc of fire will be taken as being 22° 30′ on either side of the zero line, drawn down the length of the gun's barrel.) If there is more than one target available to the gunners, the firer must state how many guns will be firing at each target. A single die is thrown for each gun firing.

Example. A saker gun (manned by three gunner figures) will throw three dice. Should two targets be selected, the firer will will announce, 'First die will be at target *A*, the other two at target *B*' (different coloured dice may be used if desired).

ARTILLERY RANGE

Heavy artillery (saker), maximum effective range	48 in (1·2 m)
Light artillery (drake), maximum effective range	32 in (800 mm)

These ranges are measured from the muzzle of the gun to any point of the enemy target and the target must not be obscured in any manner; ie, there must be a clear line of sight drawn along the barrel to the target.

CANISTER

Heavy artillery (saker), maximum effective range	12 in (300 mm)
Light artillery (drake), maximum effective range	8 in (200 mm)

Note. When firing canister, each figure will have two dice thrown for it instead of the normal one.

Method of scoring artillery hits

When deciding upon the method of scoring hits from musket-fire it was suggested that the efficiency of the unit firing was of major importance, a fact that most wargames completely ignore. So it should be with artillery fire. Each 'battery', that is, model gun representing two or three field pieces, is given an efficiency rating before the game commences (see p. 56). This it will keep throughout the game unless situations cause it to vary. These will be as follows.

1. Permanent reduction of 1 point.

(*a*) The battery is reduced to half strength. (In the case of heavy artillery, two gunners will have been removed, as the normal complement is three.)

(*b*) The battery has been routed.

Note. As the gunners represent actual guns, the model gun always moves with them and is never abandoned if they are routed.

2. Permanent increase of 1 point.
The battery forces an enemy unit into a rout due to its unaided gunfire.

3. Temporary increase of 1 point.
(*a*) The battery is stationed under cover.
(*b*) The battery is joined by a staff officer.

4. Temporary reduction of 1 point.
The battery is isolated (at least 6 in [150 mm] away from the nearest friendly unit) and is being engaged by infantry or cavalry.

When a battery is called upon to fire it will observe the following procedure.

1. Look up its current efficiency factor on the battle record chart.

2. Throw a single die for every gunner (figure manning the pieces) and consult the casualty table following.

CASUALTY TABLE

			Die thrown	
Hit in open	5, 6	4, 5, 6	3, 4, 5, 6	2, 3, 4, 5, 6
Hit under cover	6	5, 6	4, 5, 6	3, 4, 5, 6
Efficiency rating	6	2	3	4

Example. A battery of heavy artillery fires upon a regiment of infantry in the open. Its efficiency rating is 2. The number of guns in the battery is three. Therefore three dice are thrown, showing a score of 1, 3, and 5. Result, one hit upon the regiment, one figure being removed.

Artillery efficiency rating

Before the beginning of the battle, each battery (gun model) will throw a single die in order to establish the unit's efficiency. This will be decided by consulting the table following.

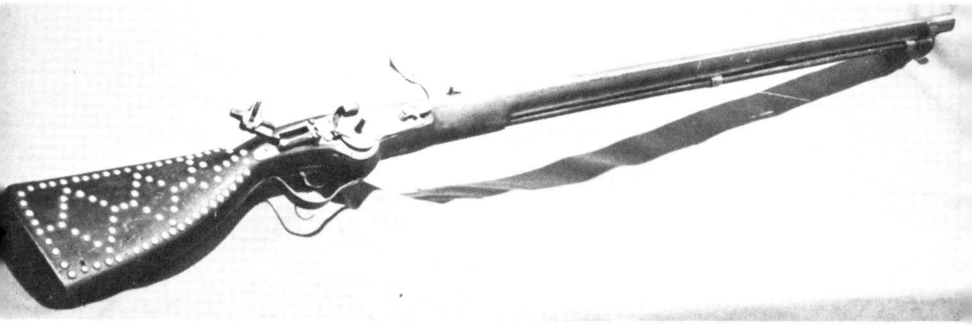

Above Combined 'wheel and matchlock' musket, with (*top*) detail of the mechanism.

Right A caltrop.

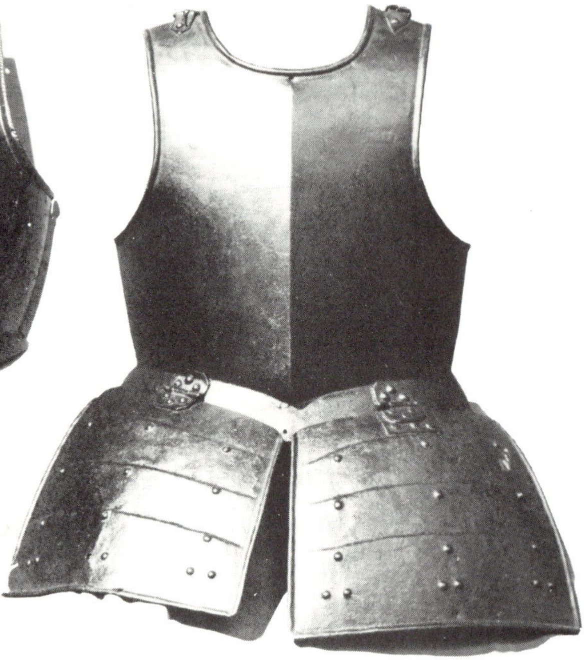

Top left Early Stuart cuirassier breastplate, with ribbed collar and arms.

Top right Pikeman's breastplate, with hinged tassets.

Above Lobster-tail helmet (the Dutch pot).

Far left Seventeenth-century English partizan.

Near left Sixteenth-century halberd.

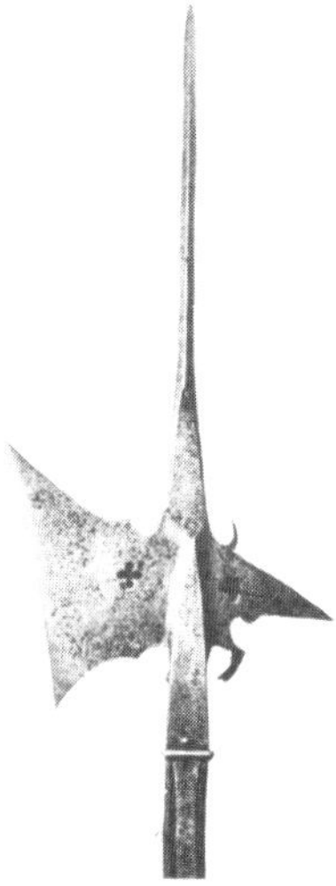

Right Lobster-tail 'siege' helmet.

Below Double-edged broadsword, with basket hilt.

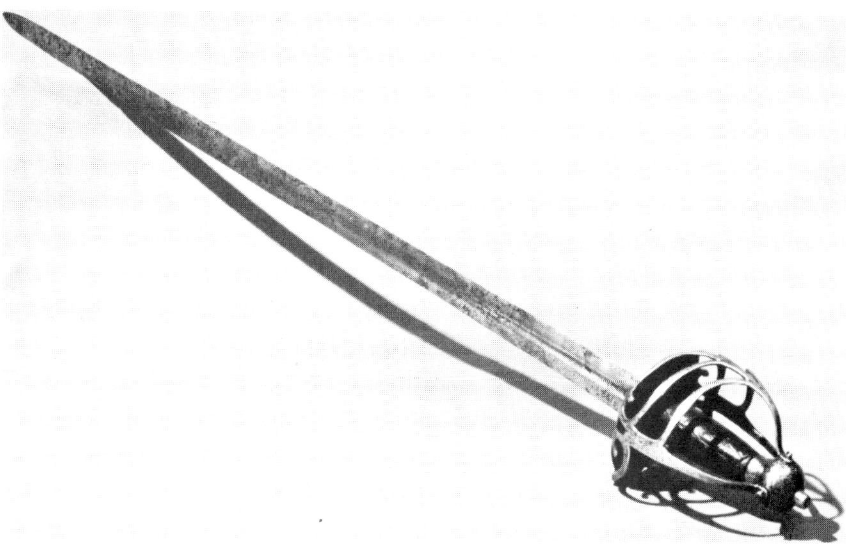

The battle of Cheriton, 29 March 1644.

Above A hill: the basic structure.

Above A hill: the finished effect.

Left A 'foam' hill.

The battle of Marston Moor, 2 July 1644.

Above Heavy artillery in action.

Above Musketeers.

Below Light artillery on the march.

The battle of Hopton Heath, 19 March 1643.

EFFICIENCY RATING TABLE

Die thrown	1, 2	3, 4	5, 6
Efficiency rating	1	2	3

Note. The maximum efficiency rating a unit may attain is 4. The minimum efficiency rating a unit may attain is 1.

PISTOL AND MUSKET FIRE

WEAPON RANGES

Pistol	30 yd (27 m)	3 in (75 mm)
Musket	150 yd (137 m)	15 in (375 mm)

Providing the enemy is within the above ranges and the firing unit is not charging nor already engaged in a mêlée, any figures in the front two ranks of the unit armed with either pistols or muskets are entitled to fire. To take into account the elaborate procedure of loading and aiming, 4 in (100 mm) will be deducted from the game move of any unit wishing to fire.

Having established who is entitled to fire, let us now decide upon a method of indicating firing. This can be done in a number of different manners. A single die could be thrown for every man with a firearm and depending upon the score on the die, so the casualties can be assessed. So let us assume that six men are to fire and it has been agreed that a throw of a 5 or a 6 will kill a man in the open, while a throw of a 6 will be needed to kill a man under cover. With six men firing, six dice will be thrown, resulting in a score of 2, 1, 6, 5, 2, and 2. If the target was in the open, then two hits would be registered; if under cover, only one. Some wargamers are prepared to add a further stage, introducing what is known as 'saving throws'. Taking our example of two men hit, the player commanding the unit suffering the casualties now throws a single die for each of his two men, attempting to throw 6s. For every 6 thrown, a figure is saved, ie, not hit.

This has always seemed to me a very odd way of going about things. Either the man was hit or he was not hit. Why waste time rethrowing dice? It is argued that this gives the defender a chance to save some of his men. Frankly, this is the last thing the attacker desires. In wargaming, advantages should be pressed home. It is war, not cricket.

The two main disadvantages to the single die per man firing system are firstly it is a time-consuming operation and secondly very unrealistic numbers of hits are often scored. In an effort to reduce the number of dice thrown, some wargamers agree to throw one die for every four, six, or eight men firing, scoring a single kill for every 5 and 6 as before. Unfortunately, using this method, the casualty rate is often even more unrealistic. Let us consider the case of one die being thrown for groups of six men and assume that eighteen men are to fire. Eighteen divided by six is three, so three dice will be thrown. Let us assume that the falls of the dice are 3, 4, and 3. This is very average throwing, no high numbers and no low ones. Yet no hits are recorded. Imagine it, average shooting by eighteen musketeers and not a hit among them!

Perhaps the answer lies in the use of casualty tables. Here the odds of hitting a target have been mathematically calculated. Down one side of the table is shown the number of men firing, say one to ten, or one to twenty. Across the top are the die scores, 1–6. The table of results based on these two lines gives an immediate answer. Take the number of men firing, say nine, throw a die, resulting in a 4, and then read off the kills, two. Easy! This method has the advantage of allowing every man to be included in the firing, the norm of hits is worked out in advance and is only slightly affected by chance (the die throw). A suggested table has been drawn up below.

MUSKET AND PISTOL FIRE TABLE

Men firing	*Target in the open* *Die throw*			*Target under cover* *Die throw*		
	1, 2	*3, 4*	*5, 6*	*1, 2*	*3, 4*	*5, 6*
1	—	—	1	—	—	1
2	—	—	1	—	—	1
3	—	1	1	—	—	1
4	—	1	2	—	1	1
5	1	1	2	—	1	2
6	1	2	2	—	1	2
7	1	2	2	—	1	2
8	2	2	3	1	1	2
9	2	2	3	1	1	2
10	2	3	4	1	2	2

It must be remembered that the weapons used were highly inefficient. The number of misfires was very high and even when the weapon did fire, the ball could only be expected to travel in the general direction of the target. The above table attempts to reflect the low hitting rate.

Unfortunately, the above methods of calculating casualties all fail to take into account the efficiency, or lack of it, displayed by the firing unit. Obviously, the more efficient the unit, the higher must be the possibility of it scoring casualties. In a previous chapter we have already seen that every unit will enter the field of battle armed with a unit efficiency rating of either 1, 2, 3, or 4. As these ratings are secret and will vary as the action proceeds, we are presented with a built-in chance factor which the enemy can only read once he has committed himself to a fire-fight. He literally has no idea whether the enemy unit he is about to engage will deliver a well-aimed, devastating volley that will destroy his own unit or merely reply to his own fire with a ragged, ineffective rumble. Below is a table which combines the number of men firing, their efficiency rating, and the anticipated number of hits. But we must allow for a slight variable. This is produced by the throw of a single die. A 1 or a 2 will indicate one kill less; a 3 or a 4 will indicate no change; while a 5 or a 6 will add one to the number of kills.

CASUALTY TABLE

Men firing	*Efficiency rating* 1	2	3	4
1	—	—	—	—
2	—	—	—	1
3	—	—	1	1
4	—	1	1	2
5	1	1	2	2
6	1	1	2	2
7	1	2	2	3
8	2	2	3	3
9	2	3	3	4
10	2	3	3	4

Example. A mixed unit of infantry, containing four musketeers, fire from cover upon an enemy unit in the open. The firing unit has an efficiency rating of 2. As it is under cover, this is temporarily raised to 3. Examining the fire table above we find that four men, with an efficiency rating of 3 score one hit. We now throw a single die, a 3 or a 4 will confirm the hit, a 5 or a 6 will increase it to two hits and a 1 or a 2 will negate it.

The above table has been drawn up for ten men firing. Should more than ten men fire, say fifteen, simply calculate the casualties for ten men and then for five and add the two scores together.

Cover

Should the target be under cover, total the number of men firing, half it, rounding *up* any fractions and read off against the new firing line. For example, should seven figures be firing at a unit under cover, then halve the seven, three and a half, rounded up to four and consult the fire table for four men firing.

The fire table has been designed for troops using matchlock muskets. However, the cavalry used the wheel-lock pistol and dragoons and a few other units, such as units detailed to guard artillery, were issued with the newer firelocks. When troops are using either of these weapons their efficiency is increased. This fact should be taken into account when determining these units' efficiency ratings. Units so armed will be treated as élite units.

11 | *Engaging in a mêlée*

THE MÊLÉE

In the pike and musket period, a set battle usually commenced with the two sides forming up within sight of one another. When the lines were properly drawn, the artillery would engage each other as if to signal the start. After much hesitation, either one, or perhaps both sides would advance. At about one hundred paces distance, the musketeers would open fire. On occasion, this may be all that was required before one side broke and ran, or simply withdrew, satisfied that it had blooded the enemy. Such engagements were rare. More often than not, having fired, the two sides closed upon each other to finish the affair with a push of the pike, a hand-to-hand mêlée between lines swaying, probing to find a weak spot that would open into a breach, a flood, a turned flank, a *coup de grâce*.

In the mêlée, as in the fire-fight, the unit's efficiency rating is the controlling factor. Naturally, the great difference between the fire-fight and the mêlée is the fact that the former is limited to figures carrying firearms, whereas every single man, no matter how armed, can partake in the latter. This is not to say that every man is in with an equal chance. Far from it. Just as certain men were trained to fire, so others were taught skills of defence and offence with the pike or the sword and buckler, how to hold off the enemy while the musketeers reloaded, to slip under the pike and kill with the sword and dagger. At certain times during the mêlée, one type of weapon would have a natural advantage, at a later stage, the same weapon could be almost useless. The rules that govern engaging in a mêlée can become extremely complicated. So let us examine the problem, analyse it and so emerge with a quick and simple solution.

The basic problem is this. In a mêlée, a variety of weapons, some more powerful than others, mixed in any proportion, are wielded by troops of differing efficiency.

We have already solved the problem involving the unit's efficiency—we simply refer to the 'unit efficiency' section on the battle record chart. This separates the units into poor, fair, good, and excellent. As to the numbers involved, again we will require a chart, drawn up in the same manner as was used when calculating musket-fire. The same chart can be used, so removing the necessity of introducing a second. This still leaves the variety and the anticipated killing power of each weapon to be considered.

A points value must be given to each type of weapon, so that the mêlée value of a force may quickly be calculated by simply totalling the number of each weapon, converting this total to points, so arriving at a final number. By looking this number up on the casualty chart, the kills will be determined. Let us therefore begin by giving each type of weapon a mêlée value.

The pike

Being such a long weapon, it follows that the pikeman was able to engage his opponent at a distance, whilst still retaining the weapon. This advantage must give the weapon a high points value. However, as we have seen, once the initial clash has taken place, the weapon loses a great deal of its purpose and should the pikeman be engaged in the flank or the rear, the weapon is virtually useless. We will, therefore, award the pike a points value of 1 in the first round of a mêlée and reduce it to half a point in subsequent rounds. In a flank attack or rear attack, it will always count as half a point.

The musket

As the bayonet had not yet been invented, the musketeer found himself saddled with a length of wood and metal, 3 or 4 ft (900 mm or 1·2 m) long according to type and era, and nothing else other than his cheap 4*s* 6*d* sword. He had the choice of this unreliable blade or of reversing his musket and using it as a club. No real advantage could be gained as the mêlée proceeded. The musketeer will be given a points value in the mêlée of half a point, irrespective of which round, flank or rear or front being attacked.

The sword and buckler

This was the weapon that finally destroyed the pike in Europe. Should the swordsman be able to parry the pike with his buckler and so close with his enemy, the poor pikeman became a chopping block. Bearing this in mind, we must reverse the points awarded to the pike. The sword and buckler, therefore, is given a points value of only half a point in the first round and a full point in all subsequent rounds.

The halberd

As we have seen, the halberd was used to cut down enemy pikemen after they had become held fast in the mêlée and was not usually to be found in the forefront of a battle line. We will, therefore, award it half a point during the first round, a full point in subsequent rounds.

The cavalry

There is one weapon which is common to all cavalrymen, namely, the horse. To be effective, the animal must be on the move, for, once brought to a halt, the horse may even become a hindrance. Half a point will be added to any rider whose horse is moving into a mêlée, but if the horse is stationary, as in the second round of a mêlée, cavalrymen will gain no advantage.

The lancer

The lancer will be treated as a mounted pikeman, that is, he will be given a first round points value of 1, plus a half for his horse, so totalling $1\frac{1}{2}$ points. As the lance becomes less useful after the first round, his value drops to a half, with nothing added for the horse. So the lancer can be seen to be a mêlée winner, providing the mêlée does not last for more than one round.

The swordsman

We have seen that the infantryman armed with a sword only comes into his own after the first round of the mêlée. He will, therefore, be awarded half a point (plus his half a point for an advancing horse). This will be increased to a full point in the second round, gaining nothing for the horse, as it will be stationary.

The dragoon

This warrior, although he rode a horse, was, in fact, merely a mounted infantryman. In other words, it was not his normal practice to seek a mêlée whilst being in the saddle. Should he be engaged whilst riding, he will score as the swordsman.

Staff officer

The staff officer normally fought with a sword and would therefore have the same points allowance as the swordsman. However, it should be recognized that such an officer was normally from the type of background where training with the weapon would have been from childhood. Half a point will be added to cover this extra training.

So we have covered the weapons that our troops will be carrying on our battlefields. They are summarized in the mêlée points table below.

MÊLÉE POINTS TABLE

	Type	*1st round*	*Subsequent rounds*
Infantry	Pikeman or standard bearer	1	½
	Musketeer	½	½
	Swordsman	½	1
	Halberdier	1	1
Cavalry	Swordsman	½ (1)	1
	Lancer	1 (1½)	½
	Dragoon	½ (1)	1
	Staff officer	1 (1½)	1½

The figures in brackets will be used if the cavalry are advancing as the mêlée is joined.

It will have been noted and no doubt with a little surprise, that gunners are nowhere mentioned in the above table. This is because no gunners as such appear on the table top. Each gunner represents a gun, not a number of men. It must be borne in mind that only two or three actual men manned these guns. In the use of the above table, one figure represents either 50 or 100 actual men (according to the battle being fought), so two or three men would not be represented in any case.

When totalling points, the final score will be rounded up to eliminate any half numbers.

Using the mêlée points table

Let us look at one or two examples of the use of the mêlée points table.

An infantry regiment of six pike, six musketeers, and a standard bearer are moving into a mêlée. Providing they suffer no casualties as they attack, their points value on impact would be: Pikemen: 6. Musketeers: 3. Standard bearer: 1. Total: 10.

Again, if they suffered no casualties during the round, their second round value would be: Pikemen: 3. Musketeers: 3. Standard bearer: ½. Total: 6½ (this would then be rounded up to 7 points).

This example illustrates the shock value of the pike.

A staff officer is leading a regiment of lancers (represented by five figures) in a cavalry charge. Translated into points, this will be expressed as follows: Five lancers: 7½. Staff officer: 1½. Total: 9 points.

Assuming they suffered no casualties in the first round, their points value would drop in subsequent rounds by half a point per horse and a further half a point per lancer, reflecting the inadequacy of the weapon at this stage of a mêlée. Five lancers: 2½ points. Staff officer: 1. Total: 3½ (again rounded up to 4 points in practice).

Point value modifications

All the above calculations have assumed a head-on clash in the open. But this is not always the case. Below are exceptions and their subsequent simple modifications.

A UNIT ENGAGED IN A MÊLÉE IN THE FLANK

When totalling the points available to such a unit, the player should use the 'subsequent rounds' column of the points value table. Thus in the example of the pikemen and musketeers quoted above, the unit would fight its first round with a points total of 7 and not 10. (Their attacker would use the 'first round' column, of course.)

A UNIT ENGAGED IN A MÊLÉE IN THE REAR

As with the flank attack, the 'subsequent rounds' column should be used *after* (1) deducting any impact casualties and then (2) checking the unit's morale to see if it will turn and fight.

A UNIT ENGAGED IN A MÊLÉE WHILST UNDER COVER

This time it is the attacking unit that is at a disadvantage, therefore the attacker will use the 'subsequent round' column, while the defender uses the 'first round' column. This applies to the first round only after which both will use the 'subsequent round' column.

A UNIT ATTACKING UP A HILL

Such a unit will merely lose its impetus (see 'Impetus').

MOVING INTO A MÊLÉE

Troops that have been well drilled and are, therefore, an efficient unit, are more likely to obey the word of command than their less efficient brethren. We can assume that all units will obey commands such as 'form line', 'about turn', etc. The order to open fire will be readily obeyed, in the hope that a well-aimed volley will cause such havoc within the enemy ranks that they will call it a day. The order to advance into a mêlée, however, is less likely to be so readily obeyed, for here the chips are well and truly down. The enemy, who until now are a mere faceless mass, are about to become individuals. It is kill or be killed.

A unit ordered to engage in a mêlée will test its reaction to the command in the following manner:

1. Consult its current efficiency rating.
2. Throw a single die.
3. Add together the score of (1) and (2).
4. Consult the reaction table below.

REACTION TABLE: ATTACKER

6 and over	Obey the order
5	Stand
4	Fall back
3	Run

Example. A unit with an efficiency rating of 2, ordered to engage in a mêlée with an enemy unit, throws a single die, scoring a 3. Two plus three equals five. The unit will ignore the command to join in the mêlée, standing muttering grave threats at the enemy, preparing to blaze away, but apparently unable to hear or understand their officers' pleas, threats, etc.

Similarly, a unit about to be engaged in a mêlée will suffer a reaction test. The enemy has decided to risk all, completed its reaction test, and is now closing at the double. Four choices are open to the unit under attack. It can:

1. Counter-attack.
2. Stand and receive.
3. Fall back, so hoping to avoid the clash.
4. Suddenly remember it is harvest time back home and run.

To ascertain which of these reactions the unit will make, simply look up the unit's efficiency rating, throw a single die, and consult the table below.

REACTION TABLE: DEFENDER

7 or over	Counter-charge
5 or 6	Stand
4	Fall back
3	Run

CALCULATING A ROUND OF A MÊLÉE

Let us assume that the attacking unit obeys the command to close and the defending unit accepts the challenge. If the counter-charge is ordered, then the casualties for both units will be calculated simultaneously.

Example. Our lancer unit of five riders and their staff officer (with their mêlée points value of 9) charges the mixed infantry unit of six pikemen, six musketeers, and a standard bearer (mêlée points value 10). The infantry unit counter-charges. Both sides will consult the casualty table simultaneously (p. 59). According to the unit's efficiency and the throw of a die, both will suffer casualties that will vary between one and five.

We will now assume that the same charge is to be made, with the difference that this time the infantry decide that they will meet the cavalry without moving. Before the cavalry close, the musketeers will fire. Should the lancers suffer casualties, they must test their morale before hitting home. Providing the ground is level, giving the infantry no hilltop advantage and they are not under cover, the cavalry will claim *impetus*.

IMPETUS

Impetus is expressed by the attacker being allowed to consult the casualty table first, casualties being removed from the defending unit before it is allowed to consult the table itself.

Example. Our cavalry with its 9 points scores, let us say, two hits. These turn out to be one pikeman and one musketeer (see 'Casualties', p. 71). The infantry now fight back as their contribution to the mêlée, but now they only have five pikemen and five musketeers and their standard bearer (5 plus $2\frac{1}{2}$ plus 1 equals $8\frac{1}{2}$, rounded up to 9). So they will fight with 9 points instead of the original 10.

THE CASUALTY CHART

The same casualty chart is used for calculating the dead in a mêlée as was used for the infantry fire-fight. It is the method of use that has been slightly altered. In the fire-fight, any figure in the unit stationed in the front two ranks of a formation and carrying a firearm was entitled to fire. The *total number* of such men was the criterion. In the mêlée, all were entitled to join in. They were converted to points and it is the *total points* that are used, not the figures.

In both cases, the die is used merely as a chance factor, giving a slight variation to the anticipated result.

Artillery in a mêlée

As the gunners manning the pieces represent guns and not men, it is not possible for the figure to be 'killed' in a mêlée. The choice open to Artillery is threefold; they can limber up and run, they can be overrun and captured, or they can be spiked.

When the enemy unit announces its intention to close into a mêlée (and it has tested its willingness so to do), the artillery must test its own desire to stand, using the following figures in conjunction with its own efficiency rating.

ARTILLERY ABOUT TO BE ENGAGED IN A MÊLÉE

6 or over	Limber up and move away.
5 and under	Stand and fire.

Should the artillery stand and fire and inflict casualties upon the attacker, that unit must test its willingness to continue the advance. Should it succeed in closing on to the piece, a further die is thrown to settle the issue.

1 or 2	The piece is spiked and the crew killed.
3 or 4	The gun is captured and may be turned upon its former side during the next game move.
5 or 6	The gunners are holding out. If the attackers are forced to withdraw the guns will be able to carry on firing during the next game move.

BREAKTHROUGH

The object of any attack is always to inflict a defeat upon the enemy, either by storming and securing a vital strongpoint, or by cutting through or round his lines, in such a manner as to throw him completely off balance. This limited victory within a battle will be termed a breakthrough.

Ours is a game of alternative moves and as such there is always a tendency for any success achieved during the first player's move to be nullified during the second player's turn. An advantage must be given to the player who has succeeded in forcing his enemy to flee. This will be achieved as follows.

Two units are engaged, either in a mêlée or in a fire-fight, when suddenly one breaks and runs. This flight is considered to be its next game move, so it will end it with its rear towards the enemy and at an agreed distance from him. This retreat will have left a gap in the line which the victor may care to exploit. He must first test his efficiency rating (which will have increased by 1 point through causing the enemy unit to run) and providing this is good, he may claim a bonus game move for the victorious unit and for any other units being within a game move distance of that unit and who have not been engaged in action during the game move.

This will enable the victor to pursue the routed unit, or attack any other enemy unit, or even to re-deploy the unit and bring up reserves to its aid. This exploitation will be continued should more enemy units break during the bonus move, always bearing in mind that only non-committed units within the game move may be employed. Once a unit has engaged an enemy and failed to rout him, that unit's turn is completed. Thus the initial collapse of a unit may lead to the rout of an entire wing before the defending general is able to respond.

12 *Casualties*

Having determined that artillery fire, musket and pistol shots, and hand-to-hand fighting results in casualties, the question remains, which figures have been hit within the unit on the receiving end. Each arm must be dealt with individually.

Cavalry
A cavalry figure is composed of two parts, the rider and the horse, either of which may be brought down as a casualty. A single die is thrown for each hit, an odd number signifying that a horse has been killed, an even that the rider is dead. Should one man and one horse be hit, remove one complete figure, not a horse from one flank and a rider from the other. The selection of the actual man will be the same as for infantrymen.

Infantry
An infantry unit will contain an officer and an undetermined number of other figures, some of whom may carry a pike, some a musket, some a bow, etc. In order to determine which has been hit, it is necessary to adopt the following procedure.

1. Agree upon the number of casualties that have been scored.

2. The firer elects to score hits either from the left or the right of the unit and informs his opponent of his decision.

3. He throws a single die and counts along the front rank of the target unit according to the fall of the die. After each hit he continues on along the row, starting again at his chosen flank each time he completes the row until all the casualties

have been removed. Should there be a gap in the front rank, a figure will be removed from the second rank.

Example. Three hits are scored on the infantry unit in the accompanying diagram. The player firing elects to score these hits starting from the left flank and he informs his opponent of his decision. The die is thrown and a 2 is recorded. Counting along the front rank beginning at the left, the figure numbered 1 is removed. Carrying on along the front for a further two, the figure numbered 2 is the next to bite the dust. This is the last figure in the line and still one casualty remains to be removed. The counting is started again from the left, but this time a count of two lands where the first kill occurred. The shot is, therefore deemed to have struck the figure in the second rank, numbered 3.

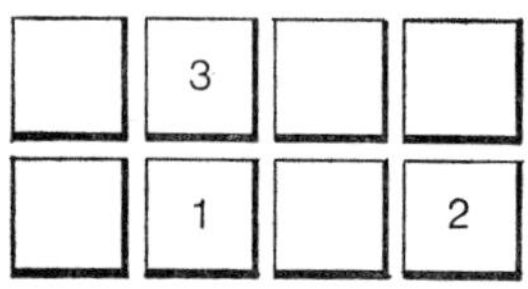

Artillery

As all gunner figures within a battery of artillery are of equal value, no dicing to select the actual casualty is necessary.

Prisoners

Prisoners are taken when a unit runs away or is forced to fall back whilst engaged in a mêlée (see p. 61).

METHOD

In a mêlée between infantry and infantry, or cavalry and cavalry, should one unit run or fall back, a single die is thrown for every man within the unit, including the standard bearer and a staff officer should he be temporarily attached. Any die showing a 1 indicates that one figure has surrendered. Commence by throwing a die for the staff officer, then one for the standard bearer, then for all the musketeers, the pike, etc.

Should infantry run or fall back in mêlée whilst fighting cavalry, a die throw of 1 or 2 will result in capture.

Captured figures are removed from the board.

Evaluating casualties

KILLED

When a figure is killed it is removed from the table and is therefore out of the game. Let us assume that a single figure represents 100 men and that the unit is made up of nine figures (900 men all told). During the game it may suffer seven casualties before it breaks and flees the field. It is unreasonable to imagine that the 700 men represented would be considered dead. A much more realistic figure is achieved simply by declaring that one-tenth are slain. Thus the regiment losing its seven figures has in fact lost 70 killed in the action.

CAPTURED

A much higher number of men must be represented when a figure surrenders when compared with those who die. When calculating the numbers captured, assume that 50 per cent are taken. Should our regiment of 900 lose seven figures, then 350 men will be in enemy hands.

13 | *The battle record chart*

By using the alternative move game, we have been able to dispense with the order sheet so dear to the heart of many wargamers. The only record that must be kept is the unit's current efficiency rating. Every unit has its own efficiency rating, which may change as the battle progresses. As every unit carries a standard or pennant, identification on the table is simple. Also, our rules state that when a unit is reduced to below half its original strength, its morale falls, it is neccessary to record its strength as it enters the field.

So the battle record chart must record the following:

1. A simple sketch of the unit's standard.
2. The original total strength of the unit.
3. The unit's current efficiency rating.

Further information may be added as desired. Players may wish to name their units after known or imaginary leaders or regiments. So we may refer to 'Norfolk's Redcoats' or 'Newcastle's Whitecoats', rather than simply saying Regiment 2' or 'Unit 4'. Some wargamers may care to record the number of pike or shot in each unit's ranks at the beginning of the battle. It will be realized by the reader that all this superfluous information can be entered and not changed, so with the only variable being the unit's efficiency rating, book-keeping is reduced to a minimum.

It is suggested that a blank column should be left on the chart. Here will be recorded the unit's performance in the battle for future reference. For example, 'ran away' or 'took no active part', or 'captured an enemy standard'. The next time the unit takes part in a battle, these facts can be examined and after recruits have been drafted in to replace any casualties, its current efficiency rating will be used for the coming battle, so giving continuity during a campaign.

A suggested layout of a battle record chart appears below.

BATTLE RECORD CHART

REGIMENTAL NAME	STANDARD	ORIG. STR.	TYPE P	TYPE M	TYPE Sw	TYPE L	EFFICIENCY FACTOR				BATTLE REPORT D	BATTLE REPORT C	PERFORMANCE
BASSETT'S HOUNDS		12	5	7	-	-	~~3~~	2			3	1	Ran away
BRETT'S MUSKETEERS		10	1	9	-	-	~~4~~	~~3~~	2		5	-	Heavily engaged
GERARD'S OWN FOOT		9	6	3	-	-	3				-	-	Not engaged
DOUBTY'S DRAGOONS		10	-	10	-	-	2	1			3	3	Surrendered

KEY
P pike, inc. s/b
M musketeer
Sw swordsman
L lancer
D dead
C captured

14 | *Battle reconstructions*

The remainder of this book is devoted to a series of actual battles in which English armies fought during the pike and musket period. The intention is to enable the wargamer to reconstruct each battle using a simplified layout, incorporating all the major features of the battlefield, scaled-down armies, and the various objectives of each army engaged. Here is the reader's chance to take command, faced with the military problems of the day and to attempt to improve on, or to change the results of history, according to his skill.

Each battle has a separate section devoted to it. Each is treated in the following manner:

1. A description of the actual events.

2. The forces engaged. These have been computed from many sources. In some cases, conflicting numbers appeared in different accounts; often the proportion of infantry to cavalry can only be estimated; artillery is mentioned, but no details given. In these instances, intelligent guesses have been made. From these the wargame equivalents have been drawn up.

3. A wargame map of the battlefield, showing all the major features. The start-lines of the armies are drawn in. Every map is accompanied by a breakdown of the number of units required (the actual number of figures in each unit is left for the reader to allocate).

4. The type of battle is detailed, along with its figure scale. The layout is described as are any special rules appertaining to the battle. Finally, the objectives of the two armies are declared.

Key to the battle maps

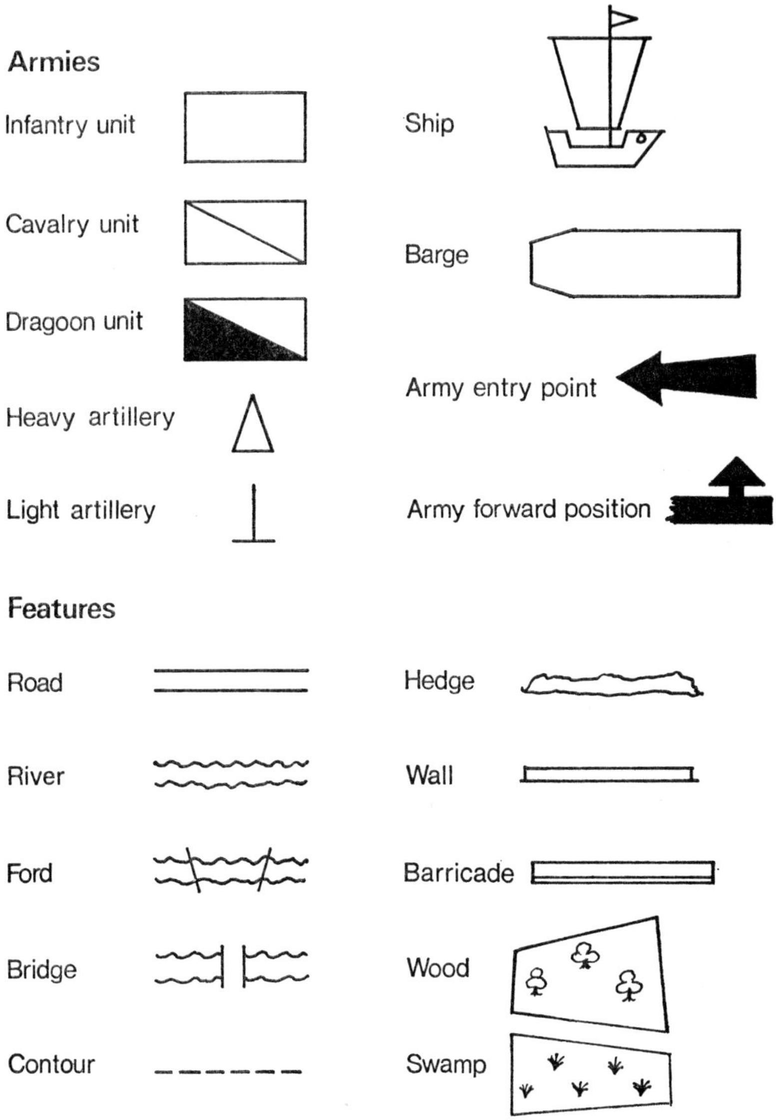

10 September 1547

THE BATTLE OF PINKIE

Henry VIII was dead. In his will he declared that his son, Edward, should marry the four-year-old Mary, Queen of Scots. But the Scots had other plans for Mary and were prepared to express them in blood if necessary. So words led to deeds as the political climate deteriorated, each country looking for an excuse to publicly rebuff the other. At sea, a small naval action was fought, Scotland losing the most prized ship in her fleet. On both sides of the Border troops began to mass. The royal 'wooing' had begun.

It was the English army that took the initiative. Led by the Duke of Somerset, about 12,000 infantry and 4,000 cavalry followed the eastern coast-line, always keeping within hailing distance of his supporting ships. Edinburgh was their objective and they were within sight of the hills guarding the City when they came across the Scottish host encamped at the small town of Musselburgh. Between the two armies ran the River Esk, fast flowing and steep banked. Each side occupied a position that was the mirror image of the other. One flank rested on the sea. The other was guarded by woods. The centre was too narrow to allow for the full deployment of the size of forces each commanded. Obviously, neither would wish to attack, both would prefer to defend.

During the evening of 9 September there occurred a small cavalry engagement as the two contestants examined each other's lines. What the English lacked in numbers of men they made up for with their superiority in artillery. The battle commenced, therefore, with a bombardment by these guns of the Scottish camp. The Scots were stung into action and they determined to rid themselves of these guns. They filtered across the bridge over the Esk and formed up to attack the heights of Inveresk, when all hell was let fly upon their cramped formations as arrows, shot, and arquebus fire thinned their ranks. To add to their discomfort, English ships joined in the bombardment. The Scottish left wing broke. The bridge became choked with dead as the entire army tried to extricate itself.

Fugitives were pursued for miles. 1,500 were taken prisoner. Some reports claim that the dead numbered 14,000.

Actual numbers engaged in the battle

English		*Scots*	
Foot	12,000	Foot	23,000
Horse	4,000	Horse	1,500
Artillery	15 heavy cannon	Artillery	A few, possibly 6
Ships	Small fleet		

Wargame figures required for reconstructing the battle

English		*Scots*	
Foot	3 Standard bearers	Foot	4 Standard bearers
	39 Pikemen		80 Pikemen
	3 Halberdiers		4 Axemen
	12 Archers		16 Sword and buckler
	3 Arquebusiers		11 Archers
Horse	20 Swordsmen	Horse	7 Lancers
Artillery	5 Heavy guns	Artillery	3 Light guns
	15 Gunners		6 Gunners
Ships	2 Warships		

Staff officers

English	*Scots*
Duke of Somerset	Earl of Arran, Regent of Scotland
Lord Grey	Earl of Angus
Earl of Warwick	Lord Hume

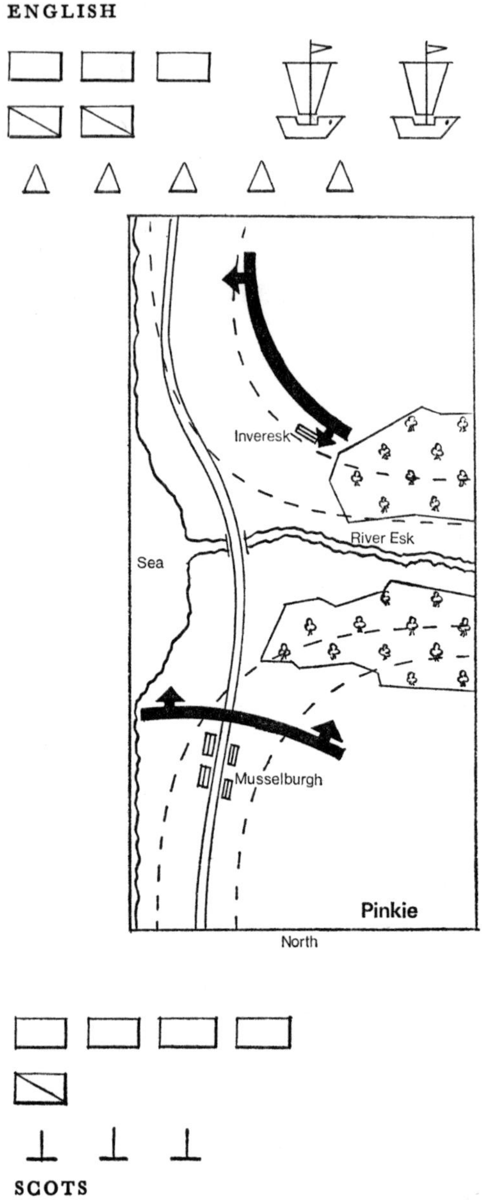
ENGLISH
Inveresk
River Esk
Sea
Musselburgh
Pinkie
North
SCOTS

Battle type. Set piece.

Scale. 1 figure represents 500 men.

Layout. The eastern baseline is the North Sea. There are two plateaux, one forming the south-western corner of the board, the other the north-west. Between runs the River Esk. Slopes are steep. (All units move at half speed when climbing these slopes.)

English. Troops are placed in position anywhere on the southern plateau. There are no reserves off the table.

Scots. All the units are placed on the board, their foremost disposition being the village of Musselburgh.

Special rules. The English ships may enter the area marked 'Sea' at the beginning of the fourth game move. Each ship is to be treated as a battery of light artillery. They will remain at anchor for the rest of the battle.

Objectives. The complete destruction of the enemy land forces.

Elite units. English: 3; Scots: 0.

14 August 1598

THE YELLOW FORD

Once again the flag of rebellion flew in Ireland, raised on this occasion by Hugh Tyrone, the Earl of Tyrone himself. Ulster became a virtual no-man's land to the English. Tyrone country began at the Blackwater River. Here the English had established a fort as an advance post from whence the re-conquest could begin. There was only one problem. The post was too far advanced and consequently this posed a problem of supplying the garrison whilst the main expedition was being assembled. Tyrone decided to force the English hand and besieged it. Without fresh supplies the fort would surely fall.

Sir Henry Bagenal, acting on behalf of the Lieutenant-General, the Earl of Ormonde, raised an army of over 4,000 men, including a small cavalry escort and a few guns, departed from Newry, moved through the town of Armagh and, on 14 August, advanced towards the Blackwater. Across his path ran the River Callan.

During the march the six infantry regiments had become over-extended, with the result that when flanking fire suddenly pounded the two leading units, those following were in no position to give immediate assistance. From the start there was chaos. One of the guns was lost in the ford. A powder waggon exploded through carelessness.

Whilst attempting to restore order, the commanding officer of the van, Colonel Richard Percy was slain, shot through the head. As the regiments of the main force tried to press forward they ran into the leading regiments moving at an equal speed in the opposite direction. The rear-guard found itself pinned down and unable to move. Inevitably panic spread, fanned on by the fact that the musketeers were running out of ammunition. The retreat, such as it was, was successfully covered by the cavalry.

Of the force of over 4,000 that had left Armagh, over a third had been lost. Within a few days, the defenders of the fort on the Blackwater surrendered.

Actual numbers engaged in the battle

English		*Irish*	
Foot	3,900	Foot	4,050
Horse	320	Horse	600
Artillery	3 or 4		

Wargame figures required for reconstructing the battle

English		*Irish*	
Foot	6 Standard bearers	Foot	12 Standard bearers
	30 Pikemen		16 Pikemen
	6 Halberdiers		6 Axemen
	36 Musketeers		29 Musketeers
Horse	6 Swordsmen		6 Archers
Artillery	2 Drakes		12 Sword and buckler
	4 Gunners	Horse	6 Swordsmen
			6 Lancers

Staff officers

English	*Irish*
Sir Henry Bagnal	Hugh Tyrone
Colonel Richard Percy	Hugh O'Donnell
Sir Thomas Wingfield	Keith Kavanagh (f)*

* (f) indicates a fictitious name.

ENGLISH

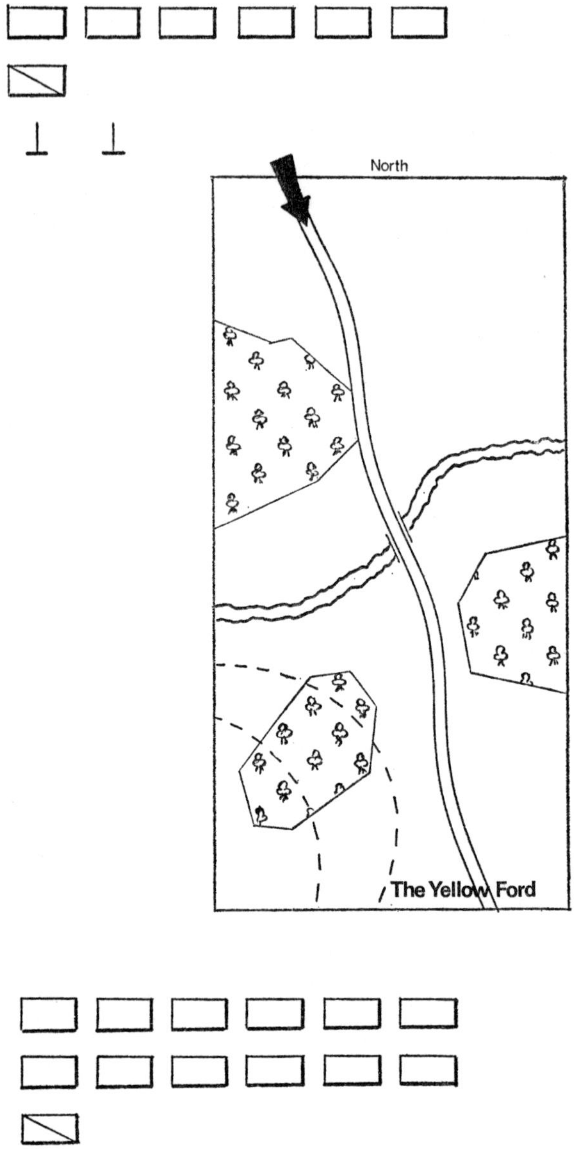

IRISH

Battle type. Ambush.

Scale. 1 figure represents 50 men.

Layout. The field is flat, except for a hill in the south-western corner. Its slopes are steep. (All units move at half speed when climbing them.) All woods are passable by any arm, except artillery. The river is fordable. (Use cards 2–8.)

English. Enter at arrow on the northern baseline. No troops are on the board at the start of the game. The order of entry must be written down before the game begins.

Irish. All units should be plotted on paper. Troops hidden in or behind the woods are only declared and placed on the board if: (1) the English try to enter the woods; (2) the English move into position enabling them to see behind the woods; (3) the Irish declare their position by firing muskets from the edge of woods.

Special rules. None.

Objectives. English. To leave the board by the road at the southern baseline. Irish. Simply to stop them achieving this objective.

Elite units. English: 4. Irish: 1.

5 August 1599

ACTION IN THE CURLIEU HILLS

In April 1599, the Earl of Essex was appointed Lord-Lieutenant of Ireland. He had inherited a war-torn country and a demoralized army with which to hold it. He campaigned to little effect, finally falling back to his main base at Dublin. One of his Irish allies, Sir Donogh O'Connor was beseiged in Collooney Castle by Hugh O'Donnell.

Upon hearing this news the Governor of Connaught, one Sir Conyers Clifford, determined to raise the seige and, having collected a force of about 1,500 men, moved out of Boyle and marched to the relief. Late on the afternoon of 4 August his little army reached the foothills of the Curlieus. Clifford, against all advice, decided to cross the hills immediately, expecting to make camp on the shores of Lough Arrow.

In spite of the fact that he had a small cavalry force which could have been used to scout ahead, he elected to leave these with the baggage and to advance his entire infantry arm straight up the pass. Sir Alexander Radcliffe led the van, the main body, which included Clifford, was commanded by Lord Dunkellin, while Sir Arthur Savage brought up the rear. The English passed with safety between two areas of bogland and then ran into heavy firing from a nearby wood. The English deployed and, advancing and firing, they drove the Irish out of the wood, only to be halted themselves by new firing from further up the slope. Panic spread through the leading formations as they began to run out of powder and within minutes it had transferred itself to the rest of the English foot. They broke. Trying desperately to rally his men, Clifford fell, run through by an Irish pike. Only a cavalry counter-attack allowed the shattered remnants of the army to fall back into Boyle. Almost one in three failed to answer the call to arms on the following morning. The Irish losses had been trifling. Clifford's severed head was sent to O'Donnell as a grim token of victory.

Actual numbers engaged in the battle

English		*Irish*	
Foot	1,500	Foot	1,800 (estimate)
Horse	205		

Wargame figures required for reconstructing the battle

English		*Irish*	
Foot	6 (6) Standard bearers	Foot	9 (6) Standard bearers
	44 (21) Pikemen		40 (15) Pikemen
	6 (6) Halberdiers		9 (9) Axemen
	94 (42) Musketeers		60 (29) Musketeers
Horse	10 (5) Swordsmen		30 (15) Archers
	10 (5) Lancers		32 (16) Sword and buckler

The numbers have been calculated to a scale of 1 figure to 10 actual men. In the brackets are the numbers required for fighting at a scale of 1 figure equals 20 men. It will be noted that the number of standard bearers and their protecting halberdiers and axemen have not been altered.

Staff officers

English	*Irish*
Sir Conyers Clifford	Brian Oge O'Rourke
Sir Alexander Radcliffe	Phelim O'Cahan (f)
Lord Dunkellin	Red MacWilliam (f)
Sir Arthur Savage	Neill Cormac (f)

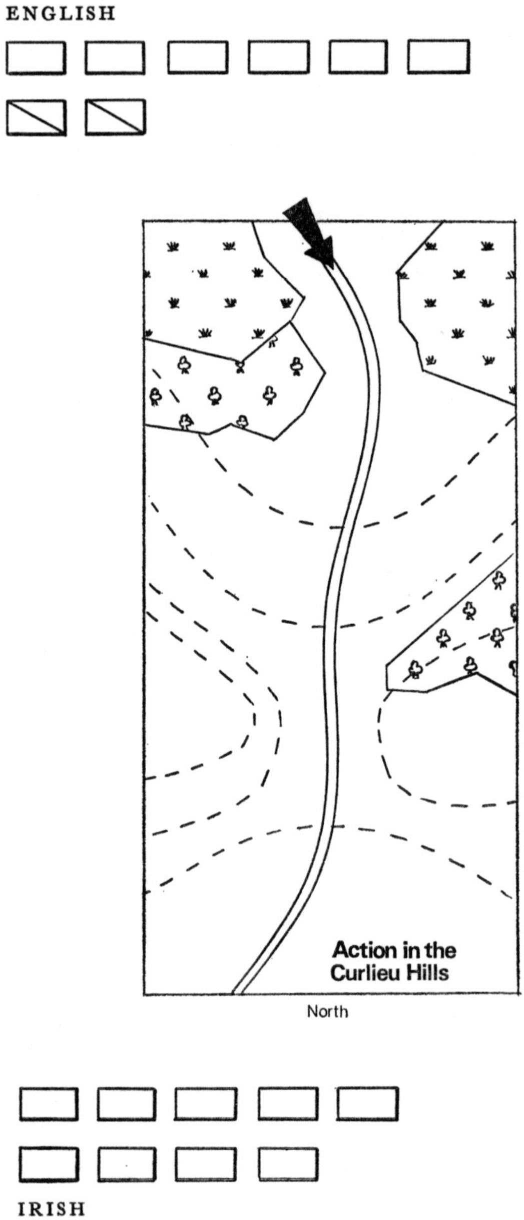
ENGLISH
Action in the Curlieu Hills
North
IRISH

Battle type. Ambush.

Scale. 1 figure represents 10 men (brackets show a scale of 1 figure representing 20 men).

Layout. A road enters the board from the south, between two bogs, one of which is bordered by a wood. It then climbs a gentle slope (no loss of movement when climbing), crosses a plateau and descends to the north. On either side of the high plateau, steep slopes rise, one of which is wooded.

English. Enter the board at arrow on the southern baseline. No troops are on the board at the start of the game. The order of entry must be written down before the game begins.

Irish. All units should be plotted on paper. Troops hidden in or behind the woods are only declared and placed on the board if: (1) the English try to enter the woods; (2) the English move into position enabling them to see behind the woods; (3) the Irish declare their position by firing muskets from the edge of woods. Troops on the plateau are only visible to the English if they have managed to climb up to it.

Special rules. None.

Objectives. English. To leave the board by the road at the northern baseline. Irish. Simply to stop them achieving this objective.

Elite units. English: 2. Irish: 0.

2 July 1600

THE BATTLE OF NIEUPORT

By 1600, the Dutch held most of the Flemish coast. To maintain her army, it was essential that Spain should keep the Channel ports of Dunkirk and Nieuport open. Prince Maurice was equally determined to cut this jugular vein. He collected his polyglot army near Bruges, a force of about 14,000 men, nearly all infantry, of whom 4,000 were English. Nieuport was selected as his first objective. Having reached the coast without incident, the army settled down to the task of beseiging the town.

The Spaniards were not going to lose such an important harbour without a fight. Archduke Albert of Austria, leading a Spanish army about equal to Maurice's, marched to the relief. Hearing of the Archduke's approach, Prince Maurice, having failed to delay him a few miles from the port, advanced along the beach to do battle. The two contestants halted about a mile apart and formed their lines.

Each had an apparently safe flank—the sea. But this very feature was to create problems and dominate the battle. Between the sand dunes and the sea stretched an area of hard sand, an area on which to manoeuvre with ease, but an area that was steadily decreasing as the tide rolled in. Bearing this in mind, both armies placed six guns on the flank furthest from the sea, the Archduke's remaining two guns facing the sea as a new danger hove into sight. Dutch warships were about to support their army.

Sir Francis Vere was given the honour of leading the van with his 4,000 English, supported by cavalry. About two o'clock the Spanish horse advanced to the attack, only to be halted by gunfire. Maurice ordered his own cavalry to charge them, routing them completely. By now, the Archduke's infantry was fully committed and was pressing back Sir Francis. Maurice refused to support him until the Spanish advance had exposed their open flank. When Maurice eventually gave the order to attack, it proved to be devastating. In the struggle the Archduke was wounded, his second-in-command was captured, and his army was destroyed. In spite of his victory, Maurice failed to take the port.

Actual numbers engaged in the battle

Anglo-Dutch		*Spanish*	
Foot	11,000	Foot	10,000
Horse	1,700	Horse	1,500
Artillery	6 guns	Artillery	8 guns

Wargame figures required for reconstructing the battle

Anglo-Dutch		*Spanish*	
Foot	8 Standard bearers	Foot	7 Standard bearers
	42 Pikemen		38 Pikemen
	52 Musketeers		48 Musketeers
	8 Halberdiers		7 Halberdiers
Horse	17 Swordsmen	Horse	15 Swordsmen
Artillery	3 Drakes	Artillery	2 Sakers
	6 Gunners		1 Drake
Ships	2 Warships		8 Gunners

Staff officers

Anglo-Dutch	*Spanish*
Prince Maurice of Nassau	Archduke Albert of Austria
Sir Francis Vere (English)	Mendoza, Marquis of Guadalete

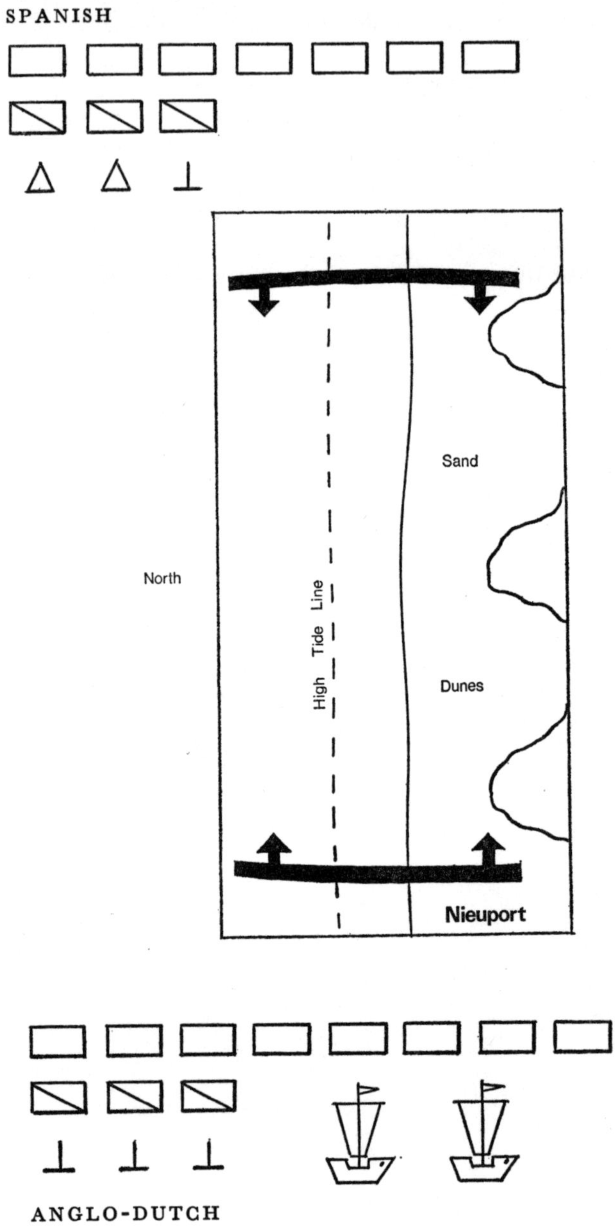
SPANISH
North
High Tide Line
Sand
Dunes
Nieuport
ANGLO-DUTCH

Battle type. Set piece.

Scale. 1 figure represents 100 men.

Layout. The table is roughly divided in half by the line of the dunes which runs from east to west. The area to the north of this line is flat, representing hard sand, to the south it is raised in gentle slopes, being sand dunes, with three low, flat areas on the southern baseline. At the beginning of the game the tide is out. It will advance towards the dunes at a rate of 3 in (75 mm) each game move to a maximum distance of 15 in (375 mm). It will remain at high tide for one game move, after which it will recede, again at 3 in (75 mm) per move.

Spanish. Troops are placed on the board anywhere along the eastern baseline, to a maximum depth of 12 in (300 mm). All units are on the board at the start of the game.

Anglo-Dutch. Troops are placed on the board anywhere along the western baseline, to a maximum depth of 12 in (300 mm). All units are on the board at the start of the game except the ships, which may appear at any point they desire or the tide allows. They may never be within 6 in (150 mm) of the tide line. They may move up to 6 in (150 mm) per game move. They are treated as a battery of light artillery and are considered sunk if the guns are destroyed (guns are considered under cover).

Special rules. Movement over the sand dunes is reduced by half for all units. Any troops standing more than 3 in (75 mm) in the water will be drowned.

Objectives. The annihilation of the enemy land forces.

Elite units. Spanish: 4. Anglo-Dutch: 4.

2 October 1600

THE BATTLE OF THE MOYRY PASS

Following the recall and disgrace of the Earl of Essex, Elizabeth appointed Charles Blount, Lord Mountjoy, as the next Lord Deputy of Ireland. Within weeks, the spirits of the army had risen considerably and reinforcements landed to swell his ranks. Mountjoy decided to settle with Tyrone once and for all.

The situation was not good. Armagh had fallen to Tyrone so Mountjoy made this his first objective as this would give him an advance base for his final assault into County Tyrone. He assembled his force at Newry, from whence they marched through Dundalk to Faughard. Before him was Moyry Pass.

Here he discovered Tyrone waiting for him, backed by an army of 3,500 men. The pass itself was well wooded and Tyrone had improved the position with a series of trenches.

On 1 October, Mountjoy made some probing attacks to test the morale fighting qualities of his small army and the determination of the enemy. These initial assaults were thrown back but the position of the earthworks had been noted. Mountjoy decided to attack in full strength the following morning. The fighting was extremely bitter, the Irish contending each trench and only falling back to the next one when overwhelmed. Finally Mountjoy stood at the head of the Pass and the remaining Irish troops melted away. There was no question of attempting to hunt them down. Mountjoy was content with the knowledge that he had defeated his enemy. He filled in the trenches, cut back the woods from the roadside to avoid any further ambushes at this point and then retreated back to Newry. He had lost over 200 men, but claimed to have inflicted more than double that number upon the enemy.

Actual numbers engaged in the battle

English		*Irish*	
Foot	3,450	Foot	3,300
Horse	375	Horse	250

Wargame figures required for reconstructing the battle

English		*Irish*	
Foot	6 Standard bearers	Foot	9 Standard bearers
	42 Pikemen		32 Pikemen
	84 Musketeers		66 Musketeers
	6 Halberdiers		9 Axemen
Horse	15 Swordsmen		16 Sword and buckler
		Horse	5 Swordsmen
			5 Lancers

Staff officers

English	*Irish*
Lord Mountjoy	Hugh, Earl of Tyrone
Sir Henry Danvers	Keith Kavanagh (f)
Sir William Godolphin	Neill Cormac (f)

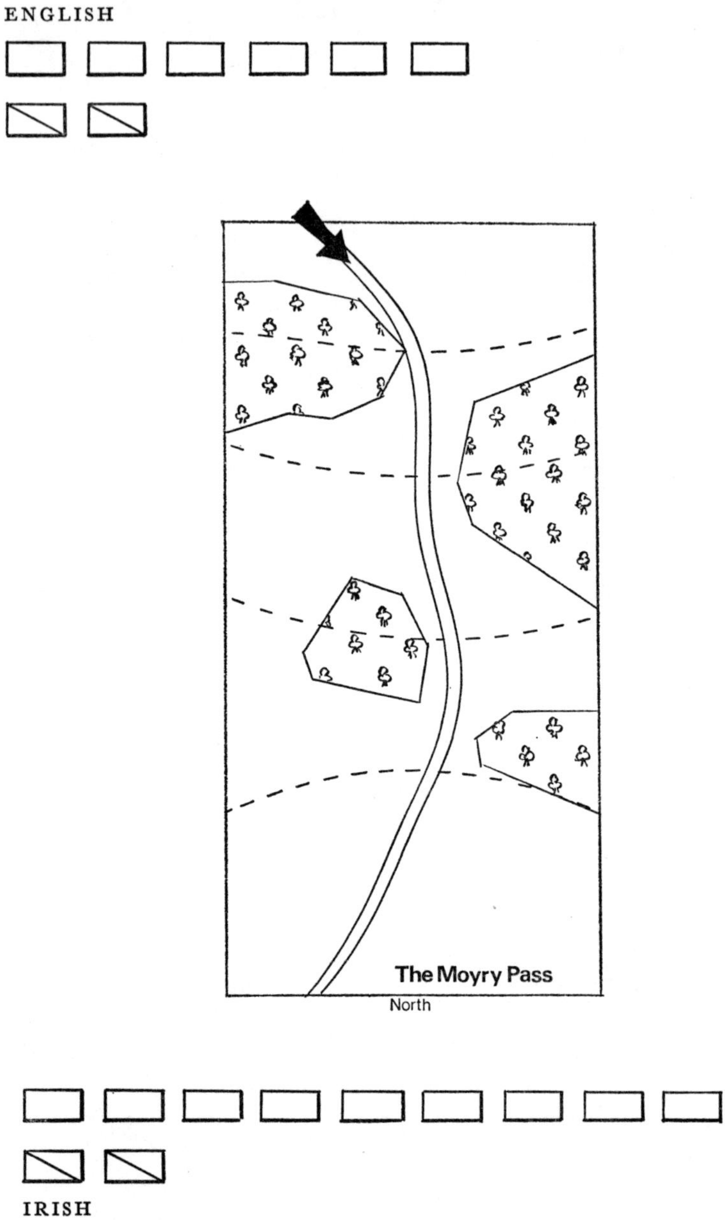
ENGLISH
The Moyry Pass
North
IRISH

Battle type. Ambush.

Scale. 1 figure represents 25 men.

Layout. The road from the south enters near the centre of that baseline and snakes over gentle slopes across the Moyry Pass. The top of the pass is a plateau. The entire area is covered by woods, all of which are passable by infantry and cavalry.

English. No units are on the board at the start of the game. They will enter by the road at the point marked by the arrow, in a predetermined order.

Irish. Units may be placed anywhere on the board. Any units in or behind woods do not have to be placed on the board, but the positions of such units must be marked on the player's map. Similarly, on or behind the plateau cannot be seen by the English until they reach the top of the pass.

Special rules. None.

Objectives. English. To leave the board by the road at the northern baseline. Irish. To hold the pass and deny the English a crossing.

Elite units. English: 2. Irish: 0.

25 August 1640

THE BATTLE OF NEWBURN

Scots across the Border! Newcastle threatened! Charles had been outwitted and out-marched. The people of Scotland were turning in ever-increasing numbers towards the Presbyterian faith, much to the alarm of the English king. All Scottish shipping in English ports was seized. Charles gathered his army at York and prepared to invade when he learnt that he had moved too slowly.

Led by Sir Alexander Leslie, a force estimated to have been about 40,000, left Coldstream in three vast divisions. The van was led by Leslie himself, the second column by Lord Almond and the third by Major-General Baillie. Marching through Northumberland, the Scots reached the River Tyne at Newburn ford, a few miles west of Newcastle. Here stood Lord Conway with a small but resolute force, with instructions from the King to deny the invader the crossing.

The Scots halted and demanded the surrender of the city, which Conway refused. He had thrown up a strongly barricaded position on the southern bank of the river and awaited Leslie's move. He had not long to wait. The Scots attacked at dawn. Under cover of his artillery fire they rushed into and across the river. Met with a salvo of musket fire, they never wavered, charging the entrenchments. Conway had placed his cavalry in the rear. As the barricades were stormed, he sounded the charge and the infantry and gunners tried to extricate themselves as the cavalry thundered forward into the enemy horse. Into the flank of this struggling mass Scottish musketeers poured a devastating fire. The English broke, their cavalry galloping away through the streets of Newcastle shouting for all to flee.

The following day the city surrendered to the victors. After Durham had also fallen and the Scots had entered Yorkshire, Charles sued for terms.

Actual numbers engaged in the battle

English		*Scots*	
Foot	3,000	Foot	12,000
Horse	2,500	Horse	1,300
Artillery	12 guns	Artillery	12 guns

Wargame figures required for reconstructing the battle

English		*Scots*	
Foot	3 Standard bearers	Foot	12 Standard bearers
	19 Musketeers		51 Musketeers
Horse	25 Swordsmen		26 Pikemen
Artillery	6 Drakes		16 Sword and buckler
	12 Gunners		15 Archers
		Horse	5 Swordsmen
			15 Lancers
		Artillery	4 Sakers
			12 Gunners

Staff officers

English	*Scots*
Lord Conway	Sir Alexander Leslie
Lord Wilmet	Lord Livingstone
Sir John Digby	The Earl of Montrose
Colonel Lunsford	Major-General William Baillie

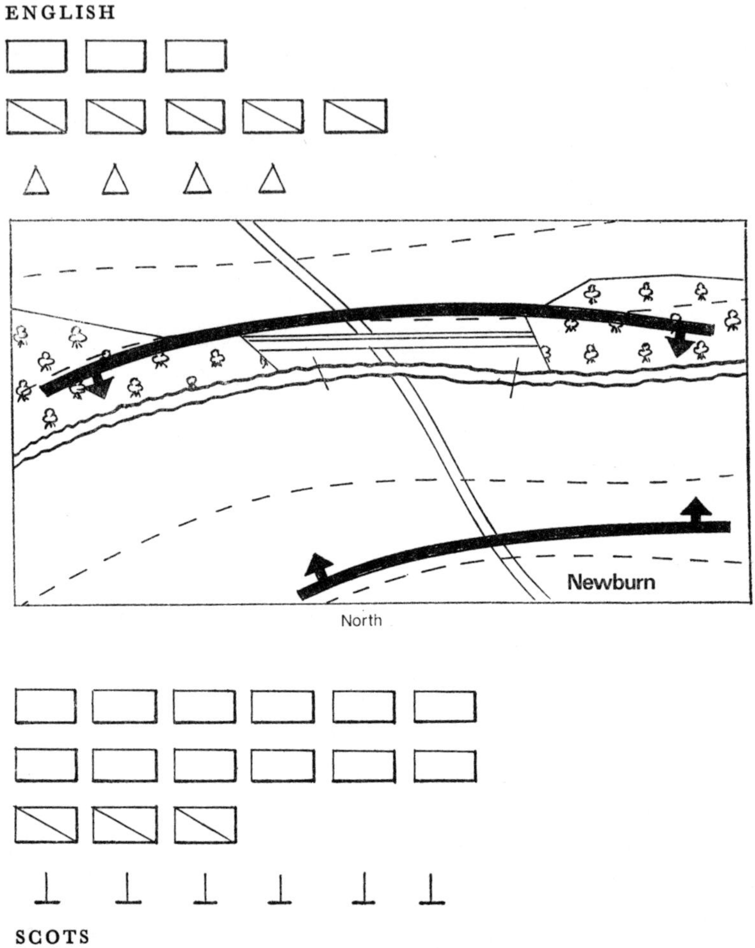
ENGLISH
Newburn
North
SCOTS

Battle type. An attack upon a prepared position.

Scale. 1 figure represents 75 men.

Layout. The River Tyne runs across the board, flowing from west to east. The slopes on either side are gentle, causing units no loss of movement when climbing them. The land at the top of the slopes is flat. On the south side of the river are two woods, between which a barricade has been erected. The central length of the river is a recognized ford (use cards 2–5; see 'Rivers', p. 26). On either side of the ford it is less fordable (use cards 6–10).

English. Units may be hidden in the woods or line the barricade, or be positioned anywhere behind this line. Troops in or behind the woods or on the plateau on the southern baseline need not be placed on the board, but must be marked in on a map.

Scots. Units may be placed on the board anywhere behind their forward line of advance as indicated on the map. Any not so placed at the start of the game must enter the board by the road.

Special rules. None.

Objectives. English. To hold the crossing. Scots. To leave the board by the southern road.

Elite units. English: 2. Scots: 0.

23 October 1642

THE BATTLE OF EDGEHILL

Edgehill was the first major clash of arms in the Civil War of 1642–6. Charles had raised his standard in August 1642 at Nottingham, moved to the west to collect further support and finally turned towards his main objective, London. South of Warwick he encountered a Parliamentary army, led by the Earl of Essex. The King took up his position on the heights of Edgehill and prepared to give battle.

Essex, holding the lower, inferior ground and awaiting the arrival of his reserves, made no attempt to close. To break the stalemate, Charles eventually ordered his army to descend the hill and by shortly after noon the two sides faced one another across half a mile of open country.

Both had adopted the same classical military formation, infantry in the centre, supported by their artillery, with the cavalry fairly evenly divided on each wing. With like facing like, the initial moves were virtually predetermined. The battle began with an exchange of gunfire, followed by a mêlée embracing the entire line. On the flanks, cavalry charged cavalry while in the centre, once the guns had had their say, the infantry settled down grimly to settle the matter with the push of the pike.

On both wings the Royalist cavalry were successful, sweeping the enemy cavalry from the field and chasing them for miles. Thus both infantry divisions were left unsupported. It was now that Essex revealed a cavalry reserve which advanced round an unprotected flank of the struggling mass of infantry and fell upon the King's own party, cutting down his gunners and capturing his personal standard and all but taking the King himself. Returning Royalist cavalry finally drove them off and the standard was retaken.

Eventually the exhausted infantry having failed to better each other, parted, bringing the battle to an indecisive end. 5,000 had fallen. Charles claimed victory and entered Oxford in triumph. Essex retreated to London.

Actual numbers engaged in the battle

Royalists		*Parliamentarians*	
Foot	10,000	Foot	11,000
Horse	2,500	Horse	2,500
Dragoons	1,000	Dragoons	1,000
Artillery	20 guns (6 heavy)	Artillery	15 guns

Wargame figures required for reconstructing the battle

Royalists		*Parliamentarians*	
Foot	9 Standard bearers	Fot	10 Standard bearers
	40 Pikemen		40 Pikemen
	51 Musketeers		60 Musketeers
Horse	25 Swordsmen	Horse	25 Swordsmen
	10 Dragoons		10 Dragoons
Artillery	3 Sakers	Artillery	1 Saker
	1 Drake		3 Drakes
	11 Gunners		9 Gunners

Staff officers

Royalists	*Parliamentarians*
Charles I	Earl of Essex
Prince Rupert	Sir John Meldrum
Sir Jacob Astley (f)	Sir Philip Stapleton
Lord Wilmot	Colonel Charles Essex
Earl of Lindsey	Sir James Ramsey

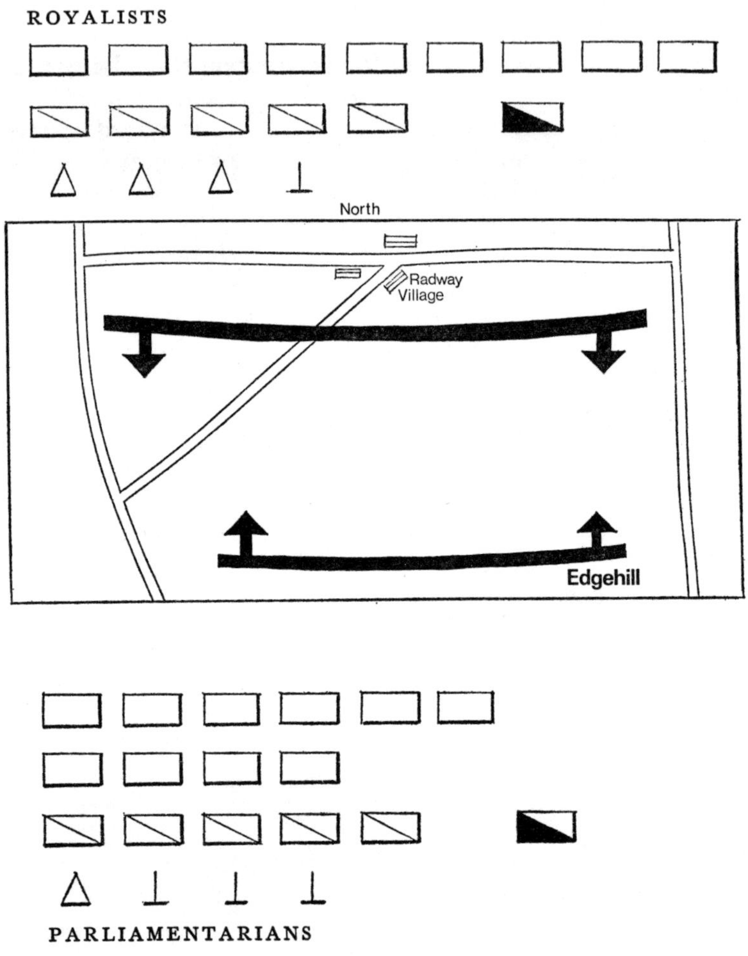
ROYALISTS
North
Radway
Village
Edgehill
PARLIAMENTARIANS

Battle type. Set piece.

Scale. 1 figure represents 100 men.

Layout. There are no physical features on the battlefield apart from the small village of Radway, which is set in the centre of the Royalist lines. It is not fortified and will not be occupied during the action. Through the village is a road running from west to east, joining two other roads which cross the field from north to south. Another road also runs from the village at an angle, meeting one of the south-running roads near the Parliamentarian lines. The mighty Edgehill runs the length of the northern baseline, but is not represented on the board.

Royalists. Units are drawn up in battle formation within 12 in (300 mm) of the northern baseline, between the two north–south roads. All units must be placed on the table at the start of the game.

Parliamentarians. Units are drawn up in battle formation within 12 in (300 mm) of the southern baseline, between the two north–south roads. All units must be placed on the table at the start of the game.

Special rules. No unit may leave the field by the northern baseline, except by the two roads. Any unit being forced to do so will disintegrate owing to the steepness of the slope, surrendering if being pursued.

Objectives. Royalists. The total destruction of the enemy army. Parliamentarian. The total destruction of the enemy army and the death or capture of the King.

Elite units. Royalists: 5. Parliamentarians: 5.

13 November 1642

THE ENGAGEMENT AT SYON HOUSE

Following the indecisive battle at Edgehill, the Earl of Essex returned to London to regroup his forces. Likewise, the King established his headquarters at Oxford, so setting the pattern for the rest of the war. Charles sent forward probing patrols to test the outer defences of London. One such reconnaissance overwhelmed a Parliamentarian position at Brentford, taking a number of guns and prisoners. Another Royalist group of about 500 men took Syon House, so giving themselves effective control of the Thames at that spot.

Further up the river, Sir James Ramsey was holding the vital bridge at Kingston when he received instructions to concentrate his force nearer to the capital. He could not have known about the capture of Syon House, for he decided to embark 13 guns, their ammunition and stores, and some 600 men on a number of barges and sail them downstream in broad daylight.

One can imagine the delight and surprise in the Royalist camp when they were presented with such a target, albeit a moving one. The Parliamentarians were quick to respond and the scene developed into a running battle with the one side attempting to knock holes in and so sink their floating targets and the other firing from moving platforms as the barge-masters tried to avoid each other, the banks and the falling shot.

Of course, it all ended in chaos. A number of the barges were holed and five sank. The others were unable to get away and were duly forced to surrender. The King's men then quietly slipped away.

Actual numbers engaged in the battle

Royalists		*Parliamentarians*	
Foot	500	Foot	600
Artillery	12 guns	Artillery	13 guns
		Barges	14

Wargame figures required for reconstructing the battle

Royalists		*Parliamentarians*	
Foot	4 Standard bearers	Foot	3 Standard bearers
	46 Musketeers		57 Musketeers
Artillery	4 Sakers	Artillery	6 Drakes
	12 Gunners		12 Gunners
			7 Barges

Staff officers

Royalists	*Parliamentarians*
Colonel John Smith	Sir William Constable
Captain Richard O'Leary	Captain James Hopton

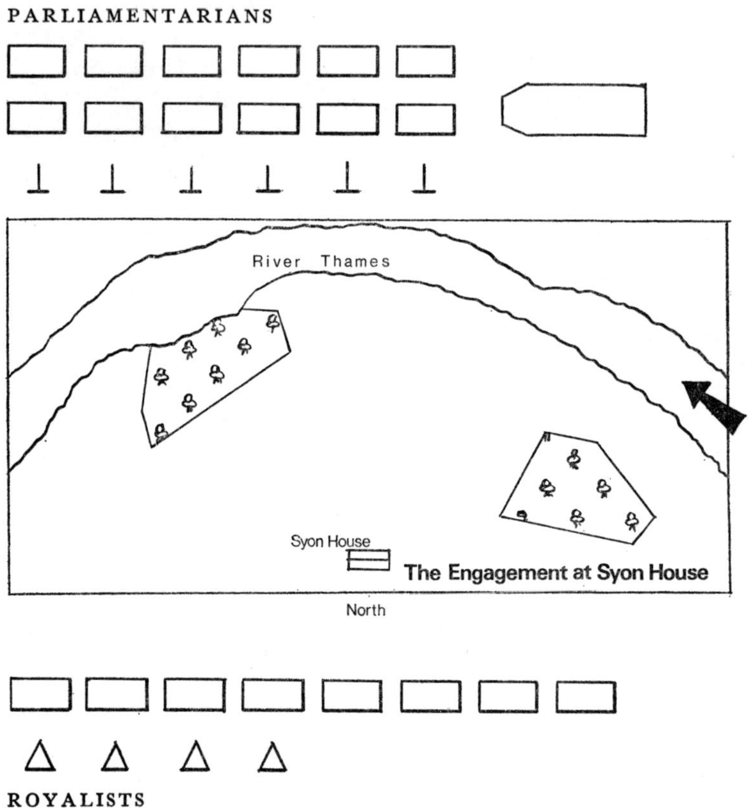
PARLIAMENTARIANS
River Thames
Syon House
The Engagement at Syon House
North
ROYALISTS

Battle type. Ambush.

Scale. 1 figure represents 10 men.

Layout. Syon House stands in the centre of the northern baseline and about 9 in (225 mm) on to the table. The River Thames flows from west to east, curving past the southern baseline. The grounds of the House are wooded.

Royalists. A Royalist force occupies the grounds, being anywhere on the northern banks of the river. Units hidden in, or behind the woods must have their position marked on a map and need not be declared.

Parliamentarians. All units must enter the board on the barges, one of which is an ammunition barge. None is on the table at the start of the game.

Special rules. Barges will move at the rate of 12 in (300 mm) per game move. Only two barges may move down the river abreast. A sunken barge will block half the width of the river. All troops and guns on barges will be considered as under cover. If a cannon-ball scores a hit upon a barge, casualties must be diced for; 1, 2, or 3, infantryman hit; 4 or 5, gun hit; 6, barge sinks (guns will sink, every man to be diced for, 1, 2, 3, drowned). The ammunition barge carries no artillery. Barges must be at anchor (costs half a move) before troops or guns may disembark or embark. (Such guns may not fire during the game move.)

Objectives. Royalists. To sink the convoy and stop the guns reaching London (leave the board by the eastern baseline). Parliamentarians. To send as many guns through to London as possible.

Note. The barges are rectangular in shape, 7 in (175 mm) long by 3 in (75 mm) wide.

Elite units. Royalists: 2. Parliamentarians: 2.

19 March 1643

THE BATTLE OF HOPTON HEATH

The King was in Oxford, his capital for the war. It was now becoming essential to form a wall of outposts around the city, a ring that would expand from the centre as when a stone is dropped into a pond, gradually and steadily the wave was to spread out until all had been affected by the energy created in the middle. The Earl of Northampton was given the task of expanding the King's control northwards. Accompanied by General Henry Hastings, he led a tiny force of about 1,200 men on his mission.

News of the progress came to the Parliamentarians and they determined to throw him back. Two small Parliamentary armies were detailed to crush the Earl between them. They were of equal size, one led by Sir John Gell, the other by Sir William Brereton. Their agreed venue was Hopton Heath. They would then attack the Earl at Stafford.

Gell was the first to arrive and found himself facing Northampton's army alone, for the Royalists had ridden out to meet him. Gell held the crest of a long ridge, too long for him to hold by himself, but confident that support would soon arrive, he took up his battle stations along it. The battle began with an exchange of shots by the artillery, followed immediately by a Royalist charge up the hill. Northampton hoping to defeat one foe before being faced by a second. During a second such charge, the Earl was cut off from his men and killed. Brereton had meanwhile arrived and taken up his position along the ridge. A number of Parliamentary guns had been taken during the mêlée and when their horse turned about and left the field, they decided to withdraw completely. This they succeeded in doing as night fell. The Royalist horses were too blown and too weak to pursue them. The Parliamentarians had lost a third of their force. Apart from the loss of the Earl, the Royalist's losses had been trifling.

Actual numbers engaged in the battle

Royalists		*Parliamentarians*	
Foot	500	Foot	(1) 600+(2) 550
Horse	700	Horse	150+200
Artillery	1 gun	Artillery	11 guns

Wargame figures required for reconstructing the battle

Royalists		*Parliamentarians*	
Foot	3 Standard bearers	Foot	9 Standard bearers
	16 Pikemen		35 Pikemen
	31 Musketeers		71 Musketeers
Horse	70 Swordsmen		35 Swordsmen
Artillery	1 Saker	Artillery	1 Saker
	3 Gunners		4 Drakes
			11 Gunners

Staff officers

Royalists	*Parliamentarians*
Earl of Northampton	Sir William Brereton
General Henry Hastings	Sir John Gell
Sir Thomas Byron	

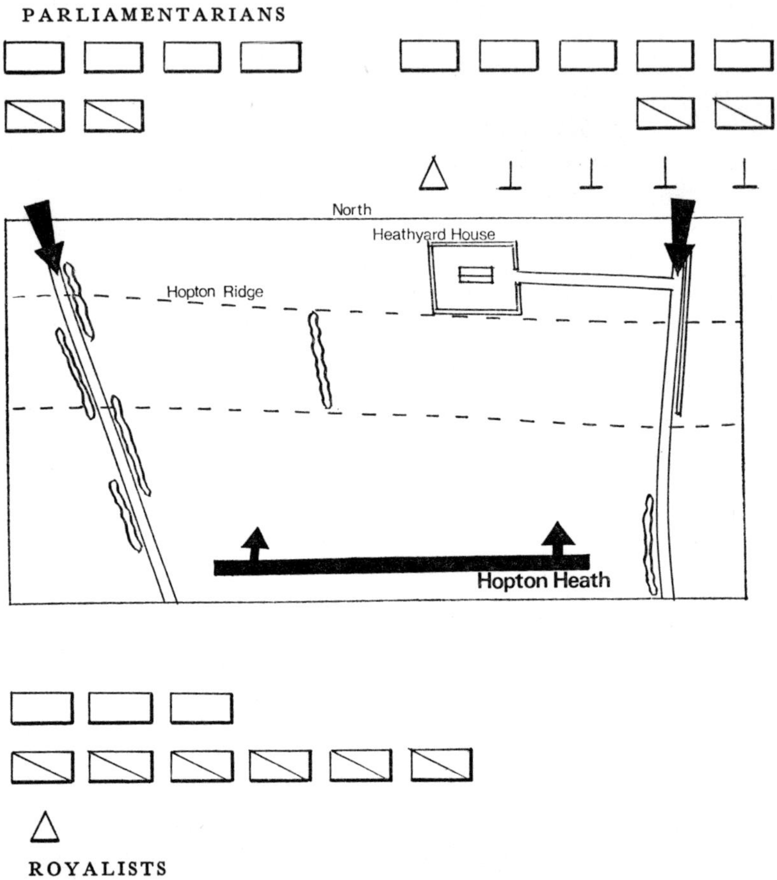
PARLIAMENTARIANS
North
Heathyard House
Hopton Ridge
Hopton Heath
ROYALISTS

Battle type. A chance engagement.

Scale. 1 figure represents 10 men.

Layout. Heathyard House is surrounded by a stone wall and stands on top of Hopton Ridge. From the ridge to the plain below is a steep slope (movement uphill is at half speed). Two roads cross the battlefield from north to south, one is hedge-lined, the other has a stone wall along much of one side.

Royalists. Units are all on the board at the beginning of the game, between the roads and within 12 in (300 mm) of the southern baseline.

Parliamentarians. No troops are on the board at the start of the game. The two Parliamentarian forces enter independently of one another, each by a different road. The force entering from the north-east will do so according to a secret die throw: 1, 2, enter first game move; 3, 4, second game move, 5, 6, third game move. The force entering from the north-west will enter according to the number on a single die throw.

Special rules. None.

Objectives. The destruction of the enemy force.

Elite units. Royalists: 5. Parliamentarians: 2.

13 April 1643

THE BATTLE OF RIPPLE FIELD

Waller had established his headquarters at Gloucester. Here, in March, he defeated the Welsh and pursued them back into Wales. On his return he was informed about the nearness of another Royalist army, this time led by Prince Maurice. The Prince had been manoeuvring to the west of the River Severn and was returning to Tewkesbury with about 2,000 men when he discovered that Waller had taken the town, so cutting his line of retreat. He was forced to turn north to find a crossing and this he made at Upton Bridge. Facing south again he had barely moved 2 or 3 miles before he became aware of Parliamentarians on the ridge to his front.

Leaving a force in Gloucester, Waller was steadily moving north and had just passed through Ripple village and climbed its hill when Maurice's army was sighted below him. Both sides prepared for battle. Naturally, Waller occupied the ridge and settled down to await the Royalist attack. As for Maurice, he divided his tiny army into three distinct groups. He was nervous about launching an all-out attack as he could not see from his position the full numbers or disposition of the enemy. Had he but known that Waller was desperately short of infantry he may have moved sooner. As it was it was Waller who advanced some cavalry units to the foot of the hill. This proved to be a foolish move as he was unable to support them. They were routed by the Royalist's first charge. Seeing the disorder, Maurice immediately sounded the attack, taking the Parliamentarians before they were able to regroup.

Waller's force dissolved in a panic. At the same moment that his frontal attack crested the ridge, Maurice's cavalry, having taken the village of Uckinghall on Waller's left flank, charged along the ridge from west to east using their sabres as they went. Waller himself escaped back into Tewkesbury. For Maurice, the road back to Oxford was open.

Actual numbers engaged in the battle

Royalists		*Parliamentarians*	
Foot	1,200	Foot	200
Horse	800	Horse	1,800
Artillery	6 guns	Artillery	6 guns

Wargame figures required for reconstructing the battle

Royalists		*Parliamentarians*	
Foot	3 Standard bearers	Foot	1 Standard bearer
	15 Pikemen		2 Pikemen
	30 Musketeers		5 Musketeers
Horse	24 Swordsmen	Horse	52 Swordsmen
	8 Dragoons		10 Dragoons
Artillery	3 Drakes		10 Heavy cavalry
	6 Gunners	Artillery	3 Drakes
			6 Gunners

Staff officers

Royalists	*Parliamentarians*
Prince Maurice	Sir William Waller
Lord Grandison	Lieutenant-Colonel Edward Massey
Major Thomas Sheldon	Sir Arthur Hazelrig

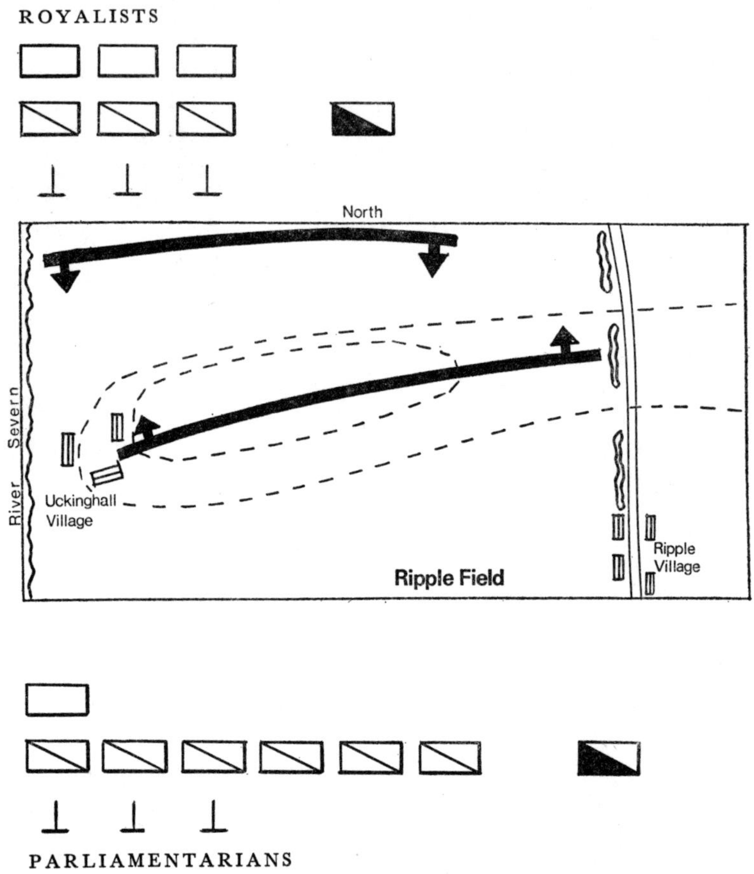
ROYALISTS
North
River Severn
Uckinghall Village
Ripple Village
Ripple Field
PARLIAMENTARIANS

Battle type. Set piece.

Scale. 1 figure represents 25 men.

Layout. The battlefield is dominated by a long spur of land running from the eastern baseline until it dips down to the River Severn which forms the western baseline. Much of the northern and southern slopes of this ridge are steep. Units will lose 50 per cent of their movement climbing them. The eastern end of the ridge has gentle slopes, as has the area around the village of Uckinghall. Ripple village stands on the southern baseline, across the road which runs due north.

Royalists. All units are in position at the beginning of the game along the northern baseline between the river and the road, to a maximum depth of 9 in (225 mm) on to the board.

Parliamentarians. The most advanced units are in position along the ridge between Uckinghall village and the road. Units hidden behind the ridge must be marked on a map if they are not placed on the board.

Special rules. None.

Objectives. The destruction of the enemy forces.

Elite units. Royalists: 2. Parliamentarians: 2.

16 May 1643

THE BATTLE OF STRATTON

If numbers of men, a strong defensive position and a superiority of artillery are all that is required to guarantee victory, then the result of the Battle of Stratton would have been a foregone conclusion. But it is in the determination of some men to win irrespective of any adverse conditions, the sheer faith of the David in his ability to win when confronted with his Goliath, that will often carry the day. Such a man was Sir Ralph Hopton, the commander of the King's army in Cornwall. He led a force of less than 3,000, while his enemy, the Earl of Stamford commanded an army of nearly 5,500 infantry, a regiment of cavalry, and 13 guns.

This Parliamentarian force had chosen itself a very strong position, being an isolated hill, with a wood covering the whole of one side and hedges running across its front. A lesser man than Hopton would have refused battle on such a ground and against such odds. However, he determined upon a dawn attack, hoping to catch his opponent at his least vigilant.

Hopton divided his small force into four units. The first attacked frontally, through the hedges, into the wood, and up the slope. The very wood that was giving cover to its defenders also blinded them to the numbers that the Royalists were using in the assault, so pinning down many of the available Parliamentarians. With his other three divisions Hopton carried out a pincer movement, two passing round one side of the position and the third round the other.

Wheeling into line they pressed on up the rise, joining before the final thrust that was to carry the day. His co-ordination had been perfect. The Parliamentary guns were quickly overrun and taken and their infantry, unable to deploy to meet the unexpected threat, broke and ran. They had lost about 2,000 killed and captured and all their cannon. Most of the south-west fell into Royalist hands.

Actual numbers engaged in the battle

Royalists		*Parliamentarians*	
Foot	2,400	Foot	5,400
Horse	500	Horse	200
Artillery	8 guns	Artillery	13 guns

Wargame figures required for reconstructing the battle

Royalists		*Parliamentarians*	
Foot	4 Standard bearers	Foot	8 Standard bearers
	16 Pikemen		36 Pikemen
	32 Musketeers		72 Musketeers
Horse	10 Swordsmen	Horse	4 Swordsmen
Artillery	4 Drakes	Artillery	3 Sakers
	8 Gunners		2 Drakes
			13 Gunners

Staff officers

Royalists	*Parliamentarians*
Sir Ralph Hopton	The Earl of Stamford
Lord Mohum	Major-General James Chudleigh
Sir John Berkeley	Sir George Chudleigh

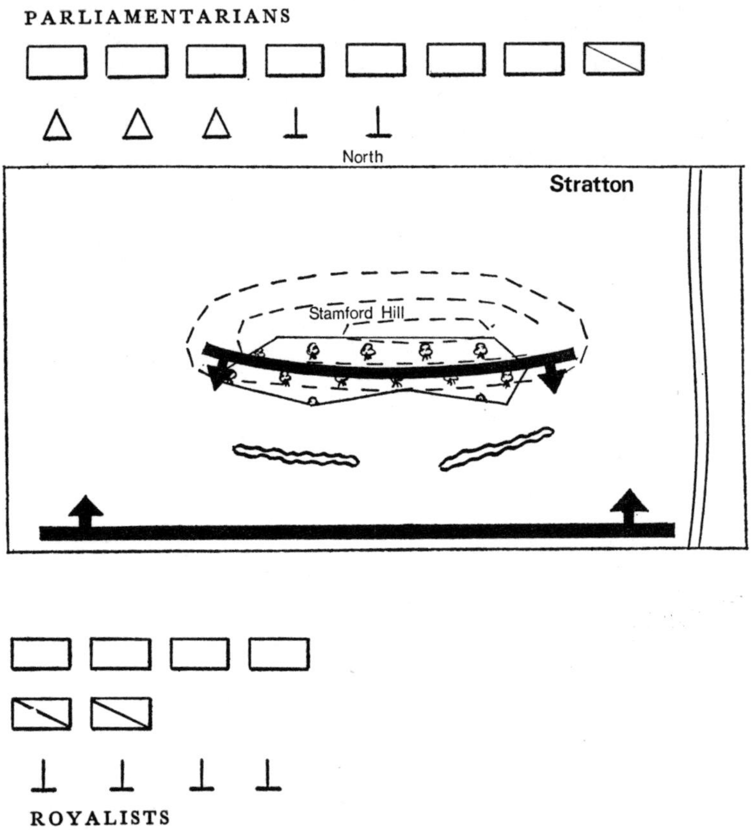
PARLIAMENTARIANS
North
Stratton
Stamford Hill
ROYALISTS

Battle type. An attack on a prepared position.

Scale. 1 figure represents 40 men.

Layout. Stamford Hill occupies the centre of the board. All sides are steep and its entire southern slope is covered with trees. To the south it is protected by hedges. A single road skirts the hill, running north to south.

Parliamentarians. All units are in position on the hill at the start of the game. Only those that would be visible from the southern baseline must be placed on the table. All others must be indicated on a map.

Royalists. Having studied the dispositions of the visible Parliamentarians the Royalist units will be set out anywhere along the southern baseline, to a maximum depth of 9 in (225 mm).

Special rules. None.

Objectives. The destruction of the enemy.

Elite units. Parliamentarians: 0. Royalists: 5.

5 July 1643

THE BATTLE OF LANSDOWN

Waller, commanding a Parliamentary army of nearly 7,000 troops, had established himself in Bath. Lieutenant-General the Marquis of Hertford and Prince Maurice, with a force of about the same size, decided to prise him out. They lay to the south of the city, but after discussing the situation, agreed upon an outflanking march. Having crossed the Chippenham road, the Royal army bivouacked about 7 miles (11 km) to the north-west of Bath, round the village of Marshfield. In the morning they proceeded west towards Lansdown Hill where they discovered Waller's force awaiting them. The Parliamentarians had decided to deny them this vantage point.

The position that Waller had chosen was an extremely strong one. His flanks were protected by woods and across his front he had quickly thrown up earthworks. To his rear ran a stone wall, giving him a second line of defence should he be ejected from his first.

The Royalists realized that this would be a difficult nut to crack, so they began by putting out a feeler to test the quality of the opposition. This took the form of a cavalry flanking attack, but this soon ground to a halt and was withdrawn. A frontal assault had been ruled out in the initial contemplations, but now it was decided that this might prove to be the only method of dislodging Waller. The cavalry were massed in the centre, with infantry on either wing. The horse were given the task of feinting at the barricade, while the infantry carried out the real attack, a push through the two woods. After some fierce hand-to-hand fighting amongst the trees, both the woods fell to the attackers. With his two flanks thus exposed, Waller found it impossible to hold the breastworks and was forced to retreat to his second line, the walls.

All was now set for stage three of the battle. However, both sides were exhausted following the mêlée in the woods and gradually the firing died down. When night fell, Waller retreated back into the city. The victorious Royalists were denied the full fruits of victory when Sir Ralph Hopton was blinded when some ammunition exploded.

Actual numbers engaged in the battle

Royalists		*Parliamentarians*	
Foot	4,000	Foot	3,800
Horse	2,300	Horse	2,900
		Artillery	7 guns

Wargame figures for reconstructing the battle

Royalists		*Parliamentarians*	
Foot	10 Standard bearers	Foot	6 Standard bearers
	26 Pikemen		26 Pikemen
	44 Musketeers		44 Musketeers
Horse	37 Swordsmen	Horse	40 Swordsmen
	9 Dragoons		8 Heavy cavalry
			10 Dragoons
		Artillery	1 Saker
			2 Drakes
			7 Gunners

Staff officers

Royalists	*Parliamentarians*
Prince Maurice	Sir William Waller
Marquis of Hertford	Colonel Robert Burrell
Sir Bevil Grenville	Sir Arthur Hazelrig
Sir Ralph Hopton	

ROYALISTS

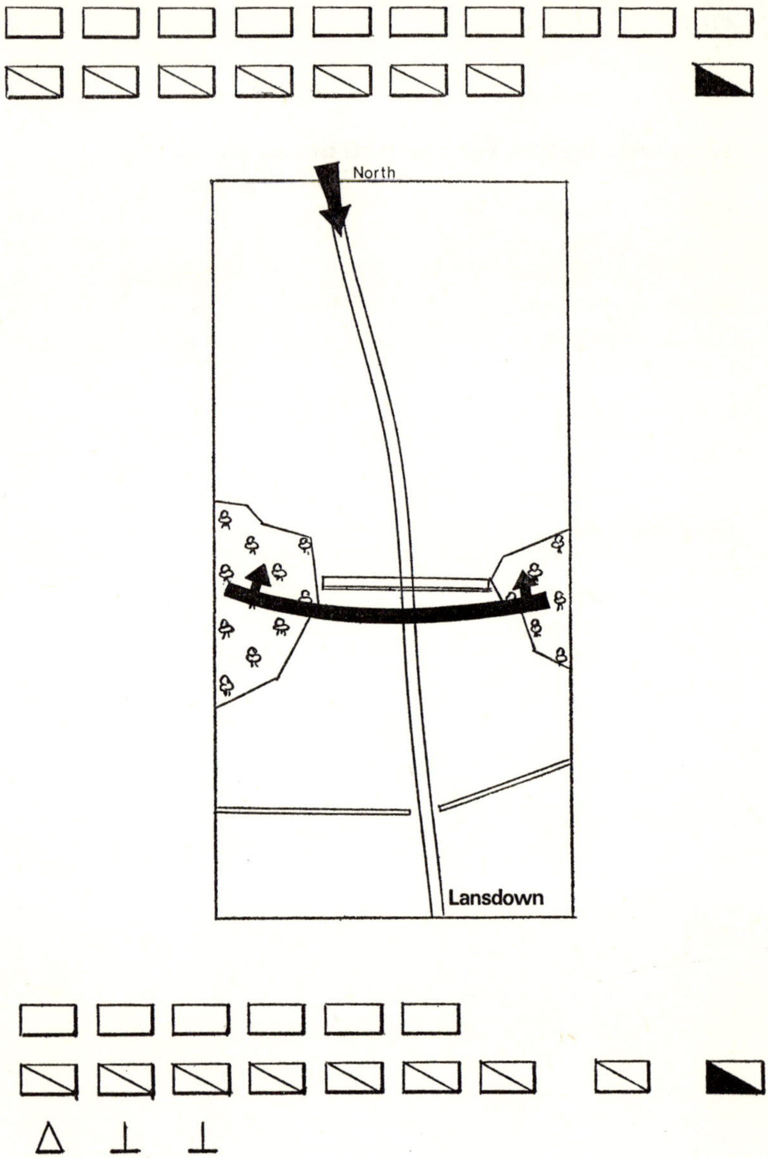

PARLIAMENTARIANS

Battle type. An attack on a prepared position.

Scale. 1 figure represents 50 men.

Layout. The main road runs down the centre of the board from north to south. Where it passes between two woods, a barricade has been thrown across the road. Still further south a stone wall crosses the field from east to west.

Parliamentarians. All units are in position at the start of the game. Their forward troops may occupy the woods and the barricade. Units within or behind the woods, or behind the stone wall, do not have to be declared, but their positions must be indicated on a map.

Royalists. No troops are on the board at the start of the game. All units enter from the north by the road.

Special rules. None.

Objectives. Royalists. To leave the board by the road where it crosses the southern baseline. Parliamentarians. To destroy the enemy.

Elite units, Parliamentarians: 3. Royalists: 5.

13 July 1643

THE BATTLE OF ROUNDWAY DOWN

After their limited success at Lansdown, the Royalist army fell back via Chippenham to the town of Devizes, closely followed by the smarting Waller at the head of 5,000 men. Prince Maurice and Lieutenant-General the Marquis of Hertford agreed that the town should be defended. General Sir Ralph Hopton was left in command while they pressed on to Oxford with the intention of raising more troops and returning to his aid. Waller assumed that they had abandoned Hopton and settled down to lay seige to the town.

For three days Waller launched attacks upon the beleaguered garrison, all to no avail. On the third evening he received word that a relief force was approaching from the north-east. He decided to deal with this before making a final assault on the town. He took up his line of battle on Roundway Down and stood ready to meet his new assailants. He placed his infantry in the centre, flanking them with his cavalry. When the enemy hove into sight, it proved to consist entirely of horsemen, about 2,000 strong and a pair of small galloper guns. They were under the command of Lord Henry Wilmot.

Completely ignoring the infantry, Wilmot's cavalry charged straight at the Parliamentary horse, completely routing both divisions and chasing them from the field. Roundway Down happens to end with a sudden drop which the fleeing cavalry was now to discover. Over this cliff-like drop they fell, crashing to their destruction. The victorious Royalist cavalry now returned to deal with the now isolated infantry.

Back on the main field of battle the situation had changed completely. Hopton had arrived from Devizes with his 2,500 infantry. The Parliamentary guns had been quickly overrun and the Royalist horse and infantry completed a savage pincer movement. Six hundred Parliamentarians fell, the survivors surrendered. Waller was not among those taken—he had left with the cavalry!

Actual numbers engaged in the battle

Royalists		*Parliamentarians*	
Foot	2,500	Foot	3,000
Horse	1,800	Horse	2,000
Artillery	2 guns	Artillery	8 guns

Wargame figures required for reconstructing the battle

Royalists		*Parliamentarians*	
Foot	7 Standard bearers	Foot	6 Standard bearers
	12 Pikemen		18 Pikemen
	31 Musketeers		36 Musketeers
Horse	36 Swordsmen	Horse	40 Swordsmen
Artillery	1 Drake	Artillery	2 Sakers
	2 Gunners		6 Gunners

Staff officers

Royalists	*Parliamentarians*
Sir Ralph Hopton	Sir William Waller
Lord Henry Wilmot	Sir Arthur Hazelrig
Sir John Byron	Colonel Robert Burrell
Earl of Crawford	

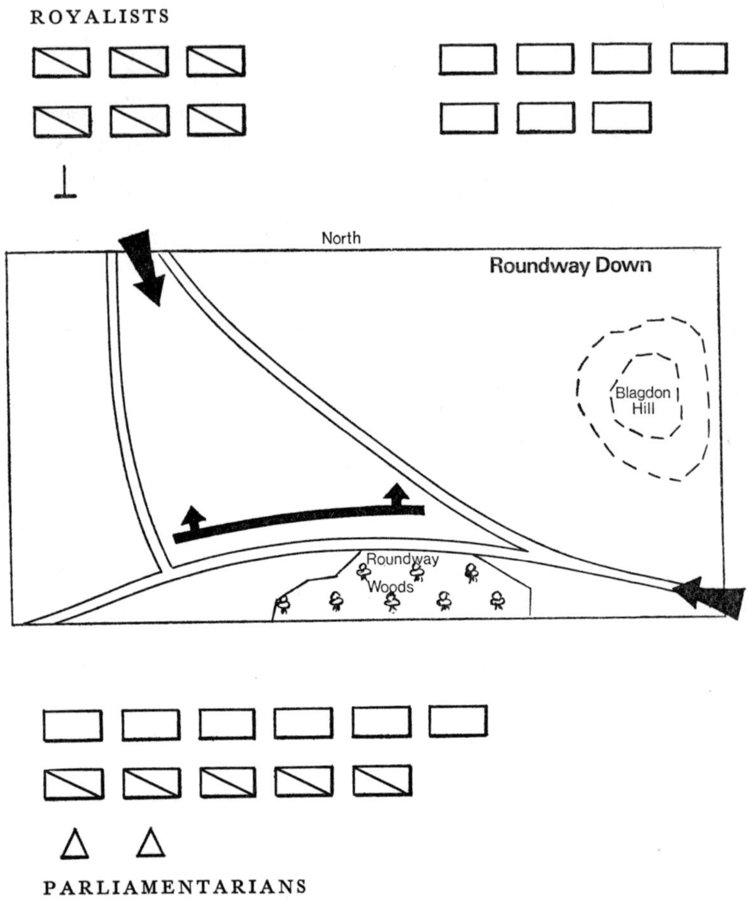
ROYALISTS
North
Roundway Down
Blagdon Hill
Roundway Woods
PARLIAMENTARIANS

Battle type. An attack on a prepared position.

Scale. 1 figure represents 50 men.

Layout. Three roads form a triangle of land which is the main feature of the field. On the eastern baseline rises Blagdon Hill, a steep-sided mound. The centre of the southern baseline is dominated by a large wood. From this wood, running west along the baseline is a cliff over which any troops attempting to leave the field at this point will fall to their destruction.

Parliamentarians. All units to be set out in position just forward of the road running east–west across the battlefield.

Royalists. The Royalists are split into two forces. All their cavalry and artillery will enter in game move one either on or between the two roads on the northern baseline. The second force, all infantry enter during the fourth game move along the road from the east.

Special rules. Units leaving the board by the southern baseline to the west of the wood are completely destroyed as they will fall over a cliff.

Objectives. The destruction of the enemy.

Elite units. Parliamentarians: 2. Royalists: 5.

20 September 1643

THE FIRST BATTLE OF NEWBURY

In July 1643, Bristol fell to the King. This gave him control of the road to the south-west. If he could take Gloucester, communications with South Wales would be open. Gloucester became his next objective. In order to thwart him, the Earl of Essex left London, entering Gloucester in early September. Having relieved the city, Essex attempted to return to London. Charles moved to intercept him, the two armies converging upon Newbury.

The King had 14,000 men at his back, with an artillery train of twenty guns. Essex commanded a similar force. The Royalist horse outnumbered the Parliamentary cavalry, while the Parliamentarians had the larger infantry host. The two armies found themselves advancing towards one another along the same bank of the River Kennet, so when they sighted each other, each had a safe flank. Across a narrow plain, much broken by hedges, there rose the low hills of Enbourne Heath.

Essex's troops were exhausted by their march and their morale fell even more when they realized that Charles had beaten them to Newbury, so capturing their supplies.

Both sides appreciated the advantage of seizing the high ground. The guns were dragged up the slopes, resulting in an artillery duel in an effort to command the heights. On the plain confusion reigned as the infantry charged and countercharged in an effort to progress through the maze of hedges. Darkness eventually brought the fighting to an end with neither side having made much impression upon the other. Short of ammunition, the King decided to withdraw again to Oxford, leaving the road to London open to Essex. The losses in the battle were not very considerable, but the death of Lord Falkland was the King's greatest lament.

Actual numbers engaged in the battle

Royalists		*Parliamentarians*	
Foot	8,000	Foot	10,000
Horse	6,000	Horse	4,000
Artillery	20 guns	Artillery	20 guns

Wargame figures required for reconstructing the battle

Royalists		*Parliamentarians*	
Foot	7 Standard bearers	Foot	9 Standard bearers
	28 Pikemen		30 Pikemen
	45 Musketeers		61 Musketeers
Horse	60 Swordsmen	Horse	40 Swordsmen
Artillery	2 Sakers	Artillery	2 Sakers
	2 Drakes		Drakes 2
	10 Gunners		10 Gunners

Staff officers

Royalists	*Parliamentarians*
Charles I	Earl of Essex
Prince Rupert	Lientenant-Colonel Edward Massey
Viscount Falkland	Sir James Ramsey
Sir John Byron	Sir John Meldrum

ROYALISTS

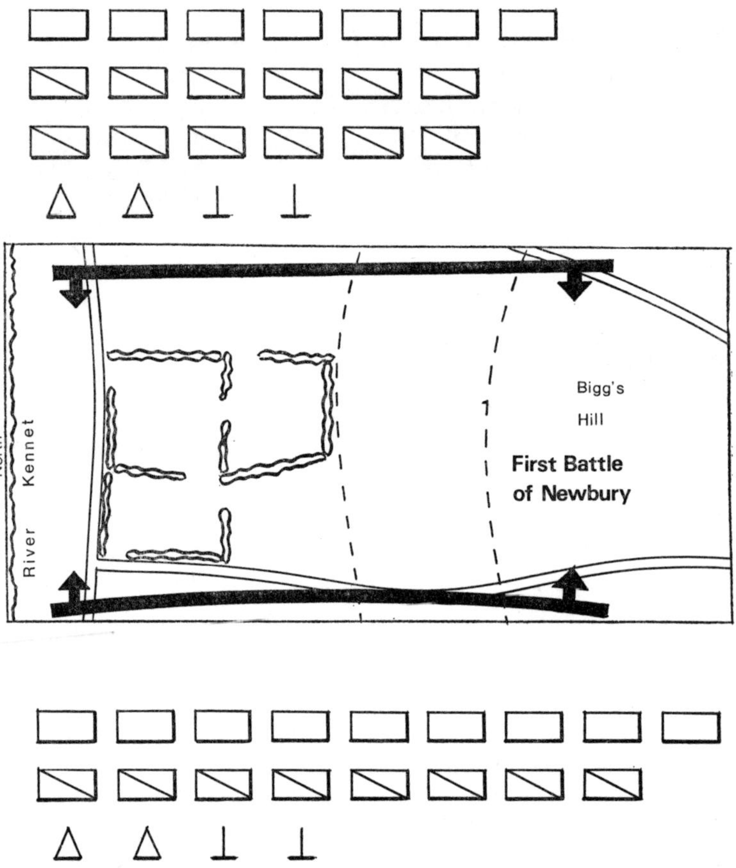

PARLIAMENTARIANS

Battle type. Set piece.

Scale. 1 figure represents 100 men.

Layout. The north edge of the battlefield is formed by the River Kennet. The most dominant feature, however, is the area known as Bigg's Hill, a plateau which covers the southern third of the board. The slope down to the plain is a gentle one. The plain itself is crisscrossed with hedges. The main road follows the river, running east to west. Along the west baseline a second road crosses the field, whilst a third road cuts across the south-east corner.

Royalists. The entire army will be set up anywhere along the eastern baseline, to a depth of 9 in (225 mm) on to the board.

Parliamentarians. The entire army will be set up anywhere along the western baseline, to a depth of 9 in (225 mm) on to the board.

Note. The layout of the armies will be simultaneous and therefore both sides must set out in detail the intended position of each unit under its command on a map before any units are placed on the board.

Special rules. Any troops being forced into the River Kennet will be individually diced for. Any scoring 1, 2, or 3 will be considered drowned.

Objectives. The destruction of the enemy force.

Elite units. Parliamentarians: 3. Royalists: 3.

11 October 1643

THE BATTLE OF WINCEBY

Edgehill had been a set-piece battle. Both sides had been fully aware of their enemy's nearness. They had taken their time in arranging their forces. There were no surprises, neither side gaining or losing a great deal. Winceby was to be one of those accidental clashes, both sides were taken by surprise, victory going to the fastest thinker and swiftest striker.

The Earl of Manchester, supported by Fairfax and Cromwell, had been beseiging Bolingbroke Castle, when he learned that a Royalist force had left Newark and was marching to the relief. Quickly collecting his cavalry and ordering the infantry to follow as fast as possible, Manchester moved to intercept them. With both sides advancing with all speed towards one another, it was inevitable that they should suddenly come face to face. The action that followed developed into a unique cavalry affair.

The Royalist forces were led by Sir William Saville and Sir John Henderson, being in the region of 1,600 horse and 800 dragoons. Manchester only had about 1,500 cavalry all told, including dragoons, but his infantry were not far behind.

A shallow hollow separated the would-be contestants. As usual, neither side appeared to be willing to take the initiative. Eventually it was the Royalist dragoons who advanced into the hollow, where they were challenged by the Parliamentary dragoons who threw them back into their own lines in considerable confusion. Seizing his chance, Fairfax charged home upon the enemy left wing, which broke and ran without a fight. Many were trapped by a line of hedges and were either slain or captured. Their remaining colleagues escaped with the Parliamentarians following close on their heels. The two towns of Gainsborough and Lincoln were lost.

Actual numbers engaged in the battle

Royalists		*Parliamentarians*	
Foot	0	Foot	Small detachment
Horse	2,400	Horse	1,500
Artillery	0	Artillery	0

Wargame figures required for reconstructing the battle

Royalists		*Parliamentarians*	
Horse	38 Swordsmen	Foot	1 Standard bearer
	10 Dragoons		3 Pikemen
			6 Musketeers
		Horse	24 Swordsmen
			6 Dragoons

Staff officers

Royalists	*Parliamentarians*
Sir John Henderson	Earl of Manchester
Sir William Widdrington	Lord Fairfax
Sir William Saville	Oliver Cromwell

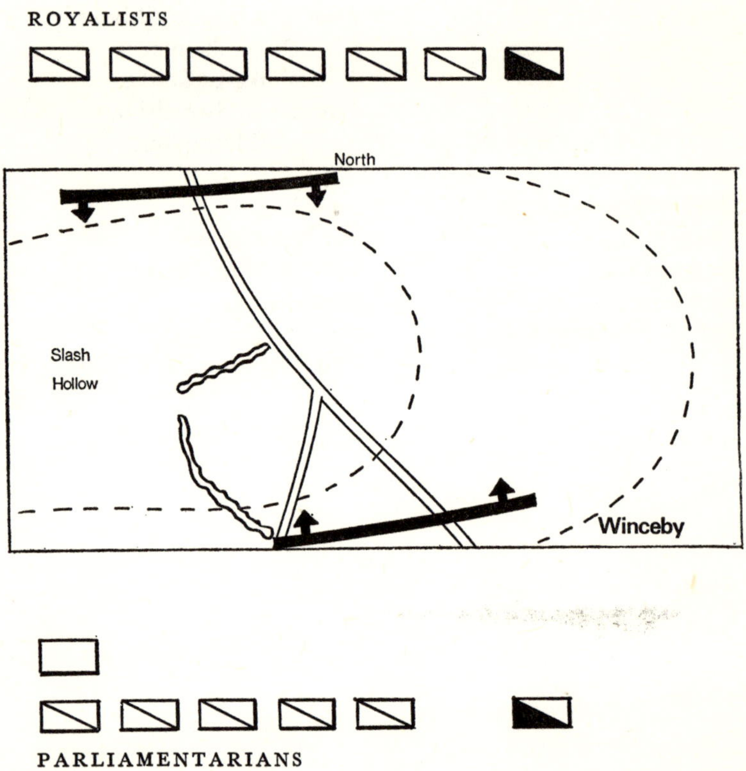
ROYALISTS
North
Slash
Hollow
Winceby
PARLIAMENTARIANS

Battle type. A chance engagement.

Scale. 1 figure represents 50 men.

Layout. Slash Hollow is a low-lying area of land, surrounded on three sides by gentle slopes. A road descends into the valley from the north, crosses it, and divides into two before ascending and leaving the board near the centre of the southern baseline. In the hollow itself is a field with hedges on its northern and western boundaries.

Armies. There no troops on the board at the start of the game. Both commanders will decide their order of march before the game begins. All units must enter by a road, the Parliamentarians having the choice of two roads and may use both.

Special rules. None.

Objectives. The destruction of the enemy.

Elite units. Parliamentarians: 2. Royalists: 2.

25 January 1644

THE BATTLE OF NANTWICH

If Nantwich fell, all Cheshire would be in Royalist hands. For a month, through the depths of an English winter, the town had resisted all assaults by the beseiging Royalist army, led by Lord Byron. He had under his command a force of over 5,000 men and for a while it looked as though the town was doomed. Sir William Brereton was in the vicinity, but with an insufficient force to risk a general engagement. Suddenly, in mid January, the scales were turned with the approach of Sir Thomas Fairfax, leading a victorious army of over 3,000 men. It was now the Parliamentarians who had the advantage in numbers. Byron was going to be forced to raise the seige and prepare to defend himself.

His infantry and artillery marched to meet Fairfax as he approached the town from the north-west. In so doing, they crossed the River Weaver and were cut off from their cavalry arm when flooding closed the bridge the following day. Byron was left with the cavalry. Realizing the nearness of the enemy to his virtually leaderless infantry, he moved rapidly north, desperately looking for a place to cross. By the time such a crossing was found, Fairfax was already south of him and within sight of the waiting infantry. These had been drawn up in battle array on a hill to the north of the village of Acton, sullenly awaiting the attack.

Realizing that Byron was approaching his left flank, Fairfax detached some of his infantry to hold back the Royalist horse, while he prepared to attack the hill. On both scores he was successful. Byron was unable to break through to the aid of his infantry, whilst they in turn were assaulted from two points at once. Not only did Fairfax charge their front, but they were also simultaneously taken in flank by the defenders of Nantwich, who rushed from the town to join in the battle. The defending infantry fell back into the village and a last stand was made around the church. The overwhelmed infantry laid down their arms and surrendered, Byron retreating and leaving them to their fate. Nantwich had been relieved.

Actual numbers engaged in the battle

Royalists		*Parliamentarians*	
Foot	3,000	Foot	3,800
Horse	2,000	Horse	2,300
Artillery	6 guns	Artillery	2 or 3 guns

Wargame figures required for reconstructing the battle

Royalists		*Parliamentarians*	
Foot	5 Standard bearers	Foot	4 Standard bearers
	18 Pikemen		24 Pikemen
	37 Musketeers		48 Musketeers
Horse	40 Swordsmen	Horse	46 Swordsmen
Artillery	3 Drakes	Artillery	2 Drakes
	6 Gunners		4 Gunners

Staff officers

Royalists	*Parliamentarians*
Lord Byron	Sir Thomas Fairfax
Major-General Richard Gibson	Colonel George Monk

PARLIAMENTARIANS

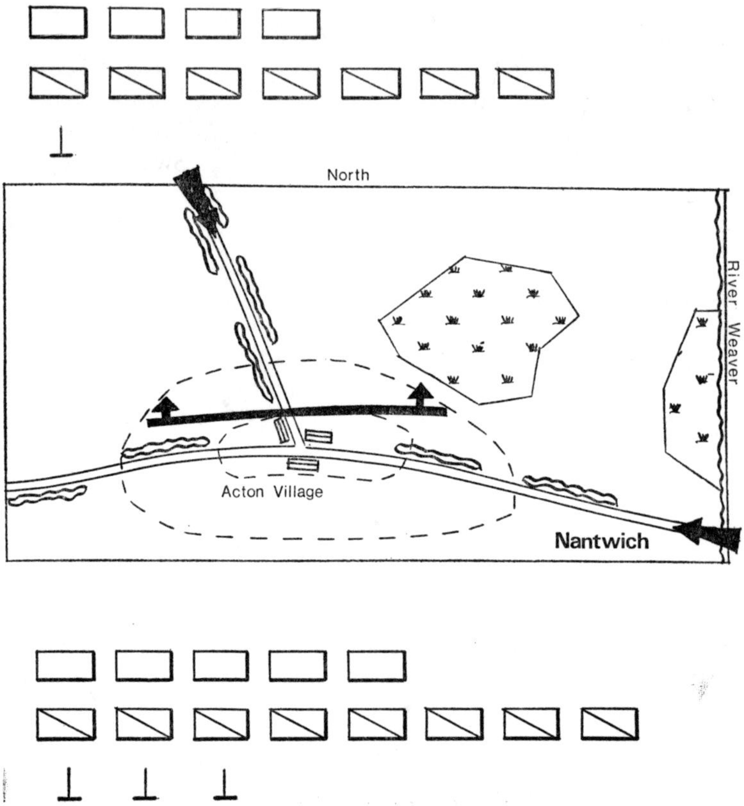

ROYALISTS

Battle type. An attack upon a prepared position.

Scale. 1 figure represents 50 men.

Layout. Acton village stands on the top of a gently rising hill and is situated near the centre of the southern baseline. The River Weaver forms the eastern baseline. Between the river and the hill are swamps. The village itself is at a road junction, one road crossing the field from east to west, the other running from the village to the north. Hedgerows line these roads.

Parliamentarians. The Parliamentarians will enter the board at two points. During the sixth game move the single infantry regiment may enter across the bridge. All their other units will enter during the first game move along or on either side of the road from the north.

Royalists. All the Royalist infantry are drawn up in position on Acton Hill. The cavalry will enter in the north-east corner during the second game move.

Special rules. Any troops being forced back into the River Weaver will be individually diced for: 1, 2, or 3 will be drowned.

Objectives. Parliamentarians. To hold the hill. Royalists. To defeat the enemy.

Note. During the sixth game move the single infantry regiment of the Parliamentarians may enter across the bridge.

Elite units. Parliamentarians: 2. Royalists: 2.

21 March 1644

THE BATTLE OF NEWARK

Two thousand Royalists held Newark for the King. They were surrounded by over three times that number under the leadership of Sir John Meldrum, an experienced Parliamentarian general who had fought successfully at Edgehill and the defence of Hull. Now he was attempting to take a town, the fall of which would alter the balance of power throughout the north. It became essential for the town to be relieved. Prince Rupert was given the command of the relieving force and set out from Shrewsbury on 13 March. He advanced via Wolverhampton, Lichfield, skirted round Nottingham and by 20 March, was within 10 miles (16 km) of his target.

Upon hearing of the Prince's approach, Meldrum withdrew his army to the north-east of the town. To his rear ran the River Trent, spanned by a bridge of boats across which he expected to retreat if faced with defeat. Rupert was told that Meldrum had moved north of the town and believed that the Parliamentarians were trying to slip away without a fight. He therefore ordered a night march in an attempt to encircle his enemy. By dawn he was looking down upon Newark from the heights of Beacon Hill. The armies were now only a mile apart. The die was cast and a battle was now inevitable.

Surprisingly, it was the Parliamentarian cavalry that began the fray by charging home against the Royalist's right wing, all but overwhelming it. Rupert's reserves were thrown in and the wing held. Meanwhile, the Parliamentarian right wing deserted without a fight. Rupert sent a mixed force round the rear of Meldrum's position in an attempt to cut the bridge, a move that failed but one that encouraged Meldrum to begin the retreat. The position that Meldrum had now adopted proved to be a trap rather than a refuge. He was on an island. The besieger was besieged. With no supplies his army rapidly disintegrated. Units mutinied. Meldrum sued for terms. These were granted. Having piled up their arms, the Parliamentarians were allowed to leave. They left behind over 200 dead.

Actual numbers engaged in the battle

Royalists		*Parliamentarians*	
Foot	3,000	Foot	4,000
Horse	3,500	Horse	3,600
Artillery	3 guns	Artillery	11 guns

Wargame figures required for reconstructing the battle

Royalists		*Parliamentarians*	
Foot	6 Standard bearers	Foot	6 Standard bearers
	54 Musketeers		48 Musketeers
Horse	60 Swordsmen		26 Pikemen
	10 Dragoons	Horse	57 Swordsmen
Artillery	1 Saker		15 Dragoons
	3 Gunners	Artillery	3 Sakers
			1 Drake
			11 Gunners

Staff officers

Royalists	*Parliamentarians*
Prince Rupert	Sir John Meldrum
Major-General George Porter	Sir Edward Hartop
Lord Loughborough	Sir Miles Hobart
Colonel Henry Tillier	Colonel Edward Rossiter

PARLIAMENTARIANS

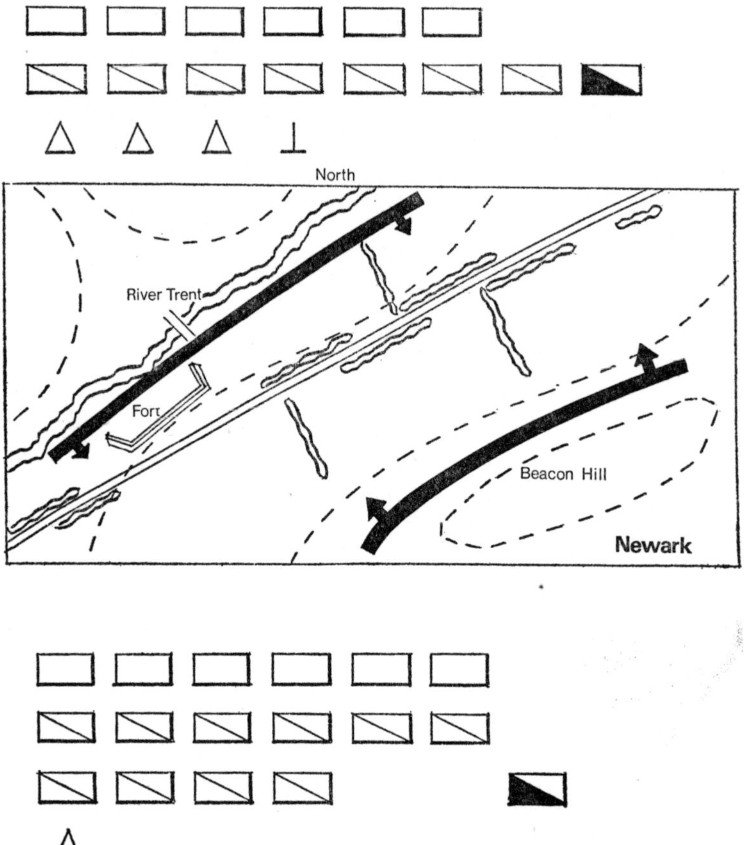

ROYALISTS

Battle type. Set piece.

Scale. 1 figure represents 50 men.

Layout. Beacon Hill occupies the south-eastern corner of the board, its gentle slopes falling down towards the River Trent. The Fosse Way follows the line of the river on its southern side. The entire area is crisscrossed with hedges. A bridge straddles the river, leading to more high ground in the north-west corner of the field. This bridge is protected by an earthen fort.

Parliamentarians. All units are on the board at the start of the game, with their advance units up to 9 in (225 mm) to the south of the river and occupying the fort.

Royalists. Having examined the layout of the Parliamentarians, the Royalists will now decide upon their layout, placing all their units on the table, anywhere in the region of Beacon Hill.

Special rules. The River Trent is crossable, using a different card on either side of the bridge (cards 6–10).

Objectives. Royalists. The destruction of the enemy. Parliamentarians. To defeat the enemy, but should the battle be going against them, to withdraw their army across the bridge and escape between the hills in the north-east corner of the board.

Elite units. Parliamentarians: 2. Royalists: 5.

29 March 1644

THE BATTLE OF CHERITON

Hopton and Waller. A battle involving one always seemed to involve the other. So it was to be again on Cheriton field.

As the King had made Oxford his capital, much of the Royalist grand policy was governed by the wish either to expand dominated territory by themselves or to attack any enemy force that attempted to enter the zone. Hopton commanded the Royalist army stationed to the south of Winchester. The force was about 8,000 strong. The Parliamentarian army reported to be assembling within his near vicinity was commanded by his old friend and enemy, Sir William Waller. Once established, the armies drifted towards one another.

By the evening of 28 March Hopton's force were camped along the northern ridge of the Cheriton arena. At dawn on the 29th, Waller lined the southern ridge facing him. Where the two ridges met, the area was covered by Cheriton Wood. It was near this wood that Hopton had massed his guns.

The wood was the key to the position and Waller decided to seize it without delay. His opponent was not slow in reacting and a fierce hand-to-hand mêlée ensued. Waller retreated in disorder. A stillness descended over the field, with neither side wishing to be the next to advance.

No command had been given when suddenly part of the Royalist centre was seen to move down into the arena. Entirely unsupported, it crossed the valley floor and was cut to pieces before it reached the Parliamentarian lines. Ignoring this grim warning, the Royalist units advanced one by one, to suffer a similar fate. With his line weakened, Hopton wavered. He was now too thin on the ground to order an all-out assault and when Waller hurled his cavalry across against his right wing, crushing it, he conceded defeat and retreated.

Following the battle of Cheriton all Hampshire was lost to the Royalist cause.

Actual numbers engaged in the battle

Royalists		*Parliamentarians*	
Foot	3,800	Foot	3,100
Horse	4,100	Horse	5,800
Artillery	11 guns	Artillery	A few

Wargame figures required for reconstructing the battle

Royalists		*Parliamentarians*	
Foot	8 Standard bearers	Foot	6 Standard bearers
	18 Pikemen		15 Pikemen
	37 Musketeers		31 Musketeers
Horse	58 Swordsmen	Horse	70 Swordsmen
	10 Dragoons		15 Dragoons
Artillery	1 Saker		12 Heavy cavalry
	4 Drakes	Artillery	2 Sakers
	11 Gunners		6 Gunners

Staff officers

Royalists	*Parliamentarians*
Sir Ralph Hopton	Sir William Waller
Lord John Stewart	Sir Arthur Hazelrig
Colonel George Lisle	Colonel Robert Burrell
Colonel Mathew Appleyard	Lieutenant-Colonel Edward Massey

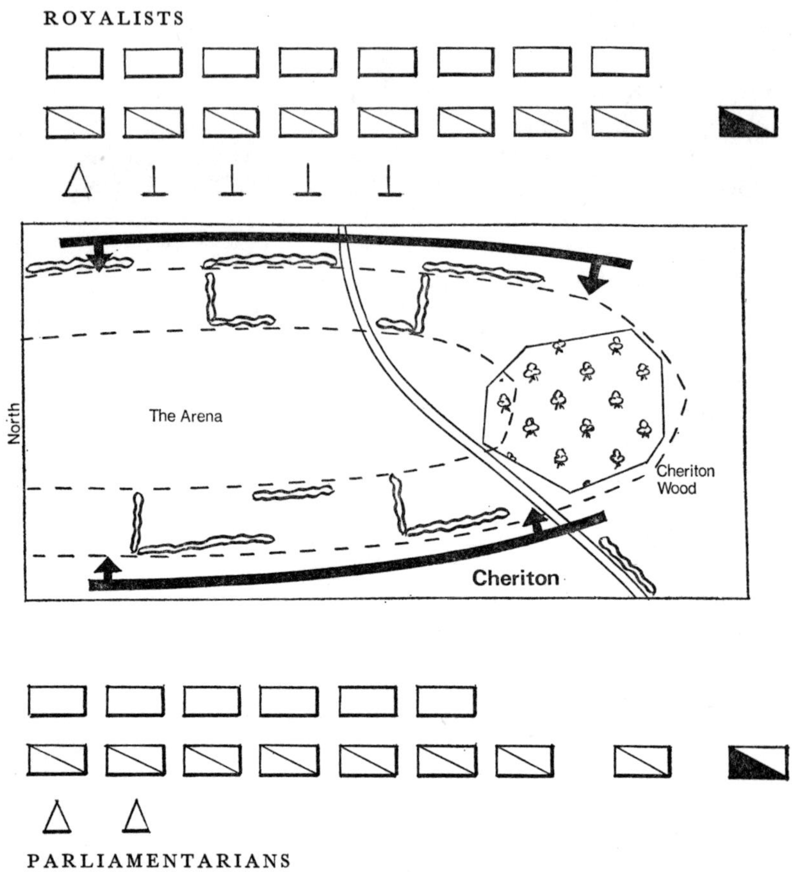
ROYALISTS
North
The Arena
Cheriton Wood
Cheriton
PARLIAMENTARIANS

Battle type. Set piece.

Scale. 1 figure represents 75 men.

Layout. The arena is a low-lying area, surrounded on three sides by high ground. All the slopes down into the valley are gentle. At the head of the valley stands Cheriton Wood, which is passable to all units except artillery. The hillsides are covered in hedgerows. A road crosses the battlefield running from north to south.

Royalists. All units are on the board at the start of the game. They are drawn up in battle array anywhere along the plateau north of the arena, but not occupying Cheriton Wood.

Parliamentarians. All units are on the board at the start of the game. They are drawn up in battle array anywhere along the plateau south of the arena, but not occupying Cheriton Wood.

Note. The layout is simultaneous, therefore each commander will sketch on a map the intended position of every unit before the layout is made.

Special rules. None.

Objectives. The destruction of the enemy.

Elite units. Parliamentarians: 4. Royalists: 4.

29 June 1644

THE BATTLE OF CROPREDY BRIDGE

Yet again the King had returned to Oxford. More supplies and new recruits were required. His enemies were still trying to break the ring surrounding the city. Waller was lurking at Banbury. Charles decided to move against him, so his newly raised force found itself marching north.

When they finally found their quarry, Waller was entrenched in a very strong position near Hanwell Castle, a mile or two out of Banbury. This position was deemed to be too strong to assault, so Charles continued moving north along the banks of the River Cherwell with the intention of turning Waller's flank, so cutting him off from his supply base. To his surprise he found that the Parliamentarian army had left its stronghold and was marching along a parallel road on the other bank of the Cherwell. The race was on to take the first bridge ahead. This happened to be Cropredy Bridge. As the vanguard of the Royalist army pressed on they were confronted by a single Parliamentary cavalry regiment that just happened to be approaching from the north.

When the van moved forward a gap appeared in the King's column of march and this was spotted by Waller. He determined to attack the main Royalist host at once, if only he could cross the river. Near where he stood was the ford at Slat Mill and across this ford he hurled his army, having sent forward a detachment to contend the bridge and so guard his flank.

Unfortunately for him, things did not go at all well. The lone cavalry regiment had been charged by the King's vanguard and put to flight. The attack across the ford was also a complete failure. The royal van captured the bridge and with it some of Waller's cannon. Waller was now on the defensive along his entire front. But the river was to prove to be too great an obstacle for the King, for he also failed in his attempt to dislodge the Parliamentarians.

For the rest of the day the cannons were allowed to growl at one another, but little damage was done. Night brought the battle to an end. The King claimed victory when Waller retired. The fact that certain Parliamentarian regiments mutinied apparently supported his claim.

Actual numbers engaged in the battle

Royalists		*Parliamentarians*	
Foot	5,000	Foot	1,000
Horse	4,000	Horse	2,500
Artillery	A few.	Artillery	11 guns

Wargame figures required for reconstructing the battle

Royalists		*Parliamentarians*	
Foot	10 Standard bearers	Foot	2 Standard bearers
	29 Pikemen		5 Pikemen
	61 Musketeers		13 Musketeers
Horse	65 Swordsmen	Horse	42 Swordsmen
	15 Dragoons		8 Dragoons
Artillery	2 Sakers	Artillery	1 Saker
	6 Gunners		4 Drakes
			11 Gunners

Staff officers

Royalists	*Parliamentarians*
Charles I	Sir William Waller
Earl of Brentford	Lieutenant-General John Middleton
Earl of Northampton	James Wemyss

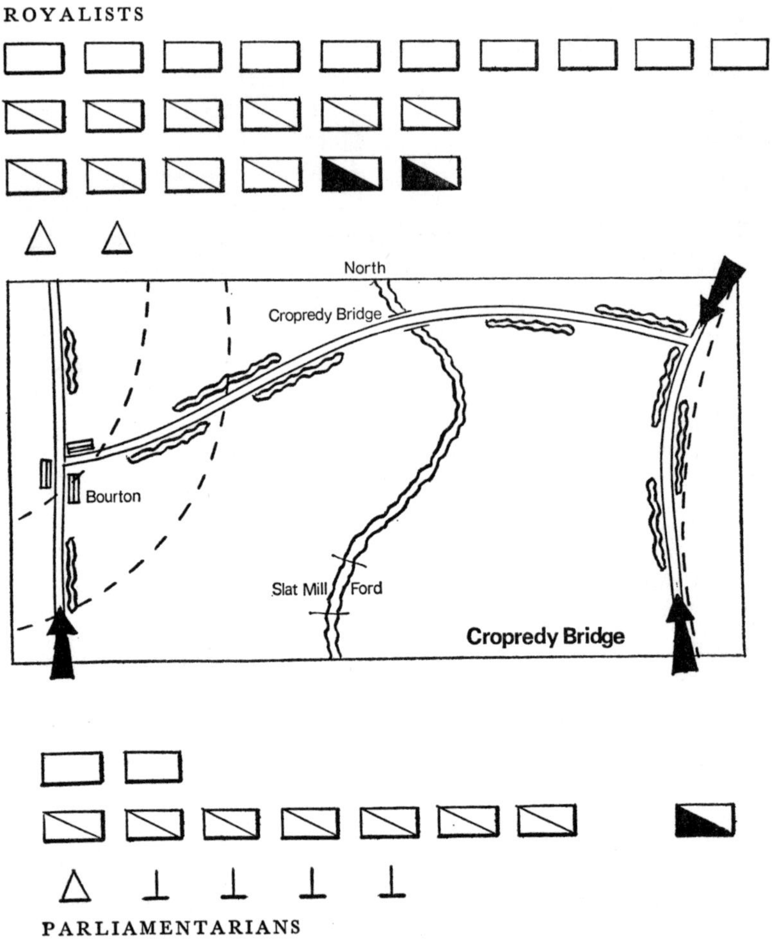
ROYALISTS
North
Cropredy Bridge
Bourton
Slat Mill
Ford
Cropredy Bridge
PARLIAMENTARIANS

Battle type. A chance engagement.

Scale. 1 figure represents 50 men.

Layout. The River Cherwell meanders across the centre of the board, running from south to north. Running parallel with it along the eastern and the western baselines are two roads. These are joined by a third road which runs from the village of Bourton, down a steep hill, then across the river near the northern baseline via Cropredy Bridge, finally forming the road junction near the north-east corner of the board. The Slat Mill ford requires cards 2–5. All other river sections cards 6–10. The hill along the eastern baseline has gentle slopes.

Royalists. There are no Royalist units on the board at the start of the game. They will all enter by the road in the south-eastern corner, using a prearranged order of march, first game move (it may be they will not all be able to come on to the board in the first move).

Parliamentarians. There are no Parliamentarian units on the board at the start of the game. All but one cavalry regiment will enter by the road at the south-west corner of the board. They will enter using a prearranged order of march, during the first game move (as many units as possible will enter during the game move). The odd cavalry regiment will enter during the second game move via the road in the north-east corner.

Special rules. None.

Objectives. To destroy the enemy.

Elite units. Parliamentarians: 4. Royalists: 2.

2 July 1644

THE BATTLE OF MARSTON MOOR

Follow the Wetherby road on its journey due west out of York and for about 6 miles (9·5 km) it rises and falls by but a few feet. Gradually one becomes aware of a ridge ahead, running across one's entire front. This is the route Rupert took after he had raised the siege of York and on this ridge he found Levan, Fairfax, and Cromwell waiting with their army drawn up in battle array. The scene was set for the biggest battle of the war.

The Parliamentary battle line stretched for 1½ miles (2·5 km), between the villages of Tockwith and Long Marston. Having initially formed up on the ridge, it was later decided to advance to the foot of the hill. They redressed along the line of the present road and waited for the battle to commence. Between the two contestants ran a ditch which was hedged on the Parliamentary side. Rupert lined this obstacle with dragoons. The standard layout of cavalry on either wing, flanking their infantry, was adopted by both armies.

For about three hours the two forces merely faced one another, neither wishing to take the initiative. Rupert and his staff had retired to eat when suddenly the entire Parliamentarian line advanced. The ditch was soon cleared of its defenders. On the right, the Parliamentary cavalry wing, under Thomas Fairfax, was held by Goring's cavalry and this became the pivot for the whole battle. The other wing proved to be more successful once Cromwell rejoined it, having been forced to leave the field early in the action to have a wound dressed. He moved behind the Royalist position and fell upon Goring's rear.

With the cavalry defeated, Rupert's infantry rapidly began to disintegrate. A final stand was made in the centre by Newcastle's Whitecoats. About 4,000 Royalists fell in the fray, the Parliamentarians claimed to have lost in the region of 1,000. A few days later, York opened its gates to the victorious Parliamentarian army.

Actual numbers engaged in the battle

Royalists		*Parliamentarians*	
Foot	11,000	Foot	20,000
Horse	6,500	Horse	7,000
Artillery	16 guns	Artillery	25 guns

Wargame figures required for reconstructing the battle

Royalists		*Parliamentarians*	
Foot	10 Standard bearers	Foot	15 Standard bearers
	40 Pikemen		52 Pikemen
	60 Musketeers		100 Musketeers
Horse	58 Swordsmen		32 Sword and Buckler
	7 Dragoons	Horse	40 Swordsmen
Artillery	3 Drakes		20 Lancers
	6 Gunners		10 Dragoons
		Artillery	3 Sakers
			9 Gunners

Staff officers

Royalists	*Parliamentarians*
Prince Rupert	Lord Leven
Earl of Newcastle	Major-General the Earl of Manchester
Sir Charles Lucas	Lord Fairfax
Lord George Goring	Oliver Cromwell
	Major-General David Leslie
	Sir Thomas Fairfax

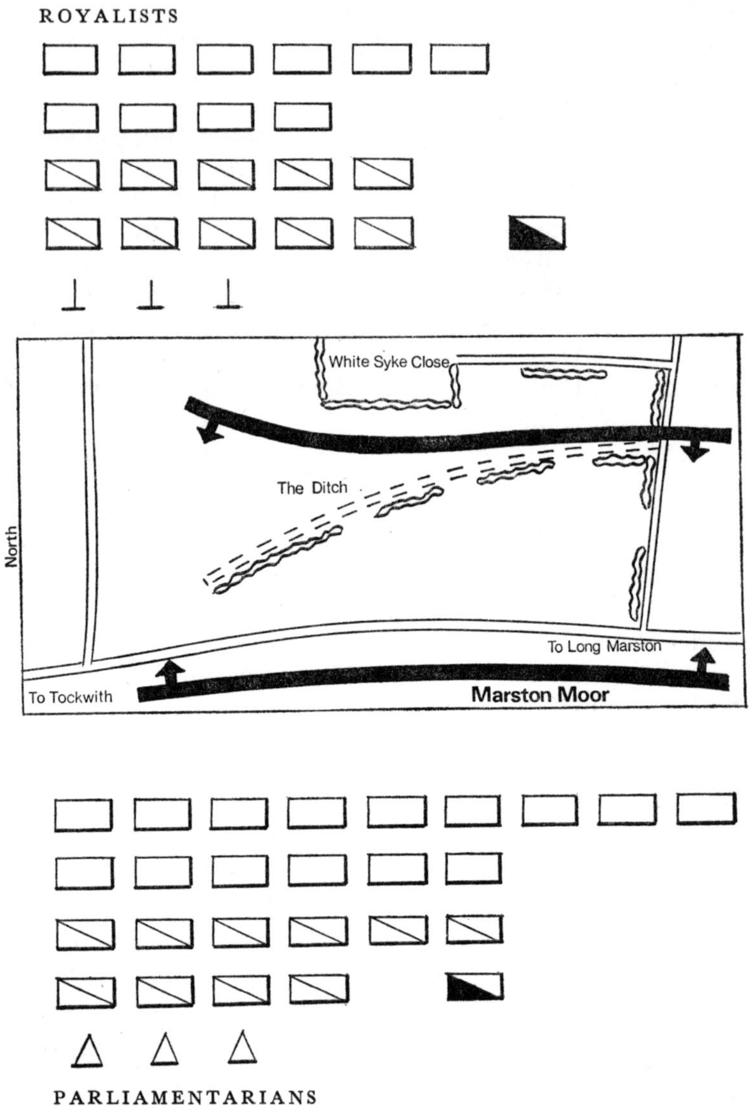
ROYALISTS
White Syke Close
The Ditch
North
To Long Marston
To Tockwith
Marston Moor
PARLIAMENTARIANS

Battle type. Set piece.

Scale. 1 figure represents 100 men.

Layout. The battlefield couldn't be flatter, although the western baseline area between Tockwith and Long Marston can be raised as a gentle slope along the line of the road which runs from north to south. Joining this road near its northern and southern extremities are two minor roads running east. In the centre of the eastern baseline is an enclosure known as White Syke Close. The main feature which cuts across the field is a ditch, with a hedge on its western flank.

Royalists. All units are set out on the board at the start of the game. They are in position along the line of the ditch and in front of White Syke Close.

Parliamentarians. All units are on the board at the start of the game. Their most advanced units may take up their positions on the Tockwith–Long Marston Road.

Special rules. Units wishing to cross the ditch will lose 25 per cent of their game move. The ditch will give cover to any troops standing in it. It should be about 2 in (50 mm) wide.

Objectives. To destroy the enemy.

Elite units. Parliamentarians: 3. Royalists: 6.

2 September 1644

THE BATTLE OF LOSTWITHIEL

Essex against the King. It sounds like Edgehill all over again. However, the conditions had completely changed. Two years of bitter fighting had turned inexperienced troops and would-be generals into veterans. At Edgehill the two sides were fairly equally balanced. At Lostwithiel, Essex was heavily outnumbered and on the defensive.

The south-west peninsular had been a thorn in the flesh of Parliament since the commencement of the war. Essex had attempted to neutralize the area. Unfortunately for him this move had had the effect of bringing the King in person upon him. At the beginning of August, Charles lay at Bodmin, with Essex a few miles to his south at Lostwithiel. Lostwithiel's importance lay in its position, as it held the key to the port of Fowey. Hold Lostwithiel and Essex may be able to evacuate his infantry and guns by sea. With luck, the cavalry may be able to break out overland. Lostwithiel must not fall.

The importance of the town was not lost upon the King and it became his major objective. He divided his army and prepared to strike from two directions at once, one from the north and one from the east. Lostwithiel was protected by Beacon Hill to the west and Restormel Castle to the north. Essex stands accused of half-hearted attempts to defend either. His mind can only have been set upon evacuation. Beacon Hill very quickly fell. The Royalists, anticipating a counter-attack spent valuable time digging in. Likewise, Restormel Castle was lost at the first assault, leaving Lostwithiel completely untenable. The King now appeared to lose control of the initiative he had so far built up. Essex was allowed to collect his forces and slip away towards the coast while Charles sat mesmerized and allowing him to go. To add insult to injury, the Parliamentary cavalry were able to ride through the Royalist lines during the night and make their escape to the east. Over 6,000 infantry and many guns were being spirited away before the King's eyes. A further attempt must be made, and made quickly.

Actual numbers engaged in the battle

Royalists		*Parliamentarians*	
Foot	11,500	Foot	8,000
Horse	3,500	Horse	2,000
Artillery	A few	Artillery	About 30 (not all actively engaged)

Wargame figures required for reconstructing the battle

Royalists		*Parliamentarians*	
Foot	11 Standard bearers	Foot	6 Standard bearers
	31 Pikemen		50 Musketeers
	73 Musketeers		24 Pikemen
Horse	35 Swordsmen	Horse	20 Swordsmen
Artillery	1 Saker	Artillery	2 Sakers
	2 Drakes		3 Drakes
	7 Gunners		12 Gunners

Staff officers

Royalists	*Parliamentarians*
Charles I	Earl of Essex
Earl of Brentford	Major-General Philip Skippon
Prince Maurice	Sir William Balfour
Sir Richard Grenville	Colonel John Weare

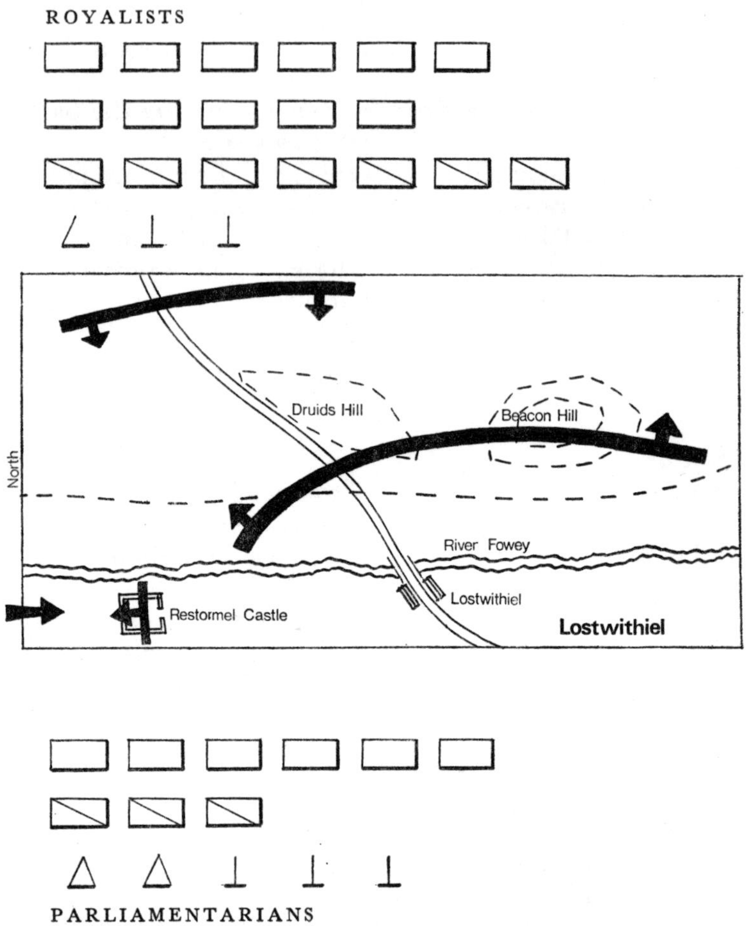
ROYALISTS
Druids Hill
Beacon Hill
North
River Fowey
Lostwithiel
Restormel Castle
Lostwithiel
PARLIAMENTARIANS

Battle type. An attack upon a prepared position.

Scale. 1 figure represents 100 men.

Layout. The River Fowey runs across the board from north to south and about 12 in (300 mm) in from the western baseline. Half-way down its course stands the village of Lostwithiel, on the western bank. On the same bank and further north is Restormel Castle. The land on the eastern bank of the river rises gradually to the eastern baseline. In the centre of its ascent are two isolated hills, Druids Hill and Beacon Hill. These are both steep-sided tors. A road enters by the north-eastern corner of the board and leaves west of Lostwithiel.

Parliamentarians. All units are on the board at the beginning of the game. They may occupy Restormel Castle and the lower slopes of the two tors.

Royalists. There are no Royalist units on the board at the start of the game. All must enter by the road from the east, starting in the first game move, with the exception a second force (maximum of four units) which will attack Restormel Castle from the north.

Special rules. The river is divided into two sections by the bridge. Cards will be used valued 4–10.

Objectives. Royalists. To destroy the enemy and capture Lostwithiel. Parliamentarians. To hold Lostwithiel for at least six game moves, after which they may attempt to withdraw west via the road.

Elite units. Parliamentarians: 3. Royalists: 2.

31 August 1644

THE BATTLE OF CASTLE DORE

On the surface it would appear that Essex's plan of campaign was succeeding in every detail. His cavalry had made its escape and was now well on the road to Exeter. He had accomplished his withdrawal from Lostwithiel having suffered few casualties, apart from a number of guns that had had to be abandoned because of the appalling road conditions. If only he could reach Fowey the evacuation could begin.

The King suddenly appeared to become aware of his intentions and was galvanized into action. Rapidly collecting his forces from their defensive positions, he pressed on after the Earl with all speed, determined to bring him to battle before he could reach the coast. A message was sent to Goring, who was stationed at St Blazey, a few miles to the west of Fowey, instructing him to march at once and to fall upon the left flank of the Parliamentarians once the King had succeeded in halting them. Essex realized that the game was up and formed up in battle array on a hilly position known as Castle Dore, a prehistoric hill fort. He was to attempt to give the King a bloody nose after which he hoped he might be allowed to withdraw in peace.

The King's initial head-on attack all but broke him but somehow he managed to hang on. His counter-attack hurled the Royalists back and as night fell, Castle Dore remained firmly in his hands. To stand or to fall back? This was now the vital decision. If he stood, perhaps the King would be reinforced. If he withdrew, perhaps he would not have time in which to embark. Unfortunately for Essex, the decision was no longer his to make. His army decided for him. They had had enough, were out of food and ammunition and were unsupported by cavalry. Six thousand men laid down their arms. Essex himself slipped away in a fishing boat. Only Major-General Philip Skippon and a handful of his men managed to fight their way out. All the artillery fell into Charles's hands. The Parliamentarians had suffered one of the major defeats of the war.

Actual numbers engaged in the battle

Royalists		*Parliamentarians*	
Foot	11,000	Foot	6,000
Horse	3,000	Horse	400
Artillery	5 or 6 guns	Artillery	42 guns (not all these were used in the battle. This is the number captured after the surrender).

Wargame figures required for reconstructing the battle

Royalists		*Parliamentarians*	
Foot	10 Standard bearers	Foot	6 Standard bearers
	33 Pikemen		14 Pikemen
	67 Musketeers		40 Musketeers
Horse	30 Swordsmen	Horse	4 Swordsmen
Artillery	1 Saker	Artillery	2 Sakers
	1 Drake		3 Drakes
	5 Gunners		10 Gunners

Staff officers

Royalists	*Parliamentarians*
Charles I	Earl of Essex
Prince Maurice	Major-General Philip Skippon
Lord Goring	Sir William Balfour
Sir Richard Grenville	Colonel John Weare

ROYALISTS

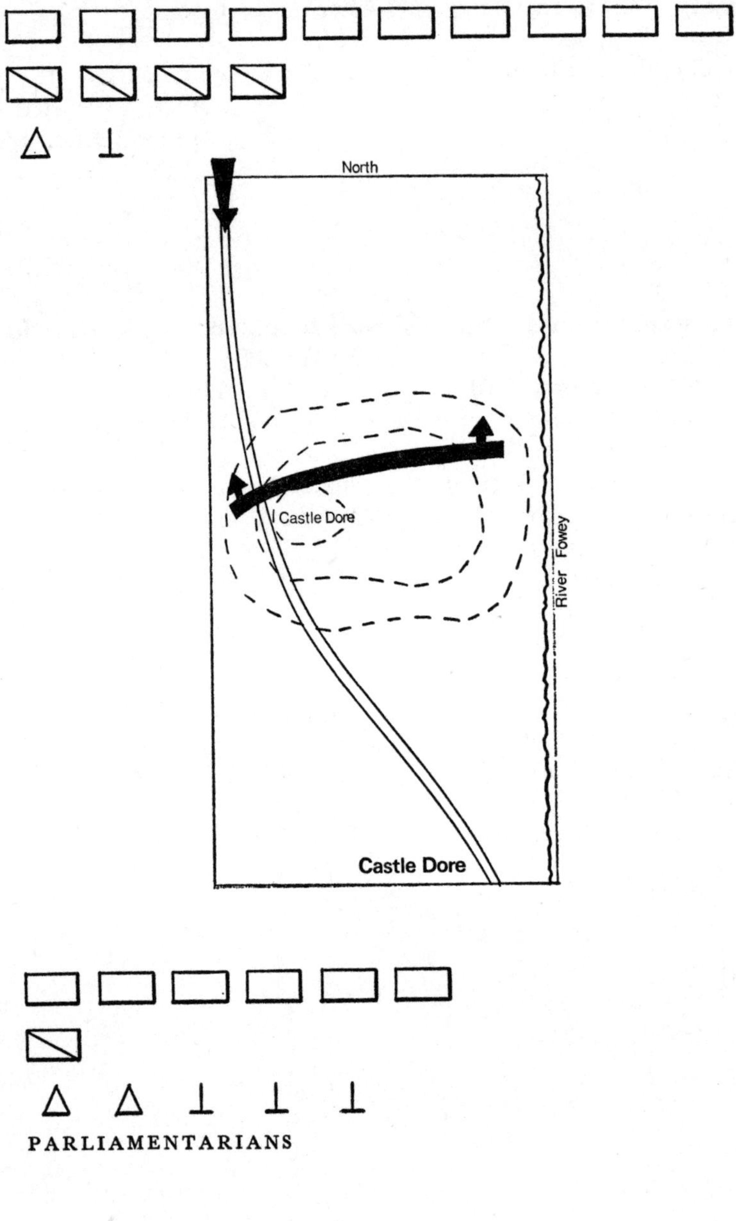

PARLIAMENTARIANS

Battle type. An attack on a prepared position.

Scale. 1 figure represents 100 men.

Layout. The centre of the board is dominated by the steep-sided hill of Castle Dore. The top of the hill is a plateau, with the exception of an area at the western summit which rises steeply over all the rest. The River Fowey runs the length of the eastern baseline. A road enters at the north-west corner and leaves by the south-west.

Parliamentarians. All the Parliamentarian units are in position on the hill of Castle Dore at the start of the game. Those behind the hill, ie on its southern slopes, do not have to be revealed on the board, but their position must be marked on a map.

Royalists. No Royalist units are on the board at the start of the game. They must enter by the road from the north in a pre-determined order.

Special rules. The River Fowey is not fordable. All troops being forced to enter the river will be individually diced for; 1, 2, or 3 will be drowned.

Objectives. Parliamentarians. To hold Castle Dore Hill. Should the Royalists break through, they must attempt to withdraw from the field via the road to the south. Royalists. To defeat the enemy and stop them retreating from the board by the road to the south.

Elite units. Parliamentarians: 2. Royalists: 2.

27 October 1644

THE SECOND BATTLE OF NEWBURY

Probably the most difficult military manoeuvre to execute is the attack by two forces, starting miles apart and out of sight of one another, yet with orders to converge simultaneously upon a single objective. This was to be the ploy attempted by the Parliamentarian army at the second battle of Newbury.

Having settled with the West Country, Charles received news of a new threat. The Earl of Manchester and Sir William Waller were assembling their forces near Reading. A fresh threat to Oxford was developing. To counter it the King moved rapidly to Salisbury. This was a good move. If the Parliamentarians moved north, London would be exposed. In chess, this would resemble an exchange of queens. The King now advanced on Newbury, with Waller avoiding contact and falling back before him to Basingstoke, where he joined Manchester. This combined force now advanced and on 26 October the opposing forces faced one another north of Newbury. The Parliamentarians had an advantage in numbers of nearly two to one. Charles sought a defensive position. He found it at the junction of the Kennet and the Lambourn rivers. With his flanks and his front secure, he settled to await the Parliamentarian attack.

Manchester and Waller decided to divide their force. Waller was given the task of marching in a huge arc completely round the Royalist positions, with the intention of falling upon their rear as Manchester launched his attack upon the front. Throughout much of the day of the 27th Waller was committed to his march, while Manchester contented himself with a show of force for the benefit of the King. When he did, after much hesitation, launch his attack it was easily repulsed. His timing was out and he failed completely to co-ordinate with Waller's attack. This proved to be the more serious assault from the King's point of view. Speen village quickly fell and was only retaken after desperate fighting. Cromwell, commanding the cavalry north of the village failed to charge home decisively and after two hours of sporadic fighting, darkness brought hostilities to an end.

During the night the King slipped away to Oxford. Manchester had lost his great opportunity to end the war on Newbury field.

Actual numbers engaged in the battle

Royalists		*Parliamentarians*	
Foot	5,000	Foot	11,000
Horse	4,000	Horse	7,000
Artillery	29 guns	Artillery	24 guns

Wargame figures required for reconstructing the battle

Royalists		*Parliamentarians*	
Foot	7 Standard bearers	Foot	10 Standard bearers
	16 Pikemen		40 Pikemen
	27 Musketeers		60 Musketeers
Horse	40 Swordsmen	Horse	70 Swordsmen
Artillery	1 Saker	Artillery	3 Sakers
	4 Drakes		9 Gunners
	11 Gunners		

Staff officers

Royalists	*Parliamentarians*
Charles I	Major-General the Earl of Manchester
Prince Maurice	Sir William Waller
Colonel George Lisle	Oliver Cromwell
General Goring	Major-General Philip Skippon
	Lieutenant-General Sir William Balfour

PARLIAMENTARIANS

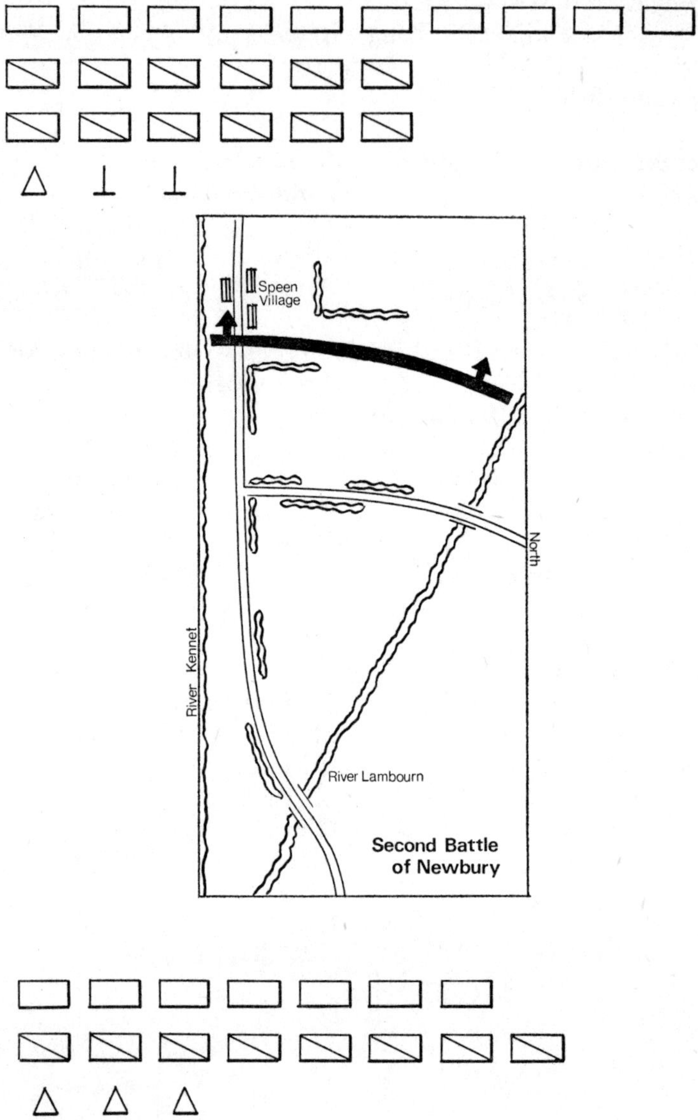

ROYALISTS

Battle type. An attack on a prepared position.

Scale. 1 figure represents 100 men.

Layout. The River Kennet forms the southern baseline of the board. Running down to join it in the south-east corner is the River Lambourn. A road from the west crosses the Lambourn near this junction, follows the northern bank of the Kennet and leaves by the western baseline, having passed through Speen village. A second road runs at right angles from this road east of the village, crosses the Lambourn, and leaves the battlefield at the centre of the northern baseline.

Royalists. All units are placed on the board at the start of the game anywhere within the triangle of land formed by the two rivers and a line drawn east of the village.

Parliamentarians. Before the Royalists set out their troops, the Parliamentarian army will be divided into two groups. The first of these forces will enter the board during the first game move, anywhere along the eastern baseline north of the River Lambourn. The second force will enter anywhere along the western baseline during game moves 1–6 according to a die throw.

Special rules. The River Kennet is unfordable. Any units being forced to enter will be subject to individual die throws; any 1, 2, or 3 will be drowned. The River Lambourn is divided into three sections, each having a card of 4–10.

Objectives. The defeat of the enemy.

Elite units. Parliamentarians: 2. Royalists: 4.

14 June 1645

THE BATTLE OF NASEBY

Essex, Manchester, and Waller had all tried and failed to defeat the King. New leaders were needed. New ideas were needed. A new army was needed. At Windsor, in the April, it was created. Fairfax was given the command. Within a few weeks, Cromwell had joined him to take over the cavalry. When June came, Fairfax decided to challenge the King. He led out his New Model Army and advanced on Oxford. Here he heard that Leicester had fallen to Rupert.

The King was lodged in Daventry. Within a week Fairfax had closed to within 10 miles (16 km) of him. Charles attempted to escape to Newark but his pursuer was too quick for him and he was overtaken at Naseby. Further retreat was impossible. Charles turned and prepared to give battle.

Charles had chosen to draw up his forces on top of Dust Hill. Half a mile (800 m) away Fairfax was forming his battle lines along the ridge of Red Hill. Each army took up about a mile (1·5 km) from flank to flank. By mid morning all was ready. Rupert commanded the Royalist right wing, Langdale the left. The King took the centre. For Parliament, Ireton faced Rupert, Cromwell commanded the cavalry on the right. Fairfax took the centre opposite the King.

Following a period of summing one another up, Charles decided to attack. With his infantry moving into a mêlée with the enemy infantry, Rupert made an all-out charge, shattering Ireton's wing. The Royalist infantry advanced up the hill, successfully pushing all before them. Only on the King's left were things going wrong. Cromwell had charged, Langdale was defeated and the King's flank was exposed. Charles committed his reserves to try to stabilize the position, only to see them surrounded by fresh Parliamentary cavalry. Cornered on three sides the Royalist infantry began to surrender. Charles turned and left the field. Rupert, seeing all was lost, fled. The battle was over. More than 4,000 Royalists and all their guns had been lost and with them, the war. A few desperate fights were still to be fought but never again was the King able to collect an army capable of taking on this New Model Army.

Actual numbers engaged in the battle

Royalists		*Parliamentarians*	
Foot	4,000	Foot	7,000
Horse	5,000	Horse	6,000
Artillery	12 guns	Artillery	13 guns

Wargame figures required for reconstructing the battle

Royalists		*Parliamentarians*	
Foot	4 Standard bearers	Foot	6 Standard bearers
	15 Pikemen		22 Pikemen
	21 Musketeers		42 Musketeers
Horse	35 Swordsmen	Horse	54 Swordsmen
	6 Dragoons		6 Dragoons
Artillery	2 Sakers	Artillery	2 Sakers
	2 Drakes		2 Drakes
	10 Gunners		10 Gunners

Staff officers

Royalists	*Parliamentarians*
Charles I	Sir Thomas Fairfax
Prince Rupert	Oliver Cromwell
Lord Jacob Astley (f)	Major-General Philip Skippon
Sir Marmaduke Langdale	General Henry Ireton

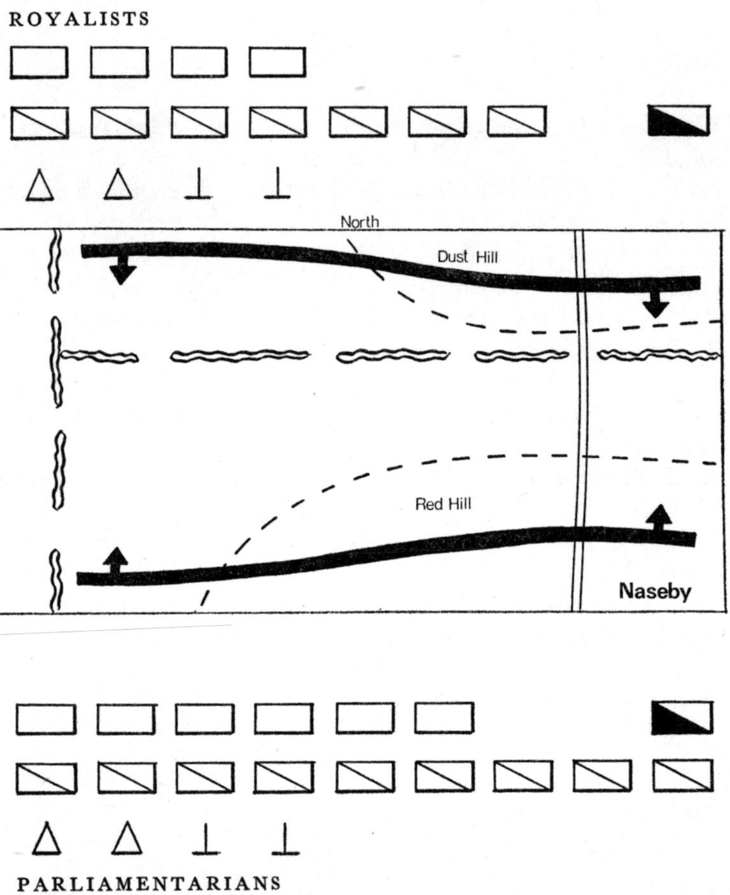
ROYALISTS
North
Dust Hill
Red Hill
Naseby
PARLIAMENTARIANS

Battle type. Set piece.

Scale. 1 figure represents 100 men.

Layout. The northeastern corner of the board is dominated by the gentle slopes of Dust Hill, whilst opposite across the valley rises the equally slight slopes of Red Hill. A single road crosses the valley running from north to south. The only other feature worthy of mention are two lines of hedges at right angles to one another, one down the centre of the valley, the other near the western baseline.

Parliamentarians. All units are on the board at the start of the game. Their most advanced units are up to 12 in. (300 mm) on to the board along the southern baseline.

Royalists. All units are on the board at the start of the game. Their most advanced units are up to 12 in (300 mm) on to the board along the northern baseline.

Special rules. None.

Objectives. The destruction of the enemy.

Elite units. Parliamentarians: 2. Royalists: 3.

24 September 1645

THE BATTLE OF ROWTON HEATH

After his crushing defeat at Naseby, Charles sought desperately for another army with which to challenge the New Model Army. But the Royalists of England were exhausted. The King had fled to Wales after the battle. To all but himself, his cause looked lost. Scotland. Of course, Scotland. As a Stuart surely he could raise a further force in the north. Montrose had been fighting a brilliant campaign on his behalf. He would join him.

Escorted by a cavalry force he headed for Chester. The town was under a half-hearted seige, and he had no difficulty in entering. He decided to route the beseigers and sent his cavalry over 3,000 strong, in a wide flanking sweep to the east of Chester. He himself would attack simultaneously against the Parliamentary front. A good plan, which unfortunately did not take into account the fact that he had been shadowed from Wales by a Parliamentary cavalry force equal to his own which was now poised ready to strike at the Royalist horse. They were led by General Poyntz.

Sir Marmaduke Langdale, having crossed the Dee, reached Rowton Heath, only to find Poyntz waiting for him. Neither was supported by infantry or artillery, but both expected these to arrive at any moment. It was the Parliamentarians who won the race and Langdale found himself being assaulted both in front and in flank. He broke. The remnants of his scattered force crashed into the friendly infantry as they came to his assistance, throwing them into disorder. Chester was filled with running men. A third of the small Royalist army had been lost. Chester was doomed and Charles had taken a further step towards the waiting axe.

Actual numbers engaged in the battle

Royalists		*Parliamentarians*	
Foot	500	Foot	800
Horse	3,500	Horse	3,500
Artillery	A few	Artillery	A few

Wargame figures required for reconstructing the battle

Royalists		*Parliamentarians*	
Foot	1 Standard bearer	Foot	1 Standard bearer
	3 Pikemen		5 Pikemen
	6 Musketeers		10 Musketeers
Horse	60 Swordsmen	Horse	60 Swordsmen
	10 Dragoons		10 Dragoons
Artillery	2 Sakers	Artillery	2 Sakers
	6 Gunners		6 Gunners

Staff officers

Royalists	*Parliamentarians*
Charles I	Colonel-General Poyntz
Earl of Lichfield	Colonel Michael Jones
Sir Marmaduke Langdale	Adjutant-General James Lothian

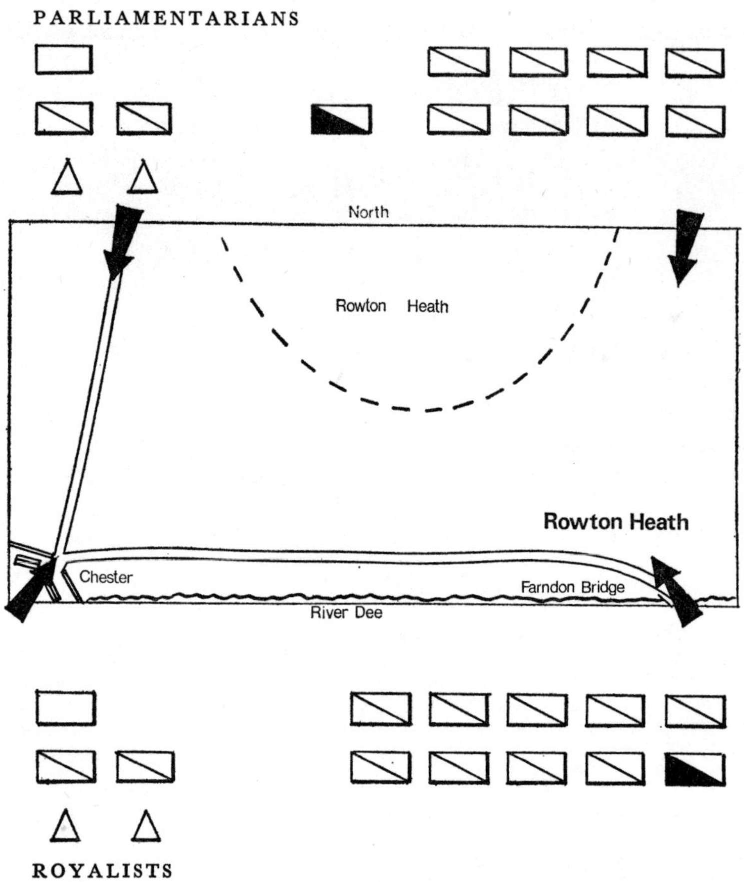
PARLIAMENTARIANS
North
Rowton Heath
Rowton Heath
Chester
Farndon Bridge
River Dee
ROYALISTS

Battle type. A chance engagement.

Scale. 1 figure represents 50 men.

Layout. The River Dee forms the southern baseline of the battlefield. The city of Chester stands in the south-western corner of the board. A road runs from the city, along the river bank, crossing in the south-eastern corner by Farndon Bridge. A second road out of Chester leaves the board by the northern baseline. Rowton Heath is a gentle rise of ground in the centre of this baseline.

Royalists. There are no Royalist units on the board at the start of the game. All the artillery, the infantry regiment, and two units of cavalry may leave Chester during the first game move. The rest of the cavalry enter at the same time over Farndon Bridge.

Parliamentarians. There are no Parliamentarian units on the board at the start of the game. All the artillery, the infantry, and two cavalry units enter along the road from the north. At the same time, the rest of the cavalry enters from the north-eastern corner of the board.

Special rules. The River Dee is unfordable. Any troops being forced into the water risk drowning. 1, 2, or 3 thrown on a die for each individual figure will indicate death.

Objectives. The destruction of the enemy.

Elite units. Royalists: 2. Parliamentarians: 2.

3 September 1650

THE BATTLE OF DUNBAR

Charles II had landed in Scotland. Cromwell was appointed Captain-General and Commander-in-Chief of all the forces in England, and ordered to put down the Scottish rebellion. Collecting an army with all speed, the Lord Protector crossed the Border at Berwick and headed for Edinburgh.

Waiting for him was a large but less well organized Scottish force, under the command of General David Leslie, about 26,000 men all told. Cromwell reached the Esk and it appeared that a second battle of Pinkie was about to be fought. However, Leslie preferred to fall back and concentrate at Leith. Cromwell's attempts to dislodge him failed. Disease spread through the English army and Cromwell's position became critical. Slowly he fell back along the coast to Dunbar. Leslie followed him and overtaking him, took up a position on Doon Hill, overlooking and commanding the harbour. The road back into England was cut. Cromwell was trapped with his back to the sea and not enough ships to take off his army. He must either fight or surrender.

Leslie was prepared to wait and allow plague to win his victory for him. But not his advisers. They demanded English blood. During the evening of 2 September the Scottish host abandoned its position on Doon Hill and formed up on the plain below. This move was to prove to be a fatal error. Cromwell recognized Leslie's mistake and determined to attack at dawn.

At first light the Parliamentarians formed column to the south of the town. They fell upon the unsuspecting Scottish right wing and smashed it. The trap had been sprung. Frantically the northerners tried to take up their battle stations, light their matches, find their horses. The shock of the first assault proved to be too great. The unformed line crumbled. Within minutes the Scots were in full flight: 3,000 were killed and 10,000 were taken prisoner. Cromwell turned back north and his army occupied Edinburgh.

Actual numbers engaged in the battle

Scots		*Parliamentarians*	
Foot	16,000	Foot	7,500
Horse	6,000	Horse	3,500
Artillery	30 guns	Artillery	A few

Wargame figures required for reconstructing the battle

Scots

Foot	16 Standard bearers
	40 Pikemen
	80 Musketeers
	16 Sword and buckler
	8 Axemen
Horse	30 Swordsmen
	20 Lancers
	10 Dragoons
Artillery	3 Sakers
	9 Gunners

Parliamentarians

Foot	6 Standard bearers
	23 Pikemen
	47 Musketeers
Horse	35 Swordsmen
Artillery	3 Drakes
	6 Gunners

Staff officers

Scots

General David Leslie
Colonel Holbourn
Lord Lorne
Major-General Sir Robert Montgomerie
Lieutenant-General Sir James Lumsdain

Parliamentarians

Oliver Cromwell
General George Monk
Lieutenant-General Charles Fleetwood
Lieutenant-General George Lambert

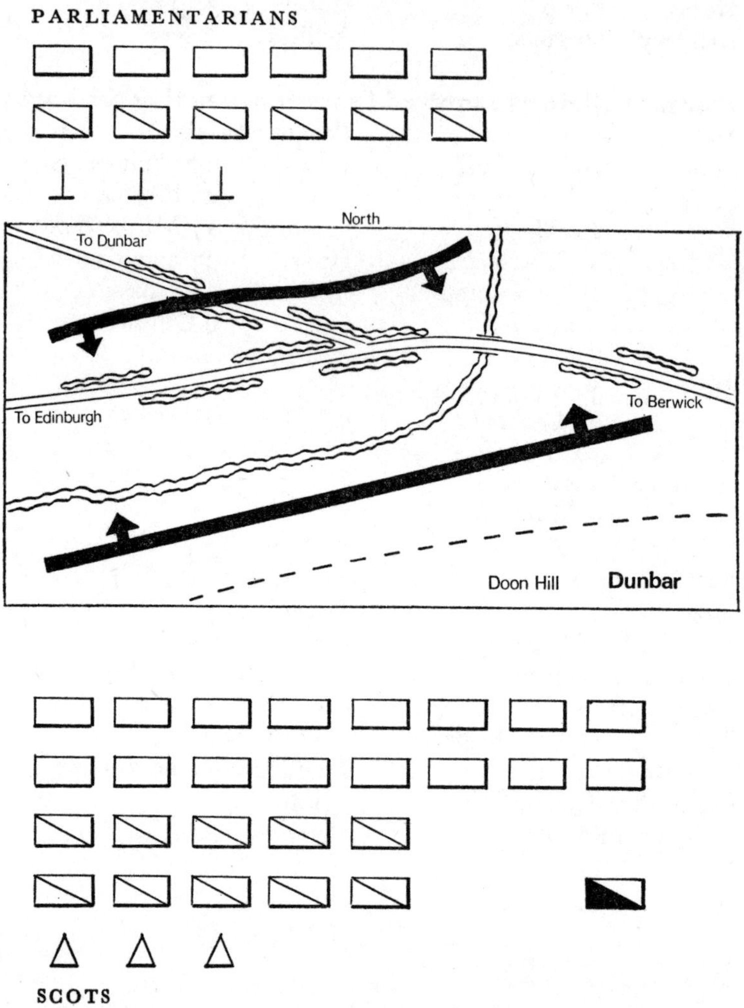
PARLIAMENTARIANS
North
To Dunbar
To Edinburgh
To Berwick
Doon Hill
Dunbar
SCOTS

Battle type. Set piece.

Scale. 1 figure represents 100 men.

Layout. Along the northern baseline runs the North Sea. Rising along the southern baseline are the gentle slopes of Doon Hill. The town of Dunbar is situated in the north-western corner. The Spott Burn enters on the western baseline and flows into the sea. The main Edinburgh to Berwick road cuts across the field from west to east, being joined by the Dunbar road just before it crosses the burn.

Scots. The entire Scottish force is on the board at the start of the game, set out to the south of the burn.

English. Having examined the layout of the Scottish army, the English lay out their entire force to the north of the Edinburgh road and west of the burn.

Special rules. The English army will move first. The Scottish host is asleep during this movement and will not reply to any English firing nor may it move during the first game move. The burn is a very small obstacle, so cards 2–5 will be used. Any troops being forced into the sea will be drowned.

Objectives. English. To leave the board by the road to Berwick. Scots. To destroy the enemy.

Elite units. Scots: 0. English: 4.

3 September 1651

THE BATTLE OF WORCESTER

Leslie had escaped from Dunbar battlefield with half his army. He at once set about recruiting and reorganizing. With Charles II already King in Scotland, the next step was to install him in London. The English had occupied Edinburgh after Dunbar and gradually their army had moved north. A number of small actions ensued. Perth fell. The outlook for Charles if he remained in Scotland was bleak. His only chance lay in England itself. If he was to march south, perhaps those who had been loyal to his father would take up arms for him. Accompanied by Leslie and leading an army of 12,000 Scots, Charles crossed the border at Carlisle. He headed for the West Country, with the hope that the Cornish and the Welsh would join him in the Gloucester area before he need turn east towards London and the inevitable fight with Cromwell for the capital.

Charles rested at Worcester. It had not been a happy march. The anticipated recruits had not been forthcoming and his Scottish troops were uneasy about being so far from their homeland, knowing that they could expect no help from the local population should they be defeated. Here Cromwell descended upon him.

The King was in a strong position, his front and west flank being covered by rivers. Over the Severn he had occupied Fort Royal. Cromwell had double the forces at his command than had Charles and he was determined not only to defeat him, but also to annihilate his army. He therefore planned a double attack, splitting his army into two parts, the one to hold down the King at Fort Royal, while the other crossed the Teme to encircle the main army and pin them against the Severn with a left hook.

To his surprise he found himself on the defensive in front of Fort Royal and for about three hours it was touch and go. Eventually the fort was taken and a final stand was made within Worcester itself. The Royalists had been defeated on the other flank and the battle ended with Scots either fleeing or surrendering in groups. Charles escaped abroad, only returning after the death of the Protector.

Actual numbers engaged in the battle

Royalists		*Parliamentarians*	
Foot	9,000	Foot	18,000
Horse	4,000	Horse	9,000
Artillery	A few	Artillery	A few

Wargame figures required for reconstructing the battle

Royalists		*Parliamentarians*	
Foot	7 Standard bearers	Foot	10 Standard bearers
	14 Pikemen		40 Pikemen
	39 Musketeers		85 Musketeers
	8 Sword and buckler	Horse	45 Swordsmen
Horse	10 Swordsmen	Artillery	2 Sakers
	10 Lancers		1 Drake
Artillery	2 Sakers		8 Gunners
	1 Drake		
	8 Gunners		

Staff officers

Royalists	*Parliamentarians*
Charles II	Oliver Cromwell
Lord Montgomery	General Fleetwood
Major-General Dalziel	General Lambert
Major-General Pitscotty	General Harrison

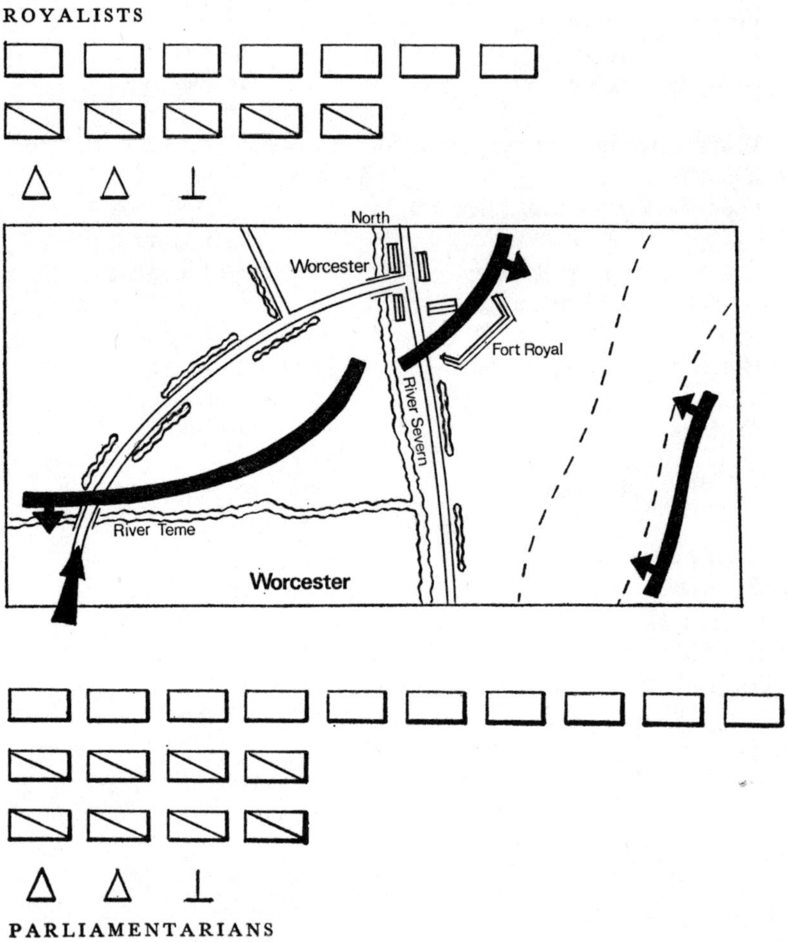
ROYALISTS
North
Worcester
Fort Royal
River Severn
River Teme
Worcester
PARLIAMENTARIANS

Battle type. Set piece.

Scale. 1 figure represents 150 men.

Layout. Down the centre of the board, running from north to south, is the River Severn. A tributary, the River Teme, flows into it from the west. In the east the ground rises gradually away from the river. The city of Worcester stands east of the River Severn near the northern baseline. The main road runs south from the city, a second road crosses the river, carrying on to bridge the River Teme near the south-east corner of the board. Worcester is protected by the stone-walled Fort Royal.

Royalists. All units are on the board at the start of the game. They are set out in position anywhere to the north of the River Teme and west of the Severn. They may also occupy Fort Royal and the City of Worcester.

Parliamentarians. The units are divided between two forces before the Royalist army is placed on the board. The force entering the game from the east will be laid out on the high land in the south-east corner during game move one. The second force will also enter during this move along the road in the south-west.

Special rules. The River Severn will be controlled by cards 6–10. The Teme will draw from cards 3–6.

Objectives. Royalists. To destroy the enemy, holding its own ground for at least six games moves, after which it may begin to fall back to the north should this become necessary.
Parliamentarians. To destroy the enemy.

Elite units. Parliamentarians: 4. Royalists: 4.

15 | *Summary of the rules of play*

Movement

	Advance	*Charge*	*Fall back*	*Run*
Pikeman	12 in (300 mm)	N/A	6 in (150 mm)	18 in (450 mm)
Musketeer	16 in (400 mm)	N/A	8 in (200 mm)	24 in (600 mm)
Sword and buckler	20 in (500 mm)	30 in	10 in (250 mm)	30 in (750 mm)
Archer	20 in (500 mm)	N/A	10 in (250 mm)	30 in (750 mm)
Light cavalry	24 in (600 mm)	36 in		
Heavy cavalry	20 in (500 mm)			
Dragoon	20 in (500 mm)			
Heavy artillery	12 in (300 mm)	Limber up or unlimber		
Light artillery	16 in (400 mm)			4 in (100 mm)

Variations

Unit about turn: deduct 50 per cent of game move.
Change of formation: deduct 50 per cent.
Unit climb a steep slope: deduct 50 per cent.
Unit move through dense wood: deduct 50 per cent.
Unit fighting through a village: deduct 50 per cent.
Artillery moving through open wood: deduct 50 per cent.
Infantry or cavalry moving through open wood: deduct 25 per cent.
Infantry or cavalry pass through hedge: deduct 3 in (75 mm).
Artillery pass through hedge: takes 1 game move.
Infantry or cavalry pass over wall: deduct 6 in. (150 mm).

Unit moving along a road: deduct 25 per cent.
Unit moving up gentle slope: no penalty.
Infantry or cavalry moving through swamps: deduct 75 per cent.
Infantry or cavalry moving through lake: deduct 75 per cent.
Artillery lost if moving through lake or swamp: deduct card value.
Unit moving through a river: deduct card value.

PRE-BATTLE EFFICIENCY

	Infantry and cavalry				*Artillery*		
Elite		1, 2	3, 4, 5	6	1, 2	3, 4	5, 6
Other	1	2, 3, 4	5, 6				
Rating	1	2	3	4	1	2	3

MÊLÉE POINTS TABLE

	1st round	*Subsequent*
Infantry		
Pikeman or standard bearer	1	½
Musketeer	½	½
Swordsman	½	1
Halberdier	1	1
Cavalry		
Swordsman	½ (1)	1
Lancer	1 (1½)	½
Dragoon	½ (1)	1
Staff officer	1 (1½)	1½

CASUALTIES FROM FIRE AND MÊLÉE

Men	*Efficiency rating* 1	2	3	4
1	—	—	—	—
2	—	—	—	1
3	—	—	1	1
4	—	1	1	2
5	1	1	2	2
6	1	1	2	2
7	1	2	2	3
8	2	2	3	3
9	2	3	3	4
10	2	3	3	4

Casualties from artillery fire

Efficiency rating	1	2	3	4
Hit in open	5	4	3	2
Hit under cover	6	5	4	3

CONTROL

Movement reaction

5 plus	Obey
4	Stand
3	Fall back
2	Run

Attack into a mêleé

6 plus	Obey
5	Stand
4	Fall back
3	Run

Defender into a mêleé

7 plus	Counter-charge
5 or 6	Stand
4	Fall back
3	Run

Bibliography

Buchan, J., *Cromwell* (London: Hodder & Stoughton, 1934).

Chandler, D., *Battlefields of Europe* (London: H. Evelyn, 1965).

Cooper, L., *British Regular Cavalry, 1644–1914* (London: Chapman & Hall, 1965).

Falls, C., *Elizabeth's Irish Wars* (London: Methuen, 1950).

Firth, Sir C., and Davies, G., *Regimental History of Cromwell's Army* (Oxford: Clarendon Press, 1940).

Fuller, Maj.-Gen. J. F. E., *The Decisive Battles of the Western World* (London: Eyre & Spottiswood, 1954).

Grant, J., *British Battles on Land and Sea* (London: Cassell).

Kinross, J. *Discovering Battlefields of England* (Princes Risborough: Shire Publications, 1974).

Montgomery of Alamein, *A History of Warfare* (London: Collins, 1968).

Oman, C. W. C., *The Art of War in the Sixteenth Century* (New York: E. P. Dutton and Co., 1937).

Peterson, H. L. ,*The Book of the Gun* (London: Hamlyn, 1963).

Potter, R., and Embleton, G. A., *The English Civil War* (London: Almark, 1973).

Treece, H., and Oakeshott, E., *Fighting Men* (Leicester: Brockhampton Press, 1963).

Wilkinson, F., *Guns* (London: Hamlyn, 1970).

Woolrych, A., *Battles of the English Civil War* (London: Batsford, 1961).

Young, Brig. P., *English Civil War Armies* (Norwich: Osprey, 1973).

Index